FILM ART

AN INTRODUCTION

FIFTH EDITION

DAVID BORDWELL

KRISTIN THOMPSON

University of Wisconsin

The McGraw-Hill Companies, Inc.

*New York   St. Louis   San Francisco   Auckland   Bogotá
Caracas   Lisbon   London   Madrid   Mexico   Milan   Montreal
New Delhi   Paris   San Juan   Singapore   Sydney   Tokyo   Toronto*

McGraw-Hill

A Division of The McGraw-Hill Companies

FILM ART: AN INTRODUCTION

3 4 5 6 7 8 9 0   VNH   VNH   9 0 9 8 7

ISBN 0-07-006634-5

This book was set in Bodoni Book by Ruttle, Shaw & Wetherill, Inc.
The editors were Cynthia Ward, Nancy Blaine, and Curt Berkowitz;
the designer was Joan E. O'Connor;
the cover was designed by Karen K. Quigley;
the production supervisor was Paula Keller.
Von Hoffmann Press, Inc., was printer and binder.

Cover Photo: © 1941 RKO Pictures, Inc. Used by permission of Turner Entertainment Co. All rights reserved.

Library of Congress Cataloging-in-Publication Data
Bordwell, David.
   Film art : an introduction / David Bordwell, Kristin Thompson.—
5th ed.
    p.   cm.
    Includes bibliographical references and index.
    ISBN 0-07-006634-5
    1. Motion pictures—Aesthetics.   I. Thompson, Kristin, (date).
II. Title.
PN1995.B617   1997
791.43'01—dc20   96-5174

ABOUT
THE AUTHORS

David Bordwell and Kristin Thompson are married and live in Madison, Wisconsin.

David Bordwell is Jacques Ledoux Professor of Film Studies at the University of Wisconsin—Madison. He holds a master's degree and a doctorate in film from the University of Iowa. His books include *The Films of Carl-Theodor Dreyer* (University of California Press, 1981), *Narration in the Fiction Film* (University of Wisconsin Press, 1985), *Ozu and the Poetics of Cinema* (British Film Institute/Princeton University Press, 1988), *Making Meaning: Inference and Rhetoric in the Interpretation of Cinema* (Harvard University Press, 1989), and *The Cinema of Eisenstein* (Harvard University Press, 1993). He has won a University Distinguished Teaching Award.

Kristin Thompson is an Honorary Fellow at the University of Wisconsin—Madison. She holds a master's degree in film from the University of Iowa and a doctorate in film from the University of Wisconsin—Madison. She has published *Eisenstein's Ivan the Terrible* (Princeton University Press, 1981), *Exporting Entertainment: America's Place in World Film Markets, 1907–1934* (British Film Institute, 1985), *Breaking the Glass Armor: Neoformalist Film Analysis* (Princeton University Press, 1988), and *Wooster Proposes, Jeeves Disposes; or, Le Mot Juste* (James H. Heineman, 1992). In her spare time she studies Egyptology.

The authors have also collaborated on *Film History: An Introduction* (McGraw-Hill, 1994) and, with Janet Staiger, on *The Classical Hollywood Cinema: Film Style and Mode to Production to 1960* (Columbia University Press, 1985).

To our parents
Marjorie and Jay Bordwell
and Jean and Roger Thompson

CONTENTS

FILM FORM

FILM STYLE

PART IV

CRITICAL ANALYSIS OF FILMS

PART V

FILM HISTORY

TWELVE / FILM FORM AND FILM HISTORY   441

PREFACE

This book seeks to introduce the reader to the aesthetics of film. It assumes that the reader has no knowledge of cinema beyond the experience of movie-going. Although some aspects of the book may prove useful for people with considerable knowledge of film, our aim is to survey the fundamental aspects of cinema as an art form.

By stressing film as art, we necessarily ignore certain aspects of the medium. Industrial documentaries, instructional filmmaking, the social history of cinema or its impact as a mass medium—all these are important dimensions of cinema, and each would require a separate book for adequate treatment. Instead, this book seeks to isolate those basic features of film which can constitute it as an art. The book therefore directs itself at the person interested in how the film medium may give us experiences akin to those offered by painting, sculpture, music, literature, theater, architecture, or dance.

As we wrote this book, we envisioned readers of three particular sorts. First is the interested general reader, who wants to know a little more about the movies. Second is the student in a course in film appreciation, introduction to film, film criticism, or film aesthetics; for this reader, the book can function as a textbook. Third is the more advanced student of film, who may find here a convenient outline of principal issues and concepts and a set of suggestions for more specialized work.

Organizationally, *Film Art: An Introduction* offers a distinct approach to studying its topic. It might be possible to survey, willy-nilly, all contemporary approaches to film aesthetics, but we judged this to be too eclectic. Instead, we have sought an approach that would lead the reader in logical steps through various aspects of film aesthetics. Crucial to this approach is an emphasis on *the whole film*. Audiences experience entire films, not snippets.

If the particular film is the irreducible center of our inquiry, we need an approach that will help us understand it. The approach we have chosen emphasizes the film as an artifact—made in particular ways, having a certain wholeness and unity, existing in history. We can outline the approach in a series of questions.

How is a film created? To understand film as an art, we must first understand how human labor creates the artifact. This leads to a study of *film production. What kinds of films result from the production process?* We shall also examine various *types* and *genres* of films (Part I).

How does an entire film function? This book assumes that like all artworks, a film may be understood as a *formal* construct. This leads to a consideration of what form is and how it affects us, of basic principles of film form, and of narrative and nonnarrative forms in cinema (Part II). Matters of film form also demand that we consider the *techniques* which are characteristic of the film medium, for such techniques function within the form of the total film. Thus we analyze the artistic possibilities of the four primary film techniques: mise-en-scene, cinematography, editing, and sound (Part III).

How may we analyze a film critically? Armed with both a conception of film form and a knowledge of film technique, we can go on to analyze *specific films* as artworks. We analyze several such films as examples (Part IV).

How does film art change through history? Although a thorough history of cinema would require many volumes, here we can suggest how the formal aspects of film do not exist outside determinable historical contexts. We survey the most noteworthy *periods and movements in film history* to show how understanding form helps us locate films within history (Part V).

This approach to the entire film came from several years of teaching introductory film courses. As teachers, we wanted students to see and hear more in the films we studied, but it was evident that simply providing the "lecturer's view" would not teach students how to analyze films on their own. Ideally, we decided, students should master a repertory of *principles* which would help them examine films more closely. We became convinced that the best way to understand cinema is to use general principles of film form to help analyze specific films. Our success with this approach led us to decide that this book should be skills-centered. By learning basic concepts of film form and technique, the reader can sharpen his or her perception of any particular film.

The stress on skills has another consequence. You will note that we refer to a great many films. We expect that very few readers will have seen all of the films we mention, and certainly no teacher of a film course could possibly show every title. But because the book stresses the acquisition of conceptual skills, the reader need not see all of the films we mention in order to grasp the general principles. Many other films can be used to make the same points. For instance, the possibilities of camera movement can be as easily illustrated with *La Ronde* as with *La Grande Illusion;* to exemplify classical Hollywood filmmaking, *My Darling Clementine* will serve as well as *North by Northwest.* Indeed, although the book can serve as a syllabus for a course in cinema, it is also possible for a teacher to use different films to illustrate the book's ideas. (It would then be a useful exercise for the class to *contrast* the text example with the film shown, so as to specify even more clearly particular aspects of the film.) The book rests not on titles, but on concepts.

Film Art: An Introduction has certain unusual features. A book on film must be heavily illustrated, and most are. Many film books, however, utilize so-called production stills—photographs taken during filming, but usually not from the position of the motion picture camera. The result is a picture that does not correspond to any image in the finished film. We have used few production stills. Instead, the illustrations in this book are virtually all frame enlargements—magnified photographs from the actual film. Most of these illustrations come from 35mm prints of the films. (For more on frame enlargements, see the Notes and Queries for Chapter 1.)

Another unusual feature is the Notes and Queries section at the end of almost every chapter. In these sections we attempt to raise issues, provoke discussion, and suggest further reading and research. As chapter supplements, the Notes and Queries sections constitute a resource for the advanced undergraduate, the graduate student, and the interested general reader.

In all, we hope that this book will help readers to watch a greater variety of films with keener attention and to ask precise questions about the art of cinema.

NEW TO THIS EDITION

When we set out to write an introduction to film in 1976, we could not have anticipated that it would have met with a welcome warm enough to carry it through five editions. This version of *Film Art: An Introduction* seeks to enrich the ideas set forth in preceding editions. We have again tried to make the book more comprehensive, flexible, and up to date.

The book's approach to film form and technique remains constant from prior editions. As in our previous edition, we have tried to expand the book's range of coverage, including more examples from non-Western filmmakers, from recent films, and from independent and minority filmmakers in North America. The discussion of film production in Chapter 1 incorporates more material about the electronic and computer-based technologies that are currently revolutionizing filmmaking. Chapter 12's treatment of film history has been somewhat recast in the light of current scholarship; we have also added a section on contemporary Hollywood cinema and dropped three sections on topics that no longer seem central to an introductory course. These topics, and a full bibliography, can be found in our companion volume, *Film History: An Introduction*. As usual, we have updated the Notes and Queries sections to reflect recent developments in cinema studies.

We have also created a new chapter. Chapter 2 covers types of films—popular genres as well as fiction, documentary, animation, and experimental cinema. Previous editions considered these topics piecemeal throughout the book, and we are thankful to those readers and instructors who suggested that the ideas be drawn together and examined more closely. To accommodate this new chapter, we have eliminated seven sample analyses, some of them discussing films which are unfortunately no longer widely available for rental. We have added analyses of *Breathless* and *Do The Right Thing*.

One of the advantages of revising a textbook is that you have chances to rethink, recast, and even rescind. In principle, this means that you have a chance to make the whole thing better.

We think we have, and we are grateful to many people who have over the last twenty years helped us greatly: David Allen, Tino Balio, John Belton, Ralph Berets, Eileen Bowser, Edward Branigan, Martin Bresnick, Michael Budd, Peter Bukalski, Elaine Burrows of the British Film Institute, Richard B. Byrne, Jerome Carolfi, Corbin Carnell, Jerry Carlson, Kent Carroll, Paolo Cherchi Usai of George Eastman House, Jeffrey Chown, Gabrielle Claes and the staff of the Cinémathèque Royale de Belgique, Bruce Conner, Mary Corliss of the Museum of Modern Art Film Stills Department, Susan Dalton of the American Film Institute, Robert E. Davis, Dorothy Desmond, Kathleen Domenig, Maxine Fleckner-Ducey of the Wisconsin Center for Film and Theater Research, Don Fredericksen, Jon Gartenberg, Ernie Gehr, Kathe Geist, Douglas Gomery, Claudia Gorbman, Ron Gottesman, Eric Gunneson, Howard Harper, Denise Hartsough, Kevin Heffernan, Linda Henzl, Richard Hincha, Jan-Christopher Horak of the Munich Film Archive, Lea Jacobs, Kathryn Kalinak, Charles Keil, Laura Kipnis, Barbara Klinger, Don Larsson, Thomas M. Leitch, Gary London, José Lopez of New Yorker Films, Patrick Loughney of the Library of Congress Motion Picture Division, Mark McClelland of Films Inc., Roger L. Mayer of MGM Inc., Norman McLaren, Jackie Morris of the National Film Archive, Kazuto Ohira of Toho Films, Badia Rahman, Paul Rayton, Leo Salzman, Rob Silberman, Charles Silver of the Museum of Modern Art Film Study Center, Joseph Evans Slate, Harry W. Smith, Jeff Smith, Michael Snow, John C. Stubbs, Dan Talbot of New Yorker Films, Edyth von Slyck, and Chuck Wolfe.

In preparing this edition, we are grateful to several of the above, as well as to Ben Brewster, Noël Carroll, Bruce Jenkins and Mike Maggiore of the Walker Art Center, and Vance Kepley. We would like to thank the reviewers who responded to our revision plan: Paul Arthur, Montclair State University; Matthew Bernstein, Emory University; Robin Blaetz, Emory University; George Butte, Colorado College; Mary Carbine, University of Chicago; John T. Casey, St. Leo's College; Christine Catanzarite, Illinois State University; Elizabeth Ellsworth, University of Wisconsin at Madison; Jane Gaines, Duke University; Tim Hirsch, University of Wisconsin, Eau Claire; Mary Hurd, East Tennessee State University; Arthur Knight, College of William and Mary; William B. Larsen, University of Tennessee, Knoxville; Julie Levinson, Babson College; William Luhr, St. Peters College; Barry Mauer, University of Florida; Joan McGettigan, Penn State University; Joan Mellen, Temple University; Gloria Monti, Yale University; Alan Nadel, Rensselaer Polytechnic Institute; Ben Nyce, University of San Diego; Ruth Prigozy, Hofstra University; Matthew D. Ramsey, Ohio State University; Shawn Rosenheim, Williams College; Rob Sabal, University of Arizona; James Shepard, Williams

College; Richard Wesley Thiede, The Defiance College; John C. Tibbetts, University of Kansas; Dee Tudor, Oakton Community College; Geoffrey Waite, Cornell University; Margaret Ward, Wellesley College; Emmett J. Winn, Auburn University; Esther Yau, Occidental College; and Shari Zeck, Illinois State University.

As always, we thank our team of editors at McGraw-Hill: Curt Berkowitz, Nancy Blaine, and Cynthia Ward (as well as past editors Peter Labella and Roth Wilkofsky).

David Bordwell
Kristin Thompson

PART I

TYPES OF
FILMMAKING,
TYPES OF FILMS

THE WORK
OF FILM
PRODUCTION

We all know that films are like buildings, books, and symphonies—artifacts made by humans for human purposes. Television news programs and cable stations reveal technical details of production with segments on "The Making of . . ." and behind-the-scenes interviews with cast and crew members. Yet, sitting in a darkened theater watching an enthralling movie, we may find it difficult to remember that what we are seeing is not a natural object, like a flower or an asteroid. Cinema is so captivating that we tend to forget that movies are *made*. An understanding of the art of cinema depends initially on a recognition that a film is produced by both machines and human labor.

TECHNICAL FACTORS IN FILM PRODUCTION

Watching a film differs from viewing a painting, a stage performance, or even a slide show. A film presents us with *images* in *illusory* motion. What creates this sense of "moving pictures"?

For cinema to exist, a series of images must be displayed in rapid succession. A mechanism presents each image for a very short period and inserts a brief interval of blackness between the images. If slightly different images of the same object are displayed under these conditions, physiological and psychological processes in the viewer will create the illusion of seeing a moving image.

What are these processes? Since the nineteenth century, a prime candidate has been the process of "persistence of vision," the phenomenon by which an image lingers on the retina for a fraction of a second after the source has vanished. But this does not in itself explain why we would see movement rather than a succession of still images. Twentieth-century research has shown the problem to be more complex. We still do not know for certain how illusory movement is generated by cinema, but at least two features of the human visual system seem to be involved.

First is what is called *critical flicker fusion,* a term that describes the results of increasing the rate at which a light is flashed. Under film projection conditions, if a beam of light is broken more than 50 times per second, the viewer no longer sees pulses or bursts but rather an illusion of continuous light. A film is usually shot and projected at a rate of 24 frames per second. The projector shutter breaks the light beam once as a new frame is moving into place and once while that frame is held still within the gate. Thus each frame is actually projected onto the screen twice. This raises the number of flashes to the threshold of flicker fusion. Early silent films were shot at a lower rate (often 16 or 20 frames per second), and until engineers devised shutters that could break the beam more than once per frame, the projected image had a pronounced flicker. Hence the early slang term for movies, "flickers," which survives today when people call a film a "flick."

A second factor in creating cinema's illusion is *apparent motion.* This is the tendency of human vision to see movement when in fact there is none. In 1912, the Gestalt psychologist Max Wertheimer discovered that when two side-by-side lights were flashed at certain intervals, viewers perceived not two flashing lights but a single moving light. (The same effect can be seen on many neon advertising signs.) For a time researchers hypothesized that the viewer might be using some process of unconscious thought in creating the illusion of movement. Recent experimental work, however, suggests that apparent motion may owe something to specific "motion analyzers" in the human visual system. Any displacements, whether real or only projected on a screen, may automatically cause certain cells in the eye or brain to attribute movement to the stimuli.

Critical flicker fusion and apparent motion are quirks of our visual system. They are rarely triggered by naturally occurring events. Humans have devised particular machines to create the conditions for cinematic perception.

First, the images must be displayed in a *series.* They might be on a row of cards, as in the Mutoscope (Fig. 1.1), and flipped past the viewer to create the illusion of movement. More commonly, the images are inscribed on a strip of some flexible material. Optical toys such as the Zoetrope put their images on strips of paper (Fig. 1.2), but cinema as we know it uses a strip of celluloid as support for the series of images, which are called *frames.* If the images are to be put on a strip of film, cinema usually requires three machines to create and display those images. All three share a basic principle: A mechanism controls how light is admitted to the film, advances the strip of film a frame at a time, and exposes it to light for the proper interval. The three machines are:

1. *The camera* (Fig. 1.3). In a light-tight chamber, a drive mechanism feeds the motion picture film from a reel (a) past a lens (b) and aperture (c)

Fig. 1.1

Fig. 1.2

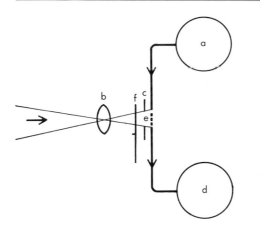

Fig. 1.3   The camera

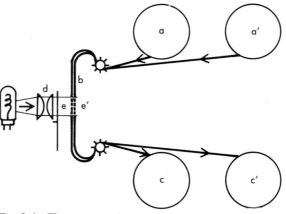

Fig. 1.4   The contact printer

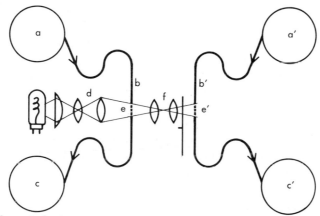

Fig. 1.5   The optical printer

to a take-up reel (d). The lens focuses light reflected from a scene onto each frame of film (e). The mechanism moves the film intermittently, with a brief pause while each frame is held in the aperture. A shutter (f) admits light through the lens only when each frame is unmoving and ready for exposure. The standard shooting rate for sound film is 24 frames per second (25 in some European productions).

2. *The printer* (Figs. 1.4, 1.5). Printers exist in various designs, but all consist of light-tight chambers that drive a negative or positive roll of film from a reel (a) past an aperture (b) to a take-up reel (c). Simultaneously, a roll of unexposed film (a', c') moves through the aperture (b or b'), either intermittently or continuously. By means of a lens (d), light beamed through the aperture prints the image (e) on the unexposed film (e'). The two rolls of film may pass through the aperture simultaneously. Figure 1.4 diagrams a printer of this sort, called a *contact printer*. Contact printers are used for making work prints and release prints, as well as for various special effects that combine portions of images filmed separately.

Alternatively, light coming through the original may be beamed to the unexposed roll through lenses, mirrors, or prisms [as in (f) in Fig. 1.5]. This

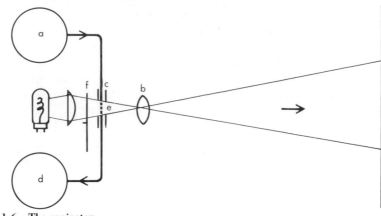

Fig. 1.6   The projector

sort of printer is known as an *optical printer* and is used for rephotographing camera images, for making prints of different gauges, and for certain special effects, such as freeze-frames.

3. *The projector* (Fig. 1.6). A drive mechanism feeds the exposed and developed film from a reel (a) past a lens (b) and aperture (c) to a take-up reel (d). Light is beamed through the images (e) and magnified by the lens for projection on a screen. Again, a mechanism moves the film intermittently past the aperture, while a shutter (f) admits light only when each frame is pausing. For the movement effect to occur, the film must display at least 12 frames per second; the shutter must also block and reveal each frame at least twice in order to reduce the flicker effect on the screen. The standard projection rate for sound film is 24 frames per second, with the shutter displaying each frame twice.

Camera, printer, and projector are all variants of the same basic machine. Both the camera and the projector control the intermittent movement of the film past a light source. The crucial difference is that the camera gathers light from outside the machine and focuses it on the film, whereas in the projector the machine produces the light which shines through the film onto a surface outside. The printer combines both other devices. Like a projector, it controls the passage of light through exposed film (the original negative or positive). Like a camera, it focuses light to form an image (on the unexposed roll of film).

The filmmaker can create *non*photographic images on the film strip by drawing, punching holes, etching, or painting. Most filmmakers, however, have relied on the camera, the printer, and other photographic technology. Thus the images that we see in movement are usually created photographically. Like photographic film, motion picture film consists of a transparent *base,* which supports an *emulsion* (layers of gelatin containing light-sensitive materials). Black-and-white film emulsion contains grains of silver halide. When light from the environment strikes them, it sets off a chemical reaction which makes the crystals cluster together to form tiny specks. Billions of these specks are formed on each frame of exposed film. Taken together, these specks comprise a latent image which corresponds to the density of light in the scene filmed. Chemical processing makes the latent image visible as a configuration of black grains on a white ground. The resulting image is either a negative one, from which positive prints can be struck, or a positive one (called a *reversal image*).

Color film emulsion consists of three additional gelatin layers, each containing a chemical dye sensitive to a primary color: red, green, or blue. During exposure and development, the silver halide crystals create an image by reacting with the dyes and other organic chemicals in the emulsion layers. With color negative film, the developing process yields an image that is complementary to the original color values. Color reversal processing yields a positive image with colors conforming to the original scene. Most professional filmmaking uses negative emulsion so as to allow better control of print quality and larger numbers of positive prints to be made. The reversal process is chiefly confined to amateur work.

In order to run satisfactorily through camera, printer, and projector, the strip of film is perforated along one or both edges, so that small teeth (sprockets) in the machines can seize the perforations (sprocket holes) and pull the film at a uniform rate and smoothness. The film strip also usually reserves space for a sound track. All these features of the physical film have been standardized around the world. The width of the film strip is called the *gauge* and is measured in millimeters (mm). Although many gauges have been experimented with, the internationally standardized ones are Super 8mm, 16mm, 35mm, and 70mm.

Super 8mm (Fig. 1.7) was for several decades a popular gauge for amateurs and experimental filmmakers, but portable video formats have largely eclipsed it in recent years. Figure 1.8 shows 16mm film, which is used for both amateur and professional film production. Most film study courses show 16mm prints of films. The standard professional gauge is 35mm, and most commercial theaters show 35mm prints. Figures 1.9 and 1.10 show frames from *On the Waterfront* and *Jurassic Park* respectively. Another pro-

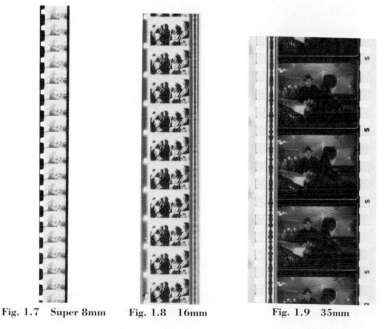

Fig. 1.7   Super 8mm   Fig. 1.8   16mm   Fig. 1.9   35mm   Fig. 1.10   35mm

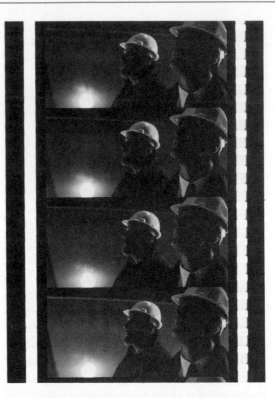

Fig. 1.11   70mm

Fig. 1.12   Imax system

fessional gauge is 70mm film, which has since the 1950s been used for spectacle-centered projects (e.g., Fig. 1.11, frames from *The Hunt for Red October*).

Usually image quality increases with the width of the film because a larger picture area yields more definition and detail. All other things being equal, 35mm provides significantly better picture quality than does 16mm, and 70mm is superior to both. The largest picture area currently available for public screenings is that offered by the Imax system. The film is 70mm gauge, but the images run horizontally along the film strip, allowing each image to be ten times larger than 35mm and triple the size of 70mm (Fig. 1.12). This enables the image to be projected on a very large screen with no loss of quality.

The print we see of a film, however, may not be in the gauge of the original. Most films studied in cinema courses were originally shot in 35mm but are shown in 16mm. During the 1950s and 1960s, several films were produced and shown in 70mm, but even archives seldom show them in that gauge today. Often, quality deteriorates when a film shot on one gauge is transferred to another. Thus a 35mm print of Keaton's *The General* will almost certainly be photographically superior to a 16mm print, whereas a film shot on Super 8 will look fuzzy and grainy if printed and projected in 35mm. Independent filmmakers who work in 16mm face the problem of blowing up their negative so as to minimize loss of photographic quality in the theatrical gauge of 35mm.

Not all transfers among gauges compromise quality. Today films released in 70mm are shot on 35mm negative film. Due to improved film stocks, there is no significant decline when the image is blown up to 70mm. Also, a format known as Super 16mm has an improved image quality if blown up to 35mm.

Usually recorded sound accompanies the images. The sound track may be either *magnetic* or *optical*. In the magnetic type, one or more strips of magnetic recording tape run along the film's edges. During projection, the film's track is "read" by a sound head similar to that on a tape recorder. The 70mm frames in Figure 1.11 have a stereophonic magnetic sound track (running along both edges of the film strip).

An optical sound track encodes sonic information in the form of patches of light and dark in a parallel line running alongside the frames. During production, electrical impulses from a microphone are translated into pulsations of light which are photographically inscribed on the moving film strip. When the film is projected, the optical track produces varying intensities of light which are translated back into electrical impulses and then into sound waves. In the first decades of sound filmmaking, the sound was recorded optically during production, but now it is recorded on magnetic tape, then optically transferred onto film late in the production process.

At present, most film prints shown in theaters and colleges have optical sound tracks. An optical sound track usually encodes the sound as *variable area*, a wavy contour of black and white within the sound strip. The 16mm frames in Figure 1.8 have a variable-area optical sound track on the right side; the 35mm strip in Figure 1.9 utilizes a variable-area optical track running down the left.

A film's sound track may be monophonic or stereophonic. The 35mm film strip in Fig. 1.9 has a monophonic optical track, whereas the 35mm strip in Fig. 1.10 has a stereophonic track, indicated by the two dark squiggles running down the left side. Some stereophonic or multichannel sound uses a digital format. To reproduce digital sound in the theater, the projector scans marks running along the film's perforations or between the picture area and the optical sound track. An example of the latter system is shown in our *Jurassic Park* strip (Fig. 1.10). Here the information encoded on the film controls a digital compact disc of the sound track.

Specific machines, then, create a film from a raw material—a photo-chemically sensitive strip of perforated celluloid of some standardized gauge, with picture and sound information imbedded in it. Important as technology is, however, it is only part of the story.

SOCIAL FACTORS IN FILM PRODUCTION

Machines don't make movies by themselves. Film production transforms raw materials into a product through the application of machinery *and* human labor. But human labor may be organized in different ways, and the options are affected by economic and social factors.

Most films go through three general phases of production.

1. *Preparation.* The idea for the film is developed and usually committed to paper in some form. At this phase, the filmmaker or filmmakers begin to acquire funds to make, publicize, and distribute the film.

2. *Shooting.* At this stage, images and sounds are created on the film strip. More specifically, the filmmaker produces *shots.* A shot is a series of frames produced by the camera in an uninterrupted operation. The filmmaker also records or creates sounds to accompany the shots.

3. *Assembly.* At this stage, which may overlap with the shooting phase, the images and sounds are put together in their final form.

Not every film goes through every step. A home movie might involve very little preparation and might never undergo any final assembly. A compilation documentary might not require the shooting of any new footage, only the assembly of existing clips from libraries and archives. On the whole, though, most films go through these production phases.

The organization of production tasks at each phase can vary significantly. It is possible for one person to do everything: plan the film, finance it, perform in it, run the camera, record the sound, and put it all together. More commonly, though, different tasks are assigned to different people, making each job more or less specialized. This is the phenomenon of *division of labor,* a process that occurs in most of the tasks any social group undertakes. Various jobs are assigned to different individuals. Even a single job may be broken down into smaller tasks, which then may be assigned to specialists. In the framework of filmmaking, the principle of division of labor yields different *modes,* or social organizations, of film production and different *roles* for individuals within those modes. The overall preparation, shooting, and assembly stages remain, but they take place within different social contexts.

■ MODES OF PRODUCTION: THE STUDIO PROCESS

We can conveniently start by looking at the most detailed and specialized division of labor—that present in the *studio* mode of production. This will allow us to trace the amazing variety of tasks that a film can require. We will

Fig. 1.13

then be in a better position to understand how those tasks can be accomplished in other modes of production.

A studio is a company in the business of manufacturing films. The most famous examples are the studios that flourished in Hollywood between the 1920s and the 1960s—Paramount, Warner Bros., Columbia, and so on. Under the classic studio system, the company owned its own filmmaking equipment and an extensive physical plant, and it retained most of its workers on long-term contract. (In Fig. 1.13, a World War II–era publicity photo, MGM studio head Louis B. Mayer, front row center, shows off his stable of contract stars.) The studio central management planned the projects, then delegated authority to individual supervisors, who in turn assembled casts and crews from the studio's pool of workers.

The classic studio system has frequently been compared to industrial assembly line manufacture, in which a manager supervises a number of workers, each repeating a particular task at a rigid rate and in fixed order. The analogy suggests that the Hollywood studios of the 1930s cranked out films the way that General Motors turned out cars. But the analogy is not exact, since each film is different, not a replica of a prototype. A better term for studio mass-production filmmaking is probably *serial manufacture*. Here skilled specialists collaborate to create a unique product while still adhering to a blueprint prepared by management.

The centralized studio production system remains viable in some parts of the world (such as China and Hong Kong) and for some types of film (especially animated films). But the American production companies of today do not manufacture films so much as acquire them. Each film is planned as a unique "package," with director, actors, staff, and technicians gathered specifically for this project. The studio may have contractual relations with a prized director, star, or producer, but any particular film starts with the creation of a particular package around free-lance workers. The production company may own a physical plant which can be used for the project, as some of the surviving studios do, but in most cases the producer rents or acquires facilities for the project. The producer will also subcontract particular tasks to other firms, such as special-effects companies.

Despite the growth of the package system, however, the specific production stages and the assignment of roles remain similar to what they were in the heyday of more centralized studio production.

■ THE PREPRODUCTION PHASE

In studio filmmaking, the preparation phase is known as *preproduction*. At this point, two roles emerge as most critical: that of producer and that of writer.

The role of the *producer* is chiefly financial and organizational. She or he may be an "independent" producer, unearthing film projects and trying to convince production companies or distributors to finance the film. Or the producer may work for a studio and generate ideas for films. A studio may also hire a producer to put together a particular package.

The producer's job is to develop the project through the script process, to obtain financial support, and to arrange for the personnel who will work on the film. During shooting and assembly, the producer usually acts as the liaison between the writer or director and the company that is financing the film. After the film is completed, the producer will often have the task of arranging the distribution, promotion, and marketing of the film and of monitoring the paying back of the funds that underwrite the project.

Outside Hollywood, a single producer may take on all these tasks, but in the contemporary American film industry the producer's work is further subdivided. The *executive producer* is usually remote from the day-to-day process, being the individual who arranged the financing for the project or obtained the literary property. Subordinate to the executive producer is the *line producer.* She or he is the actual organizer of the film, monitoring phases of production. The line producer is assisted by an *associate producer,* who acts as a liaison with laboratories or technical personnel.

The chief task of the *writer* is to prepare the script. Sometimes the writer will set the process in motion by sending a script to his or her agent, who submits it to an independent producer or a production company for consideration. Alternatively, an experienced screenwriter meets with a producer in a "pitch session," where the writer can propose several ideas that might become scripts. And sometimes the producer or the director has an idea for a film and hires a script writer to work it up. The latter course of action is particularly common if the producer, ever on the lookout for ideas, has bought the rights to a novel or play and wants it *adapted* into a film.

Fig. 1.14

The script goes through several stages. These stages include a *treatment*, a synopsis of the action; one or more full-length scripts; and a final version, the *shooting script*. Extensive rewriting is common. Often the director will want to reshape the script. For example, in the original script of *Witness* the protagonist was Rachel, the Amish widow with whom police detective John Book falls in love. The romance, and Rachel's confused feelings about Book, formed the central plot line. But the director, Peter Weir, wanted to emphasize the clash between pacifism and violence. So William Kelley and Earl Wallace revised their script to emphasize the mystery plot line and to center the action on Book, whose investigation draws urban crime into the peaceful Amish community.

Even the shooting script is seldom identical to the finished film. It is often altered during the shooting phase. During the filming of the 1954 *A Star Is Born*, the scene in which Judy Garland sings "The Man That Got Away" was reshot at several points in the production, each time with different dialogue supplied by the script writer, Moss Hart. Script scenes that have been shot may also be condensed, rearranged, or dropped entirely in the assembly stage. Figure 1.14 is a publicity still for Alfred Hitchcock's *Notorious,* showing a scene which was eliminated from the final film. (Indeed, the actress sitting next to Cary Grant does not appear in the film at all.)

If the producer or director finds one writer's script unsatisfactory, other writers may be hired to revise it. As you may imagine, this often leads to conflicts about which writer or writers deserve screen credit for the film. In the American film industry, these disputes are adjudicated by the Screen Writers' Guild.

As the script reaches its final state, the executive producer has been arranging the film's finances. He or she has sought out a director and perhaps also stars to make the package a promising·investment. The producer must now prepare a budget spelling out *above-the-line costs* (the costs of literary property, script writer, director, and cast) and *below-the-line costs* (the expenses allocated for the crew, the shooting and assembly phases, insurance, and publicity). The sum of above- and below-the-line costs is called the *negative cost* (that is, the total cost of producing the film's master negative). In 1994, the average Hollywood negative cost ran to about $35 million, with advertising and print costs adding about $15 million more per picture.

The producer, or the line producer, must also prepare a daily schedule for shooting and assembling the film. This will be done with an eye on the budget. For example, since the film will be shot out of continuity, all shots using a certain setting or certain personnel can be filmed during one stretch of time. If a star is forced to join the production late or leave it at intervals, the producer must plan to "shoot around" the performer. Keeping all such contingencies in mind, the producer and his or her staff are expected to come up with the most efficient schedule of several weeks or months that juggles cast, crew, locations, and even seasons and geography.

■ THE PRODUCTION PHASE

In Hollywood parlance, the shooting phase is frequently called *production*, even though "production" is also the term for the entire process of making a film.

Although the *director* is often involved in preproduction, he or she is primarily responsible for overseeing the shooting and assembly phases. Traditionally, the director puts the script on film by coordinating the various aspects of the film medium. Within most film industries, the director is considered the single person most responsible for the look and sound of the finished film.

Because of the specialized division of labor in large-scale production, many aspects of the task of shooting the film must be delegated to other workers who consult with the director.

1. In the preparation phase, the director has already begun work with the *set* unit, or *production design* unit. This is headed by a *production designer*. The production designer is in charge of visualizing the film's settings. This unit creates drawings and plans that determine the architecture and the color schemes of the sets. Under the production designer's supervision, an *art director* supervises the construction and painting of the sets. The *set decorator*, often someone with experience in interior decoration, modifies the sets for specific filming purposes, supervising a staff who finds props and a *set dresser* who arranges things on the set during shooting. The *costume designer* is in charge of planning and executing the wardrobe for the production. A *location scout* may find settings which the art director will incorporate into the film.

Working with the production designer, a graphic artist may be assigned to produce a *storyboard*, a series of comic-strip-like sketches of the shots in each scene, including notations about costume, lighting, camera work, and other matters. Figure 1.15 is taken from the storyboard for Hitchcock's film *The Birds.* Most filmmakers do not storyboard every scene, but action sequences and shots using special effects and complicated camera work tend to be storyboarded in detail. In such instances, the storyboard gives the cinematography unit and the special-effects unit a preliminary sense of what the finished shots should look like. Before shooting *Godfather III,* Francis Ford Coppola had his storyboard videotaped, with extras' voices supplying the dialogue. Some films may use computer-generated storyboards to "previsualize" stunts or special effects.

2. During the shooting, the director relies on what is called the *director's crew.* This includes:

a. The *script supervisor,* known in the classic studio era as a "script girl." (Today one-fifth of Hollywood script supervisors are male.) The script supervisor is in charge of all details of *continuity* from shot to shot. The script supervisor keeps track of details of performers' appearance (in the last scene, was the carnation in the left or right buttonhole?), props, lighting, movement, camera position, and the running time of each scene.

b. The *first assistant director,* who, with the director, plans out each day's shooting schedule and sets up each shot for the director's approval.

c. The *second assistant director,* who is the liaison among the first assistant director, the camera crew, and the electricians' crew.

d. The *third assistant director,* who serves as messenger for director and staff.

e. The *dialogue coach,* who feeds performers their lines and speaks the lines of offscreen characters during shots of other performers.

f. The *second unit director,* who films stunts, location footage, action scenes, and the like, at a distance from where principal shooting is taking place.

3. The most publicly visible group of workers is the *cast.* The cast likely includes *stars,* well-known players assigned to major roles and likely to attract audiences. Figure 1.16 shows 1930s star Greta Garbo in a *screen test,* a procedure used to determine casting and to try out lighting, costume, makeup, and camera positions in relation to the actor. The cast also includes *supporting players,* or performers in secondary roles; *minor players;* and *extras,* those anonymous persons who pass by in the street, come together for crowd scenes, and fill distant desks in large office sets. One of the director's major jobs is to shape the performances of the cast. Most directors will spend a good deal of time explaining how a line or gesture should be rendered, reminding the actor of the place of this scene in the overall film, and helping the actor create a coherent performance. The first assistant director usually works with the extras and takes charge of arranging crowd scenes.

On some productions, more specialized cast members require particular coordination. *Stunt persons* will probably be supervised by a *stunt coordinator;* professional dancers will work with a *choreographer.* If animals join the cast, they will be handled by a *wrangler.* (*Mad Max beyond Thunderdome* carries the memorable credit line "Pig Wrangler.")

Fig. 1.15

Fig. 1.16

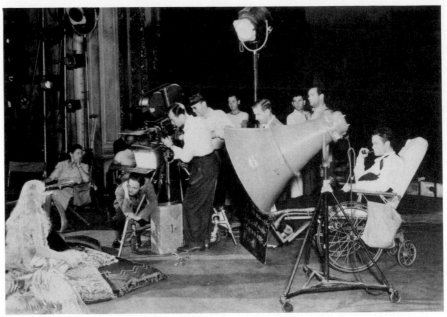

Fig. 1.17

4. Another unit of specialized labor is the *photography unit.* The leader here is the *cinematographer,* also known as the *director of photography* or *DP.* The cinematographer is an expert on photographic processes, lighting, and manipulation of the camera. He or she consults with the director on how each scene will be lit and filmed. In Figure 1.17, on the set of *Citizen Kane,* Orson Welles directs from his wheelchair on the far right, cinematographer Gregg Toland crouches below the camera, and actress Dorothy Comingore kneels at the left. (The script supervisor is in the background left.)

The cinematographer supervises:

a. The *camera operator,* who runs the machine and who may also have assistants to load the camera, adjust and follow focus, push a dolly, and so on.

b. The *key grip,* the person who supervises the *grips.* These workers carry and arrange equipment, props, and elements of the setting and lighting.

c. The *gaffer,* the head electrician who supervises the placement and rigging of the lights. In Hollywood production the gaffer's assistant is called the *best boy.*

5. Parallel to the photography unit is the *sound unit.* This is headed by the *production recordist* (also called the *sound mixer*). The recordist's principal responsibility is to record dialogue during shooting. Typically the recordist will use a portable tape recorder, several sorts of microphones, and a console to balance and combine the inputs from various microphones. The recordist will also attempt to tape some ambient sound when no actors are speaking. These bits of "room tone" will later be inserted to fill pauses in the dialogue.

The recordist's staff includes:

a. The *boom operator*, who manipulates the boom microphone and conceals radio microphones on the actors.

b. The *"third man,"* who places other microphones, lays sound cables, and is in charge of controlling ambient sound.

Some productions have a "sound designer" who enters the process during the preparation phase and who, like the production designer, plans a "sonic style" appropriate for the entire film.

6. A *special-effects* unit is charged with preparing and executing process shots, miniatures, matte work, computer-generated graphics, and other technical shots. Figure 1.18 shows a miniature used in the making of *The Comedians.* During the planning phase, the director and the production designer will have determined what effects will be needed, and the special-effects unit consults with the director and the cinematographer on an ongoing basis.

7. A miscellaneous unit includes a *make-up staff,* a *costume staff, hairdressers,* and *drivers* (who transport cast and crew).

8. During shooting, the producer is represented by a unit often called the *producer's crew.* This consists of the *production manager,* also known as the *production coordinator* or the *associate producer.* This person will manage daily organizational business, such as arranging for meals and accommodations. A *production accountant* (or *production auditor*) monitors expenditures, a *production secretary* coordinates telephone communication among units and with the producer, and *production assistants* (PAs) run errands. Newcomers to the film industry often start out working as production assistants.

All this coordinated effort, involving perhaps hundreds of workers, results in many thousands of feet of exposed film and recorded sound-on-tape. Every shot called for in the script or storyboard or decided on by the director usually has several *takes,* or unique versions, of that shot. For instance, if the finished film requires one shot of an actor saying a line, the director may

Fig. 1.18

shoot several takes of the speech, each time asking the actor to vary the expression or posture. Not all takes are printed, and probably only one of those becomes the shot included in the finished film.

In shooting, the separate shots are often filmed "out of continuity"—that is, in the most convenient order. If a family's home is to be seen at both the beginning and the ending of the film, it is easier and cheaper to photograph all shots in the home at one time. Sometimes this constraint can help the film. For *Diner* Barry Levinson filmed all the diner scenes last, hoping that the actors had come to know each other well and could give more natural performances than they could at the beginning of the shoot. Lawrence Bender, producer of Quentin Tarentino's controversial *Reservoir Dogs,* scheduled the most conventional scenes to be shot first, so that the initial screenings of footage would increase the backers' confidence in the project.

Because shooting usually proceeds out of continuity, the director and crew must have some way of labeling each take. During filming, one of the cinematographer's staff holds a *clapboard* up before the camera at the start of each shot. The clapboard records the production, scene, shot, and take. The clapboard's hinged arm makes a cracking sound that helps the editor to synchronize sound and picture later. (See Fig. 1.19, from Jean-Luc Godard's *La Chinoise.* The white "X" marks this as the exact frame with which the cracking sound should synchronize.) Thus every take is identified for future reference. A more advanced method of synchronization involves automatically fogging the frame just as the take starts, while a tone is sent to the audiotape recording the sound.

Fig. 1.19

In the course of filming, most directors and technicians follow an organized procedure. Assume that a scene is to be filmed. While crews set up the lighting and test the sound recording, the director rehearses the actors and instructs the cinematographer. The director then supervises the filming of a *master shot.* The master shot records the entire action and dialogue of the scene. There may be several takes of the master shot. Then portions of the scene are restaged and shot in closer views or from different angles. These other shots are called *coverage,* and each of them may require many takes. Contemporary practice is to shoot a great deal of coverage, occasionally by using two or more cameras filming at the same time. The script supervisor checks to ensure that continuity details are consistent within coverage shots.

When special effects are to be included, the shooting phase must carefully plan for them. In many cases actors will be filmed against neutral blue backgrounds so that their figures may be inserted into footage shot elsewhere. (This process is called *matte work* or *composite work.*) Or the director will film performers with the understanding that other material will be composited into the frame. For the climax of *Jurassic Park,* the actors were shot in the set of the visitor center's rotunda, but the velociraptors and the tyrannosaurus rex were computer-generated images added later (Fig. 1.20).

Fig. 1.20

■ POSTPRODUCTION

Members of the film industry today call the assembly phase of filmmaking *postproduction.* Yet this phase does not begin simply when shooting is com-

SOME TERMS AND ROLES
IN FILM PRODUCTION

The rise of "packaged" productions, pressures from unionized workers, and other factors have led producers to credit everyone who worked on a film. (The credits for *Who Framed Roger Rabbit?* contained 771 names.) Moreover, the specialization of mass-production filmmaking has created its own jargon. Some of the most colorful terms ("gaffer," "best boy") are explained in the text. Here are some other terms that you might see in a film's credits.

ACE: After the name of the editor; abbreviation for the American Cinema Editors, a professional association.

ASC: After the name of the director of photography; abbreviation for the American Society of Cinematographers, a professional association. The British eqivalent is the BSC.

Additional photography: A crew shooting footage apart from the *principal photography* supervised by the director of photography.

Casting director: Searches for and auditions performers for the film.

Clapper boy: Crew member who operates the clapboard that identifies each take.

Dialogue editor: Sound editor specializing in making sure recorded speech is audible.

Dolly grip: Crew member who pushes the dolly that carries the camera, either from one setup to another or during a take for moving camera shots.

Foley artist: A sound-effects specialist who creates sounds of body movement by walking or by moving materials across large trays of different substances (sand, earth, glass, and so on). Named for Jack Foley, a pioneer in postproduction sound.

Greenery man: Crew member who chooses and maintains trees, shrubs, and grass in settings.

Lead man: Member of set crew responsible for tracking down various props and items of decor for the set.

Loader: Member of photography unit who loads and unloads camera magazines, as well as logging the shots taken and sending the film to the laboratory.

Matte artist: Member of special-effects unit who paints backdrops which are then photographically incorporated into a shot in order to suggest a particular setting.

Model maker: (1) Member of production design unit who prepares architectural models for sets to be built. (2) Member of the special-effects unit who fabricates scale models of locales, vehicles, or characters to be filmed as substitutes for full-size ones.

Optical effects: Laboratory workers responsible for such effects as fades and dissolves, as well as matte shots and other special photographic processes.

Property master: Member of set crew who supervises the use of all *props,* or movable objects, in the film.

Publicist, Unit publicist: Member of producer's crew who creates and distributes promotional material regarding the production. The publicist may arrange for press and television interviews with the director and stars, and for coverage of the production in the mass media.

Scenic artist: Member of set crew responsible for painting surfaces of set.

Steadicam operator: Camera operator responsible for making shots with the gyroscopically balanced body rig patented as the Steadicam.

Still photographer: Member of crew who takes photographs of scenes and "behind-the-scenes" shots of cast members and others. These photographs may be used to check lighting or set design or color, and many will be used in promoting and publicizing the film.

Timer, Color timer: Laboratory worker who inspects the negative film and who adjusts the printer light to achieve consistency of color across the finished product.

Video assist: The use of a video camera mounted alongside the motion picture camera to check lighting, framing, or performances. In this way, the director and the cinematographer can try out a shot or scene on tape before committing it to film.

pleted. Postproduction staff members work steadily, if sometimes behind the scenes, throughout shooting.

Before the shooting has begun, the director or producer has probably hired an *editor* (also known as the *supervising editor*). This person has the responsibility of cataloguing and assembling the various takes produced during shooting.

Because each shot usually exists in several takes, because the film is shot out of continuity, and because the master-shot/coverage approach yields so much footage, the editor's job can be a vast one. A 90-minute 35mm feature, which comprises about 8000 feet of film, may have been carved out of 500,000 feet of exposed footage. For this reason, postproduction on major Hollywood pictures has become a lengthy process. Sometimes several editors and assistants will be brought in.

Typically, the editor receives the processed footage from the laboratory as quickly as possible. This footage is known as the *dailies,* or the *rushes.* The editor inspects the dailies, leaving it to the *assistant editor* to synchronize image and sound and to sort the takes by scene. The editor will meet with the director to examine the dailies or, if the production is filming far away, the editor will call to inform the director of how the footage looks. Since retaking shots is costly and troublesome, constant checking of the dailies is important for spotting any problems with focus, exposure, framing, or other visual factors.

As the footage accumulates, the editor assembles the shots into a *rough cut*—the film loosely strung in sequence, without sound effects or music. Some films are notorious for having gargantuan rough cuts: That of *Heaven's Gate* ran over six hours, that of *Apocalypse Now* seven and a half. Still, even the average rough cut is significantly longer than the finished film. From this the editor, in consultation with the director, builds a *fine cut,* or *final cut.* The material not used comprises the *outtakes.*

Until the mid-1980s, editors cut and spliced the *work print,* footage printed from the camera negative. In trying out their options, editors were obliged to rearrange the shots physically. Now many films are edited electronically. The dailies are transferred to videotape, then to laserdisc or to a hard drive. The editor enters notes on each take directly into a computer database. Such electronic editing systems, usually known as *nonlinear* systems, permit random access to the entire store of footage. The editor can call up any shot, paste it alongside any other shots, trim it, or junk it. Some systems allow special effects and music to be tried out as well. Although nonlinear systems have speeded up the process of cutting, the editor usually asks for a work print of key scenes in order to check for color, details, and pacing.

While the editor, director, and staff are shaping a final cut, a *second unit* may be shooting footage to fill in certain spots. Another specialized unit will be preparing superimposed titles, to be used in the opening and perhaps elsewhere in the film. Further laboratory or special-effects work may also be necessary. Computers may erase the wires holding "flying" players aloft or increase the size of crowds by reduplicating a patch of a shot. Digitally generated imagery can be used to cover mistakes in shooting. After Brandon

Lee's demise interrupted filming of the *The Crow*, digital compositers copied his image from certain scenes and inserted it into sequences filmed after his death.

Once the shots are arranged in something approaching final form, the *sound editor*, also known as the *sound effects editor*, takes charge of building up the sound track. With the editor, the director, and the composer, the sound editor goes through the film and chooses where music and effects will be placed, a process known as *spotting*. The sound editor may have a staff whose members specialize in recording or cutting dialogue, music, or sound effects.

One of the sound editor's principal duties is supervising the rerecording of dialogue after filming. This has become known as *automated dialogue replacement* (ADR for short). Although dialogue is recorded on the set, this may serve only as a guide track. Then the actors are brought into the sound studio to rerecord their lines (a process called *dubbing*, or *looping*). In addition, if there is a recording error or muffled line in the original recording, dubbing is used to replace it. Nonsynchronized dialogue, such as the babble of a crowd, will also be added. In addition, the sound editor will loop alternative lines of dialogue that eliminate phrases that may be found offensive; this sanitized track will be used in broadcast television and airline versions of the film.

The sound editor also adds sound effects. Most of the sound effects the audience hears in a studio-produced film are not recorded at the moment the image is shot. The sound editor draws on a library of stock sounds, utilizes effects recorded "wild" on location, and creates particular effects for this film. Sound editors routinely manufacture footsteps, cars crashing, doors closing, pistol shots, a fist thudding into flesh (often produced by whacking a watermelon with an axe). In *Terminator 2*, for example, the sound of the T-1000 cyborg passing through cell bars is that of dog food sliding slowly out of a can.

Like picture editing, sound editing has been greatly assisted by computer technology. Now the editor can store recorded sounds in a database, classifying and rearranging them in any way desired. A sound's qualities can be modified digitally—clipping off high or low frequencies, changing pitch, reverberation, equalization, or speed. The boom and throb of underwater action in *The Hunt for Red October* were slowed down and reprocessed from such mundane sources as a diver plunging into a swimming pool, water bubbling from a garden hose, and the hum of Disneyland's air-conditioning machinery. One technician on the film calls digital editing "sound sculpting."

During the spotting of the sound track, the film's *composer* has entered the assembly phase as well. Reviewing a fairly advanced cut of the film, the composer decides, along with the director and sound editor, where music should be inserted. The composer then compiles cue sheets that list exactly where the music will go and how long it should run. The composer proceeds to write the score, although she or he will probably not orchestrate it personally. While the composer is working, the rough cut will be synchronized with a "temp dub," musical accompaniment from preexisting sources that approximates the sort of music that will eventually be written. With the aid of a "click track," which synchronizes the beat of the music to the finished film, the score will be recorded and form part of the sound editor's material.

All these sounds are recorded on different pieces of magnetic tape. Each person's voice, each musical passage, and each sound effect may occupy a separate track. At a final mixing session, the director, editor, and sound-effects editor put dozens of such separate tracks together into a single master track on 35mm magnetic film. The sound specialist who performs the task is the *rerecording mixer*. Often the dialogue track is organized first, then sound effects are balanced with that, and then music is added to create the final mix. Often there will need to be equalization, filtering, and other adjustments to the track. Once fully mixed, the master track is transferred onto sound recording film, which encodes the magnetic sound as optical sound.

The film's *camera negative*, which was used to make the dailies and the work print, is normally too precious to serve as the source for final prints. Instead, from the camera negative footage the laboratory draws an *interpositive*, which in turn furnishes an *internegative*. This negative footage is assembled in accordance with the final cut and becomes the source for future copies. Then the master sound track is synchronized with it.

The positive prints, complete with picture and sound, are called *answer prints*. The producer, director, and cinematographer check the answer print for exposure, color values, and other qualities. If they are dissatisfied, an adjusted answer print is made. Once an answer print has been approved, *release prints* are made for distribution. These are the copies shown in theaters.

In contemporary Hollywood practice, the work of production does not end with the final theatrical version. In consultation with the producer and director, the postproduction staffs prepare airline and broadcast television versions of the film. In some cases, particular versions may be prepared for different countries. The European version of David Lynch's *Wild at Heart* contained footage that was believed to be too violent for American audiences, and Sergio Leone's *Once Upon a Time in America* was completely rearranged for its American release because its American producers considered the original plot too complicated. At the same time, laboratory personnel, often working with the director and the cinematographer, may transfer the film to a master videotape, which will form the basis of videocassette and laserdisc versions. This video transfer process often involves new judgments about color quality and sound balance.

The studio mode of production is characterized by a minute breakdown of labor. With this comes an attempt to control every aspect of the filmmaking process by means of paper records. At the start there will be versions of the script; during shooting reports will be written on camera footage, sound recording, special-effects work, and laboratory results; in the assembly phase there will be logs of shots catalogued in editing, and a variety of cue sheets for music, mixing, looping, and title layout. Once planning and execution are committed to paper, the production workers can control, or at least adjust to, unplanned events.

This is never wholly successful. Every case study of a large-scale studio production will attest to the compromises, accidents, and foul-ups that plague the process. Weather may throw the shooting off schedule. Disagreements about the script may result in a director's being fired. Last-minute changes demanded by the producer or director may require that some scenes be reshot. Studio production is a constant struggle between the desire to plan the film completely and the inevitable "noise" created by the sheer complexity of such a detailed division of labor.

Many fictional films, such as *Singin' in the Rain*, have been made about the studio mode of production. Some films set their action at particular phases of the process. Federico Fellini's *8½* concerns itself with the preparation, or preproduction, stage of a film that is abandoned before shooting starts. François Truffaut's *Day for Night* takes place during the shooting phase of a production marred by the death of one of the cast. The action of Brian De Palma's *Blow Out* occurs during the sound editing process of a low-budget slasher movie.

■ INDEPENDENT PRODUCTION

Not all films that use the studio mode of production are large-budget projects financed by major companies. Many so-called "independent" films are made in similar ways, though on a smaller scale.

For example, very low-budget "exploitation" filmmaking (so called because it "exploits" sensational material) tailors its product to a particular market, such as home videocassette rentals. The independent exploitation film, often a horror film or teenage sex comedy, may have a budget as low as $100,000. Nonetheless, the production roles are parceled out in ways which roughly conform to mass-production practices. Because of cost constraints, however, many tasks may be carried out by amateurs, students, friends, and relatives. And in such circumstances people often double up on jobs: the director might produce the film and write the script as well, the picture editor might cut sound as well.

To take an extreme example, Robert Rodriguez made *El Mariachi* as an exploitation film for the Spanish-language video market. The twenty-one-year-old director functioned as producer, scriptwriter, cinematographer, camera operator, still photographer, and sound recordist and mixer. Rodriguez's friend Carlos Gallardo starred, co-produced, and co-scripted; he also served as unit production manager and grip. Gallardo's mother fed the cast and crew. *El Mariachi* wound up costing only about $7000.

The label "independent production" also covers low-budget projects that seek to go beyond the exploitation market. Often regionally based, these films may find success with wide audiences, as did Robert Townsend's *Hollywood Shuffle*, Richard Linklater's *Slacker*, and Kevin Smith's *Clerks*. In these more ambitious low-budget efforts, a small staff and crew fulfill the production functions of the studio model. And trimming costs often stimulates the filmmaker's imagination. Charles Lane's *Street Stories* saved money on synchronized sound by including virtually no dialogue. In making *Just Another Girl on the IRT*, Leslie Harris used locations and available lighting in order to shoot rapidly (Fig. 1.21); she completed filming in just seventeen days.

Fig. 1.21

Some prominent mainstream filmmakers are considered "independents" because they work at budgets significantly below the industry norm. Oliver Stone's *Platoon* and Spike Lee's *School Daze* each cost $6 million. Although Quentin Tarentino's *Pulp Fiction* featured major stars, their willingness to accept reduced salaries kept the budget around $8 million. In Chapter 10, we will analyze one such project, Spike Lee's *Do The Right Thing* (pp. 393–399).

In this type of independent production, the director usually initiates the project and works with a producer to get it realized. As we would expect, these industry-based independents organize production in ways very close to the full-fledged studio mode. Nonetheless, because they require less financing, such independents can demand more flexibility and control in the production process. Woody Allen, for instance, is allowed by his contract to rewrite and reshoot extensive portions of his film after he has assembled an initial rough cut. In shooting *School Daze*, Lee was able to create an off-camera tension between performers portraying conflicting factions of African-American college students. Lee assigned each group's cast to separate living quarters, different meals, and different hairstyling treatments. "It's a very sensitive subject, class and color," reflected one actor. "And I think the majority of the people on the shoot thought they were beyond it. They were forced to examine it, though, and many realized they weren't as far removed from the subject as they thought." Lee's status as an independent allowed him to control the production circumstances in ways that he believed would benefit both the film and its personnel.

◼ MODES OF PRODUCTION: INDIVIDUAL AND COLLECTIVE

Our survey of the studio mode of production demonstrates how precisely production tasks can be broken down. But not all filmmaking demands such a detailed division of labor. In general, two alternative modes of production treat the preparation, shooting, and assembly phases differently.

In *individual* film production the filmmaker functions as an artisan. He or she may own or rent the necessary equipment. Financial backing can be obtained on a film-by-film basis, and the production is generally on a small scale. The preferred format is 16mm. There is very little division of labor: The filmmaker oversees every production task, from obtaining financing to final editing, and will actually perform many of them. Although technicians or performers may make distinct contributions, the principal creative decisions rest with the filmmaker.

Documentary production offers many examples of the individual mode. Jean Rouch, a French anthropologist, has made several films alone or with a small crew in his efforts to document the lives of marginal people, often members of minorities, living in an alien culture. Rouch wrote, directed, and photographed *Les Maîtres fous* (1955), his first widely seen film. Here he examined the ceremonies of a Ghanian cult whose members lived a double life: Most of the time they worked as low-paid laborers, but in their rituals they passed into a frenzied trance and assumed the identities of their colonial rulers. Other documentary filmmakers work on a scale only somewhat larger than that of Rouch. Frederick Wiseman, whose *High School* we examine in Chapter 11, produces, plans, and distributes his own films. During filmmaking he often serves as sound recordist while a cinematographer runs the camera.

Politically activist documentary offers another example of individual film production. Barbara Koppel devoted four years to the production stages of *Harlan County, U.S.A.*, a record of Kentucky coal miners' struggles for union representation. After eventually obtaining funding from foundations, she and a very small crew spent thirteen months living with miners during the workers' strike. A large crew was ruled out not only by Koppel's budget but also by the need to be absorbed as naturally as possible into the community. Koppel acted as sound recordist, working with cameraman Hart Perry and sometimes also a lighting person. Like the miners, the filmmakers were threatened with violence from strikebreakers. Some of these incidents were recorded on film, as when the driver of a passing truck fired a gun at the crew (Fig. 1.22).

Fig. 1.22

The individual mode of film production is also exemplified by the work of many experimental filmmakers. Maya Deren, one of the most important American experimentalists, made several films in the 1940s (*Meshes of the Afternoon, Choreography for Camera, Ritual in Transfigured Time*, Fig. 1.23) which she scripted, directed, performed in, and edited. In some cases the shooting was done by her husband, Alexander Hammid.

A comparable example is the work of Stan Brakhage, whose films are among the most directly personal ever made. Some, like *Window Water Baby Moving* and *Scenes from under Childhood*, are lyrical studies of his family life; others, such as *Dog Star Man*, are mythic treatments of nature; still others, such as *23rd Psalm Branch* and *The Act of Seeing with One's Own Eyes*, are quasi-documentary studies of war and death. Funded by grants and his personal finances, Brakhage prepares, shoots, and edits his films virtually unaided. For a time, while he was working in a film laboratory, he also personally developed and printed his footage. The work of Brakhage, which now comprises over 150 films, demonstrates that in the individual mode of production the filmmaker can become an artisan, a solitary worker executing all the basic production tasks. In later chapters, we will be examining films by other artisanal experimental directors, such as Bruce Conner, Michael Snow, and Ernie Gehr.

Fig. 1.23

In *collective* film production several film workers participate equally in the project. Like individual filmmakers, the group may own or rent its equipment. The production is on a small scale, and financing may come from foundations or members' personal resources. But although there may be a detailed division of labor, the group shares common goals and makes production decisions collectively. Roles may also be rotated: The sound recordist one day may serve as cinematographer on the next. The collective mode of production attempts to replace the authority vested in the producer and director with a more broadly distributed responsibility for the film.

Not surprisingly, the left-wing political movements of the late 1960s fostered many efforts toward collective film production. In France, several such groups were formed, the most noteworthy being SLON (an acronym for a name that translates as Society for the Launching of New Works). SLON was a cooperative that sought to make films about contemporary political struggles around the world. Financed chiefly by television companies, SLON filmmakers often collaborated with factory workers in documenting strikes and union activities.

In the United States, the most famous and long-lived collective unit has been the Newsreel group, which was founded in 1967 as an effort to document the student protest movement. Newsreel attempted to create not only a collective production situation, with a central coordinating committee answerable to the complete membership, but also a community distribution network that would make Newsreel films available for local activists around the country. During the late 1960s and early 1970s, the collective produced dozens of works, including *Finally Got the News* and *The Woman's Film.* Newsreel branches sprang up in many cities, with those in San Francisco (now known as California Newsreel) and in New York (known as Third World Newsreel) surviving into the 1990s. After the mid-1970s, Newsreel moved somewhat away from purely collective production, but it retained certain policies characteristic of the collective mode, such as equal pay for all participants in a film. Important Newsreel films of recent years are *Controlling Interests, The Business of America . . .* (funded largely by American public television), and *Chronical of Hope: Nicaragua.* Members of Newsreel such as Robert Kramer, Barbara Koppel, and Christine Choy have gone on to work as individual filmmakers.

The catchall label of "independent filmmaking" thus includes not only small-budget filmmaking modeled on the studio mode but also individual production and collective production. The drawbacks of independent production consist chiefly in financing, distribution, and exhibition. Studios and large distribution firms have ready access to large amounts of capital and usually can ensure the distribution and exhibition of the films they decide to back. The independent filmmaker or group often has trouble gaining access to money and to audiences.

But many filmmakers believe the advantages of independence outweigh the drawbacks. Independent production can treat subjects that large-scale studio production ignores. Few film studios would have initiated Sayles's *Matewan,* and no film studio would have made Jim Jarmusch's *Stranger Than Paradise* or Harris's *Just Another Girl on the IRT.* Because the independent film does not need as large an audience to repay its costs, it can be more personal, more unusual, and perhaps more controversial. The filmmaker need not tailor the script to the Hollywood pattern. (Indeed, the independent filmmaker may not use a script at all.) Independent filmmaking thus often explores new possibilities of the film medium.

IMPLICATIONS OF DIFFERENT MODES OF FILM PRODUCTION

Since much of cinema's uniqueness rests on the technical and social factors that produce it, the modes and stages of film production have considerable implications for the study of film as an art. For one thing, film production is tied to modes of production in the society as a whole. Because of the technological requisites of production, cinema began in the most highly industrialized societies—the United States, Germany, France, and England. In these countries filmmaking quickly became a business for both individual filmmakers and firms. Studio film production tends to occur when countries have achieved division of labor in other manufacturing industries. In American and European industry, for instance, the separation of production planning from execution had been accomplished by 1900, and the same separation emerged in the film industry in the subsequent decade.

Once film and equipment become more widely available, alternative modes of production are possible. With access to 16mm and portable video equipment, people can engage in individual and collective film production. But this access rests in turn on the existence of social groups that can afford to purchase such machines and that know how to operate them. Just as MGM could not have developed in the Middle Ages, so independent film production cannot indigenously spring up among preindustrial societies today. Film production has historically modeled its practices on economic production in other industries, and the overall economic nature of a society constrains the modes of film production which can develop there.

Finally, the mode of film production affects how we view the filmmaker as artist. This is the issue of authorship. Who, it is often asked, is the "author," the artist responsible for the film?

For some modes of film production, the question is easily answered. In individual production the author must be the solitary filmmaker—Stan Brakhage, Louis Lumière, yourself. Collective film production creates collective authorship; the author is the entire group (Third World Newsreel or SLON). The question of authorship becomes difficult to answer only when asked about studio production.

In the earlier instances authorship is defined by control and decision making, whether by an individual or a collective. But studio film production assigns tasks to so many individuals that it is often difficult to determine who decides what. Is the producer the author? In the prime years of the Hollywood studio system, the producer might have had little or nothing to do with shooting. The writer? Again, in Hollywood, the writer's script might be completely transformed in filming. So is this situation like collective production, with group authorship? No, since studio division of labor denies film workers common goals and shared decision making. Moreover, if we consider not only control and decision making but also "individual style," it must be admitted that certain studio workers leave recognizable and unique traces on the films they make. Cinematographers such as Hal Mohr and Gregg Toland, set designers such as Hermann Warm, costumers such as Edith Head, choreographers such as Michael Kidd—the contributions of these people stand out within the films they made. So where does the studio-produced film leave the idea of authorship?

In recent years the most commonly accepted solution has been to regard the director as the "author" of most studio films. Although the writer prepares a script, that script does not define the finished film, since later phases of production can modify the script beyond recognition. (Indeed, writers are famous for complaining about how directors mutilate scripts.) In general, the director's role comes closest to orchestrating all of those stages of production which most directly affect how a movie looks and sounds.

For a director to orchestrate the labor of shooting and assembly does not mean that he or she is expert at every job or even overtly orders this or that. Within the studio mode of production, the director can delegate tasks to trusted and competent personnel; hence the tendency of directors to work habitually with certain actors, cinematographers, composers, and so on. Alfred Hitchcock reportedly sat on the set during filming, never looking through the camera's viewfinder. Yet he sketched out every shot beforehand and thoroughly explained to his cinematographer what he wanted. Even in the assembly phase, the director can exercise remote-control power. Most Hollywood studios did not permit the director to supervise the editing of the film. But John Ford, for example, got around this by simply making only one take of each shot whenever possible, with very little overlap of action from shot to shot. By precutting the film "in his head," Ford gave the editor the bare minimum and had no need to set foot in an editing room. Finally, the importance of the director's role is confirmed by the recent trend for the director to operate on a free-lance basis, organizing his or her chosen project.

For all of these reasons, in the rest of this book we will generally identify the director as the worker responsible for the film in question. There are exceptions, but usually it is through the director's control of the shooting and assembly phases that the film's form and style crystallize. These two aspects of a film are central to film art and thus to the concerns of the rest of this book.

Film production requires some division of labor, but how that division is carried out, and how power is allocated to various roles, differs from project to project. The process of film production thus reflects different conceptions of what a film is, and the finished film inevitably bears traces of the mode of production within which it was created.

AFTER PRODUCTION: DISTRIBUTION AND EXHIBITION

Film production has been our principal concern, but the social institution of cinema also depends on distribution and exhibition. Feature films are distributed through companies set up for this purpose, and most exhibition occurs within theater circuits. When a firm owns the production facility, a distribution company, and exhibition outlets, it is said to be *vertically integrated.* Vertical integration is a common business practice in most film-producing countries. In the 1920s, for example, Paramount already consisted of production and distribution branches, and it went on to buy and build hundreds of theaters, thus guaranteeing itself a market for its products. In 1948, United States courts declared vertical integration monopolistic, but in this country the major production firms have remained the most important distributors. Recently some theater chains, such as Cineplex Odeon, have become involved in distribution.

Production has always affected exhibition and distribution. In the heyday of Hollywood, studios produced a variety of short films (cartoons, comedies, newsreels) which accompanied the feature film and made up a package with specific exhibition appeal. Nowadays the extra material on a cinema program is more likely to include advertisements, movie previews, announcements of no-smoking laws, and pleas for patrons not to litter the theater or talk during the film.

The way in which a theater exhibits a film can have a profound effect on our movie-going experience. Most patrons are aware that it is more rewarding to see a film made with a stereophonic sound track in a theater equipped with a stereophonic sound system, and so theaters add "in stereo" to their advertisements. Throughout cinema history, the individual exhibitor has controlled how the patrons see films. In the earliest days of the cinema, when films were only a few minutes long, the exhibitor could arrange a program in a certain order and might even lecture during some of the films. With the move to longer features in the 1910s and 1920s, some exhibitors found ways to squeeze in an extra show or two a day—by having the projectionist either cut out portions of the print or run the hand-cranked projector a bit faster than standard speed.

The introduction of sound discouraged such practices, but we should not assume that today we always see the film exactly as its makers intended. For one thing, since the 1950s, films have been shot in a variety of shapes, or *aspect ratios.* Some are very wide rectangles, others slightly narrower, and some are closer to the shape of a television screen. Theater projectors are equipped with a variety of *aperture plates,* whose rectangular slots enable the film to be projected in various proportions. In Figure 1.24, from a 35mm print of *Beetlejuice,* you can see that the top of the set has been left unfinished. When the print is projected, the aperture plate conceals this portion of the image. The screen is also usually framed by a dark masking, which can be adjusted to match the shape of the image. Sometimes, however, projectionists do not bother to change their projector's plates or move the masking to suit the film. If you see a film that, say, cuts off the tops of the actors' heads, the problem is most likely in the projection, not in the original cinematographer's work.

Fig. 1.24

One reason why such mistakes occur is that in recent years theaters have tried to cut expenses by redefining the projectionist's job. In a "multiplex" cinema complex, a single projectionist might be responsible for supervising a half dozen films running simultaneously, from one central booth or from several. This works well as long as nothing goes wrong, but if the film goes out of focus, there may be no one in the projection booth to notice the problem for minutes on end. On the other hand, more and more theater chains are striving to improve the quality of their screenings, and many projectionists take immense pride in smoothly run shows. It is worth noticing which theaters provide the best presentation of films and trying to patronize them whenever possible.

Broadly speaking, there are three types of exhibition of new films in the

United States. Mainstream commercial cinemas are the most common, showing popularly oriented feature films. Films with a more limited appeal are more likely to show in "art houses," which cater to those interested in foreign-language films, feature-length documentaries, festivals of animation, independently produced films, and the like. Like mainstream commercial theaters, art theaters are oriented toward making a profit, and they do so by appealing to a steady, loyal audience in such places as large cities and college towns. Finally, small-budget independent and experimental films may be shown in very specialized exhibition situations. Museums and archives often sponsor film series, as do local filmmaking cooperatives. Virtually all such venues depend upon outside support—from grants, foundations, corporate sponsors, and the like—to supplement ticket sales.

Three comparable types of distributors supply these various exhibition sites. The large national distribution firms cater to the commercial cinemas. Smaller distributors may pick up independent productions or imported films for the art-house market. Experimental films also have their own alternative distribution system, consisting of outlets such as the Film-Makers' Cooperative in New York and Canyon Cinema in San Francisco.

These distinctions among types of exhibition and distribution are not hard and fast. A few art cinemas show experimental films as shorts before their features. Independent filmmakers may try to break into the studio distribution and exhibition structure, as Robert Rodriguez did with *El Mariachi* and Michael Moore did with *Roger and Me*. In recent years there has been a trend toward taking foreign films that are initially very successful in an art-house context and moving them into mainstream commercial cinemas for a second run; this has happened, for example, with the Mexican film *Like Water for Chocolate*. Italian director Bernardo Bertolucci's *The Last Emperor* ordinarily might have played in art cinemas, but its spectacular sets and costumes helped it get a wide release in commercial cinemas instead, and its subsequent sweep of the Oscar awards made it a considerable popular success.

Mainstream theaters, art houses, and venues for experimental cinema are all instances of *theatrical* exhibition. *Nontheatrical* exhibition includes screenings in viewers' homes, classrooms, hospitals, military institutions, public libraries, and similar circumstances.

■ FILM AND VIDEO

By far the most significant nontheatrical means of exhibition is video, in the form of broadcast, cable or satellite transmission, and home formats like videocassette and laserdisc. Since 1988, the American film industry has garnered twice as much income from nontheatrical video as from domestic theater returns. Because of the widespread use of this new exhibition format, we should recognize the important differences between film and video.

Certain differences depend on technological factors. Video images are created by bombarding light-sensitive phosphors on the surface of the monitor's picture tube. A "gun" at the rear of the tube scans the surface horizontally, rapidly activating the phosphors one by one. In North America, the broadcast standard is established at 525 scan lines, each with about 600 separate points, or picture elements (pixels). (In practice, the number of lines available on a home television monitor is around 425.) In Europe, the standard is 625 scan lines.

Motion picture film can carry far more visual information than the standard video image. Estimates vary, but a 16mm color image offers the equivalent of at least 500 video scan lines, while 35mm positive film offers color resolution equivalent to over 2000 scan lines. Moreover, American-standard video has a total of about 350,000 pixels per frame, but 35mm color negative film has the equivalent of about 7 million. This should not be surprising. We can see the tiny flickering pixels on a video monitor, but on 35mm a grain of silver halide may support a distinct image point no bigger than four atoms!

Another disparity between film and video involves *contrast ratio,* the relation between the brightest area and the darkest area of the image. While the video camera can reproduce a maximum contrast ratio of 20:1, 35mm color film can reproduce a contrast ratio of over 100:1. As a result of these factors, the 35mm film image can display a much greater range of tonalities. When a film is transferred to video, engineers typically handle the narrower contrast ratio by lightening the image, thereby losing the richness of shadow areas. "The versions of *The Dead Zone* and *The Fly* that you find on video carry my name," observes director David Cronenberg, "and they are the films that I made, but I hate the way they look on tape. Too bright."

A film on video may fall prey to other defects as well. Video color is likely to smear, with sharp-edged reds and oranges particularly difficult to render. There is also the problem of "comet tailing," streaks of light that trail movements of objects against a dark background. Highly patterned clothing and closely packed horizontal stripes produce moiré, or "herringbone," oscillation in the picture.

There are other important differences between film and television. An obvious one is scale. A 35mm film image is designed to be displayed on a screen area of hundreds of square feet. Video images look faint and stippled when projected on even a 6-by-8-foot area. Another difference between the two media is long-term storage capacity. Film has been a notably perishable medium, but it can last far longer than videotape. By current estimates, images on a tape in the 1-inch format can start to degrade in 10 to 15 years, and images on a 1/2-inch videocassette may fall into jeopardy in half that time.

More than technological differences separate the two media. A video version of a film may have a different musical background than does the original, often because producers could not obtain the video rights to existing songs. Broadcast television habitually alters films, reediting them and reworking the sound tracks to eliminate potentially offensive dialogue. Sometimes the filmmakers shoot material solely for the broadcast versions of the film. The U.S. network broadcast of *The Silence of the Lambs* contained some alternate versions of shots seen in the theatrical version. Video "colorization" uses computer analysis to add color to black-and-white films. Broadcasters also utilize "time compression," speeding up the film past its original 24 fps

Fig. 1.25

Fig. 1.26

Fig. 1.27

so that more commercial advertising can be inserted. Broadcast and home-video versions sometimes present a "semi-squeezed" image that distorts faces and bodies in order to fit widescreen information onto the television screen.

The most widespread alteration of the original film comes in the process of "panning and scanning." Here a film made in a widescreen ratio is cropped to fit the narrower television frame. A controller decides what portions of the image to show and what to eliminate. When important action takes place at opposite ends of the widescreen frame, a computer-controlled scanning mechanism pans across the image. Since most films made after about 1955 have been intended to be shown in some wide format, pan-and-scan is very common. It can be seen on films that are broadcast and cablecast, as well as those available on home video.

Pan-and-scan processes are highly unfaithful to the original film. The moviegoer who sees *River of No Return* in a widescreen film print sees an image like that in Figure 1.25. The home-video viewer sees what is in Figure 1.26. Sometimes the results can be quite hilarious, as when the television image includes an actor's nose sticking into the frame. (See Fig. 1.27, from a 16mm television print of Douglas Sirk's *Tarnished Angels.*) To avoid such awkward compositions, panning and scanning will sometimes make separate shots out of what is actually a single shot. In any case, the video frame may eliminate up to 50 percent of the original image.

All of which is not to say that motion pictures should not be watched on video. Video copies of films are very convenient to use, widely accessible, and comparatively inexpensive. Video has aroused viewers' interest in a wider range of films than is available in local theaters. If a film is no longer in circulation or is prohibitively expensive to rent, watching it on video is usually better than not seeing it at all.

And some video formats are superior to others. A VHS videocassette offers only about 200 lines of resolution and seldom respects the film's original image proportions. Laserdisc video offers much improved image quality (400 or more lines). Laserdisc versions also sometimes approximate widescreen compositions by putting black bands at the top and bottom of the screen ("letterboxing"). In addition, the digital sound track of laserdisc versions, offering stereophonic and surround channels, far exceeds the quality of videocassette and 16mm film. True, there are problems with the laserdisc format: Often the letterboxing does not recapture the full width of the original, and only the CAV disc format allows the viewer to stop at a single film frame and examine it. Nevertheless, the laserdisc format is currently the most preferable video approximation to the original film.

A video version can be useful in film study, but we suggest that it serves best as an adjunct to a film copy. Ideally, the first viewing of a film should be in a film-exhibition situation, and close analysis should be done using a film print. If a print is unavailable for study, the scholar or student can utilize a laserdisc version. While a videocassette can give some idea of a film's visual qualities, it remains chiefly valuable for examining dialogue, music, performances, script construction, and similar factors.

As the television image improves, chiefly through the development of high-definition video, it may compete with 16mm (see Notes and Queries). Like all media technologies, video has advantages as well as disadvantages, and in studying film, we need to be aware of both.

NOTES AND QUERIES

■ THE ILLUSION OF MOVEMENT IN THE CINEMA

Most people are surprised to learn that for much of the time that a film is running, the screen is completely dark. At 24 frames per second, a projected film advances one frame every 42 milliseconds. (A millisecond is a thousandth of a second.) Since the shutter breaks the projector beam twice—once while the film is moving, once while it is stationary—each frame is actually shown twice during that 42-millisecond interval. Each of the two displays is on the screen for 8.5 milliseconds, with 5.4 milliseconds of darkness between each one. During a film that lasts a hundred minutes, the audience is sitting in total darkness for almost forty minutes! We do not, however, perceive the brief intervals of darkness because of critical flicker fusion and apparent-motion processes within our visual system.

A useful introduction to visual perception is John P. Frisby, *Seeing: Illusion, Brain and Mind* (New York: Oxford University Press, 1980). A technical treatment of the illusion of movement in film is offered in Julian E. Hochberg, "Representation of Motion and Space in Video and Cinematic Displays," in Kenneth R. Boff, Lloyd Kaufman, and James P. Thomas, eds., *Handbook of Perception and Human Performance*, vol. 1, "Sensory Processes and Perception" (New York: Wiley, 1986), chap. 22. Stuart Liebman uses the perceptual mechanisms of illusion to analyze an experimental film in "Apparent Motion and Film Structure: Paul Sharits' *Shutter Interface*," *Millennium Film Journal* **1**, 2 (Spring–Summer 1978): 101–109.

■ THE TECHNICAL BASIS OF CINEMA

André Bazin suggests that humankind dreamed of cinema long before it actually appeared: "The concept men had of it existed so to speak fully armed in their minds, as if in some platonic heaven" [*What Is Cinema?* vol. 1 (Berkeley: University of California Press, 1967), p. 17]. Still, whatever its distant antecedents, the cinema became technically feasible only in the nineteenth century.

Motion pictures depended on many discoveries in various scientific and industrial fields: optics and lens making, the control of light (especially by means of arc lamps), chemistry (involving particularly the production of cellulose), steel production, precision machining, and other areas. The cinema machine is closely related to other machines of the period. For example, engineers in the nineteenth century designed machines that could intermittently unwind, advance, perforate, advance again, and wind up a strip of material at a constant rate. The drive apparatus on cameras and projectors is a late development of a technology which had already made feasible the sewing machine, the telegraph tape, and the machine gun. The nineteenth-century origins of film are even more apparent today; compare cinema technology's mechanical and chemical basis with image systems such as television, holography, and "virtual reality," which depend on electronics, lasers, and computer imaging, respectively.

On the history of film technology, see Barry Salt's *Film Style and Technology: History and Analysis* (London: Starword, 1992); David Bordwell, Janet Staiger, and Kristin Thompson's *The Classical Hollywood Cinema: Film Style and Mode of Production to 1960* (New York: Columbia University Press, 1985); and many essays in Elisabeth Weis and John Belton, eds., *Film Sound: Theory and Practice* (New York: Columbia University Press, 1985). Primary sources of technological information are included in Raymond Fielding, ed., *A Technological History of Motion Pictures and Television* (Berkeley: University of California Press, 1967). Douglas Gomery has pioneered the economic history of film technology: for a survey, see Robert C. Allen and Douglas Gomery, *Film History: Theory and Practice* (New York: Knopf, 1985). In *Basic Motion Picture Technology* (New York: Hastings House, 1975), L. Bernard Happé includes some historical background; the book as a whole constitutes a solid introduction to the technical basis of cinema. The most comprehensive and up-to-date reference book on the subject is Ira Konigsberg, *The Complete Film Dictionary* (New York: New American Library, 1987). An entertaining appreciation of film technology is Nicholson Baker's essay "The Projector," *New Yorker* (March 21, 1994): 148–152.

■ MODES OF FILM PRODUCTION

Many "how-to-do-it" books discuss basic stages and roles of film production. Especially good are William B. Adams, *Handbook of Motion Picture Production* (New York: Wiley, 1977); Lenny Lipton, *Independent Filmmaking* (San Francisco: Straight Arrow, 1972); and Kris Malkiewicz, *Cinematography*, 2d ed. (New York: Prentice-Hall, 1989). Steven Bernstein's *The Technique of Film Production* (London: Focal Press, 1988) reflects contemporary British practice.

There are many informative discussions of the studio mode of production as it currently exists in the United States. Good recent ones are Alexandra Brouwer and Thomas Lee Wright, *Working in Hollywood: 64 Film Professionals Talk about Moviemaking* (New York: Crown, 1990) and Roy Paul

Madsen, *Working Cinema: Learning from the Masters* (Belmont, Calif.: Wadsworth, 1990). Jason E. Squire's *The Movie Business Book,* 2d ed. (New York: Simon & Schuster, 1992) is a comprehensive guide to the state of the industry today. An outstanding reference work is Harvey Rachlin's *TV and Movie Business: An Encyclopedia of Careers, Technologies and Practices* (New York: Crown, 1991).

Entire books have been devoted to particular tasks within production. On the work of the producer, see Paul N. Lazarus III, *The Film Producer* (New York: St. Martin's, 1992). On production design see Vincent LoBrutto, *By Design: Interviews with Film Production Designers* (Westport, Conn.: Praeger, 1992). The details of organizing preparation and shooting are explained thoroughly in Alain Silver and Elizabeth Ward's *The Film Director's Team: A Practical Guide for Production Managers, Assistant Directors, and All Filmmakers* (Los Angeles: Silman-James, 1992).

Storyboarding is extensively discussed in Steven D. Katz, *Film Directing Shot by Shot: Visualizing from Concept to Screen* (Studio City, Calif.: Wiese, 1991). Several "Making of" promotional books include examples of storyboarding; see in particular Don Shay and Jody Duncan, *The Making of "Jurassic Park"* (New York: Ballantine, 1993).

Boston's Focal Press has published a series of useful handbooks to various specialities, including Pat P. Miller, *Script Supervising and Film Continuity* (1986); Marvin M. Kerner, *The Art of the Sound Effects Editor* (1989); and Dan Carlin, Sr., *Music in Film and Video Productions* (1991).

Norman Hollyn's *The Film Editing Room Handbook* (New York: Arco, 1984) offers a detailed account of traditional assembly procedures. Newer video- and computer-based methods are discussed in Michael Rubin, *Nonlinear: A Guide to Electronic Film and Video Editing,* 2d ed. (Gainesville: Triad, 1992) and in Thomas Ohanian, *Digital Nonlinear Editing: New Approaches to Editing Film and Video* (Boston: Focal Press, 1993). On sound editing, see Vincent LoBrutto, *Sound-on-Film: Interviews with Creators of Film Sound* (Westport, Conn.: Praeger, 1994); our quotation on p. 21 is derived from p. 225. Special effects are covered in a richly designed magazine, *Cinefex.*

The craft of contemporary screenwriting is discussed in Syd Field, *Screenplay: The Foundations of Screenwriting* (New York: Delta, 1979); Linda Seeger, *Making a Good Script Great* (New York: Dodd, Mead, 1987); Michael Hauge, *Writing Screenplays that Sell* (New York: HarperCollins, 1988); Andrew Horton, *Writing the Character-Centered Screenplay* (Berkeley: University of California Press, 1994); and Ken Dancyger and Jeff Rush, *Alternative Scriptwriting: Writing Beyond the Rules* (Boston: Focal Press, 1991).

Several recent books explain the financing, production, and sale of independent low-budget films. The most serious and wide-ranging are David Rosen and Peter Hamilton, *Off-Hollywood: The Making and Marketing of Independent Films* (New York: Grove Weidenfeld, 1990) and Renée Harmon, *The Beginning Filmmaker's Business Guide* (New York: Walker, 1994). Two entertaining how-to guides are Rick Schmidt, *Feature Filmmaking at Used-Car Prices* (New York: Penguin, 1988), and John Russo, *Making Movies: The Inside Guide to Independent Movie Production* (New York: Dell, 1989). Lessons from a low-budget master are available in Roger Corman's *How I Made a Hundred Movies in Hollywood and Never Lost a Dime* (New York: Random House, 1990). A sample passage: "In the first half of 1957 I capitalized on the sensational headlines following the Russians' launch of their Sputnik satellite. . . . I shot *War of the Satellites* in a little under ten days. No one even knew what the satellite was supposed to look like. It was whatever I said it should look like" (pp. 44–45).

Several useful magazines treat independent cinema in the United States and elsewhere: *The Independent, Filmmaker,* and *Visions.*

Many contemporary scholars have researched the history of production practices. For the American film industry we have economic accounts such as Douglas Gomery's *The Hollywood Studio System* (London: Macmillan, 1985), which deals with production in relation to distribution and exhibition. Bordwell, Staiger, and Thompson's *The Classical Hollywood Cinema* (cited in the previous section) discusses the history of studio production practices and their relation to the development of American industry. On screenwriting, a historical overview is Tom Stempel, *FrameWork: A History of Screenwriting in the American Film* (New York: Continuum, 1988). Pat McGilligan has collected reminiscences of script writers in *Backstory: Interviews with Screenwriters of Hollywood's Golden Age* (Berkeley: University of California Press, 1986) and *Backstory 2: Interviews with Screenwriters of the 1940s and 1950s* (Berkeley: University of California Press, 1991).

Anecdotal biographies and chatty memoirs of stars, directors, producers, and other personnel offer some insight into historical aspects of production. But there are some excellent detailed case studies of the making of particular films. See Rudy Behlmer, *America's Favorite Movies: Behind the Scenes* (New York: Ungar, 1982); Aljean Harmetz, *The Making of "The Wizard of Oz"* (New York: Limelight, 1984); François Truffaut's "Diary of the Making of *Fahrenheit 451,"* in *Cahiers du cinéma in English* **5, 6,** and **7** (1966); Ronald Haver, *"A Star is Born": The Making of the 1954 Movie and Its 1985 Restoration* (New York: Knopf, 1988); Stephen Rebello, *Alfred Hitchcock and the Making of "Psycho"* (New York: Dembuer, 1990); John Sayles, *Thinking in Pictures: The Making of the Movie "Matewan"* (Boston: Houghton Mifflin, 1987); and Julie Salamon, *The Devil's Candy: "The Bonfire of the Vanities" Goes to Hollywood* (Boston: Houghton Mifflin, 1991). Most of Spike Lee's productions have been documented with published journals and production notes; see, for example, Spike Lee, *Uplift the Race: The Construction of "School Daze"* (New York: Simon & Schuster, 1988) and *Do The Right Thing: A Spike Lee Joint* (New York: Simon & Schuster, 1989). Our quotation on p. 24 comes from p. 85 of the former.

There are fewer studies of individual and collective film production, but here are some informative works. On Jean Rouch, see Mick Eaton, ed., *Anthropology—Reality—Cinema: The Films of Jean Rouch* (London: British Film Institute, 1979). The makers of *Harlan County, U.S.A.,* and other independent documentaries discuss their production methods in Alan Rosenthal, *The Documentary Conscience: A Casebook in Film Making* (Berkeley: University of California Press, 1980). Maya Deren's work is scrutinized in P. Adams Sitney, *Visionary Film: The American Avant-Garde, 1943–1978,* 2d ed. (New York: Oxford University Press, 1979). Stan Brakhage ruminates on his approach to filmmaking in *Brakhage Scrapbook: Collected Writings* (New Paltz, N.Y.: Documentext, 1982). For information on other experimentalists, see Scott MacDonald, *A Critical Cinema: Interviews with Independent Film-makers* (Berkeley: University of California Press, 1988) and David E. James, *Allegories of Cinema: American Film in the Sixties* (Princeton: Princeton University Press, 1989).

Collective film production is the subject of Guy Hennebelle, *"SLON: Working Class Cinema in France," Cinéaste* **5,** 2 (Spring 1972): 15–17; Bill Nichols, *Newsreel: Documentary Filmmaking on the American Left* (New York: Arno, 1980); and Michael Renov, "Newsreel: Old and New—Towards an Historical Profile," *Film Quarterly* **41,** 1 (Fall 1987): 20–33. Collective production in film and other media is discussed in John Downing, *Radical Media: The Political Experience of Alternative Communication* (Boston: South End Press, 1984).

The relation between modes of film production and social organization as a whole has been explored very little. Ian Jarvie's *Movies and Society* (New York: Basic Books, 1970) compares methods of socialization in studio film production with those in other areas of life. A good introduction to twentieth-century modes of production is Harry Braverman's *Labor and Monopoly Capital* (New York: Monthly Review Press, 1974).

For a detailed study of contemporary film distribution, see Suzanne Mary Donahue, *American Film Distribution: The Changing Marketplace* (Ann Arbor: UMI Research Press, 1987). Issues of reception are addressed in Bruce A. Austin's *Immediate Seating: A Look at Movie Audiences* (Belmont, Calif.: Wadsworth, 1988). Douglas Gomery's *Shared Pleasures: A History of Moviegoing in America* (Madison: University of Wisconsin Press, 1992) offers a history of exhibition.

■ PRODUCTION STILLS VERSUS FRAME ENLARGEMENTS

A film may live in our memory as much through still photographs as through our experience of seeing the movie. These photographs are typically of two sorts. The photograph may be a copy of a single frame of the finished film, as it exists on the film strip. Such a copy is usually called a *frame enlargement*. Most photographs from the film, however, are *production stills*—that is, photographs made while the film is being shot. Typically production stills are used for publicizing the film in newspapers and magazines, but they are also used in many books on motion pictures.

Production stills are usually photographically sharper than frame enlargements, and they can be useful for studying details of setting or costume. Unfortunately, they differ from the image on the film strip. Usually the photographer rearranges and relights the actors and takes the still from an angle and distance not comparable to that shown in the finished film. Frame enlargements therefore offer a much more faithful record of the finished film.

For example, both Figures 1.28 and 1.29 have been used to illustrate discussions of Jean Renoir's *Rules of the Game*. Figure 1.28 is a production still in which the actors have been posed. It is not, however, faithful to the

Fig. 1.28

Fig. 1.29

finished film. Figure 1.29 shows the actual shot in the film. The frame enlargement reveals that Renoir uses the central doorway to present action taking place in depth. Here, as often happens, a production still does not capture important features of the director's visual style.

Virtually all of the photographs in this book are frame enlargements.

■ AUTHORSHIP

On what grounds may we say that a director is the "author" of a studio-produced film? Three possibilities seem to be available.

Author as production worker. This is the concern of this chapter. Some film scholars believe that the director of a studio film cannot be the author unless he or she seeks to fulfill every major role personally. (An example is Charles Chaplin, who was producer, writer, director, composer, and star of his later films.) Other scholars maintain that although the director cannot perform all those tasks, he or she must at least have overt veto control at every stage of production (as, say, Jacques Tati and Federico Fellini did). In the view of still other scholars, the director's role provides the closest thing to a grasp of the totality of the shooting and assembly phases. Not that the director can do everything or make every choice, but the director's role is defined as a synthetic one, combining the participants' contributions into a whole. This is the position we have taken in this book. A defense of the "director as orchestrator" view may be found in V. F. Perkins's *Film as Film* (Baltimore: Penguin, 1972), chap. 8.

Author as personality. In France in the 1950s young writers grouped around the magazine *Cahiers du cinéma* began to discover traces of "personal style" in Hollywood films. Attributing this personality to the director, they stressed the "Howard Hawks" flavor (love of action and professional stoicism), the "Alfred Hitchcock" flavor (suspense but also a brooding Catholic guilt), and so on. This became known as the *politique des auteurs,* the "position of being for authors." The idea was taken up by Andrew Sarris in a series of now famous essays. "The strong director imposes his own personality on a film" [*The American Cinema* (New York: Dutton, 1968), p. 31]. Auteurism also became an evaluative method, enabling the *Cahiers du cinéma* critics and Sarris to rank auteurs against nonauteurs. (Sarris: Fred Zinnemann has only a superficial "personal commitment" to direction, David Lean's *Doctor Zhivago* is a work of "the most impeccable impersonality.")

The *politique des auteurs* made a major step toward our understanding of film as art, but according to this conception, what constitutes "personality"? Film form and style? Certain preferred themes, stories, actors, genres? Anglo-American auteur criticism has tended to speak of the director's "personal vision" and recurrent "concerns." For a vigorous statement, see William Cadbury and Leland Poague, *Film Criticism: A Counter Theory* (Ames: Iowa State University Press, 1983). The major progenitor of this emphasis is Robin Wood's remarkable body of work on various directors; he defends his stance in *Personal Views* (London: Gordon Fraser, 1976).

Author as a group of films.   In reaction to the notion of "personality," some have suggested that we regard the idea of the "author" as simply a critical construct. On this account, the critic would group films by *signature* of director, producer, screenwriter, or whatever. Thus *Citizen Kane* could belong to the "Orson Welles" group *and* to the "Herman Mankiewicz" group *and* to the "Gregg Toland" group, and so on. The critic would then analyze the patterns of relations within a given group. This would mean that certain aspects of *Citizen Kane* interact with aspects of other films directed by Welles, or of other films written by Mankiewicz, or of other films photographed by Toland. The "author" is no longer a person, but, for the sake of analysis, a system of relations among several films bearing the same signature. Peter Wollen develops this idea in *Signs and Meanings in the Cinema* (Blooming-ton: Indiana University Press, 1972). This approach, of course, could be applied to independent works as well as to studio-produced films.

The 1960s and 1970s saw a great many disputes over the concept of authorship, such as the argument between proponents of the "director as auteur," led by Andrew Sarris (in *The American Cinema* and elsewhere) and proponents of the "screenwriter as auteur," led by Richard Corliss [in *The Hollywood Screenwriters* (New York: Avon, 1972) and *Talking Pictures* (New York: Penguin, 1974)]. It is interesting that the Sarris-Corliss disagreement does not distinguish among author as production worker, as personality, or as critical label, so at times the two critics are not talking about the same thing. After the initial interest in authorship in the cinema, many critics have taken a step back to differentiate and compare assumptions as we have here. John Caughie's useful anthology *Ideas of Authorship* (London: Routledge & Kegan Paul, 1981) and Steve Crofts's "Authorship and Hollywood," *Wide Angle* **5,** 3 (1983): 16–22, both categorize various approaches to authorship. Despite the difficulties and varieties of approach, some version of the director-as-author position remains probably the most widely shared assumption in film studies today. Most critical studies of cinema put the director at center stage.

A detailed consideration of how the personal life of the independent filmmaker can be a source of creative material is P. Adams Sitney, "Auto-biography in Avant-Garde Film," *Millennium Film Journal* **1,** 1 (Winter 1977–78:) 60–105.

■ FILM AND VIDEO

Detailed comparisons of film and video technology can be found in Harry Mathias and Richard Patterson, *Electronic Cinematography: Achieving Photographic Control over the Video Image* (Belmont, Calif.: Wadsworth, 1985) and Richard H. Kallenberger and George D. Cvjetnicanin, *Film into Video* (Boston: Focal Press, 1994). See also Tim Lucas, *The Video Watchdog Book* (Cincinnati: Video Watchdog, 1992); our quote from David Cronenberg on p. 31 comes from p. 223 of this book.

On using video to help plan shots during production, the Polish director Andrzej Wajda remarks: "For a director who has grown up with and been formed by film, video is a technique that offers no resistance. The lighting is always sufficient, the camera movement incredibly light and facile—too facile—and what is more, if you don't like what you just did you can simply erase it and start again from scratch, which means the possibilities are infinite. This means you work without tension, without the familiar atmosphere of being on the edge, constantly at risk. The problem, of course, is that that tension, that sense of risk, is precisely what characterizes the work in a good film" [Wajda, *Double Vision: My Life in Film,* trans. Rose Medina (New York: Holt, 1989), pp. 43–44].

John Belton has written several essays on pan-and-scan practices; two of the most informative are "Pan and Scan Scandals," *The Perfect Vision* **1,** 3 (Indian summer 1987): 40–49, and "The Shape of Money," *Sight and Sound* **56,** 3 (Summer 1987): 170–174. Three contemporary filmmakers discuss the relation of cinema to video in Roger Ebert and Gene Siskel, *The Future of the Movies: Interviews with Martin Scorsese, Steven Spielberg, and George Lucas* (Kansas City, Mo.: Andres and McMeel, 1991).

The boundaries between cinema and video are blurring in several ways. Several well-established directors are moving into television (following the precedent of Alfred Hitchcock, whose television series ran from 1955 to 1962). Francis Ford Coppola revised and melded his first two *Godfather* films to create a vehicle designed for network broadcast. Steven Spielberg's *Amazing Stories* and David Lynch's *Twin Peaks* marked the entry of the "film-brat" generation into series television. Since then Oliver Stone, Woody Allen, and Paul Schrader have filmed programs for the small screen. Spike Lee, John Sayles, Martin Scorsese, and other filmmakers direct television commercials and music videos. A "video look" influenced by commercials and MTV clips has been prominent in such recent films as *Reality Bites* and *The Crow.*

Debate on the technological relations between film and television currently centers on high-definition video. In 1981, the Japanese broadcasting company NHK demonstrated a video system composed of 1125 lines, a remarkable gain in sharpness and detail. Several different high-definition TV (HDTV) systems were then developed. Some cable, satellite, and broadcast transmissions in Europe and Japan utilized one or another HDTV system. In the fall of 1988, the United States Federal Communications Commission announced that any high-definition system to be used in broadcast must be compatible with the 525-line standard. This seems to have increased competition among different incompatible systems, with the result that a compromise system of moderate quality may be adopted in the United States, perhaps one utilizing 1050 lines.

Some form of digital HDTV is likely to emerge in the 1990s, perhaps one designed for flat liquid-crystal screens rather than for orthodox tube monitors. Although HDTV will improve the video image significantly, any system currently under consideration falls short of the quality available on 35mm color film. Furthermore, most HDTV systems utilize a 1.77:1 aspect ratio, which will pose problems in reproducing the compositions of many films. In addition, film technology will continue to advance; today's 16mm stocks have the quality of 35mm stocks of a decade ago.

For a valuable overview of HDTV's past and prospects, see Jean-Luc Renaud, "Towards Higher Definition Television," in *Future Visions: New Technologies of the Screen*, Philip Hayward and Tana Wollen, eds. (London: British Film Institute, 1993), pp. 46–71. A nontechnical summary is offered in Seth Shostak, "HDTV: Defining the Future of Broadcasting and Film?" *American Cinematographer* **72,** 8 (August 1991): 55–60.

On the overall relation between the U.S. film industry and television, see Tino Balio, ed., *Hollywood in the Age of Television* (Boston: Unwin Hyman, 1990) and Janet Wasko, *Hollywood in the Information Age: Beyond the Silver Screen* (London: Polity, 1994).

TWO

TYPES OF FILMS

Anyone who visits video stores knows that the staff file films under different headings—by star, by period ("silent movies"), by place of origin ("foreign films"). In order to understand how films work, we need a preliminary sense of some significant ways audiences, filmmakers, and film scholars sort them into groups.

BASIC TYPES

Some of the most basic types of film line up as distinct alternatives. We commonly distinguish documentary from fiction, live-action from animation, and "mainstream" from experimental or avant-garde filmmaking. Yet these categories are not watertight; they often mix and combine.

■ DOCUMENTARY VERSUS FICTION

Before we see a film we nearly always have some sense whether it is a documentary or a piece of fiction.

Documentary.   A documentary film purports to present factual information about the world outside the film. For example, *Primary* asks us to take it as a factual account of John Kennedy and Hubert Humphrey campaigning to win the 1960 Democratic presidential nomination (Fig. 2.1). Documentary films are typically contrasted with fiction films (more about them shortly).

What justifies our belief that a film is a documentary? For one thing, a documentary typically comes to us labeled as such. This in turn leads us to assume that the persons, places, and events exist and that the information presented about them is trustworthy.

In carrying out its purpose of presenting factual information, a documentary may utilize many devices. The filmmaker may record events as they actually occur, as the cameramen did in filming the Democratic campaigns in *Primary*. But a documentary may convey information in other ways as well. The filmmaker might supply charts, maps, or other visual aids. In addition, the documentary filmmaker may stage certain events for the camera to record.

Fig. 2.1

It is worth pausing on this last point. Some viewers tend to suspect that a documentary is unreliable if it manipulates the events that are filmed. It is true that, very often, the documentary filmmaker records an event without scripting or staging it. For example, in interviewing an eyewitness, the documentarist typically controls where the camera is placed, what is in focus, and so on; the filmmaker likewise controls the final editing of the images. But the filmmaker does not tell the witness what to say or how to act. The filmmaker may also have no choice about setting or lighting.

Still, both viewers and filmmakers regard some staging as legitimate in a documentary if the staging serves the larger purpose of presenting information. Suppose you are filming a farmer's daily routines. You might ask him or her to walk toward a field in order to frame a shot showing the whole farm. Similarly, the cameraman who is the central figure in Dziga Vertov's documentary *Man with a Movie Camera* is clearly performing for Vertov's camera (Fig. 2.2; see also pp. 415–420).

In some cases, staging may intensify the documentary value of the film. Humphrey Jennings made *Fires Were Started* during the German bombardment of London during World War II. Unable to film during the air raids, Jennings found a group of bombed-out buildings and set them afire. He then filmed the fire patrol battling the blaze (Fig. 2.3). Although the event was staged, the actual fire fighters who took part judged it an authentic depiction of the challenges they faced under real bombing. Similarly, after Allied troops liberated the Auschwitz concentration camp near the end of World War II, a newsreel cameraman assembled a group of children and had them roll up their sleeves to display the prisoner numbers tattooed on their arms. This staging of an action arguably enhanced the film's reliability.

Fig. 2.2

Staging events for the camera, then, need not consign the film to the realm of fiction. Regardless of the details of its production, the documentary film asks us to assume that it presents trustworthy information about its subject. Even if the filmmaker asks the farmer to wait a moment while the camera operator frames the shot, the film suggests that the farmer's morning visit to the field is part of the day's routine, and it is this suggestion which is set forth as reliable.

As a type of film, documentaries present themselves as factually trustworthy. Still, any one documentary may not prove reliable. Throughout film history, many documentaries have been challenged as inaccurate. A recent controversy involved Michael Moore's *Roger and Me*. The film presents, in

Fig. 2.3

sequences ranging from the heartrending to the absurd, the response of the people of Flint, Michigan, to a series of layoffs at General Motors plants during the 1980s. Much of the film shows inept efforts of the local government to revive the town's economy. Ronald Reagan visits, a television evangelist holds a mass rally, and the city officials launch expensive new building campaigns, including AutoWorld, an "indoor theme park" that is supposed to lure tourists to Flint.

No one disputes that all these events took place. The controversy arose when critics claimed that *Roger and Me* leads the audience to believe that the events occurred in the *order* in which they are shown. Ronald Reagan came to Flint in 1980, the TV evangelist in 1982; AutoWorld opened in 1985. These events could not have been responses to the plant closings shown early in the film because the plant closings started in 1986. Moore falsified the actual chronology, critics charged, in order to make the city government look foolish.

Moore's defense is discussed in Notes and Queries at the end of this chapter. The point for our purposes is that his critics accused his film of presenting unreliable information. Even if this charge were true, however, *Roger and Me* would not therefore turn into a fiction film. An unreliable documentary is still a documentary. Just as there are inaccurate and misleading news stories, there are inaccurate and misleading documentaries.

A documentary may take a stand, state an opinion, advocate a solution to a problem. As we shall see in Chapter 5, documentaries often use rhetorical form to persuade an audience. But, again, simply taking a stance does not turn the documentary into fiction. In order to persuade us, the filmmaker marshalls evidence, and this evidence is put forth as being factual and reliable. A documentary may be strongly partisan, but as a documentary it nonetheless presents itself as providing trustworthy information about its subject. *Roger and Me* offers criticisms of social policies, but the criticisms are presented as based upon facts.

Types of documentary. Viewers readily recognize types of documentary. A common type is the *compilation* film, produced by assembling images from archival sources. *The Atomic Cafe* compiles newsreel footage and instructional films to suggest how 1950s American culture reacted to the proliferation of nuclear weapons (Fig. 2.4). The *interview* or "talking heads" documentary records testimony about events or social movements. *Word Is Out* consists largely of interviews with lesbians and gay men discussing their lives.

Fig. 2.4

The *direct-cinema* documentary characteristically records an ongoing event "as it happens," with minimal interference by the filmmaker. Direct cinema emerged fully in the 1950s and 1960s, when portable camera and sound equipment became available and allowed films like *Primary* to follow an event as it unfolds. For this reason, such documentaries are also known as *cinéma-vérité*, French for "cinema-truth." A recent example is *Hoop Dreams*, which traces two aspiring basketball players through high school and into college. In Chapter 11 we analyze one direct-cinema documentary, Frederick Wiseman's *High School* (pp. 409–415).

Very often a documentary pursues several of these options at once. A film may mix archival footage, interviews, and material shot on the fly, as do *Roger and Me*, *Harlan County, U.S.A.*, and *In the Year of the Pig*. This "synthetic" documentary format is also common in television journalism.

Fiction. By contrast with documentary, we assume that a fictional film presents imaginary beings, places, or events. We take it for granted that Don Vito Corleone and his family never existed, and that their activities, as depicted in *The Godfather*, never took place. Bambi's mother did not really get shot by a hunter because Bambi, his mother, and their forest companions are imaginary.

If a film is fictional, that does not mean that it is completely unrelated to actuality. For one thing, not everything shown or implied by a fiction film need be imaginary. *The Godfather* alludes to World War II and the building of Las Vegas, both historical events; it takes place in New York City and in Sicily, both real locales. Nonetheless, the characters and their activities remain fictional, with history and geography providing a context for the made-up elements.

Fictional films are tied to actuality in another way: They often comment on the real world. *Dave*, about an imaginary U.S. president and his corrupt administration, criticizes contemporary political conduct. In 1943 some viewers took Carl Dreyer's *Day of Wrath*, a film about witch-hunts and prejudice in seventeenth-century Denmark, as a covert protest against the Nazis currently occupying the country. Through theme, subject, characterization, and other means, a fictional film can directly or obliquely present ideas about the world outside the film.

Sometimes our response to a fictional film is shaped by our assumptions about how it was made. The typical fictional film *stages* its events; they are designed, planned, rehearsed, filmed, and refilmed. The studio mode of production is well-suited to creating fiction films, since it allows stories to be scripted and action to be staged until what is captured on film satisfies the decision makers. Similarly, in a fictional film the agents are portrayed or depicted by an intermediary, not photographed directly (as in a documentary). The camera films not Vito Corleone but Marlon Brando portraying the Don (Fig. 2.5).

This assumption about how the film was made typically comes into play when we consider historical films or biographies. *Apollo 13* and *Schindler's List* base themselves on actual events, while *Malcolm X*, *Heart Like a Wheel*, and other "biopics" trace the careers of people who really existed. Are these documentaries or fictional films? In practice most such films add purely make-believe characters, speeches, or actions. But even if the films did not tamper with the record in this way, they would remain fictional according to our assumptions about how they were produced. Their events are wholly staged and the historical agents are portrayed through actors' performances. Like plays or novels based on real-life events, historical and biographical movies convey ideas about history by means of fictional portrayal.

Fig. 2.5

Sometimes, however, the ways in which the images and sounds were produced will not distinguish sharply between a fiction film and a documentary. Documentaries may include shots of prearranged or staged events, while fictions can incorporate unstaged material. Some fictional films include newsreel footage to bolster their stories. *Invaders from Mars* includes authentic footage of Army and Navy forces readying for battle, but the context makes the fictional point that the U.S. armed forces are preparing to repel Martians. Some filmmakers have made fictional films almost completely out of documentary footage. Craig Baldwin's *Tribulation 99: Alien Anomalies under America* draws extensively on newsreel footage to present a conspiracy involving space aliens living within the earth and controlling international politics. As with documentary, the overall purpose and point of the fictional film—to present imaginary actions and events—governs how we will take even documentary footage seen within it.

Mixtures and hybrids.   As you might expect, filmmakers have sometimes sought to blur the lines separating documentary and fiction. A notorious example is Mitchell Block's *No Lies*, which purports to present an interview with a woman who has been raped. Audiences are typically disturbed by the woman's emotional account and by the callousness of the offscreen filmmaker questioning her. A final title, however, reveals that the film was scripted and that the woman was an actor. Part of Block's purpose was apparently to show how the look and sound of *cinéma-vérité* documentary can elicit viewers' uncritical belief in what they are shown.

A film may fuse documentary and fiction in other ways. For *JFK*, Oliver Stone inserted compilation footage into scenes in which actors played historical figures such as Lee Harvey Oswald. Stone also staged and filmed the assassination of Kennedy in a pseudo-documentary manner. This material was then intercut with genuine archival footage, creating constant uncertainty about what was staged and what was filmed spontaneously. An even more extreme example is *Forrest Gump*, which uses special effects to allow its hero to meet John F. Kennedy, Lyndon Johnson, and Richard Nixon (Fig. 2.6).

Fig. 2.6

Errol Morris's *The Thin Blue Line*, a documentary investigation into a murder, mixes interviews and archival material with episodes performed by actors. The sequences, far from being the jittery reenactments of television true-crime shows, are shot with smooth camera work, dramatic lighting, and vibrant color (Color Plate 1). Several of these staged sequences dramatize witnesses' alternative versions of how the crime took place. The result is a film that not only seeks to identify the real killer but also raises questions about how fact and fiction may intermingle.

■ ANIMATED FILM

Most fiction and documentary films photograph people and objects in full-sized, three-dimensional spaces. As we have seen, the standard shooting speed for such *live-action* filmmaking is typically 24 frames per second.

Animated films are distinguished from live-action ones by the unusual kinds of work that are done at the production stage. Instead of continuously filming an ongoing action in real time, animators create a series of images by shooting one frame at a time. Between the exposure of each frame, the

Fig. 2.7

animator changes the subject being photographed. Daffy Duck does not exist to be filmed, but a carefully planned and executed series of slightly different drawings of Daffy can be filmed as single frames. When projected, the images create illusory motion comparable to that of live-action filmmaking. Anything in the world—or indeed the universe—that the filmmaker can manipulate can be animated by means of two-dimensional drawings, three-dimensional objects, or electronic information stored in a computer.

There are several distinct types of animation. The most familiar is *drawn* animation. From almost the start of cinema, animators drew and photographed long series of cartoon images. At first they drew on paper, but copying the entire image, including the setting, over and over proved too time-consuming. During the 1910s, studio animators introduced clear rectangular sheets of celluloid, nicknamed "cels." Characters and objects could be drawn on different cels (Fig. 2.7), and these could then be layered like a sandwich on top of an opaque painted setting. The whole stack of cels would then be photographed. New cels showing the characters and objects in slightly different positions could then be placed over the same background, creating the illusion of movement. Figure 2.7 shows two layered cels from a Road Runner cartoon. Wile E. Coyote is on one cel, the patches of flying dust on another. The cel process allowed animators to save time and to split up the labor among assembly lines of people doing drawing, coloring, photography, and other jobs.

This system, with a few additional labor-saving techniques, is still in use today. Big-budget studio cartoons have used "full" animation, with lots of movement and detailed drawing styles. (See Color Plates 38 and 39, as well as Figs. 7.134–7.136.) Cheaper productions use "limited" animation, with only small sections of the image moving from frame to frame. Limited animation is mainly used on television, although Japanese theatrical features, such as *Silent Möbius* (Fig. 2.8), have exploited it to create flat, poster-like images.

Some independent animators have continued to draw on paper. Robert Breer, for example, uses ordinary white index cards for his witty, quasi-abstract animated films.

Fig. 2.8

Fig. 2.9

Fig. 2.10

Fig. 2.11

Fig. 2.12

Cels and drawings are photographed, but an animator can work without a camera as well. He or she can draw directly on the film, scratch on it, attach flat objects to it. Stan Brakhage taped moths' wings to film stock in order to create *Mothlight*. The innovative animator Norman McLaren made *Blinkety Blank* by engraving the images frame by frame, using knives, needles, and razor blades (Fig. 2.9).

Another type of animation that works with two-dimensional images involves *cut-outs*. Sometimes filmmakers make flat puppets with movable joints. Lotte Reiniger specialized in lighting her cut-outs in silhouette to create delicate, intricate fairy tales, as in Figure 2.10, from *The Adventures of Prince Achmed*, the first feature-length animated film (1926). Animators could also manipulate cut-out images frame by frame to create moving collages; Frank Mouris's exuberant *Frank Film* presents a flickering dance of popular-culture imagery (Color Plate 2).

Three-dimensional objects can also be shifted and twisted frame by frame to create apparent movement. Animation of objects falls into three closely related categories: clay, model, and pixillation. *Clay* animation, often termed "claymation," sometimes actually does involve modelling clay. But more often, plasticine is used, since it is less messy and can be made in a wider range of colors. Sculptors create objects and characters of plasticine, and the animator then presses the flexible material to change it slightly between exposures. Although clay animation has been used occasionally since the early years of the twentieth century, it has grown enormously in popularity since the mid-1970s. Nick Park's *Creature Comforts* (Fig. 2.11) parodies the "talking heads" documentary by creating droll interviews with the inhabitants of a zoo.

Model or *puppet* animation is often very similar to clay animation. As the name implies, it involves the use of figures which can be moved, using bendable wires, joints, and the like. Historically the master of this form of animation was Ladislav Starevich, who as early as 1910 baffled Russian audiences with realistic insect models acting out human dramas and comedies. In his later *The Mascot* (1934) Starevich's puppets display intricate movements and detailed facial expressions (Fig. 2.12). Perhaps the most famous animated puppet was the "star" of *King Kong*, a small, bendable gorilla doll. If you watch *King Kong* closely, you can see the gorilla's fur rippling—the traces of the animator's fingers touching it as he shifted the puppet between exposures. The most famous feature-length puppet film of recent years is Tim Burton's *The Nightmare before Christmas.*

Pixillation is a term applied to frame-by-frame movement of people and of ordinary objects. For example, in 1908 Arthur Melbourne-Cooper animated toys in a miniature set to create dense layers of movement in *Dreams of Toyland* (Fig. 2.13). Although actors ordinarily move freely and are filmed in "real time," occasionally an animator "pixillates" them. That is, the actor freezes in a pose for the exposure of one image, then moves slightly and freezes again for another frame, and so on. The result is a jerky, unnatural motion quite different from ordinary acting. The innovative animator Norman MacLaren uses this approach to tell the story of a feud, *Neighbors*, and to show a man struggling to tame a rebellious piece of furniture in *A Chairy Tale.* Dave Borthwick's *The Secret Adventures of Tom Thumb* animates a tiny plasticine figure of Tom as well as eerie giants played by real actors. (The humans are pixillated even in scenes without Tom.)

Fig. 2.13

Computer imaging has begun a revolution in animation. On a mundane level, the computer can perform the repetitive task of making the many slightly altered images needed to give a sense of movement. On a creative level, software can be devised that enables filmmakers to create images of things that could not be filmed in the real world.

The earliest computer animation depended on intensive hand labor and could not create convincing three-dimensional compositions. James Whitney used an analogue computer to generate the elaborate and precise abstract patterns for his *Lapis* (1963–1966), but he still had to hand-prick cards to create the myriad dots of light for each frame (Color Plate 3).

It was not until the 1980s that computer technology advanced far enough to be used extensively in feature production. Graphic manipulation of frame-by-frame images requires enormous amounts of computer memory, and firms like George Lucas's Industrial Light & Magic developed banks of powerful computers for creating animated imagery. Images generated on computers are transferred to film either by filming directly off a high-resolution monitor or by using a laser to imprint individual pixels of the images onto each frame.

In 1989 James Cameron's thriller *The Abyss* popularized computer animation in live-action features by creating a shimmering water creature. Since then, computer animation has allowed Forrest Gump to meet past presidents (Fig. 2.6) and has created dinosaurs for *Jurassic Park* (Fig. 1.20). Animation, which was formerly used primarily in shorts to accompany a feature-length film, is now supplying special-effects imagery for the features themselves.

Animation can be combined with other types of filmmaking. For example, some documentaries contain animation. An instructional film may show the inner working of a car's engine, while war documentaries often use animated attack maps to show troop movements. Similarly, experimental filmmakers can create abstract or bizarre imagery using animation techniques, as we saw with Whitney's *Lapis* (Color Plate 3). Cel animation is sometimes combined with live-action footage in fiction films, as in *Who Framed Roger Rabbit?* (Color Plate 20).

Fig. 2.14

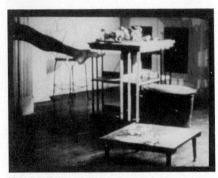

Fig. 2.15

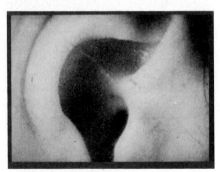

Fig. 2.16

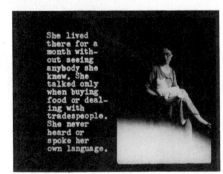

Fig. 2.17

■ EXPERIMENTAL AND AVANT-GARDE FILM

Another basic type of filmmaking is wilfully nonconformist. In opposition to "dominant" or "mainstream" cinema, some filmmakers set out to create films which challenge orthodox notions of what a movie can show and how it can show it. These filmmakers work independently of the studio system, and often they work alone. Their films are hard to classify, but usually they are called *experimental* or *avant-garde*.

Experimental films are made for many reasons. The filmmaker may wish to express personal experiences or viewpoints in ways that would seem eccentric in a mainstream context. In *Mass for the Dakota Sioux*, Bruce Baillie suggests a despair at the failure of America's optimistic vision of history. Su Friedrich's *Damned If You Don't*, a story of a nun who discovers her sexuality, presents the theme of release from religious commitment. Alternatively, the filmmaker may seek to convey a mood or a physical quality. Maya Deren's *Choreography for Camera* frames and cuts a dancer's movements to suggest graceful passage across different times and places (Figs. 2.14, 2.15).

The filmmaker may also wish to explore some possibilities of the medium itself. Experimental filmmakers have tinkered with the medium in myriad ways. They have presented cosmic allegories, such as Stan Brakhage's *Dog Star Man*, and highly private japes, as in Ken Jacobs's *Little Stabs at Happiness*. Robert Breer's *Fist Fight* experiments with shots only one or two frames long (Color Plate 4); by contrast, the shots in Andy Warhol's *Eat* last until the camera runs out of film. An experimental film might be improvised or built according to mathematical plan. For *Eiga-zuke* ("Pickled Film") Japanese-American Sean Morijiro Sunada O'Gara applied pickling agents to negative film and then handprinted the blotchy abstractions onto positive stock.

The experimental filmmaker may tell no story, creating poetic reveries like Willard Maas's *Geography of the Body* (Fig. 2.16) or pulsating visual collages like *Ballet mécanique*, which we will examine later (pp. 148–154 and 373–376). Alternatively, the filmmaker may create a fictional story, but it will usually challenge the viewer. Yvonne Rainer's *Film about a Woman Who* presents its story partly through a series of slides which a group of men and women are watching. At the same time, on the sound track, we hear anonymous voices carry on a dialogue, but we cannot confidently assign any voice to a particular character. Rainer thus forces us to weigh everything we see and hear on its own terms, outside any involvement with characters. Thanks to Rainer's combination of pictures, sounds, and captions (Fig. 2.17), the viewer is left free to imagine several possible stories.

Any sort of footage may be used for an avant-garde film. Images that a documentarist might take as fragments of actuality can be mobilized for quite different purposes. Marjorie Keller draws on home-movie footage in *Daughters of Chaos* to evoke childhood memories (Fig. 2.18), while Bruce Conner pulls footage from travelogues and newsreels to create a sweeping image of the destruction of civilization in *A Movie* (pp. 157–163 and 376–379). Within the experimental mode, such scavenged works are often called *found-footage films*.

Experimentalists have also used staging to express distinct feelings or ideas. James Broughton's *Mother's Day* offers static pictures of adults playing children's games (Fig. 2.19). By superimposing different portions of a kitchen scene from a fiction film, Ivan Galeta's *Two Times in One Space* creates cycles of people splitting or drifting like phantoms. There is avant-garde animation as well, seen in Breer's *Fuji* and Stan Van Der Beek's *Science Friction* (Fig. 2.20).

Fig. 2.18

The freedom available to experimental film is on flamboyant display in Kenneth Anger's *Scorpio Rising*. Anger takes as his subject the motorcycle culture of the 1960s, and he includes scenes of bikers working on their machines, dressing, reveling, and racing. Alongside footage of bikers glimpsed on the streets or in parties, there are many staged incidents—chiefly around Scorpio, a James Dean figure. Anger also cuts in still photos, comic strips, old movies, and Nazi posters. In addition, each segment is accompanied by a rock-and-roll song that adds an ironic or ominous tone to the images. For example, as one young man fetishistically tunes up his bike, Anger shows the figure of death looming over him (Fig. 2.21) and on the sound track we hear "My boyfriend's back . . . and he's coming after you." This sequence links biking to a death wish, an idea that returns in cartoons and other imagery. In such ways, *Scorpio Rising* creates elusive but powerful associations, suggesting the homoerotic dimensions of bike culture, comparing its rituals to fascism and Christianity, and evoking the possibility that people often model their behavior on images supplied by mass media.

Fig. 2.19

Impossible to define in a capsule formula, avant-garde cinema is recognizable by its efforts at self-expression or experimentation outside mainstream cinema. Yet the boundary lines can be breached. Techniques associated with the avant-garde have been deployed in music videos; Conner, Anger, Derek Jarman, and other experimentalists were early pioneers of the format. And mainstream features have been continually drawing upon the avant-garde for ideas and techniques. Over the history of film, the basic types have cross-fertilized each other constantly.

Fig. 2.20

FILM GENRES

Filmmakers and viewers also categorize films by *genre*. A genre is easier to recognize than to define. The Western, the musical film, the action picture, the horror movie, the comedy, the romance—all these are genres. The popular cinema of most countries rests upon genre filmmaking. Germany has its *Heimatfilm,* the tale of small-town life. The Hindi cinema of India produces "devotionals," films centering on the lives of saints and religious figures, as well as "mythologicals" derived from legend and literary classics. Mexican filmmakers developed the *cabaretera,* a type of melodrama centering on prostitutes.

Fig. 2.21

Since most popular filmmaking is fictional, fictional genres come to mind most readily. But there are genres of documentary as well, such as the propaganda film or the instructional film. Experimental film has genres too;

the "found-footage" film is a common one. And in many cases genre categories cut across the basic types. The animated film *Beauty and the Beast* is also a musical, and the Japanese cartoon *Akira* is a science-fiction film.

Defining a genre.   Audiences know the genres of their culture very well, and so do filmmakers. The intriguing problem comes in defining just what a genre is. What makes a group of films a genre?

Most scholars now agree that no genre can be defined in a single hard and fast way. Some genres stand out by their subjects or themes. A gangster film centers on large-scale urban crime. A science-fiction film features a technology beyond the reach of contemporary science. A Western is usually about life on some frontier (not necessarily the West, as *North to Alaska* and *Drums Along the Mohawk* suggest).

Yet subject matter or theme is not so central to defining other genres. Musicals are recognizable chiefly by their manner of presentation: singing, dancing, or both. The detective film is partly defined by the plot pattern of an investigation that solves a mystery. And some genres are defined by the distinctive emotional effect they aim for: amusement in comedy, tension in the thriller. Apparently no strictly logical distinctions can capture the variety of factors which create the genres we have.

Within any one genre, things are also fairly loose. A genre is best thought of as a rough category intuitively shared by audience and filmmaker. That category contains both undeniable instances and fuzzier examples as well. *Singin' in the Rain* is a prime example of a musical, but David Byrne's *True Stories,* with its ironic presentation of musical numbers, is more of a borderline case. And an audience's sense of the core cases can change over history. For today's audiences, a gory film like *The Silence of the Lambs* probably exemplifies the thriller, whereas for audiences of the 1950s a prime example would have been an urbane Hitchcock exercise like *North by Northwest.*

Despite the flexibility of genre categories, we usually have no trouble identifying coherent groups of films within a genre—what are usually called *subgenres.* There is, for example, the "backstage" musical, which centers on professionals putting on entertainment (as in *Fame* or *42nd Street*). This subgenre can be distinguished from the "folk" musical, in which ordinary people sing or dance their way through the story (*Meet Me in St. Louis* or *Hair*). Subgenres of comedy include romantic comedy, slapstick comedy, and parody.

Genre mixing is common throughout popular filmmaking. We can have musical Westerns (the Roy Rogers singing-cowboy movies), musical melodramas (*Yentl* and *A Star Is Born*), and a musical horror movie (*The Rocky Horror Picture Show*). *Alien* merges the horror film, science fiction, and the thriller; *Aliens* combines horror and science fiction with the war movie. *Blade Runner* mixes science fiction and the detective story, while *Billy the Kid vs. Dracula* links the Western and the horror film, two genres that seem pretty incompatible. Comedy, it seems, can combine with anything.

The fact that genres can intermingle does not, however, mean that there are no distinctions among them. Instead of abstract definition, the best way to identify a genre is to recognize how audiences and filmmakers, at different historical periods and places, have intuitively distinguished one sort of movie from another.

Analyzing a genre.   Genres are based on a tacit agreement between film-makers and audiences. What gives films of a type some common identity are shared *genre conventions* which reappear in film after film.

Certain plot elements may be conventional. We expect an investigation in a mystery film, a revenge motive in a Western, and a song-and-dance situation in a musical. The gangster film usually centers on the gangster's rise and fall as he struggles against police and rival gangs. We expect a biographical film to trace the main character's entire life. In a cop thriller, certain characters are conventional: the shifty informer, the comic sidekick, the impatient captain who despairs of getting the squad detectives to follow procedure.

Other genre conventions are more thematic, involving general meanings that are summoned up again and again. The Hong Kong martial arts film commonly celebrates loyalty and obedience to one's teacher. A standard theme of the gangster film has been the price of criminal success, with the gangster's rise to power portrayed as a hardening into egotism and brutality. The screwball comedy traditionally sets up a thematic opposition between a stiff, unyielding social milieu and characters' urges for freedom and innocent zaniness.

Still other genre conventions involve characteristic film techniques. Sombre lighting is standard in the horror film and the thriller, as in Fig. 2.22, from *I Walked with a Zombie*. The action picture often relies on rapid cutting and slow-motion violence. In the melodrama, an emotional twist may be underscored by a sudden burst of pathetic music.

Fig. 2.22

As a visual medium, cinema can also define genres through conventional *iconography*. A genre's iconography consists of recurring symbolic images that carry meaning from film to film.

Objects and settings often furnish iconography for a genre. A close-up of a tommygun lifted out of a 1920s Ford would probably be enough to identify a film as a gangster movie, while a shot of a long, curved sword hanging from a kimono would place us in the world of the samurai. The war film takes place in battle-scarred landscapes, the backstage musical in the-aters and nightclubs, the space-travel film in starships and on distant planets. Even stars can become iconographic—Judy Garland for the musical, John Wayne for the Western, Arnold Schwarzenegger for the action picture, Bill Murray for comedy.

By knowing conventions, the viewer has a pathway into the film. Such landmarks allow the genre movie to communicate information quickly and economically. When we see the weak sheriff, we strongly suspect that he will not stand up to the gunslinger. We can then focus attention on the cowboy hero as he gets slowly drawn into helping the townspeople defend themselves.

Alternatively, a film can revise or reject the conventions associated with its genre. *Bugsy Malone* is a gangster-musical in which children play all the traditional adult roles. *2001: A Space Odyssey* violated several conventions of the science-fiction genre: beginning with a lengthy sequence set in prehistoric times, synchronizing classical music to outer-space action, and ending with an enigmatically symbolic fetus drifting through space. Filmmakers may seek to surprise or shock viewers by breaking their expectations that a certain convention will be followed.

Audiences expect the genre film to offer something familiar, but they also demand fresh variations on it. The filmmaker may devise something mildly or radically different, but it will still be based on tradition. The interplay of convention and innovation, familiarity and novelty, is central to the genre film.

Genre history and social function. Most film genres originate by borrowing from other media. The melodrama has clear antecedents in stage plays and novels like *Uncle Tom's Cabin.* Types of comedy can be traced back to stage farces or comic novels.

Once a genre is launched, there seems to be no fixed pattern of development. We might expect that the earliest films in the genre are the "purest," with genre mixing coming at a late stage. But genre mixing can take place very soon. *Whoopee!* (1930), a musical from the beginning of talking pictures, is also a Western. *Just Imagine* (1930), one of the first sound science-fiction films, contains a comic song. Some historians have also speculated that a genre inevitably passes from a phase of maturity to one of parody, when it begins to mock its own conventions. Yet an early Western, *The Great K & A Train Robbery* (1926) is an all-out parody of its own genre. Early slapstick comedies often take moviemaking as their subjects and ruthlessly poke fun at themselves, as in Charlie Chaplin's farcical *His New Job* (1915).

Across a genre's history, subgenres get marked out. Some filmmakers innovate, either by treating conventions in unique ways or by forging new conventions that get picked up by other filmmakers. At the same time, *cycles* emerge.

A cycle is a batch of genre films that enjoys intense popularity and influence over a distinct period. Cycles can occur when a successful film produces a burst of imitations. *The Godfather* triggered a brief spate of gangster movies. During the 1970s there was a cycle of "disaster movies" (*Earthquake, The Poseidon Adventure*). More recently there have been cycles of comedies centering on spaced-out teenagers (*Wayne's World* and *Bill and Ted's Excellent Adventure*), buddy-cop movies (*Lethal Weapon* and its clones), movies adapted from comic books (*Batman, Judge Dredd*), romantic thrillers aimed at a woman's audience (*Dead Again, Single White Female*), and dramas describing coming of age in African-American neighborhoods (*Boyz N the Hood, Menace II Society*).

Genres also rise and fall in popularity. The Hollywood musical, once the most consistently successful genre, is now waning in live-action filmmaking; it seems to flourish chiefly in animated films like *The Lion King* and *Pocahontas.* Few observers would have predicted that science-fiction movies would return in the 1970s, but *Star Wars* created a long-lasting cycle. It seems likely that a genre never dies. It may pass out of fashion for a time, only to return in updated garb.

The fact that every genre has fluctuated in popularity reminds us that genres are tightly bound to cultural factors. Why do audiences enjoy seeing the same conventions over and over? Many film scholars believe that genres are ritualized dramas resembling holiday celebrations—ceremonies which are satisfying because they reaffirm cultural values with little variation. And just as one can see these ceremonies as helping participants forget the more disturbing aspects of the world, the familiar characterizations and plots of genres may also serve to distract the audience from genuine social problems.

Some scholars would argue that genres go further and actually exploit ambivalent social values and attitudes. The gangster film, for instance, makes it possible for audiences to relish the mobster's swaggering freedom while still feeling satisfied when he receives his punishment. Seen from this standpoint, genre conventions arouse emotion by touching upon deep social uncertainties but then channel those emotions into approved attitudes.

Because of the contract between filmmaker and audience, the promise of something new based on something familiar, genres may also respond quickly to broad social trends. During the economic depression of the 1930s, for instance, the Warner Bros. musical films introduced social commentary into stage numbers; in *Gold Diggers of 1933* a singer asks the Depression-era audience to remember "my forgotten man," the unemployed war veteran. Recently Hollywood producers have tried to shape romantic comedies and dramas to the emergence of "Generation X" tastes. In Chapter 11, we will consider how another musical, *Meet Me in St. Louis,* reflects concerns of the U.S. home front during World War II.

It is common to suggest that at different points in history, the stories, themes, values, or imagery of the genre harmonize with public attitudes. For instance, do the science-fiction films of the 1950s, with hydrogen bombs creating Godzilla and other monsters, reveal fears of technology run amok? The hypothesis is that genre conventions, repeated from film to film, display the audience's pervasive doubts or anxieties. Many film scholars would argue that this "reflectionist" approach helps explain why genres vary in popularity.

Social processes can also be reflected in genre innovations. Ripley, the female protagonist of *Aliens,* is a courageous, even aggressive warrior who also has a warm maternal side. This is something of a novelty in the science-fiction genre. Many commentators saw Ripley as a product of attitudes derived from the Women's Movement of the 1970s. Feminist groups argued that women could be seen as active and competent without losing positive qualities associated with feminine behavior, like gentleness and sympathy. As these ideas spread through mainstream media and social opinion, films like *Aliens* could turn traditionally "masculine" roles over to female characters.

Some critics would argue that such "reflectionist" readings of genre can become oversimplified. Once we look closely at a genre film, we usually discover complexities that nuance a reflectionist account. For instance, if we look beyond Ripley, the protagonist of *Aliens,* we find that all the characters lie along a continuum running between "masculine" and "feminine" values, and the survivors of the adventure seem to blend the best of both gender identities. Moreover, often what seems to be social reflection is simply the film industry's effort to exploit the day's headlines. A genre film may reflect not the audience's hopes and fears but the filmmakers' guess about what will sell.

Whether we study a genre's history, its cultural functions, or its reflection of social trends, conventions remain our best point of departure. As examples, we look briefly at two significant genres of American fictional filmmaking.

■ THE WESTERN

The Western emerged early in the history of cinema, becoming well-established by the early 1910s. It is partly based on historical reality, since in the American West there were cowboys, outlaws, settlers, and tribes of Native Americans. Films also based their portrayal of the frontier on songs, popular fiction, and "Wild West" shows. Early actors sometimes mirrored this blend of realism and myth: cowboy star Tom Mix had been a Texas Ranger, a Wild West performer, and a champion rodeo rider.

Quite early the central theme of the genre became the conflict between civilized order and the lawless frontier. From the East and the city come the settlers who want to raise families, the schoolteachers who aim to spread learning, and the bankers and government officials. In the vast natural spaces, by contrast, thrive those outside "civilization"—not only the American Indians but also outlaws, trappers and traders, and greedy cattle barons.

Iconography reinforces this basic duality. The covered wagon and the railroad are set against the horse and canoe; the schoolhouse and church contrast with the lonely campfire in the hills. As in most genres, costume is iconographically significant too. The settlers' starched dresses and Sunday suits stand out against Indians' tribal garb and the cowboys' jeans and Stetsons.

Interestingly, the typical Western hero stands between the two thematic poles. At home in the wilderness but naturally inclined toward justice and kindness, the cowboy is often poised between savagery and civilization. William S. Hart, one of the most popular early Western stars, crystalized the character of the "good bad man" as the most common protagonist. In *Hell's Hinges* (1916) a minister's sister tries to reform him; one shot represents the pull between two ways of life as Hart reads the Bible, a bottle of whisky at his elbow (Fig. 2.23).

The in-between position of the hero affects common Western plots. He may start out on the side of the lawless, or he may simply stand apart from the conflict. In either case, he will become uneasily attracted to the life offered by the newcomers to the frontier. Eventually the hero decides to join the forces of order, helping them fight hired gunmen, bandits, or whatever the film presents as a threat to stability and progress.

As the genre developed, it adhered to a social ideology implicit in its conventions. White populations' progress westward was considered a historic mission, while the conquered indigenous cultures were usually treated as primitive and savage. Western films are full of racist stereotypes of Native Americans and Hispanics. Yet on a few occasions filmmakers treated Native

Fig. 2.23

American characters as tragic figures, ennobled by their closeness to nature but facing the extinction of their way of life. The best early example is probably *The Last of the Mohicans* (1920).

Moreover, the genre was not wholly optimistic about taming the wilderness. The hero's eventual commitment to "civilized" values was often tinged with regret for his loss of freedom. In John Ford's *Straight Shooting* (1917), Cheyenne Harry (played by Harry Carey) is hired by a villainous rancher to evict a farmer, but he falls in love with the farmer's daughter and vows to reform. Rallying the farmers, Harry helps defeat the rancher. Still, he is reluctant to settle down with Molly. One shot frames him within the farmhouse doorway, halfway between the lure of civilization and the call of the wilderness (Fig. 2.24).

Within this set of values a great many conventional scenes became standardized—the Indians' attack on forts or wagon trains, the shy courting of a woman by the rough-hewn hero, the hero's discovery of a burned settler's shack, the outlaws' robbery of bank or stagecoach, the climactic gunfight on dusty town streets. Writers and directors could distinguish their films by novel handlings of these elements. In Sergio Leone's flamboyant Italian Westerns, every convention is stretched out in minute detail or amplified to a huge scale, as when the climactic shootout in *The Good, the Bad, and the Ugly* (1966) is filmed to resemble a bullfight (Color Plate 5).

There were narrative and thematic innovations as well. After such "liberal" Westerns of the 1950s as *Broken Arrow* (1950), native cultures began to be treated with more respect. In *Little Big Man* (1970) and *Soldier Blue* (1970), the conventional thematic values were reversed, depicting Indian life as civilized and white society as marauding. Some films played up the hero's "uncivilized" side, showing him perilously out of control (*Winchester 73*, 1950), even psychopathic (*The Left-Handed Gun*, 1958). The heroes of *The Wild Bunch* (1969) would have been considered unvarnished villains in early Westerns.

The new complexity of the protagonist is evident in John Ford's *The Searchers* (1956). After a Comanche raid on his brother's homestead, Ethan Edwards sets out to find his kidnapped niece Debbie. He is driven primarily by family loyalty but also by his secret love for his brother's wife, who has been raped and killed by the raiders. Ethan's sidekick, a young man who is part Cherokee, realizes that Ethan plans not to rescue Debbie but to kill her for becoming a Comanche wife. Ethan's fierce racism and raging vengeance culminate in a raid on the Comanche village. At the film's close, Ethan returns to civilization but pauses on the cabin's threshold (Fig. 2.25) before turning back to the desert.

The shot eerily recalls Ford's *Straight Shooting* (Fig. 2.24); Ford even has John Wayne repeat Harry Carey's characteristic gripping of his forearm (Fig. 2.26). Now, however, it seems that the drifting cowboy is condemned to live outside civilization because he cannot tame his grief and hatred. More savage than citizen, he seems condemned, as he says of the souls of dead Comanches, "to wander forever between the winds" (Fig. 2.25). This bitter treatment of a perennial theme illustrates how drastically a genre's conventions can change across history.

Fig. 2.24

Fig. 2.25

Fig. 2.26

■ THE HORROR FILM

While the Western is most clearly defined by subject, theme, and iconography, the horror genre is most recognizable by its intended emotional effect on the audience. The horror film aims to shock, disgust, repel—in short, to horrify. This impulse is what shapes the genre's other conventions.

What can horrify us? Typically, a monster. In the horror film, the monster is a dangerous breach of nature, a violation of our normal sense of what is possible. The monster might be unnaturally large, as King Kong is. The monster might violate the boundary between the dead and the living, as vampires and zombies do. Or the monster might manifest a biology unknown to science, as with the creature in the *Alien* films. The genre's horrifying emotional effect, then, is usually created by a character convention: a threatening, unnatural monster.

Other conventions follow from this one. Our reaction to the monster may be guided by other characters who react to it in the properly horrified way. In *Cat People*, a mysterious woman can, apparently, turn into a panther. Our revulsion and fear are confirmed by the reaction of the woman's husband and his coworker (Fig. 2.27). By contrast, we know that *E. T.* is not a horror film because, although the alien is unnatural, he is not threatening and the children do not react to him as if he is.

The horror plot will often start from the monster's attack on normal life. In response, the other characters must discover that the monster is at large and try to destroy it. This plot can be developed in various ways—by having the monster launch a series of attacks, by having people in authority resist believing that the monster exists, or by blocking the characters' efforts to destroy it. In *The Exorcist*, for example, the characters only gradually discover that Regan is possessed; even after they realize this, they still must struggle to drive the demon out.

The genre's characteristic themes also stem from the intended response. If the monster horrifies us because it violates the laws of nature we know, the genre is well-suited to suggest the limits of human knowledge. It is probably significant that the skeptical authorities who must be convinced of the monster's existence are often scientists.

History. Like the Western, the horror film emerged in the era of silent moviemaking. Some of the most important works in the genre were German—notably *The Cabinet of Dr. Caligari* (1920) and *Nosferatu* (1922), the earliest adaptation of the novel *Dracula*. The angular performances and distorted settings characteristic of German Expressionist cinema conveyed an ominous, supernatural atmosphere. In *Nosferatu*, Max Schreck's make-up and acting made his Count Orlock eerily like a rat or bat (Fig. 2.28).

Because a horror film can create its emotional impact with make-up and other low-technology special effects, the horror genre has long been favored by low-budget filmmakers. During the 1930s, a secondary Hollywood studio, Universal, launched a cycle of horror films. *Dracula* (1931), *Frankenstein* (1931), and *The Mummy* (1932; Fig. 2.29) proved enormously popular and helped the studio become a major company. A decade later, RKO's B-picture

Fig. 2.27

Fig. 2.28   Fig. 2.29

unit under Val Lewton produced a cycle of literate, somber films on minuscule budgets. Lewton's directors proceeded by hints, keeping the monster off-screen and bathing the sets in darkness. In *Cat People* (1942), for instance, we never see the heroine transform herself into a panther, and we only glimpse the creature in certain scenes. The film achieves its effects through shadows, offscreen sound, and character reaction (Fig. 2.27).

In later decades, other low-budget filmmakers were drawn to the genre. Horror became a staple of 1960s U.S. independent production, with many films targeted at the teenage market. Similarly, George Romero's *Night of the Living Dead* (1968) was budgeted at only $114,000, but its success on college campuses helped revive the genre. Today, the horror film is one of the most popular types of cheap, straight-to-video filmmaking.

During the 1970s, the genre acquired a new respectability, chiefly because of the prestige of *Rosemary's Baby* (1968) and *The Exorcist* (1973). These films innovated by presenting violent and disgusting actions with unprecedented explicitness. When the possessed Regan vomited in the face of the priest bending over her, a new standard for horrific imagery was set.

The big-budget horror film entered on a period of popularity which has not yet ended. Many major Hollywood directors have worked in the genre, and several horror films—from *Jaws* (1975) and *Carrie* (1976) to *Jurassic Park* (1993) and *Interview with the Vampire* (1994)—have become huge hits. The genre's iconography pervades contemporary culture, decorating lunch boxes and theme park rides. Horror classics have been remade (*Cat People*, *Dracula*), and the genre conventions have been parodied (*Young Franken-stein, Beetlejuice*).

While the Western declined in popularity during the 1970s, the horror film has sustained an audience for twenty years. Its longevity has set scholars looking for cultural explanations. Many critics suggest that the subgenre of "family horror" films, such as *The Exorcist* and *Poltergeist*, reflect social concerns about the breakup of American families. Others suggest that the genre's questioning of normality and traditional categories is in tune with the post-Vietnam era: viewers may be uncertain of their fundamental beliefs about the world and their place in it. For whatever reason, filmmakers working in the horror film have maintained that dynamic of convention and innovation which is basic to every film genre.

In studying film we often need to make explicit some things we take for granted—those assumptions which are so fundamental that we no longer even notice them. Genres, along with more basic types of film like fiction and documentary, animation, and live action, mainstream and experimental film, are just such taken-for-granted categories. At the back of our minds whenever we watch a film, these categories shape what we expect to see and hear. They guide our reactions. They press us to make sense of a movie in certain ways. Shared by filmmakers and viewers alike, these categories are a condition for film art as we know it. So too, as Part II will suggest, are another set of deep-seated assumptions: those involving film form.

NOTES AND QUERIES

■ BASIC TYPES OF FILM

For histories of documentary, see Richard Meran Barsam, *Nonfiction Films: A Critical History* (Bloomington: Indiana University Press, 1992) and Erik Barnouw, *Documentary: A History of the Nonfiction Film* (New York: Oxford University Press, 1974). A history of the compilation film may be found in Jay Leyda, *Films Beget Films* (New York: Hill & Wang, 1964). More general approaches are exemplified in Michael Renov, ed., *Theorizing Documentary* (New York: Routledge, 1993).

Much contemporary work on documentary has stressed the areas of overlap between documentary and fiction. Bill Nichols's *Representing Reality* (Bloomington: Indiana University Press, 1991) explores this question. See also the essays by Noël Carroll and Carl Plantinga in *Post-Theory: Reconstructing Film Studies* (Madison: University of Wisconsin Press, 1996). We borrow the idea that documentary films come to us "indexed" as such from Carroll's essay, "From Real to Reel: Entangled in Nonfiction Film," *Philosophic Exchange*, no. 14 (1983): 5–45.

Although many scholars have reflected on what makes documentary film factual, few have explained what might make a movie fictional. One theory of fiction that includes film is set forth by Kendall L. Walton in *Mimesis as Make-Believe: On the Foundations of the Representational Arts* (Cambridge: Harvard University Press, 1990). See also Gregory Currie, "Visual Fictions," *The Philosophical Quarterly* **41,** 163 (April 1991): 129–143.

Historical studies of animation include Gianalberto Bendazzi's wide-ranging *Cartoons: One Hundred Years of Cinema Animation* (London: John Libbey, 1994), Donald Crafton's *Before Mickey: The Animated Film, 1898–1928* (1982; 2d ed., Chicago: University of Chicago Press, 1993), and Leonard Maltin's *Of Mice and Magic: A History of American Animated Cartoons* (New York: New American Library, 1980). Roger Noake's *Animation: A Guide to*

Animated Film Techniques (London: MacDonald Orbis, 1988) provides a clear introduction to the various techniques and includes a wide variety of illustrated examples. Useful studies of individual types of animation include Robert Russett and Cecile Starr, eds., *Experimental Animation: An Illustrated Anthology* (New York: Van Nostrand Reinhold, 1976), Michael Frearson's *Clay Animation: American Highlights 1908 to the Present* (New York: Twayne, 1994), and Christopher W. Baker's *How Did They Do It? Computer Illusion in Film and TV* (Indianapolis: Alpha Books, 1994).

On avant-garde cinema, good general studies are P. Adams Sitney, *Visionary Film: The American Avant-Garde 1943–1978*, 2d ed. (New York: Oxford University Press, 1979); Scott MacDonald's *Avant-Garde Film: Motion Studies* (Cambridge: Cambridge University Press, 1993); and James Peterson, *Dreams of Chaos, Visions of Order: Understanding the American Avant-Garde Cinema* (Detroit: Wayne State University Press, 1993). Found-footage film is discussed in William C. Wees, *Recycled Images* (New York: Anthology Film Archives, 1993).

Many fiction films interlard their scenes with documentary footage; examples are the openings of *Road Warrior, JFK,* and *True Stories.* What sorts of effects does the filmmaker seem to be trying to achieve in each case?

ON *ROGER AND ME*

Upon its release *Roger and Me* was hailed as one of the best films of 1989, winning large audiences in the United States and abroad. It seemed a likely contender for an Academy Award until a series of articles pointed out that the film diverged from the actual chronology of events. The major revelations appeared in Harlan Jacobson's interview with director Michael Moore ["Michael and Me," *Film Comment* **25,** 6 (November–December 1989): 16–30]. This often heated conversation explores different conceptions of documentary accuracy.

When challenged by Jacobson about the order of events, Moore granted that "the chronology skips around a bit. That's why I don't use dates in the film" (p. 23). He claimed that he had sought to portray the entire 1980s and that the chronology of the film was not intended to be exact. Moore also said that rearranging events made the film more entertaining and allowed him to condense a decade down to a manageable viewing length.

The controversy is discussed in Carley Cohan and Gary Crowdus, "Reflections on *Roger and Me,* Michael Moore, and His Critics," *Cinéaste* **17,** 4 (1990): 25–30. Carl Plantinga finds *Roger and Me* an example of an "expressive" documentary, a trend that also includes the work of Errol Morris ["The Mirror Framed: A Case for Expression in Documentary," *Wide Angle* **13,** 2 (April 1991): 40–53].

GENRES AND SOCIETY

The "ritual" conception of a genre's social function (p. 55) derives from the anthropological theory of Claude Lévi-Strauss. One version of the ritual model is Thomas Schatz, *Hollywood Genres* (New York: Random House, 1981). See also Jane Feuer, *The Hollywood Musical* (London: British Film Institute, 1982) and Rick Altman, *The American Film Musical* (Bloomington: Indiana University Press, 1987).

Another conception of a genre's social function holds that genre films are centrally concerned with social groups—particularly women and racial minorities—which are oppressed and feared by many in a society. The genre's stories and iconography portray those groups as threatening "normal" life. The film's action will then work to contain and defeat these elements. One argument for this approach can be found in Robin Wood, "An Introduction to the American Horror Film," in Bill Nichols, ed., *Movies and Methods*, vol. II (Berkeley: University of California Press, 1985), pp. 195–220. For a criticism of the theory, see Noël Carroll's *The Philosophy of Horror; or, Paradoxes of the Heart* (New York: Routledge, 1990), pp. 168–206.

■ SPECIFIC GENRES

The vast array of conventions in the Western genre have been codified, along with major films and figures, in two useful reference books: *The Western*, Phil Hardy, ed. (London: Aurum, 1991) and *The BFI Companion to the Western*, Edward Buscombe, ed. (New York: Atheneum, 1988). Our discussion of the conventions of the Western has been shaped by John Cawelti's *The Six-Gun Mystique* (Bowling Green, Ohio: Bowling Green Popular Press, 1975).

Noël Carroll explores the "affective aesthetics" of the horror film in *The Philosophy of Horror,* cited above. Carroll's analysis, which has guided our discussion of the genre, is complemented by the social account offered by Andrew Tudor's *Monsters and Mad Scientists: A Cultural History of the Horror Movie* (Oxford: Blackwell, 1989). Phil Hardy, ed., *Horror* (London: Aurum, 1985) is a comprehensive reference book.

PART II

FILM FORM

Chapter 1 outlined some ways in which people, working with technology, make films. In Chapter 2, we looked at some typical products of that activity—broad types of films, as well as film genres.

Now we can get a little more abstract and ask other questions. By what principles is a film put together? How do the various parts relate to one another to create a whole? Answering these questions will help us understand how we respond to individual movies and how cinema works as an artistic medium.

In the next three chapters we will start to answer such aesthetic questions. We assume that a film is not a random collection of elements. If it were, viewers would not care if they missed the beginnings or endings of films or if films were projected out of sequence. But viewers do care. When you describe a book as "hard to put down" or a piece of music as "absorbing," you are implying that a pattern exists there, that an internal system governs the relations among parts and engages your interest. This system of relationships among parts we shall call *form*. Chapter 3 examines form in film to see what makes that concept so important to the understanding of cinema as an art.

One formal feature that commonly seizes our interest while viewing a film is its "story." Chapters 4 and 5 examine the different types of form that may occur in films—both *narrative* and *nonnarrative* form. We shall see that not all films tell stories, and that whether or not a film does, we can examine that film's form. We can, that is, analyze how its parts relate to one another to create the spectator's overall experience.

THE
SIGNIFICANCE
OF FILM FORM

THE CONCEPT OF FORM IN FILM

If you are listening closely to a song on a tape and the tape is abruptly switched off, you are likely to feel frustrated. If you start reading a novel, become engrossed in it, and then misplace the book, you will probably feel the same way.

Such feelings arise because our experience of artworks is patterned and structured. The human mind craves form. For this reason, form is of central importance in any artwork, regardless of its medium. The entire study of the nature of artistic form is the province of the aesthetician, and it is too large a question for us to deal with extensively here. (See the first part of the Notes and Queries to this chapter for pertinent readings.) But some ideas about aesthetic form are indispensable in analyzing films.

■ FORM AS SYSTEM

Artistic form is best thought of in relation to a perceiver, the human being who watches the play, reads the novel, listens to the piece of music, or views the film. Perception in all phases of life is an *activity*. As you walk down the street, you scan your surroundings for salient aspects—a friend's face, a familiar landmark, a sign of rain. The mind is never at rest. It is constantly seeking order and significance, testing the world for breaks in the habitual pattern.

Artworks rely on this dynamic, unifying quality of the human mind. They provide organized occasions in which we exercise and develop our ability to pay attention, to anticipate upcoming events, to draw conclusions, and to construct a whole out of parts. Every novel leaves something to the imagination; every song asks us to expect certain developments in the melody; every film coaxes us to connect sequences into a larger whole. But how does this process work? How does an inert object, the poem on a piece of paper or the sculpture in the park, draw us into such activities?

Some answers to this question are clearly inadequate. Our activity cannot be *in* the artwork itself. A poem is only words on paper; a song, just acoustic vibrations; a film, merely patterns of light and dark on a screen. Objects do nothing. Evidently, then, the artwork and the person experiencing it depend on one another.

The best answer to our question would seem to be that the artwork *cues* us to perform a specific activity. Without the artwork's prompting, we could not start the process or keep it going. Without our playing along and picking up the cues, the artwork remains only an artifact. A painting uses color, line, and other techniques to invite us to imagine the space portrayed, to compare color and texture, to run our eye over the composition in a certain direction. A poem's words may guide us to imagine a scene, or to notice a break in rhythm, or to expect a rhyme. A sculpture's shape, volume, and materials prompt us to move around it, noticing how its mass fills the space it occupies. In general, any work of art presents cues that can elicit a particular activity from the perceiver.

We can go further in describing how an artwork cues us to perform activities. These cues are not simply random; they are organized into *systems*. Let us take a system as any set of elements that depend on and affect one another. The human body is one such system; if one component, the heart, ceases to function, all of the other parts will be in danger. Within the body there are individual, smaller systems, such as the nervous system or the optical system. A single small malfunction in a car's workings may bring the whole machine to a standstill; the other parts may not need repair, but the whole system depends on the operation of each part. More abstract sets of relationships also constitute systems, such as a body of laws governing a country, or the ecological balance of the wildlife in a lake.

As with each of these instances, a film is not simply a random batch of elements. Like all artworks, a film has *form*. By film form, in its broadest sense, we mean the overall system of relations that we can perceive among the elements in the whole film. In this part of the book and in Part III (on film style), we shall be surveying the sorts of elements a film may possess. Since the viewer makes sense of the film by recognizing these elements and reacting to them in various ways, we shall also be considering how form and style participate in the spectator's experience.

This description of form is still very abstract, so let us draw some examples from one film that many people have seen. In *The Wizard of Oz* the perceiver can notice many particular elements. There is, most obviously, a set of *narrative* elements. These comprise the film's story. Dorothy dreams that a tornado blows her to Oz, where she encounters certain characters. The narrative continues to the point when Dorothy awakens from her dream to find herself home in Kansas. We can also pick out a set of *stylistic* elements: the way the camera moves, the patterns of color in the frame, the use of music, and other devices. Stylistic elements derive from the various film techniques we will be considering in later chapters.

Because *The Wizard of Oz* is a system and not just a hodgepodge, the perceiver actively relates the elements within each set to one another. We link and compare narrative elements. We see the tornado as causing Dorothy's trip to Oz; we identify the characters in Oz as similar to characters in Dorothy's Kansas life. Various stylistic elements can also be connected. For instance, we recognize the "We're Off to See the Wizard" tune whenever Dorothy picks up a new companion. We attribute unity to the film by positing two subsystems—a narrative one and a stylistic one—within the larger system of the total film.

Moreover, our minds seek to tie these subsystems to one another. In *The Wizard of Oz*, the narrative subsystem can be linked to the stylistic subsystem. Film colors identify prominent landmarks, such as Kansas (in black and white) and the Yellow Brick Road. Movements of the camera call our attention to story action. And the music serves to describe certain characters and actions. It is the overall pattern of relationships among the various elements that makes up the form of *The Wizard of Oz*.

■ "FORM VERSUS CONTENT"

Very often people assume that "form" as a concept is the opposite of something called "content." This assumption implies that a poem or a musical piece or a film is like a jug. An external shape, the jug, *contains* something that could just as easily be held in a cup or a pail. Under this assumption, form becomes less important than whatever it is presumed to contain.

We do not accept this assumption. If form is the total system which the viewer attributes to the film, there is no inside or outside. Every component *functions as part of* the overall pattern that is perceived. Thus we shall treat as formal elements many things that some people consider content. From our standpoint, subject matter and abstract ideas all enter into the total system of the artwork. They may cue us to frame certain expectations or draw certain inferences. The perceiver relates such elements to one another dynamically. Consequently, subject matter and ideas become somewhat different from what they might be outside the work.

For example, consider a historical subject, such as the United States Civil War. The real Civil War may be studied, its causes and consequences disputed. But in a film such as D. W. Griffith's *The Birth of a Nation*, the Civil War is not neutral "content." It enters into relationships with other elements: a story about two families, political ideas about Reconstruction, and the epic film style of the battle scenes. Griffith's film depicts the Civil War in a way that is coordinated with other elements in the film. A different film by another filmmaker might draw on the same subject matter, the Civil War, but there the subject would play a different role in a different formal system. In *Gone with the Wind* the Civil War functions as a backdrop for the heroine's romance, but in *The Good, the Bad, and the Ugly* the war aids three cynical men in their search for gold. Thus subject matter is shaped by the film's formal context and our perceptions of it.

■ FORMAL EXPECTATIONS

We are now in a better position to see how film form guides the audience's activity. An interrupted song or an uncompleted story brings frustration because of our urge for form. We realize that the system of relationships within the work has not yet been completed. Something more is needed to make the form whole and satisfying. We have been caught up in the inter-relations among elements and want to understand how the cues prompt us to develop and complete the patterns.

One way in which form affects our experience, then, is to create the sense that "everything is there." Why is it satisfying when a character glimpsed early in a film reappears an hour later or when a shape in the frame is balanced by another shape? Because such relations among parts suggest that the film has its own organizing laws or rules—its own system.

Moreover, an artwork's form creates a special sort of involvement on the part of the spectator. In everyday life, we perceive things around us in a practical way. But in a film the things that happen on the screen serve no such practical end for us. We can see them differently. In life if a person fell down on the street, we would probably hurry to help the person up. But in a film when Buster Keaton or Charlie Chaplin falls, we laugh. We shall see in Chapter 7 how even as basic an act of filmmaking as framing a shot creates a new way of seeing. We watch a pattern which is no longer just "out there" in the everyday world, but which has become a calculated part within a self-contained whole. Film form can even make us perceive things anew, shaking us out of our accustomed habits and suggesting fresh ways of hearing, seeing, feeling, and thinking.

To get a sense of the ways in which purely formal features can involve the audience, try the following experiment (suggested by Barbara Herrnstein Smith). Assume that "A" is the first letter of a series. What follows?

AB

"A" was a cue, and on this basis you made a formal hypothesis, probably that the letters would run in alphabetical order. Your expectation was confirmed. What follows AB? Most people say "C." But form does not always follow our initial expectation.

ABA

Here form takes us by surprise, puzzles us. If we are puzzzled by a formal development, we readjust our expectations and try again. What follows ABA?

ABAC

Here the possibilities were chiefly two: ABAB or ABAC. (Note that your expectations *limit* possibilities as well as select them.) If you expected ABAC, your expectation was gratified and you can confidently predict the next letter. If you expected ABAB, you still should be able to make a strong hypothesis about the next letter.

ABACA

Simple as this game is, it illustrates the involving power of form. You as a viewer or listener don't simply let the parts parade past you. You enter into an active participation with them, creating and readjusting expectations about form as the experience develops.

Now consider a story in a film. *The Wizard of Oz* begins with Dorothy clutching her dog, Toto, and running down a road (Fig. 3.1). Immediately we form expectations. Perhaps she will meet another character or arrive at her destination. Even such a simple action asks that the audience participate actively in the ongoing process by making certain hypotheses about "what will happen next" and readjusting expectations accordingly. Eventually we come to expect that Dorothy will get her wish to return to Kansas. Indeed, the settings of the film give *The Wizard of Oz* a large-scale ABA form, or in this case Kansas-Oz-Kansas.

Fig. 3.1

Expectation pervades our experience of art. In reading a mystery story, we expect that a solution will be offered at some point, usually the end. In listening to a piece of music, we expect repetition of a melody or a motif. (Many musical pieces, in fact, follow the AB, ABA, and ABACA patterns we have just outlined.) In looking at a painting, we search for what we expect to be the most significant features, then scan the less prominent portions. From beginning to end, our involvement with a work of art depends largely on expectations.

This does not mean that the expectations must be immediately satisfied. The satisfaction of our expectations may be *delayed*. In our alphabet exercise, instead of presenting ABA we might have presented this:

AB . . . .

The series of periods postpones the revelation of the next letter, and you must wait to find it out. What we normally call *suspense* involves a delay in fulfilling an established expectation. As the term implies, suspense leaves something "suspended"—not only the next element in a pattern but also our urge for completion.

Expectations may also be cheated, as when we expect ABC but get ABA. In general, *surprise* is a result of an expectation that is revealed to be incorrect. We do not expect that a gangster in 1930s Chicago will find a rocket ship in his garage; if he does, our reaction may require us to readjust our assumptions about what can happen in this story. (The example suggests that comedy often depends on cheating expectations.)

One more pattern of our expectations needs tracing. Sometimes an artwork will cue us to hazard guesses about what has come *before* this point in the work. When Dorothy runs down the road at the beginning of *The Wizard of Oz,* we wonder not only where she is going but where she has been and what she is fleeing from. Similarly, a painting or photograph may depict a scene that asks the viewer to speculate on some earlier event. Let us call this ability of the spectator to frame hypotheses about prior events *curiosity*. As Chapter 4 will show, curiosity is an important factor in narrative form.

Already we have several possible ways in which the artwork can actively engage us. Artistic form may cue us to make expectations and then gratify them, either quickly or eventually. Or form may work to disturb our expectations. We often associate art with peace and serenity, but many artworks offer us conflict, tension, and shock. An artwork's form may even strike us as unpleasant because of its imbalances or contradictions. Many people find atonal music, abstract or surrealist painting, and experimental writing highly disturbing. Similarly, experimental films may jar rather than soothe us. Viewers frequently feel puzzled or shocked by *Eat, Scorpio Rising*, and other avant-garde works (pp. 50–51). And we shall encounter similar problems when we examine the editing of Eisenstein's *October* (Chapter 8) and the style of Godard's *Breathless* (Chapter 11).

Yet even in disturbing us, such films still arouse and shape formal expectations. For example, on the basis of our experience of most movie stories, we expect that the voices we hear can be clearly assigned to the characters whom we see. Yet we cannot do this in Rainer's *Film about a Woman Who . . .* (p. 50). When our expectations are thwarted, we may feel disoriented, but we are also urged to try out anticipations more appropriate to this particular film.

Indeed, if we can adjust our expectations to a disorienting work, it may involve us deeply. Our uneasiness may lessen as we get accustomed to the work's unique formal system. Hollis Frampton's *Zorns Lemma*, for example, slowly trains the viewer to associate a series of images with the letters of the alphabet. Viewers often become quite absorbed in watching the series take shape as a cinematic picture puzzle.

As *Film about a Woman Who . . .* and *Zorns Lemma* also suggest, a disturbing work can also reveal to us our normal expectations about form. Such films are valuable because they coax us to reflect on our taken-for-granted assumptions about how a movie must behave.

There is no limit to the number of ways in which a film can be organized. Some films will ask us to recast our expectations in drastic ways. Still, our enjoyment of the cinema can increase if we welcome the unfamiliar experiences offered by formally challenging films.

■ CONVENTIONS AND EXPERIENCE

Our ABAC example illustrates still another point. One guide to your hunches was *prior experience*. Your knowledge of the English alphabet makes ABA an unlikely alternative. This fact suggests that aesthetic form is not a pure activity isolated from other experiences. The idea that our perception of form depends on prior experience has important implications for both artist and spectator.

Precisely because artworks are human artifacts and because the artist lives in history and society, he or she cannot avoid relating the work, in some way, to other works and to aspects of the world in general. A tradition, a dominant style, a popular form—some such elements will be common to several different artworks. Such common traits are usually called conventions. Genres, as we have already seen in Chapter 2, depend heavily upon conventions. It is a convention of the musical film that characters sing and dance, as in *The Wizard of Oz*. It is one convention of narrative form that the narrative solves the problems which the characters confront, and *Wizard* likewise accepts this convention by letting Dorothy return to Kansas. Bodies of conventions constitute *norms* of what is appropriate or expected in a particular tradition. Through obeying or violating norms, artists relate their works to other works.

From the spectator's standpoint, the perception of artistic form will arise from cues within the work and from prior experiences. But although our *ability* to recognize formal cues may be innate, the *particular* habits and expectations we bring to the artwork will be guided by other experiences— experiences derived from everyday life and from other artworks. You were able to play the ABAC game because you had learned the alphabet. You may have learned it in everyday life (in a classroom, from your parents) or from an artwork (as some children now learn the alphabet from television cartoons). Similarly, we are able to recognize the "journey" pattern in *The Wizard of Oz* because we have taken trips and because we have seen other films organized around this pattern (e.g., *Stagecoach* or *North by Northwest*), and because the pattern is to be found in other artworks, such as the *Odyssey* or *Alice's Adventures in Wonderland*. Our ability to spot cues, to see them as forming systems, and to create expectations is guided by our real-life experiences and our knowledge of formal conventions.

In recognizing film form, then, the audience must be prepared to understand formal cues through knowledge of life and of other artworks. But what if the two principles come into conflict? In ordinary life people don't simply start to sing and dance, as they do in *The Wizard of Oz*. Very often conventions demarcate art from life, saying implicitly, "In artworks of this sort the laws of everyday reality don't operate. By the rules of *this* game, something 'unreal' *can* happen." All stylized art, from opera, ballet, and pantomime to comedy and other genres, depends on the audience's willingness to suspend the laws of ordinary experience and to accept particular conventions. It is simply beside the point to insist that such conventions are unreal or to ask why Tristan sings to Isolde or why Buster Keaton doesn't smile. Very often the most relevant prior experience for perceiving form is not everyday experience but previous encounters with works having similar conventions.

Finally, artworks can create new conventions. A highly innovative work can at first seem odd because it refuses to conform to the norms we expect. Cubist painting, twelve-tone music, and the French "New Novel" of the 1950s seemed difficult initially because of their refusal to adhere to conventions. But a closer look may show that an unusual artwork has its own rules, creating an unorthodox formal system, which we can learn to recognize and respond to. Eventually, the new systems offered by such unusual works may themselves furnish conventions and thus create new expectations.

■ **FORM AND FEELING**

Certainly emotion plays a large role in our experience of form. To understand this role, let us distinguish between emotions *represented in* the artwork and an emotional *response felt by* the spectator. If an actor grimaces in agony, the emotion of pain is *represented within the film*. If, on the other hand, the viewer who sees the painful expression laughs (as the viewer of a comedy might), the emotion of amusement is *felt by the spectator*. Both types of emotion have formal implications.

Emotions represented within the film interact as parts of the film's total system. For example, that grimace of pain might be consistent with the character's response to bad news. A character's sly expression may prepare us for the later revelation of his or her villainous side. Or a cheerful scene might stand in contrast to a mournful one. A tragic event might be undercut by light-hearted music. All emotions present in a film may be seen as systematically related to one another through that film's form.

The spectator's emotional response to the film is related to form as well. We have just seen how cues in the artwork interact with our prior experience, especially our experience of artistic conventions. Often form in artworks appeals to ready-made reactions to certain images (for example, sexuality, race, social class). But form can create new responses instead of harping on old ones. Just as formal conventions often lead us to suspend our normal sense of real-life experience, so form may lead us to override our everyday emotional responses. People whom we would despise in life may become spellbinding as characters in a film. We can be enthralled by a film about a subject that normally repels us. One cause of these experiences lies in the systematic way we become involved in form. In *The Wizard of Oz* we might, for example, find the land of Oz far more attractive than Kansas. But because the film's form leads us to sympathize with Dorothy in her desire to go home, we feel great satisfaction when she finally returns to Kansas.

It is first and foremost the dynamic aspect of form that engages our feelings. Expectation, for instance, spurs emotion. To make an expectation about "what happens next" is to invest some emotion in the situation. Delayed fulfillment of an expectation—suspense—may produce anxiety or sympathy. (Will the detective find the criminal? Will boy get girl? Will the melody return?) Gratified expectations may produce a feeling of satisfaction or relief. (The detective solves the mystery, boy does get girl, the melody returns one more time.) Cheated expectations and curiosity about past material may produce puzzlement or keener interest. (So he isn't the detective? This isn't a romance story? Has a second melody replaced the first one?)

Note that all of these possibilities *may* occur. There is no general recipe by which a novel or film can be concocted to produce the "correct" emotional response. It is all a matter of context—that is, of the particular system that is each artwork's overall form. All we can say for certain is that the emotion felt by the spectator will emerge from the totality of formal relationships she or he perceives in the work. This is one reason why we should try to notice as many formal relations as possible in a film; the richer our perception, the deeper and more complex our response may become.

Taken in context, the relations between the feelings represented in the film and those felt by the spectator can be quite complicated. Let us take an example. Many people believe that no more sorrowful event can occur than the death of a child. In most films this event would be represented so as to summon up the sadness we would also feel in life. But the power of artistic form can alter the emotional tenor of even this event. In Jean Renoir's *The Crime of M. Lange* the cynical pubisher Batala rapes and abandons Estelle, a young laundress. After Batala disappears, Estelle becomes integrated into the courtyard community and returns to her former fiancé. But Estelle is pregnant by Batala and bears his child. The scene when Estelle's employer, Valentine, announces that the child was born dead is one of the most emotionally complex in cinema. The first emotions represented are solemnity and sorrow; the characters display grief. Suddenly Batala's cousin remarks, "Too bad. It was a relative." In the film's context this is taken as a joke, and the other characters break out in smiles and laughter. The shift in the emotion represented in the film catches us off guard. Since these characters are not heartless, we must readjust our reaction to the death and respond as they do—with relief. That Estelle has survived is far more important than the death of Batala's child. The film's formal development has rendered appropriate a reaction that might be perverse in ordinary life. This is a daring, extreme example, but it dramatically illustrates how both emotions onscreen and our responses depend on the context created by form.

■ FORM AND MEANING

Like emotion, meaning is important to our experience of artworks. As an active perceiver, the spectator is constantly testing the work for larger significance, for what it says or suggests. The sorts of meanings that the spectator attributes to the work may vary considerably. Let us look at four things we might say about the meaning of *The Wizard of Oz.*

1. *In the Depression, a cyclone takes a girl from her family's Kansas farm to the mythical land of Oz. After a series of adventures, she returns home.*

This is very concrete, close to a bare-bones plot summary. Here the meaning depends on the spectator's ability to identify specific items: a period of American history called the Depression, a place known as Kansas, features of Midwestern climate. A viewer who was unacquainted with such information would miss some of the meanings cued by the film. We can call such tangible meanings *referential,* since the film refers to things or places already invested with significance.

A film's subject matter—in *The Wizard of Oz,* American Midwestern farm life in the 1930s—is often established through referential meaning. And, as one would expect, referential meaning functions within the film's overall form, in the way that we have argued that the subject of the Civil War functions within *The Birth of a Nation.* Suppose that instead of having Dorothy live in flat, spare, rural Kansas, the film made Dorothy a child living in Beverly Hills. When she got to Oz (transported there, perhaps, by a hillside flash flood), the contrast between the crowded opulence of Oz and her home would not be nearly so sharp. Here the referential meanings of "Kansas" play a definite role in the overall contrast of settings that the film's form creates.

2. *A girl dreams of leaving home to escape her troubles. Only after she leaves does she realize how much she loves her family and friends.*

This assertion is still fairly concrete in the meaning it attributes to the film. If someone were to ask you the point of the film—what it seems to be trying to get across—you might answer with something like this. Perhaps you would also mention Dorothy's closing line, "There's no place like home," as a summary of what she learns. Let us call this sort of openly asserted meaning an *explicit meaning.*

Like referential meanings, explicit meanings function within the film's overall form. They are defined by context. For instance, we are inclined to take "There's no place like home" as a statement of the meaning of the entire film. But, first, *why* do we feel that as a strongly meaningful line? In ordinary conversation it is a cliché. In context, however, the line is uttered in close-up, it comes at the end of the film (a formally privileged moment), and it refers back to all of Dorothy's desires and ordeals, recalling the film's narrative development toward the achievement of her goal. It is the *form* of the film that gives the homily an unfamiliar weight.

This example suggests that we must examine how explicit meanings in a film interact with other elements of the overall system. If "There's no place like home" adequately and exhaustively summarizes the meaning of *The Wizard of Oz,* no one need ever see the film; the summary would suffice. But like feelings, meanings are formal entities. They play a part along with other elements to make up the total system. We usually cannot isolate a particularly significant moment and declare it to be *the* meaning of the whole film. Even Dorothy's "There's no place like home," however strong as a summary of *one* meaningful element in *The Wizard of Oz,* must be placed in the context of the film's entire beguiling Oz fantasy. If "There's no place like home" were the whole point of the film, why is there so much that is pleasant in Oz? The explicit meanings of a film arise from the *whole* film and are set in dynamic formal relation to one another.

In trying to see the meaningful moments of a film as parts of a larger whole, it is useful to set individually significant moments against one another. Thus Dorothy's final line could be juxtaposed to the scene of the characters getting spruced up after their arrival at the Emerald City. We can try to see the film as not "about" one or the other but rather about the relation of the two—the risk and delight of a fantasy world versus the comfort and stability of home. Thus the film's total system will be larger than any one explicit meaning we can find in it. Instead of asking "What is this film's meaning?" we can ask, "How do *all* the film's meanings interrelate formally?"

3. *An adolescent who must soon face the adult world yearns for a return to the simple world of childhood, but she eventually accepts the demands of adulthood.*

This is considerably more abstract than the first two statements. It assumes something that goes beyond what is explicitly stated in the film: that *The Wizard of Oz* is in some sense "about" the passage from childhood to adulthood. In this view, the film suggests or *implies* that, in adolescence, people may desire to return to the apparently uncomplicated world of childhood. Dorothy's frustration with her aunt and uncle and her urge to flee to a place "over the rainbow" become examples of a general conception of adolescence. Let us call this suggested meaning an *implicit* one. When perceivers ascribe implicit meanings to an artwork, they are usually said to be *interpreting* it.

Clearly, interpretations vary. One viewer might propose that *The Wizard of Oz* is really about adolescence. Another might suggest that it is really about courage and persistence, or that it is a satire on the adult world. One of the appeals of artworks is that they seem to ask us to interpret them, often in several ways at once. Again, the artwork cues the spectator to perform certain activities—here, building up implicit meanings. But once again the artwork's overall form shapes the viewer's sense of implicit meanings.

Some viewers approach a film expecting to learn valuable lessons about life. They may admire a film because it conveys a profound or relevant message. Important as meaning is, though, this attitude often errs by splitting the film into the content portion (the meaning) and the form (the vehicle for the content). The abstract quality of implicit meanings can lead to very broad concepts (often called *themes*). A film may have as its theme courage or the power of faithful love. Such descriptions have some value, but they are very general; hundreds of films fit them. To summarize *The Wizard of Oz* as being simply about the problems of adolescence does not do justice to the specific qualities of the film as an experience. We suggest that the search for implicit meanings should not leave behind the *particular* and *concrete* features of a film.

This is not to say that we should not interpret films. But we should strive to make our interpretations precise by seeing how each film's thematic meanings are suggested by the film's total system. In a film, both explicit and implicit meanings depend closely on the relations between narrative and style. In *The Wizard of Oz* the visual element called "the Yellow Brick Road" has no meaning in and of itself. But if we examine the function it fulfills in relation to the narrative, the music, the colors, and so on, we can argue that the Yellow Brick Road does indeed function meaningfully. Dorothy's strong desire to go home makes the Road represent that desire. We want Dorothy to be successful in getting to the end of the Road, as well as in getting back to Kansas; thus the Road participates in the theme of the desirability of home.

Interpretation need not be an end in itself. It also helps in understanding the overall form of the film. Nor does interpretation exhaust the possibilities of a device. We can say many things about the Yellow Brick Road other than how its meaning relates to the film's thematic material. We could analyze how the Road becomes the stage for dances and songs along the way. We could see how it is narratively important because an indecision at a crossroads delays Dorothy long enough to meet the Scarecrow. We could work out a color scheme for the film, contrasting the yellow road, the red slippers, the green Emerald City, and so forth. From this standpoint, interpretation may be seen as one kind of formal analysis, one that seeks to analyze a film's implicit meanings. Those meanings should be constantly tested by placing them within the concrete texture of the whole film.

4. *In a society where human worth is measured by money, the home and the family may seem to be the last refuge of human values. This belief is especially strong in times of economic crisis, such as that in the United States in the 1930s.*

Like the third statement, this is abstract and general. It situates the film within a trend of thought which is assumed to be characteristic of American society during the 1930s. The claim could apply equally well to many other films, as well as to many novels, plays, poems, paintings, advertisements, radio shows, political speeches, and a host of cultural products of the period.

But there is something else worth noticing about the statement. It treats an explicit meaning in *The Wizard of Oz* ("There's no place like home") as a manifestation of a wider set of values characteristic of a whole society. We could treat implicit meanings the same way. If we say the film implies something about adolescence as a crucial time of transition, we could suggest that this emphasis on adolescence as a special period of life is also a recurrent concern of American society. In other words, it is possible to understand a film's explicit or implicit meanings as bearing traces of a particular set of social values. We can call this sort of meaning *symptomatic* meaning, and the set of values that get revealed can be considered to be a social *ideology*.

The possibility of noticing symptomatic meanings reminds us that meaning, whether referential, explicit, or implicit, is largely a social phenomenon. Many meanings of films are ultimately ideological; that is, they spring from systems of culturally specific beliefs about the world. Religious beliefs, political opinions, conceptions of race or sex or social class, even our most unconsciously held, deep-seated notions of life—all these constitute our ideological frame of reference. Although we may live as if our beliefs were the only true and real explanations of how the world is, we need only compare our own ideology with that of another group or culture or historical period to see how historically and socially shaped those views are. In other times or places, "Kansas" or "home" or "adolescence" do not carry the meanings they carry in t.ventieth-century America.

Films, like other artworks, can be examined for their symptomatic meanings. Again, however, the abstract and general quality of such meanings can lead us away from the concrete form of the film. As when analyzing implicit meanings, the viewer should strive to ground symptomatic meanings in the film's specific aspects. A film *enacts* ideological meanings through its particular and unique formal system. We shall see in Chapter 11 how the narrative and stylistic systems of *Meet Me in St. Louis* and *Raging Bull* can be analyzed for ideological implications.

In short, films "have" meaning because we attribute meanings to them. We cannot therefore regard meaning as a simple product to be extracted from the film. Our minds will probe an artwork for significance at several levels, seeking referential meanings, explicit meanings, implicit meanings, and symptomatic meanings. The more abstract and general our attributions of meaning, the more we risk loosening our grasp on the film's specific formal system. As analysts, we must balance our concern for that concrete system with our urge to assign it wider significance.

■ EVALUATION

In talking about an artwork, people often *evaluate* it; that is, they make claims about its goodness or badness. Reviews in popular magazines exist almost solely to tell us whether a film is worth seeing; our friends often urge us to go to their latest favorite. But all too often we discover that the film that someone else esteemed appears only mediocre to us. At that point we may complain that most people evaluate films only on the basis of their own, highly personal, tastes.

How, then, are we to evaluate films with any degree of objectivity? We can start by realizing that there is a difference between personal taste and evaluative judgment. To say "I liked this film" or "I hated it" is not equal to saying "It's a good film" or "It's wretched." Very few people in the world limit their enjoyment only to the greatest works. Most people can enjoy a film they know is not particularly good. This is perfectly reasonable—unless they start trying to convince people that these pleasant films actually rank among the undying masterpieces. At that point others will probably stop listening to their judgments at all.

We may set aside, therefore, personal preference as the sole basis for judging a film's quality. Instead, the critic who wishes to make a relatively objective evaluation will use specific *criteria*. A criterion is a standard which can be applied in the judgment of many works. By using a criterion, the critic gains a basis for comparing films for relative quality.

There are many different criteria. Some people evaluate films on "realistic" criteria, judging a film good if it conforms to their view of reality. Aficionados of military history might judge a film entirely on whether the battle scenes use historically accurate weaponry; the narrative, editing, characterization, sound, and visual style might be of little interest to them.

Other people condemn films because they don't find the action plausible. They will dismiss a scene by saying, "Who'd really believe that X would meet Y just at the right moment?" We have already seen, though, that artworks often violate laws of reality and operate by their own conventions and internal rules.

Viewers can also use moral criteria to evaluate films. Most narrowly, aspects of the film can be judged outside their context in the film's formal system. Some viewers might feel any film with nudity or profanity is bad, while other viewers might find just these aspects praiseworthy. More broadly, viewers and critics may employ moral criteria to evaluate a film's overall significance, and here the film's complete formal system becomes pertinent. A film might be judged good because of its overall view of life, its willingness to show opposed points of view, or its emotional range.

While "realistic" and moral criteria are well-suited to particular purposes, this book will suggest criteria that assess films as artistic wholes. Such criteria should allow us to take each film's form into account as much as possible. *Coherence* is one such criterion. This quality, often conceived as unity, has traditionally been held to be a positive feature of artworks. So too has *intensity of effect*. If an artwork is vivid, striking, and emotionally engaging, it may be considered more valuable.

Another criterion is *complexity*. We can argue that, all other things being equal, complex films are good. A complex film engages our perception on many levels, creates a multiplicity of relations among many separate formal elements, and tends to create interesting formal patterns.

Yet another formal criterion is *originality*. Originality for its own sake is pointless, of course. Just because something is different does not mean that it is good. But if an artist takes a familiar convention and uses it in a way that makes it fresh again or creates a new set of formal possibilities, then (all other things being equal) the resulting work may be considered good from an aesthetic standpoint.

Note that all these criteria are matters of degree. One film may be more complex than another, but the second film may be more complex than a third one. Moreover, there is often a give and take among the criteria. A film might be very complex but lack coherence or intensity. Ninety minutes of a black screen would make for an original film but not a very complex one. A "slasher" movie may create great intensity in certain scenes but be wholly unoriginal, as well as disorganized and simplistic. In applying the criteria, the analyst must often weigh one against another.

Evaluation can serve many useful ends. It can call attention to neglected artworks or make us rethink our attitudes toward accepted classics. But just as the discovery of meanings is not the only purpose of formal analysis, we suggest that evaluation is most fruitful when it is backed up by a close examination of the film. General statements ("This is a masterpiece") seldom enlighten us very much. Usually an evaluation is helpful insofar as it points to aspects of the film and shows us relations and qualities we have missed. Like interpretation, evaluation is most useful when it drives us back to the film itself as a formal system, helping us to understand that system better.

In reading this book, you will find that we have generally minimized evaluation. We think that most of the films and sequences we analyze are more or less good on the formal criteria we mentioned, but the purpose of this book is not to persuade you to accept a list of masterpieces. Rather, we believe that if we show in detail how films may be understood as artistic systems, you will have an informed basis for whatever evaluations you wish to make.

PRINCIPLES OF FILM FORM

Because film form is a system—that is, a unified set of related, interdependent elements—there must be some principles which help create the relationships among the parts. In disciplines other than the arts, principles may be sets of rules or laws. In the sciences principles may take the form of physical laws or mathematical propositions. In practical work, such principles provide firm guidelines about what is possible. For example, engineers designing an airplane must obey fundamental laws of aerodynamics.

In the arts, however, there are no absolute principles of form which all artists must follow. Artworks are products of culture. Thus many of the principles of artistic form are matters of convention. We have already seen (pp. 53–54) that various genres can have very different conventions. A Western is not in error if it does not follow the conventions of, say, a horror film. The artist obeys (or disobeys) norms—bodies of conventions, not laws.

But within these social conventions, each artwork tends to set up its own specific formal principles. The forms of different films can vary enormously. We can distinguish, however, five general principles which the spectator perceives in a film's formal system: function, similarity and repetition, difference and variation, development, and unity/disunity.

■ FUNCTION

If form in cinema is the overall interrelation among various systems of elements, we can assume that every element in this totality has one or more *functions*. That is, every element will be seen as fulfilling one or more roles within the whole system.

Of any element within a film we can ask: What are its functions? In our example of *The Wizard of Oz*, every element in the film fulfills one or more roles. For instance, Miss Gulch, the woman who wants to take Toto from Dorothy, reappears in the Oz section as the Witch. In the opening portion of the film Miss Gulch frightens Dorothy into running away from home. In Oz the Witch seeks to prevent Dorothy from returning home by keeping her away from the Emerald City and by trying to seize the ruby slippers.

Even an element as apparently minor as the dog Toto serves many functions. The dispute over Toto causes Dorothy to run away from home and to get back too late to take shelter from the cyclone. Later, Toto's chasing of a cat makes Dorothy jump out of the ascending balloon and miss her chance to go back to Kansas. Toto's gray color, set off against the brightness of Oz, creates a link to the black and white of the Kansas episodes at the film's beginning. Functions, then, are almost always multiple; both narrative and stylistic elements have functions.

One useful way to grasp the function of an element is to ask what other elements demand that it be present. For instance, the narrative requires that Dorothy run away from home, so Toto functions to motivate this action. Or, to take another example, Dorothy must seem completely different from the Wicked Witch, so costume, age, voice, and other characteristics function to contrast the two. Finally, the switch from black-and-white to color film functions to signal the arrival in the bright fantasy land of Oz.

Note that the concept of function does not always depend on the filmmaker's intention. Often discussions of films get bogged down in the question of whether the filmmaker really knew what he or she was doing in including a certain element. In asking about function, we do not ask for a production history. From the standpoint of intention, Dorothy may sing "Over the Rainbow" because MGM wanted Judy Garland to launch a hit song. From the standpoint of function, however, we can say that Dorothy's singing that song fulfills certain narrative and stylistic functions. It establishes her desire to leave home, its reference to the rainbow foreshadows her trip through the air to the color Oz sequences, and so forth. In asking about formal function, therefore, we ask not, "How did this element get there?" but rather, "What is this element *doing* there?" and "How does it cue us to respond?"

One way to notice the functions of an element is to consider the element's *motivation.* Because films are human constructs, we can expect that any one element in a film will have some justification for being there. This justification is the motivation for that element. For example, when Miss Gulch appears as the Witch in Oz, we justify her new incarnation by appealing to the fact that early scenes in Kansas have established her as a threat to Dorothy. When Toto jumps from the balloon to chase a cat, we motivate his action by appealing to notions of how dogs are likely to act when cats are around.

Sometimes people use the word "motivation" to apply only to reasons for characters' actions, as when a murderer acts from certain motives. Here, however, we will use "motivation" to apply to any element in the film which the viewer justifies on some grounds. A costume, for example, needs motivation. If we see a man in beggar's clothes in the middle of an elegant society ball, we will ask why he is dressed in this way. He could be the victim of practical jokers who have deluded him into believing that this is a masquerade. He could be an eccentric millionaire out to shock his friends. Such a scene does occur in *My Man Godfrey.* The motivation for the beggar's presence at the ball is a scavenger hunt; the young society people have been assigned to bring back, among other things, a beggar. An event, the hunt, *motivates* the presence of an inappropriately dressed character.

Motivation is so common in films that spectators tend to take it for granted. Shadowy, flickering light on a character may be motivated by the presence of a candle in the room. (We may be aware that in production the light is provided by offscreen lamps, but the candle purports to be the source and thus motivates the pattern of light.) The movement of a character across a room may motivate the moving of the camera to follow the action and keep the character within the frame. When we study principles of narrative form (Chapter 4) and nonnarrative form (Chapter 5), we will look more closely at how motivation works to give elements specific functions.

■ SIMILARITY AND REPETITION

In our example of the ABACA pattern, we saw how we were able to predict the next steps in the series. One reason for this was a regular pattern of repeated elements. Like beats in music or meter in poetry, the repetition of the A's in our pattern established and satisfied formal expectations. Similarity and repetition, then, comprise an important principle of film form.

Repetition is basic to our understanding any film. For instance, we must be able to recall and identify characters and settings each time they reappear. More subtly, throughout any film we can observe repetitions of everything from lines of dialogue and bits of music to camera positions, characters' behavior, and story action.

Fig. 3.2

Fig. 3.3

Fig. 3.4

It is useful to have a term to help describe formal repetitions, and the most common term is *motif*. We shall call *any significant repeated element in a film* a motif. A motif may be an object, a color, a place, a person, a sound, or even a character trait. We may call a pattern of lighting or camera position a motif if it is repeated through the course of a film. The form of *The Wizard of Oz* utilizes all of these kinds of motifs. Even in such a relatively simple film, we can see the pervasive presence of similarity and repetition as formal principles.

Film form utilizes general similarities as well as exact duplication. To understand *The Wizard of Oz*, we must see the similarities between the three Kansas farmhands and the Scarecrow, Tin Man, and Cowardly Lion. We must notice that the itinerant Kansas fortune teller (Fig. 3.2) bears a striking resemblance to the old charlatan posing as the Wizard of Oz (Fig. 3.3). We should realize that Miss Gulch's bicycle (Fig. 3.4) becomes the Witch's broom (Fig. 3.5). The duplication is not perfect, but the similarity is very strong. Such similarities are called *parallelism*, the process whereby the film cues the spectator to compare two or more distinct elements by highlighting some similarity. For example, at one point Dorothy says she feels that she has known the Scarecrow, Tin Man, and Cowardly Lion before. At another point, as the Lion describes his timidity, the characters are lined up to form a mirror-reversal image (Fig. 3.6) of the earlier scene where the others had taunted Zeke about being afraid of the pigs (Fig. 3.7).

Motifs can assist in creating parallelism. The viewer will notice, and even come to expect, that every time Dorothy meets a character in Oz, the scene will end with the song "We're Off to See the Wizard." Our recognition of parallelism provides part of our pleasure in watching a film, much as the echo of rhymes contributes to the power of poetry.

Fig. 3.5

Fig. 3.6

▮ DIFFERENCE AND VARIATION

The form of a film could hardly be composed only of repetitions. AAAAAA is pretty boring. There must also be some changes or variations, however small. Thus difference is another fundamental principle of film form.

We can readily understand the need for variety, contrast, and change in films. Characters must be distinguished, environments must be delineated,

Fig. 3.7

different times or activities must be established. Even within the image, we must distinguish differences in tonality, texture, direction and speed of movement, and so on. Form needs its stable background of similarity and repetition, but it also demands that differences be created.

This means that although motifs (scenes, settings, actions, objects, stylistic devices) may be repeated, those motifs will seldom be repeated *exactly*. Variation will appear. In our chief example, *The Wizard of Oz*, the three Kansas hired hands are not exactly the same as their "twins" in Oz. Parallelism thus requires a degree of difference as well as striking similarity. Similarly, Dorothy's determination to return home is a stable and recurrent motif, but it expresses itself in varied ways because of the different obstacles she encounters. Even the repeated motif of Toto's disruption of a situation does not always function in the same way. In Kansas it disturbs Miss Gulch and induces Dorothy to take Toto away from home, but in Oz Toto's disruption prevents Dorothy from returning home.

Differences among the elements may often sharpen into downright opposition among them. We are most familiar with formal oppositions as clashes among characters. In *The Wizard of Oz* Dorothy's desires are opposed, at various points, by the differing desires of Aunt Em, Miss Gulch, the Wicked Witch, and the Wizard, so that the film's formal system derives many dynamics from characters in conflict. But character conflict is not the only way the formal principle of difference may manifest itself. Settings, actions, and other elements may be opposed. *The Wizard of Oz* also presents color oppositions: black-and-white Kansas versus colorful Oz, Dorothy in red, white, and blue versus the Witch in black, and so on. Settings are opposed as well—not only Oz versus Kansas but also the various locales within Oz and especially the Emerald City (Fig. 3.8) versus the Witch's castle (Fig. 3.9). Voice quality, musical tunes, and a host of other elements play off against one another, demonstrating that any motif may be opposed by any other motif.

Fig. 3.8

Not all differences are simple oppositions, of course. Dorothy's three Oz friends—the Scarecrow, the Tin Woodman, and the Lion—are distinguished not only by external features but by means of a three-term comparison of what they lack (brains, a heart, courage). Other films may rely on less sharp differences, suggesting a scale of gradations among the characters, as in Jean Renoir's *Rules of the Game*. At the extreme, an abstract film may create minimal variations among its parts, such as in the slight changes that accompany each return of the same footage in J. J. Murphy's *Print Generation*.

Repetition and variation are two sides of the same coin. To notice one is to notice the other. In analyzing films, we ought to look for similarities *and* differences. Shuttling between the two, we can point out motifs and contrast the changes they undergo, recognize parallelisms as a repetition, and still spot crucial variations.

Fig. 3.9

■ DEVELOPMENT

One way to keep ourselves aware of how similarity and difference operate in film form is to look for principles of development from part to part. Development will constitute some patterning of similar and differing elements. Our pattern ABACA is based not only on repetition (the recurring motif of A) and difference (the varied insertion of B and C) but also on a principle of *progression* which we could state as a rule: alternate A with successive letters in alphabetical order. Though simple, this is a principle of *development*, governing the form of the whole series.

Think of formal development as *a progression moving from X through Y to Z*. For example, the story of *The Wizard of Oz* shows development in many ways. It is, for one thing, a *journey:* from Kansas through Oz to Kansas. The good witch Glinda emphasizes this formal pattern by telling Dorothy that "It's always best to start at the beginning." We see Dorothy put her feet on the literal beginning of the Yellow Brick Road, as it widens out from a thin line (Fig. 3.10). Many films possess such a journey plot. *The Wizard of Oz* is also a *search*, beginning with an initial separation from home, tracing a series of efforts to find a way home, and ending with home being found. Within the film there is also a pattern of *mystery*, which usually has the same from-X-through-Y-to-Z pattern. We begin with a question (Who is the Wizard of Oz?), pass through attempts to answer it, and conclude with the question answered (the Wizard is a fraud). Most feature-length films are composed of several developmental patterns.

Fig. 3.10

In order to analyze a film's pattern of development, it is usually a good idea to make a *segmentation*. A segmentation is simply a written outline of the film that breaks it into its major and minor parts, with the parts marked by consecutive numbers or letters. If a narrative film has ten scenes, then we can label each scene with a number running from one to ten. It may be useful to divide some parts further (for example, scenes 6a and 6b). Segmenting a film enables us not only to notice similarities and differences among parts but also to plot the overall progression of the form. A diagram may be a further help. In Chapters 4 and 5 we will consider how to segment different types of films.

Another way to size up how a film develops formally is to *compare the beginning with the ending*. By looking at the similarities and differences between the beginning and ending, we can start to understand the overall pattern of the film. We can test this advice on *The Wizard of Oz*. A comparison of the beginning and ending on the level of narrative reveals that Dorothy's journey ends with her return home; the journey has been a search for an ideal place "over the rainbow" and has turned into a search for a way back to Kansas. The final scene repeats and develops the narrative elements of the opening. Stylistically, the beginning and ending are the only parts that use black-and-white film stock. This repetition supports the contrast the narrative creates between the dreamland of Oz and the bleak landscape of Kansas.

Fig. 3.11

At the film's end, the fortune teller, Professor Marvel, comes to visit Dorothy (Fig. 3.11), reversing the situation of her visit to him when she had tried to run away. At the beginning he had convinced her to return home; then, as the Wizard in the Oz section, he had also represented her hopes of returning home. Finally, when she recognizes Professor Marvel and the farmhands as the basis of the characters in her dream, she remembers how much she had wanted to come home from Oz.

Earlier, we suggested that film form engages our emotions and expectations in a dynamic way. Now we are in a better position to see why. The constant interplay between similarity and difference, repetition and variation, leads the viewer to an active, developing awareness of the film's formal system. It may be handy to visualize the film's development in static terms, but we ought not to forget that formal development is a *process*.

■ UNITY/DISUNITY

All of the relationships among elements in a film create the total filmic system. Even if an element seems utterly out of place in relation to the rest of the film, we cannot really say that it "isn't part of the film." At most, the unrelated element is enigmatic or incoherent. It may be a flaw in the otherwise integrated system of the film—but it *does affect* the whole film.

When all of the relationships we perceive within a film are clear and economically interwoven, we say that the film has *unity*. We call a unified film "tight," because there seem to be no gaps in the formal relationships. Every element present has a specific set of functions, similarities and differences are determinable, the form develops logically, and there are no superfluous elements.

Unity is, however, a matter of degree. Almost no film is so tight as to leave no end dangling. For example, at one point in *The Wizard of Oz,* the Witch refers to her having attacked Dorothy and her friends with insects, yet we have never seen them, and the mention becomes puzzling. In fact, a sequence of a bee attack was originally shot but then cut from the finished film. The Witch's line about the insect attack now lacks motivation. More striking is a dangling element at the film's end. We never find out what happens to Miss Gulch; presumably she still has her legal order to take Toto away, but no one refers to this in the last scene. The viewer may be inclined to overlook this disunity, however, because Miss Gulch's parallel character, the Witch, has been killed off in the Oz fantasy and we do not expect to see her alive again. Since perfect unity is scarcely ever achieved, we ought to expect that a "unified" film may still contain some unintegrated elements or unanswered questions.

Such disunities may become particularly noticeable when the film as a whole is striving for unity. If we look at unity as a criterion of evaluation, we may judge the film a failure. But unity and disunity may be looked at nonevaluatively as well, as the results of particular formal conventions.

Suppose we saw a film in which several characters die mysteriously, and we never find out how or why. This film leaves a number of loose ends, but the repetition suggests that the omission of clear explanations is not just a mistake. Our impression of a deliberate disunity would be reinforced if other elements of the film also failed to relate clearly to one another. Some films, then, create disunity as a positive quality of their form. This does not mean that these films become incoherent. Their disunity is *systematic,* and it is brought so consistently to our attention as to constitute a basic formal feature of the film. Inevitably such films will be formally disunified only to a relative degree.

SUMMARY

If one issue has governed our treatment of aesthetic form, it might be said to be *concreteness.* Form is a specific system of patterned relationships that we perceive in an artwork. Such a concept helps us understand how even elements of what is normally considered "content"—subject matter, or abstract ideas—take on particular functions within any work.

Our experience of an artwork is also a concrete one. Picking up cues in the work, we can create specific expectations which are aroused, guided, delayed, cheated, satisfied, or disturbed. We undergo curiosity, suspense, and surprise. We compare the particular aspects of the artwork with general conventions which we know from life and from art. The concrete context of the artwork expresses and stimulates emotions and enables us to construct many types of meanings. And even when we apply general criteria in evaluating artworks, we ought to use those criteria to help us discriminate more, to penetrate more deeply into the particular aspects of the artwork. The rest of this book is devoted to studying these properties of aesthetic form in cinema.

We can summarize the principles of film form as a set of questions which you can ask about any film.

1. Of any element in the film, you can ask: What are its functions in the overall form? How is it motivated?
2. Are elements or patterns repeated throughout the film? If so, how and at what points? Are motifs and parallelisms asking us to compare elements?
3. How are elements contrasted and differentiated from one another? How are different elements opposed to one another?
4. What principles of progression or development are at work throughout the form of the film? More specifically, how does a comparison of the beginning and ending reveal the overall form of a film?
5. What degree of unity is present in the film's overall form? Is disunity subordinate to the overall unity, or does disunity dominate?

In this chapter we have examined some major ways in which films as artworks can engage us as spectators. We have also reviewed some broad principles of film form. Armed with these general principles, we can press on to distinguish more specific *types* of form, which are central for understanding film art.

NOTES AND QUERIES

■ FORM IN VARIOUS ARTS

Many of the ideas in this chapter are based on ideas of form to be found in other arts. All of the following constitute helpful further reading: Monroe Beardsley, *Aesthetics* (New York: Harcourt Brace and World, 1958), especially chaps. 4 and 5; Rudolf Arnheim, *Art and Visual Perception* (Berkeley: University of California Press, 1974), especially chaps. 2, 3, and 9; Leonard Meyer, *Emotion and Meaning in Music* (Chicago: University of Chicago Press, 1956); E. H. Gombrich, *Art and Illusion* (Princeton: Princeton University Press, 1961).

■ THE CONCEPT OF FORM IN FILM

On the relation of form to the audience, see the book by Meyer mentioned above. The ABACA example is borrowed from Barbara Herrnstein Smith's excellent study of literary form, *Poetic Closure* (Chicago: University of Chicago Press, 1968). Compare Kenneth Burke's claim: "Form is the creation of an appetite in the mind of the auditor and the adequate satisfying of that appetite." [See Kenneth Burke, "Psychology and Form," *Counter-Statement* (Chicago: University of Chicago Press, 1957), pp. 29–44.] Gestalt psychology posited that the mind has innate form-making capacities, and this has made Gestalt thinkers strong contributors to conceptions of film form that stress audience response. See Rudolf Arnheim, *Film as Art* (Berkeley: University of California Press, 1957). For a more updated survey, see Julian Hochberg and Virginia Brooks, "The Perception of Motion Pictures," in Edward C. Carterette and Morton P. Friedman, eds., *Handbook of Perception,* vol. 10: *Perceptual Ecology* (New York: Academic Press, 1978), pp. 259–304.

Cognitive psychology, with its assumption that humans seek to make sense out of their environment by testing hypotheses and drawing inferences, offers many intriguing leads for an account of the spectator's activity. See Edward Branigan, *Point of View in the Cinema* (New York: Mouton, 1984), chap. 3, and David Bordwell, *Narration in the Fiction Film* (Madison: University of Wisconsin Press, 1985), chap. 3. Another psychological paradigm for the spectator's absorption in the process of film form derives from Freudian psychoanalysis or its offshoots. Dudley Andrew provides a rapid overview of such theories in *Concepts of Film Theory* (New York: Oxford University Press, 1984).

This chapter presupposes that any filmmaker utilizes basic formal principles. But is the filmmaker fully aware of doing so? Many filmmakers use formal principles intuitively, but others apply them quite deliberately. Spike Lee's cinematographer Ernest Dickerson remarks: "A motif we used throughout [*School Daze*] was two people in profile, 'up in each other's face.' That was a conscious decision" [*Uplift the Race: The Construction of "School Daze"* (New York: Simon & Schuster, 1988), p. 110].

FORM, MEANING, AND FEELING

Some psychoanalytical theories of the spectator characterize the emotional appeal of cinema as involving "pleasure" and "unpleasure": an example is Laura Mulvey, "Visual Pleasure and Narrative Cinema," *Screen* **16,** 3 (Autumn 1975): 6–18. A somewhat different line of argument is pursued in Charles Affron, *Cinema and Sentiment* (Chicago: University of Chicago Press, 1982), which concentrates on how narrative structures create identification with the characters or their situations.

Many critics concentrate upon ascribing implicit and symptomatic meanings to films—that is, interpreting them. A survey of interpretive approaches is offered in R. Barton Palmer, *The Cinematic Text: Methods and Approaches* (New York: AMS Press, 1989). David Bordwell's *Making Meaning: Inference and Rhetoric in the Interpretation of Cinema* (Cambridge, Mass.: Harvard University Press, 1989) reviews trends in film interpretation.

SIMILARITY AND DIFFERENCE

No systematic study has been made of how films may be based on repetitions and variations, but most critics implicitly recognize the importance of these processes. A valuable exercise would be to read a critical essay on a film you have seen and to ask how the critic points out similarities and differences crisscrossing the whole film.

Some theorists have pointed out the play of similarity and difference quite explicitly. After an analysis of one sequence from *The Big Sleep,* Raymond Bellour ["The Obvious and the Code," *Screen* **15,** 4 (Winter 1975): 7–17] concludes that a specific pattern of similarities and differences of shots makes the narrative intelligible to us. Stephen Heath attributes a great importance to the "rhyming" effect of certain scenes in *Jaws* ["*Jaws,* Ideology and Film Theory," *Times Higher Education Supplement,* no. 231 (March 16, 1976): 11].

The strangeness of some films may come from their playing up of *differences* within their formal systems. Two theorists have devoted considerable attention to the functions of tension and conflict in cinematic form. See S. M. Eisenstein, *Writings, 1922–34,* vol. 1, edited and translated by Richard Taylor (London: British Film Institute, 1988), and Noël Burch's *Theory of Film Practice,* trans. Helen R. Lane (Princeton: Princeton University Press, 1981). Both theorists use the term *dialectics* of form, but in different ways. How would you define the differences between these theorists?

LINEAR SEGMENTATION AND DIAGRAMMING

Dividing a film into sequences in order to analyze its form is usually called *segmentation.* It is usually not difficult to do, though most often we do it intuitively. Recent film theory has devoted some consideration to the principles by which we segment a film. See Raymond Bellour, "To Analyze, to Segment," *Quarterly Review of Film Studies* **1,** 3 (August 1976): 331–354.

The most influential explanation of how to segment a narrative film has been Christian Metz's famous "Grand Syntagmatic of the Image Track." Metz suggests that there are eight basic sorts of sequences (with some subdivisions and exceptions). See Christian Metz, *Film Language,* translated by M. Taylor (New York: Oxford University Press, 1974), and Stephen Heath, "Film/ Cinetext/Text," *Screen* **14,** 1/2 (Spring/Summer 1973): 102–127.

Usually a feature-length film will have no more than 40 sequences and no fewer than 5, so if you find yourself dividing the film into tiny bits or huge chunks, you may want to shift to a different level of generality. Of course, sequences and scenes can also be further subdivided into subsegments. In segmenting any film, an outline format or a linear diagram may help you visualize formal relations (beginnings and endings, parallels, patterns of development, etc.). We employ an outline format in discussing the nonnarrative films in Chapter 5 (pp. 134, 141, 149, 158) and in discussing *Citizen Kane* (pp. 113, 116).

NARRATIVE
AS A
FORMAL SYSTEM

Stories surround us. In childhood we learn fairy tales and myths. As we grow up, we read short stories, novels, history, and biography. Religion, philosophy, and science often present their doctrines through exemplary stories: the Judeo-Christian tradition's Bible and Torah are huge collections of narratives, while a scientific discovery is often presented as the tale of an experimenter's trials and breakthroughs. Plays tell stories, as do films, television shows, comic books, paintings, dance, and many other cultural phenomena. Much of our conversation is taken up with stories of one sort or another—recalling an event from the past or telling a joke. Even newspaper articles are called "stories," and when we ask for an explanation of something, we may say, "What's the story?" We cannot escape even by going to sleep, since we often experience our dreams as little narratives, and we recall and retell the dreams in the shape of stories. Perhaps narrative is a fundamental way that humans make sense of the world.

The prevalence of stories in our lives is one reason that we need to take a close look at how films may embody *narrative form*. When we speak of "going to the movies," we almost always mean that we are going to see a narrative film—a film that tells a story.

Narrative form is most common in fictional films, but it can appear in all other basic types. For instance, documentaries often employ narrative form. *Primary* tells the story of how Hubert Humphrey and John F. Kennedy campaigned in the Wisconsin presidential primary of 1960. Many animated films, such as Disney features and Warner Bros. short cartoons, also tell stories. Some experimental and avant-garde films use narrative form, although the story or the way it is told may be quite unusual, as in *Film about a Woman Who . . .* and *Scorpio Rising* (pp. 50–51).

Because stories are all around us, spectators approach a narrative film with definite expectations. We may know a great deal about the particular story the film will tell. Perhaps we have read the book on which a film is based, or we have seen the film to which this is a sequel. More generally, though, we have anticipations that are characteristic of narrative form itself. We assume that there will be characters and some action that will involve them with one another. We expect a series of incidents that will be connected in some way. We also probably expect that the problems or conflicts arising in the course of the action will achieve some final state—either they will be resolved, or at least a new light will be cast on them. A spectator comes prepared to make sense of a narrative film.

As the viewer watches the film, she or he picks up cues, recalls information, anticipates what will follow, and generally participates in the creation of the film's form. The film shapes particular expectations by summoning up curiosity, suspense, and surprise. The ending has the task of satisfying or cheating the expectations prompted by the film as a whole. The ending may also activate memory by cueing the spectator to review earlier events, possibly considering them in a new light. As we examine narrative form, we will consider at various points how it engages the viewer in a dynamic activity.

■ PLOT AND STORY

We can consider a narrative to be *a chain of events in cause-effect relationship occurring in time and space*. A narrative is thus what we usually mean by the term "story," although we shall be using that term in a slightly different way later. Typically, a narrative begins with one situation; a series of changes occurs according to a pattern of cause and effect; finally, a new situation arises that brings about the end of the narrative.

All the components of our definition—causality, time, and space—are important to narratives in most media, but causality and time are central. A random string of events is hard to perceive as a story. Consider the following actions: "A man tosses and turns, unable to sleep. A mirror breaks. A telephone rings." We have trouble grasping this as a narrative because we are unable to determine the causal or temporal relations among the events.

Consider a new description of these same events. "A man has a fight with his boss; he tosses and turns that night, unable to sleep. In the morning, he is still so angry that he smashes the mirror while shaving. Then his telephone rings; his boss has called to apologize."

We now have a narrative. We can connect the events spatially: The man is in the office, then in his bed; the mirror is in the bathroom; the phone is somewhere else in his home. More important, we can understand that the three events are part of a series of causes and effects. The argument with the boss causes the sleeplessness and the broken mirror. A phone call from the boss resolves the conflict; the narrative ends. In this example, time is also important. The sleepless night occurs before the breaking of the mirror, which in turn occurs before the phone call; all of the action runs from one day to the following morning. The narrative develops from an initial situation of conflict between employee and boss, through a series of events caused by the conflict, to the resolution of the conflict. Simple and minimal as our example is, it shows how important causality, space, and time are to narrative form.

The fact that a narrative relies on causality, time, and space does not mean that other formal principles cannot govern the film. For instance, a narrative may make use of parallelism. As Chapter 3 points out (pp. 81–82), parallelism posits a similarity among different elements. Our example was the way that *The Wizard of Oz* made the three Kansas farmhands parallel to Dorothy's three Oz companions. A narrative may cue us to draw parallels among characters, settings, situations, times of day, or any other elements. In Věrá Chytilová's *Something Different*, scenes from the life of a housewife and from the career of a gymnast are presented in alternation. Since the two women never meet and lead entirely separate lives, there is no way that we can connect the two stories causally. Instead, we compare and contrast the two women's actions and situations—that is, we draw parallels. In *Primary*, scenes of Humphrey making speeches and shaking hands alternate with scenes of Kennedy's efforts, thus comparing the two candidates' campaign styles.

Another documentary, *Hoop Dreams*, makes even stronger use of parallels. Two high-school students from Chicago's black ghetto dream of becoming professional basketball players, and the film follows each one through his athletic career. The film's form invites us to compare and contrast their personalities, the obstacles they face, and the choices they make. In addition, the film creates parallels between their high schools, their coaches, their parents, and older male relatives who vicariously live their own dreams of athletic glory. Parallelism allows the film to become richer and more complex than it might have been had it concentrated on only one protagonist.

Yet *Hoop Dreams*, like *Something Different* and *Primary*, is still a narrative film. Each of the two lines of action is organized by time, space, and causality. The film suggests some broad causal forces as well. Both young men have grown up in urban poverty, and because sports is the most visible sign of success for them, they turn their hopes in that direction.

We make sense of a narrative, then, by identifying its events and linking them by cause and effect, time, and space. As viewers, we do other things as well. We often infer events that are not explicitly presented, and we recognize the presence of material that is extraneous to the story world. In order to describe how we perform such activities, we can draw a distinction between *story* and *plot* (sometimes called "story" and "discourse"). Since this distinction is basic to understanding narrative form, we need to examine it in a little more detail.

We often make assumptions and inferences about events in a narrative. For instance, at the start of Alfred Hitchcock's *North by Northwest* we know we are in Manhattan at rush hour. The cues stand out clearly: skyscrapers, congested traffic, hurrying pedestrians. Then we watch Roger Thornhill as he leaves an elevator with his secretary, Maggie, and strides through the lobby, dictating memos as she takes them down. On the basis of these cues, we start to draw some conclusions. Thornhill is an executive who leads a busy life. We assume that before we saw Thornhill and Maggie, he was also dictating to her; we have come in on the middle of a string of events in time. We also assume that the dictating began in the office, before they got on the elevator. In other words, we infer causes, a temporal sequence, and another locale even though none of this information has been directly presented. We are probably not aware of having made these inferences, but they are no less firm for going unnoticed.

The set of *all* the events in a narrative, both the ones explicitly presented and those the viewer infers, comprises the *story*. In our example the story would consist of at least two depicted events and two inferred ones. We can list them, putting the inferred events in parentheses:

(Roger Thornhill has a busy day at his office.)
Rush hour hits Manhattan.
(While dictating to his secretary Maggie, Roger leaves the office and they take the elevator.)
Still dictating, Roger gets off the elevator with Maggie and they stride through the lobby.

The total world of the story action is sometimes called the film's *diegesis* (the Greek word for "recounted story"). In the opening of *North by Northwest*, the traffic, streets, skyscrapers, and people we see, as well as the traffic, streets, skyscrapers, and people we assume to be offscreen, are all diegetic because they are assumed to exist in the world that the film depicts.

The term *plot* is used to describe everything visibly and audibly present in the film before us. The plot includes, first, all the story events that are directly depicted. In our *North by Northwest* example, only two story events are explicitly presented in the plot: rush hour and Roger Thornhill's dictating to Maggie as they leave the elevator.

Secondly, the film's plot may contain material that is extraneous to the story world. For example, while the opening of *North by Northwest* is portraying rush hour in Manhattan, we also see the film's credits and hear orchestral music. Neither of these elements is diegetic, since they are brought in from *outside* the story world. (The characters cannot read the credits or hear the music.) Credits and such extraneous music are thus *nondiegetic* elements. In Chapters 8 and 9 we will consider how editing and sound can function nondiegetically. At this point, we need only notice that the film's plot—the totality of the film—can bring in nondiegetic material.

Nondiegetic material may occur elsewhere than in credit sequences. In *The Band Wagon*, we see the premiere of a hopelessly pretentious musical play. Eager patrons file into the theater; there then appears a pair of black-and-white drawings of bleak landscapes, followed by a third drawing of an egg. The three images are accompanied by a brooding chorus. These images and sounds are clearly nondiegetic, inserted from outside the story world in order to signal that the production was catastrophic and "laid an egg." The plot has added material to the story for comic effect.

In sum, story and plot overlap in one respect and diverge in others. The plot explicitly presents certain story events, so these events are common to both domains. The story goes beyond the plot in suggesting some diegetic events which we never witness. The plot goes beyond the story world by presenting nondiegetic images and sounds which may affect our understanding of the story. A diagram of the situation would look like this:

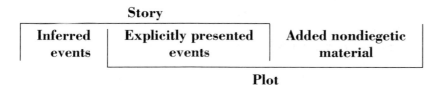

We can think about these differences between story and plot from two perspectives. From the standpoint of the storyteller, the filmmaker, the story is the sum total of all the events in the narrative. The storyteller can present some of these events directly (that is, make them part of the plot), can hint at events that are not presented, and can simply ignore other events. For instance, though we learn later in *North by Northwest* that Roger has a mother, we never learn what happened to his father. The filmmaker can also add nondiegetic material, as in the example from *The Band Wagon*. In a sense, then, the filmmaker makes a story into a plot.

From the perceiver's standpoint, things look somewhat different. All we have before us is the plot—the arrangement of material in the film as it stands. We create the story in our minds on the basis of cues in the plot. We also recognize when the plot presents nondiegetic material.

The story-plot distinction suggests that if you want to give someone a synopsis of a narrative film, you can proceed in two ways. You can summarize the story, starting from the very earliest incident which the plot cues you to infer and running straight through to the end. Or you can tell the plot, starting with the first incident you encountered in watching the film.

Our initial definition and the distinction between plot and story constitute a set of tools for analyzing how narrative works. We shall see that the plot-story distinction affects all three aspects of narrative: causality, time, and space.

■ CAUSE AND EFFECT

If narrative depends so heavily on cause and effect, what kinds of things can function as causes in a narrative? Usually the agents of cause and effect are *characters*. By triggering and reacting to events, characters play roles within the film's formal system.

If narrative depends so heavily on cause and effect, what can function as a cause? Most often, persons, or at least entities like persons—Bugs Bunny or E. T. the extraterrestrial or even the singing teapot in *Beauty and the*

Beast. To avoid creating clumsy terms, let us simply call any personlike agent in a narrative a character. For our purposes here Michael Moore is a character in *Roger and Me* no less than Roger Thornhill is in *North by Northwest*, even though Moore is a real person and Thornhill is fictional. In any narrative film, either fictional or documentary, characters create causes and register effects. Within the film's formal system, they make things happen and react to the twists and turns of events.

In film narrative, characters have several properties. They usually have a body (though sometimes a character is only a ghostly voice, as when the dead Obi-Wan Kenobi urges the Jedi master Yoda to train Luke Skywalker in *The Empire Strikes Back*). Characters also often possess character *traits*. When we say that a character in a film was "complex" or "well developed," we really mean that the character was a collection of several or varying traits. A minor character may have only one or two traits. A memorable character such as Sherlock Holmes is a mass of traits, some bearing on his habits (his love of music, his addiction to cocaine) and others reflecting his basic nature (his penetrating intelligence, his disdain for stupidity, his professional pride, his occasional gallantry).

In general, a character's traits are designed to play a causal role in the narrative. The second scene of Alfred Hitchcock's *The Man Who Knew Too Much* (1934) shows that the heroine, Jill, is an excellent shot with a rifle. For much of the film, this trait seems irrelevant to the narrative, but in the last scene Jill is able to shoot one of the villains when a police marksman cannot do it. This skill with a rifle is not a natural part of a person named Jill; it is a trait that helps make up a character named Jill, and it serves a particular narrative function. Character traits can involve attitudes, skills, preferences, psychological drives, details of dress and appearance, and any other specific quality the film creates for a character.

Not all causes and effects in narratives originate with characters. In the so-called disaster movies, an earthquake or tidal wave may precipitate a series of actions on the parts of the characters. The same principle holds when the shark in *Jaws* terrorizes a community. (The film may "personify" these natural causes by assigning them human traits like malevolence. In *Jaws*, the shark is seen as vengeful and cunning.) Still, once these natural occurrences set the situation up, human desires and goals usually enter the action to develop the narrative. A man escaping from a flood may be placed in the situation of having to decide whether to rescue his worst enemy. In *Jaws*, the townspeople pursue a variety of strategies to deal with the shark, propelling the plot as they do so.

In general, the spectator actively seeks to connect events by means of cause and effect. Given an incident, we tend to hypothesize what might have caused it, or what it might in turn cause. That is, we look for causal motivation. We have mentioned an instance of this in Chapter 3: In the scene from *My Man Godfrey*, a scavenger hunt serves as a cause that justifies the presence of a beggar at a society ball (see p. 80). Causal motivation often involves the "planting" of information in advance of a scene. In one climactic scene of John Ford's *Stagecoach*, there is a last-minute rescue from Indians by a cavalry troop. If these soldiers appeared from nowhere, we would most likely find the rescue a weak resolution of the battle scene. But *Stagecoach* begins with a scene of the cavalry discovering that Geronimo is on the attack. Several later scenes involve the cavalry, and at one of their stops the passengers on the coach learn that the soldiers have had a skirmish with the Indians. These previous scenes of cavalry troops causally motivate their appearance in the final rescue scene.

Most of what we have said about causality pertains to the plot's direct presentation of causes and effects. In *The Man Who Knew Too Much*, Jill is shown to be a good shot, and because of this she can save her daughter. The townsfolk in *Jaws* respond to the shark attack that is shown at the start of the film. But the plot can also lead us to *infer* causes and effects and thus build up a total story. The detective film furnishes the best example of how this active construction of the story may work.

A murder has been committed. That is, we know an effect but not the causes—the killer, the motive, perhaps also the method. The mystery tale thus depends strongly on curiosity, our desire to know events that have occurred before the plot action begins. It is the detective's job to disclose, at the end, the missing causes—to name the killer, explain the motive, and reveal the method. That is, in the detective film the climax of the plot (the action that we see) is a revelation of prior incidents in the story (events which we did not see). We can diagram this.

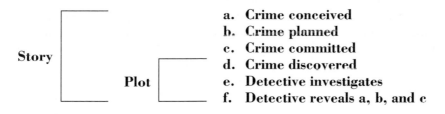

Story   Plot

a. **Crime conceived**
b. **Crime planned**
c. **Crime committed**
d. **Crime discovered**
e. **Detective investigates**
f. **Detective reveals a, b, and c**

Although this pattern is most common in detective narratives, any film's plot can withhold causes and thus arouse our curiosity. Horror and science-fiction films often leave us in the dark about what forces lurk behind certain events. We shall see that the plot of *Citizen Kane* delays revealing what causes the hero to say "Rosebud" on his deathbed. In general, whenever any film creates a mystery, it does so by suppressing certain story causes and by presenting only effects in the plot.

The plot may also present causes but withhold story effects, prompting the viewer to imagine them. During the final battle in *Jaws*, the young scientist, Hooper, is last seen hiding on the ocean bottom after the shark has smashed open his protective cage. Although we are not shown the outcome, we might assume that Hooper is dead. Later, after Sheriff Brody has destroyed the shark, Hooper surfaces, revealing that he has escaped after all.

A plot's withholding of effects is perhaps most disruptive at the end of a film. A famous example occurs in the final moments of François Truffaut's *The 400 Blows*. The boy Antoine Doinel has escaped from a reformatory and runs along the seashore. The camera zooms in on his face and the frame

Fig. 4.1

freezes (Fig. 4.1). The plot does not reveal whether he is captured and brought back, leaving us to speculate on what might happen next.

■ TIME

Causes and their effects are basic to narrative, but they take place in time. Here again our story-plot distinction is of some help in clarifying how time shapes our understanding of narrative action.

As we watch a film, we construct story time on the basis of what the plot presents. For example, the plot may present events out of chronological order. In *Citizen Kane*, we see a man's death before we see his youth, and we must build up a chronological version of his life. Alternatively, the plot may present only certain periods of time; the viewer thus infers that some story duration has been skipped over. Still another possibility is to have the plot present the same story event many times, as when a character repeatedly recalls a traumatic incident. This means that in constructing the film's story out of its plot, the viewer tries to put events in chronological *order* and to assign them some *duration* and *frequency*. We can look at each of these temporal factors separately.

Temporal order. We are quite accustomed to films that present events out of story order. A flashback is simply a portion of a story that the plot presents out of chronological order. Suppose we see a shot of a woman thinking about her childhood, then a second shot depicting her as a girl; we understand that the second shot actually shows an earlier story event than the first one did. This does not confuse us because we mentally rearrange the events into the order in which they would logically have to occur: Childhood comes before adulthood. From the plot order, we infer the story order. If story events can be thought of as ABCD, then the plot that uses a flashback presents something like BACD. Similarly, a flashforward—that is, moving from present to future then back to the present—would also be an instance of how plot can shuffle story order. A flashforward could be represented as ABDC.

Our example of the detective film is also pertinent here. A detective film not only manipulates story causality by holding back key events, the film also juggles story order. The plot presents events surrounding the crime only when the detective reveals them at the climax.

One common pattern for reordering story events is an alternation of past and present in the plot. In the first half of Terence Davies's *Distant Voices, Still Lives* we see scenes set in the present during a young woman's wedding day. These alternate with flashbacks to a time when her family lived under the sway of an abusive, mentally disturbed father. Interestingly, the flashback scenes are arranged out of chronological story order: Childhood episodes are mixed with scenes of adolescence.

Sometimes a fairly simple reordering of scenes can create complicated effects. The plot of Quentin Tarentino's *Pulp Fiction* begins with a couple deciding to rob the diner in which they are eating breakfast. This scene takes place somewhat late in the story, but the viewer doesn't learn this until near the end of the film, when the robbery interrupts a dialogue involving other, more central characters eating breakfast in the same diner. Just by pulling a scene out of order and placing it at the start, Tarentino creates a surprise. Later in *Pulp Fiction* a hired killer is killed. But he reappears alive in subsequent scenes, which show him and his partner trying to dispose of a dead body. Tarentino has simply shifted a block of scenes from the middle of the story (before the man was killed) to the end of the plot. By coming at the film's conclusion these portions receive an emphasis they would not have if they had remained in their chronological story order.

Temporal duration. The plot of *North by Northwest* presents four crowded days and nights in the life of Roger Thornhill. But the story stretches back far before that, since information about the past is revealed in the course of the plot. The story events include Roger's past marriages, the U.S. Intelligence Agency's plot to create a false agent named George Kaplan, and Van Damm's series of smuggling activities.

In general, a film's plot selects certain stretches of story duration. This could involve concentrating on a short, relatively cohesive time span, as *North by Northwest* does, or by highlighting significant stretches of time from a period of many years, as *Citizen Kane* does when it shows us the protagonist in his youth, skips over some time to show him as a young man, skips over more time to show him middle-aged, and so forth. The sum of all these slices of story duration yields an overall plot duration.

But we need one more distinction. Watching a movie takes time—twenty minutes, two hours, eight hours (for example, Hans Jürgen Syberberg's *Our Hitler: A Film from Germany*). There is thus a third duration involved in a narrative film, which we can call *screen duration*. The relationships among story duration, plot duration, and screen duration are complex (see Notes and Queries for further discussion), but for our purposes we can say that the filmmaker can manipulate screen duration independently of the overall story duration and plot duration. For example, *North by Northwest* has an overall story duration of several years (including all relevant prior events), an overall plot duration of four days and nights, and a screen duration of about 136 minutes.

Just as plot duration selects from story duration, so screen duration selects from overall plot duration. In *North by Northwest*, only portions of the film's four days and nights are shown to us. An interesting counterexample is *Twelve Angry Men*, the story of a jury deliberating a murder case. The 95 minutes of the movie approximate the same time in its characters' lives.

At a more specific level, the plot can use screen duration to override story time. For example, screen duration can *expand* story duration. A famous instance is that of the raising of the bridges in Sergei Eisenstein's *October*. Here an event that takes only a few moments in the story is stretched out to several minutes of screen time by means of the technique of film editing. As a result, this action gains a tremendous emphasis. The plot can also use screen duration to compress story time, as when a lengthy process is condensed into a rapid series of shots. These examples suggest that film techniques play a central role in creating screen duration. We shall consider this in more detail in Chapters 7 and 8.

Temporal frequency.   Most commonly, a story event is presented only once in the plot. Occasionally, however, a single story event may appear twice or even more in the plot treatment. If we see an event early in a film and then there is a flashback to that event later on, we see that same event twice. Some films use multiple narrators, each of whom describes the same event; again, we see it occur several times. This may allow us to see the same action in several ways. The plot may also provide us with more information, so that we understand the event in a new context when it reappears. This occurs in *Pulp Fiction*, when the robbery of the diner, shown at the start of the film, takes on its full significance only when it is repeated at the climax. In our examination of *Citizen Kane* we shall see another example of how repetition can recontextualize old information.

The various ways that a film's plot may manipulate story order, duration, and frequency illustrate how the spectator must actively participate in making sense of the narrative film. The plot supplies cues about chronological sequence, the time span of the actions, and the number of times an event occurs, and it is up to the spectator to make inferences and form expectations.

Often we must motivate manipulations of time by the all-important principle of cause and effect. For instance, a flashback will often be justified as caused by some incident that triggers a character's recalling some event in the past. The plot may skip over years of story duration if they contain nothing important to the chains of cause and effect. The repetition of actions may also be motivated by the plot's need to communicate certain key causes very clearly to the spectator.

■ SPACE

In some media, a narrative might emphasize only causality and time. Many anecdotes do not specify where the action takes place. In film narrative, however, space is usually an important factor. Events tend to occur in particular locales, such as Kansas or Oz, the Flint, Michigan of *Roger and Me*, or the Manhattan of *North by Northwest*. We shall consider setting in more detail when we examine mise-en-scene in Chapter 6, but we ought briefly to note how plot and story can manipulate space.

Normally, the place of the story action is also that of the plot, but sometimes the plot leads us to infer other locales as part of the story. We never see Roger Thornhill's office or the colleges that kicked Kane out. Thus the narrative may ask us to imagine spaces and actions that are never shown. In Otto Preminger's *Exodus*, one scene is devoted to Dov Landau's interrogation by a terrorist organization he wants to join. Dov reluctantly tells his questioners of life in a Nazi concentration camp. Although the film never shows this locale through a flashback, much of the scene's emotional power depends on our using our imagination to fill in Dov's sketchy description of the camp.

Finally, we can introduce an idea akin to the concept of screen duration. Besides story space and plot space, cinema employs *screen space*: the visible space within the frame. We shall consider screen space and offscreen space in more detail in Chapter 7, when we analyze framing as a cinematographic technique. For now, it is enough to say that just as screen duration selects certain plot spans for presentation, so screen space selects portions of plot space.

■ OPENINGS, CLOSINGS, AND PATTERNS OF DEVELOPMENT

In Chapter 3 our discussion of formal development within the film suggested that it is often useful to compare beginnings and endings. This holds true for narrative form as well, since a narrative's use of causality, time, and space usually involves a change from an initial situation to a final situation.

A film does not just start, it *begins*. The opening provides a basis for what is to come and initiates us into the narrative. Typically, the plot will seek to arouse curiosity by bringing us into a series of actions that has already started. (This is called opening *in medias res*, a Latin phrase meaning "in the middle of things.") The viewer speculates on possible causes of the events presented. Typically, some of the actions that took place before the plot started will be stated or suggested so that we can start to connect up the whole story. The portion of the plot that sets out story events and character traits important in the opening situation is called the *exposition*. In general, the opening raises our expectations by setting up a specific range of possible causes for and effects of what we see.

No film can explore all the possibilities hovering in our mind at the start. As the plot proceeds, the causes and effects will define narrower patterns of development. There is no exhaustive list of possible plot patterns, but several kinds crop up frequently enough to be worth mentioning.

Most patterns of plot development depend heavily upon the ways that causes and effects create a change in a character's situation. The most common general pattern is a *change in knowledge*. Very often, a character learns something in the course of the action, with the most crucial knowledge coming at the turning point of the plot.

A little more specifically, there are *goal-oriented* plots, in which a character takes steps to achieve a desired object or state of affairs. Plots based on *searches* would be instances of the goal plot. In *Raiders of the Lost Ark*, the protagonists try to find the Ark of the Covenant; in *Le Million*, characters search for a missing lottery ticket; in *North by Northwest*, Roger Thornhill looks for George Kaplan. A variation on the goal-oriented plot pattern is the *investigation*, so typical of detective films, in which the protagonist's goal is not an object, but information, usually about mysterious causes. In more strongly psychological films such as Fellini's *8½*, the search and the investigation become internalized when the protagonist, a noted film director, attempts to discover the source of his creative problems.

Time or space may also provide plot patterns. A framing situation in the present may initiate a series of flashbacks showing how events led up to the present situation, as in *Citizen Kane*'s flashbacks. *Hoop Dreams* is organized around the two main characters' high-school careers, with each part of the film devoted to a year of their lives. The plot may also create a specific duration for the action, a deadline. In *Back to the Future*, the hero must synchronize his time machine with a bolt of lightning at a specific moment in order to return to the present. Or the plot may create patterns of repeated action via cycles of events: the familiar "here we go again" pattern. Such a pattern occurs in Woody Allen's *Zelig*, where the chameleonlike hero repeatedly loses his own identity by imitating the people around him.

Space can also become the basis for a plot pattern. This usually happens when the action is confined to a single locale, such as a train (Anthony Mann's *The Tall Target*) or a home (Sidney Lumet's *Long Day's Journey into Night*).

A given plot can, of course, combine these patterns. Any film built around a journey, such as *The Wizard of Oz* or *North by Northwest*, involves both a timetable and an itinerary. Jacques Tati's *Mr. Hulot's Holiday* uses both spatial and temporal patterns to structure its comic plot. The plot confines itself to a beachside resort and its neighboring areas, and it consumes one week of a summer vacation. Each day certain routines recur: morning exercise, lunch, afternoon outings, dinner, evening entertainment. Much of the film's humor relies on the way that Mr. Hulot alienates the other guests by disrupting their too-habitual routines. Although cause and effect still operate in *Mr. Hulot's Holiday*, time and space are central to the plot's formal patterning.

For any pattern of development, the spectator will create specific expectations. As the film "trains" the viewer in its particular form, these expectations become more and more precise. Once we comprehend Dorothy's desire to get home, we see her every action as furthering or delaying her progress toward her goal. Thus her trip through Oz is hardly a sightseeing tour. Each step of her journey (to the Emerald City, to the Witch's castle, to the Emerald City again) is governed by the same principle—her desire to go home.

In any film, the pattern of development in the middle portion may delay an expected outcome. When Dorothy at last reaches the Wizard, he sets up a new obstacle for her by demanding the Witch's broom. Similarly, in *North by Northwest*, Hitchcock's journey plot constantly postpones Roger Thornhill's discovery of the Kaplan hoax, and this, too, creates suspense. The pattern of development may also create surprise, the cheating of an expectation, as when Dorothy discovers that the Wizard is a fraud or when Thornhill sees the minion Leonard fire point-blank at his boss Van Damm. Patterns of development encourage the spectator to form long-term expectations which can be delayed, cheated, or gratified.

A film does not simply stop; it *ends*. The narrative will typically resolve its causal issues by bringing the development to a high point, or *climax*. In the climax, the action is presented as having a narrow range of possible outcomes. At the climax of *North by Northwest*, Roger and Eve are dangling off Mount Rushmore, and there are only two possibilities: They will fall, or they will be saved.

Because the climax focuses possible outcomes so narrowly, it typically serves to settle the causal issues that have run through the film. *Primary*'s climax takes place on election night; both Kennedy and Humphrey await the voters' verdict and finally learn the winner. In *Jaws* several battles with the shark climax in the collapse of the boat, the death of Captain Quint, the apparent death of Hooper, and Brody's final victory. In such films the ending resolves, or "closes off," the chains of cause and effect.

Emotionally, the climax aims to lift the viewer to a high degree of tension or suspense. Since the viewer knows that there are relatively few ways the action can develop, she or he can hope for a fairly specific outcome. In the climax of many films, formal resolution coincides with an emotional satisfaction.

A few narratives, however, are deliberately anticlimactic. Having created expectations about how the cause-effect chain will be resolved, the film scotches them by refusing to settle things definitely. One famous example is the last shot of *The 400 Blows* (p. 96). Another can be seen in Michelangelo Antonioni's *L'Eclisse* ("The Eclipse"), in which the two lovers vow to meet for a final reconciliation but in fact never do.

In such films, the ending remains relatively "open." That is, the plot leaves us uncertain about the final consequences of the story events. Our response becomes less firm than it does when a film has a clear-cut climax and resolution. The form may encourage us to imagine what might happen next or to reflect on other ways in which our expectations might have been fulfilled.

NARRATION: THE FLOW OF STORY INFORMATION

A plot presents or implies story information. The opening of *North by Northwest* presents Manhattan at rush hour and Roger Thornhill as an executive; it also suggests that he has been busily dictating before we see him. Filmmakers have long realized that the spectator's interest can be aroused and manipulated by carefully divulging story information at various points. In general, when we go to a film, we know relatively little about the story; by the end we know a lot more, usually the whole story. What happens in between?

The plot may arrange cues in ways that withhold information for the sake of curiosity or surprise. Or the plot may supply information in such a way as to create expectations or increase suspense. All these processes constitute *narration,* the plot's way of distributing story information in order to achieve specific effects. Narration is the moment-by-moment process that guides us in building the story out of the plot. Many factors enter into narration (see Notes and Queries), but the most important ones for our purposes involve the *range* and the *depth* of story information that the plot presents.

■ RANGE OF STORY INFORMATION

The plot of D. W. Griffith's *The Birth of a Nation* begins by recounting how slaves were brought to America and how people debated the need to free them. The plot then shows two families, the northern Stoneman family and the southern Camerons. The plot also dwells on political matters, including Lincoln's hope of averting civil war. From the start, then, our range of knowledge is very broad. The plot takes us across historical periods, regions of the country, and various groups of characters. This breadth of story information continues throughout the film. When Ben Cameron founds the Ku Klux Klan, we know about it at the moment the idea strikes him, long before the other characters learn of it. At the climax, we know that the Klan is riding to rescue several characters besieged in a cabin, but the besieged people do not know this. On the whole, in *The Birth of a Nation* the narration is very *unrestricted:* We know more, we see and hear more, than any or all of the characters can. Such extremely knowledgeable narration is often called *omniscient narration.*

Now consider the plot of Howard Hawks's *The Big Sleep.* The film begins with the detective Philip Marlowe visiting General Sternwood, who wants to hire him. We learn about the case as he does. Throughout the rest of the film, Marlowe is present in every scene. With hardly any exceptions, we don't see or hear anything that he cannot see and hear. The narration is thus *restricted* to what Marlowe knows.

Each alternative offers certain advantages. *The Birth of a Nation* seeks to present a panoramic vision of a period in American history (seen through peculiarly racist spectacles). Omniscient narration is thus essential to creating the sense of many destinies intertwined with the fate of the country. Had Griffith restricted narration the way *The Big Sleep* does, we would have learned story information solely through one character—say, Ben Cameron. We could not witness the prologue scene or the scenes in Lincoln's office or most of the battle episodes or the scene of Lincoln's assassination, since Ben is present at none of these events. The plot would now concentrate on one man's experience of the Civil War and Reconstruction.

Similarly, *The Big Sleep* derives functional advantages from its restricted narration. By confining our range of knowledge to Marlowe's, the film can create curiosity and surprise. Restriction is important to mystery films, since the films engage our interest by hiding certain important causes. Confining the plot to an investigator's range of knowledge realistically motivates concealing other story information. *The Big Sleep* could have been less restricted by, say, alternating scenes of Marlowe's investigation with scenes that show the gambling boss, Eddie Mars, planning his crimes, but this would have given away some of the mystery. In each of the two films, the narration's range of knowledge functions to achieve specific effects on the viewer.

Unrestricted and restricted narration are not watertight categories but rather two ends of a continuum. Range is a matter of degree. A film may present a broader range of knowledge than does *The Big Sleep* and still not attain the omniscience of *The Birth of a Nation.* In *North by Northwest,* for instance, the early scenes confine us pretty much to what Roger Thornhill sees and knows. After he flees from the United Nations building, however, the narration moves to Washington, where the members of the United States Intelligence Agency discuss the situation. In this scene the viewer learns something that Roger Thornhill will not learn for some time: The man he seeks, George Kaplan, does not exist. Thereafter, we have a greater range of knowledge than Roger does. In at least one important respect we also know more than the Agency's staff: We know exactly how the mix-up took place. But we still do not know many other things that the narration could have divulged in this particular scene. For instance, the Intelligence Agency's staff do not identify the agent they do have working under Van Damm's nose. In this way, any film may oscillate between restricted and unrestricted presentation of story information. (For more on narration in *North by Northwest,* see pp. 389–393.)

In fact, across a whole film, narration is never completely unrestricted. There is always something we are not told, even if it is only how the film will end. Usually, therefore, we think of a typical unrestricted narration as operating in the way that it does in *The Birth of a Nation:* The plot shifts constantly from character to character to change our source of information. Similarly, a completely restricted narration is not common. Even if the plot is built around a single character, the narration usually includes a few scenes that the character is not present to witness.

The plot's range of story information creates a *hierarchy of knowledge,* and this may vary somewhat depending on the film. At any given moment, we can ask if the viewer knows more than, less than, or as much as the characters do. For instance, here is how hierarchies would look for the three films we have been discussing. The higher someone is on the scale, the greater his or her range of knowledge:

The Birth of a Nation	*The Big Sleep*	*North by Northwest*
(unrestricted narration)	(restricted)	(mixed and fluctuating)
viewer	viewer—Marlowe	the Agency
all characters		viewer
		Thornhill

An easy way to analyze the range of narration is to ask, "Who knows what when?" The spectator must be included among the "whos," not only because we may get more knowledge than any one character but also because we may get knowledge that *no* character possesses. We shall see this happen at the end of *Citizen Kane*.

Our examples suggest the powerful effects that narration can achieve by manipulating the range of story information. Restricted narration tends to create greater curiosity and surprise for the viewer. For instance, if a character is exploring a sinister house and we see and hear no more than the character does, a sudden revelation of a hand thrusting out from a doorway will startle us. By contrast, as Alfred Hitchcock pointed out, a degree of unrestricted narration helps build suspense. He explained it this way to François Truffaut:

> We are now having a very innocent little chat. Let us suppose that there is a bomb underneath this table between us. Nothing happens, and then all of a sudden, "Boom!" There is an explosion. The public is surprised, but prior to this surprise, it has seen an absolutely ordinary scene, of no special consequence. Now, let us take a suspense situation. The bomb is underneath the table and the public knows it, probably because they have seen the anarchist place it there. The public is aware that the bomb is going to explode at one o'clock and there is a clock in the decor. The public can see that it is a quarter to one. In these conditions this innocuous conversation becomes fascinating because the public is participating in the scene. The audience is longing to warn the characters on the screen: "You shouldn't be talking about such trivial matters. There's a bomb beneath you and it's about to explode!"
>
> In the first case we have given the public fifteen seconds of surprise at the moment of the explosion. In the second case we have provided them with fifteen minutes of suspense. The conclusion is that whenever possible the public must be informed. [François Truffaut, *Hitchcock* (New York: Simon & Schuster, 1967), p. 52.]

Hitchcock lived up to his belief. In *Psycho*, Lila Crane explores the Bates mansion in much the same way as our hypothetical character is doing above. There are isolated moments of surprise as she discovers odd information about Norman and his mother. But the overall effect of the sequence is built on suspense because we know, as Lila does not, that Mrs. Bates is in the house, possibly in the fruit cellar, or possibly stalking Lila. (Actually, as in *North by Northwest*, our knowledge is not completely accurate, but during Lila's investigation we believe it to be.) As in Hitchcock's anecdote, our superior range of knowledge creates suspense because we can anticipate effects that the character cannot.

■ DEPTH OF STORY INFORMATION

A film's narration not only manipulates degrees of knowledge, it manipulates the depth of our knowledge. Here we are referring to how "deeply" the plot plunges into a character's psychological states. Just as there is a spectrum between restricted and unrestricted narration, so is there a continuum between objectivity and subjectivity.

A plot might confine us wholly to information about what characters say and do: their external behavior. Here the narration is relatively *objective*. Or a film's plot may give us access to what characters see and hear. We might see shots taken from a character's optical standpoint (the *point-of-view shot*) or hear sounds as the character would hear them (what sound recordists call "sound perspective"). This would offer a greater degree of subjectivity, one we might call *perceptual subjectivity.* There is the possibility of still greater depth if the plot plunges into the character's mind. We might hear an internal voice reporting the character's thoughts, or we might see the character's "inner images," representing memory, fantasy, dreams, or hallucinations. This can be called *mental subjectivity.* In short, narrative films can present story information at various depths of the character's psychological life.

You might think that the more restricted the narration's range of knowledge is, the greater the subjective depth. This is not necessarily true. *The Big Sleep* is quite restricted in its range of knowledge, but we very seldom see or hear things from Marlowe's perceptual vantage point, and we never get direct access to his mind. *The Big Sleep* uses almost completely objective narration. The omniscient narration of *The Birth of a Nation,* on the other hand, plunges to considerable depth with optical point-of-view shots, flash-backs, and the hero's final fantasy vision of a world without war. Hitchcock delights in giving us greater knowledge than his characters have, but then at certain moments he confines us to their perceptual subjectivity (for instance, through point-of-view shots). Range and depth of knowledge are independent variables.

Incidentally, this is one reason why the term "point of view" is ambiguous. It can refer to range of knowledge (as when a critic speaks of an "omniscient point of view") or to depth (as in the term "subjective point of view"). In this book, we will use "point of view" only to refer to perceptual subjectivity, as in the phrase "optical point-of-view shot."

Manipulating the depth of knowledge can have many functions and effects. Plunging to the depths of mental subjectivity can increase our identification with a character and can cue stable expectations about what the characters will later say or do. The memory sequences in Alain Resnais's *Hiroshima mon amour* and the fantasy sequences in Fellini's *8½* yield information about the protagonists' traits and possible future actions that would be less vivid if presented objectively. A subjectively motivated flashback can create parallels among characters, as does the flashback shared by mother and son in Kenji Mizoguchi's *Sansho the Bailiff.* A plot can create curiosity about a character's motives and then use some degree of subjectivity—for example, inner commentary, or subjective flashback—to explain the cause of the behavior.

On the other hand, objectivity can be an effective way of withholding information. One reason that *The Big Sleep* does not treat Marlowe subjectively is that the detective genre demands that the detective's reasoning be concealed from the viewer. The mystery is more mysterious if we do not know his inferences and conclusions before he reveals them at the end. At any moment in a film we can ask "How deeply do I know the characters' perceptions, feelings, and thoughts?" The answer will point directly to how the narration is presenting or withholding story information in order to achieve a formal function or a specific effect on the viewer.

Fig. 4.2

Fig. 4.3

Fig. 4.4

One final point about the depth of knowledge that the narration presents: Most films insert subjective moments into an overall framework of objectivity. For instance, in *North by Northwest,* we see Roger Thornhill crawl up to Van Damm's window and look in (objective narration); cut to a shot from Roger's point of view (perceptual subjectivity); cut back to a shot of Roger looking (objectivity again). (See Figs. 4.2–4.4.) Similarly, a dream sequence will often be bracketed by shots of the sleeper in bed.

Flashbacks offer a fascinating instance of the overarching power of objective narration. They are usually motivated as mental subjectivity, since the events we see are triggered by a character's recalling the past. Yet, once we are "inside" the flashback, events will typically be presented from a wholly objective standpoint. They will usually be presented in an unrestricted fashion too, and may even include action that the remembering character could have no way of knowing!

In other words, most films take "objective" narration as a baseline from which we may depart in search of subjective depth but to which we will return. There are, however, other films which refuse this convention and which mix objectivity and subjectivity in ambiguous ways. *8½,* Buñuel's *Belle du jour* and *That Obscure Object of Desire,* and Resnais's *Last Year at Marienbad* are good examples. Here, as elsewhere, the manipulation of story information is not just a matter of what action takes place in the film. Any choice about range or depth has concrete effects on how the spectator thinks and feels about the film as it progresses.

■ THE NARRATOR

Narration, then, is the process by which the plot presents story information to the spectator. This process may shift between restricted and unrestricted ranges of knowledge, and greater and lesser degrees of subjectivity. Narration may also utilize a *narrator,* some specific agent who purports to be telling us the story. The narrator may be a *character* in the story. We are familiar with this convention from literature, as when Huck Finn or Jane Eyre recounts a novel's action. Edward Dmytryk's film *Murder, My Sweet* makes the detective tell his story in flashbacks, addressing the information to inquiring policemen. In the documentary *Roger and Me,* Michael Moore frankly acknowledges his role as a character narrator. He starts the film with his reminiscences of growing up in Flint, Michigan, and he appears on camera in interviews with workers and in confrontations with General Motors security staff.

A film can also use a *noncharacter narrator.* Noncharacter narrators are common in documentary. We never learn who belongs to the anonymous "voice of God" we hear in *The River, Primary,* or *Hoop Dreams.* A fictional film may employ this device as well. *Jules and Jim* uses a dry, matter-of-fact commentator to lend a flavor of objectivity, while other films might call on this device to lend a sense of realism, as in the urgent voice-over we hear during *The Naked City.*

A film may play between the character/noncharacter distinction by making the source of a narrating voice uncertain. In *Film about a Woman Who . . . ,* we might assume that a character is the narrator, but we cannot be sure because we cannot tell which character the voice belongs to. In fact, it may be coming from an external commentator.

Note that either sort of narrator may present various sorts of narration. A character narrator is not necessarily restricted and may tell of events that she or he did not witness. A noncharacter narrator need not be omniscient and could confine the commentary to what a single character knows. A character narrator might be highly subjective, telling us details of his or her inner life, or might be objective, confining his or her recounting strictly to externals. A noncharacter narrator might give us access to subjective depths (as in *Jules and Jim*), or might stick simply to surface events (as does the impersonal voice-over commentator in *The Killing*). In any case, the viewer's process of picking up cues, erecting expectations, and constructing an ongoing story out of the plot will be governed by what the narrator tells or does not tell.

■ SUMMARY

We can summarize the shaping power of narration by considering George Miller's *The Road Warrior* (also known a *Mad Max II*). The film's plot opens with a voice-over commentary by an elderly male narrator who recalls "the warrior Max." After presenting an exposition telling of the worldwide wars that led society to degenerate into gangs of scavengers, the narrator falls silent. The question of his identity is left open.

The rest of the plot is organized around Max's encounter with a group of peaceful desert people. They want to flee to the coast with the gasoline they have refined, but they are under siege by a horde of vicious marauders. The cause-and-effect chain involves Max's agreement to work for the settlers in exchange for gasoline. Later, after a brush with the gang leaves him wounded, his dog dead, and his car demolished, Max commits himself to helping the people escape their compound. The struggle against the encircling gangs comes to its climax in an attempt to escape with a tanker truck, with Max at the wheel.

Max is at the center of the plot's causal chain. Moreover, after the anonymous narrator's prologue, most of the film is restricted to his range of knowledge. Like Philip Marlowe in *The Big Sleep*, Max is present in every scene, and almost everything we learn gets funneled through him. The depth of story information is also consistent. The narration provides optical point-of-view shots as Max drives his car or watches a skirmish through a telescope. When he is rescued after his car crash, his delirium is rendered as mental subjectivity, using the conventional cues of slow-motion, superimposed imagery, and slowed-down sound. All of these narrational devices encourage us to identify with Max.

At certain points, however, the narration becomes more unrestricted. This occurs principally during chases and battle scenes, where we witness events Max probably does not know about. In such scenes, unrestricted narration functions to build up suspense by showing both pursuers and pursued, or different aspects of the battle. At the climax, Max's truck successfully draws the gang away from the desert people, who escape to the south. But when his truck overturns, Max—and we—learn that the truck holds only sand. It has been a decoy. Thus our restriction to Max's range of knowledge creates a surprise.

There is still more to learn, however. At the very end, the elderly narrator's voice returns to tell us that he was the feral boy whom Max had befriended. The desert people drive off, and Max is left alone in the middle of the highway. The film's final image—a shot of the solitary Max receding into the distance as we pull back—suggests both a perceptual subjectivity (the boy's point of view as he rides away from Max) and a mental subjectivity (the memory of Max dimming for the narrator).

In *The Road Warrior,* then, the plot's form is achieved not only by causality, time, and space but by a coherent use of narration. The middle portion of the film channels our expectations through an identification with Max, alternating with more unrestricted portions. And this middle section is "framed" by the mysterious narrator who puts all the events into the distant past. The narrator's presence at the opening leads us to expect him to return at the end, perhaps explaining who he is. Thus both the cause-effect organization and the narrational patterning help the film achieve coherence and closure.

THE CLASSICAL HOLLYWOOD CINEMA

The number of possible narratives is unlimited. Historically, however, fictional cinema has tended to be dominated by a single mode of narrative form. In the course of this book we shall refer to this dominant mode as the "classical Hollywood cinema"—"classical" because of its lengthy, stable, and influential history, "Hollywood" because the mode assumed its definitive shape in American studio films. The same mode, however, governs many narrative films made in other countries. For example, *The Road Warrior,* though an Australian film, is constructed along classical Hollywood lines. And many documentaries, such as *Primary,* rely upon conventions derived from Hollywood's fictional narratives.

This conception of narrative depends on the assumption that the action will spring primarily from *individual characters as causal agents.* Natural causes (floods, earthquakes) or societal causes (institutions, wars, economic depressions) may serve as catalysts or preconditions for the action, but the narrative invariably centers on personal psychological causes: decisions, choices, and traits of character.

Often an important trait that functions to get the narrative moving is a *desire.* The character wants something. The desire sets up a goal, and the course of the narrative's development will most likely involve the process of achieving that goal. In *The Wizard of Oz* Dorothy has a series of goals, as we have seen: first to save Toto from Miss Gulch, then to get home from Oz. The latter goal creates short-term goals along the way: getting to the Emerald City and then killing the Witch.

If this desire to reach a goal were the only element present, there would be nothing to stop the character from achieving the goal immediately. But there is a counterforce in the classical narrative: an opposition that creates conflict. The protagonist comes up against a character whose traits and goals are opposed to his or hers. As a result, the protagonist must seek to change the situation so that he or she can achieve the goal. Dorothy's desire to return to Kansas is opposed by the Wicked Witch, whose goal is to obtain the ruby slippers. Dorothy must eventually eliminate the Witch before she is able to use the slippers to go home. We shall see in *His Girl Friday* how the two main characters' goals conflict until the final resolution (pp. 385–386).

Cause and effect imply *change*. If the characters did not desire something to be different from the way it is at the beginning of the narrative, change would not occur. Therefore characters and their traits, particularly desire, are a strong source of causes and effects.

But don't all narratives have protagonists of this sort? Actually not. In 1920s Soviet films, such as Sergei Eisenstein's *Potemkin, October,* and *Strike,* no *individual* serves as protagonist. More recently, Jacques Rivette's *L'Amour Fou* and Robert Altman's *Nashville* experiment with eliminating protagonists. In films like those of Eisenstein and Yasujiro Ozu, many events are seen as caused not by characters, but by larger forces (social dynamics in the former, an overarching Nature in the second). In narrative films such as Michelangelo Antonioni's *L'Avventura,* the protagonist is not active but passive. So the active, goal-oriented protagonist, though common, does not appear in every narrative film.

In the classical Hollywood narrative the chain of actions that results from predominantly psychological causes tends to motivate most or all other narrative events. Time is subordinated to the cause-effect chain in a host of ways. The plot will omit significant durations in order to show only events of causal importance. (The hours Dorothy and her entourage spend walking on the Road are omitted, but the moments during which she meets a new character are presented.) The plot will order story chronology so as to present the cause-effect chain most strikingly. Thus if a character acts peculiarly, we may get a flashback to reveal the cause of the odd behavior. Specific devices weld plot time to the story's cause-effect chain: the appointment (which motivates characters' encountering each other at a specific moment) and the deadline (which makes plot duration dependent on the cause-effect chain). Motivation in the classical narrative film will strive to be as clear and complete as possible—even in the fanciful genre of the musical, in which song and dance numbers become motivated as either expressions of the characters' emotions or stage shows mounted by the characters.

Narration in the classical Hollywood cinema exploits a variety of options, but there is a strong tendency for it to be "objective" in the way discussed on p. 106. That is, there is a basically "objective" story reality, against which various degrees of perceptual or mental subjectivity can be measured. Classical cinema also tends to put narration on the unrestricted end of the scale. Even if we follow a single character, there are portions of the film giving us access to things the character does not see, hear, or know. (*North by Northwest* and *The Road Warrior* remain good examples of this tendency.) This weighting is overridden only in genres that depend heavily on mystery, such as the detective film, with its reliance on the sort of restrictiveness we saw at work in *The Big Sleep.*

Finally, most classical narrative films display a strong degree of closure at the end. Leaving no loose ends unresolved, these films seek to complete their causal chains with a final effect. We usually learn the fate of each character, the answer to each mystery, and the outcome of each conflict.

Again, none of these features is necessary to narrative form in general. There is nothing to prevent a filmmaker from presenting the "dead time" or narratively unmotivated intervals between more significant events. (François Truffaut, Jean-Luc Godard, Carl Dreyer, and Andy Warhol do this frequently, albeit in very different ways.) The filmmaker's plot can also reorder story chronology to make the causal chain *more* perplexing. For example, Jean-Marie Straub and Danièle Huillet's *Not Reconciled* moves back and forth among three widely different time periods without clearly signaling the shifts. Dušan Makavejev's *Love Affair, or the Case of the Missing Switchboard Operator* uses flashforwards interspersed with the main plot action; only gradually do we come to understand the causal relations of these flashforwards to the "present-time" events.

The filmmaker can also include material that is unmotivated by narrative cause and effect, such as the chance meetings in Truffaut's films, the political monologues and interviews in Godard's films, the "intellectual montage" sequences in Eisenstein's films, the transitional shots in Ozu's work, and so on. Narration may be completely subjective, as in *The Cabinet of Dr. Caligari*, or it may hover ambiguously between objectivity and subjectivity as in *Last Year at Marienbad.* Finally, the filmmaker need not resolve all of the action at the close; films made outside the classical tradition sometimes have quite "open" endings.

We shall see in Chapter 8 how the classical Hollywood mode also makes cinematic space subservient to causality by means of continuity editing. For now we can simply note how the classical mode tends to treat narrative elements and narrational processes in specific and unique ways. The classical Hollywood mode is, however, only one system among many that have been and could be used for constructing films.

NARRATIVE FORM IN *CITIZEN KANE*

Citizen Kane is a useful film with which to begin film analysis, because it is unusual in form and varied in style. In what follows we shall examine *Citizen Kane* to discover how principles of narrative form may function in a particular film. *Kane*'s investigation plot carries us toward analyzing how causality and goal-oriented characters may operate in narratives. The film's manipulations of our knowledge shed light on the story-plot distinction. *Kane* also shows how ambiguity may arise when certain elements are not clearly motivated. Furthermore, the comparison of *Kane*'s beginning with its ending indicates how a film may deviate from the patterns of classical Hollywood narrative construction. Finally, the film's use of narration clearly shows how our experience can be shaped by the way that narration governs the flow of story information.

■ OVERALL NARRATIVE EXPECTATIONS

We have seen in Chapter 3 that our experience of a film depends heavily upon the expectations we bring to it and the extent to which the film confirms them. Before you saw *Citizen Kane,* you may have known only that it is regarded as a film classic. Such an evaluation would not give us a very specific set of expectations. A 1941 audience would have had a keener sense of anticipation. For one thing, the film was widely regarded as a disguised version of the life of the newspaper publisher William Randolph Hearst. Spectators would thus be looking for events and references keyed to Hearst's life. Moreover, the advertising campaign for the film (see Fig. 4.5), while not specifying any real-life correspondences, does prepare us for a story about a single man, a colossus seen from different vantage points.

Fig. 4.5

After a few minutes of the film have gone by, the viewer can form more specific expectations about pertinent genre conventions. The early "News on the March" sequence suggests that this film may be a fictional biography, and this hint is confirmed once the reporter, Thompson, begins his inquiry into Kane's life. The film does indeed follow the conventional outline of the biography, which typically covers an individual's whole life and dramatizes certain episodes in the period. Examples of this genre would be *Anthony Adverse* (1936) and *The Power and the Glory* (1933). (The latter film is often cited as an influence on *Citizen Kane* because of its complex use of flashbacks.)

The viewer can also quickly identify the film's use of conventions of the newspaper-reporter genre. Thompson's colleagues resemble the wisecracking reporters in *Picture Snatcher* (1933), *Five Star Final* (1931), and *His Girl Friday* (1940). In this genre, the action usually depends on a reporter's dogged pursuit of a story against great odds. We are therefore prepared to expect not only Thompson's investigation but also his triumphant discovery of the truth. In the scenes devoted to Susan, there are also some conventions typical of the musical film: frantic rehearsals, backstage preparations, and, most specifically, the montage of her opera career, which parodies the conventional montage of singing success in films like *Maytime* (1937). More broadly, the film evidently owes something to the detective genre, since Thompson is aiming to solve a mystery (what is "Rosebud"?) and his interviews resemble those of a detective questioning suspects in search of clues.

Note, however, that *Kane*'s use of genre conventions is somewhat equivocal. Unlike many biographical films, *Kane* is more concerned with psychological states and relationships than with the hero's public deeds or adventures. As a newspaper film, *Kane* is unusual in that the reporter does not get his story. And *Kane* is not exactly a standard mystery, since it answers some questions but leaves others unanswered. *Citizen Kane* is a good example of a film that relies on genre conventions but often thwarts the expectations they arouse.

The same sort of equivocal qualities can be found in *Kane*'s relation to the classical Hollywood cinema. Even without specific prior knowledge about this film, we expect that, as an American studio product of 1941, it will obey norms and rules of that tradition. In most ways it does. We shall see that desire propels the narrative, causality is defined around traits and goals, conflicts lead to consequences, time is motivated by plot necessity, and narration is objective, mixing restricted and unrestricted passages. We shall also see some ways in which *Citizen Kane* is more ambiguous than most films in this tradition. Desires, traits, and goals are not always spelled out; the conflicts sometimes have an uncertain outcome; at the end, the narration's omniscience is emphasized to a rare degree. The ending in particular does not provide the degree of closure that one would expect in a classical film. Our analysis will show how *Citizen Kane* draws upon Hollywood narrative conventions but also violates some of the expectations that we have in watching a Hollywood film.

■ PLOT AND STORY IN *CITIZEN KANE*

In analyzing a film, it is often helpful to begin by segmenting it into sequences. Sequences are often demarcated by cinematic devices (fades, dissolves, cuts, black screen, and so on) and form meaningful units. In a narrative film, the sequences constitute the parts of the plot.

Most sequences in a narrative film are called *scenes*. The term is used in its theatrical sense, to refer to distinct phases of the action occurring within a relatively unified space and time. We present our segmentation of *Citizen Kane* below. (In segmenting films, we will label the opening credits with a "C," the end title with an "E," and all other segments with numbers.) In this outline, Arabic numerals refer to major parts, some of which are only one scene long. In most cases, however, the major parts consist of several scenes, and each of these is identified by a lowercase letter. Many of these segments could be further divided, but this segmentation suits our immediate purposes.

Our segmentation lets us see at a glance the major divisions of the plot and how scenes are organized within them. The outline also helps us notice how the plot organizes story causality and story time. Let us look at these factors more closely.

■ *CITIZEN KANE*'S CAUSALITY

In *Citizen Kane*, two distinct sets of characters cause events to occur. On the one hand, a group of reporters seeks information about Kane. On the other hand, Kane and the characters who know him provide the subject of the reporters' investigations.

The initial causal connection between the two groups is Kane's death, which leads the reporters to make a newsreel summing up his career. But the newsreel is already finished when the plot introduces the reporters. The boss, Rawlston, supplies the cause that initiates the investigation of Kane's life. Thompson's newsreel fails to satisfy him. Rawlston's desire for "an angle" for the newsreel gets the search for "Rosebud" underway. Thompson thus

CITIZEN KANE: PLOT SEGMENTATION

C.   **Credit title**
1.   **Xanadu: Kane dies**
2.   **Projection room:**
        a. "News on the March"
        b. Reporters discuss "Rosebud"
3.   **El Rancho nightclub: Thompson tries to interview Susan**
4.   **Thatcher library:**
        a. Thompson enters and reads Thatcher's manuscript

First flashback
        b. Kane's mother sends the boy off with Thatcher
        c. Kane grows up and buys the *Inquirer*
        d. Kane launches the *Inquirer*'s attack on big business
        e. The Depression: Kane sells Thatcher his newspaper chain
        f. Thompson leaves library

5.   **Bernstein's office:**
        a. Thompson visits Bernstein

Second flashback
        b. Kane takes over the *Inquirer*
        c. Montage: the *Inquirer*'s growth
        d. Party: the *Inquirer* celebrates getting the *Chronicle* staff
        e. Leland and Bernstein discuss Kane's trip abroad
        f. Kane returns with his fiancée Emily
        g. Bernstein concludes his reminiscence

6.   **Nursing home:**

Third flashback
        a. Thompson talks with Leland
        b. Breakfast table montage: Kane's marriage deteriorates
        c. Leland continues his recollections

Third flashback (cont.)
        d. Kane meets Susan and goes to her room
        e. Kane's political campaign culminates in his speech
        f. Kane confronts Gettys, Emily, and Susan
        g. Kane loses election and Leland asks to be transferred
        h. Kane marries Susan
        i. Susan's opera premiere
        j. Because Leland is drunk, Kane finishes Leland's review
        k. Leland concludes his reminiscence

7.   **El Rancho nightclub:**
        a. Thompson talks with Susan

Fourth flashback
        b. Susan rehearses her singing
        c. Susan's opera premiere
        d. Kane insists that Susan go on singing
        e. Montage: Susan's opera career
        f. Susan attempts suicide and Kane promises she can quit singing
        g. Xanadu: Susan bored
        h. Montage: Susan plays with jigsaw puzzles
        i. Xanadu: Kane proposes a picnic
        j. Picnic: Kane slaps Susan
        k. Xanadu: Susan leaves Kane
        l. Susan concludes her reminiscence

8.   **Xanadu:**
        a. Thompson talks with Raymond

Fifth flashback
        b. Kane destroys Susan's room and picks up paperweight, murmuring "Rosebud"
        c. Raymond concludes his reminiscence; Thompson talks with the other reporters; all leave
        d. Survey of Kane's possessions leads to a revelation of Rosebud; exterior of gate and of castle; the end

E.   **End credits**

gains a goal, which sets him delving into Kane's past. His investigation constitutes one main line of the plot.

Another line of action, Kane's life, has already taken place in the past. There too a group of characters has caused actions to occur. Many years before, a poverty-stricken boarder at Kane's mother's boardinghouse has paid her with a deed to a silver mine. The wealth provided by this mine causes Mrs. Kane to appoint Thatcher as young Charles's guardian. Thatcher's guardianship results (in somewhat unspecified ways) in Kane's growing up into a spoiled, rebellious young man.

Citizen Kane is an unusual film in that the object of the investigator's search is a set of character traits. Thompson seeks to know what aspects of Kane's personality led him to say "Rosebud" on his deathbed. This mystery motivates Thompson's detective-like investigation. Kane, a very complex character, has many traits that influence the other characters' actions. As we shall see, however, *Citizen Kane*'s narrative does not ultimately define all of Kane's character traits.

Kane himself has a goal; he too seems to be searching for something related to "Rosebud." At several points characters speculate that Rosebud was something that Kane lost or never was able to get. Again, the fact that Kane's goal remains so vague makes this an unusual narrative.

Other characters in Kane's life provide causal material for the narrative. The presence of several characters who knew Kane well makes Thompson's investigation possible, even though Kane himself has died. Significantly, the characters provide a range of information that spans Kane's entire life. This is important if we are to be able to reconstruct the progression of story events in the film. Thatcher knew Kane as a child; Bernstein, his manager, knew his business dealings; his best friend, Leland, knew of his personal life (his first marriage in particular); Susan Alexander, his second wife, knew him in middle age; and the butler, Raymond, managed Kane's affairs during his last years. Each of these characters has a causal role in Kane's life, as well as in Thompson's investigation. Note that Kane's wife, Emily, does not tell a story, since Emily's story would simply duplicate Leland's and would contribute no additional information to the "present-day" part of the narrative, the investigation. Hence the plot simply eliminates her (via a car accident).

■ TIME

The order, duration, and frequency of events in the story differ greatly from the way the plot of *Citizen Kane* presents those events. Much of the film's power arises from the complex ways in which the plot cues us to construct the story.

To understand the story in its chronological order and assumed duration and frequency, the spectator must follow an intricate tapestry of plot events. For example, in the first flashback, Thatcher's diary tells of a scene in which Kane loses control of his newspapers during the Depression (4e). By this time Kane is a middle-aged man. Yet in the second flashback Bernstein describes Kane's youthful arrival at the *Inquirer* and his engagement to Emily

(5b, 5f). We mentally sort these plot events into a correct chronological (story) order, then continue to rearrange other events as we learn of them.

Similarly, the earliest *story* event about which we learn is Mrs. Kane's acquisition of a deed to a valuable mine. We get this information during the newsreel, in the second sequence. But the first event in the *plot* is Kane's death. Just to illustrate the maneuvers we must execute to construct the film's story, let us assume that Kane's life consists of these phases:

> Boyhood
> Youthful newspaper editing
> Life as a newlywed
> Middle age
> Old age

Significantly, the early portions of the plot tend to roam over many phases of Kane's life, while later portions tend to concentrate more on particular periods. The "News on the March" sequence (2a) gives us glimpses of all periods, and Thatcher's manuscript (4) shows us Kane in boyhood, youth, and middle age. Then the flashbacks become primarily chronological. Bernstein's recounting (5) concentrates on episodes showing Kane as newspaper editor and fiancé of Emily. Leland's recollections (6) run from newlywed life to middle age. Susan (7) tells of Kane as a middle-aged and an old man. Raymond's perfunctory anecdote (8b) concentrates on Kane in old age.

The plot becomes more "linear" in its ordering as it goes along, and this aids the viewer's effort to understand the story. If every character's flashback skipped around Kane's life as much as the newsreel or Thatcher's account does, the story would be much harder to reconstruct. As it is, the early portions of the plot show us the results of events we have not seen, while the later portions confirm or modify the expectations that we formed earlier.

By arranging story events out of order, the plot cues us to form very specific anticipations. In beginning with Kane's death and the newsreel version of his life, the plot creates strong curiosity about two issues. What does "Rosebud" mean? And what could have happened to make so powerful a man so solitary at the end of his life?

There is also a degree of suspense. We already have quite firm knowledge when the plot goes back to the past. We know that neither of Kane's marriages will last, that his friends will drift away, and so on. The plot encourages us to focus our interest on *how and when* a particular thing will happen. Thus many scenes function to delay an outcome that we already know is certain. For example, we know that Susan will abandon Kane at some point, so we are constantly expecting her to do so each time he bullies her. For several scenes (7b–7j) she comes close to leaving him, though after her suicide attempt he mollifies her. The plot could have shown her walking out (7k) much earlier, but then the ups and downs of their relations would have been less vivid, and there would have been no suspense.

This process of mentally rearranging plot events into story order might be quite difficult in *Citizen Kane* were it not for the presence of the "News on the March" newsreel. The first sequence in Xanadu disorients us, for it shows the death of a character about whom we so far know almost nothing. But the newsreel gives us a great deal of information quickly. Moreover, the newsreel's own structure uses parallels with the main film to supply a miniature introduction to the film's overall plot:

A. Shots of Xanadu
B. Funeral; headlines announcing Kane's death
C. Growth of financial empire
D. Silver mine and Mrs. Kane's boardinghouse
E. Thatcher testimony at congressional committee
F. Political career
G. Private life; weddings, divorces
H. Opera house and Xanadu
I. Political campaign
J. Depression
K. 1935: Kane's old age
L. Isolation at Xanadu
M. Death announced

A comparison of this outline with the one for the whole film shows some striking formal similarities. "News on the March" begins by emphasizing Kane as "Xanadu's Landlord"; a short segment (A) presents shots of the house, its grounds, and its contents. This is a variation on the opening of the whole film (1), which consisted of a series of shots of the grounds, moving progressively closer to the house. That opening sequence had ended with Kane's death; now the newsreel follows the shots of the house with Kane's funeral (B). Next comes a series of newspaper headlines announcing Kane's death. In a comparison with the plot diagram of *Citizen Kane*, these headlines occupy the approximate formal position of the whole newsreel itself (2a). Even the title card that follows the headlines ("To forty-four million U.S. news buyers, more newsworthy than the names in his own headlines was Kane himself . . .") is a brief parallel to the scene in the projection room, in which the reporters decide that Thompson should continue to investigate Kane's "newsworthy" life.

The order of the newsreel's presentation of Kane's life roughly parallels the order of scenes in the flashbacks related to Thompson. "News on the March" moves from Kane's death to summarize the building of Kane's newspaper empire (C), with a description of the boardinghouse deed and the silver mine (including an old photograph of Charles with his mother, as well as the first mention of the sled). Similarly, the first flashback (4) tells how Thatcher took over the young Kane's guardianship from his mother and how Kane first attempted to run the *Inquirer*. The rough parallels continue: The newsreel tells of Kane's political ambitions (F), his marriages (G), his building of the opera house (H), his political campaign (I), and so on. In the main plot Thatcher's flashback describes his own clashes with Kane on political matters. Leland's flashback (6) covers the first marriage, the affair with Susan, the political campaign, and the premiere of *Salammbo*. These are not all of the similarities between the newsreel and the overall film. You can tease out many more by comparing the two closely.

In general, the newsreel provides us with a "map" at the beginning of the investigation into Kane's life. As we see the various scenes of the flashbacks, we already expect certain events and have a rough chronological basis for fitting them into our story reconstruction.

Kane's plot not only manipulates story order, it also cues us to construct story duration and frequency. The total *story duration* which the viewer infers consists of the 75 years of Kane's life plus a week after his death. This entire period is presented in a *plot duration* consisting of the week of Thompson's investigation. The use of flashbacks allows the plot to concentrate its revelation of story material into so short a period. But there is also *screen duration,* or running time—almost exactly 120 minutes.

As in most films, ellipsis has been used. The plot skips over years of story time, and the running time omits even more, skipping over many hours of Thompson's week of investigation. But screen duration also compresses time, through "montage sequences," such as those showing the *Inquirer*'s campaign against big business (4d), the growth of the paper's circulation (5c), Susan's opera career (7e), and Susan's bored playing with jigsaw puzzles (7h). Here long passages of story time are condensed into brief summaries quite different from ordinary narrative scenes. We will discuss montage sequences in more detail in Chapter 8, but we can already see the value of such segments in clarifying story duration for the spectator.

Citizen Kane also provides a clear demonstration of how events that occur only once in the story may appear several times in the plot. In their respective flashbacks, both Leland and Susan Alexander describe the latter's debut in the Chicago premiere of *Salammbo.* Watching Leland's account (6i), we see the performance from the front; we witness the audience reacting with distaste. Susan's version (7c) shows us the performance from behind and on the stage, to suggest her humiliation. This repeated presentation of Susan's debut in the plot does not confuse us, for we recognize the two scenes as depicting the same story event. ("News on the March" has also referred to Susan's opera career, in parts G and H.)

Overall, *Citizen Kane*'s narrative dramatizes Thompson's search by means of flashbacks that encourage us to seek the sources of Kane's failure and to try to identify "Rosebud." As in a detective film, we must locate missing causes and arrange events into a coherent story pattern. Through manipulations of order, duration, and frequency, the plot both assists our search and complicates it in order to provoke curiosity and suspense.

■ MOTIVATION

Some critics have argued that Welles's use of the search for "Rosebud" is a flaw in *Citizen Kane,* because the identification of the word proves it to be a trivial gimmick. If indeed we assume that the whole point of *Citizen Kane* is really to identify "Rosebud," this charge might be valid. But in fact, "Rosebud" serves a very important motivating function in the film. It creates Thompson's goal and focuses our attention on his delving into the lives of

Kane and his associates. *Citizen Kane* becomes a mystery story; but instead of investigating a crime, the reporter investigates a character. So the "Rosebud" clues provide the basic motivation necessary for the plot to progress. (Of course, the "Rosebud" device serves other functions as well; for instance, the little sled provides a transition from the boardinghouse scene to the cheerless Christmas when Thatcher gives Charles a new sled.)

Citizen Kane's narrative revolves around an investigation into traits of character. As a result, these traits provide many of the motivations for events. (In this respect, the film obeys principles of the classical Hollywood narrative.) Kane's desire to prove that Susan is really a singer and not just his mistress motivates his manipulation of her opera career. His mother's overly protective desire to remove her son from what she considers to be a bad environment motivates her appointment of Thatcher as the boy's guardian. Dozens of actions are motivated by character traits and desires.

At the end of the film, Thompson gives up his search for the meaning of "Rosebud," saying he doesn't "think any word can explain a man's life." Up to a point Thompson's statement motivates his acceptance of his failure. But if we as spectators are to accept this idea that no key can unlock the secrets of a life, we need further motivation, and the film provides this. In the scene in the newsreel projection room, Rawlston suggests that "maybe he told us all about himself on his deathbed." Immediately, one of the reporters says, "Yeah, and maybe he didn't." Already the suggestion is planted that "Rosebud" may not provide any adequate answers about Kane. Later Leland scornfully dismisses the "Rosebud" issue and goes on to talk of other things. These brief references to "Rosebud" help justify Thompson's pessimistic attitude in the final sequence.

The presence of the scene in which Thompson first visits Susan Alexander at the El Rancho nightclub (3) might seem puzzling at first. Unlike the other scenes in which he visits people, no flashback occurs here. Thompson learns from the waiter that Susan knows nothing about "Rosebud"; he could easily learn this on his second visit to her. So why should the plot include the scene at all? One reason is that it evokes curiosity and deepens the mystery around Kane. Moreover, Susan's story, when she does tell it, covers events relatively late in Kane's career. As we have seen, the flashbacks go through Kane's life roughly in order. If Susan had told her story first, we would not have all of the material necessary to understand it. But it is plausible that Thompson should start his search with Kane's ex-wife, presumably the surviving person closest to him. In Thompson's first visit, Susan's drunken refusal to speak to him motivates the fact that her flashback comes later. By that point, Bernstein and Leland have filled in enough of Kane's personal life to prepare the way for Susan's flashback. This first scene functions partly to provide motivation for postponing Susan's flashback until a later part of the plot.

Motivation makes us take things for granted in narratives. Mrs. Kane's desire for her son to be rich and successful motivates her decision to entrust him to Thatcher, a powerful banker, as his guardian. We may be inclined to think it is just natural that Thatcher is a rich businessman. Yet this feature is necessary to motivate other events. It motivates Thatcher's presence in the newsreel; he is powerful enough to have been asked to testify at a congressional hearing. More important, Thatcher's success motivates the fact that he has kept a journal now on deposit at a memorial library that Thompson visits. This, in turn, justifies the fact that Thompson is able to find information from a source who knew Kane as a child.

Despite its reliance on psychological motivation, *Citizen Kane* also departs somewhat from the usual practice of the classical Hollywood narrative by leaving some motivations ambiguous. The ambiguities relate primarily to Kane's character. The other characters who tell Thompson their stories all have definite opinions of Kane, but these do not always tally. Bernstein still looks on Kane with sympathy and affection, whereas Leland is cynical about his own relationship with Kane. The reasons for some of Kane's actions remain unclear. Does he send Leland the $25,000 check in firing him because of a lingering sentiment over their old friendship or from a proud desire to prove himself more generous than Leland? Why does he insist on stuffing Xanadu with hundreds of artworks which he never even unpacks?

■ PARALLELISM

Parellelism does not provide the entire basis of *Citizen Kane*'s narrative form, but several parallel structures are present. We have already seen important formal parallels between the newsreel and the film's plot as a whole. We have also noticed a parallel between the two major lines of action: Kane's life and Thompson's search. "Rosebud" serves as a summary of the things Kane strives for through his adult life. We see him repeatedly fail to find love and friendship, living alone at Xanadu in the end. His inability to find happiness parallels Thompson's failure to locate the significance of the word "Rosebud." This parallel does not imply that Kane and Thompson share similar character traits. Rather, it allows both lines of action to develop simultaneously in similar directions.

Another narrative parallel juxtaposes Kane's campaign for the governorship with his attempt to build up Susan's career as an opera star. In each case he seeks to inflate his reputation by influencing public opinion. In trying to achieve success for Susan, Kane forces his newspaper employees to write favorable reviews of her performances. This parallels the moment when he loses the election and the *Inquirer* automatically proclaims fraud at the polls. In both cases Kane fails to realize that his power over the public is not great enough to hide the flaws in his projects: first his affair with Susan, which ruins his campaign, then her lack of singing ability, which Kane refuses to admit. The parallels stress that Kane continues to make the same kinds of mistakes throughout his life.

■ PATTERNS OF PLOT DEVELOPMENT

The progression from beginning to ending in *Citizen Kane* leads us through two lines of action, as we have seen: Kane's life story and Thompson's investigation of it. Each of Thompson's visits during his investigation leads to a flashback that gives us a further look at Kane.

The order of Thompson's visits allows the series of flashbacks to have a clear pattern of progression. Thompson moves from people who knew Kane early in his life to those who knew him as an old man. Moreover, each flashback contains a distinct type of information about Kane. Thatcher establishes Kane's political stance; next Bernstein gives an account of the business dealings of the newspaper. These provide the background to Kane's early success and lead into Leland's stories of Kane's personal life, where we get the first real indications of Kane's failure. Susan continues the description of his decline with her account of how he had manipulated her life. Finally, in Raymond's flashback Kane becomes a pitiable old man.

Thus even though the order, duration, and frequency of events in the story vary greatly from those in the plot, *Citizen Kane* presents Kane's life through a steady pattern of development. The present-day portions of the narrative—Thompson's scenes—also follow their own pattern of a search. By the ending this search has failed (as Kane's own search for happiness or personal success had also failed).

Because of this failure, the ending of *Citizen Kane* remains somewhat more open than was the rule in Hollywood in 1941. True, Thompson does resolve the question of "Rosebud" for himself by saying that it would not have explained Kane's life. To this extent, we have the common pattern of action leading to greater knowledge. But in most classical narrative films, the main character reaches his or her initial goal, and Thompson is the main character of this line of action.

The line of action involving Kane himself has even less closure. Not only does Kane apparently not reach his goal, but the film never specifies what that goal is to start with. Most classical narratives create a situation of conflict. The character must struggle with a problem and solve it by the ending. Kane begins his adult life in a highly successful position (happily running the *Inquirer*), then gradually falls into a barren solitude. We are invited to speculate about exactly what, if anything, would make Kane happy. *Citizen Kane*'s lack of closure in this line of action made it a very unusual narrative for its day.

The search for "Rosebud" does lead to a certain resolution at the end. We the audience discover what "Rosebud" was. The ending of the film, which follows this discovery, strongly echoes the beginning. The beginning had moved past fences toward the mansion. Now a series of shots takes us away from the house and back outside the fences, with the "No Trespassing" sign and large K insignia.

But even at this point, when we learn the answer to Thompson's question, a degree of uncertainty remains. Just because we have learned what Kane's dying word meant, do we now have the key to his entire character? Or is Thompson's final statement *correct*—that no one word can explain a person's life? It is tempting to declare that all of Kane's problems arose from the loss of his sled and his home life as a child, but the film also suggests that this is too easy a solution. It is the kind of solution that the slick editor Rawlston would pounce on as an "angle" for his newsreel.

For years critics have debated whether the "Rosebud" solution does give us a key that resolves the entire narrative. This debate itself suggests the ambiguity at work in *Citizen Kane*. The film provides much evidence for both views and hence avoids complete closure. (You might contrast this slightly open ending with the tightly closed narratives of *His Girl Friday* and *North by Northwest* in Chapter 11. You might also compare *Citizen Kane*'s narrative with another partially open-ended film, *Do The Right Thing*, also discussed in Chapter 11.)

■ NARRATION IN *CITIZEN KANE*

In analyzing how *Kane*'s plot manipulates the flow of story information, it is useful to consider a remarkable fact: The only time we see Kane directly and in the present is when he dies. On all other occasions, he is presented at one remove—in the newsreel, in various characters' memories. This unusual treatment makes the film something of a portrait, a study of a man seen from different perspectives.

The film employs five narrators, the people whom Thompson tracks down: Thatcher (whose account is in writing), Bernstein, Leland, Susan, and the butler, Raymond. The plot thus motivates a series of more or less restricted views of Kane. In Thatcher's account (4b–4e), we see only scenes at which he is present. Even Kane's newspaper crusade is rendered as Thatcher learns of it, through buying copies of the *Inquirer*. In Bernstein's flashback (5b–5f), there is some deviation from what Bernstein witnesses, but in general his range of knowledge is respected. At the *Inquirer* party, for example, we are confined to following Bernstein and Leland's conversation while Kane dances in the background. Similarly, we never see Kane in Europe, we merely hear the contents of Kane's telegram, which Bernstein delivers to Leland.

Leland's flashbacks (6b, 6d–6j) deviate most markedly from the narrator's range of knowledge. Here we see Kane and Emily at a series of morning breakfasts, Kane's meeting with Susan, and the confrontation of Kane with Boss Gettys at Susan's apartment. In scene 6j, Leland is present but unconscious most of the time. (The plot motivates Leland's knowledge of Kane's affair with Susan by having Leland suggest that Kane told him about it, but the scenes present detailed knowledge that Leland is unlikely to possess.) By the time we get to Susan's flashback (7b–7k), however, the range of knowledge fits the character more snugly. (There remains one scene, 7f, in which Susan is unconscious for part of the action.) The last flashback (8b) is recounted by Raymond and plausibly accords with his range of knowledge; he is standing in the hallway as Kane wrecks Susan's room.

Using different narrators to transmit story information fulfills several functions. It offers itself as a "realistic" depiction of the process of investigation, since we expect any reporter to hunt down information through a series of inquiries. More deeply, the plot's portrayal of Kane himself becomes more complex by showing somewhat different sides of him, depending on who's talking about him. Moreover, the use of multiple narrators makes the film like one of Susan's jigsaw puzzles. We must put things together piece by piece. The pattern of gradual revelation enhances curiosity—what is it in Kane's past that he associates with Rosebud?—and suspense—how will he lose his friends and his wives?

This strategy has important implications for film form. While Thompson uses the various narrators to gather data, the plot uses them both to furnish us with story information and to *conceal* information. The narration can motivate gaps in knowledge about Kane by appealing to the fact that no informant can know everything about anyone. If we were able to enter Kane's consciousness, we might discover the meaning of "Rosebud" much sooner. The multiple-narrator format thus appeals to expectations we derive from real life in order to motivate the gradual and piecemeal transmission of story information, the withholding of key pieces of information, and the arousing of curiosity and suspense.

Although each narrator's account is predominantly restricted to his or her range of knowledge, the plot does not treat each flashback in much subjective depth. Most of the flashbacks are rendered objectively. Some transitions from the framing episodes use a voice-over commentary to lead us into the flashbacks, but these do not represent the narrators' subjective states. Only in Susan's flashbacks are there some attempts to render subjectivity. In scene 7c we see Leland as if from her optical point of view on stage, and the phantasmagoric montage of her career (7e) suggests some mental subjectivity that renders her fatigue and frustration.

On the whole, however, the film adheres to the classical Hollywood convention of objective presentation. This, too, is functional. If we are to pursue the Rosebud mystery and to watch the unraveling of Kane's personal relationships, we need to believe that what we see and hear actually occurred.

Against the five character narrators, the film's plot sets another purveyor of knowledge, the "News on the March" short. We have already seen the crucial function of the newsreel in introducing us both to Kane's story and to its plot construction, with the newsreel's parts echoing the parts of the film as a whole. The newsreel also gives us a broad sketch of Kane's life and death that will be filled in by the more restricted behind-the-scenes accounts offered by the narrators. The newsreel is also highly "objective," even more so than the rest of the film; it reveals nothing about Kane's inner life. Rawlston acknowledges this: "It isn't enough to tell us what a man did, you've got to tell us who he was." In effect, Thompson's aim is to add depth to the newsreel's superficial version of Kane's life.

Yet we are still not through with the narrational manipulations in this complex and daring film. For one thing, all the localized sources of knowledge—"News on the March" and the five narrators—are linked together by the shadowy reporter Thompson. To some extent, he is our surrogate in the film, gathering and assembling the puzzle pieces.

Note too that Thompson is barely characterized; we cannot even identify his face. This, as usual, has a function. If we saw him clearly, if the plot gave him more traits or a background or a past, he would become the protagonist. But *Citizen Kane* is less about Thompson than about his *search*. The plot's handling of Thompson makes him a neutral conduit for the story information that he gathers (though his conclusion at the end, "I don't think any word can explain a man's life," suggests that he has been changed by his investigation).

Thompson is not, however, a perfect surrogate for us because the film's narration inserts the newsreel, the narrators, and Thompson within a still broader range of knowledge. The flashback portions are predominantly restricted, but there are other passages that reveal an overall narrational omniscience. From the very start we are given a god's-eye-view of the action. We move into a mysterious setting that we will later learn is Kane's estate, Xanadu. We might have learned about this locale through a character's journey, the way we acquaint ourselves with Oz by means of Dorothy's adventures there. Here, however, an omniscient narration conducts the tour. Eventually we enter a darkened bedroom. A hand holds a paperweight, and over this is superimposed a flurry of snow (Fig. 4.6). The image teases us. Is the narration making a lyrical comment, or is the image subjective, a glimpse into the dying man's mind or vision? In either case, the narration reveals its ability to command a great deal of story information. Our sense of omniscience is enhanced when, after the man dies, a nurse strides into the room. Apparently no character knows what we know.

Fig. 4.6

At other points in the film the omniscient narration calls attention to itself. For instance, during Susan's opera debut in Leland's flashback (6i), we see stagehands high above her reacting to her performance. (Such omniscient "asides" tend to be associated with camera movements, as we shall see in Chapter 10.) Most vivid, however, is the omniscient narration at the very end of the film. Thompson and the other reporters leave, never having learned the meaning of "Rosebud." But we linger in the vast storeroom of Xanadu. And, thanks to the narration, we learn that "Rosebud" is the name of Kane's childhood toy. We can now associate the opening's emphasis on the little paperweight with the scene's revelation of the sled.

This narration is truly omniscient. It "knew" a key piece of story information at the outset, teased us with hints (the snow, the tiny cottage in the paperweight), and has finally revealed at least part of the answer to the question posed at the outset. A return to the "No Trespassing" sign reminds us of our point of entry into the film. Like *The Road Warrior*, then, the film derives its unity not only from principles of causality and time but also from a patterned narration that arouses curiosity and suspense and yields a surprise at the very end.

SUMMARY

Not every narrative analysis goes through the categories of cause-effect, story-plot differences, motivations, parallelism, progression from opening to closing, and narrational range and depth in that exact order, as we have done here. Our purpose in this examination of *Citizen Kane* has been as much to illustrate these concepts as to analyze the film's narrative. With practice, the critic becomes more familiar with these analytical tools and can use them flexibly, suiting his or her approach to the specific film at hand.

In looking at any narrative film, such questions as these may help in understanding its formal structures:

1. Which story events are directly presented to us in the plot, and which must we infer? Is there any nondiegetic material given in the plot?
2. What is the earliest story event of which we learn? How does it relate through a series of causes and effects to later events?
3. What is the temporal relationship of story events? Has temporal order, frequency, or duration been manipulated in the plot to affect our understanding of events?
4. Does the closing reflect a clear-cut pattern of development that relates it to the beginning? Do all narrative lines achieve closure, or are some left open?
5. How does the narration present story information to us? Is it restricted to one or a few characters' knowledge, or does it range freely among the characters in different spaces? Does it give us considerable depth of story information by exploring the characters' mental states?
6. How closely does the film follow the conventions of the classical Hollywood cinema? If it departs significantly from those conventions, what formal principle does it use instead?

Though narrative films are the type we see most often when we "go to the movies" in a theater, many other possibilities exist for structuring the overall form in a film. We shall explore the basic types of nonnarrative form in the next chapter.

NOTES AND QUERIES

■ NARRATIVE FORM

An overview of the history and functions of narrative in human culture is Robert Scholes and Robert Kellogg, *The Nature of Narrative* (New York: Oxford University Press, 1966). Most conceptions of narrative are drawn from literary theory, which in the last two decades has made remarkable contributions to the study of this type of form. Good introductions are Seymour Chatman, *Story and Discourse: Narrative Structure in Fiction and Film* (Ithaca: Cornell University Press, 1978), and *Coming to Terms: The Rhetoric of Narrative in Fiction and Film* (Ithaca: Cornell University Press, 1990); Gerald Prince, *Narratology: The Form and Function of Narrative* (Berlin: Mouton, 1982); and Shlomith Rimmon-Kenan, *Narrative Fiction: Contemporary Poetics* (New York: Methuen, 1983). The concepts we discuss in this chapter are congruent with this trend of contemporary theory. See also "Film-Narratology," in Robert Stam, Robert Burgoyne, and Sandy Flitterman-Lewis, *New Vocabularies in Film Semiotics: Structuralism, Post-Structuralism, and Beyond* (New York: Routledge, 1992), pp. 69–122.

For discussions centered on film narrative's debt to literature and other arts, see John L. Fell, *Film and the Narrative Tradition* (Norman: University of Oklahoma Press, 1974) and "Film/Narrative/The Novel," special number of *Ciné-tracts* **13** (Spring 1981). For a discussion emphasizing the theoretical aspects of film narrative, see Roy Armes, *Action and Image: Dramatic Structure in Cinema* (Manchester: Manchester University Press, 1994).

■ THE SPECTATOR

What does the spectator *do* in making sense of a narrative? Various theorists have sought to characterize the perceiver's activity. In literature, two valuable studies are Horst Ruthrof, *The Reader's Construction of Narrative* (London: Routledge & Kegan Paul, 1981), and Peter Brooks, *Reading for the Plot: Design and Intention in Narrative* (New York: Knopf, 1984). Meir Sternberg emphasizes expectation, hypotheses, and inference in his *Expositional Modes and Temporal Ordering in Fiction* (Baltimore: Johns Hopkins University Press, 1978). Sternberg's approach is close to our own assumptions in this chapter. In "Styles of Reading," *Poetics Today* **3,** 3 (Spring 1982): 77–88, George L. Dillon distinguishes among the "Character-Action-Moral" approach, the "Digger for secrets" approach, and the "Anthropologist" approach. David Bordwell proposes a model of the spectator's story-comprehending activities in chapter 3 of *Narration in the Fiction Film* (Madison: University of Wisconsin Press, 1985). Compare Edward Branigan, *Narrative Comprehension in Film* (New York: Routledge, 1992).

■ NARRATIVE TIME

Most theorists agree that cause-effect relations and chronology are central to narrative. The books by Chatman, Sternberg, and Rimmon-Kenan cited above provide useful analyses of causality and temporality. For specifically cinematic discussions, see Jan Mukařovskỳ, "Time in Film," in John Burbank and Peter Steiner, eds., *Structure, Sign, and Function: Selected Essays by Jan Mukařovskỳ* (New Haven, Conn.: Yale University Press, 1977), pp. 191–200; Brian Henderson, "Tense, Mood, and Voice in Film (Notes After Genette)," *Film Quarterly* **26,** 4 (Summer 1983): 4–17; and Maureen Turim, *Flashbacks in Film: Memory and History* (New York: Routledge, 1989).

Our discussion of the differences between plot duration, story duration, and screen duration is necessarily simplified. The distinctions hold good at a theoretical level, but the differences may sometimes vanish in particular cases. Story and plot duration differ most drastically at the level of the *whole* film, as when two years of action (story duration) are shown or told about in scenes that occur across a week (plot duration) and then that week is itself rendered in two hours (screen duration). At the level of a smaller *part*, say a shot or a scene, we usually assume story and plot duration to be equal, and screen duration may or may not be equal to them. These nuances are discussed at greater length in chap. 5 of Bordwell, *Narration in the Fiction Film* (cited above).

■ NARRATION

One approach to narration has been to draw analogies between film and literature. Novels have first-person narration ("Call me Ishmael") and third-person narration ("Maigret puffed his pipe as he walked along slowly, hands clasped behind his back"). Does film have first-person or third-person narration too? The argument for applying the linguistic category of "person" to cinema is discussed most fully in Bruce F. Kawin, *Mindscreen: Bergman, Godard and First-Person Film* (Princeton: Princeton University Press, 1978). Kawin does not confine his discussion to character narrators, such as Kane's associates, who are obviously telling their tale in the first person. He suggests that entire films can be seen as proceeding from the mind of a narrator and thus warrant the label "first person." This analogy seems to assume the more basic categories of range and depth, which we discuss in this chapter.

Another literary analogy is that of "point of view." The best survey in English is Susan Snaider Lanser, *The Narrative Act: Point of View in Prose Fiction* (Princeton: Princeton University Press, 1981). The applicability of point of view to film is discussed in detail in Edward Branigan, *Point of View in the Cinema: A Theory of Narration and Subjectivity in Classical Film* (New York: Mouton, 1984). See also Kristin Thompson's "Closure within a Dream? Point-of-view in *Laura*," in *Breaking the Glass Armor: Neoformalist Film Analysis* (Princeton: Princeton University Press, 1988), pp. 162–194. A special issue of *Film Reader* **4** (1979) considers various meanings of the concept.

In "A Scene at the 'Movies'," *Screen* **23,** 2 (July–August 1982), Ben Brewster discusses how the hierarchy of knowledge can operate in a single "simple" film. The implicit moral values at work in narration are considered in George Wilson, *Narration in Light* (Baltimore: Johns Hopkins University Press, 1986). For general discussion, see Bordwell, *Narration in the Fiction Film* (cited above).

■ NARRATIVE ANALYSES OF FILMS

Sample narrative analyses of films may be found in Alan Williams, "Narrative Patterns in *Only Angels Have Wings*," *Quarterly Review of Film Studies* **1,** 4 (November 1976): 357–372; Kristin Thompson, *Breaking the Glass Armor*, cited above; Joyce Nelson, "*Mildred Pierce* Reconsidered," *Film Reader* **2** (1977): 65–70; and Roy Armes, *The Films of Alain Robbe-Grillet* (Amsterdam: John Benjamins B. V., 1981). Analyses which highlight specific problems of film narrative are found in Noël Burch, *Life to Those Shadows,* translated and edited by Ben Brewster (Berkeley: University of California Press, 1990); Tom Gunning, *D. W. Griffith and the Origins of the American Narrative Film: The Early Years at Biograph* (Urbana: University of Illinois Press, 1991); and Robert Burgoyne, *Bertolucci's "1900": A Narrative and Historical Analysis* (Detroit: Wayne State University Press, 1991).

For advanced study, see Stephen Heath's essay on Welles's *Touch of Evil*, "Film and System: Terms of Analysis," *Screen* **16,** 1 (Spring 1975): 7–77, and **16,** 2 (Summer 1975): 91–113.

■ "ROSEBUD"

Critics have scrutinized few films as closely as *Citizen Kane*. For a sampling, see Joseph McBride, *Orson Welles* (New York: Viking, 1972); Charles

Higham, *The Films of Orson Welles* (Berkeley: University of California Press, 1970); David Bordwell, *"Citizen Kane,"* in Bill Nichols, ed., *Movies and Methods* (Berkeley: University of California Press, 1976); Robert Carringer, "Rosebud, Dead or Alive: Narrative and Symbolic Structure in *Citizen Kane*," *PMLA* (March 1976): 185–193; and James Naremore, *The Magic World of Orson Welles* (New York: Oxford University Press, 1978).

Pauline Kael, in a famous essay on the making of the film, finds "Rosebud" a naïve gimmick. Interestingly, her discussion emphasizes *Citizen Kane* as part of the journalist-film genre and tends not to go beyond the detective-story aspect. See *The Citizen Kane Book* (Boston: Little, Brown, 1971), pp. 1–84. In contrast, other critics find "Rosebud" an incomplete answer to Thompson's search; compare particularly the Naremore, Bordwell, and Carringer analyses above. A very different account of the film is offered by Peter Bogdanovich, in "The Kane Mutiny," *Esquire* **78,** 4 (October 1972): 99–105, 180–190. For a balanced assessment of *Kane*'s classical and modern features, see Peter Wollen, "Introduction to *Citizen Kane*," *Film Reader* **1** (1975): 9–15. Half of this issue of *Film Reader* is devoted to analyzing *Citizen Kane*. Robert Carringer's *Making of Citizen Kane* (Berkeley: University of California Press, 1985) offers the most extensive account of the film's production.

FIVE

NONNARRATIVE FORMAL SYSTEMS

In examining the general characteristics of film form in Chapter 3, we took *The Wizard of Oz* as our main example. The formal principles we saw at work in it—function and motivation, similarity and repetition, difference and variation, development, and unity and disunity—apply to all films. Because narrative films are so important in our film-viewing experience, we devoted Chapter 4 to this type of form, using *Citizen Kane* as our specimen.

But there are other types of film form, and these are as important as narrative form. Instructional films, political advertisements, the experimental films we may watch in a local art museum auditorium—such films may not contain any stories at all. They have *nonnarrative* formal systems.

We can distinguish four broad types of nonnarrative form: *categorical, rhetorical, abstract,* and *associational.* In this chapter we will look at the traits of each type of form, examining one example of each type closely.

How do these four types of nonnarrative form differ from each other? Before looking at each of these types in detail, let us differentiate them briefly by showing how each could treat the same subject matter. Suppose we are setting out to make a film about our local grocery store and are considering different ways of organizing its form. We could use narrative form by, say, showing a typical day in the store. But there are other, nonnarrative ways of constructing such a film.

Categorical films, as the name suggests, divide a subject into parts, or categories. In our hypothetical film, the grocery store would be our overall subject. We could go through the store and film each portion, showing what sorts of things the store contains. We might present the meat section, the produce section, the checkout counters, and other parts of the store.

But this is not the only way to treat the subject. We might instead set out to convince our audience of something about the grocery store. In that case we would employ *rhetorical* form, which presents an argument and lays out evidence to support it. We might state the idea that a locally owned grocery store gives its customers better service than does a chain store. For this version, we might film the owner of the store giving the customers personal help; we might interview him or her about the services that the store tries to provide; we might interview customers about their opinions on the store; we might try to show that the food carried by the store is of superior quality. Overall, we could organize our film to give our audience reasons to believe that this locally owned store is a better place to shop.

We could, however, decide on a third alternative. We could make a film about the grocery store using *abstract* form. In this type of organization, the audience's attention is drawn to abstract visual and sonic qualities of the things depicted—shape, color, aural rhythm, and the like. Hence we would try to film the store, which most people would consider quite mundane, in interesting and striking ways. Unusual camera positions could distort the shapes of cans and boxes on the shelves, close framings could bring out areas of bright color, an incongruous musical track could affect the audience's reaction to the images, and so on.

Finally, we might wish to express an attitude toward the store, or to evoke a mood. *Associational* form would be appropriate here, for it juxtaposes loosely connected images to suggest an emotion or a concept to the spectator. Perhaps we find grocery stores cramped and oppressive. We could film the store's contents to look bleak, and we could insert metaphorical material to cue the audience to respond negatively to what they see. For example, a shot of long lines of shopping carts at a checkout counter might be compared to a shot of a rush-hour traffic jam. Through a series of such associations between aspects of the store and other phenomena, the film could create a certain tone or attitude toward the store.

We do not intend to suggest that filmmakers typically choose a subject and then cast about for an appropriate sort of organization. Usually the type of form chosen arises from the filmmaker's purposes and the choices available in a production context. The point is that each of these films would create a very different view of the same grocery store.

Like narrative form, these four sorts of nonnarrative form may appear in all of the basic types of films we surveyed in Chapter 2. Our grocery store movie employs live action, but we could make an animated film about the store using any of these formal patterns. The independent animator Bill Plympton has made categorically organized films, *How to Kiss* and *25 Ways to Quit Smoking*. An experimental filmmaker can likewise utilize any sort of form: We shall see that *Ballet mécanique* is a model of abstract form, while Bruce Conner's *A Movie* organizes its imagery associationally. You could structure a fictional film rhetorically if you made a movie arguing for giving Martians colonization rights on the moon. Peter Greenaway's *The Falls* surveys the effects of an unnamed disaster on a series of fictitious people named Fall; the film is organized categorically, with each person's case considered in alphabetical order. And the merrily offbeat documentaries of Les Blank have utilized narrative form *(Burden of Dreams,* about the making of a film), categorical form *(Gap-Toothed Women),* and associational form *(Garlic Is As Good As Ten Mothers).*

The differences among varieties of nonnarrative form are important because each type will call upon different viewing conventions and will prompt different types of expectations in the spectator. If we know we are watching a rhetorical film that is trying to convince us to support a certain governmental policy, we may adopt a skeptical attitude, testing the evidence and perhaps ultimately rejecting it. But as we watch an abstract film, we may become more contemplative, watching shapes and colors pass before us. Even though we may seldom consciously classify the films we watch as "rhetorical" or "associational," we do differentiate among types of films, and we have a range of viewing skills upon which we can draw.

With our basic distinctions among the four types of nonnarrative form, we are ready to look at each in greater detail. For each type, we examine a typical film, segmenting it as described in Chapter 3. Our analysis will then emphasize how these parts relate to each other in each type of nonnarrative organization.

CATEGORICAL FORMAL SYSTEMS

■ PRINCIPLES OF CATEGORICAL FORM

Categories are groupings which individuals or societies create to organize their knowledge of the world. Some categories are based on scientific research, and these will often attempt to account exhaustively for all the data in question. For example, scientists have developed an elaborate system to classify every known animal and plant into genus and species.

Most of the categories we use in our daily life are less strict, less neat, and less exhaustive. We tend to group the things around us based on a common-sense, practical approach, or on ideological views of the world. Ordinarily, for example, we do not sort animals we see by genus and species. We use such rough categories as "pets," "wild animals," "farm animals," "zoo animals," and so on. Such groupings are not logically exclusive or exhaustive (at one time or another, some animals might fit into most or all of these categories), yet they suffice for our usual purposes. Ideologically based categories are also seldom strictly logical. Societies do not naturally fall into such categories as "primitive" or "advanced," for example. These are groupings that have been developed out of complex sets of beliefs, and they may not stand up well to scrutiny.

If a filmmaker wants to convey some information about the world to audiences, categories and subcategories may provide a basis for organizing the film's form. A documentary film about butterflies might use scientific classification, showing one type of butterfly and giving information about its habits, then showing another, with more information, and so on. Similarly, a travelogue about Switzerland might offer a sampling of local sights and customs. Often the categories chosen will be loose, common-sense ones that audiences can easily recognize.

A lively example of a categorically organized film is Harrod Blank's *Wild Wheels*. The subject is the decorated automobile. Within this realm Blank traces out many subcategories. There are decorated vans, limousines, buses, and taxicabs. There are painted cars and cars sporting glued-on marbles, mirrors, beads, buttons, sculpture, and even grass. There are cars made of wrought iron, cars based on animal motifs, and cars that light up like neon signs. Blank also surveys the sorts of people who decorate their cars. Some wish to attract attention, others to express their personalities; some hope to contact aliens or to convert people to Christianity, others to overcome personal problems. Blank organizes his film as an overview of aspects of "Car Art"—not as a strictly logical set of instances but as a cluster of rough, common-sense groupings that most viewers can grasp.

As this example indicates, the categorically organized film typically bases each segment upon one category or subcategory. A stereotyped travelogue about Switzerland might devote one sequence to clock making, another to alpine skiing. *Wild Wheels* uses less predictable categories, such as vehicles with Christian messages or cars decorated by women who are self-consciously announcing their femininity.

The categorical film often begins by identifying its subject. Our clichéd travelogue might start with a map of Switzerland. *Wild Wheels* opens by showing an ordinary small-town parade before dwelling on a procession of decorated cars. Typically the ending of a categorical film will return to the general topic as a summary. *Wild Wheels* concludes with a sequence in which all the cars we have seen in detail are identified by name and owner. This itemization recalls the parade of autos at the beginning while reaffirming both the general category and the diversity of Car Art.

Patterns of development will usually be simple. The film might move from small to large, local to national, personal to public, and so on. The film on butterflies, for example, might begin with smaller species and work up to large ones, or it might go from drab to colorful types. *Wild Wheels* saves its most flamboyant cars and most moving stories for late in the film.

Because categorical form tends to develop in fairly simple ways, it risks boring the spectator. If the progression from segment to segment depends too much on repetition ("And here's another example . . ."), our expectations will be easily satisfied. The challenge to the filmmaker using categorical form is to introduce variations and to make us adjust our expectations.

For example, the filmmaker may look for ways in which certain categories overlap. Because most categorical films are based on common-sense sortings of examples, some instances fit into several categories. In *Wild*

Wheels a "Coltmobile" decorated with dozens of horse statuettes is shown at the end of a segment devoted to animal motifs. But after the owner comments that creating the car helped him overcome alcoholism, Blank shifts to a grieving husband explaining that his car, covered with jewelry and gems, is his tribute to his dead wife. And this is followed by a tale of how a car encased in toys compensates for its owner's unhappy childhood. The overlap between categories lets Blank move from a fairly amusing segment to one which engages the viewer's sympathy.

Another way in which the filmmaker can maintain our interest and vary the segments is by mixing categorical organization with other types of formal systems: abstract, rhetorical, associational, or narrative. The butterfly film might exploit the colors and shapes of the various examples to add abstract visual interest. Similarly, a rhetorical argument could be made within a segment. One sequence might deal with an endangered species of butterfly, arguing that certain governmental policies had created the threat.

The categorical film could also call on narrative form in one segment or another. After the brief parade prologue, *Wild Wheels* provides a narrative episode. Blank receives a parking ticket and feels that he has been singled out because his Volkswagen is elaborately decorated. He then drives through the United States with a goal: "I wish I could find somebody I could relate to." However, after a quick series of shots of signs and landmarks from different states, the film abruptly halts the story of his trip. The rest of *Wild Wheels* follows categorical form, with Blank presenting the car decorators categorically rather than in a causal-chronological string of events. One might also argue that the film makes a quiet plea for tolerating outrageous self-expression. But even if we find an implicit rhetorical point in the movie, the overall organizational scheme remains categorical.

Categorical form is simple in principle, but filmmakers can use it to create complex and interesting films. Our extended example, the documentary *Olympia*, Part 2, helps us understand how.

■ AN EXAMPLE OF CATEGORICAL FORM: *OLYMPIA*, PART 2

Today we are used to seeing the Olympic games broadcast live on television, with the cameras and announcers picking out certain events from the several that are going on simultaneously. The series of broadcasts takes place over days and therefore has a somewhat loose organization. It takes the form of the Olympic games themselves, with opening and closing ceremonies to mark the beginning and end, and a series of events between. But even with such a rough formal scheme, we can reasonably expect certain patterns of repetitions: previews before events, instant replays after events, interviews with the winners, and so on.

Olympia, the two-part film made of the 1936 Olympic games held in Berlin, has a more careful and varied formal structure than television broadcasts of the Olympic games. Its director, Leni Riefenstahl, had to take the vast amount of footage of many events, shot by over 40 cameras, and reduce it to two films of under two hours each. Since the events were not being shown live, her films could contain patterns of development that would link the individual events together into a unified whole.

We will be analyzing only Part 2 of *Olympia* here, because its formal organization is more complex and varied than Part 1, which shows a series of games with little development across the film. Part 2, on the other hand, has distinct patterns of development. It is also a self-contained film that one can follow without having seen the first part.

In presenting the 1936 Olympics Riefenstahl had many options. She could, for example, have gone chronologically through the games from their beginning to their end, as television does now. Instead, Riefenstahl rearranged events according to an ABA pattern.

Making *Olympia* and hosting the 1936 Olympic games were among the Nazi government's last efforts to present a friendly face to the world. To placate the International Olympic Committee and to avoid adverse reactions and boycotts by other countries, Hitler agreed to suppress anti-Semitic campaigns in Germany (though these campaigns resumed after the games ended). To demonstrate this apparent cooperativeness, the film stresses the comradeship among the athletes of different countries, and its pattern of development supports this explicit meaning.

The early part of the film concentrates on the games as such, rather than on the competition among athletes and countries. Gradually, toward the middle and latter parts of the film, we begin to learn the identities of the players, and suspense builds up about who will win the events. Finally, in the diving sequence at the end, the form turns back to the beginning, and we watch the diving without any differentiation being made among the participants, simply for the sheer beauty of the event itself. The film thus achieves variety and also places the competition in the context of the games themselves as the main focus of attention.

Parallel changes reinforce this ABA arc of development. Most notably, the film begins by showing the athletes and crowds in an impersonal way during the games; individuals' appearances and reactions are not stressed. Then, as the competition becomes more important, we begin to see a personalized view of the athletes—even, at one point, a subjective one. Then, in the diving sequence, the personal emphasis drains away once more, and we watch a series of abstract, birdlike bodies fly through the air. Similarly, the athletes' participation in the events is at first made to look effortless. Then, as the athletes are personalized, we see more of the stress and struggle. Finally, the diving sequence returns us to the effortlessness of the original segments.

The film also develops from nonnarrative form toward the insertion of little narratives within segments. Some of the central segments present the athletes as characters, and the film builds suspense as to which of them will win. But such plot structures also disappear by the film's end.

Despite the simplicity of its subject, then, *Olympia*, Part 2, is a highly structured film which presents its categories in a variety of ways. Its segments are clearly marked off within the film by fade-outs and frequently by musical fanfares as well.

C. Credits, with Olympic flag
1. Nature and the Olympians: morning exercise and swimming
2. Gymnastics
3. Yacht races
4. Pentathlon
5. Women's calisthenics
6. Decathlon
7. Field games: field hockey, polo, soccer
8. Bicycle race
9. Cross-country riding
10. Crew
11. Diving and swimming
12. Epilogue in stadium

The individual games provide one set of categories for the film. Since the nationalities of the participants are also a set of categories, Riefenstahl can vary the relative emphasis placed upon each set in the course of the film. The participating countries are of less importance in the opening and closing games, but they come forward strongly in the central, personalized segments. Again, the result is a considerable degree of variety in a film that potentially could have become quite repetitious.

The opening credits introduce the main category of the film in a direct way, not only by the film's title itself but with flags bearing the Olympic emblem (Fig. 5.1). Yet the first segment of the film seems initially to cheat our expectations. Instead of athletes or a stadium, we see lyrical, almost static shots of foliage and a pond. Slow, Wagnerian music complements this passage. Soon we see a line of running figures in the misty morning air, and our expectations are belatedly fulfilled. Riefenstahl links the Olympian athletes to nature by introducing them in this woodland setting, and she also plays down their different nationalities. The whole first segment, in the woods and bathhouse, and later by the Olympians' club, centers around preparations for the games, rather than on the games themselves. The filmmaker has chosen to begin with a prologue centering around the one element that joins together all the athletes, whatever their sport—exercise. Thus the initial emphasis is on camaraderie rather than competition.

Fig. 5.1

At the same time, we begin to see indications of the athletes' nationalities. Shirts with "Italia" on them (Fig. 5.2) and other similar cues introduce one set of categories—the countries represented at the games. The motif of comparing the athletes with nature continues as well, with shots of athletes exercising juxtaposed with shots of animals. The scene's ending brings all the segment's motifs together. A shot with flowers in the foreground (Fig. 5.3) shifts its focus to reveal an athlete in the background (Fig. 5.4), thus comparing nature and the games once more. In the next, and final, shot of the segment, a row of flags (Fig. 5.5) summarizes the categories of nations participating.

Segment 2, the gymnastics event, opens by picking up a motif from Segment 1. A branch in the foreground is juxtaposed with the crowded stadium at the rear (Fig. 5.6). A parade of athletes with flags develops the

Fig. 5.2

Fig. 5.3

Fig. 5.4

Fig. 5.5

Fig. 5.6

Fig. 5.7

Fig. 5.8

motif of nations. But, as the competition begins, we do not learn the participants' nationalities or names. The emphasis here is on skill, not the competition among countries, and this, too, develops a motif in Segment 1. Of all
the events shown, gymnastics most resembles the calisthenics that we have
just seen the athletes executing. The men seem to be cooperating rather than
competing. The emotional reactions of both participants and onlookers are
deemphasized. We see the crowds only at a distance, as the backdrop for the
action (Fig. 5.7). And the next shot places the gymnast against the sky (Fig.
5.8), seeming to move with easy grace. Indeed, in the final shot of the segment,
an athlete goes soaring off the bar in slow motion (Fig. 5.9), with a fade-out
as he drifts gracefully out of the frame to the right. In this and other shots of
this segment, we see athletes flying off the bar, but not landing. The soaring,
effortless action by bodies suspended in space will be a motif central to the
diving sequence at the end.

Fig. 5.9

The emphasis on the event itself continues in Segment 3, the yacht
races. Quick shots of the individual crews and boats do not enable us to
distinguish one crew from another. But now the film begins slightly to emphasize the competition among individual countries and athletes. While the
boats are still skimming across the water, an announcer's voice tells us which
country won each event. Still, we do not see the ends of the races, the winners'
reactions, or anything else that would individualize this international competition.

Olympia's tactics change more noticeably in Segment 4, the pentathlon.

Fig. 5.10

Fig. 5.11

Fig. 5.12

Fig. 5.13

Now the announcer's voice supplies more information about the countries involved in the event: "Swedish officers have monopolized it since 1912." The contestants are introduced to us by name: Handrick the German, Leonhard the American, and so on. Shots of each with the names repeated come in at intervals during the various races, so that we can for the first time recognize the individuals. Moreover, the events of the pentathlon are shown in chronological order (though some are skipped and just summarized by the announcer). Thus we follow the event as a narrative. The participants become characters, and we are in suspense about who will win. When the German wins the gold medal and the American the silver, the film stresses their reactions during the awards ceremony. Moreover, we see the crowd's reaction, as boys in uniform applaud (Fig. 5.10), and then we see the winners and officials at the ceremony (Fig. 5.11).

We should note that, in spite of *Olympia*'s being a Nazi-financed film, its ideology downplays racism to a surprising extent. In a film destined for screenings around the world, the Nazis wanted to put on a show of international cooperation. (Different versions of *Olympia* were distributed with German, French, and English sound tracks; according to historians, these differed only slightly. Riefenstahl made no attempt to deemphasize the fact that many black athletes won medals in Berlin in 1936. Despite Hitler's disapproval, in Part 1 she chose to concentrate on Jesse Owens more than any other athlete.) In some segments, however, a considerable amount of militarism is in evidence. The comparison of the uniformed boys to German officers in these two shots (Figs. 5.10, 5.11) is particularly striking. Both the pentathlon and the riding events in Segment 9 involve military officers as participants and officials, and an occasional swastika armband is visible. Thus, though Nazi ideology is muted in the film, it could be treated as an implicit meaning.

After the highly dramatic pentathlon, Riefenstahl provides an interlude, a brief series of shots of thousands of women doing calisthenics in unison on a field before the stadium. Beginning with close views of a few women, the scene takes us through a series of more distant views to a point high above the field, gradually revealing the enormous number of people taking part. This impressive segment depends upon the abstract patterns of the dancelike movements and reiterates the exercise motif of the opening. For a short span the emphasis returns to cooperation among countries, before the film goes on to the next segment, which deals again with competition.

Segment 6, the decathlon, uses narrative form to a greater extent than any other part of the film. An announcer is shown standing before microphones (Fig. 5.12), and a voice (dubbed into English in American prints) introduces the participants. Although there are a number of athletes named, our attention is focused from the start on Glen Morris, described as "a hitherto unknown American." The "hitherto" cues us that he might win the event, and the rest of the segment concentrates on him. In each field event shown, the camera favors Morris, and suspense is generated by our sense of his great tension and effort. The announcer emphasizes this; over a shot of Morris's intense preparation for the shot put (Fig. 5.13), the voice declares: "He must try to catch up on Clark," the player currently ahead. We see Morris and his

Fig. 5.14

Fig. 5.15

Fig. 5.16

competitors' facial reactions to their performances in each event. This treatment is very different from the distant, objective, noncompetitive treatment of the gymnastics in Segment 2, and the decathlon marks the height of this attempt to involve us with the athletes as characters. The segment ends by reiterating the flag motif, with Morris's laurel-crowned face superimposed briefly over an American flag.

Segment 7, the field games, goes back to a simple categorical presentation of three events. Yet even within a straightforward segment, the film manages to introduce variation to maintain our interest. Over general shots of field hockey, an announcer tells us the winning country. By contrast, polo is accompanied only by music, without our knowing who is playing. The soccer game is presented as a chronological series of highlights of the game from beginning to end.

Fig. 5.17

Segment 8, the bike race, is shorter than the pentathlon or decathlon segments, but here too there is some attempt to dramatize events. At first we see only general shots of the race, but as the end approaches, the announcer tells us that various national teams are striving to pull ahead. This generates suspense, and the film involves us in the finish by actually giving us hints of the subjective experiences of the cyclists. We see a French cyclist (Fig. 5.14), then a tree whizzing by, as he might be seeing it (Fig. 5.15), and then a tree and road superimposed over a close view of a cyclist (Fig. 5.16). From the distant, depersonalized view of the athletes in the early parts of the film, we have progressed to a point where we are right with the cyclists, seeing things as they do. The ending of the segment brings back the flag motif as the cyclists are given their awards in the stadium (Fig. 5.17).

Fig. 5.18

The next segments retreat from this strong subjectivity. The cross-country riding events are handled in Segment 9 in a fashion somewhat parallel to the pentathlon. We see the individual riders and know their nationalities, but there is little treatment of them as individuals. (The militarism of the pentathlon segment also returns here.) Similarly, the rowing races in Segment 10 put the stress on the teams' nationalities and the winners. We see close shots of crew members (Fig. 5.18) and onlookers, but no particular characters emerge as Glen Morris had. In these segments, the film moves further along its pattern of development, shifting back toward a more objective, depersonalized treatment.

The final segment climaxes this pattern. We see women's diving and get

Fig. 5.19

Fig. 5.20

Fig. 5.21

Fig. 5.22

brief views of the winners' reactions. One woman is embraced by her father and signs autographs. Similarly, the swimming races, though mostly covered by distant moving camera shots, yield glimpses of the athletes' emotions, as when a Japanese contestant learns that he has won (Fig. 5.19). By the final diving sequence, the emphasis on the competition between individuals and countries is nearly gone. Early in the diving sequence, we briefly see the faces of the divers and the audience (Fig. 5.20). But soon the divers' bodies simply plunge in a long series, into or toward the water. As in the gymnasts' segment, there is no announcer's voice, no information on identity or country—simply a sense of the beauty and dynamism of the sport itself. As with the gymnasts, we see less and less of the crowd; later shots isolate the divers as shapes against the sky (Fig. 5.21). Thus the film comes full circle in its pattern of development: back to treating the event as graceful, impersonal, and effortless action, drained of any sense of competition or narrative progress toward a winner. The emphasis rests wholly on the mastery of the body and on a feeling of flight.

In Segment 12, a brief epilogue again summarizes the overall topic— the Olympics—and brings back some motifs. The sky behind the final divers changes to billowing clouds, and the camera moves down to reveal the stadium, with floodlights beaming into the sky. The Olympic flame, a bell, and rows of flags (Fig. 5.22) combine to reiterate the general idea of the Olympics, and the cloudy sky suggests once more the initial linking of the games to nature. The film ends as the camera moves up the beams of the searchlights to the bright point where they meet in the clouds. And, although this triumphant moment brings the Olympics themselves to a climax, it also suggests the propaganda purpose behind the film itself: a display of Nazi power disguised by a show of cooperation with other nations.

Because of *Olympia*'s double purpose—as a record of the games and as subtle Nazi propaganda—the film provides a good example of all four types of meaning discussed in Chapter 3. On its referential level, we recognize it as coverage of the games, and some of its segments are straightforward accounts of who participated and won. The fact that we are often not given this information, added to the beauty of the treatment of the events, also cues us to build an explicit meaning: These games involve a peaceful, cooperative struggle among athletes of different countries to discipline their bodies and carry on a great international tradition.

There are further meanings involving the Nazi sponsorship of the games. We can see the film's treatment of them as reflecting an underlying Nazi ideology. (The Nazi government financed the film, but to avoid antagonizing the International Olympic Committee, the film was treated as an independent production by Riefenstahl.) The implicit meaning, which we can interpret fairly easily from a modern perspective, involves an emphasis on Nazi power. In *Olympia*, Part 1, there had been numerous reaction shots of Hitler in the audience; in Part 2, as we have seen, the militarism and swastika armbands frequently remind us of the powers behind these games.

More generally, we can find symptomatic meaning in the film's whole treatment of the Olympics. Traces of the Nazi ideology can be found in the film's stress of discipline, on regimenting mass activity (especially the calisthenics in Segments 2 and 5), on a mystical bond between humans and nature, and on a cult of the heroic body. As we shall see in Chapter 10, the film's style supports all these levels of meaning. These meanings show that a categorically organized film can be as subject to ideological coloring as can any other sort of film.

RHETORICAL FORMAL SYSTEMS

■ PRINCIPLES OF RHETORICAL FORM

Another type of film uses *rhetorical* form, in which the filmmaker presents a persuasive argument. The goal in such a film is to make the audience hold an opinion about the subject matter and perhaps to act upon that opinion. This type of film goes beyond the categorical type in that it tries to convince the viewer of something of practical consequence.

Rhetorical form is common in all the media. We encounter it frequently in daily life, not just in formal speeches but also in conversation. People often try to persuade each other by argument. Salespeople use persuasion in their jobs, and friends may argue politics over lunch. Television bombards us with one of the most pervasive uses of rhetorical form in film—commercials, which try to persuade viewers to buy products or vote for candidates.

We can define rhetorical form in film by four basic attributes. First, it addresses the viewer openly, trying to move him or her to a new intellectual conviction, to a new emotional attitude, or to action. (In the latter case, we may already believe something but may need to be persuaded that the belief is important enough to act upon.)

Second, the subject of the film will usually not be an issue of scientific truth but a matter of opinion, toward which a person may take a number of equally plausible attitudes. The filmmaker will try to make his or her position seem the most plausible by presenting different types of arguments and evidence. Yet, because the issue cannot be absolutely proven, we may decide upon our opinion simply because the filmmaker has made a convincing case for one position. Because rhetorical films deal with beliefs and arguments, they involve the expression of ideology; indeed, perhaps no type of film form centers so consistently around explicit meaning and ideological implications.

A third aspect of rhetorical form follows from this. If the conclusion cannot be proven beyond question, the filmmaker often appeals to our emotions, rather than presenting only factual evidence. And, fourth, the film will often attempt to persuade the viewer to make a choice that will have an effect on his or her everyday life. This may be as simple as what shampoo to use, or it may involve decisions about which political candidate to support, or even whether a young person will fight in a war.

Films can use all sorts of arguments to persuade us to make such choices. Often, however, these arguments are not presented to us *as* arguments. The film will frequently present arguments as if they were simply observations or factual conclusions. Nor will the film tend to point out other opinions. There are three main types of arguments the film may use: relating to the source, to the subject, and to the viewer.

Arguments from source.   Some of the film's arguments will usually present the film as a reliable source of information. The people who made it and those who narrate it try to give the audience the impression that they are intelligent, well informed, sincere, trustworthy, and so on. These seem just to be objective traits, but they imply an argument: This film comes from reliable people; therefore you should allow yourself to be persuaded by it. For example, a film may use a narrator whose voice is strong and clear, rather than soft and hesitating, because if we hear a voice that seems to carry conviction, we may be more likely to take it as a reliable source of information.

Subject-centered arguments.   The film will also employ arguments about its subject matter. Sometimes the film appeals to beliefs common at the time in a given culture. For example, in contemporary America, a large segment of the population is said to believe that most politicians are cynical and corrupt. This may or may not be true of any one politician, but someone running for public office may appeal to that belief and tell potential voters that he or she will bring a new honesty to government.

A second approach the film may take is to use examples that support its point. Such evidence may be more or less strong. A taste-test commercial that shows one person choosing the advertiser's product seems to imply that the product really tastes better; yet there is no mention of the other people— perhaps a majority—who prefer other brands.

Finally, filmmakers can back up an argument by exploiting familiar, easily accepted argumentative patterns. Students of rhetoric call such patterns *enthymemes,* arguments that rely on widespread opinion and usually conceal some crucial premises.

For example, we might make a film to persuade you that a problem has been solved correctly. We would show that the problem had existed, then show that some action had been taken which solved it. The movement from problem to solution is such a familiar pattern of inference that you might assume that we had proven reasonably that the right thing was done. On closer analysis, however, you might discover that the film had a hidden premise, such as "On the assumption that this was the best solution, a particular course of action was taken." Perhaps other solutions would have been better, but those were judged inadequate, and the film does not examine them. The solution presented is not as strictly necessary as the problem-solution pattern would seem to suggest. Shortly we shall see such enthymematic patterns at work in *The River.*

Viewer-centered arguments.   Lastly, the film may make an argument that appeals to the emotions of the viewer. We are all familiar with politicians who pose with flag, family, and pets to rouse potential voters. Appeals to patriotism, romantic sentimentality, and other emotions are common in rhetorical films. Filmmakers often draw conventions from other films to provoke the desired reaction. Sometimes such appeals can disguise the weakness of other arguments of the film and can persuade the more susceptible audience members to accept the film's outlook.

Rhetorical form in a film can organize these arguments and appeals in a variety of ways. Some filmmakers will present their basic arguments first, then go on to show evidence of the problems and how they would be addressed by the solutions argued for in the film. Other films will start with the problem and describe it in detail, then let the viewer know late in the film what change is being advocated. This second approach may create more curiosity and suspense, leading the viewer to reflect on and anticipate possible solutions. Which overall approach the filmmaker chooses will depend on judgments about how the subject can be most effectively presented.

One standard description of rhetorical form suggests that it begins with an introduction of the situation, goes on to a discussion of the relevant facts, then presents proofs that a given solution fits those facts, and ends with an epilogue that summarizes what has come before. *The River*, a documentary made in 1937 by Pare Lorentz, will be our main example of rhetorical form. In laying out its overall form, the film adheres to the four-part structure just outlined.

■ AN EXAMPLE OF RHETORICAL FORM: *THE RIVER*

Lorentz made *The River* for the U.S. government's Farm Security Administration. In 1937, the country was making progress toward pulling out of the Depression. Under the administration of Franklin Delano Roosevelt, the federal government used its powers extensively to create public works programs in order to provide jobs for the large number of unemployed workers, as well as to correct various social problems. Although many people tend now to think of Roosevelt's policies as the right ones and to credit him with bringing America out of the Depression, we should not foget that there was much political opposition to those policies at the time. *The River* hails the Tennessee Valley Authority (TVA) as the solution to problems of flooding, argicultural depletion, and electrification. The film had a definite ideological slant: promoting Roosevelt's policies. Thus the film's argument was controversial at the time. Let us look at how this film sets out to persuade its audience that the TVA is a good program.

The River has eleven segments:

C. The credits
1. A prologue title setting forth the subject of the film
2. A description of the rivers that flow into the Mississippi and then into the Gulf of Mexico
3. A history of the early agricultural use of the river
4. The problems caused in the South by the Civil War
5. A section on lumbering and steel mills in the North and the building of urban areas
6. The flooding caused by careless exploitation of the land
7. The current effects of these cumulative problems on people: poverty and ignorance
8. A map and description of the TVA project
9. The dams of the TVA and the benefits they bring
E. An end title

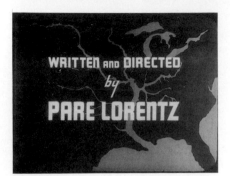

Fig. 5.23

Fig. 5.24

The film seems at first just to be giving us information about the Mississippi. The film proceeds for quite a while before its argument becomes apparent. But, by the careful use of repetition, variation, and development, Lorentz builds up a case that really depends on all the segments working together as a unified whole.

The opening credits of the film are shown over an old-fashioned picture of steamboats on the Mississippi, then over a map of the United States with the Mississippi River and its tributaries exaggerated in size (Fig. 5.23). The film immediately suggests to the audience that its makers are reliable and knowledgeable and that this will be an account based on both historical and geographical facts. The same map returns under the prologue writing in the brief opening segment, which states, "This is the story of a river." Such a statement disguises the rhetorical purpose of the film, implying that the film will be an objectively told "story"—that is, it will have features of narrative form.

Segment 2 continues the introduction with images of the sky, mountains, and rivers, with a man's voice telling us facts about how water flows into the Mississippi from as far away as Idaho and Pennsylvania. The narrator's voice is deep and authoritative, playing on culturally conventional notions of what a trustworthy person sounds like. (The narrator, who was carefully chosen for these qualities, was Thomas Chalmers, formerly a baritone with the Metropolitan Opera.) As the images show the rivers growing in size as they join together (Fig. 5.24), the narrator begins to intone: "Down the Yellowstone, the Milk, the White, and Cheyenne . . . the Cannonball, the Musselshell, the James, and the Sioux." Many other river names follow in a rhythmically declaimed roll-call. (The technique is based on the work of Walt Whitman and other American poets.) Moreover, the voice combines at most points in the film with the distinctively American musical score written by Virgil Thomson, often employing familiar folk songs. Thus the film deliberately adopts an "American" tone throughout. This not only appeals to the spectator's patriotic and sentimental feelings, but also implies that the whole country should be united in dealing with problems that seem merely regional.

Segment 2 has established an idyllic situation, with its beautiful images of mountain and river landscapes. The overall development of the film will be toward a restoration of this beauty, but with a difference. The scene also sets up techniques to be repeated and varied in other segments.

With Segment 3, we move into the section of the film's form devoted to facts of American history relating to the Mississippi and the problems it causes. Segment 3 begins much as Segment 2 had, with a view of clouds. But now things begin to change. Instead of the mountains we saw earlier, we see mule teams and drivers. Again the narrator's voice begins a list: "New Orleans to Baton Rouge . . . Baton Rouge to Natchez . . . Natchez to Vicksburg." This list is part of the brief recounting of the history of the dikes built along the Mississippi in pre–Civil War days to control flooding. The narrator is confirmed as trustworthy and knowledgeable, giving us facts and dates in the nation's history. We see cotton bales loaded onto steamboats, giving a sense of the country's early strength as an exporter of goods.

So far the film has seemed to follow its initial purpose of telling a story of the river. But in Segment 4, it begins to introduce the problems that the TVA will eventually solve. The film shows the results of the Civil War: destroyed houses and dispossessed landowners, the land worn out by the cultivation of cotton, and people forced to move west. The moral tone of the film becomes apparent, and it is an appealing one. Over images of impoverished people, bleak music plays. It is based on a familiar folk tune, "Go Tell Aunt Rhody," which, with its line, "The old gray goose is dead," underscores the losses of the farm dwellers. The narrator's voice expresses compassion as he speaks of the South's "tragedy of land impoverished." This attitude of sympathy may incline us to accept as true other things which the film tells us. The narrator also refers to the people of the period as "we": "We mined the soil for cotton until it would yield no more." Here the film's persuasive intent becomes evident. It was not literally *we*, you and I and the narrator, who grew this cotton. The use of the word "we" is a rhetorical strategy to make us feel that all Americans have a responsibility for this problem and for finding a solution.

Later segments repeat the strategies of these earlier ones. In Segment 5 the film again uses the poetically repetitious narration to describe the lumbering industry's growth after the Civil War, listing "Black spruce and Norway pine" and other trees. In the images, we see the pines against the sky, echoing the cloud motif that had opened Segments 2 and 3 (Fig. 5.25). This creates a parallel between the riches of the agricultural and the industrial areas. A sprightly sequence of logging, accompanied by music based on the tune "Hot Time in the Old Town Tonight," again gives us a sense of America's strength. A section on coal mining and steel mills follows and enhances this impression. This segment ends with references to the growing urban centers: "We built a hundred cities and a thousand towns," and we hear a list of some of their names.

Fig. 5.25

Up to this point we have seen the strengths of America associated with the river valley, with just a hint of the problems that growth has sparked. But Segment 6 switches over and creates a lengthy series of contrasts to the earlier parts. It begins with the same list of trees—"Black spruce and Norway pine"—but now we see stumps against fog instead of trees against clouds (Fig. 5.26). Another line returns, but with a new phrase added: "We built a hundred cities and a thousand towns . . . but at what a cost." Beginning with the barren hilltops, we are shown how melting ice runs off, and how the runoff gradually erodes hillsides and swells rivers into flooding torrents. Once more we hear the list of rivers from Segment 2, but now the music is sombre and the rivers are no longer idyllic. Again there is a parallel presented between the soil erosion here and the soil depletion in the South after the Civil War.

The film has gradually taken us away from a situation of natural beauty and developed the central problem around which its argument is based. Now we see scenes of real flooding, with sandbagging, destruction, people rescued and living in tent camps, and other flood problems. And, as we watch these scenes, we hear sirens and the turbulent roar of water, building up a sense

Fig. 5.26

Fig. 5.27

of onrushing disaster. There is a considerable emotional appeal here, as we are given a sense of the people being utterly unable to control the water.

By this point we understand the information the film is presenting about flooding and erosion. Still, the film withholds the solution and presents the effects of the floods on people's lives in contemporary America. Segment 7 describes government aid to flood victims in 1937 but points out that the basic problem still exists. *The River* employs a striking enthymeme here: "And poor land makes poor people—poor people make poor land." This sounds reasonable on the surface, but upon examination its meaning becomes unclear. (Didn't the rich southern plantation owners whose ruined mansions we saw in Segment 4 have a lot to do with the impoverishment of the soil?) Such statements are employed more for their poetic neatness and emotional appeal than for any rigorous reasoning they may contain. Scenes of tenant farmer families (Fig. 5.27) appeal directly to our emotional response to such poverty. This segment picks up on motifs introduced in Segment 4, on the Civil War. Now, the film tells us, these people cannot go west, because there is no more open land there.

Now the problem has been introduced and discussed, and emotional appeals have prepared the audience to accept a solution. Segment 8 presents that solution and begins the part of the film devoted to the proofs that this solution is an effective one. In Segment 8, the map of the opening titles returns, and the narrator says, "There is no such thing as an ideal river in nature, but the Mississippi River is out of joint." Here we have another example of an enthymeme—an inference assumed to be logically valid and factually accurate. The Mississippi may be "out of joint" for certain uses, but would it present a problem to the animals and plants in its ecological system? This statement assumes that an "ideal" river would be one perfectly suited to *our* needs and purposes. The narrator goes on to give the film's most clear-cut statement of its argument: "The old River *can* be controlled. We had the power to take the Valley apart. We have the power to put it together again."

Now we can see why the film's form has been organized as it has. In early segments, especially 3 and 5, we saw how the American population built up great agricultural and industrial strengths. At the time, we might have just taken these events as simple facts of history. But now they turn out to be crucial to the film's argument. That argument might be summarized this way: We have seen that the American people have the power to build and to destroy; therefore they have the power to build again. This argument is yet another enthymeme. Perhaps the people destroyed something incapable of being rebuilt, or maybe they have lost their former power. But the film does not consider these possibilities.

The narrator continues: "In 1933 we started . . . ," going on to describe how Congress formed the TVA. This segment presents the TVA as an already implemented solution to the problem and presents no other possible solutions. Thus something that was actually controversial seems to be a matter of straightforward implementation. Here is a case where one solution, because it has been effective in dealing with a problem, is taken to be *the* solution. Yet, in retrospect, it is not certain that the massive series of dams built by the TVA was the single best solution to flooding. Perhaps a less radical plan combining reforesting with conservation-oriented farming would have created fewer new problems (such as the displacement of people from the land flooded by the dams). Perhaps local governments rather than the federal government would have been more efficient problem solvers. *The River* does not bother to rebut these alternatives, relying instead on our habitual inference from problem to solution.

Fig. 5.28

Segment 9 contains similarities to and differences from several earlier parts of *The River*. It begins with a list of dams, which we see in progress or finished. This echoes the lists of rivers, trees, towns, and so on, that we have heard at intervals. The serene shots of the artificial lakes that follow link the ending to the beginning, recalling the lyrical river shots of Segment 2 (Fig. 5.28). The displaced, flooded-out, and unemployed people from Segment 6 seem now to be happily at work, building planned model towns on government loans. Electricity generated by the dams links these rural communities to those "hundred cities and thousand towns" we heard about earlier, bringing to the countryside "the advantages of urban life." Many motifs planted in a simple fashion are now picked up and woven together to act as proofs of the TVA's benefits. The ending shows life as being parallel to the way it was in the beginning—beautiful nature, productive people—but enhanced by modern government planning.

An upswell of music and a burst of views of the dams and rushing water create a brief epilogue summarizing the factors that have brought about the change—the TVA dams. Under the ending titles and credits, we see the map again. A list tells us the names of the various government agencies that sponsored the film or assisted in its making. These again seem to lend authority to the source of the arguments in the film.

The River was successful in achieving its purposes. Favorable initial response led a major American studio, Paramount, to agree to distribute the film, a rare opportunity for an independently made short documentary at that time. Reviewers and public alike greeted the film enthusiastically. A contemporary critic's review testifies to the power of the film's rhetorical form. After describing the early portions, Gilbert Seldes wrote, "And so, without your knowing it, you arrive at the Tennessee Valley—and if this is propaganda, make the most of it, because it is masterly. It is as if the pictures which Mr. Lorentz took arranged themselves in such an order that they supplied their own argument, not as if an argument conceived in advance dictated the order of the pictures."

President Roosevelt himself saw *The River* and liked it. He helped get congressional support to start a separate government agency, the U.S. Film Service, to make other documentaries like it. But not everyone was in favor of Roosevelt's policies or believed that the government should set itself up to make films that essentially espoused the views of the administration currently in office. By 1940, the Congress had taken away the U.S. Film Service's support, and documentary films were once again made only within the separate sections of the government. Such a series of results shows that rhetorical films can lead both to direct action and to controversy.

ABSTRACT FORMAL SYSTEMS

■ PRINCIPLES OF ABSTRACT FORM

In categorical and rhetorical form, the pictorial aspects of the images are a means to inform or persuade. But it is also possible to organize a film around purely visual features. The filmmaker might arrange the images so as to compare or contrast qualities like color, shape, rhythm, and size.

As viewers, when we confront a film exhibiting abstract form, we do not look for causally linked events that make up a narrative or for propositional claims that might add up to an argument, as in rhetorical organization. Similarly, the motifs used in an abstract film will not necessarily fit into substantive categories. A ball and a balloon might be put side by side, not because they are both toys but because they are both round or both of an orange color. To see the connection between the ball and the balloon, we must recognize the similarity of the abstract qualities of the objects.

Of course, all films contain objects with color, shape, and size, and their sounds have rhythm and other sonic qualities. We have seen how *Olympia* contains some segments, like the diving sequence, where our attention is drawn to abstract elements of the actions shown. Similarly, the lyrical beauty of the river and lake shots in *The River* functions to create parallels, and the rhythm of its musical score enhances our emotional involvement in the argument being made. But in each of these cases, an abstract pattern becomes a means to an end, always subordinate to the overall purposes—categorical or rhetorical—of the films. They are not organized around abstract qualities but emphasize such qualities only occasionally. In abstract form, the *whole* film's system will be determined by such qualities.

Abstract films are often organized in a way that we might call "theme and variations." This term usually applies to music, where a melody or other type of motif is introduced, and then a series of different versions of that same melody follows—often with such extreme differences of key and rhythm that the original melody becomes difficult to recognize. An abstract film's form may work in a similar fashion. An introductory section will typically show us in a relatively simple way the kinds of relationships the film will use as its basic material. Then other segments will go on to present similar kinds of relationships but with changes. The changes may be slight, depending on our noticing that the similarities are still greater than the differences. But abstract films also usually depend on building up greater and greater differences from the introductory material. Thus we may find considerable contrast coming into the film, and sudden differences can help us to sense when a new segment has started. If the film's formal organization has been created with care, the similarities and differences will not be random. There will be some underlying principle that runs through the film.

Sometimes that principle will be a very precise idea. In making *Print Generation*, J. J. Murphy took a random series of color shots, then rephotographed them over and over on a contact printer. Each succeeding duplication lost photographic quality, until the final images were unrecognizable. *Print Generation* repeats the footage twenty-five times, starting with the most abstract images and moving to the most recognizable ones. Then the process is reversed and the images gradually move back toward abstraction. On the sound track the progression is exactly the opposite. Murphy rerecorded the sound twenty-five times, but the film begins with the most clearly audible version. As the image clarifies, the sound deteriorates; as the image slips back into abstraction, the sound clarifies. Part of the fascination of this experimental film derives from seeing blobs of abstract color become slowly defined as people and landscapes before passing back into abstraction. The film also teases us to discover its overall formal pattern.

Other abstract films use a more general idea as an organizing principle. Stan Brakhage's *Mothlight* was made by taping dead moths' wings to a strip of clear film, then duplicating the results on a negative. No mathematical principle lies behind this. Rather, the varied and random positions of the wings from frame to frame create a vibrant effect of flicker and changing shapes. Some animators, such as Oskar Fischinger and Norman McLaren, choose a piece of music and draw shapes that move in rhythm to the sound track. There is an infinite number of ways of organizing an abstract film, but most filmmakers will consider not just how to string images together but how to create overall forms for their films. Abstract films gain much of their complexity from their organization, and part of their interest for the viewer comes in discovering how the individual motifs function in relation to the overall organization.

When we call a film's form abstract, we do not mean that the film has no recognizable objects in it. It is true that many abstract films use pure shapes and colors, created by the filmmaker by drawing, cutting out pieces of colored paper, animating clay shapes, and the like. There is an alternative approach, however, and that is to use real objects and to isolate them from their everyday context in such a way that their abstract qualities come forward. After all, shapes, colors, rhythmic movements, and every abstract quality that the filmmaker uses exist both in nature and in human-made objects. Markings on animals, bird songs, cloud formations, and other such natural phenomena often attract us because they seem beautiful or striking— qualities similar to those that we look for in artworks. Moreover, even those objects that we create for very practical and mundane uses may have pleasing contours or textures. Chairs are made to sit on, but we will usually try to furnish our home with chairs that also look attractive to us.

Because abstract qualities are common in the world, filmmakers often start by photographing real objects. But, since the filmmakers then juxtapose the images to create relations of shape, color, and so on, the film is still using abstract organization in spite of the fact that we can still recognize the object as a bird, a face, or a spoon. And, because the abstract qualities in films do resemble those present in real objects, such films call upon skills we use in everyday life. Normally we use our ability to recognize shapes and colors in very practical ways, as when we drive and have to interpret traffic signs and lights quickly. But, in watching an abstract film, we do not need to use the shapes, colors, or repetitions that we see and hear for practical purposes.

Fig. 5.29

Consequently we can notice them more fully and see relationships that we would seldom bother to look for during the practical activities of everyday life. In a film these abstract qualities become interesting for their own sake.

For example, a turnbridge over a river serves an eminently practical purpose. A section of railroad tracks swivels on a central column to clear space for tall boats passing through the waterway. The sculptor Richard Serra set up a camera at the center of a turnbridge and filmed the process. The surprising onscreen result is that the bridge framework seems monumentally unmoving while the landscape rotates majestically around it. The slowly changing background obliges the viewer to notice the symmetrical geometry of the bridge's design (Fig. 5.29). Without the title *Railroad Turnbridge* we might not recognize that this abstract imagery was created out of a very concrete piece of engineering.

This abstract, impractical interest has led some critics and viewers to think of abstract films as frivolous. Critics may call them "art for art's sake," since all they seem to do is present us with a series of interesting shapes and sounds. Yet in doing so, such films often make us more aware of such shapes and sounds, and we may be better able to notice them in the everyday world as well—in nature and in practical objects. In this sense we perceive not only the film but the world around us more fully through an awareness of pictorial qualities. In talking about abstract films, we might amend the phrase to "art for life's sake"—for such films enhance our lives as much as do the films of other formal types.

■ AN EXAMPLE OF ABSTRACT FORM: *BALLET MÉCANIQUE*

Ballet mécanique ("Mechanical Ballet"), one of the earliest abstract films ever made, was also one of the most influential. It remains a highly enjoyable avant-garde film and a classic example of how mundane objects can be transformed when their abstract qualities are used as the basis for a film's form.

Two filmmakers collaborated on *Ballet mécanique* during 1923–1924. They were Dudley Murphy, a young American journalist and aspiring film producer, and Fernand Léger, a major French painter. Léger had developed his own distinctive version of Cubism in his paintings, often using stylized machine parts. His interest in machines transferred well into the cinema, and it contributed to the central formal principles of *Ballet mécanique*.

This title suggests the paradox the filmmakers employ in creating their film's thematic material and variations. We expect a ballet to be flowing, with human dancers performing it. A classical ballet seems the opposite of a machine's movements, yet the film creates a mechanical dance. Relatively few of the many objects we see in the film are actually machines; it mostly uses hats, faces, bottles, kitchen utensils, and the like. But through juxtaposition with machines and through visual and temporal rhythms, we are cued to see even a woman's moving eyes and mouth as being like machine parts.

We cannot segment *Ballet mécanique* by tracing its arguments or dividing it into scenes of narrative action. Rather, we must look for changes in abstract qualities being used at different points in the film. Going by this principle, we can find nine segments in *Ballet mécanique:*

C. A credits sequence with a stylized, animated figure of Charlie Chaplin introducing the film's title (The word "Charlot" in this introduction is Chaplin's character's name in France.)

1. The introduction of the film's rhythmic elements

2. A treatment of similar elements with views taken through prisms

3. Rhythmic movements

4. A comparison of people and machines

5. Rhythmic movements of intertitles and pictures

6. More rhythmic movements, mostly of circular objects

7. Quick dances of objects

8. A return to Charlot and the opening elements

Fig. 5.30

Ballet mécanique uses the theme-and-variations approach in a complex way, introducing many individual motifs in rapid succession, then bringing them back at intervals and in different combinations. There is a definite pattern of development built from elements of the earlier segments. Each new segment picks up on a limited number of the abstract qualities from the previous one and plays with these for a while.

The last segments use elements from early in the film once again, and the ending strongly echoes the opening. The film throws a great deal of material at us in a short time, and we must actively seek to make connections among motifs if we are to perceive the film's repetitions and variations.

As we have suggested, the introductory portion of an abstract film will usually give us strong cues as to what we can expect to see developed later. *Ballet mécanique's* animated Chaplin begins this process. The figure is highly abstract—recognizably human, but also made up of abstract shapes that move about in a jerky fashion (Fig. 5.30). Already we have the human figure as an object.

Segment 1 surprises us by beginning with a woman swinging in a garden (Fig. 5.31). Yet the film's title may lead us to notice the regular rhythm of the swinging, and the puppetlike gestures as the woman repeatedly lifts her eyes and head, then lowers them, a fixed smile on her face. Certain abstract qualities already have become prominent. Suddenly a rapid succession of images appears, passing too quickly for us to be able to do more than glimpse a hat, bottles, an abstract white triangle, and other objects. Next a woman's mouth appears, smiling, then not smiling, then smiling again. The hat returns, then the smiling mouth again, then some spinning gears, then a shiny ball circles close to the camera. Next we see the woman in the swing and the camera moves back and forth with her—but now she is upside down (Fig. 5.32). This segment ends with the shiny ball, now swinging back and forth directly toward the camera, and we are invited to compare its movement with that of the woman in the swing. We are thus confirmed in our expectation that she is not a character but an object, like the bottle or the shiny ball. The same is true of that smiling mouth, which does not suggest an emotion as much as a regularly changing shape. Shapes of objects (a round hat,

Fig. 5.31

Fig. 5.32

Fig. 5.33

Fig. 5.34

vertical bottles), direction of movement (the swing, the shiny ball), textures (the shininess of both the ball and the bottles), and the rhythms of the objects' movements and the changes from object to object will be qualities which the film calls to our attention.

With these expectations set up in the short introduction section, the film goes on to vary its elements. Segment 2 sticks fairly closely to the elements just introduced by beginning with another view of the shiny ball, now seen through a prism. There follow other shots of household objects, similar to the ball in that they are also shiny and are seen through a prism. One of these is recognizable as a pot lid (Fig. 5.33), its round shape picking up that of both the ball and the hat of the previous segment. Here is a good example of how a mundane object can be taken out of its everyday use and its abstract qualities can create formal relations.

In the middle of the series of prism shots, we see a rapid burst of shots, alternating a white circle and white triangle. This is yet another motif that will return at intervals, with variations. In a sense, these shapes, which are not recognizable objects, contrast with the kitchen utensils of the other shots. But they also invite us to make comparisons: The pot lid is also round, the prismatic facets are somewhat triangular. During the rest of Segment 2 we see more prism shots, interspersed with another rapid series of circles and triangles, and also with views of a woman's eyes opening and closing, a woman's eyes partially masked off by dark shapes (Fig. 5.34), and finally the smiling/unsmiling mouth from Segment 1.

Segment 2 has further confirmed our expectations that the film will concentrate on comparisons of shapes, rhythms, or textures. We also begin to see a pattern of surprising interruptions of the segments with brief bursts of short shots. In Segment 1 interruptions had been created by shots alternating objects and a single triangle. Now we have twice seen a circle and triangle alternate. The rhythm of changing views is as important as the rhythm of movement within individual shots.

Now that such patterns are well established, the film begins to introduce greater variations to complicate and sometimes overturn our expectations. Segment 3 begins with shots of rows of platelike discs, alternating with spinning shapes reminiscent of a fairground game wheel. Will round shapes and movements provide the main principle of development in this segment? Suddenly the camera is moving rapidly down a twisting fairground slide. We see elements such as marching feet, cars going over the camera, and rapid shots of a carnival ride's cars spinning past. Here different rhythms succeed each other, and common shape seems less important. Relatively few of the elements from Segments 1 and 2 return. We do not see the parts of the woman's face, and many of the objects are new ones, seen out of doors. Yet, after the carnival cars, we see a relatively lengthy shot of a spinning, shiny object—not in a prism view but at least recalling the image of the kitchen utensils seen earlier. The segment ends with the familiar rapid alternation of circle and triangle.

Segment 4 gives us the film's most explicit comparison of humans and machines. We first see a carnival slide from above, picking up on an element from Segment 3 (though here the camera does not move down the slide). The slide stretches horizontally across the screen, and in quick succession a man's silhouette whizzes down it four times (Fig. 5.35). This may seem a continuation of Segment 3's concentration on rhythm, but next we see a machine part, strongly vertical on the screen (Fig. 5.36), with a piston moving up and down rhythmically. Again we see similarities—a tubelike object with another object moving along it—and differences—the compositions use opposing directions, and the four movements of the man are done in different shots, while the camera holds as the piston moves up and down within one shot. More shots compare the slide and machine parts, ending with one machine seen through a prism.

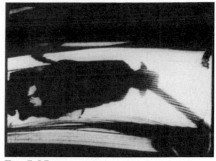
Fig. 5.35

The familiar alternating circle and triangle return, but with differences: Now the triangle is sometimes upside down, and each shape remains on the screen slightly longer. The segment continues with more spinning shiny objects and machine parts, then reintroduces the motif of the woman's masked eye (similar to Fig. 5.34). Now the motions of this eye are compared to machine parts.

Segment 4 closes with one of *Ballet mécanique*'s most famous and daring moments. After a shot of a rotating machine part (Fig. 5.37), we see seven identically repeated shots of a laundry woman climbing a stair and gesturing (Fig. 5.38). The segment returns to the smiling mouth, then gives us eleven more shots of the same view of the laundry woman, a shot of a large piston, and five more repetitions of the laundry woman shot. This insistent repetition makes the woman's movements as precise as those of the machine. Even though she is seen in a real place, we cannot see her as a character but must concentrate on her movements' rhythms. (The filmmakers have taken advantage of the cinema's own mechanical ability to multiply the same image.) Segment 4 is quite different from earlier ones, but it does bring back motifs: The prism recurs briefly (from Segment 2), spinning shiny objects recall those of Segment 3, and the woman's eyes and mouth (Segments 1 and 2) return, having been absent from Segment 3.

Fig. 5.36

Segment 4 has been the culmination of the film's comparison of mechanical objects with people. Now Segment 5 introduces a strong contrast by concentrating on printed intertitles. Unlike other segments, this one begins with a black screen, which is gradually revealed to be a dark card upon which a white zero is painted. We see this first as a prismed shot (once again recalling Segment 2). An unprismed view of the zero shows it shrinking.

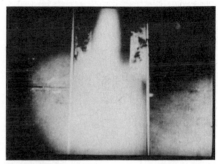
Fig. 5.37

Unexpectedly, an intertitle appears: "ON A VOLÉ UN COLLIER DE PERLES DE 5 MILLIONS" ("A pearl necklace worth 5 million has been stolen"). In a narrative film this might give us story information, but the filmmakers use the printed language as one more visual motif for rhythmic variation. There follows a series of quick shots, with large zeros, sometimes one, sometimes three, appearing and disappearing, shrinking and growing. Parts of the intertitle appear in isolation ("ON A VOLÉ"), participating in this "dance" of letters. The film plays with an ambiguity: Is the zero really an "O," the first letter of the sentence, or is it part of the number 5,000,000, or is it a stylized representation of the pearl necklace itself? Beyond this sort of play with a visual pun, the zero recalls and varies the circle motif that has been so prominent in the film.

Fig. 5.38

More punning occurs as the zero gives way to a picture of a horse collar—which resembles the zero visually but also refers to the word "*collier*" (which in French can mean either "necklace" or "collar"). The collar bobs about in its own little dance, and alternates with moving zeros and parts of the intertitle sentence, sometimes printed backward—to emphasize their graphic, rather than informative, function. This segment has been very different from earlier ones, but even here a couple of motifs are repeated. Just before the horse collar is introduced, we see the masked woman's eye briefly, and in the course of the rapid flashes of intertitles, one tiny shot of a machine part is inserted.

After this point, the film begins to move toward variations that are closer to the elements of the opening segments. Segment 6 shows us rhythmic movements involving mostly circular shapes. It begins with a woman's head, eyes closed, turning (Fig. 5.39). Directly after this we see a wooden statue swing toward and away from the camera (Fig. 5.40). Once again the comparison of person and object comes forward. An abstract circular shape grows, cueing us to watch for the recurrence of this shape. A woman's face appears in a prismed view; she passes a cardboard with holes cut in it before her face, with her expression continually changing in a mechanical fashion. We see the circles and triangles alternate again, but this time these shapes are presented in four different sizes. A quick series of shots of rows of shiny kitchen utensils follows (Fig. 5.41), with short bursts of black film interspersed. This blackness picks up and varies the dark backgrounds of the intertitles in Segment 5, and the shiny pots and other utensils reintroduce a motif which has appeared in every segment *except* 5. The motif of rows of objects had come in Segment 3, while the swinging motion of the utensils in many of these shots echoes the swinging of the woman and the shiny ball from way back in Segment 1. With this sequence and the next segment the film's development is turning back toward its beginning.

Segment 7 begins with a shot of a display window, with spiral shapes that seem to freeze the gyrating motions that have made up so much of the film's rhythmic play (Fig. 5.42). The circle motif returns, leading into a series of "dances" that vary key motifs. Short shots make a pair of mannequin legs seem to dance (Fig. 5.43); then the legs begin to spin within the shots. The shiny ball motif returns, but now two balls spin in opposite directions. Two very different shapes—a hat and a shoe—alternate quickly (Fig. 5.44), creating a conflict of shapes similar to the juxtaposition of circle and triangle earlier. The prismed shot of a woman changing expressions follows, then a profile shot similar to the one in Figure 5.39. Two slightly different views of a face (Fig. 5.45) quickly alternate, inducing us to see the head as nodding mechanically. Finally, quick shots of bottles make them seem to change position in another dancelike rhythm.

Interestingly, the motifs used in Segment 7 come primarily from Segments 1 and 2 (the shiny balls, hat, bottles) and from Segment 6 (the prismed face, the growing circle). Here, where the "mechanical ballet" becomes most explicit, the film draws together elements from its beginning, and from the previous segment, where the recapitulation of the earlier segments had begun. Segment 7 avoids motifs from the center of the film—3 through 5—and thus

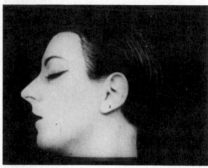

Fig. 5.39

Fig. 5.40

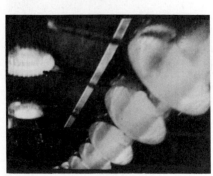

Fig. 5.41

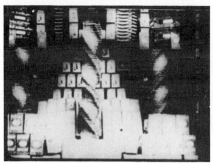

Fig. 5.42

Fig. 5.43

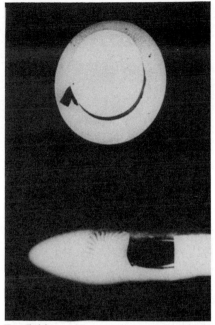

Fig. 5.44

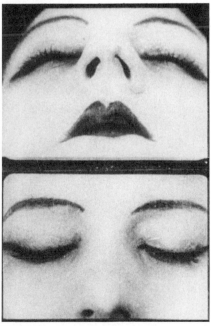

Fig. 5.45

Fig. 5.46

gives us a sense both that the film is continuing to develop and that it is coming full circle.

The final segment makes this return more obvious by showing us the Chaplin figure again. Now its movements are even less "human," and at the end most of its parts seem to fall away, leaving the head alone on the screen. The spinning head may remind us of the woman's profile (Fig. 5.39) seen earlier. But the film is not quite over yet. Its last shot brings back the woman from the swing in Segment 1, now standing in the same garden smelling a flower and looking around. Seen in another context, her gestures might seem ordinary to us (Fig. 5.46). But by now the film has trained us sufficiently for us to make the connection between this shot and what has preceded it. Our expectations have been so strongly geared to seeing rhythmic, mechanical movement that we will probably see her smiles and head gestures as *un*natural, like other motifs we have seen in the film. Léger and Murphy end their abstract film by emphasizing how much they have altered our perception of ordinary objects and people.

ASSOCIATIONAL FORMAL SYSTEMS

■ PRINCIPLES OF ASSOCIATIONAL FORM

Associational formal systems suggest expressive qualities and concepts by grouping images. What the images represent will not necessarily belong to the same category, as in categorical systems. They will not add up to an argument, as in rhetorical systems. And their purely pictorial qualities need not be the basis for the comparison, as in abstract systems. But the very fact that the images and sounds are juxtaposed prods us to look for some connection—an *association* that binds them together.

Godfrey Reggio's *Koyaanisqatsi* is a very clear example of associational form. The film is built out of shots of widely different things—airplanes and buttes, subways and clouds, rockets and pedestrians. At one point, rows of frankfurters are seen pumped out of a machine and fed onto an assembly line. Reggio then cuts to fast-motion shots of commuters riding escalators. The juxtaposition has no narrative connection, and the pictorial qualities are not as stressed as they would be in *Ballet mécanique.* Instead, the shots evoke the idea of impersonal, routine sameness, perhaps suggesting that modern life makes people into standardized units. The filmmaker has created an association among unlike things.

This process is somewhat comparable to the techniques of metaphor and simile used in lyric poetry. When the poet Robert Burns says, "My love is like a red, red rose," we do not leap to the conclusion that his love is prickly to the touch, bright red, or vulnerable to aphids. Rather, we look for the possible conceptual links: Her beauty is the most likely reason for the comparison.

A similar process goes on in associational films. Here the imagery and the metaphorical connections which poetry conveys through language are presented in a more direct fashion. A filmmaker could film a woman he loved in a garden and suggest by visual juxtaposition that she is like the flowers that surround her. (Indeed, this might be an implicit meaning which viewers could assign to *Ballet mécanique*'s last shot, if it were taken out of context.)

The imagery used in associational form may range from the conventional to the strikingly original, and the conceptual connections can be readily apparent or downright mystifying. These possibilities are not necessarily linked: A highly original juxtaposition might have an obvious emotional or conceptual implication. Again, poetry offers examples. Many religious, patriotic, romantic, and laudatory poems use strings of images to create an expressive tone. In "America the Beautiful," the images of "spacious skies," "purple mountains' majesty," and "fruited plain" add up to suggest the patriotic fervor expressed in the chorus, "God shed his grace on thee."

Another poem might be more elusive in its effect, giving us less explicit statements of the associative qualities of its imagery. The Japanese poetic form called the *haiku* usually juxtaposes two images in a brief three-line form, in order to create an immediate emotion in the reader. Here, for example, is a *haiku* by Bashō:

The eleventh moon—
Storks listlessly
Standing in a row

Here the images used are less obviously meaningful and the purpose for connecting them somewhat mysterious. Yet, if we are willing to fill in with our imaginations, as one is supposed to do with *haiku,* the effect should be a mood or emotional tone—one which is not present in either individual image but which results from the juxtaposition of the two.

So far we have looked at associational form working at a fairly "local" level: the side-by-side juxtaposition of images. Associational form also creates larger-scale patterns which can organize an entire film. Yet because associational formal systems are so unlimited in their subjects and means of organization, it is impossible to define a conventional set of parts into which an associational film will fall. In categorical form, the individual categories must be distinct, or the purpose is defeated. If we cannot follow the stages of a rhetorical film's argument, it would be pointless. And an abstract film's variations on a theme present us with visual and sonic qualities that are directly perceivable as such.

Associational form, however, can be much more loose. Many associational films will build their own particular pattern with little attention paid to conventions. Some films will show us a series of amusing images, while others may offer us frightening ones. Still, we can make a start at understanding associational form by noticing that it usually accords with two general principles.

First, the filmmaker typically groups images together in larger sets, each of which creates a distinct, unified part of the film. Each group of images can then contrast with other groups of images. This principle of grouping is also seen in abstract form, as our *Ballet mécanique* analysis shows. Secondly, as in other types of form, the film will use repeated motifs to reinforce associational connections. To see how these two principles work, let us return briefly to *Koyaanisqatsi*.

The film breaks fairly easily into seven longish parts, framed by a prologue and an epilogue. Each part is based upon associational links. For instance, the second segment emphasizes the majesty and beauty of untamed nature by showing rugged cliffs, canyons, clouds, and waterways. The next part, however, introduces a sharp contrast. Now the images show pipes, power lines, factories, and dams sprawling across the land. This section culminates in images of detonating bombs. The film's subsequent segments depict the huge scale and frantic pace of modern urban life. In all cases, each segment's images are grouped primarily by an emotion-laden idea: natural majesty, destructive plundering of the earth, and so on. The associations are emphasized by Philip Glass's musical score, which gives each segment a distinctive melodic and rhythmic identity.

We know that the repetition of motifs is a basic principle of any type of form, but it is particularly important in the associational film. Lacking the clear-cut organization of narrative, categorical, and rhetorical types, associational form relies on our noticing recurrent elements. Like abstract form, associational form requires the audience to remember motifs and to unify the film around them.

For example, *Koyaanisqatsi*'s prologue presents three motifs that will be used throughout the film. We see simplified paintings of human figures on a rock, possibly deriving from a premodern society. As the camera pulls back from the paintings, the image dissolves into flames and smoke as an unidentified blast showers fragments of metal into the air. The following sequence will use rock, stone, and other mineral elements as central images of unspoiled nature. The sequence after that will present fire as the chief force in destroying nature. Later the mineral structures of buttes and valleys will be replaced by skyscrapers and glass-and-steel canyons. Human figures will also recur throughout the film, often filmed in very slow motion so that they seem as frozen as the paintings in the prologue.

At the film's end, the initial blast is repeated, but it is now revealed to be that of a huge rocket taking off from a launch pad. The camera follows it up into the sky, where it explodes. It falls slowly, turning endlessly in midair, a final image of technological destruction and futility. The film ends with the paintings seen in the first shot, perhaps inviting us to reflect on the prospects for human life. In these ways motivic elements play a prominent role in unifying *Koyaanisqatsi*'s associational form.

Koyaanisqatsi illustrates the unique aspects of associational form. The film surely presents a process, but it does not tell a story in the manner of narrative filmmaking. It offers no continuing characters, no specific causal connections, and no temporal order among the scenes. The film has a point, perhaps several, but it does not attempt to persuade us of it through an argument, giving reasons and offering evidence to lead us to a conclusion. There is no voice-over narrator as in *The River* to define problems and marshall evidence. Nor does the film explore a clear-cut set of categories: The concepts of majestic nature and destructive technology are very loose and open-ended. But *Koyaanisqatsi* is not purely a pictorial exercise either, in the manner of abstract form. The connections we make among its images sometimes involve visual qualities, but these qualities are associated with broader concepts and emotions.

As even our brief discussion of *Koyaanisqatsi* indicates, associational form strongly invites interpretation, the assigning of general meanings to the film. Most viewers, for instance, would probably agree that at the very least the film criticizes modern life for its destruction of nature, its inhuman mechanization, and its frantic, thoughtless pace. The film also seems to propose that we heed ancient wisdom and adopt ways of living associated with less "advanced" civilizations. These would seem to be among the film's explicit meanings, yet there is no voice-over narrator to announce them. The film has suggested its meanings chiefly through associations created by the juxtaposition of imagery.

The associational small-scale connections, the distinct large-scale parts, the repeated motifs, and the cues for interpretation—all these factors indicate that associational organization puts demands on the viewer. For this reason, many films which use associational form are experimental, made by independent directors working outside the mainstream industry. When watching such films, we must be prepared to change our expectations frequently and to speculate on possible connections.

Nevertheless, we are not completely lost when reflecting on an associational film. Although it may use striking, original, even puzzling, juxtapositions, it may still elicit a fairly familiar emotion or idea. The explicit point of *Koyaanisqatsi* is not particularly subtle or novel. Here, as in many associational films, the purpose is to make a familiar emotion or concept vivid by means of new imagery and fresh juxtapositions.

Other associational films are more complex and evocative. The filmmaker will not necessarily give us obvious cues to the appropriate expressive qualities or concepts. He or she may simply create a series of unusual and striking combinations and leave it up to us to tease out their relations. Kenneth Anger's *Scorpio Rising*, for instance, explicitly associates motorcycle gangs with traditional religious groups and with Nazi violence, but it also suggests, more elusively, that gang regalia and rituals have homoerotic aspects. Like other sorts of film form, associational form can offer implicit meanings as well as more explicit ones.

■ AN EXAMPLE OF ASSOCIATIONAL FORM: *A MOVIE*

Bruce Conner's film *A Movie* illustrates how associational form can confront us with evocative and mysterious juxtapositions, yet can at the same time create a coherent film and an intense impact on the viewer.

Conner made *A Movie*, his first film, in 1958. Like Léger, he worked in the visual and plastic arts and was noted for his "assemblage" pieces—collages built up of miscellaneous found objects. Conner takes a comparable approach to filmmaking. He typically uses footage from old newsreels, Hollywood movies, soft-core pornography, and the like. As a result, Conner can find two shots from widely different sources that apparently have nothing in common. Yet, if we see the two shots together, we will strive to find some connection between them. From a series of juxtapositions, our activity can create an overall emotion or concept.

A Movie uses a musical accompaniment that helps establish these emotions and ideas. As with the images, Conner chose music that already existed: three portions of Respighi's well-known tone poem *The Pines of Rome.* The music is important to the film's form, since it has distinct sections. Moreover, the overall tone of each segment is different, corresponding to the music.

We can break *A Movie* into four large-scale segments. As in *Koyaanisqatsi,* each segment consists of related images, marked off from other segments by a shared expressive idea and by a distinct musical accompaniment.

1. An introductory portion with the film's title and director's name and projectionists' markings
2. Quick, dynamic music with images of moving animals and vehicles on land
3. A more mysterious, tense section stressing precariously balanced objects in air and water
4. Frightening images of disaster and war interspersed with more lyrical, mysterious scenes

In only 12 minutes, *A Movie* leads us through a range of emotionally charged ideas and qualities. It also creates a distinct developmental thread. In Segments 2, 3, and 4 many shots emphasize accidents or aggressive actions, and while some of these seem funny or trivial at first, they gradually accumulate and become more serious. By Segment 4 a series of war scenes and natural disasters presents practically an apocalyptic vision. *A Movie*'s tone finally eases in its closing underwater scenes.

Segment 1. This segment does far more than give us the title and film-maker's name, and for that reason we have numbered it as the first segment rather than separating it off as a credits sequence. At first we see blank black leader, over which the dynamic, quick opening of *The Pines of Rome* begins. This stresses the importance of the music in the film, since we hear it before seeing any images. Then the words "Bruce Conner" appear, remaining on the screen for many seconds. As we do not need that much time to read the name, we may begin to sense that this film will playfully thwart our expectations.

After the name we see black leader, then white leader, then a quick flicker effect rapidly alternating two frames of the word "A" with blank white leader, and then the word "Movie." The word "By" appears, with more white frames, then "Bruce Conner," as before. Now a black leader appears, with markings that usually appear on the first portion of the film strip, but which are seldom projected on the screen for the audience to see: splice cues, dots, and other signs. Then, suddenly, "End of Part Four," flashes on the screen.

We might think that Conner is simply playing with the graphic qualities of titles and leader marks, as Léger and Murphy had done in Segment 5 of *Ballet mécanique* with their "dance" of intertitles and zeros. But here Conner uses graphics with conventional meanings: Leaders and credits usually signal the beginning, while "End of Part Four" implies we have already seen a considerable part of the film. Once again *A Movie* signals us that it will not be a conventional film—not one where the parts will follow in logical order. We must prepare our expectations for odd juxtapositions.

Moreover, the flicker and leader markings stress the physical qualities of the film medium itself. The title *A Movie* reinforces this reference to the medium, cueing us to watch this assemblage of shots *as* bits of film. This segment also suggests the implicit meaning that this opening is mocking the opening portions of most films.

The opening continues with a countdown leader, beginning with "12" and flashing other numbers at one-second intervals—again, more signals to the projectionist, but seldom seen by the audience. Is *this* the beginning, then? But after "4," we are startled to see the film's first moving image: a "nudie" shot of a woman taking off her stockings. The shot is very worn, with lines and scratches, and we surmise that Conner took it from an old stag film. Here *A Movie* helps us to focus our expectations by suggesting that it will involve more "found footage" of this type. After the nude shot, the countdown leader continues to "1," then the words "The End" appear. Another joke: This is the end of the leader, not of the film. Yet even this is untrue, since more leader appears, with "Movie" backward, more projectionists' signals, and a repeating number "1" that flickers in time to the music's quick tempo, then goes to black.

Segment 2.   Although the music runs continuously over the transition, in Segment 2 we begin to see a very different kind of image. A series of twelve shots shows us mounted Indians on a hill, then chasing a fleeing wagon train, with Hopalong Cassidy recognizable as one of the cowboys. More old film footage follows, this time a clip suggesting a story situation that will continue from shot to shot: a fight between Indians and settlers. But Conner shows us this scene only to refer briefly to the conventional kind of movie he is *not* making. Suddenly, from a shot of galloping horses pulling a wagon (Fig. 5.47), he cuts to similar horses, but now pulling a fire engine on a city street (Fig. 5.48). The association here seems clear enough; we move from horses to more horses, all in rapid motion. The next change, moving toward imagery of cavalry, confirms this association among horse-drawn vehicles.

Fig. 5.47

There follows a shaky shot of a charging elephant. Now we must stretch our associations to account for this: Maybe the link is through a series of rapidly moving animals? This seems safe enough to assume, as we see two more shots of horses' running legs. But the next shot shows a speeding locomotive's wheels. We must generalize the terms of the association still further—the rapid motion of animals and vehicles on land. (The "on land" idea may not seem important at this point, but it will become significant in contrast to the later segments, which often emphasize air and water.) The next series of shots, repeating these motifs and introducing a military tank, seems to confirm this overall idea of rushing movement. The segment so far has been very dynamic, with short shots, fast-moving objects, and a loud musical accompaniment in a quick tempo.

Fig. 5.48

Fig. 5.49

Fig. 5.50

Fig. 5.51

Fig. 5.52

This sense of rapid activity continues into the later part of Segment 2, which moves from the tank to a series of shots of race cars speeding around tracks. Since these shots initially confirm our expectations about moving animals and vehicles, they are less challenging to us—at first. Then one race car crashes, followed by two other similar crashes; and the segment ends with the long, spectacular fall of an old-fashioned car off a cliff. The sense of movement has become less funny and exhilarating, more uncontrolled and frightening in these final shots. During the crashes the music has built up to a frenzied climax, and it cuts off abruptly as a "The End" title flashes on the screen. This parody of the ending of a conventional film suggests that the crashes have resulted from all that rushing motion earlier in the segment.

At this point, we might begin to sense that there was an underlying tone of threatening aggression and danger from the start: the attacking Indians, the cavalry, the charging elephant, the tank, and so on. This element will be intensified in Segments 3 and 4.

Segment 3.   More black leader continues the transition set up by the "The End" title, and there is a pause before the music of Segment 3 begins. (As at the film's opening, it plays at first over the darkness.) But this time the music is slow, bleak, and slightly ominous. The "Movie" title and more black leader move us into a series of shots very different from those of Segment 2. Two Polynesian women carry large totemlike objects on their heads. Leader and a title interrupt once more, introducing a short series of shots of a large dirigible in flight (Fig. 5.49) and of an acrobat couple performing on a small platform and tightrope high above a street (Fig. 5.50). If the women and the dirigible are associated through balancing, the dirigible is linked to the acrobats not only by that but by an emphasis on heights and danger. This portion of the segment ends with a shot of a small plane plunging downward through fleecy clouds, as if, having lost its balance, it is falling. Slow, ominous music has cued us how to react to these floating and falling objects; without the music, we might take them to be lyrical, but in context they suggest a vague threat. This passage ends with more titles: "A," "Movie," "By," and "Bruce Conner," followed by black leader.

The next part of the segment begins with an apparent incongruity between music and image. A series of shots shows parts of a submarine, including an officer looking through a periscope (Fig. 5.51). The next shot seems to suggest that he sees a bikini-clad woman (Fig. 5.52). This shot picks up the stag-film motif from Segment 1 and points out the paradox of this juxtaposition. We know the shots of the officer and the woman come from different films—yet at the same time we cannot help but interpret the shots as showing him "looking" at her, and thus we find the moment comic.

The same principle underlies the next shots, as the officer orders a torpedo fired, and we see it seeming to race toward the woman, creating a sexual pun. This, too, is funny, as is the atomic-bomb orgasm that seems to result. But, as in the first segment, there is an overtone of threat and aggression—now specifically sexual aggression—in these images. They move quickly from humor to disaster as additional mushroom-cloud shots undercut the joke. Moreover, the music that plays through the submarine-woman series is slow, quiet, and ethereal—*not* appropriate to the silly punning scene, but more suited to the images of the bomb blasts.

This music carries us into a series of shots of waves and wavelike movements that seem to result from the bomb: a ship engulfed by fog or smoke, surfers and rowing teams battered by heavy waves, water skiers and motorboaters falling during stunts. During this, the music's ethereal quality gives way to a slow melody with a dynamic tempo, played on low stringed instruments; this creates a more ominous tone. The first accidents seem trivial, as when water skiers fall over. But gradually things become more disturbing. A motorboat driver plows into a pile of debris and is hurled out.

Fig. 5.53

Abruptly, people are seen riding odd bicycles (Fig. 5.53). The move from the boat to the bikes takes us briefly away from the "accident" series to a string of shots showing people deliberately doing things that look grotesque. Additional shots show motorcyclists riding through mud and water and a plane trying to land on a lake and flipping over.

The whole segment has developed steadily, introducing tension at the beginning and then juxtaposing the humorous (the submarine-woman scene) with the disastrous (the bomb), and trivial accidents with grotesque actions. The sequence ends in an odd way. Black leader appears after the plane crash, with the music building up toward a climax. This is followed by a close view of Theodore Roosevelt speaking vigorously, seemingly angry, with bared teeth (Fig. 5.54). Immediately, there follows a shot of a collapsing suspension bridge, with the music swelling up as the pieces fall (Fig. 5.55) and then fading down. Although these shots are difficult to interpret, the association of human-caused disasters with one of America's most belligerent presidents would seem to link even the toppling bridge to human, especially political, aggression.

Fig. 5.54

Segment 4.   Once more *A Movie* marks off its segments clearly, with black leader again accompanying the opening of the third portion of *The Pines of Rome*. An eerie gong and low, slow chords create a distinctly ominous mood. Segments 2 and 3 had both built up toward accidents and disasters. Now Segment 4 begins with a series of images of military planes being shot out of the sky and firing on the ground, followed by a series of explosions against a dark sky.

Fig. 5.55

Yet the next passage juxtaposes shots of disasters with some shots that are inexplicable in this context. All the images of planes and explosions seem associated with war and disaster. Now we see two planes flying past an Egyptian pyramid (Fig. 5.56). As with so many of the earlier juxtapositions, we must abruptly switch our assumptions about how these shots relate to one another, since now we see *nonmilitary* planes. But immediately two shots of an erupting volcano appear. Clearly, the connection between them and the previous shot is mainly created by the pictorial similarity of mountains and pyramids. Are we back to disasters again? Seemingly not, for we next see an elaborate church ceremony of a coronation, and all our expectations are thwarted. But the disaster motif returns as strongly as ever: the burning dirigible *Hindenburg*, tanks, more race car crashes, and tumbling bodies.

All these images create tension, but the next shots we see are of people

Fig. 5.56

Fig. 5.57

Fig. 5.58

Fig. 5.59

Fig. 5.60

parachuting from a plane. Interestingly, this action is not threatening, and the people here are not hurt. Yet in the context of the earlier accidents and because of the ominous music, we have begun to expect some sort of disaster as the most likely subject of each shot. Now even these innocent actions seem threatening and again may be seen as linked to military and political aggression.

The next series of shots is equally innocent in itself but takes on mysterious and ominous overtones as part of the overall segment. We see a burning balloon floating to earth, reminding us of the floating dirigible and *Hindenburg* footage. Shots of palm trees, cattle, and other glimpses follow, suggesting some idyllic Middle Eastern or African setting (Fig. 5.57). This brief respite, however, leads into one of the film's eeriest and most striking moments, three shots of a suspension bridge writhing and buckling as if shaken by a giant hand (Fig. 5.58). This is followed by the most intense disaster images in the whole film, including the burning *Hindenburg*, a sinking ship (Fig. 5.59), a firing-squad execution, bodies hanging on a scaffold, dead soldiers, and a mushroom cloud. A shot of a dead elephant and hunters introduces a brief series of shots of suffering Africans. The music has built up during this, becoming steadily less ominous and more triumphant with fanfares of brass instruments.

After the climactic series of disaster shots, the tone shifts one more time. A relatively lengthy series of underwater shots follows a scuba diver. He explores a sunken wreck encrusted with barnacles (Fig. 5.60). It recalls the disasters just witnessed, especially the sinking ship (Fig. 5.59). The music builds to a triumphant climax as the diver swims into the ship's interior. The film ends on a long-held musical chord over more black leader and a final shot looking up toward the surface of the sea. Ironically, there is no "The End" title at this point.

A Movie has taken us through its disparate footage almost entirely by means of associations. There is no argument about why we should find these images disturbing or why we should link volcanos and earthquakes to sexual or military aggression. There are no categorical similarities between many of the things juxtaposed and no story told about them. Occasionally, as we shall see in Chapter 10, Conner does use abstract qualities to compare objects, but this is only a small-scale strategy, not one that organizes the whole film.

In building its associations, *A Movie* uses the familiar formal principles of repetition and variation. Even though the images come from different films, certain elements are repeated, as with the series of horse shots in Segment 1 or the different airplanes. These repetitions form motifs that help unify the whole film.

Moreover, there is a distinct pattern to the return of those motifs. We have seen how the titles and leader of the opening come back in some way in all the segments, and how the "nudie" shot of Segment 1 is similar to the one used with the submarine footage in Segment 3. Interestingly, not a single motif that appears in Segment 2 returns in Segment 3, creating a strong contrast between the two. But then Segment 4 picks up and varies many of the motifs of both 2 and 3. As in so many films, the ending thus seems a development of and return to earlier portions. The dead elephant, the tanks, and the race cars all hark back to Segment 2, while the natives, the *Hindenburg* disaster, the planes, the ships, and the bridge collapse all continue motifs begun in 3. The juxtapositions that have obvious links play on repetition, while startling and obscure ones create contrast. Thus Conner has created a unified work from what would seem to be a disunified mass of footage.

The pattern of development is also strikingly unified. Segment 1 is primarily amusing, and a sense of play and exhilaration also carries through most of Segment 2, up to the car crashes. But we have seen that the subjects of all the shots in Segment 2 could also suggest aggression and violence, and they all relate in some way to the disasters to come. Segment 3 makes this more explicit, but uses some humor and playfulness as well. By Segment 4, the mixture of tones has largely disappeared, and an intensifying sense of tension and doom replaces it. Now even odd or neutral events seem ominous.

Unlike the more clear-cut *Koyaanisqatsi*, *A Movie* withholds explicit meanings. Still, *A Movie*'s constantly shifting associations invite us to reflect on a range of implicit meanings. From one standpoint, the film can be interpreted as presenting the devastating consequences of unbridled aggressive energy. The horrors of the modern world—warfare and the hydrogen bomb—are linked with more trivial pastimes, like sports and risky stunts. We are asked to reflect on whether both may spring from the same impulse, perhaps a kind of death wish. This impulse may in turn be tied to sexual drives (the pornographic motif) and political repression (the recurring images of people of developing countries).

Another interpretation might see the film as commenting on how cinema stirs our emotions through sex, violence, and exotic spectacle. In this sense, *A Movie* is "a movie" like any other, with the important difference that its thrills and disasters are actual parts of our world.

What of the ending? The scuba diver epilogue also offers a wide range of implicit meanings. It returns to the beginning in a formal sense: Along with the Hopalong Cassidy segment, it is the longest continuous action we get. It might offer a kind of hope, perhaps an escape from the world's horrors. Or the images may suggest humankind's final death. After despoiling the planet, the human can only return to the primeval sea. Like much of *A Movie*, the ending is ambiguous, saying little but suggesting much. Certainly we can say that it serves to relax the tension aroused by the mounting disasters. In this respect, it demonstrates the power of an associational formal system: Its ability to guide our emotions and to arouse our thinking simply by juxtaposing different images and sounds.

SUMMARY

As we have seen in looking at some of our individual examples, films may mix types of form. *Olympia* uses categorical form but creates short narratives within a few of its segments. *The River* has some sections that employ associations between music and imagery to cue the spectator to adopt a certain attitude. *A Movie* exploits some abstract links between objects in different shots.

Usually, however, one type of form dominates, providing the overall organization. In trying to identify a film's basic organizational principle, it is often helpful to look at the beginning and ending. This is because films tend to put their strongest cues at these points. In addition, the development that has occurred between the beginning and end will usually help to define the large-scale formal relations within the work.

In looking at different types of films, you can ask questions like these:

1. What sort of response does the film seem to call forth? Is it trying to inform its audience about categories of things? to make a convincing argument? to elicit the contemplation of pictorial properties? to evoke an emotion or concept?

2. If the form is categorical, what is the overall subject, and how is it introduced? What are the categories, and how does the film progress from the first to the last?

3. If the form is rhetorical, what is the argument being made? What pieces of evidence are given, and how convincing are they? How does the film make itself seem authoritative and reliable? How do the parts move toward the conclusion that the viewer is to arrive at?

4. If the form is abstract, what are the main visual motifs set forth and varied? What is the pattern of their recurrence?

5. If the form is associational, how are different parts marked out according to emotional or conceptual qualities? What are the shifts in emotions or concepts through the course of the film? What types of imagery cue us to respond in a certain way?

In this portion of the book, we have tried to show how narrative and nonnarrative patterns work within the total film. Understanding both kinds of form becomes important as we move into a consideration of film techniques. As we shall see, cinematic techniques work with narrative or nonnarrative structure to create the overall formal system of a film. The analytical tools presented here in Part II, in combination with an ability to analyze the function of the techniques to be defined in Part III, should help us understand whole films. At the end of our survey of film techniques, we shall return to the films considered in the last two chapters and analyze how they use resources of the film medium.

NOTES AND QUERIES

■ TYPES OF FORM

Of all the types of formal organization, categorical structure has received the least discussion. It is very pervasive, forming the basis of many instructional and promotional films, and it deserves further analysis.

Rhetorical form can be seen as a variant of verbal argument, and we can understand it through such studies of rhetoric as Stephen Toulmin's *The Uses of Argument* (Cambridge: Cambridge University Press, 1958). Many films may have a "layout of arguments" similar to Toulmin's. For a concrete analysis of one film's rhetorical form, see Steve Neale, "Propaganda," *Screen* **18,** 3 (Autumn 1977): 9–40. Categorical and rhetorical form seem to be subsumed under "expository form" in Bill Nichols's discussion of documentary films in chaps. 6–8 of *Ideology and the Image* (Bloomington: Indiana University Press, 1981).

Associational form may be studied by comparison to such poetic genres as the lyric; see Northrop Frye, "The Rhythm of Association: Lyric," in his *Anatomy of Criticism* (Princeton: Princeton University Press, 1957), and Paul Goodman, "Lyrical Poems: Speech, Feeling, Motion of Thought," in his *Structure of Literature* (Chicago: University of Chicago Press, 1954). A good example of a critic's discussion of associational form is Ken Kelman, "The Anti-Information Film (Conner's *Report*)," in P. Adams Sitney, ed., *The Essential Cinema: Essays on the Films in the Collection of Anthology Film Archives* (New York: New York University Press, 1975), pp. 240–244.

Abstract form is often best examined in the light of principles of musical form or abstract visual design. For the former, see Parts 3 and 4 of William S. Newman's *Understanding Music* (New York: Harper, 1967). For the latter, see E. H. Gombrich, *The Sense of Order: A Study in the Psychology of Decorative Art* (Ithaca: Cornell University Press, 1979), and Rudolph Arnheim, *Art and Visual Perception,* 2d ed. (Berkeley: University of California Press, 1974). Noël Carroll considers qualities of abstract form in "Causation, the Ampliation of Movement and Avant-Garde Film," *Millennium Film Journal* **10/11** (Fall/Winter 1981/82): 61–82. Malcolm Le Grice, *Abstract Film and Beyond* (Cambridge, Mass.: MIT Press, 1977), surveys the history of abstract film.

Both associational and abstract form are commonly found in experimental and avant-garde filmmaking. Several of the books we referred to in the Notes and Queries for Chapter 2 (pp. 60–62) discuss these types of organization; see in particular Sitney's *Visionary Film* and Peterson's *Dreams of Chaos, Visions of Order.* Another valuable work is P. Adams Sitney, ed., *The Avant-Garde Film: A Reader of Theory and Criticism* (New York: New York University Press, 1978), in which you will find this suggestion by Peter Kubelka: Cinema is not essentially movement but rather "the quick projection of light impulses" (p. 140). It would be hard to come closer to a purely abstract aesthetic.

PART III

FILM STYLE

We are still seeking to understand the principles by which a film is put together. Chapter 3 showed that the concept of film form offers a way to do this. Chapters 4 and 5 went on to look at two sorts of formal systems operating in films—narrative and nonnarrative.

When we see a film, though, we do not engage with only a narrative or a nonnarrative pattern. We experience a *film*—not a painting or a novel. Analyzing a painting demands a knowledge of color, shape, and composition; analyzing a novel demands knowledge of language. To understand form in any art, we must be familiar with the medium which that art utilizes. Consequently, our understanding of a film must also include features of the *film medium*. Part III of this book investigates just this area. We shall look at four sets of cinematic techniques: two techniques of the shot, mise-en-scene and cinematography; the technique that relates shot to shot, editing; and the relation of sound to film images.

Each chapter will introduce a single technique, surveying the choices it offers to the filmmaker. We will suggest how you can recognize the technique and its uses. Most importantly, we shall concentrate on the formal functions of each technique. We will try to answer such questions as these: How may a technique guide expectations or furnish motifs for the film? How may it develop across a film? How may it direct our attention, clarify or emphasize meanings, shape our emotional response?

In Part III, we will also discover that in any film, certain techniques tend to create a formal system of their own. Every film develops specific techniques in patterned ways. This unified, developed, and significant use of particular technical choices we shall call *style*. In our study of certain films, we shall see how each filmmaker creates a distinctive stylistic system. We can visualize the result in a diagram:

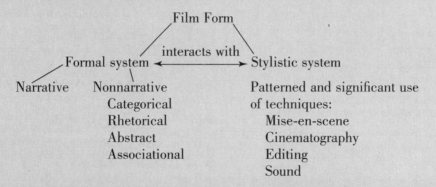

The use a film makes of the medium—the film's style—cannot be studied apart from the film's use of narrative or nonnarrative form. We shall find that film style interacts with the formal system. Often film techniques support and enhance nonnarrative or narrative form. In a narrative film, style can function to advance the cause-effect chain, create parallels, manipulate story-plot relations, or sustain the narration's flow of information. But also, film style may become separate from narrative or nonnarrative form, attracting our attention in its own right. Some uses of film technique can call attention to patterns of style. In either event, the chapters that follow will continually return to the problem of relations between narrative and nonnarrative formal systems and the stylistic system.

THE SHOT: MISE-EN-SCENE

Of all the techniques of cinema, mise-en-scene is the one with which we are most familiar. After seeing a film, we may not recall the cutting or the camera movements, the dissolves or offscreen sound. But we do remember the costumes in *Gone with the Wind* or the bleak, chilly lighting in Charles Foster Kane's Xanadu. We retain vivid memories of the rainy, gloomy streets in *The Big Sleep* or the cozy family home in *Meet Me in St. Louis*. We recall Harpo Marx clambering over Edgar Kennedy's peanut wagon *(Duck Soup)* and Katharine Hepburn defiantly splintering Cary Grant's golf clubs *(The Philadelphia Story)*. In short, many of our most sharply etched memories of the cinema turn out to center on mise-en-scene.

WHAT IS MISE-EN-SCENE?

In the original French, *mise-en-scene* (pronounced "meez-ahn-sen") means "staging an action," and it was first applied to the practice of directing plays. Film scholars, extending the term to film direction, use the term to signify the director's control over what appears in the film frame. As you would expect from the term's theatrical origins, mise-en-scene includes those aspects of film that overlap with the art of the theater: setting, lighting, costume, and the behavior of the figures. In controlling the mise-en-scene, the director *stages the event* for the camera.

As we've seen in Chapter 2, staging an event to be filmed is characteristic of fictional films, so our examples will be drawn largely from films of this type. Staging also appears to some extent in documentary, with vivid examples including *The Thin Blue Line* (Color Plate 1). Animated and abstract films may control mise-en-scene to a degree impossible with live performers shot in real time—as is seen not only in drawn or puppet animation but also in computer graphics.

Mise-en-scene usually involves some planning, but the filmmaker may be open to unplanned events as well. An actor may add a line on the set, or an unexpected change in lighting may enhance a dramatic effect. While filming a cavalry procession through Monument Valley for *She Wore a Yellow Ribbon*, John Ford took advantage of an approaching lightning storm to create a dramatic backdrop for the action. The storm remains part of the film's mise-en-scene even though Ford neither planned it nor controlled it; it was a lucky accident that he decided to incorporate into his story. Jean Renoir, Robert Altman, and other directors have allowed their actors to improvise their performances, making the films' mise-en-scene more spontaneous and unpredictable.

REALISM

Before we analyze mise-en-scene in detail, one preconception must be brought to light. Just as viewers often remember this or that bit of mise-en-scene from a film, so viewers often judge mise-en-scene by standards of realism. A car may seem to be realistic for the period the film depicts, or a gesture may not seem realistic because "real people don't act that way."

Realism as a standard of value, however, raises several problems. Notions of realism vary across cultures, through time, and even among individuals. Marlon Brando's acclaimed "realist" performance in the 1954 film *On the Waterfront* looks stylized today. American critics of the 1910s praised William S. Hart's Westerns for being realistic, but equally enthusiastic French critics of the 1920s considered the same films to be as artificial as a medieval epic. Moreover, realism has become one of the most problematic issues in the philosophy of art. (See Notes and Queries for examples.) Most important, to insist rigidly on realism for all films can blind us to the vast range of mise-en-scene possibilities.

Look, for instance, at the frame from *The Cabinet of Dr. Caligari* (Fig. 6.1). The jagged rooftops and slanted chimneys certainly do not accord with our conception of normal reality. Yet to condemn the film for lacking realism would be inappropriate, because the film uses stylization to present a madman's fantasy. *The Cabinet of Dr. Caligari* borrows conventions of Expressionist painting and theater and then assigns them the function of suggesting the madman's delusion.

It is better, then, to examine the *functions* of mise-en-scene than to dismiss this or that element that happens not to match our conception of realism. The filmmaker may use *any* system of mise-en-scene, and we should

Fig. 6.1

analyze its function in the total film—how mise-en-scene is motivated, how it varies or develops, how it works in relation to narrative and nonnarrative forms.

THE POWER OF MISE-EN-SCENE

To confine the cinema to some notion of realism would indeed impoverish mise-en-scene. This technique has the power to transcend normal conceptions of reality, as we can see from a glance at the cinema's first master of the technique, Georges Méliès. Méliès's mise-en-scene enabled him to create a totally imaginary world on film.

A caricaturist and magician, Méliès became fascinated by the Lumière brothers' demonstration of their short films in 1895. (For more on the Lumières, see pp. 226–227 and 443–444.) After building a camera based on an English projector, Méliès began filming unstaged street scenes and moments of passing daily life. One day, the story goes, he was filming at the Place de l'Opéra and his camera jammed as a bus was passing. After some tinkering, he was able to resume filming, but by this time the bus had gone and a hearse was passing in front of his lens. When Méliès screened the film, he discovered something unexpected: a moving bus seemed to transform itself instantly into a hearse. The anecdote may be apocryphal, but it at least illustrates Méliès's recognition of the magical powers of mise-en-scene. He would devote most of his efforts to cinematic conjuring.

But to do so would require preparation, since Méliès could not count on lucky accidents like the bus-hearse transformation. He would have to plan and stage action for the camera. Drawing on his experience in theater, Méliès built one of the first film studios—a small, crammed affair bristling with theatrical machinery, balconies, trapdoors, and sliding backdrops. He sketched shots beforehand and designed sets and costumes. Figures 6.2 and 6.3 illustrate the correspondence between his detailed drawings and the finished shots. As if this were not enough, Méliès starred in his own films (often in several roles per film). His desire to create magical effects led Méliès to control every aspect of his films' mise-en-scene.

Fig. 6.2

Fig. 6.3

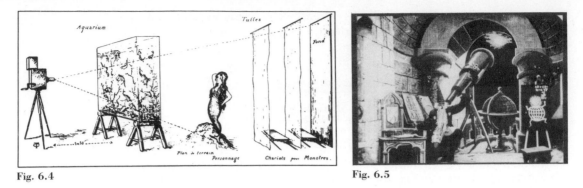

Fig. 6.4   Fig. 6.5

Such control was necessary to create the fantasy world he envisioned. Only in a studio could Méliès produce *The Mermaid,* in which an undersea world is created out of an actress in costume, a fish tank placed in front of the camera, some sets, and "carts for monsters" (see Fig. 6.4). He could also surround himself (playing an astronomer) with a gigantic array of cartoonish cut-outs like the telescope, globe, and blackboard in *La Lune à un mètre* (Fig. 6.5).

Méliès's "Star-Film" studio made hundreds of short fantasy and trick films based on such a control over every element in the frame, and the first master of mise-en-scene demonstrated the great range of technical possibilities it offers. The legacy of Méliès's magic is a delightfully unreal world wholly obedient to the whims of the imagination.

ASPECTS OF MISE-EN-SCENE

What possibilities for selection and control does mise-en-scene offer the filmmaker? We can mark out four general areas and indicate some potential uses of each.

■ SETTING

Since the earliest days of cinema, critics and audiences have understood that setting plays a more active role in cinema than in most theatrical styles. André Bazin writes:

> The human being is all-important in the theatre. The drama on the screen can exist without actors. A banging door, a leaf in the wind, waves beating on the shore can heighten the dramatic effect. Some film masterpieces use man only as an accessory, like an extra, or in counterpoint to nature, which is the true leading character.

Cinema setting, then, can come to the forefront; it need not be only a container for human events but can dynamically enter the narrative action. (See Color Plates 33, 42, 62, and 63 for examples of settings without characters.)

The filmmaker may control setting in many ways. One way is to select an already existing locale in which to stage the action, a practice stretching back to the earliest films. Louis Lumière shot his short comedy *L'Arroseur arrosé* ("The Waterer Watered," Fig. 6.6) in a garden, and Victor Sjöström filmed *The Outlaw and His Wife* in the splendor of the Swedish countryside (Fig. 6.7). At the close of World War II, Roberto Rossellini shot *Germany Year Zero* in the rubble of Berlin (Fig. 6.8). Today filmmakers often go "on location" to shoot.

On the other hand, the filmmaker may choose to construct the setting. Méliès understood the increased control yielded by shooting in a studio, and many filmmakers followed his lead. In France, Germany, and especially the United States, the possibility of creating a wholly artificial world on film led to the development of several approaches to constructing setting. Some directors have emphasized historical authenticity. For example, Erich von Stroheim prided himself on meticulous research into details of locale, as the shot from *Greed* (1924) illustrates (Fig. 6.9). *All the President's Men* (1976) took a similar tack, seeking to duplicate the *Washington Post* office on a sound stage by reproducing every detail of the original newsroom (Fig. 6.10). Even waste paper from the actual office was scattered around the set. We should remember, however, that realism in settings is partly a matter of viewing conventions. What strikes us as realistic today might seem highly stylized to future audiences.

Fig. 6.6

Fig. 6.7

Fig. 6.8

Fig. 6.9

Fig. 6.10

Fig. 6.11

Fig. 6.12

Fig. 6.13

Fig. 6.14

Other films have been less committed to historical verisimilitude. Though D. W. Griffith studied the various historical periods presented in *Intolerance,* his Babylon—part Assyrian, part Egyptian, part American—constitutes a personal image of that city (Fig. 6.11). Similarly, in *Ivan the Terrible* Sergei Eisenstein freely stylized the decor of the czar's palace to harmonize with the lighting, costume, and figure movement, so that characters crawl through doorways that resemble mouseholes and stand frozen before allegorical murals.

Setting can overwhelm the actors, as in the confetti-festooned shot from Josef von Sternberg's *Underworld* (Fig. 6.12), or it can be reduced to zero, as in Godard's *Le Gai savoir* (Fig. 6.13) and Dreyer's *La Passion de Jeanne d'Arc* (Fig. 6.14). Settings need not possess realistic-looking buildings, as witness the contorted streets and convulsively twisted architecture of *The Cabinet of Dr. Caligari* (a film heavily influenced by German Expressionist art).

The overall design of a setting can significantly shape how we understand story action. In Louis Feuillade's silent crime serial *The Vampires,* a criminal gang has killed a courier on his way to a bank. The gang's confederate, Irma Vep, is also a bank employee, and just as she tells her superior that the courier has vanished, an imposter, in beard and bowler hat, strolls in behind them (Fig. 6.15). They turn away from us in surprise as he comes forward (Fig. 6.16). Working in a period when cutting to closer shots was rare in a French film, Feuillade draws our attention to the man by putting him in the center of the shot. The office set enhances his importance by framing him neatly in the doorway.

So far our examples have been taken from black-and-white films, but color can also be an important component of settings. Robert Bresson's *L'Argent* creates parallels among its various settings—home, school, and prison—by the recurrence of drab green backgrounds and cold blue props and costumes (Color Plates 6–8). By contrast, Jacques Tati's *Play Time* displays sharply changing color schemes. In the first portion of *Play Time,*

Fig. 6.15

Fig. 6.16

Fig. 6.17

the settings and costumes are mostly gray, brown, and black—cold, steely colors. Later in the film, however, beginning in the restaurant scene, the settings start to sport cheery reds, pinks, and greens. This change in the settings' colors supports a narrative development which shows an inhuman city landscape that is transformed by vitality and spontaneity.

A full-size setting need not always be built. To save money or to create fantasy effects, the filmmakers may build miniature settings, and these too have the range of possibilities we have discussed for normal sets. (See Fig. 1.18 for an example of a miniature set.) Parts of settings may also be done as paintings which are then photographed to combine with full-size objects. Since this process involves cinematography, we look at it in the next chapter.

In manipulating a shot's setting, the filmmaker may create *props*— another term borrowed from theatrical mise-en-scene. When an object in the setting is motivated to operate actively within the ongoing action, we can call it a "prop." Films teem with examples: the snowstorm paperweight that shatters at the beginning of *Citizen Kane*, the little girl's balloon in *M*, the cactus rose in *The Man Who Shot Liberty Valance*, Cesare's coffin in *The Cabinet of Dr. Caligari*. Luis Buñuel's films teem with the surrealistic use of props, as when a blind man uses a dove to cure a woman's illness (Fig. 6.17, from *Los Olvidados*).

Fig. 6.18

In the course of a narrative, a prop may become a motif. The shower curtain in *Psycho* is at first an innocuous part of the setting, but when the killer enters the bathroom the curtain screens her (?) from our sight. Later, after the murder, Norman Bates uses the curtain to wrap up the victim's body. In *The Crime of M. Lange* a poster outside Batala's publishing house advertises its new dime-novel series "Javert" (Fig. 6.18), but after the tyrannical Batala has left the company, Lange and his associates pull the poster down to reveal the window and room that have for so long been blocked from sunlight (Figs. 6.19, 6.20).

When the filmmaker uses color to create parallels among elements of setting, a color motif may become associated with several props. Souleymane Cissé's *Finye (The Wind)* begins with a woman carrying an orange calabash as the wind rustles through weeds (Color Plate 9). Later, in a fantasy sequence, a boy carries water in an orange-brown bowl to the main male and female characters. Still later, the vengeful grandfather prepares to stalk his

Fig. 6.19

Fig. 6.20

Fig. 6.21

Fig. 6.22

Fig. 6.23

grandson's persecutor by dressing in orange and making magic before a fire (Color Plate 10). At the film's end, the little boy passes his bowl to someone offscreen—possibly the couple seen earlier (Color Plate 11). The recurrent color creates a cluster of nature motifs around the drama. Later in this chapter we shall examine in more detail how elements of setting can weave through a film to form motifs within the narrative.

■ COSTUME AND MAKE-UP

Like setting, costume can have specific functions in the total film, and the range of possibilities is huge. Erich von Stroheim, for instance, was as passionately committed to authenticity of dress as of setting, and he was said to have created underwear that would instill the proper mood in his actors even though it was never to be seen in the film. In Griffith's *Musketeers of Pig Alley* Lillian Gish appears in a faded and threadbare dress, which summarizes the poverty in which her character lives.

On the other hand, costumes may be quite stylized, calling attention to their purely graphic qualities. In *The Cabinet of Dr. Caligari* the somnambulist Cesare wears a jet-black leotard, whereas the woman he abducts wears a white nightgown. Throughout *Ivan the Terrible* costumes are carefully orchestrated with one another in their colors, their textures, and even their movements. One shot of Ivan and his adversary gives their robes a plastic sweep and dynamism (Fig. 6.21). In *Freak Orlando*, Ulrike Ottinger (herself a costume designer) boldly uses costumes to display the spectrum's primary colors in maximum intensity (Color Plate 12).

Like settings, costume may furnish props for the film's ongoing narrative system. The film director Guido in Fellini's *8¹/₂* persistently uses his sunglasses to shield himself from the world. To think of Dracula is to think of how his billowing cape enwraps him, unfolds, and closes decisively around a victim. In cinema any portion of a costume may become a prop: a pair of spectacles *(Potemkin)*, shoes *(Strangers on a Train, The Wizard of Oz)*, a cross pendant *(Ivan the Terrible)*, a jacket *(Le Million)*. When Hildy Johnson, in *His Girl Friday*, switches from her role of aspiring housewife to that of reporter, her stylish hat with its low-dipping brim is replaced by a "masculine" hat with its brim pushed up, journalist-style (Figs. 6.22, 6.23). In Roberto Rossellini's *Rise to Power of Louis XIV* the King wants to keep his nobles indebted to him, so he creates outlandish, expensive fashions in dress (Color Plate 13).

Film genres make extensive use of costume props—the frontier six-gun, the gangster's automatic pistol, the dancer's top hat and cane. Every major film comedian has turned a specific costume into a panoply of props: Chaplin's cane and derby, Fields's cigar and top hat, Laurel and Hardy's derbies and too-tight suits, Harpo Marx's capacious pockets.

As we have already seen in *L'Argent* and *Play Time* (p. 174), costume is often coordinated with setting. Since the filmmaker usually wants to emphasize the human figures, setting may provide a more or less neutral background, while costume helps pick out the characters. Color design is particularly important here. The *Freak Orlando* costumes (Color Plate 12) stand out boldly against the neutral gray background of an artificial lake. In the climactic skirmish of *The Night of the Shooting Stars*, luminous wheat fields set off the hard black-and-blue costumes of the fascists and the peasants (Color Plate 14). The director may instead choose to match the color values of setting and costume more closely. One shot in Fellini's *Casanova* (Color Plate 15) creates a color gradation that runs from bright red costumes to paler red walls, the whole composition set off by a small white accent in the distance. This "bleeding" of the costume into the setting is carried to a kind of limit in the prison scene of *THX 1138*, in which George Lucas strips both locale and clothing to stark white on white (Color Plate 16).

Ken Russell's *Women in Love* affords a clear example of how costume and setting can coordinate and contribute to a film's overall narrative progression. The opening scenes portray the characters' shallow middle-class life by means of highly saturated primary and complementary colors in costume and setting (Color Plate 17). In the middle portions of the film, as the characters discover love on a country estate, pale pastels predominate (Color Plate 18). The last section of *Women in Love* takes place around the Matterhorn, and the characters' ardor has cooled. Now the colors have become even paler, dominated by pure black and white (Color Plate 19). By integrating itself with setting, costume may function to reinforce the film's narrative and thematic patterns.

All these points about costume apply equally to a closely related area of mise-en-scene, the actors' make-up. Make-up was originally necessary because actors' faces would not register well on early film stocks. And, up to the present, it has been used in various ways to enhance the appearance of actors on the screen. Over the course of film history, a wide range of possibilities has emerged. Dreyer's *La Passion de Jeanne d'Arc* was famous for its complete avoidance of make-up (Fig. 6.14). This film relied on close-ups and tiny facial changes to create an intense religious drama. On the other hand, Nikolai Cherkasov did not look particularly like Eisenstein's conception of Czar Ivan IV, so he wore a wig and false beard, nose, and eyebrows for *Ivan the Terrible*. Changing actors to look like historical personages has been one common function of make-up.

Make-up can aim at complete realism. When Laurence Olivier blackened his skin and hair to make a film of *Othello*, he strove to be as convincing a Moor as possible. Women often wear make-up that looks like the ordinary street cosmetics currently in fashion, and most men's make-up is designed to look as if they were not wearing any. Yet it is equally possible to use make-up in nonrealistic ways. Bizarre make-up plays a major role in the conventions of the horror genre. In *The Cabinet of Dr. Caligari* (Fig. 6.24), the actors' faces are heavily painted with unshaded areas of light and dark colors, and this fits in with a similar treatment of the other aspects of mise-en-scene in that film.

In recent years the craft of make-up has developed in response to the popularity of horror and science-fiction genres. Rubber and plasticene compounds create bumps, bulges, extra organs, and layers of artificial skin in

Fig. 6.24

Fig. 6.25

Fig. 6.26

Fig. 6.27

Fig. 6.28

such films as David Cronenberg's *The Fly* (Fig. 6.25) and Tim Burton's *Edward Scissorhands*. In such contexts, make-up, like costume, becomes important in creating character traits or motivating plot action.

■ LIGHTING

Much of the impact of an image comes from its manipulation of lighting. In cinema, lighting is more than just illumination that permits us to see the action. Lighter and darker areas within the frame help create the overall composition of each shot and thus guide our attention to certain objects and actions. A brightly illuminated patch may draw our eye to a key gesture, while a shadow may conceal a detail or build up suspense about what may be present. Lighting can also articulate textures: the soft curve of a face, the rough grain of a piece of wood, the delicate tracery of a spider's web, the sheen of glass, the sparkle of a faceted gem.

Lighting shapes objects by creating highlights and shadows. A highlight is a patch of relative brightness on a surface. The man's face in Figure 6.26 (from Cecil B. De Mille's *The Cheat*) and the edge of the fingers in Figure 6.27 (from Robert Bresson's *Pickpocket*) display highlights. Highlights provide important cues to the texture of the surface. If the surface is smooth, like glass or chrome, the highlights tend to gleam or sparkle; a rougher surface, like a coarse stone facing, yields more diffuse highlights.

There are two basic types of shadows, each of which is important in film composition: *attached* shadows, or *shading*, and *cast* shadows. An attached shadow occurs when light fails to illuminate part of an object because of the object's shape or surface features. If a person faces a candle in a darkened room, patches of the face and body will fall into darkness. This phenomenon is shading, or attached shadow. But the candle also projects a shadow on the wall behind. This is a cast shadow, because the body blocks out the light. The shadows in Figure 6.26, for example, are cast shadows, made by bars between the actor and the light source. But, in Figure 6.27 the small dark patches on the hand are attached shadows, for they are caused by the three-dimensional curves and ridges of the hand itself.

As these examples suggest, highlights and shadows help create our sense of a scene's space. In Figure 6.26, a few shadows imply an entire prison cell. Animated films can utilize the same cues to one degree or another. In Color Plate 20, from *Who Framed Roger Rabbit?*, human and cartoon figures display both cast shadows and attached shadows, or shading.

Lighting also shapes a shot's overall composition. One shot from John Huston's *Asphalt Jungle* welds the gang members into a unit by the pool of light cast by a hanging lamp (Fig. 6.28). At the same time, it sets up a scale of importance, emphasizing the protagonist by making him the most frontal and clearly lit figure.

Lighting also affects our sense of the shape and texture of the objects depicted. If a ball is lit straight from the front, it will appear round. If the same ball is lit from the side, we will see it as a half-circle. Hollis Frampton's short film *Lemon* consists primarily of light moving around a lemon, and the shifting shadows create dramatically changing patterns of yellow and black. This film almost seems designed to prove the truth of a remark made by Josef

Plate 1   *The Thin Blue Line*

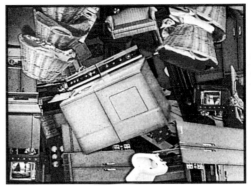

Plate 2   *Frank Film*

Plate 3   *Lapis*

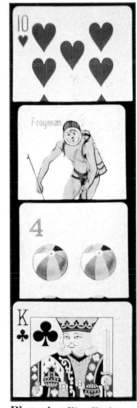

Plate 5   *The Good, the Bad, and the Ugly*

Plate 4   *Fist Fight*

Plate 6   *L'Argent*

Plate 7   *L'Argent*

Plate 8   *L'Argent*

Plate 9   *Finye (The Wind)*

Plate 10   *Finye (The Wind)*

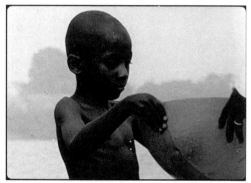

Plate 11   *Finye (The Wind)*

Plate 12   *Freak Orlando*

Plate 13   *The Rise to Power of Louis XIV*

Plate 14   *The Night of the Shooting Stars*

Plate 15   *Casanova*

Plate 16 *THX 1138*

Plate 17 *Women in Love*

Plate 18 *Women in Love*

Plate 19 *Women in Love*

Plate 20 *Who Framed Roger Rabbit?*

Plate 21 *La Chinoise*

Plate 22 *La Chinoise*

Plate 23 *The Purple Rose of Cairo*

Plate 24 *The Purple Rose of Cairo*

Plate 25 *El Sur*

Plate 26 *The Green Room*

Plate 27 *Written on the Wind*

Plate 28 *Ivan the Terrible*

Plate 29 *Ivan the Terrible*

Plate 30 *Larks on a String*

Plate 31 *Yol*

Plate 32 *A*

Plate 33 *The Draughtsman's Contract*

Plate 34 *A Better Tomorrow III*

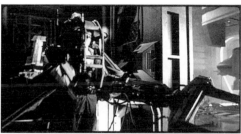

Plate 35 *Aliens*

Plate 36 *Life on a String*

Plate 37 *Sambizanga*

Plate 38 *One Froggy Evening*

Plate 39 *Bambi*

Plate 40 *The Wall*

Plate 41 *An Autumn Afternoon*

Plate 42 *An Autumn Afternoon*

Plate 43 *Lancelot du Lac*

Plate 44 *Meet Me in St. Louis*

Plate 45 *Meet Me in St. Louis*

Plate 46 *Stalker*

Plate 47 *Rainbow Dance*

Plate 48   *The Wrath of the Gods*

Plate 49   *Cenere*

Plate 50   *Viva la Muerte!*

Plate 51   *Daisies*

Plate 52   *Innocence Unprotected*

Plate 53   *Kasba*

Plate 54   *Kasba*

Plate 55   *Last Tango in Paris*

Plate 56 *Last Tango in Paris*

Plate 57 *Vertigo*

Plate 58 *Parsifal*

Plate 59 *Rumble Fish*

Plate 60 *Paris, Texas*

Plate 61 *Paris, Texas*

Plate 62 *Ohayu*

Plate 63 *Ohayu*

Fig. 6.29

Fig. 6.30

Fig. 6.31

von Sternberg, one of the cinema's masters of film lighting: "The proper use of light can embellish and dramatize every object."

For our purposes, we can isolate four major features of film lighting: its *quality, direction, source,* and *color.*

Lighting *quality* refers to the relative intensity of the illumination. "Hard" lighting creates clearly defined shadows, whereas "soft" lighting creates a diffused illumination. In nature, the noonday sun creates hard light, while an overcast sky creates soft light. The terms are relative, and many lighting situations will fall in between the extremes, but we can in practice easily recognize the differences.

Hard lighting creates bold shadows and crisp textures and edges. In Figure 6.29, from Satyajit Ray's *Aparajito,* Apu's mother and the globe she holds are emphasized by the hard lighting. In Figure 6.30, from the same film, softer lighting blurs contours and textures and makes for more diffusion and gentler contrasts between light and shade.

The *direction* of lighting in a shot refers to the path of light from its source or sources to the object lit. "Every light," wrote von Sternberg, "has a point where it is brightest and a point toward which it wanders to lose itself completely. . . . The journey of rays from that central core to the outposts of blackness is the adventure and drama of light." For convenience we can distinguish among frontal lighting, sidelighting, backlighting, underlighting, and top lighting.

Frontal lighting can be recognized by its tendency to eliminate shadows. In Color Plate 21, a shot from Godard's *La Chinoise,* the result of such frontal lighting is a fairly flat-looking image.

Fig. 6.32

In *Touch of Evil,* Welles uses a hard *sidelight* (also called a *crosslight*) to sculpt the character's features. Note the sharp shadows cast by nose, cheekbones, and lips, as well as the long shadows cast on the left wall (Fig. 6.31).

Backlighting, as the name suggests, comes from behind the subject filmed. It can be positioned at many angles: high above the figure, at various angles off to the side, pointing straight at the camera, or from below. Used with no other sources of light, backlighting tends to create silhouettes, as in Figure 6.32, a frame from Welles's *Citizen Kane.* Combined with more frontal sources of light, the technique can create an unobtrusively illuminated contour. In Figure 6.33, from *Wings,* a narrow line of light makes each actor's

Fig. 6.33

Fig. 6.34

Fig. 6.35

Fig. 6.36

Fig. 6.37

body stand out from the background. This use of backlighting is called *edge lighting* or *rim lighting*.

Underlighting suggests that the light comes from below the subject. In Figure 6.34 (from Ivan Mosjoukin's *Le Brasier ardent*), the underlighting suggests an offscreen fire. Since underlighting tends to distort features, it is often used to create dramatic horror effects, but it may also simply indicate a realistic light source, such as a fireplace. As usual, a particular technique can function differently according to context.

Top lighting is exemplified by Figure 6.35, from von Sternberg's *Shanghai Express.* Here the spotlight shines down from almost directly above Marlene Dietrich's face. Von Sternberg frequently used such a high frontal light to bring out the line of his star's cheekbones. (Our earlier example from *Asphalt Jungle* in Figure 6.28 provides a less glamorous instance of top lighting.)

Lighting can also be characterized by its *source.* In making a documentary, the filmmaker may be obliged to shoot with the light available in the actual surroundings. Most fictional films, however, use extra light sources to obtain greater control of the image's look. In most fictional films, the table lamps and street lights you see in the mise-en-scene are not the principal sources of illumination for the filming. Such visible sources of light, however, will serve to motivate the lighting decisions made in production. The filmmaker will usually strive to create a lighting design that is consistent with the sources in the setting. In Figure 6.36, from *The Miracle Worker,* the window in the rear and the lantern in the right foreground are purportedly the sources of illumination, but you can see the many studio lights used in this shot reflected as tiny white dots in the glass lantern.

Directors and cinematographers manipulating the lighting of the scene will start from the assumption that any subject normally requires two light sources: a *key light* and a *fill light.* The key light is the primary source, providing the dominant illumination and casting the strongest shadows. A fill is a less intense illumination which "fills in," softening or eliminating shadows cast by the key light. By combining key and fill, and by adding other sources, lighting can be controlled quite exactly.

The key lighting source may be aimed at the subject from any angle, as our examples of lighting direction have indicated. Color Plate 28, from *Ivan the Terrible,* shows underlighting as the key source, while a softer and dimmer fill falls on the setting behind the figure.

Figure 6.37 shows a frame from Abel Gance's *La Roue.* The bold backlighting is complemented by a key light from the left side. This casts attached shadows on the left side of the actress's face, notably by the nose and eye. The fill light comes from the right, thus ensuring that this side of her face will not appear completely dark, as does part of the face in Figure 6.31.

Figure 6.38 shows a shot from *Bezhin Meadow,* in which Eisenstein uses a number of light sources and directions. The key light falling on the figures comes from the left side, but it is hard on the face of the old woman in the foreground and softened on the face of the man because a fill light comes in from the right. This fill light falls on the woman's forehead and nose.

Classical Hollywood filmmaking developed the custom of using at least three light sources per shot: key light, fill light, and backlight. Figure 6.39 shows the most basic arrangement of these lights on a single figure. The backlight comes from behind and above the figure, the key light comes diagonally from the front, and a fill light comes from a position near the camera. The key will usually be closer to the figure or brighter than the fill. Typically, each major character in a scene will have his or her own key, fill, and backlight. If another actor is added (as in the dotted figure in Figure 6.39), the key light for one can be altered slightly to form the backlight for the other and vice versa, with a fill light on either side of the camera.

In Figure 6.40, the Bette Davis character in *Jezebel* is the most important figure, and the three-point lighting centers attention on her. A bright backlight from the rear upper right highlights her hair and edge-lights her left arm. The key light is off left, making her right arm brightly illuminated. A fill light comes from just to the right of the camera. It is less bright than the key. This balanced lighting creates mild shading, modeling Davis's face to suggest volume rather than flatness. (Note the slight shadow cast by her nose.) Davis's backlight and key light serve to illuminate the woman behind her at the right, but less prominently. Other fill lights, called *background* or *set lighting,* fall on the setting and on the crowd at the left rear.

Three-point lighting emerged during the studio era of Hollywood filmmaking, and it is still widely used. In Color Plate 23, from Woody Allen's *Purple Rose of Cairo,* the two figures are modeled by a strong key light from the left side, a fill light from off right of the camera, and a trace of edge lighting to pick out their clothes. The office behind the couple is lit more dimly and softly, as is typical with background light.

You may have already noticed that this "three-point" lighting system demands that the lamps be rearranged virtually every time the camera shifts to a new framing of the scene. This is, in fact, the case. In spite of the great cost involved, most Hollywood films will have a different lighting arrangement for each camera position. Such variations in the light sources do not conform to reality, but they do enable filmmakers to create clear compositions for each shot.

Three-point lighting was particularly well-suited for the *high-key lighting* used in classical Hollywood cinema and other filmmaking traditions.

Fig. 6.38

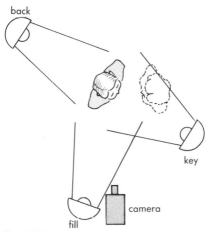

Fig. 6.39

Fig. 6.40

Fig. 6.41

Fig. 6.42

Fig. 6.43

Fig. 6.44

High-key lighting refers to an overall lighting design which uses fill and backlight to create low contrast between brighter and darker areas. Usually, the light quality is soft, making shadow areas fairly transparent. The frames from *Jezebel* (Fig. 6.40) and from *The Purple Rose of Cairo* (Color Plate 23) exemplify high-key lighting. Hollywood directors and cinematographers have relied on this for comedies, adventure films, and most dramas.

High-key lighting is not used simply to render a brightly lit situation, such as a dazzling ballroom or a sunny afternoon. High-key lighting is an overall approach to illumination that can suggest different lighting conditions or times of day. Consider, for example, two frames from *Back to the Future*. The first shot (Fig. 6.41) uses high-key illumination matched to daylight and a brightly lit malt shop. The second frame (Fig. 6.42) is from a scene set in a room at night, but it still uses the high-key approach, as can be seen from the lighting's softness, its low contrast, and its detail in shadow areas.

Low-key illumination creates stronger contrasts and sharper, darker shadows. Often the lighting is hard, and fill light is lessened or eliminated altogether. The effect is of *chiaroscuro*, or extremely dark and light regions within the image. An example is Figure 6.43, from Andrzej Wajda's *Kanal*. Here, the fill light and background light are significantly less intense than in high-key technique. As a result, shadow areas on the left third of the screen remain hard and opaque. In Figure 6.44, a low-key shot from Welles's *Touch of Evil*, the key light is hard and comes from the side. Welles eliminates both fill and background illumination, creating very sharp shadows and a dark void around the characters.

As our examples indicate, low-key lighting has usually been applied to somber or mysterious scenes. It was common in horror films of the 1930s and *films noirs* ("dark films") of the 1940s and 1950s. The low-key approach was revived in the 1980s in such films as *Blade Runner* and *Rumble Fish*. In *El Sur* (Color Plate 25) Hector Erice's low-key lighting yields dramatic chiaroscuro effects that portray the adult world as a child imagines it, full of mystery and danger.

When the actors move, the director must decide whether to alter the lighting. There are advantages to maintaining a constant lighting, even if this is not particularly realistic. At the end of Fellini's *Nights of Cabiria*, the heroine moves diagonally toward us, accompanied by a band of singing young people. As she walks, lighting on her face does not change, enabling us to notice slight changes in her expression (Figs. 6.45, 6.46). Alternatively, the filmmaker may have his or her figures move through patches of light and shadow. The swordfight in *Rashomon* is intensified by the contrast between the ferocious combat and the cheerfully dappled lighting pouring into the glade (Fig. 6.47).

Like any technique, lighting can become a motif in the course of a film. Woody Allen's *Purple Rose of Cairo* presents a woman torn between a brutal, abusive marriage and her fantasy of a movie hero (who steps down from the screen to meet her). Scenes with her fictional hero are presented in moderately high-key, using the three-point system we have just mentioned (Color Plate 23). But scenes with her husband at her home are given the harsh, hard-edged treatment characteristic of low-key technique (Color Plate 24).

We tend to think of film lighting as limited to two colors—the white of sunlight or the soft yellow of incandescent interior lamps. In practice, film-makers who choose to control lighting typically work with as purely white a light as they can. By use of filters placed in front of the light source, the filmmaker can color the onscreen illumination in any fashion. There may be a realistic source in the scene to motivate the hue of the light. For example, cinematographers often use filters to suggest the orange tint of candlelight, as in François Truffaut's *The Green Room* (Color Plate 26). In Douglas Sirk's *Written on the Wind,* purplish-blue lighting is motivated as the color of night (Color Plate 27). But colored light can also be unrealistic in its motivation. Eisenstein's *Ivan the Terrible,* Part 2, uses a blue light suddenly cast on an actor, nondiegetically, to suggest the character's terror and uncertainty (see Color Plates 28 and 29). Such a shift in stylistic function—using colored light to perform a function usually confined to acting—is all the more effective because it is so unexpected.

We are used to ignoring the illumination of our everyday surroundings, so film lighting is also easy to take for granted. Yet the look of a shot is centrally controlled by light quality, direction, source, and color. The film-maker can manipulate and combine these factors to shape the viewer's experience in a great many ways. No component of mise-en-scene is more important than "the drama and adventure of light."

■ FIGURE EXPRESSION AND MOVEMENT

The director may also control the behavior of various figures in the mise-en-scene. Here the word "figures" covers a wide range of possibilities, since the figure may represent a person but could also be an animal (Lassie, the donkey Balthasar, Donald Duck), a robot (R2D2 and C3PO in the *Star Wars* series), an object (as in *Ballet mécanique*'s choreography of bottles, straw hats, and kitchen utensils), or even a pure shape (as in *Ballet mécanique*'s circles and triangles). Mise-en-scene allows such figures to express feelings and thoughts; it can also dynamize them to create various kinetic patterns.

In Figure 6.48 (from *Seven Samurai*) the samurai have won the battle with the bandits. Virtually the only movement in the frame is the driving rain, but the slouching postures of the men leaning on their spears express their tense weariness. By contrast, in *White Heat* explosive movement and

Fig. 6.45

Fig. 6.46

Fig. 6.47

Fig. 6.48

Fig. 6.49

Fig. 6.50

Fig. 6.51

ferocious facial expression present an image of psychotic rage. In Figure 6.49 Cody Jarrett (James Cagney), after learning of his mother's death, bursts up from the prison mess table.

In cinema, facial expression and movement are not restricted to human figures. As mentioned in Chapter 2, by means of animation, drawings or three-dimensional objects can be endowed with highly dynamic movement. For example, in science-fiction and fantasy films, monsters and robots may be given expressions and gestures through the technique of *stop-action* (also called "stop-motion"). Typically a small-scale model is made with articulated parts. In filming, it is posed as desired, and a frame or two is shot. Then the figure is adjusted slightly and another frame or two is exposed, and so on. The result on screen is a continuous, if sometimes jerky, movement. The horrendous onslaught of ED-209, the crimefighting robot in *Robocop,* was created by means of a twelve-inch miniature filmed in stop-action (Fig. 6.50). (A full-scale but unmoving model was also built for long shots.) Stop-action can also be used for more abstract and unrealistic purposes, as in the clay animation in one portion of Jan Švankmajer's *Dimensions of Dialogue* (Fig. 6.51).

The filmmaker can stage action without three-dimensional figures or objects. Cel animation presents us with drawings of Aladdin or Daffy Duck. Filmmakers may also blend photographed action with animated mise-en-scene. Highly detailed computer-generated animation made it possible for James Cameron to create the outrageous metamorphoses of the cyborg in *Terminator 2: Judgment Day.* (See Notes and Queries for more on computer-generated mise-en-scene.)

Acting and actuality.   Although abstract shapes and animated figures can become important in the mise-en-scene, the most intuitively familiar cases of figure expression and movement are actors playing roles. Like other aspects of mise-en-scene, the performance is created in order to be filmed. An actor's performance consists of visual elements (appearance, gestures, facial expressions) and sound (voice, effects). At times, of course, an actor may contribute only visual aspects, as in the silent period of film history. Similarly, an actor's performance may sometimes exist only on the sound track of the film; in *A Letter to Three Wives,* Celeste Holm's character, Addie Ross, speaks a narration over the images but never appears on the screen.

Acting is often approached as a question of realism. While some broad conception of realistic behavior is probably indispensable as a first step to understanding acting, we cannot stop there. It is not always fruitful to judge an actor's performance by what would be likely behavior in the world outside the movie theater, and this is for several reasons.

For one thing, conceptions of realistic acting have changed over film history. Today we may think that the performances of Dustin Hoffman and Tom Cruise in *Rain Man* or those given by Susan Sarandon and Geena Davis in *Thelma and Louise* are reasonably close to people's real-life behavior. Yet in the early 1950s, the New York Actors Studio style, as exemplified by Marlon Brando's performances in *On the Waterfront* and *A Streetcar Named Desire,* was also thought to be extremely realistic. Fine though we may still find Brando's work in these films, it seems deliberate, heightened, and quite unrealistic. The same might be said of the performances, by professional and amateur actors alike, in post–World War II Italian neorealist films, which were hailed when they first appeared as almost documentary depictions of Italian life but many of which now seem to us to contain polished performances suitable to Hollywood films. (In fact, one of the main neorealist actors, Anna Magnani, went to Hollywood and won an Oscar there.) Already major naturalistic performances of the 1970s, such as Robert DeNiro's protagonist in *Taxi Driver,* are coming to seem quite stylized. Who can say what the acting in *Rain Man, Thelma and Louise,* and other recent films will look like in a few decades?

Changing views of realism are not the only reason to be wary of this as a concept for analyzing acting. Often when people call a performance "unrealistic," they are evaluating it as bad. But not all films try to achieve realism. Since the performance an actor creates is part of the overall mise-en-scene, films contain a wide variety of acting styles. Instead of assuming that acting must be realistic, we should try to understand what kind of acting style the film is aiming at. If the functions of acting in the film are best served by a nonrealistic performance, that is the kind that the skillful actor will strive to present. Obvious examples of nonrealistic acting style occur constantly in *The Wizard of Oz,* for fantasy purposes. (How would a "realistic" Wicked Witch behave?) Moreover, "realistic" performance will always be only one option in film acting. In mass-production filmmaking such as Hollywood, India, Hong Kong, and other traditions, overblown performances are a crucial source of the audience's pleasure. Typically viewers do not expect narrowly realistic acting from Jim Carrey or from martial arts stars like Bruce Lee or Jackie Chan.

Finally, when we watch any fictional film, we are to some degree aware that the performances on the screen are the results of the actors' skills and decisions. When we use the phrase "larger than life" to describe an effective performance, we seem to be tacitly acknowledging the actor's deliberate craft. In analyzing a particular film, it is usually necessary to go beyond assumptions about realism and consider the functions and purposes which the actor's craft serves.

Acting: Functions and motivation. In 1985 a considerable controversy arose in Hollywood because Steve Martin was not nominated for an Academy Award for his acting in *All of Me.* In that film, Martin portrays a man whose body is suddenly inhabited on the right side by the soul of a woman who has just died. Martin used sudden changes of voice, along with acrobatic pantomime, to suggest a "split" body. His performance is not realistic in the narrow sense, since the situation he portrays could not exist in the real world. Yet in the context of this fantasy-comedy, Martin's acting is not only virtuosic but completely appropriate.

In a film like *All of Me,* a more muted and superficially "realistic" performance would clearly be inappropriate to the context established by the genre, the film's narrative, and the overall mise-en-scene. This suggests that in order to determine the acting's functions, we need to determine overall

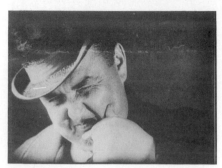

Fig. 6.52

Fig. 6.53

Fig. 6.54

Fig. 6.55

formal factors, such as narrative causality and genre conventions. In addition, if we want also to evaluate the actors' performances, we might set forth this criterion: If the actor looks and behaves in a manner *appropriate* to his or her character's *function* in the context of the film, the actor has given a good performance—whether or not he or she looks or behaves as a real person would.

As a first approximation, we can consider performance styles along two dimensions. The performance will be more or less *individualized,* and it will be more or less *stylized.* Often we have both in mind when we think of a "realistic" performance: It will create a unique character, and it will not seem too exaggerated or too underplayed. Yet less individualized and more stylized performances may also be appropriate to the context of a particular film's mise-en-scene.

Although we often think of good acting as creating highly individualized roles, many filmmaking traditions emphasize the creation of broader, more anonymous *types.* Classical Hollywood narrative was built upon ideologically stereotyped roles: the Irish cop on the beat, the black servant, the Jewish pawnbroker, the wisecracking waitress or showgirl. Through "typecasting," actors were selected and directed to conform to type. Often, however, skillful performers gave these conventions a freshness and vividness.

In the Soviet cinema of the 1920s, several directors used a similar principle, called *typage.* Here the actor was expected to portray a typical representative of a social class or historical movement. The opening of Eisenstein's *Strike* presents the cartoonish cliché of the top-hatted capitalist (Fig. 6.52), who will in the course of the film be contrasted with the earnest, resolute workers (Fig. 6.53).

Whether more or less "typed," the performance can also be located on a continuum of stylization. A long tradition of film acting strives for a resemblance to what is thought of as realistic behavior. This is often motivated by appealing to the character's psychological states. The introspective performances of Woody Allen and Diane Keaton in *Annie Hall* (Fig. 6.54), built around vague gestures and small changes of expression, suit a film about characters trying to define and articulate their feelings. More intense and explicit emotions dominate *Winchester 73,* in which James Stewart plays a man driven by a desire for revenge. Stewart's mild manner sometimes erupts into explosions of anger revealing him as on the brink of psychosis (Fig. 6.55).

Psychological motivation is less important in a film like *Trouble in Paradise,* a sophisticated comedy of manners in which the main concern is with more stereotypical characters in a comic situation. In Figure 6.56 two women competing for the same man pretend to be friendly. Their exaggerated smiles and polite gestures are amusing because we know that each is trying to deceive the other. Again, the performances are perfectly appropriate to the genre, narrative, and overall style of the film.

Comedy does not provide the only motivation for greater stylization. *Ivan the Terrible* is a film that heightens every element—music, costume, setting—to create a larger-than-life portrait of its hero. Nikolai Cherkasov's broad, abrupt gestures fit in perfectly with all of these other elements to create an overall unity of composition (Fig. 6.57).

Some films may combine different degrees of stylization. *Amadeus* contrasts a grotesque, giggling performance by Tom Hulce as Mozart with the reserved playing of Murray Abraham's suave Salieri. Here the acting sharpens the contrast between the older composer's decorous, boring music and the young man's irrepressible but offensive genius.

Films like *Caligari, Ivan the Terrible,* and *Amadeus* create stylized performances through extroversion and exaggeration. The director can also explore the possibilities of very muted performances. Compared to normal practice, highly restrained acting can seem quite stylized. Robert Bresson is noted for such restrained performances. Using nonprofessional actors and drilling them in the details of the characters' physical actions, Bresson makes his actors quite inexpressive by conventional standards. Although these performances often upset our expectations, we soon realize that such restraint focuses our attention on tiny gestures.

Jean-Marie Straub and Danièle Huillet go even further in this direction. Their *Not Reconciled* and *Chronicle of Anna Magdalena Bach* also utilize nonactors, and these players often speak their lines in a rather wooden fashion or simply have no lines at all. Straub and Huillet films invite us to consider the actors not as psychological beings but as reciters of written dialogue. We thus become actively aware of our own conventional expectations about film acting, and perhaps those expectations are broadened a bit.

Acting in the context of other techniques. By examining how an actor's performance functions in the context of the overall film, we can also notice how acting cooperates with other film techniques. For instance, the actor is always a graphic element in the film, but some films underline this fact. In *The Cabinet of Dr. Caligari,* Conrad Veidt's dancelike portrayal of the somnambulist Cesare makes him blend in with the graphic elements of the setting. His body echoes the tilted tree trunks, his arms and hands their branches and leaves (Fig. 6.58). As we shall see in our examination of the history of film styles, the graphic design of this scene in *Caligari* typifies the systematic distortion characteristic of German Expressionism.

In *Breathless,* director Jean-Luc Godard juxtaposes Jean Seberg's face with a print of a Renoir painting (Fig. 6.59). We might think that Seberg is giving a wooden performance, for she simply poses in the frame and turns her head. Indeed, her acting in the entire film may seem flat and inexpressive. Yet her face and general demeanor are visually appropriate for her role, a rather mysterious American woman unfathomable to her Parisian boyfriend.

The context of a performance may also be shaped by the technique of film editing. Sometimes film acting is denigrated because its practitioners do not have to sustain a performance. In the theater, the actor must be able to give a single, often lengthy presentation of a character. But a film, because it is shot over a period of time, breaks that performance up into bits. This can work to the filmmaker's advantage, since these bits can be selected and combined to build up a performance in ways that could never be accomplished on the stage. Most simply, if a scene has been filmed in several shots, with alternate takes of each shot, the editor may select the best gestures and expressions and create a composite performance better than any one sus-

Fig. 6.56

Fig. 6.57

Fig. 6.58

Fig. 6.59

tained performance could be. Through the addition of sound and the combination with other shots, the performance can be built up still further. The director may simply tell an actor to widen his or her eyes and stare offscreen. If the next shot shows a hand with a gun, we are likely to think the actor is depicting fear. As we will see in more detail in Chapter 8, editing plays a key role in shaping a performance.

Camera techniques also create a controlling context for acting. Film acting, as most viewers know, differs from theatrical acting. At first glance, that suggests that cinema always calls for more "underplaying," since the camera can closely approach the actor. But actually cinema calls for a stronger interplay between restraint and emphasis.

In a theater, we are usually at a considerable distance from the actor on the stage. We certainly can never get as close to the theater actor as the camera can put us in a film. In watching a film, however, we are not necessarily seeing close views of the actor at every moment. The camera can be at *any* distance from the figure. Filmed from very far away, the actor is a dot on the screen—much tinier than an actor on stage seen from the back of the balcony. Filmed from very close, the actor's tiniest eye movement may be revealed.

Thus the film actor must behave differently than the stage actor does, but not always by being more restrained. Rather, she or he must be able to adjust to each type of camera distance. If the actor is far from the camera, he or she will have to gesture broadly or move around to be seen as acting at all. But, if the camera and actor are inches apart, a twitch of a mouth muscle will come across clearly. In between these extremes, there is a whole range of adjustments to be made.

Fig. 6.60

Basically, a scene can concentrate on either the actor's facial expression or on pantomimic gestures of the body. Clearly, the closer the actor is to the camera, the more the facial expression will be visible and the more important it will be (although the filmmaker may choose to concentrate on another part of the body, excluding the face and emphasizing gesture). But if the actor is far away from the camera, or turned to conceal the face, his or her gestures become the center of the performance.

Thus both the staging of the action and the camera's distance from it determine how we will see the actors' performances. Many shots in Bernardo Bertolucci's *The Spider's Stratagem* show the two main characters from a distance, so that their manner of walking, combined with such details as the stiff, upright way in which the heroine holds her parasol, constitute the actors' performances in the scene (Fig. 6.60). In conversation scenes, however, we see their faces clearly, as in Figure 6.61.

Fig. 6.61

Turning back to some earlier examples, we see that in Figure 6.6, the actors are placed at either side of the garden, far back from the camera. The actors are so distant in Figure 6.11 that we see each one only as part of a moving crowd. Figures 6.20, 6.32, 6.48, 6.57, and 6.58 are all shots in which bodily behavior rather than facial expression forms the basis for the acting. Contrast these with Figures 6.14, 6.22, 6.33, 6.35, 6.37, 6.38, 6.49, 6.53, 6.55, and 6.56, where the faces are close enough for small changes to be visible. A performance typically combines facial expression with bodily gesture, as is evident in Figure 6.61; see also Figures 6.13, 6.31, 6.49, 6.53, 6.54, 6.55, and 6.56. In Figure 6.27, small gestures become crucial.

Such factors of context are particularly important when the performers are not actors, or even human beings. Framing, editing, and other film techniques can make trained animals give appropriate performances. Jonesy, the cat in *Aliens,* seems threatening because his hissing movement has been emphasized by lighting, framing, editing, and the sound track (Fig. 6.62). In animated films, the filmmaker's manipulation must go farther, as in Ladislav Starevich's *Mascot.* There a conversation between a devil and a thief includes subtle facial expressions and gestures, all created through the frame-by-frame manipulation of puppets (Fig. 2.12).

As with every element of a film, acting offers an unlimited range of quite distinct possibilities. It cannot be judged on a universal scale that is separate from the concrete context of the entire film's form.

Fig. 6.62

MISE-EN-SCENE IN SPACE AND TIME

Setting, costume, lighting, and figure expression and movement—these are the components of mise-en-scene. Yet one element seldom appears in isolation. Each usually combines with others to create a specific system in every film. The general formal principles of unity, disunity, similarity, difference, and development will guide us in analyzing how specific elements of mise-en-scene can function together. What are some ways in which mise-en-scene affects our attention? What pulls our eye to a portion of the frame at a given moment?

Most basically, our visual system is attuned to perceiving *change*, both in time and space. Our eyes and brains are better suited for noticing differences than for concentrating on uniform, prolonged stimuli. Thus aspects of mise-en-scene will attract our attention by means of changes in light, shape, movement, and other aspects of the image.

Moreover, looking is purposeful; what we look *at* is guided by our assumptions and expectations about what to look *for*. These, in turn, are based upon our previous experiences of artworks and of the real world. In viewing a film image, we make hypotheses on the basis of many factors.

One general factor is the total organization of the film's form. In a narrative film, characters and their actions offer strong cues. If a shot shows a crowd, we will tend to scan it looking for a character we recognize from earlier scenes. Similarly, sound can become an important factor controlling our attention. As we shall see in Chapter 9, sound can draw attention to areas of the image in various ways. Written language can also shape the viewer's expectations, as when an intertitle cues us what to look for in the next shot. In what follows, we shall concentrate on another source of hypotheses: the elements and patterns in the mise-en-scene itself. Mise-en-scene contains a host of purely spatial and temporal factors to guide our expectations and hence shape our viewing of the image.

■ SPACE

We already know that cinema is involved with different sorts of space. The image projected on a screen is flat, of course, and it displays a composition within a frame, just as a still photograph or a painting would. The arrangement of the mise-en-scene creates the composition of the *screen space*. That two-dimensional composition consists of the organization of shapes, textures, and patterns of light and dark. In most films, though, the composition also represents a *three-dimensional space* in which the action occurs. Since the image projected on the screen is flat, the mise-en-scene must give the audience cues that will enable us to infer the three-dimensionality of the scene. The filmmaker uses mise-en-scene to guide our attention across the screen, shaping our sense of the space that is represented and emphasizing certain parts of it.

In cinema, our vision is attuned to changes of several kinds: *movement, color differences, balance of distinct components,* and *variations in size.* Our sensitivity to these changes allows the filmmaker to direct our notice across the two-dimensional space of the frame.

Almost invariably, a *moving* item draws our attention more quickly than a static item does. We are sensitive to even the slightest activity within the frame. Normally, for instance, we ignore the movement of scratches and dust on a film. But in David Rimmer's *Watching for the Queen,* in which the first image is an absolutely static photograph (Fig. 6.63), the jumping bits of dust on the film draw our attention.

Fig. 6.63

Fig. 6.64

Fig. 6.65

In Figure 6.64 (from Yasujiro Ozu's *Record of a Tenement Gentleman*), many items compete for our attention. But the moment that a scrap of newspaper flaps, it immediately attracts the eye because it is the only motion in the frame. When several moving elements appear on the screen, as in a ballroom dance, we are likely to shift our attention among them, according to other cues or depending on our expectations about which one is most salient to the narrative action. In Figure 6.65, from John Ford's *Young Mr. Lincoln,* Lincoln is moving much less than the dancers we see in front of him. Yet he is framed centrally; he is the major character; and the dancers pass rapidly through the frame. As a result, we are likely to concentrate on his gestures and facial expressions, however slight they might be compared to the energetic action in the foreground.

The filmmaker, like the painter, can also exploit principles of *color contrast* to shape our sense of screen space. For instance, bright colors set against a more subdued background are likely to draw the eye. Jiří Menzel exploits this principle in *Larks on a String,* where the junkyard setting provides earthy grays and blacks against which the characters' lighter clothes stand out sharply (Color Plate 30).

Another pertinent principle is that when lightness values are equal, "warm" colors in the red-orange-yellow range tend to attract attention, while "cool" colors like purple and green are less prominent. In Yilmaz Güney's *Yol,* for example, the setting and the characters' outfits are already quite warm in hue, but the hot pink vest of the man in the central middle ground helps make him the primary object of attention (Color Plate 31).

Sometimes the filmmaker will treat color design in terms of what painters call a "limited palette." This involves a few noncontrasting colors, perhaps along with white, browns, grays, and black. An extreme example of a limited palette is Jan Lenica's animated film *A*, which uses fine-point black and white before enlivening its absurd comedy with the brief appearance of pastel flowers (Color Plate 32).

The limited palette allows the viewer to make finer distinctions of intensity or saturation in the composition. Our earlier example from Fellini's *Casanova* (Color Plate 15) uses various shades of red. A limited palette drawing on the cooler end of the spectrum is seen in Peter Greenaway's *The Draughtsman's Contract* (Color Plate 33).

Fig. 6.66

An extreme use of the "limited palette" principle is sometimes called *monochromatic* color design. Here the filmmaker emphasizes a single color, varied only in purity or lightness. We have already seen an example of monochromatic mise-en-scene in the white-on-white scene of *THX 1138* (Color Plate 16). A more common usage can be found in 1970s and 1980s action films, which often envelop battle sequences in a silver or blue-gray haze. (See Color Plate 34, from Tsui Hark's *A Better Tomorrow III*). In a monochromatic design, even the slightest fleck of a contrasting color will catch the viewer's attention. The color design of *Aliens* is dominated by metallic tones, so even a dingy yellow can mark the stiltlike loader as an important prop within the narrative (Color Plate 35).

Fig. 6.67

Black-and-white films also rely on our sensitivity to changes in tonalities. The colors of setting, costumes, lighting, and figures register on the film in shades of black, white, and gray. The differences among these provide cues for us as we scan the image. Usually lighter shapes leap to our notice while darker ones recede. Note how in Figure 6.66, from Pudovkin's *Mother*, your eye concentrates on the man's face rather than on the darkness surrounding it. The same principle works in Figures 6.31 through 6.38. All things being equal, if several light areas compete in the composition (Figs. 6.54 and 6.59), we will tend to shift our attention back and forth. Dark shapes may become prominent, however, if they are clearly defined and placed against a light background. In Figure 6.58, the actor and the trees draw our eyes instantly because they stand out so starkly from the lighter area.

Compositional *balance* refers to the extent to which the areas of screen space have equally distributed masses and points of interest. Filmmakers often assume that the spectator will concentrate more on the upper half of the frame (probably because in most shots that is where characters' faces are placed). Thus because of viewers' prior expectations the upper half needs less "filling up" than the lower.

Since the film shot is composed within a horizontal rectangle, the director usually takes care to balance the left and right halves. The extreme type of such balancing is bilateral symmetry. In the wedding banquet of *Ivan the Terrible*, Eisenstein stages the action symmetrically (Fig. 6.67). A more grandiose example is the battle scene of Chen Kaige's *Life on a String* (Color Plate 36).

More common than such near-perfect symmetry is a loose balancing of

Fig. 6.68

Fig. 6.69

Fig. 6.70

Fig. 6.71

the shot's left and right regions. The simplest way to achieve compositional balance is to center the frame on the human body. Filmmakers often place a single figure at the center of the frame and minimize distracting elements at the sides, as in Figure 6.68, from *The Rules of the Game.* Many of our earlier illustrations display this sort of balance (for example, Figs. 6.14, 6.35, 6.37, and 6.40). Other shots may balance two or more elements, encouraging our eye to move back and forth as in Figure 6.69, also from *The Rules of the Game.* (For other examples, see Figs. 6.38, 6.56, and 6.59.) The balance can be roughly equal, as in Figure 6.56, or more unequal. In Figure 6.48 we will most likely pick out the two standing men first, since they are at the center, before we notice the crouching villagers at the far left. These examples suggest that compositional balance helps shape our expectations about where significant action will be located on the screen.

Balanced composition is the norm, but unbalanced shots can also strongly govern our sense of screen space. A mild example comes from Vittorio de Sica's *Bicycle Thieves,* which emphasizes the father's new job by massing most of the composition on the right (Fig. 6.70). A bolder example comes from Michelangelo Antonioni's *Il Grido* (Fig. 6.71). Instead of balancing the husband and wife, the composition centers the husband. If there were no tree in the frame, the shot would be somewhat weighted to the right side, but the unexpected vertical of the tree trunk makes that side even heavier. In Chapter 8, we will see how editing can balance two relatively unbalanced compositions.

Our vision's effort to monitor differences also affects our sense of on-screen *size.* Looking at a static shot, we will register the larger shapes first and then discriminate smaller ones. In Figure 6.11, the huge pillars and statues of the Babylon set contribute more to our sense of the overall composition than do either the individual actors or the light and dark patches on the steps near the bottom. In Figure 6.31 we are likely to look first at the actor's face and the paper he holds, rather than at the small white labels on the file drawers—even though the labels are just as bright and in the same centered area of the screen. Nevertheless movement, color, or balance can override size as a compositional cue and can draw our attention quickly to very small areas of the screen. For example, if one of the file-drawer labels suddenly fluttered to the floor, we would almost certainly notice it.

Such compositional qualities do not only guide our attention across the flat screen space. In virtually all films, mise-en-scene functions to suggest a three-dimensional space, abstract or representational, real or fictitious.

The factors in the image which help create such a sense of space are broadly called *depth cues.* There is no real space extending behind the screen, of course, but depth cues prompt us to imagine that space, to construct a three-dimensional world in which the film's action takes place. Again, we develop our understanding of depth cues from our experience of space in the real world and from conventions of space in such arts as painting and theater. In cinema, depth cues are largely provided by lighting, setting, costumes, and figure behavior.

The depth cues suggest that a space has both *volume* and several distinct *planes.* When we speak of an object as having volume, we mean that it is solid and occupies a three-dimensional area. A film suggests volume by shape, shading, and movement. In Figures 6.59 and 6.72 (the latter from Dreyer's *La Passion de Jeanne d'Arc*), we do not think of the actors' faces as flat cutouts, like paper dolls. The shapes of those heads and shoulders suggest solid people. The attached shadows on the faces suggest the curves and recesses of the actors' features and give a modeling effect. We assume that if the actor in Figure 6.59 turned her head, we would see a profile. Thus we use our knowledge of objects in the world to discern volume in filmic space.

Fig. 6.72

An abstract film, because it can use shapes that are not everyday objects, can create compositions without a sense of volume. The shapes in Figure 6.73, a frame from Norman McLaren's *Begone, Dull Care*, give us no depth cues for volume—they are unshaded, do not have a recognizable shape, and do not move in such a way as to reveal new views which suggest roundness.

Depth cues also pick out *planes* within the image. Planes are the layers of space occupied by persons or objects. Planes run into depth, from foreground through middle ground to background.

Only a completely blank screen has a single plane. Whenever a shape—even an abstract one—appears, we will perceive it as being in front of a background. In Figure 6.73, the four dark S shapes are actually painted right on the frame surface along with the lighter, textured area. Yet the textured area seems to be behind the four shapes. The space here has only two planes, as in an abstract painting. This example suggests that one of the most basic depth cues is *overlap* of edges. The curling S shapes have edges which overlap the background plane, block our vision of it, and thus seem to be closer to us.

Fig. 6.73

Through overlap a great many planes can be defined. Color Plate 21, from Jean-Luc Godard's *La Chinoise*, displays three distinct planes: the background of fashion cutouts, the woman's face that overlaps that background, and her hand which overlaps her lower face. In the three-point lighting approach, "edge-lighting" accentuates the overlap of planes by emphasizing the contour of the object, thus sharply distinguishing it from the background. (See again Figs. 6.33, 6.38, and 6.40.)

Color differences also create overlapping planes. Because cool or pale colors tend to recede, filmmakers commonly use them for background planes such as setting. Similarly, because warm or saturated colors tend to come forward, such hues are often employed for costumes or other foreground elements. In Sarah Maldoror's *Sambizanga* (Color Plate 37), the heroine's dress has very warm and fairly saturated colors, making it stand out distinctly against the pale background. (See also Color Plates 9, 12, 13, and 35.)

Animated films can achieve brighter and more saturated color than most live-action filming, so depth effects can be correspondingly more vivid. In Chuck Jones's *One Froggy Evening* (Color Plate 38), the luminous yellow of the umbrella and the frog's brilliant green skin make him stand out against the darker red of the curtain and the earth tones of the stage floor. In Color Plate 39, from *Bambi*, spatial layers are defined by contrasting pastels and darker hues: light yellow in the foreground, then pure black and white for the skunk, then milder pastels for the flowers behind him, and finally darker green and black for the backgrounds.

Because of the eye's sensitivity to differences, even quite muted color contrasts can suggest three-dimensional space. In *L'Argent* (Color Plates 6–8) Bresson uses a limited, cool palette and relatively flat lighting. Yet the compositions pick out several planes by means of overlapping slightly different masses of black, tan, and light blue. Our shot from *Casanova* (Color Plate 15) articulates planes by means of slightly differing shades of red. In the *Draughtsman's Contract* example (Color Plate 33), much of our sense of distant space is created by strong black verticals and by horizontal strips of various shades of green. Together these colors define distinct layers in the scene.

Color Plate 22, from *La Chinoise*, suggests another depth-producing factor: the *movement* of the cigarette smoke in the foreground. In cinema, movement is one of the most important depth cues, since it strongly suggests both planes and volumes. Note also the *cast shadow* in the background of Color Plate 22, which is another depth cue.

Aerial perspective, or the hazing of more distant planes, is yet another depth cue. Typically, our visual system assumes that sharper outlines, clearer textures, and purer colors belong to foreground elements. In landscape shots, the blurring and graying of distant planes can be caused by actual atmospheric haze, as in Güney's *The Wall* (Color Plate 40). Even when such haze is a minor factor, our vision typically assigns strong color contrasts to the foreground, as in the *Sambizanga* shot (Color Plate 37). In addition, very often lighting is manipulated in conjunction with lens focus to blur the background planes. In Michael Curtiz's *Charge of the Light Brigade*, for example, aerial perspective is artificially created through diffused lighting of the background and a lack of clear focus (Fig. 6.74).

In Figure 6.75, from Straub and Huillet's *Chronicle of Anna Magdalena Bach*, the mise-en-scene provides several depth cues: overlap of edges, cast shadows, and *size diminution*. That is, figures and objects farther away from us are seen to get proportionally smaller; the smaller the figure appears, the farther away we believe it to be. This reinforces our sense of there being a deep space with considerable distances between the various planes.

The same illustration dramatically displays *linear perspective*. We will consider perspective relations in more detail in the next chapter, since they derive as much from properties of the camera lens as they do from mise-en-scene. For now, we can simply note that a strong impression of depth emerges when parallel lines converge at a distant vanishing point. Figure 6.75 illustrates *off-center* linear perspective, where the vanishing point is not the geometrical center. Color Plate 33, from *The Draughtsman's Contract*, exemplifies *central* perspective.

In many of the examples already given, you may have noticed that mise-en-scene serves not simply to direct our attention to foreground elements but rather to create a dynamic relation between foreground and background. In Color Plates 21 and 22, for instance, Godard keeps our attention on the whole composition by using prominent backgrounds. In Color Plate 21, the pictures behind the actress's head lead us to scan the various small shapes quickly, while the bright red wall in Color Plate 22 comes forward strongly, making us aware of the background even if we concentrate on the actor's face.

Fig. 6.74

Fig. 6.75

The last two instances both exemplify *shallow-space* compositions. In such shots, the mise-en-scene suggests comparatively little depth, and the closest and most distant planes seem only slightly separated. The opposite tendency is *deep-space* composition, in which a significant distance seems to separate planes. Our earlier example from *Chronicle of Anna Magdalena Bach* (Fig. 6.75) exemplifies deep-space mise-en-scene. Often a director creates a deep-space composition by making the foreground plane quite large and the background plane quite distant, as Wajda does in several scenes of *Ashes and Diamonds* (Fig. 6.76).

Fig. 6.76

"Shallow" and "deep" mise-en-scene are relative terms. Most compositions present a moderately deep space, falling in between the extremes we have just considered. Sometimes a composition will present a relatively deep space but then control depth cues in order to flatten it. For example, Leos Carax's shallow space in *Boy Meets Girl* makes his foreground figure seem to blend into the advertisement on the wall behind (Fig. 6.77).

Fig. 6.77

At this point, you might want to return to shots illustrated earlier in this chapter. You will notice that these images use depth cues of overlap, movement, cast shadows, aerial perspective, size diminution, and linear perspective to create distinctive foreground/background relations.

The fact that our vision is sensitive to differences allows filmmakers to guide our understanding of the mise-en-scene. All the cues to story space interact with one another, working to emphasize narrative elements, direct our attention, and set up dynamic relations among areas of screen space. We can see this interaction clearly in two shots from Carl Dreyer's *Day of Wrath*.

In the first shot, the heroine Anne is standing before a grillwork panel (Fig. 6.78). She is not speaking, but since she is a major character in the film, the narrative already directs us to her. Setting, lighting, costume, and figure expression create pictorial cues that confirm our expectations. The setting yields a screen pattern of horizontal and vertical lines which intersect in the delicate curves of Anne's face and shoulders. The lighting yields a patch of brightness on the right half of the frame and a patch of darkness on the left, creating pictorial balance. Anne is the meeting point of these two areas. Her face becomes modeled by the relatively strong key lighting from the right, a little top lighting on her hair, and relatively little fill light. Coordinated with the lighting in creating the pattern of light and dark is Anne's costume—a black dress punctuated by white collar, a black cap edged with white—which again emphasizes her face.

Fig. 6.78

The shot is comparatively shallow, displaying two major planes with little distance between them. The background sets off the more important element, Anne. The rigid geometrical grid in the rear makes Anne's slightly sad face the most expressive element in the frame, thus encouraging our eye to pause there. In addition, the composition divides the screen space horizontally, with the grid pattern running across the top half and the dark, severe vertical of Anne's dress dominating the lower half. As is common, the upper zone is the stronger because the character's head and shoulders occupy it. Anne's figure is positioned slightly off center, but with her face turned so as to compensate for the vacant area on the right. (Imagine how unbalanced the

Fig. 6.79

shot would look if she were turned to face us squarely and the same amount of space were left empty on the right.) Thus compositional balance reinforces the shot's emphasis on Anne's expression. In all, without using motion, Dreyer has channeled our attention through the lines and shapes, the lights and darks, and the foreground and background relations in the mise-en-scene.

In the second example, Dreyer coaxes our attention into a to-and-fro movement (Fig. 6.79). Again, the plot guides us, since the characters and the cart are crucial narrative elements. Sound helps too, since Martin is at the moment explaining to Anne what the cart is used for. But mise-en-scene also plays a role. Size diminution and cast shadows establish basic foreground/background relations, with Anne and Martin on the front plane and the cart of wood in the background. The space is comparatively deep (though the foreground is not as exaggeratedly close as that in *Ashes and Diamonds*, Fig. 6.76). The prominence of the couple and the cart is reinforced by line, shape, and lighting contrasts. The figures are defined by hard edges and by dark costumes within the predominantly bright setting. Unlike most shots, this puts the human figures in the lower half of the frame, which gives that zone an unusual importance. The composition thus creates a vertical balance, counterweighting the cart with the couple. This encourages us to glance up and down between the two objects of our attention.

Similar processes are at work in color films. In one shot of Yasujiro Ozu's *An Autumn Afternoon* (Color Plate 41), our attention is concentrated on the woman in the center foreground. Here many depth cues are at work. Overlap locates the two figures in two foreground planes, setting them against a series of more distant planes. Aerial perspective makes the tree foliage somewhat out of focus. Movement creates depth when the bride lowers her head. Perspective diminution makes the more distant objects smaller. The figure and the bright silver, red, and gold bridal costume stand out strikingly against the muted, cool colors of the background planes. Moreover, the colors bring back a red-and-silver motif that began in the very first shot of the film (Color Plate 42).

In all these cases, compositional elements and depth cues have functioned to focus our attention on the narrative elements. But this need not always be the case. Bresson's *Lancelot du Lac* uses a limited palette of dark and metallic hues, and warmer colors tend to stand out. In one scene (Color Plate 43), a group of conversing knights is centered and balanced in the foreground planes. Yet a pale purple saddle blanket on a passing horse momentarily draws our eyes *away* from this action. Such a "distracting" use of color becomes a stylistic motif in the film.

■ TIME

So far we have examined some spatial factors that guide our viewing of an image. In addition, both the shot and our viewing of it take place in time.

As we will see in more detail when we consider editing (Chapter 8), the filmmaker decides how long the shot will last on the screen. Within the confines of the shot's duration, the director can control the rhythm of time as it unfolds. Although the issue of rhythm in cinema is enormously complex and still not well understood, we can say roughly that it involves, at least, a *beat* or pulse, a pace (what musicians call *tempo*), and a pattern of *accents*, or stronger and weaker beats.

We are most familiar with these factors in the filming of dance. When Fred Astaire or Ann Miller performs, the bodily movements obey strongly patterned rhythms. We should recognize, though, that any movement within the mise-en-scene may involve the same rhythmic components. Movement on the screen can have a distinctive visual beat, such as the flashing of a neon sign or the steady rocking of a ship. Movement can also have a marked pace, such as the acceleration of a car in a chase scene. And visual movement can create distinctive, accented instants as well.

These factors combine to create a sense of the shot's overall rhythm. In Figure 6.80, from Chantal Akerman's *Jeanne Dielman, 23 quai du Commerce, 1080 Bruxelles,* the protagonist simply prepares a meal. This feminist film emphasizes the daily routine of a Belgian housewife, and many of its shots show small movements carried out slowly. Because there are no competing movements on the screen, her gestures create accented moments. Overall, the film's rhythm concentrates attention on minute variations in her habits.

Fig. 6.80

A far busier shot is Figure 6.81, from Busby Berkeley's *42nd Street.* Here we find strongly opposed movements. The central and outer rings of dancers circle in one direction, while the second ring turns in a contrary direction. The dancers also swing strips of shiny cloth back and forth. The result is a partially abstract composition, emphasized by a steady beat, rapid tempo, and strong accents—all appropriate to the shot's placement as part of a musical number.

The dancers in *42nd Street* are synchronized to a considerable degree, but Figure 6.82, from Tati's *Play Time,* contains movements of differing speeds, with different visual accents. Moreover, they occur on different planes and follow contrasting trajectories. These diverse movements accord with Tati's tendency to cram his compositions with gags which compete for our attention.

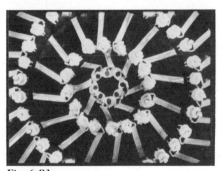

Fig. 6.81

As we have already seen, we scan any film frame for information. This scanning brings time sharply into play. Only a very short shot forces us to try to take in the image all at once. In most shots we get an initial overall impression that creates formal expectations. These expectations are quickly modified as our eye roams around the frame.

Once again, our scanning of the shot is strongly affected by the presence of movement. A static composition, such as our first shot from *Day of Wrath* (Fig. 6.78), may keep pulling our attention back to a single element (here, Anne's face). By contrast, a composition emphasizing movement becomes more "time-bound" because our glance may be directed from place to place by various speeds, directions, and rhythms of movements. In the second image from *Day of Wrath* (Fig. 6.79) Anne and Martin are turned from us (so that expression and gesture are minimized), and they are standing still. Thus the single movement in the frame—the cart—catches our attention. But when Martin speaks and turns, we look back at the couple, then back at the cart, and so on, in a shuttling, dynamic shift of attention. In such ways mise-en-scene can control not only *what* we look at but also *when* we look at it.

Fig. 6.82

Our time-bound process of scanning involves not only looking to and fro across the screen but also, in a sense, looking "into" its depths. A deep-space composition will often use background events to create expectations about what is about to happen in the foreground. "Composing in depth isn't simply a matter of pictorial richness," British director Alexander Mackendrick has remarked. "It has value in the narrative of the action, the pacing of the scene. Within the same frame, the director can organize the action so that preparation for what will happen next is seen in the background of what is happening now."

In one scene of *La Terra trema*, Luchino Visconti's deep-space composition prepares us for activity in the left foreground by having women in the family come forward to stare at the picture hanging there (Figs. 6.83, 6.84). Kenji Mizoguchi appeals to a different principle in *Naniwa Elegy*. Here, at the height of the drama, the heroine moves *away* from us, into depth. As she passes through patches of distant darkness, our curiosity about her emotional state intensifies (Figs. 6.85, 6.86).

Another fairly straightforward way to guide the viewer's attention over time is to adjust *frontality* of figure placement. All other things being equal, the viewer expects that more story information will come from a character's face than from a character's back. The viewer's attention will thus usually pass over figures which are turned away and fasten on figures which are positioned frontally. We have already seen this cue at work in our second still from *Day of Wrath* (Fig. 6.79), as well as in our *Vampires* examples (Figs.

Fig. 6.83

Fig. 6.84

Fig. 6.85

Fig. 6.86

Fig. 6.87

Fig. 6.88

Fig. 6.89

Fig. 6.90

Fig. 6.91

6.15, 6.16, p. 175). In *La Terra trema* (Fig. 6.87), this deep-space composition favors the far background plane by turning the foreground and middleground figures away from the viewer. This shifts our attention to the most frontally positioned characters, even though they are the most distant. In our *Naniwa Elegy* examples (Figs. 6.85, 6.86), both figures are turned from us, so other cues, such as the centrality and movement, drive our attention to the woman.

The frontality cue can shift the viewer's attention according to what the filmmaker wants to stress. At one point in a conversation in *The Bad and the Beautiful*, our attention is fastened on the studio executive on the right because the other two characters are turned away from us (Fig. 6.88). But when the producer turns to the camera, his centered position and the frontality of his posture emphasize him (Fig. 6.89). A more striking instance occurs in *L'Avventura*, when the characters alternate turning their backs on the camera (Figs. 6.90, 6.91). Like movements through a lighted volume and the filling of empty zones, the frontality cue shows mise-en-scene's indebtedness to theatrical staging.

As a set of techniques, mise-en-scene helps compose the film shot in space and time. Setting, lighting, costume, and figure behavior interact to create patterns of movement, of color and depth, line and shape, light and dark. These patterns define and develop the space of the story world and emphasize salient story information. The director's use of mise-en-scene not only guides our perception from moment to moment but also helps create the overall form of the film.

NARRATIVE FUNCTIONS OF MISE-EN-SCENE: *OUR HOSPITALITY*

Up to now we have looked at the general stylistic possibilities offered by mise-en-scene. Its potential for creating graphic compositions is vital to the abstract film, and can be useful as well to the other types of formal organization. Categorical, rhetorical, and associational films use mise-en-scene to guide our attention, our understanding, and our inferences about what we see. The rest of this chapter considers how mise-en-scene can function in narrative films.

In order to understand story information presented to us in a narrative film, we must perform such activities as comparing locales, identifying characters by their appearances, and noticing salient gestures as the mise-en-scene presents them to us. Many motifs that recur in the course of the plot's unfolding are visual elements of the mise-en-scene, and such motifs can contribute significantly to the fundamental formal principles of the film's overall organization: its unity and its patterns of similarity, difference, and development.

Mise-en-scene contributes to the plot action, of course, because events we see directly constitute the plot. But elements of mise-en-scene can also imply story information. If a detective discovers a corpse, we may imagine the murder. If a woman tells a friend about an important event in her past and shows the friend a picture of her parents, the picture contributes information about earlier story events not dramatized in the film. Similarly, mise-en-scene can help present a more or less restricted narration. This may go to an extreme, as when all the mise-en-scene elements of *The Cabinet of Dr. Caligari* show us the distorted outlook of a madman's subjective vision (see Figs. 6.1 and 6.58). Few films go this far, but many occasionally show us something only one character knows about, thus restricting our knowledge to that character's visual subjectivity—as when we see the words written in a diary or letter, or a view from a window.

Mise-en-scene cues our expectations about narrative events. If we watch someone hide a box of jewelry early in the story, we wait to see if someone will eventually discover it. Such expectations often depend on genre conventions: A bakery full of pies in a slapstick comedy suggests that a sticky fight will break out at some point; a piano tucked away in the corner of a room in a Judy Garland–Mickey Rooney musical will almost certainly be played to accompany a song. But there are no hard-and-fast rules, and a narrative film may also frequently surprise us with unconventional mise-en-scene.

Mise-en-scene functions not only in isolated moments, but in relation to the narrative organization of the entire film. *Our Hospitality*, like most of Buster Keaton's films, exemplifies how mise-en-scene can economically advance the narrative and create a pattern of motifs. Since the film is a comedy, the mise-en-scene also creates gags. *Our Hospitality*, then, exemplifies what we will find in our study of every film technique: An individual element almost always has *several* functions, not just one.

Consider, for example, how the settings function within the plot of *Our Hospitality*. For one thing, they help divide the film into scenes and to contrast those scenes. The film begins with a prologue showing how the feud between the McKays and the Canfields results in the deaths of the young Canfield and the husband of the McKay family. We see the McKays living in a shack and are left in suspense about the fate of the baby, Willie. Willie's mother flees with her son from their southern home to the North (action narrated to us mainly by an intertitle).

The plot skips over several years to begin the main action, with the grown-up Willie living in New York. There are a number of gags concerning early nineteenth-century life in the metropolis, contrasting sharply with the prologue scene. We are led to wonder how this locale will relate to the southern scenes, and soon Willie receives word that he has inherited his parents' home in the South. A series of amusing short scenes follows as he takes a primitive train back to his birthplace. During these scenes Keaton uses real locales, but by laying out the railroad tracks in different ways, he exploits the landscapes for surprising and unusual comic effects we shall examine shortly.

The rest of the film deals with Willie's movements in and around the southern town. On the day of his arrival he wanders around and gets into a number of comic situations. That night he stays in the Canfield house itself. Finally, an extended chase occurs the next day, moving through the country-side and back to the Canfield house for the settling of the feud. Thus the action depends heavily on shifts of setting that establish Willie's two journeys, as baby and as man, and later his wanderings to escape his enemies' pursuit. The narration is relatively unrestricted once Willie reaches the South, moving between him and members of the Canfield family. We usually know more about where they are than Willie does, and the narrative generates suspense by showing them coming toward the places where Willie is hiding.

Specific settings fulfill distinct narrative functions. The McKay "estate," which Willie envisions as a mansion, turns out to be a tumbledown shack. The McKay house is contrasted with the Canfields' palatial plantation home. In narrative terms the Canfield home gains even more functional importance when the Canfield father forbids his sons to kill Willie on the premises: "Our code of honor forbids us to shoot him while he is a guest in our house." (Once Willie overhears this, he determines *never* to leave.) Ironically the home of Willie's enemies becomes the only safe spot in town, and many scenes are organized around the Canfield brothers' attempts to lure Willie outside. At the end of the film another setting takes on significance: the landscape of meadows, mountains, river banks, rapids, and waterfalls across which the Canfields pursue Willie. Finally, the feud ends back in the Canfield house itself, with Willie now welcomed as the daughter's husband. The pattern of development is clear: from the opening shootout at the McKay house that breaks up Willie's home, to the final scene in the Canfield house with Willie becoming part of a new family. In such ways every setting becomes highly motivated by the narrative's system of causes and effects, parallels and contrasts, and overall development.

The same narrative motivation marks the film's use of costume. Willie is characterized as a city boy through his dandified suit, whereas the southern gentility of the elder Canfield is represented through his white planter's suit. Props become important here: Willie's suitcase and umbrella succinctly summarize his role as visitor and wanderer, and the Canfields' ever-present pistols remind us of their goals of continuing the feud. Note also that a change of costume (Willie's disguising himself as a woman) enables him to escape from the Canfield household. At the end, the putting aside of the various guns by the characters signals the end of the feud.

Like setting, lighting in *Our Hospitality* has both general and specific functions. The film systematically alternates scenes in darkness with scenes in daylight. The feuding in the prologue takes place at night; Willie's trip south and wanderings through the town occur in daylight; that night Willie

Fig. 6.92

Fig. 6.93

Fig. 6.94

Fig. 6.95

Fig. 6.96

comes to dinner at the Canfields' and stays as a guest; next day, the Canfields pursue him; and the film ends that night with the marriage of Willie and the Canfield daughter. More specifically, the bulk of the film is evenly lit in the three-point method. Yet the somber action of the prologue takes place in hard sidelighting. When the elder McKay flings off his hat to douse the lamp, the illumination changes from a soft blend of key, fill, and backlight to a stark key light from the fireplace (see Figs. 6.92 and 6.93). Later, the murder scene is played out in flashes of light—lightning, gunfire—which fitfully punctuate the overall darkness. Because this sporadic lighting hides part of the action from us, it helps build suspense. The gunshots themselves are seen only as flashes in the darkness, and we must wait to learn the outcome—the deaths of both opponents—until the next flash of lightning.

Most economically of all, virtually every bit of the behavior of the figures functions to support and advance the cause-effect chain of the narrative. The way Canfield sips and savors his julep establishes his southern ways; his southern hospitality in turn will not allow him to shoot a guest in his house. Similarly, Willie's every move expresses his diffidence or resourcefulness.

Even more concise is the way the film uses the arrangement of figures and setting in depth to present two narrative events simultaneously. While the engineer drives the locomotive, the other cars pass him on a parallel track (Fig. 6.94). In the same frame we see both cause (the engineer's cheerful ignorance, made visible by frontality) and effect (the runaway disconnected cars). Or, in another shot, the Canfield boys in the foreground make plans to shoot Willie, while in the background Willie overhears them (Fig. 6.95). In yet another shot, while Willie ambles along unsuspectingly in the background, one Canfield waits in the foreground to ambush him (Fig. 6.96). Thanks to depth in the spatial arrangement, Keaton is able to pack together two story events, resulting in a tight narrative construction and in a relatively unrestricted narration. In Figure 6.95, we know what Willie does and we expect that he will probably flee now that he understands the sons' plans. But in Figure 6.96, we are aware, as Willie is not, that danger lurks around the corner; suspense results, as we wonder whether the Canfield boys' ambush will succeed.

All of these devices for narrative economy considerably unify the film, but some other elements of mise-en-scene function as specific motifs. For one thing, there is the repeated squabble between the anonymous husband

and wife. On his way to his "estate," Willie passes a husband throttling his wife. Willie intervenes to protect her; the wife proceeds to thrash Willie for butting in. On Willie's way back, he passes the same couple, still fighting, but studiously avoids them. Nevertheless, the wife aims a kick at him as he passes. The mere repetition of the motif strengthens the film's narrative unity, but it functions thematically, too, as another joke on the contradictions surrounding the idea of hospitality.

Other motifs recur. Willie's first hat is too tall to wear in a jouncing railway coach. (When it gets crushed, he trades it for the familiar flat Keaton trademark hat.) Willie's second hat serves to distract the Canfields when Willie coaxes his dog to fetch it. There is also a pronounced water motif in the film. Water as rain conceals from us the murders in the prologue and later saves Willie from leaving the Canfield home after dinner ("It would be the death of anyone to go out on a night like this!"). Water as a river functions significantly in the final chase. And water as a waterfall appears soon after Willie's arrival in the South; after an explosion demolishes a dam, the water spills over a cliff and creates a waterfall (Fig. 6.97). This waterfall initially protects Willie by hiding him (Figs. 6.98, 6.99) but later threatens both him and the Canfield daughter as they are nearly swept over it (Fig. 6.105).

Fig. 6.97

Two specific motifs of setting powerfully unify the narrative. First there is the recurrence of an embroidered sampler hanging on the Canfield wall: "Love Thy Neighbor." It appears initially in the prologue of the film, when seeing it motivates Canfield's attempt to stop the feud. It then plays a significant role in linking the ending back to the beginning. The sampler reappears at the end when Canfield, enraged that Willie has married his daughter, glances at the wall, reads the inscription, and resolves to halt the years of feuding. His change in attitude is motivated by the earlier appearance of the motif.

Fig. 6.98

The film also uses gun racks as a motif. In the prologue each feuder goes to his mantelpiece to get his pistol. Later, when Willie arrives in town, the Canfields hurry to their gun rack and begin to load their pistols. Near the end of the film, when the Canfields return home after failing to find Willie, one of the sons notices that the gun rack is now empty. And in the final shot, when the Canfields accept the marriage and lay down their arms, Willie produces from all over his person a staggering assortment of pistols taken as a precaution from the Canfields' own supply. Thus mise-en-scene motifs unify the film through their repetition, variation, and development.

Fig. 6.99

Yet *Our Hospitality* is more than a film whose narrative system relates economically to patterns of mise-en-scene. It is a comedy, and one of the funniest. We should not be surprised to find, then, that Keaton uses mise-en-scene for gags. Indeed, so unified is the film that most of the elements that create narrative economy also function to yield comic effects.

The mise-en-scene bristles with many individually comic elements. Settings are exploited for amusement—the ramshackle McKay estate, the Broadway of 1830, the specially cut train tunnel that just fits the old-fashioned train and its smokestack (Fig. 6.100). Costume gags also stand out. Willie's disguise as a woman is divulged by a gap in the rear of his skirt; later, Willie puts the same costume on a horse to distract the Canfields. Most

Fig. 6.100

Fig. 6.101

Fig. 6.102

Fig. 6.103

Fig. 6.104

strongly, comedy arises from the behavior of the figures. The railroad engineer's high kick unexpectedly swipes off his conductor's hat (Fig. 6.101). (Keaton's father, Joe, played this role, and the gag was one of his famous vaudeville stunts.) The elder Canfield sharpens his carving knife with ferocious energy, just inches from Willie's head. When Willie lands at the bottom of the river, he stands there looking left and right, his hand shading his eyes, before he realizes where he is. Later, Willie scuds down the river, leaping out of the water like a fish and skidding across the rocks.

Perhaps the only aspect of mise-en-scene that competes with the comic brilliance of the figures' behavior is the film's use of deep space for gags. Many of the shots we have already examined function to create comedy as well: The engineer stands firmly oblivious to the separation of train cars from the engine (see Fig. 6.94) just as Willie is unaware that the Canfield boy is lurking murderously in the foreground (see Fig. 6.96).

Even more striking, though, is the deep-space gag that follows the demolition of the dam. The Canfield boys have been searching the town for Willie. In the meantime, Willie sits on a ledge, fishing. As the water bursts from the dam and sweeps over the cliff, it completely engulfs Willie (Fig. 6.98). At that very instant, the Canfield brothers step into the foreground from either side of the frame, still looking for their victim (Fig. 6.99). The water's concealment of Willie reduces him to a neutral background for the movement of the Canfields. This sudden eruption of new action into the scene surprises us, rather than generating suspense, since we were not aware that the Canfield sons were so close by. Here surprise is crucial to the comedy.

However appealing the individual gags are, *Our Hospitality* patterns its comic aspects as strictly as it does its other motifs. The film's journey pattern often arranges a series of gags according to a formal principle of theme and variations. For instance, during the train trip south, a string of gags is based on the idea of people encountering the train. Several people turn out to watch it pass, a tramp rides the rods, and an old man chucks rocks at the engine. Another swift series of gags takes the train tracks themselves as its "theme." The variations include a humped track, a donkey blocking the tracks, curled and rippled tracks, and finally no tracks at all.

But the most complex theme-and-variations series can be seen in the motif of "the fish on the line." Soon after Willie arrives in town, he is angling and hauls up a minuscule fish. Shortly afterward, a huge fish yanks him into the water (Fig. 6.102). Later in the film, through a series of mishaps, Willie becomes tied by a rope to one of the Canfield sons. Many gags arise from this umbilical-cord linkage, especially one that results in Canfield's being pulled into the water as Willie was earlier.

Perhaps the single funniest shot in the film occurs when Willie realizes that since the Canfield boy has fallen off the rocks (Fig. 6.103), so must he (Fig. 6.104). But even after Willie gets free of Canfield, the rope remains tied around his waist. So in the film's climax Willie is dangling from a log over the waterfall like the fish on the end of his fishing pole (Fig. 6.105). Here again, one element fulfills multiple functions. The fish-on-the-line device advances the narrative, becomes a motif unifying the film, and takes its place in a pattern of parallel gags involving variations of Willie on the rope.

In such ways *Our Hospitality* becomes an outstanding example of the integration of cinematic mise-en-scene with narrative form.

Fig. 6.105

SUMMARY

The viewer who wants to study mise-en-scene should look for it systematically. Watch, first of all, for how setting, costume, lighting, and the behavior of the figures present themselves in a given film. As a start, try to trace only one sort of element—say, setting or lighting—through an entire film.

We should also reflect on the patterning of mise-en-scene elements. How do they function? How do they constitute motifs that weave their ways through the film? In addition, we should notice how mise-en-scene is patterned in space and time to attract and guide the viewer's attention through the process of watching the film, and to create suspense or surprise.

Finally, we should try to relate the system of mise-en-scene to the large-scale form of the film. Hard-and-fast prejudices about realism are of less value here than an openness to the great variety of mise-en-scene possibilities. Awareness of those possibilities will better help us to determine the functions of mise-en-scene.

NOTES AND QUERIES

◼ ON THE ORIGINS OF MISE-EN-SCENE

As a concept, mise-en-scene reaches back into the nineteenth-century theater. For a historical introduction that is relevant to film, see Oscar G. Brockett and Robert R. Findlay, *Century of Innovation* (Englewood Cliffs, N.J.: Prentice-Hall, 1973). More specialized are Brooks McNamara, "The Scenography of Popular Entertainment," *The Drama Review* **18,** 1 (March 1974): 16–24; and Martin Meisel, *Realizations: Narrative, Pictorial, and Theatrical Arts in Nineteenth-Century England* (Princeton: Princeton University Press, 1983). The standard film work remains Nicolas Vardac, *Stage to Screen* (Cambridge, Mass.: Harvard University Press, 1949).

◼ ON REALISM IN MISE-EN-SCENE

Many film theorists have seen film as a realistic medium par excellence. For such theorists as Siegfried Kracauer, André Bazin, and V. F. Perkins, cinema's power lies in its ability to present a recognizable reality. The realist theorist thus often values authenticity in costume and setting, "naturalistic" acting, and unstylized lighting. "The primary function of decor," writes V. F. Perkins, "is to provide a believable environment for the action" [*Film as Film* (Baltimore: Penguin, 1972), p. 94]. André Bazin praises the Italian neorealist films of the 1940s for "faithfulness to everyday life in the scenario, truth to his part in an actor" [*What is Cinema?* vol. 2 (Berkeley: University of California Press, 1970), p. 25].

Though mise-en-scene is always a product of selection and choice, the realist theorist may value the filmmaker who creates a mise-en-scene that *appears* to be reality. Kracauer suggests that even apparently "unrealistic" song and dance numbers in a musical can seem impromptu [*Theory of Film* (New York: Oxford University Press, 1965)], and Bazin considers a fantasy film such as *The Red Balloon* realistic because here "what is imaginary on the screen has the spatial density of something real" [*What is Cinema?* vol. 1 (Berkeley: University of California Press, 1966), p. 48].

These theorists, then, set the filmmaker the task of representing some historical, social, or aesthetic reality through the selection and arrangement of mise-en-scene. Though this book postpones the consideration of this problem—it lies more strictly in the domain of film theory—the "realist" controversy is worth your examination. For arguments against a realist theory of mise-en-scene, see Noël Burch, *Theory of Film Practice* (Princeton: Princeton University Press, 1981), and Sergei Eisenstein, "An Unexpected Juncture," in Richard Taylor, ed., *Writings 1922–1934* (Bloomington: Indiana University Press, 1988), pp. 115–122. Christopher Williams, in *Realism and the Cinema* (London: Routledge & Kegan Paul, 1980), reviews many issues in the area.

■ COMPUTER IMAGING AND MISE-EN-SCENE

In recent years, the filmmaker's control of mise-en-scene has been extended by means of computer technology. *Digital* computer animation uses a program that will itself create images. *Analog image synthesis* enables a full blend of live-action footage with computer-generated image transformations. A drawing, photograph, or videotape is scanned with a video camera, which yields an image that can be manipulated by computer. An object can be pulled out of the image and recolored, or even rotated or extended by being plotted through a series of movements. The resulting animation is rescanned onto a high-resolution television monitor, which is then filmed by a 35mm motion-picture camera. A general survey of these processes is offered by Neil Weinstock's *Computer Animation* (Reading, Mass.: Addison-Wesley, 1986).

Another technique is *digital compositing,* utilized for the T-1000 cyborg in *Terminator 2: Judgment Day.* Here a grid was painted on the actor's body, and the actor was filmed executing movements. As the film was scanned, the changing grid patterns were translated into a digital code similar to that used on compact discs. Then new actions could be created on the computer frame by frame. For a discussion, see Jody Duncan, "A Once and Future War," *Cinefex* **47** (August 1991): 4–59. Since *Terminator 2,* sophisticated software programs have enabled directors to create "actors" wholly from models which can be scanned into a computer and then animated. The most famous example is the gallimimus herd in *Jurassic Park.* The phases of the imaging process for this film are explained in Jody Duncan, "The Beauty in the Beasts," *Cinefex* **55** (August 1993): 42–95.

The combination of live-action filming with computer animation promises to make possible a fresh range of cinematic effects. Méliès's urge to dazzle the audience with the magical powers of mise-en-scene continues to bear fruit.

■ PARTICULAR ASPECTS OF MISE-EN-SCENE

On costume, see Elizabeth Lees, *Costume Design in the Movies* (London: BCW, 1976), and Edward Maeder, ed., *Hollywood and History: Costume Design in Film* (New York: Thames and Hudson, 1987). Léon Barsacq, with careful assistance by Elliott Stein, has produced the best history of setting to date, *Caligari's Cabinet and Other Grand Illusions: A History of Film Design* (New York: New American Library, 1976). Other major studies of decor in the cinema are Charles Affron and Mirella Jona Affron, *Sets in Motion: Art Direction and Film Narrative* (New Brunswick, N.J.: Rutgers University Press, 1995), and Beverly Heisner, *Hollywood Art: Art Direction in the Days of the Great Studios* (Jefferson, N.C.: McFarland, 1990). A special issue of *Film Comment* (May/June 1978) deals with the work of the art director. The memoirs of a major set designer who worked extensively with Jean Renoir have been published: Eugene Lourie's *My Work in Films* (San Diego: Harcourt Brace Jovanovich, 1985).

The most commonly discussed type of figure behavior is, as we might expect, acting. A wide-ranging analysis of performance in film is Richard Dyer, *Stars* (London: British Film Institute, 1979). This book is complemented by Charles Affron, *Star Acting: Gish, Garbo, Davis* (New York: Dutton, 1977), and James Naremore, *Acting in the Cinema* (Berkeley: University of California Press, 1988). Michael Caine's *Acting in Film: An Actor's Take on Movie Making* (New York: Applause Books, 1990) offers excellent and detailed discussion; see also the accompanying videotape, *Michael Caine on Acting in Film.*

A fine survey of lighting is Kris Malkiewicz, *Film Lighting: Talks with Hollywood's Cinematographers and Gaffers* (New York: Prentice-Hall, 1986). (Our quotation from Alexander Mackendrick on p. 198 comes from this book, p. 16.) John Alton's *Painting with Light* (New York: Macmillan, 1949) and Gerald Millerson's *Technique of Lighting for Television and Motion Pictures* (New York: Hastings House, 1972) are useful older discussions, with emphasis on classical Hollywood practices.

One of the cinema's masters of lighting, Josef von Sternberg, has much to say on the subject in his entertaining autobiography, *Fun in a Chinese Laundry* (New York: Macmillan, 1965). Raoul Coutard discusses a different approach to lighting in "Light of Day," in Toby Mussmann, ed., *Jean-Luc Godard* (New York: Dutton, 1968), pp. 232–239. Hollywood cinematographers recall their lighting experiments in Malkiewicz, mentioned above, and in Charles Higham, *Hollywood Cameramen* (London: Thames & Hudson, 1970).

■ DEPTH

Art historians have long studied how a two-dimensional image can be made to suggest a deep space. A comprehensive introductory survey is William V.

Dunning, *Changing Images of Pictorial Space: A History of Spatial Illusion in Painting* (Syracuse: Syracuse University Press, 1991). Dunning's history of Western painting emphasizes the manipulation of five techniques we have considered in this chapter: linear perspective, shading, the separation of planes, atmospheric perspective, and "color perspective."

Though film directors have of course manipulated the image's depth and flatness since the beginning of cinema, critical understanding of these spatial qualities did not emerge until the 1940s. It was then that André Bazin called attention to the fact that certain directors staged their shots in unusually deep space. Bazin singled out F. W. Murnau (for *Nosferatu* and *Sunrise*), Orson Welles (for *Citizen Kane* and *The Magnificent Ambersons*), William Wyler (for *The Little Foxes* and *The Best Years of Our Lives*), and Jean Renoir (for practically all of his 1930s work). Today we would add Kenji Mizoguchi (for *Osaka Elegy, Sisters of Gion,* and others) and even Sergei Eisenstein (for *Old and New, Ivan the Terrible,* and the unreleased *Bezhin Meadow*). By offering us depth and flatness as analytical categories, Bazin increased our understanding of mise-en-scene. (See "The Evolution of the Language of Cinema," in *What is Cinema?* vol. 1.) Interestingly, Sergei Eisenstein, who is often contrasted with Bazin, explicitly discussed principles of deep-space staging in the 1930s, as recorded by his faithful pupil, Vladimir Nizhny, in *Lessons with Eisenstein* (New York: Hill & Wang, 1962). Eisenstein asked his class to stage a murder scene in a single shot and without camera movement; the result was a startling use of extreme depth and dynamic movement toward the spectator. For a discussion, see David Bordwell, *The Cinema of Eisenstein* (Cambridge: Harvard University Press, 1993), chaps. 4 and 6. A general discussion of deep space and deep focus is Charles Henry Harpole, *Gradients of Depth in the Cinema Image* (New York: Arno, 1978).

■ COLOR DESIGN

Two clear and readable discussions of color aesthetics in general are Luigina De Grandis, *Theory and Use of Color,* trans. John Gilbert (New York: Abrams, 1986), and Paul Zelanski and Mary Pat Fisher, *Colour for Designers and Artists* (London: Herbert Press, 1989).

Filmmakers have long considered color to be an important aspect of mise-en-scene, capable of furnishing motifs that will develop across the film. Believing that color evokes definite emotions, Rouben Mamoulian claimed that the director must develop "a complete chromatic plan for the film" ["Color and Light in Films," *Film Culture* **21** (Summer 1960): 68–79.] Carl Dreyer agreed, stressing the necessity for the director to plan the color scheme to flow smoothly, "which creates the effect of persons and objects being in constant motion and causes the colors to glide from one place to another in changing rhythms, creating new and surprising effects when they collide with other colors or melt into them" ["Color Film and Colored Films," *Dreyer in Double Reflection* (New York: Dutton, 1973), pp. 168–173].

For Stan Brakhage, cinema must break down our normal sense of color, as "closed-eye visions" produce purely subjective tonalities: "I am stating my given ability, prize of all above pursuing, to transform the light sculpted shapes of an almost dark-blackened room to the rainbow-hued patterns of light without any scientific paraphernalia" [*Metaphors on Vision* (New York: Film Culture, 1963)]. The filmmaker who theorized most extensively about color was Sergei Eisenstein. See especially "Color and Meaning," in *The Film Sense* (New York: Harcourt, Brace, 1947), pp. 113–153.

For general discussion of the aesthetics of film color, see Raymond Durgnat, "Colours and Contrasts," *Films and Filming* **15,** 2 (November 1968): 58–62; and William Johnson, "Coming to Terms with Color," *Film Quarterly* **20,** 1 (Fall 1966): 2–22. Two essays on Jean-Luc Godard exemplify how the analyst can examine a film's color system: Paul Sharits, "Red, Blue, Godard," *Film Quarterly* **19,** 4 (Summer 1966): 24–29; and Edward Branigan, "The Articulation of Color in a Filmic System," *Wide Angle* **1,** 3 (1976): 20–31. The latter contains an excellent bibliography.

■ FRAME COMPOSITION AND THE VIEWER'S EYE

The film shot is in a sense like the painter's canvas: It must be filled up, and the spectator must be cued to notice certain things (and not to notice others). For this reason, composition in film owes much to principles developed in the graphic arts. A good basic study of composition is Donald L. Weismann, *The Visual Arts as Human Experience* (Englewood Cliffs: Prentice-Hall, 1974), which has many interesting things to say about depth as well. More elaborate discussions are to be found in Rudolf Arnheim, *Art and Visual Perception: A Psychology of the Creative Eye,* rev. ed. (Berkeley: University of California Press, 1974), and his *The Power of the Center: A Study of Composition in the Visual Arts,* 2d ed. (Berkeley: University of California Press, 1988). Maureen Turim's "Symmetry/Asymmetry and Visual Fascination," *Wide Angle* **4,** 3 (1980): 38–47 applies such principles to film.

André Bazin suggested that shots staged in depth and shot in deep focus give the viewer's eye greater freedom than do flatter, shallower shots: The viewer's eye can roam across the screen. [See Bazin, *Orson Welles* (New York: Harper & Row, 1978).] Noël Burch takes issue: "All the elements in any given film image are perceived as equal in importance" (*Theory of Film Practice,* p. 34). Psychological research on pictorial perception suggests, however, that viewers do indeed scan images according to specific cues. A good review of the subject, with bibliography, may be found in Julian Hochberg, "The Representation of Things and People," in E. H. Gombrich et al., *Art, Perception, and Reality* (Baltimore: Johns Hopkins University Press, 1972), pp. 47–94. In cinema, static visual cues for "when to look where" are reinforced or undermined by movement of figures or of camera, by sound track and editing, and by the overall form of the film. The psychological research is outlined in Robert L. Solso, *Cognition and the Visual Arts* (Cambridge, Mass.: MIT Press, 1994), pp. 129–156.

THE SHOT:
CINEMATOGRAPHY

In controlling mise-en-scene the filmmaker stages an event to be filmed. But a comprehensive account of cinema as a medium cannot stop with simply what is put in front of the camera. The "shot" does not exist until light and dark patterns are inscribed on a strip of film. The filmmaker also controls what we will call the *cinematographic qualities* of the shot—not only what is filmed but also *how* it is filmed. Cinematographic qualities involve three factors: (1) the photographic aspects of the shot; (2) the framing of the shot; and (3) the duration of the shot. This chapter surveys these three areas of control.

THE PHOTOGRAPHIC IMAGE

Cinematography (literally, "writing in movement") depends to a large extent on photography ("writing in light"). Sometimes the filmmaker eliminates the camera and simply works on the film itself; but even when drawing, painting, or scratching directly on film, punching holes in it, or growing mold on it, the filmmaker is creating patterns of light on celluloid. Most often the filmmaker uses a camera to regulate how light from some object will be photochemically registered on the sensitized film. In any event, the filmmaker can select the range of tonalities, manipulate the speed of motion, and transform perspective.

■ THE RANGE OF TONALITIES

An image may seem all grays or stark black and white. It may display a range of colors. Textures may stand out clearly or recede into a haze. The filmmaker may control all these visual qualities by manipulating film stock, exposure, and developing procedures.

Types of *film stocks* are differentiated by the chemical qualities of the emulsion. The choice of film stock has many artistic implications. For one thing, the image will have more or less *contrast* depending partly on the stock used. "Contrast" refers to the degree of difference between the darkest and lightest areas of the frame. A high-contrast, or "contrasty," image displays bright white highlights, stark black areas, and a narrow range of grays in between. A low-contrast image possesses a wide range of grays with no true white or black areas.

As we have already seen in Chapter 6, human vision is highly sensitive to differences in color, texture, shape, and other pictorial properties. Contrasts within the image enable filmmakers to guide the viewer's eye to important parts of the frame. Filmmakers control the degree of contrast in the image in various ways. In general, a very "slow" stock, one which is not very sensitive to reflected light, will produce a contrasty look, while a faster, more light-sensitive one will be low in contrast. The amount of light used on the set during shooting will also affect the image's degree of contrast. Moreover, the cinematographer may choose to use particular developing procedures that heighten or decrease contrast. The strength and temperature of the chemicals and the length of time the film is left in the developing bath also affect contrast.

By manipulating the film stock, lighting factors, and developing procedures, filmmakers can achieve enormous variety in the look of the film image. Most black-and-white films employ a balance of grays, blacks, and whites, as in Renoir's *Crime of M. Lange* (Fig. 7.1). By contrast, the dream sequence at the start of Ingmar Bergman's *Wild Strawberries* uses a combination of film stock, overexposure, and laboratory processing to create a bleached-out look (Fig. 7.2).

Fig. 7.1

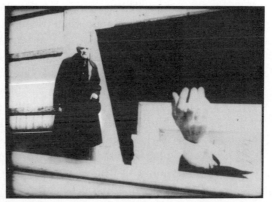

Fig. 7.2

Fig. 7.3

Jean-Luc Godard's *Les Carabiniers* (Fig. 7.3) offers a good example of what post-filming manipulations of film stock can accomplish. The shot's newsreel-like quality is heightened by both the film stock and lab work that increased contrast. "The positive prints," Godard has explained, "were simply made on a special Kodak high contrast stock. . . . Several shots, intrinsically too gray, were duped again sometimes two or three times, always to their highest contrast." The effect suggests old war footage that has been recopied or shot under bad lighting conditions; for a film about the grubbiness of war, the high-contrast look was exactly what Godard wanted.

Different color film stocks yield varying color contrasts. Technicolor became famous for its sharply distinct, heavily saturated hues, as seen in such films as *Meet Me in St. Louis* (Color Plates 44 and 45). The richness of Technicolor was achieved by means of a specially designed camera and a sophisticated printing process. To take another example, Soviet filmmakers long used a domestically made stock that tends to lower contrast and give the image a murky greenish-blue cast. Andrei Tarkovsky exploited just these qualities in the monochromatic color design of his shadowy *Stalker* (Color Plate 46), where the action seems almost to be taking place underwater. Len Lye's abstract *Rainbow Dance* utilizes specific features of the English stock Gasparcolor to create pure, saturated silhouettes that split and recombine with one another (Color Plate 47).

The tonalities of color stock may also be altered by laboratory processes. The person assigned the role of *color timer* or *grader* has a wide choice about the color range of a print. A red patch in the image may be printed as crimson, pink, or almost any shade in between. Often the timer consults with the director to select a key tone that will serve as a reference point for color relations throughout the film. In addition, some prints can be made for purposes that require a different color balance. Today, most prints made for 35mm exhibition are printed somewhat dark, to create rich shadows and darker colors. But prints struck for transfer to video are made on special low-contrast stock in order to compensate for television's tendency to heighten contrast. The resulting image often has a lighter, brighter color range than seen in any theatrical print.

Certain procedures may also add color to footage originally shot in black and white. The most widely used of these processes have been tinting and toning. *Tinting* is accomplished by dipping the already developed film into a bath of dye. The dark areas remain black and gray, while the lighter ones pick up the color. (See Color Plate 48.) *Toning* works in an opposite fashion. The dye is added during the developing of the positive print. The darker areas of the frame are colored, while the brighter portions of the frame remain white or only faintly colored. (See Color Plate 49.)

Both tinting and toning were common in the silent cinema. Night scenes, as in Color Plate 49 (from *Cenere,* a 1916 Italian film) were often colored blue. Firelight was frequently colored red, while interiors were commonly amber. Color Plate 48 (from *The Wrath of the Gods,* 1914) uses a pink tint to suggest the glow of an erupting volcano. Some contemporary filmmakers have revived these processes. Arrabal's *Viva la Muerte!* uses a vibrant yellow-orange tint (Color Plate 50), while Verá Chytilová employs crimson toning in *Daisies* (Color Plate 51).

A rarer method of adding color is the difficult process of *hand coloring.* Here portions of black-and-white images are painted in colors, frame by frame. The ship's flag in Eisenstein's *Potemkin* was originally hand colored red against a blue sky. A modern use of hand coloring may be seen in Makavejev's *Innocence Unprotected* (Color Plate 52).

Many other sorts of post-filming manipulation of tonalities are possible. In *Reflections on Black,* Stan Brakhage scratches off the emulsion in certain parts of the image, creating a graphic design that emphasizes the eye motif that runs through the film (Fig. 7.4).

Fig. 7.4

The range of tonalities in the image is most crucially affected by the *exposure* of the image during filming. The filmmaker usually controls exposure by regulating how much light passes through the camera lens, though images shot with "correct" exposure can also be overexposed or underexposed in developing and printing. We commonly think that a photograph should be "well exposed"—neither underexposed (too dark, not enough light admitted through the lens) or overexposed (too bright, too much light admitted through the lens). But even "correct exposure" usually offers some latitude for choice; it is not an absolute.

The filmmaker can manipulate exposure for specific effects. American *films noirs* of the 1940s sometimes underexpose shadowy regions of the image in keeping with low-key lighting techniques. In *Ordet,* Carl Dreyer overexposes the windows behind the minister in order to create a mystical religious atmosphere (Fig. 7.5). By contrast, in *Vidas Secas,* Nelson Pereira dos Santos overexposes the windows of the prison cell to sharpen the contrast between the prisoner's confinement and the world of freedom outside (Fig. 7.6).

Fig. 7.5

Choices of exposure are particularly critical in working with color. For shots of *Kasba,* Kumar Shahani chooses to emphasize tones within shaded areas, and so he exposes for them and lets sunlit areas bleach out somewhat. In Color Plate 53, the vibrant hues of the store's wares stand out, while the countryside glimpsed in the background is overexposed. At other moments, Shahani underexposes the shaded porches, in order to emphasize the central outdoor area (Color Plate 54).

Exposure can in turn be affected by *filters*—slices of glass or gelatin put in front of the lens of the camera or printer to reduce certain frequencies of light reaching the film. Filters thus alter the range of tonalities in quite

Fig. 7.6

radical ways. A filter can block out part of the light and thus make footage shot in daylight seem to be shot by moonlight. This technique is called "day-for-night" filming. Hollywood cinematographers since the 1920s sought to add glamour to close-ups, especially of women, by means of diffusion filters and silks. Filters applied during shooting or during printing can also alter the color image.

Finally, exposure can be altered by the process called *flashing*. Here the film is exposed to light (often a white or gray card) before shooting or before processing. Flashing adjusts contrast, since it can make shadows grayer and more transparent. Francis Ford Coppola's *Tucker* flashed each reel differently, changing the color scheme as the film progressed. In such ways, both in filming and in laboratory work the manipulation of film stock and exposure powerfully affects the image that we see on the screen.

■ SPEED OF MOTION

A gymnast's performance seen in slurred slow-motion, ordinary action accelerated to comic speed, a tennis serve stopped in a freeze-frame—we are all familiar with the effects of the control of the speed of motion. Of course, the filmmaker who stages the event to be filmed can (within limits) dictate the pace of the action. But that pace can also be controlled by a photographic power unique to cinema: the control of the depicted speed of movement.

The speed of the motion we see on the screen depends on the relation between the rate at which the film was shot and the rate of projection. Both rates are calculated in frames per second. In the silent era, films were shot at a variety of speeds, usually ranging from 16 to 20 frames per second, gradually getting a bit faster in the mid-1920s. Once sound was adopted in the late 1920s, it was necessary to record both sound and image at a standardized and uniform speed, so that they could be synchronized. The rate of shooting and projection for the sound cinema was standardized at 24 frames per second.

For depicted movement to look accurate, the rate of shooting must correspond to the rate of projection. For example, we are so used to seeing silent films having jerky, accelerated movements that we assume that the films always looked that way. But the jerkiness of the images is usually a result of projecting a film shot at 16 to 20 frames per second at 24 frames per second, or "sound speed." When shown at the proper rate, silent films look completely normal. For this reason, it is best to project silent films on projectors that can run at 16 or 18 frames per second or, better, on "variable speed" projectors that can tailor the speed precisely to the film.

Projection usually lies outside the filmmaker's control, but he or she can control the rate of the film's movement through the camera. The camera's drive mechanism can be adjusted to vary the shooting rate. A common range on 35mm cameras today is between 8 and 64 frames per second.

Assuming a constant projection speed, the fewer frames per second shot, the greater the acceleration of the screen action. We are used to this *fast-motion* effect in comedies. The most famous example of it for noncomic purposes occurs in F. W. Murnau's *Nosferatu*, in which the vampire's accelerated mobility represents his supernatural power. In Godfrey Reggio's

Koyaanisqatsi, a delirious fast-motion renders the hectic rhythms of urban life (Fig. 7.7).

Fig. 7.7

On the other hand, the more frames per second shot, the slower the screen action will appear. The resulting *slow-motion* effect is used notably in Dziga Vertov's *Man with a Movie Camera* to render sports events in detail, a function that continues to be important today. The technique can also be used for expressive purposes. In Rouben Mamoulian's *Love Me Tonight* the members of a hunt decide to ride quietly home to avoid waking the sleeping deer; their ride is filmed in slow-motion to create a comic depiction of noiseless movement. Today slow-motion footage often functions to suggest that the action takes place in a dream or fantasy; or to express a lyrical quality; or to convey enormous power, as in a martial-arts film. Slow-motion is also increasingly used for emphasis, becoming a way of dwelling on a moment of spectacle or high drama. The slow-motion scene of violence has become a cliché of the modern cinema.

To enhance expressive effects, filmmakers can change the speed of motion in the course of a shot. In *Die Hard* a fireball bursts up an elevator shaft toward the camera. During filming, the fire at the bottom of the shaft was filmed at 100 fps, slowing down its progress, and then shot at faster speeds as it erupted upward, giving the impression of an explosive acceleration. For *Bram Stoker's Dracula,* director Francis Ford Coppola wanted his vampire to glide toward his prey with supernatural suddenness. Cinematographer Michael Ballhaus used a computer program to control the shutter and the speed of filming, allowing smooth and instantaneous changes from 24 fps to 8 fps and back again.

Extreme forms of fast- and slow-motion alter the speed of the depicted material even more radically. *Time-lapse* cinematography permits us to see the sun set in seconds or a flower sprout, bud, and bloom in a minute. For this a very low shooting speed is required—perhaps one frame per minute, hour, or even day. For *high-speed* cinematography, which may seek to record a bullet shattering glass, the camera may expose hundreds, even thousands of frames per second. Most cameras can be used for time-lapse shooting, but high-speed cinematography requires specially designed cameras.

After filming, the filmmaker can still control the speed of movement on the screen through various laboratory procedures. The most common means used is the optical printer (see Fig. 1.5). This device rephotographs a film, copying all or part of each original frame onto another reel of film. Assuming a constant speed of projection, the filmmaker can use the optical printer to skip frames (accelerating the action when projected), reprint a frame at desired intervals (slowing the action by *stretch printing*), stop the action (repeating a frame over and over, to freeze the projected image for seconds or minutes), or reverse the action. Nowadays some silent films are stretch-printed with every other frame repeated, so that they may run more smoothly at sound speed. We are familiar with freeze-framing, slow-motion, and reverse-motion printing effects from the "instant replays" of sports films and investigative documentaries. Many experimental films have made striking use of the optical printer's possibilities, such as Ken Jacobs' *Tom Tom the Piper's Son,* which explores the images of an early silent film by enlarging portions of its shots.

Fig. 7.8

Fig. 7.9

Fig. 7.10

Fig. 7.11

■ PERSPECTIVE RELATIONS

You are standing on railroad tracks, looking toward the horizon. The tracks not only recede but also seem to meet at the horizon. You glance at the trees and buildings along the tracks. They diminish by a simple, systematic rule: the closer objects look larger, the farther objects look smaller—even if they are actually of uniform size. The optical system of your eye, registering light rays reflected from the scene, supplies a host of information about scale, depth, and spatial relations among parts of the scene. Such relations are called *perspective* relations.

The lens of a photographic camera does roughly what your eye does. It gathers light from the scene and transmits that light onto the flat surface of the film to form an image that represents size, depth, and other dimensions of the scene. One difference between the eye and the camera, though, is that photographic lenses may be changed and each type of lens will render perspective relations in different ways. If two different lenses photograph the same scene, the perspective relations in the resulting images could be drastically different. A wide-angle lens could exaggerate the depth you see down the track or could make the trees and buildings seem to bulge; a telephoto lens could drastically reduce the depth, making the trees seem very close together and nearly the same size.

The lens: Focal length. Control of perspective relations in the image is obviously very important to the filmmaker. The chief variable in the process is the *focal length* of the lens. In technical terms the focal length is the distance from the center of the lens to the point where light rays converge to a point of focus on the film. The focal length of the lens can affect perspective relations in several ways.

The focal length alters the perceived magnification, depth, and scale of things in the image. We usually distinguish three sorts of lenses on the basis of their effects on perspective:

1. The *short-focal-length (wide-angle) lens.* In 35mm-gauge cinematography, a lens of less than 35mm in focal length is considered a "wide-angle" lens. Such lenses tend to distort straight lines lying near the edges of the frame, bulging them outward. Note the distortion in two frames from a shot in Nicholas Roeg's *Don't Look Now* (Figs. 7.8, 7.9). As the camera swivels to follow the character, the lens makes a street lamp he passes appear to lean rightward, then leftward. When a wide-angle lens is used for a medium shot or close-up, the distortion of shape may become very evident. (See Fig. 7.10, from Mikhail Kalatozov's *Cranes Are Flying.*)

The lens of short focal length has the property of exaggerating depth. In Figure 7.11, from *The Little Foxes,* the lens makes the characters seem farther from each other than we would expect in so relatively small a locale. Because distances between foreground and background seem greater, the wide-angle lens also makes figures moving to or from the camera seem to cover ground more rapidly.

2. *The middle-focal-length ("normal") lens.* A lens of medium focal length is 35 to 50mm. This "normal" lens seeks to avoid noticeable perspective distortion. With a normal lens, horizontal and vertical lines are rendered

Fig. 7.12

Fig. 7.13

as straight and perpendicular. (Compare the bulging effect of the wide-angle lens.) Parallel lines should recede to distant vanishing points, as in our railroad-tracks example. Foreground and background should seem neither stretched apart (as with the wide-angle lens) nor squashed together (as with the telephoto lens). Figure 7.12, from *His Girl Friday*, is a shot made with the normal lens; contrast the sense of distance among the figures achieved in Figure 7.11.

3. *The long-focal-length (telephoto) lens.* Whereas wide-angle lenses distort space laterally, longer lenses flatten the space along the camera axis. Cues for depth and volume are reduced. The planes seem squashed together, much as when you look through a telescope or binoculars. In Figure 7.13, from Chen Kaige's *Life on a String*, the long lens pushes the crowd members almost to the same plane. It also makes the rapids behind the men virtually a two-dimensional backdrop.

Today, the focal length of such lenses typically ranges from around 75 to 250mm or more. They are commonly used in the filming or televising of sports events, since they allow the cinematographer to magnify action at a distance. (For this reason, long lenses are also called "telephoto" lenses.) In a baseball game there will invariably be shots taken from almost directly behind the umpire. You have probably noticed that such shots make catcher, batter, and pitcher look unnaturally close to one another. What a very long lens can do to space is dramatically illustrated throughout Godfrey Reggio's *Koyaanisqatsi*. In one sequence, an airport is filmed from a great distance, and the long lens makes it appear that a plane is landing on a crowded highway (Fig. 7.14).

Fig. 7.14

Akira Kurosawa relies heavily on long lenses, using them for all shot scales. In Figure 7.15, a medium shot from *Seven Samurai*, the figures seem very close together and almost the same size, even though the two facing front are actually quite far behind the third.

A long-focal-length lens also affects subject movement. Its tendency to flatten depth makes a figure moving toward the camera take more time to cover what seems to be a small distance. The clichéd "running-in-place" shots in *The Graduate* and other films of the 1960s and 1970s were produced by lenses of very long focal length. In Allen Fong's *Father and Son,* an extreme telephoto shot shows the two main characters walking toward the camera. Between the two stages of the shot illustrated here (Figs. 7.16, 7.17), they take sixteen steps toward us, but they seem only slightly closer in the later frame.

Fig. 7.15

Fig. 7.16   **Fig. 7.17**

Lens length can distinctly affect the spectator's experience. For example, expressive qualities can be suggested by lenses which distort objects or characters. We tend to see the man in Figure 7.18 (from Ilya Trauberg's *China Express*) as looming, even aggressive. Moreover, choice of the lens can make a character or object blend into the setting (Fig. 7.17) or stand out in sharp relief (Fig. 7.18). Filmmakers may exploit the flattening effects of the long-focal-length lens to create solid masses of space (Fig. 7.19, from Marco Ferreri's *The Last Woman*), as in an abstract painting.

A director can use lens length to surprise us, as Kurosawa does in *Red Beard*. When the mad patient comes into the intern's room, a long-focal-length lens filming from behind him initially makes her seem to be quite close to him (Fig. 7.20). But a cut to a more perpendicular angle shows that the patient and the intern are actually several feet apart, and that he is not yet in danger (Fig. 7.21).

Fig. 7.18   **Fig. 7.19**

Fig. 7.20   **Fig. 7.21**

There is one sort of lens that offers the director a chance to manipulate focal length and to transform perspective relations during a single shot. A *zoom lens* is optically designed to permit the continuous varying of focal length. Originally designed for aerial and reconnaissance photography, zoom lenses gradually became a standard tool for newsreel filming. It was not, however, the general practice to zoom during shooting. The camera operator varied the focal length as desired and then started filming. In the late 1950s, however, the increased portability of cameras led to a trend toward zooming while filming.

Fig. 7.22

Now the zoom lens is sometimes used to substitute for moving the camera forward or backward. Onscreen, the zoom shot magnifies or demagnifies the objects filmed, excluding or including surrounding space. In the opening of Francis Ford Coppola's *The Conversation,* a long zoom-in arouses considerable uncertainty about its target (Figs. 7.22, 7.23). A zoom-out ends *Barravento,* as the protagonist leaves his village and the film shows him poised before a looming, uncertain future (Figs. 7.24, 7.25).

Although the zoom shot presents a mobile framing, it is not a genuine movement of the camera. During a zoom, the camera remains stationary and the lens simply increases or decreases its focal length. Nevertheless, the zoom can produce interesting and peculiar transformations of scale and depth, as we shall see when we examine Michael Snow's *Wavelength.*

The impact that focal length can have on the image's perspective qualities is dramatically illustrated in Ernie Gehr's abstract experimental film *Serene Velocity.* The scene is an empty corridor. Gehr shot the film with a zoom lens, but he did not zoom while filming the shot. Instead, the zoom permitted him to change the lens's focal length between takes. Gehr explains that he

Fig. 7.23

divided the mm range of the zoom lens in half and starting from the middle I recorded changes in mm positions. . . . The camera was not moved at all. The zoom lens was not moved during recording either. Each frame was recorded individually as a still. Four frames to each position. To give an example: I shot the first four frames at 50mm. The next four frames I shot at 55mm. And then, for a certain duration, approximately 60 feet, I went back and forth, four frames at 50mm, four frames at 55mm; four frames at 50mm, four frames at 55mm; etc. . . . for about 60 feet. Then I went to 45–60 [mm] and did the same for about 60 feet. Then to 40–65, and so on.

Fig. 7.24

Fig. 7.25

Fig. 7.26

Fig. 7.27

Fig. 7.28

Fig. 7.29

The resulting film presents an image whose perspective relations pulsate rhythmically—first with little difference in size and scale, but gradually with a greater tension between a telephoto image and a wide-angle one (see Figs. 7.26, 7.27). In a sense *Serene Velocity* takes as its subject the effect of focal length on perspective.

The lens: Depth of field and focus. Focal length not only affects how shape and scale are magnified or distorted. It also affects the lens's *depth of field*. Depth of field is the range of distances before the lens within which objects can be photographed in sharp *focus*. A lens with a depth of field of ten feet to infinity will render any object in that range clearly, but the sharpness of the image will decrease when the object moves closer to the lens (say, to four feet). All other things being equal, a short-focal-length (wide-angle) lens has a relatively greater depth of field than does a long-focal-length (telephoto) lens.

Depth of field should not be confused with the concept of deep space, used in Chapter 6. "Deep space" is a term for the way the filmmaker has staged the action on several different planes, *regardless of whether or not all of these planes are in focus.* In the case of *Our Hospitality* those planes usually are in sharp focus, but in other films not every plane of deep space is in focus. Consider Figure 7.28. In this shot from *The Crime of M. Lange,* the action is staged in three planes of deep space: Valentine in the foreground, Batala going out the door, and the concierge passing in the distance. But the shot does not display great depth of field. The foreground plane (Valentine) is markedly out of focus, the middle ground (Batala) is slightly out of focus, and the distant plane (the concierge) is in sharp focus. Deep space is a property of mise-en-scene, depending on how the image is composed. Depth of field is a property of the photographic lens, affecting what planes of the image are in focus.

If depth of field controls perspective relations by determining what planes will be in focus, what choices are open to the filmmaker? He or she may opt for what is usually called selective focus—choosing to focus on only one plane and letting the other planes blur. This is what Renoir does in the *M. Lange* instance.

Before 1940 it was common Hollywood practice to shoot close-ups in selective focus, making the faces sharp and the foreground and background planes hazy. (See Fig. 7.29, in which Harpo Marx burns the candle at both ends in *Horse Feathers.*) Sometimes objects near the camera were thrown out of focus so that the sharper middle ground would claim the viewer's attention. The same stylistic choice is common today, especially when long-focal-length lenses are used. In Figure 7.30, from *The Godfather,* the telephoto lens allows only Michael's face to be in focus; both the foreground plane (his hand with the gun) and the background area lie outside the depth of field. Selective focus typically draws the viewer's attention to the main character or object [Fig. 7.31, from Agnès Varda's *Vagabonde* (originally titled *Sans toi ni loi*)]. The technique can be used for a more abstract compositional effect as well, as in Leos Carax's *Boy Meets Girl* (Fig. 7.32).

In Hollywood during the 1940s, partly due to the influence of *Citizen Kane,* Hollywood filmmakers began using faster film, shorter-focal-length

Fig. 7.30

Fig. 7.31

Fig. 7.32

lenses, and more intense lighting to yield a greater depth of field. The contract-signing scene from *Citizen Kane* (Fig. 7.33) offers a famous example: From one plane near the lens (Bernstein's head) through several planes in the middle ground to the wall far in the distance, everything is in sharp focus. This practice came to be called *deep focus*.

Deep-focus cinematography became a major stylistic option throughout the 1940s and 1950s. Figure 7.34, from Samuel Fuller's *Underworld USA*, illustrates a typical usage. The technique was even imitated in animated cartoons. (See Color Plate 38, from Chuck Jones's *One Froggy Evening*.) During the 1970s deep-focus cinematography was revived in Steven Spielberg's work, notably *Jaws* and *Close Encounters of the Third Kind*, and in the films of Brian De Palma (Fig. 7.35, from *Blow-Out*).

Fig. 7.33

Since the lens may be refocused at various points, the filmmaker may also adjust perspective relations while filming by *racking focus*, or *pulling focus*. A shot may begin on an object close to the lens and rack-focus so that something in the distance springs into crisp focus. Alternatively, the focus can rack from background to foreground, as in Color Plates 55–56, from Bernardo Bertolucci's *Last Tango in Paris*.

Special effects. The image's perspective relations may also be created by means of certain "special effects." We have already seen (p. 17) that the filmmaker can create setting by use of models and miniatures. The filmmaker

Fig. 7.34

Fig. 7.35

Fig. 7.36

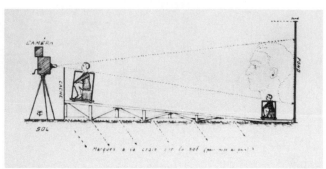

Fig. 7.37

Fig. 7.38

can also use a *glass shot.* Here portions of the setting are painted onto a pane of glass and the camera shoots through it to film action supposedly occurring in the painted setting. Glass shots were principally used in the silent era.

Alternatively, separately photographed planes of action may be combined on the same strip of film to create the illusion that the two planes are adjacent. The simplest way to do this is through *superimposition.* Either by double exposure in the camera or in laboratory printing, one image is laid over another. Méliès, whom we have already studied as an early master of mise-en-scene, was well aware of this device. Superimposition allowed him to present the illusion of *The Man with the Rubber Head,* in which Méliès inflates the disembodied head of Méliès. Figures 7.36 and 7.37 show that the trick depended on double exposure and Méliès in a cart rolling toward the camera. In his time and since, filmmakers most commonly employed double exposure to depict ghosts or to display characters' thoughts.

More complex techniques for combining strips of film to create a single shot are usually called *process,* or *composite, shots.* These techniques can be divided into *projection* process work and *matte* process work.

In projection process work, the filmmaker projects footage of a setting onto a screen, then films actors performing in front of the screen. Classical Hollywood filmmaking began this process in the late 1920s, as a way to avoid taking cast and crew on location. The Hollywood technique involved placing the actors against a translucent screen and projecting a film of the setting from behind the screen. The whole ensemble could then be filmed from the front. (See Fig. 7.38, from *The Sands of Iwo Jima.*)

Rear projection, as this system was known, is still widely used, but it does not create very convincing depth cues. Foreground and background tend to look starkly separate, partly because of the absence of cast shadows from foreground to background, partly because all background planes tend to seem equally diffuse. (See Color Plate 57, from Hitchcock's *Vertigo.*)

Front projection, which came into use in the late 1960s, projects the setting onto a two-way mirror, angled to throw the image onto a high-reflectance screen. The camera photographs the actors against the screen by shooting through the mirror (Fig. 7.39). The results of front projection can be

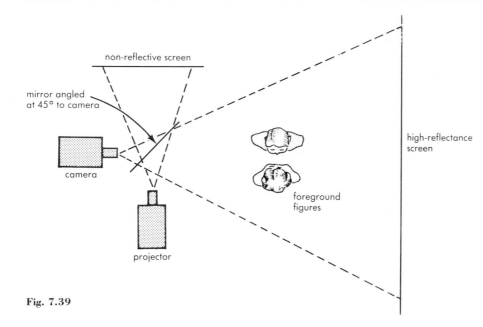

Fig. 7.39

clearly seen in the "Dawn of Man" sequence of *2001: A Space Odyssey*, the first film to use front projection extensively. (At one moment, a saber-toothed tiger's eyes glow, reflecting the projector's light.) Because of the sharp focus of the projected footage, front projection blends foreground and background planes fairly smoothly. The nonrealistic possibilities of front projection have been recently explored by Hans-Jürgen Syberberg. In his film of Wagner's opera *Parsifal* front projection conjures up colossal, phantasmagoric land-scapes (Color Plate 58).

Composite filming can also be accomplished by matte work. A *matte* is a portion of the setting photographed on a strip of film, usually with a part of the frame empty. Through laboratory printing, the matte is joined with another strip of film containing the actors. One sort of matte involves a painting of the desired areas of setting, which is then filmed. This footage is combined with footage of action, segregated in the blank portions of the painted scenery. In this way, a matte can create an entire imaginary setting for the film (Figs. 7.40, 7.41, showing the live action and the finished frame

Fig. 7.40   **Fig. 7.41**

from *Her Jungle Love*). Stationary mattes of this sort have made glass shots virtually obsolete and are so widely used in commercial cinema that the matte painter has become a mainstay of production. Figure 7.42 shows a shot from *Blade Runner,* which uses a matte painting of the sky in the background.

With a matte painting, however, the actor cannot move into the painted portions of the frame without seeming to disappear. To solve this problem, the filmmaker can use a *traveling matte.* Here the actor is photographed against a blank, usually blue, background. In laboratory printing, the moving outline of the actor is "cut out" of footage of the desired background. After further lab work, the shot of the actor is "jigsawed" into the moving gap in the background footage. It is traveling mattes that present shots of Superman's flight or of spaceships hurtling through space. In Figure 7.43, a production still from *2001,* the spacecraft visible through the porthole is a model that has been matted into a shot of the astronaut in the control cabin. In Figure 6.50 (p. 184), the robot is combined with live action in the background by means of a traveling matte. The animated figures in our shot from *Who Framed Roger Rabbit?* (Color Plate 20) were matted into live-action footage shot separately.

You can often detect traveling mattes on the screen, because even the most expensive and carefully executed special effects do not always join the

Fig. 7.42

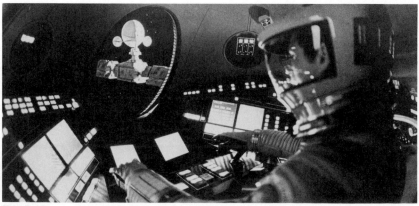

Fig. 7.43

various portions of the shot perfectly. A dark contour, called a *matte line*, may shimmer around the moving sections. In *The Empire Strikes Back*, matte lines are particularly evident during the battle with the Imperial Walkers.

Although traveling mattes are virtually a necessity in science-fiction and fantasy films, they are commonly used in all genres of mainstream cinema. Usually they function to create a realistic-looking locale or situation. But they can also generate an abstract, deliberately unrealistic image. In *Rumble Fish*, a black-and-white film, Francis Ford Coppola uses traveling mattes to color the fish in an aquarium (Color Plate 59).

For many films, different types of special effects will be combined. Our earlier illustration from *Blade Runner* (Fig. 7.42) includes a large set with actors, front projection of the pyramids appearing outside the window, matted details of the foreground columns, a matte painting of the sky behind, and an animated sun. A single shot of a science-fiction film might animate miniatures or models through stop-action, convey their movements by a traveling matte, and add animated ray bursts in superimposition while a matte painting supplies a background. For the train crash in *The Fugitive*, both front and rear projection were used simultaneously within certain shots.

You may have noticed that glass shots, superimpositions, projection process work, and matte work all straddle two general bodies of film techniques. These special effects all require arrangement of the material before the camera, so to some extent they are aspects of mise-en-scene. But since they also require control of photographic choices (e.g., refilming, laboratory adjustments) and affect perspective relations, these special effects involve cinematography as well. We have considered them here because, unlike effects employing models and miniatures, these illusions are created through specifically photographic tricks. Their photographic base is hinted at in Hollywood terminology, which describes them as "optical effects."

With the rise of computer-generated effects, the fusion of mise-en-scene and cinematography becomes even more seamless. Digital compositing allows the filmmaker to shoot some action with performers and then add backgrounds, shadows, or movement that would previously have required photographed mattes, multiple exposures, or optical printing. In *Speed*, the audience sees a city bus leap a broken freeway. The stunt was performed on a ramp designed for the jump, and the highway background was "drawn" digitally—the computer equivalent of a matte painting. Such digital effects have proven as convincing as traditional optical tricks, and they are much easier to manipulate.

Like other film techniques, photographic manipulations of the shot are not ends in themselves. They function within the overall context of the film. Specific treatments of tonalities, speed of motion, or perspective should be judged less on criteria of "realism" than on criteria of function. For instance, many Hollywood filmmakers strive to make their rear-projection shots unnoticeable. But in Jean-Marie Straub and Danièle Huillet's *The Chronicle of Anna Magdalena Bach*, the perspective relations are yanked out of kilter by an inconsistent rear projection (Fig. 7.44). Bach stands playing a harpsichord, shot straight-on. Yet the building behind him is seen from a low angle. Since the film's other shots have been filmed on location in correct perspective,

Fig. 7.44

Fig. 7.45

this blatantly artificial rear projection calls our attention to the visual style of the entire film.

Similarly, Figure 7.45, a shot from *Daisies,* looks unrealistic, unless we posit the man as being about two feet long. But Chytilová has used setting, character position, and deep focus to make a comic point about the two women's treatment of men. The filmmaker chooses not only how to register light and movement photographically but also how those photographic qualities will function within the overall formal system of the film. But the fact that the man seems to lie directly on top of the screen against which the women are leaning depends upon another factor as well: the precise *framing* of the image.

FRAMING

It may seem odd to talk of something as elusive as the border of the image, since it may seem a sheerly negative feature, a simple edge or break. (After all, literary critics do not talk of the margins of the pages in *Moby Dick.*) But, in a film, the frame is not simply a neutral border; it produces a *certain vantage point* onto the material within the image. In cinema the frame is important because it actively *defines* the image for us.

Fig. 7.46

If proof were required of the power of framing, we need only turn to the first major filmmaker in history, Louis Lumière. An inventor and business-man, Lumière and his brother Auguste devised one of the first practical cinema cameras (Fig. 7.46). The Lumière camera, the most flexible of its day, also doubled as a projector. Whereas the bulky American camera in-vented by W. K. L. Dickson was about the size of an office desk (Fig. 7.47), the Lumière camera weighed only 12 pounds and was small and portable. As a result of its lightness, the Lumière camera could be taken outside and could be simply and quickly set up. Louis Lumière's earliest films presented simple events—workers leaving his father's factory, a game of cards, a family meal. But even at so early a stage of film history, Lumière was able to use framing to transform everyday reality into cinematic events.

Fig. 7.47

Consider one of the most famous Lumière films, *The Arrival of a Train at La Ciotat Station* (1895). Had Lumière followed theatrical practice, he might have framed the shot by setting the camera perpendicular to the platform, letting the train enter the frame from one side, broadside to the spectator. Instead, Lumière positioned the camera at an oblique angle. The result is a dynamic composition, with the train arriving on a diagonal (Fig. 7.48). If the scene had been shot perpendicularly, we would have seen only a string of passengers' backs climbing aboard. Here, however, Lumière's oblique angle brings out many aspects of the passengers' bodies and several planes of action. We see some figures in the foreground, some in the distance. Simple as it is, this single-shot film, less than a minute long, aptly illustrates how choosing a position for the camera makes a drastic difference in the framing of the image and how we perceive the filmed event.

Consider another Lumière short, *Baby's Meal* (1895) (Fig. 7.49). Lu-mière selected a camera position that would emphasize certain aspects of the

Fig. 7.48

event. A long shot would have situated the family in its garden, but Lumière frames the figures at a medium distance, which downplays the setting but emphasizes the family's gestures and facial expressions. The frame's control of the scale of the event has also controlled our understanding of the event itself.

Framing can powerfully affect the image by means of (1) the size and shape of the frame; (2) the way the frame defines onscreen and offscreen space; (3) the way framing controls the distance, angle, and height of a vantage point onto the image; and (4) the way framing can move in relation to the mise-en-scene.

Fig. 7.49

■ FRAME DIMENSIONS AND SHAPE

We are so accustomed to the frame as a rectangle that we should remember that it need not be one. In painting and photography, of course, images have frames of various sizes and shapes: narrow rectangles, ovals, vertical panels, even triangles and parallelograms. In cinema the choice has been more limited.

The ratio of frame width to frame height is called the *aspect ratio*. The rough dimensions of the ratio were set quite early in the history of cinema by Edison, Dickson, Lumière, and other inventors. The film frame was to be rectangular, its proportion approximately three to two, yielding an aspect ratio of 1.33:1. Nonetheless, in the silent period, some filmmakers felt that this standard was too limiting. Abel Gance shot and projected sequences of *Napoleon* (1927) in a format he called "triptychs." This was a widescreen effect composed of three normal frames side by side. Gance sometimes used the effect to show a single huge expanse, sometimes to put three distinct images side by side (Fig. 7.50). In contrast, the Soviet director Sergei Eisenstein argued for a square frame, which would make compositions along horizontal, vertical, and diagonal directions equally feasible.

The coming of sound in the late 1920s altered the frame somewhat. Adding the sound track to the film strip required adjusting either the shape or the size of the image. At first, some films were printed in virtually a square format, usually about 1.17:1. (See Fig. 7.51, from *Public Enemy*.) But in the early 1930s, the Hollywood Academy of Motion Picture Arts and Sciences established the so-called *Academy ratio* of 1.33:1. (Strictly speaking, on most

Fig. 7.50

prints this works out to 1.37:1, but 1.33:1 is still referred to as the standard.) The Academy ratio was standardized throughout the world until the mid-1950s (see Fig. 7.52, from Renoir's *The Rules of the Game*). Outside North America and Western Europe, many films are still shot in this format. Standard television screens also are in the 1.33:1 ratio.

Since the mid-1950s, a variety of *widescreen* ratios have dominated 35mm filmmaking. The most common format in North America today is that of 1.85:1 (Fig. 7.55, from *Aliens*). The 1.66:1 ratio (Fig. 7.53, from *Lancelot du Lac*) is more frequently used in Europe than in North America, although Steven Spielberg intended *E.T.: The Extraterrestrial* to be shown in this format. A less common ratio, also widely used in European films, is 1.75:1 (Fig. 7.54, from *Last Tango in Paris*). A 2.35:1 ratio (Fig. 7.57, from King Hu's *The Valiant Ones*) was standardized by the CinemaScope anamorphic process during the 1950s. (In contemporary practice, the 2.35:1 ratio is usually projected at 2.40:1.) The 2.2:1 ratio is currently used for 70mm presentation (Fig. 7.56, from *Ghostbusters*), although many projectionists prefer to present 70mm at 2:1.

COMMON ASPECT RATIOS OF 35mm FILM

1.17:1

Fig. 7.51

1.33 (1.37):1

Fig. 7.52

1.66:1

Fig. 7.53

1.75:1

Fig. 7.54

1.85:1

Fig. 7.55

2.2:1
(70mm)

Fig. 7.56

2.35:1
(35mm anamorphic)

Fig. 7.57

The simplest way to create a widescreen image is by masking it at some stage in production or exhibition. The frame from Jean-Pierre Melville's *Le Samourai* (Fig. 7.58) was masked during filming or printing. This masking is usually called a *hard matte*.

Alternatively, many contemporary films are shot "full-frame" (that is, between 1.33:1 and 1.17:1) in the expectation that they will be masked when the film is shown. Sometimes this results in lights or sound equipment being visible in the full-frame image. In Figure 7.59, from Martin Scorsese's *Raging Bull*, you can clearly see the microphone bobbing down into the shot. This would not be seen in the theater, where the top and bottom of the frame would be masked by the aperture plate in the projector. The colored lines in our illustration show a projection framing at 1.85:1.

Another way to create a widescreen image is by using an *anamorphic* process. Here a special lens "squeezes" the image horizontally, either during filming or in printing. A comparable lens is necessary to unsqueeze the image during projection. Figure 7.60, from Jean-Luc Godard's *Made in USA,* shows the image on the 35mm film strip, while Figure 7.61 shows the image as projected on the screen. The aspect ratio is 2.35:1, that of CinemaScope

Fig. 7.58

Fig. 7.59

Fig. 7.60

Fig. 7.61

Fig. 7.62

Fig. 7.63

Fig. 7.64

previously and that of anamorphic processes today. Godard's film was photographed in Techniscope, a popular European process; the most frequently used anamorphic process in the United States today is Panavision.

Widescreen cinema, either masked or anamorphic, has significant visual effects. The screen becomes a band or strip, emphasizing horizontal compositions. The format was initially associated with genres of spectacle—Westerns, travelogues, musicals, historical epics—in which sweeping settings were important. But directors quickly learned that widescreen has value for more intimate subjects, too. Figure 7.62, from Kurosawa's *Red Beard*, shows how an anamorphic process (Tohoscope, the Japanese equivalent of CinemaScope) can be used to create significant foreground and background areas in a confined setting.

Fig. 7.65

In some widescreen compositions, the director will draw the audience's attention to only one area of the image. A common solution is to put the important information slightly off center (Fig. 7.63, from Jean-Pierre Melville's *Armée des Ombres*), or even sharply off center (Fig. 7.64, from John McTiernan's *Die Hard*). Or the director may use the widescreen format to multiply points of interest. Many scenes in Chantal Akerman's *Golden Eighties* fill the frame with bustle and movement. Our eye shuttles around the frame according to who is speaking, who is facing us, and who responds to the speaker (Fig. 7.65). Similarly, though less hectically, the shipboard sequences in Michelangelo Antonioni's *L'Avventura* pepper the frame with several points of interest (Fig. 7.66).

Fig. 7.66

On occasion, widescreen processes have attempted to "surround" view-

Fig. 7.67

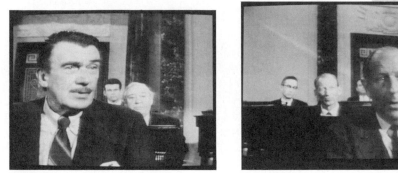

Fig. 7.68   Fig. 7.69

Fig. 7.70

Fig. 7.71

ers by activating peripheral vision. Cinerama, introduced commercially in 1952, presents us with the rectangular screen slightly curved on the edges, a tactic that increases our sense of immersion in the image. Originally a process involving three separate frames projected side by side, Cinerama later became another amamorphic process, with the image squeezed onto a single frame.

More recently, a process called Omnimax, related to the Imax format (Fig. 1.12, p. 8) has been featured in museums and other special venues. In a specially built auditorium, the audience sits in reclining seats and faces up toward a dome-shaped screen. The screen covers the entire field of vision and gives the image a greater sense of depth. Films made for such presentations are shot with anamorphic lenses that compress the image from top to bottom as well as from side to side.

A comparable approach to engaging peripheral vision comes with experiments in 360° cinema (seen at various world's fairs and international expositions, as well as at Disneyland and Disney World). In wraparound cinema ratios, the frame runs in a complete circle around the audience.

As we noted in Chapter 1 (p. 32), widescreen films shown in the theater may differ markedly from what we see on television. Most video versions utilize a "pan-and-scan" process, which picks out of the wide-film image a portion that fills the roughly 1.33:1 format of the television screen. Thus in *Advise and Consent*, a single shot in the original (Fig. 7.67) becomes two shots in the video version (Figs. 7.68, 7.69). An even more drastic solution is to leave anamorphic images still partly "squeezed" in the transfer to video, a decision which yields elongated, skinny people.

To avoid such problems, widescreen films are often shot with eventual television presentation in mind. Cinematographers' camera viewfinders are marked with rectangles representing alternative widescreen ratios. Many cinematographers try to compose their shots for both widescreen and video. A simple solution is to leave empty space in the widescreen frame that can be eliminated in the transfer to the squarer video format. (Compare Figs. 7.70 and 7.71, from a 35mm print and a VHS videocassette of *Aliens*.)

SAME FILM, DIFFERENT RATIOS

Today it is normal for 35mm films to be shot in one aspect ratio but shown in others. For example, *Speed* was filmed in anamorphic 35mm, and some prints were exhibited in the corresponding 2.35:1 ratio. 70mm prints were also made from the 35mm negative, and here the aspect ratio was 2.2:1.

The most common situation occurs when an image is filmed "full-frame" but projected at 1.85:1 by means of masking plates in the projector. Filmmakers record the Academy-ratio image so that prints for television broadcast and videocassette may be drawn from a squarer image. Sometimes, however, a film will be released on laserdisc video in a "letterbox" format which simulates the wider image shown in the theater.

Compare versions of a shot in Robert Zemeckis's *Back to the Future*. Figure 7.72 is from the 35mm full-frame image, which would have been masked to a 1.85:1 ratio during projection. The VHS videocassette (Fig. 7.73) preserves much of the full-frame ratio. The widescreen laserdisc version (Fig. 7.74) uses a hard matte to mask the image in a way similar to a theatrical presentation.

If a film is originally shot in a wider format, such as 1.85:1 or 2.35:1, video presentation poses a problem. Some video versions are presented in letterbox format, which preserves at least some of the widescreen proportions. (Results vary considerably here: Much letterboxing is not as wide as the original frame.) Most video versions, however, utilize the "pan-and-scan" technique to frame only portions of the wide image.

In addition, aspect ratios may change when prints are in different gauges. 35mm anamorphic frames (2.35:1 ratio) lose some picture area at the top and bottom when transferred to 16mm anamorphic (Figs. 7.62 and 7.67 are from 16mm anamorphic prints).

The variation in screen proportions sometimes raises questons about which version of a film is the original. Few filmmakers have been as insistent as Hans-Jürgen Syberberg, whose *Parsifal* (Color Plate 58) begins with an admonition: "This film was shot on Academy format (aperture gate 1:1.33) and may not be shown on widescreen."

Fig. 7.72

Fig. 7.73

Fig. 7.74

Fig. 7.75

Fig. 7.76

Fig. 7.77

Fig. 7.78

Fig. 7.79

The rectangular frame, while by far the most common, has not prevented filmmakers from experimenting with other frame shapes. This has usually been done by attaching *masks* over either the camera's or the printer's lens to block the passage of light. Masks were quite common in the silent cinema. A moving circular mask that opens to reveal or closes to conceal a scene is called an *iris*. In *La Roue*, Gance employed a variety of circular and oval masks (Fig. 7.75). In Figure 7.76, a shot from Griffith's *Intolerance*, most of the frame is boldly blocked out to leave only a thin vertical slice, emphasizing the soldier's fall from the rampart. A number of directors in the sound cinema have revived the use of irises and masks. In *The Magnificent Ambersons* (Fig. 7.77), Orson Welles uses an iris to close a scene; the old-fashioned device adds a nostalgic note to the sequence.

Finally, we should mention experiments with *multiple-frame* imagery, often called *split-screen* imagery. In this process, two or more different images, each with its own frame dimensions and shape, appear within the larger frame. From the early cinema onward, this device has been used to present scenes of telephone conversations; Figure 7.78, from Philips Smalley's 1913 *Suspense*, provides an example. The device was revived for phone conversations in *Bye Bye Birdie* and other 1960s widescreen comedies. Multiple-frame imagery is also useful for building suspense, as Brian De Palma has shown in such films as *Sisters*. We gain a godlike omniscience as we watch two or more actions at exactly the same moment. In Robert Aldrich's *Twilight's Last Gleaming*, the moments before guided missiles are about to be launched are made more tense by splitting the frame into several images and giving us an unrestricted range of knowledge. Some portions of the frame show the desperate men who have commandeered a missile silo, while other portions show an attack launched on the silo by officials in Washington (Fig. 7.79).

As usual, the filmmaker's choice of screen format can be an important factor in shaping the viewer's experience. Frame size and shape can guide the spectator's attention. It can be concentrated through compositional patterns or masking, or it can be dispersed by use of various points of interest or sound cues. The same possibilities exist with multiple-frame imagery, which must be carefully coordinated either to focus the viewer's notice or to send it ricocheting from one image to another.

■ ONSCREEN AND OFFSCREEN SPACE

Whatever its shape, the frame makes the image finite. The film image is bounded, limited. From an implicitly continuous world, the frame selects a slice to show us. Even in those early films so heavily dependent on theater, the characters enter the image *from* somewhere and go off *to* another area—*offscreen space*. Even in an abstract film, we cannot resist the sense that the shapes and patterns that burst into the frame come from somewhere. If the camera leaves an object or person and moves elsewhere, we will assume that the object or person is still there, outside the frame.

Noël Burch has pointed out six zones of offscreen space: the space beyond each of the four edges of the frame, the space behind the set, and the space behind the camera. It is worth considering how many ways a filmmaker can imply the presence of things in these zones of offscreen space. A character can direct looks or gestures at something offscreen. As we shall see in Chapter 9, sound can offer potent clues about offscreen space. And, of course, something from offscreen can protrude partly into the frame. Virtually any film could be cited for examples of all these possibilities, but attractive instances are offered by films that utilize offscreen space for surprise effects.

In William Wyler's *Jezebel* the heroine, Julie, greets some friends in medium shot (Fig. 7.80) when suddenly a huge fist holding a glass appears in the center foreground (Fig. 7.81). Julie looks off at its owner and comes forward, the camera retreating slightly to frame her with the man who had toasted her (Figs. 7.82, 7.83). The intrusion of the hand abruptly signals us to the man's presence; Julie's glance, the camera movement, and the sound track confirm our new awareness of the total space. The director has used the selective powers of the frame to exclude something of great importance and then introduce it with startling effect.

More systematically, D. W. Griffith's *Musketeers of Pig Alley* makes use of sudden intrusions into the frame as a motif developing across the whole film. When a gangster is trying to slip a drug into the heroine's drink, we are not aware that the Snapper Kid has entered the room until a plume of his cigarette smoke wafts into the frame (Fig. 7.84). At the film's end, when the Snapper Kid receives a payoff, a mysterious hand thrusts into the frame to

Fig. 7.80

Fig. 7.81

Fig. 7.82

Fig. 7.83

Fig. 7.84

Fig. 7.85

Fig. 7.86

Fig. 7.87

Fig. 7.88

Fig. 7.89

offer him money (Fig. 7.85). Griffith has exploited the surprise latent in our sudden awareness that figures are offscreen.

The use of the fifth zone of offscreen space, that behind the set, is of course common; characters go out a door and are now concealed by a wall or a staircase. Somewhat rarer is the use of a sixth zone—the offscreen space behind and near the camera. One famous example occurs in Jean Renoir's *Rules of the Game,* in the context of a shot in which characters virtually explode into the frame from offscreen space. André and Robert are embroiled in a fistfight; during the melee, André is flung back onto and over a divan (Fig. 7.86). Then magazines start flying at him from over the top of the frame, from "behind us," as it were (Fig. 7.87). In such ways the director can turn the necessary limitations of the frame edge to advantage.

■ ANGLE, LEVEL, HEIGHT, AND DISTANCE OF FRAMING

The frame implies not only space outside itself but also a position from which the material in the image is viewed. Most often, of course, such a position is that of the camera filming the event, but this need not always be true. In an animated film, the position implied by the drawn frames is not necessarily the same position that the camera occupies during the making of the film. Shots in an animated film may be framed as high or low angles, or long shots or close-ups, all of which simply result from the perspective of drawings selected to be photographed. Still, in what follows, we shall continue to speak of "camera angle," "camera level," "camera height," and "camera distance," with the understanding that these terms refer simply to what we see on the screen and need not always conform to what occurred during production.

Angle. The frame implies an *angle of framing* with respect to what is shown. It thus positions us at some angle onto the shot's mise-en-scene. The number of such angles is infinite, since there is an infinite number of points in space that the camera might occupy. In practice, we typically distinguish three general categories: the straight-on angle, the high angle, and the low angle. The straight-on angle is the most common. Figure 7.88 shows a straight-on angle from Straub and Huillet's *Chronicle of Anna Magdalena Bach.* The high angle positions us "looking down" at the material within the frame, as in Figure 7.89, a shot from *Ivan the Terrible.* The low-angle framing

Fig. 7.90

Fig. 7.91

Fig. 7.92

positions us as "looking up" at the framed material (as in Fig. 7.90, again from *Ivan the Terrible*).

Level. We can also distinguish the degree to which the frame is "level." This ultimately bears on the sense of gravity governing the filmed material and the frame. Assume that we are filming telephone poles. If the framing is level, the horizontal edges of the frame will be parallel to the horizon of the shot and perpendicular to the poles. If horizon and poles are at diagonal angles, the frame is *canted* in one manner or another.

The canted framing is relatively rare, although a few films make heavy use of it, such as Orson Welles's *Mr. Arkadin* and Carol Reed's *The Third Man* (see Fig. 7.91). In Christopher Maclaine's *The End*, a canted framing makes a steep street in the foreground appear level and renders the houses in the background grotesquely out of kilter (Fig. 7.92).

Height. Sometimes it becomes important to indicate that the framing gives us a sense of being stationed at a certain *height*. Camera angle is, of course, partly related to height: To frame from a high angle entails being at a vantage point higher than the material in the image.

But camera height is not simply a matter of camera angle. For instance, the Japanese filmmaker Yasujiro Ozu often positions his camera close to the ground to film characters or objects on the floor (see Color Plates 41, 62, and 63). Note that this is not a matter of camera angle, for the angle is straight on; we still see the ground or floor. Filming from such a low height with a straight-on angle is an important quality of Ozu's visual style, as we shall see in Chapter 11.

Distance. Finally, the framing of the image stations us not only at a certain angle and height and on a level plane or at a cant but also with respect to distance. Framing supplies a sense of being far away from or close to the mise-en-scene of the shot. This aspect of framing is usually called camera distance. In what follows, we shall use the standard measure—the scale of the human body—but any other filmed material would do as well. The examples are all from *The Third Man*.

In the *extreme long shot*, the human figure is barely visible (Fig. 7.93). This is the framing for landscapes, bird's-eye views of cities, and other vistas.

Fig. 7.93

Fig. 7.94

Fig. 7.95

Fig. 7.96

Fig. 7.97

Fig. 7.98

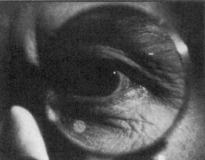

Fig. 7.99

Fig. 7.100

In the *long shot,* figures are more prominent, but the background still dominates (Fig. 7.94). The *plan américain* ("American shot") is very common in Hollywood cinema. Here, as in Figure 7.95, the human figure is framed from about the knees up. This shot permits a nice balance of figure and surroundings. Shots at the same distance of nonhuman subjects are called *medium long shots.*

The *medium shot* frames the human body from the waist up (Fig. 7.96). Gesture and expression now become more visible. The *medium close-up* frames the body from the chest up (Fig. 7.97). The *close-up* is traditionally the shot showing just the head, hands, feet, or a small object. It emphasizes facial expression, the details of a gesture, or a significant object (Fig. 7.98). The *extreme close-up* singles out a portion of the face (eyes or lips), isolates a detail, and magnifies the minute (Fig. 7.99).

Note that the size of the photographed material within the frame is as important as any real "camera distance." From the same "camera distance," you could film a long shot of a person or a close-up of King Kong's elbow. We would not call the shot in Figure 7.100 (from *La Passion de Jeanne d'Arc*) a close-up just because only Jeanne's head appears in the frame; the framing is that of a long shot because in scale her head is relatively small. (If the framing were simply adjusted downward, her whole body would be visible.) In judging camera distance, the relative proportion of the material framed provides the basic determinant.

Common confusions exist about framing. First, categories of framing are obviously matters of degree. There is no universal measure of camera angle or distance. No precise cut-off point distinguishes between a long shot and an extreme long shot, or a slightly low angle and a straight-on angle. Moreover, filmmakers are not bound by terminology. They rightly do not worry if a shot does not fit into traditional categories. Nevertheless, the concepts are clear enough for us to use them in talking about films. It is not of great importance whether the shot that cuts John Wayne off slightly above his waist is to be called a "true" medium shot or a "true" medium close-up. What is important is that we use the term in ways that enable us to analyze how that framing functions in the particular film and to share our insights with others.

Functions of framing.   Another problem is more important. Sometimes we are tempted to assign absolute meanings to angles, distances, and other qualities of framing. It is tempting to believe that framing from a low angle automatically "says" that a character is powerful and that framing from a high angle presents him or her as dwarfed and defeated. Verbal analogies are especially seductive: A canted frame seems to mean that "the world is out of kilter."

The analysis of film as art would be a lot easier if technical qualities automatically possessed such hard-and-fast meanings, but individual films would thereby lose much of their uniqueness and richness. The fact is that framings have no absolute or general meanings. In *some* films angles and distances carry such meanings as mentioned above, but in other films— probably most films—they do not. To rely on such formulas is to forget that meaning and effect always stem from the total film, from its operation as a system. The context of the film will determine the function of the framings, just as it determines the function of mise-en-scene, photographic qualities, and other techniques. Consider three examples.

Fig. 7.101

At many points in *Citizen Kane,* low-angle shots of Kane do convey his looming power, but the lowest angles occur at the point of Kane's most humiliating defeat—his miscarried gubernatorial campaign. In this context the low angle functions to isolate Kane and his friend against an empty background, his deserted campaign headquarters (Fig. 7.101). Note that angles of framing affect not only our view of the main figures but also the background against which those figures may appear.

If the cliché about high-angle framings were correct, Figure 7.102, a

Fig. 7.102

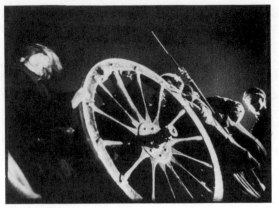

Fig. 7.103

Fig. 7.104

Fig. 7.105

Fig. 7.106

shot from *North by Northwest,* would express the powerlessness of Van Damm and Leonard. In fact, Van Damm has just decided to eliminate his mistress by pushing her out of a plane, and he is saying: "I think that this is a matter best disposed of from a great height." The angle and distance of Hitchcock's shot wittily prophesy how the murder is to be carried out.

Similarly, the world is hardly out of kilter in the shot from Eisenstein's *October* shown in Figure 7.103. The canted frame dynamizes the effort of pushing the cannon.

These three examples should demonstrate that we cannot reduce the richness of cinema to a few recipes. We must, as usual, look for the *functions* the technique performs in the particular *context* of the total film.

Camera distance, height, level, and angle often take on clear-cut narrative functions. Camera distance can establish or reestablish settings and character positions, as we shall see in the next chapter when we examine the editing of the first sequence of *The Maltese Falcon.* A framing can isolate a narratively important detail—the tears of Henriette in *A Day in the Country* (Fig. 7.104), or the snips of Jeanne's hair in *La Passion de Jeanne d'Arc* (Fig. 7.105).

Framing also contributes to cueing us to take a shot as "subjective." In Chapter 4, we saw that a film's narration may present story information with some degree of psychological depth (p. 104), and one option is a perceptual subjectivity that renders what a character sees or hears. When a shot's framing prompts us to take it as a character's vision, we call it an optically subjective shot, or a *point-of-view shot* (abbreviated as POV shot). In Figure 7.106, a shot from Fritz Lang's *Fury,* the hero in his jail cell is seen through the bars at a slightly low angle. The next shot (Fig. 7.107), a high angle through the window toward the street outside, shows us what he sees, from his point of view.

Less obviously, camera distance and angle can situate us in one area of the narrative's space. The angle and distance of Figure 7.108, a shot from *Sergeant York,* do not show the preacher from any specific character's vantage point, but we are generally situated in the congregation's position. (An alternative distance and angle might view the preacher from a high angle and from the rear, with the congregation beyond him.) A canted framing may

Fig. 7.107

Fig. 7.108

Fig. 7.109

serve the narrative function of marking certain shots or sequences as distinctly different from the rest of the film. Note the canted framing in Figure 7.109, a shot from a montage sequence in *The Roaring Twenties,* showing a routine action rather than a specific scene.

Framings may serve the narrative in yet other ways. Across an entire film the repetitions of certain framings may associate themselves with a character or situation. That is, framings may become motifs unifying the film. In *The Maltese Falcon* Casper Gutman is frequently photographed from a low angle emphasizing his obesity (Fig. 7.110). Throughout *La Passion de Jeanne d'Arc* Dreyer returns obsessively to extreme close-up shots of Jeanne (Fig. 6.14).

Fig. 7.110

Alternatively, certain framings in a film may stand out by virtue of their rarity. The ominously calm effect of the shot of the birds descending on Bodega Bay (in Hitchcock's film *The Birds*) arises from the abrupt shift from straight-on medium shots to an extreme long shot from very high above the town. (See Figs. 8.38 and 8.39, p. 278.) In a film composed primarily of long shots and medium shots, an extreme close-up will obviously have considerable force. Similarly, the early scenes of Ridley Scott's *Alien* present few shots depicting any character's point of view. But when Kane approaches the alien egg, we see close views of it as if through his eyes, and the creature leaps straight out at us. This not only provides a sudden shock; the abrupt switch to framings that restrict us to one character's range of knowledge emphasizes the main turning point in the plot.

Even within a single sequence, camera angle, level, and distance may develop significantly. In the final sequence from Hitchcock's *Saboteur,* at the top of the Statue of Liberty, the hero is holding the coatsleeve of the saboteur, who dangles precariously. The sleeve's stitching starts to tear. Hitchcock cuts from extreme long shots, high- and low-angled, canted this way and that, of the statue to extreme close-ups of the threads ripping out one by one. The scene's suspense derives principally from the drastic difference between the broad view (emphasizing the saboteur's danger) and the near-microscopic enlargement (his fate hangs by a thread).

Framings do not function only to emphasize narrative form. They can have their own intrinsic interest as well. Close-ups can bring out textures and details we might otherwise ignore. We can see the smallest surreptitious gestures of a pickpocket in the medium close-up from Robert Bresson's

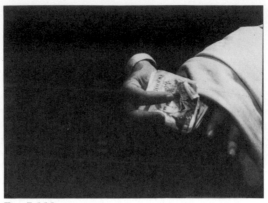

Fig. 7.111

Fig. 7.112

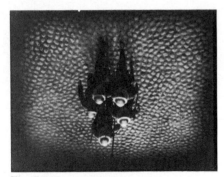

Fig. 7.113

Fig. 7.114

Pickpocket (Fig. 7.111); a series of similar close shots makes up a dazzling, balletlike scene in this film. Long shots can permit us to explore expansive spaces. Much of the visual delight of Westerns, of *2001*, or of *Seven Samurai* arises from long shots that make huge spaces manifest.

Our eye also enjoys the formal play presented by unusual angles on familiar objects, as when René Clair in *Entr'acte* frames a ballerina from straight below, transforming the figure into an expanding and contracting flower (Fig. 7.112). In *La Passion de Jeanne d'Arc* the upside down framings (Fig. 7.113) are not motivated as a character's point of view; they exist as an exploration of framing in its own right. "By reproducing the object from an unusual and striking angle," writes Rudolf Arnheim, "the artist forces the spectator to take a keener interest, which goes beyond mere noticing or acceptance. The object thus photographed sometimes gains in reality, and the impression it makes is livelier and more arresting."

Framing may be used for comic effect, as Charlie Chaplin, Buster Keaton, and Jacques Tati have all shown. We have seen that in *Our Hospitality* Keaton stages many gags in depth. Now we can see that well-chosen camera angles and distances are also vital to the gags' success. For example, if the railroad scene shown in Figure 6.94 (p. 202) were shot from the side and in extreme long shot, we would not see so clearly that the two parts of the train are on parallel tracks. Moreover, we could not see the engineer's unconcerned posture, which indicates his failure to realize what has happened. Similarly, the use of framing to create offscreen space is vital to the gag shown in Figures 6.103 and 6.104 (p. 204). Here the gag is laid out in time rather than space. First Willie tugs on the rope, then an unseen effect of that tug becomes visible as the Canfield son hurtles past and disappears. Finally Willie reacts and is himself dragged down into the abyss below the frameline. Try to imagine these moments and others in *Our Hospitality* framed in a different way, and you will see how our reaction to Keaton's humor depends on the careful combination of mise-en-scene and framing.

Similarly, in Tati's *Play Time* mise-en-scene and camera position co-operate to create humorous visual patterns. At one point, M. Hulot reacts with a start when he sees that a doorman locking a door seems suddenly to have sprouted horns (the door handles; see Fig. 7.114). The visual pun issues from the precisely chosen camera angle and distance. We cannot classify all the nonnarrative functions of framing; we can only suggest that camera distance, angle, height, and level have the constant possibility of sharpening our perception of purely visual qualities.

■ THE MOBILE FRAME

All of the features of framing we have examined are present in paintings, photographs, comic strips, and other sorts of pictures. All framed images furnish instances of aspect ratios, in-frame and out-of-frame relations, angle, height, level, and distance of the frame's vantage point. But there is one resource of framing that is specific to cinema (and video). In film it is possible for the frame to *move* with respect to the framed material.

"Mobile framing" means that within the confines of the image we see, the framing of the object changes. The mobile frame thus produces changes of camera height, distance, angle, or level *within* the shot. Further, since the framing orients us to the material in the image, we often see ourselves as moving *along with* the frame. Through such framing we may approach the object or retreat from it, circle it or move past it.

Types of mobile framing. We usually refer to the ability of the frame to be mobile as "camera movement." Very often the term is accurate, for usually mobility of framing is achieved by moving the camera physically during production. The camera, as we know, usually rests on a support while filming, and this support may be designed to move the camera. There are several kinds of camera movement, each one of which creates a specific effect onscreen.

The *pan* (short for "panorama") movement rotates the camera on a vertical axis. The camera as a whole does not displace itself. Onscreen, the pan gives the impression of a frame horizontally scanning space. It is as if the camera "turns its head" right or left. In Figures 7.115 and 7.116, shots from Dreyer's *Ordet*, the camera pans right to keep the figures in frame as they cross a room.

The *tilt* movement rotates the camera on a horizontal axis. It is as if the camera's "head" were swiveling up or down. Again, the camera itself does not change position. Onscreen, the tilt movement yields the impression of

Fig. 7.115

Fig. 7.116

Fig. 7.117

Fig. 7.118

Fig. 7.119

Fig. 7.120

unrolling a space from top to bottom or bottom to top. François Truffaut's *The Bride Wore Black* begins a sequence with a tilt down a church (Figs. 7.117, 7.118).

In the *tracking* (or *dolly* or *trucking*) *shot*, the camera as a whole does change position, traveling in any direction along the ground—forward, backward, circularly, diagonally, or from side to side. Figures 7.119 and 7.120 show two stages of a lateral tracking shot in Erich von Stroheim's *Greed*. Note how the figures remain in the same basic relationship to the frame as they stroll along a sidewalk, while the front of the house which they hope to buy remains visible behind them.

In the *crane shot* the camera moves above ground level. Typically, it rises or descends, often thanks to a mechanical arm which lifts and lowers it. The mourning scene in *Ivan the Terrible* begins with a crane down from a high view of the bier (Fig. 7.121) to a lower position, ending with a framing on Ivan seated at the bier's base (Fig. 7.122). A crane shot may move not only up and down, like an elevator, but forward and backward or from side to side. At the end of Karel Reisz's *Morgan!*, the camera cranes diagonally up and back to reveal that the hero's apparently innocuous flower garden proclaims his communist sympathies (Figs. 7.123, 7.124). Variations of the crane shot are helicopter and airplane shots.

Pans, tilts, tracking shots, and crane shots are the most common framing movements, but virtually any kind of camera movement can be imagined (somersaulting, rolling, and so on). Only a few camera movements might be

Fig. 7.121

Fig. 7.122

mistaken for each other. The pan resembles a lateral tracking shot, and the tilt resembles a vertical crane shot. But a little practice in viewing makes the differences easy to spot. In both the pan and the tilt, the body of the camera does not change position; it simply swivels left or right, up or down. For example, in Figure 7.115 the framing is fairly close to the central man, showing him in profile. If the camera were tracking along with him, it would continue to show him roughly in profile—yet Figure 7.116 shows him at a greater distance and from behind—indicating that the camera has turned but not moved along with the character. In the lateral tracking shot and the vertical crane shot, the camera moves horizontally or vertically, as if you were gliding along with a character or swooping up over a landscape. As we shall see, though, types of camera movements can be combined.

Camera movements have held an appeal for filmmakers and audiences since the beginnings of cinema. Why? Visually, camera movements have several arresting effects. They often increase information about the space of the image. Objects' positions become more vivid and sharp than in stationary framings. New objects or figures are usually revealed. Tracking shots and crane shots supply continually changing perspectives on passing objects as the frame constantly shifts its orientation. Objects appear more solid and three-dimensional when the camera arcs (i.e., tracks along a curved path) around them. Pan and tilt shots present space as continuous, both horizontally and vertically.

Moreover, it is difficult not to see camera movement as a substitute for *our* movement. The objects do not seem to swell or shrink. We seem to approach or retreat from them. This is not, of course, the case in a literal sense: We never forget that we are watching a film in a theater. But camera movement provides several convincing cues for movement through space. Indeed, so powerful are these cues that filmmakers often make camera movements *subjective*—motivated narratively to represent the view through the eyes of a moving character. That is, camera movement can be a powerful cue that we are watching a POV shot. Narratively subjective or not, the roving camera eye, the mobile framing of the shot, acts as a surrogate for our eye and our attention.

In commercial film production today, many camera movements are made with the camera on a dolly, which may be moved on tracks or other specially designed supports. An increasingly popular means is a gimbal-balanced camera mount patented as the Steadicam. This mount attaches the camera to the operator's body by means of a brace. The operator can walk with the camera, guiding the framing by minimal hand movements while viewing the image on a video monitor. Another operator adjusts focus by radio remote control.

The balancing mechanism allows the Steadicam to produce mobile shots of great smoothness. It allows fluidity in tracking with actors climbing stairs, entering rooms, and riding bicycles or motorcycles. In Martin Scorsese's *Raging Bull*, the Steadicam follows the protagonist out of his dressing room, down a long corridor (Fig. 7.125), up a flight of steps (Fig. 7.126), and through a crowd up to the boxing ring. Recently directors have used a Steadicam on the set to supplement the principal camera by providing moving shots which can be cut into longer views.

Fig. 7.123

Fig. 7.124

Fig. 7.125

Fig. 7.126

Fig. 7.127

Fig. 7.128

Fig. 7.129

In creating certain special effects, the camera's movement may be governed by other electronic means. *Motion-control* techniques use computer programs to plot the camera's movements and execute them precisely. The movements can then be repeated for different elements of a composite shot. For example, a track toward a spacecraft can be repeated to enlarge the background within which the miniature will be matted. Motion control can also blend camera movements filmed on location with those made in a studio. When the makers of *Clear and Present Danger* could not get permission to film Harrison Ford in a car inside the White House gates, a motion-control device recorded the pan from the deserted gate to the building. Back in California, Ford was filmed in a car beside a replica of the gate, and the motion-control program reproduced the original panning movement. The two shots were then blended by digital compositing.

Sometimes the filmmaker does not want smooth camera movements, preferring a bumpy, jiggling image. Commonly this sort of image is achieved through use of the *hand-held* camera. That is, the operator does not anchor the machine on a tripod or dolly but instead uses his or her body to act as the support without benefit of compensating equipment. In Figure 7.127 Don Pennebaker hand holds the camera during the filming of his *Keep on Rocking.* This sort of camera movement became common in the late 1950s, with the growth of the *cinéma-vérité* documentary. One of the most famous early hand-held traveling shots was in *Primary*, when a cameraman held the camera above his head and followed John F. Kennedy through a milling crowd (see Fig. 2.1).

Hand-held shots have appeared in many fiction films as well. Often the hand-held camera movement functions to create subjective point of view, as in Figure 7.128, from Samuel Fuller's *The Naked Kiss.* Sometimes the hand-held shot intensifies a sense of abrupt violence, as if the action were glimpsed on the fly. Manuel Octavio Gomez's *First Charge of the Machete* is set in 1868, well before cinema was invented, but it presents its story of a peasant rebellion as a documentary, complete with interviews and mock newsreel footage. Episodes of guerrilla fighting are given a sense of urgent immediacy by being filmed with the hand-held camera (Fig. 7.129).

Fig. 7.130

Fig. 7.131

Fig. 7.132

Camera movement is the most common way of making the frame mobile, but it is not the only way. In animation, the camera stays in one position, but through the drawing of individual cels frame by frame, the animator can create the effect of camera movement, as in a pan shot from *The Old Grey Hare* (Figs. 7.130–7.132). Alternatively, a mobile frame effect can be achieved by photographing a still picture or a stopped frame of film and gradually enlarging or reducing any portion of that image, as is frequently done in optical printing. Iris masking can open up to reveal a vista or close down to isolate a detail. Finally, the zoom lens, as we have already mentioned, can be used to provide a mobile framing.

The differences between the laboratory or zoom sorts of mobile framing and some kinds of mobile framing created by camera movement during filming are difficult to illustrate on the printed page. No one will think an iris-in or a circular tracking shot is a zoom. But how, for instance, can we as viewers distinguish between a zoom-in and a forward tracking shot, or a crane shot back and a change in framing created on the optical printer? In general, animation, special effects, and the zoom lens make the frame mobile by reducing or blowing up some portion of the image. Although the tracking shot and the crane shot do enlarge or reduce portions of the frame, this is not *all* that they do. In the genuine camera movement, static objects in different planes pass one another at different rates, displaying *different aspects* to us; backgrounds gain volume and depth.

Consider some examples. In Alain Resnais's *La Guerre est finie,* a tracking shot (Figs. 7.133, 7.134) gives the objects considerable volume. The wall has lost none of its bulk or solidity. Moreover, the street sign has not simply been enlarged; its orientation has changed with respect to the camera's vantage point. Similarly, in Figures 7.135–7.137, a diagonal track-in from

Fig. 7.133

Fig. 7.134

Fig. 7.135

Fig. 7.136

Fig. 7.137

Fig. 7.138

Fig. 7.139

Fig. 7.140

Fig. 7.141

Fig. 7.142

Bertolucci's *Last Tango in Paris*, the figures retain their three-dimensional volume but change somewhat in angle and aspect.

With the zoom and optical printer enlargement, however, the mobile frame does not alter the aspects or positions of the objects filmed. In the accompanying shot from Stanley Kubrick's *Barry Lyndon* (Figs. 7.138, 7.139), the marching troops are simply demagnified by the zoom-out. That is, our vantage point on the soldiers and their background is exactly the same at the end of the zoom-out. But depth cues do change as the focal length of the lens decreases. In the beginning of the shot, the telephoto image makes the troops seem closer to the trees in the background than they seem at the end of the shot, and the zoom-out discloses a group of spectators in the foreground. In sum, when the camera moves, we sense our own movement through the space. When the lens zooms, a bit of the space seems magnified or demagnified.

So far, we have isolated these different sorts of mobile framings in fairly pure states. But filmmakers frequently combine such framings within a single shot: The camera may track and pan at the same time or crane up while zooming. Still, every instance can be identified as a combination of the basic types.

Functions of frame mobility. Our catalog of the types of mobile framings is of little use without a consideration of how such framing strategies function systematically within films. How does mobile framing relate to cinematic space? To cinematic time? How do mobile framings create certain patterns of their own? Such questions demand that we examine how mobile framing interacts with the form of the film.

1. *The mobile frame and space.* The mobile frame affects onscreen and offscreen space considerably. A forward tracking shot or zoom puts onscreen space offscreen. Other camera movements and optical effects may reveal fresh offscreen areas. In many films, the camera moves back from a detail and brings something unexpected into the shot's space. This is what happens in our earlier example from *Jezebel* (Figs. 7.80–7.83); after the hand with the glass intrudes into close-up, the camera tracks back to frame the man standing in the foreground. The mobile frame also continually affects the distance, angle, height, or level of the framing. A track-in may change the distance from long shot to close-up; a crane up may change the angle from a low one to a high one.

We can, in general, ask several questions of how the mobile frame relates to space. Do the frame's movements depend on figure movement? For example, one of the commonest functions of camera movement is *reframing*. If a character moves in relation to another character, very often the frame will slightly pan or tilt to adjust to the movement. In *His Girl Friday* director Howard Hawks strives to balance his compositions through reframing. When Hildy moves, the camera pans right to reframe her; when Walter swivels in his chair, the camera reframes slightly leftward—each time guiding our attention and maintaining a balanced composition (see Figs. 7.140–7.142). Since reframings are motivated by figure movement, they tend to be relatively unnoticeable. When you do start to notice them, you may be surprised at how frequently they appear.

Reframing is only one way that the mobile frame may depend on figure movement. The camera may also displace itself in order to follow figures or moving objects. A pan may keep a racing car centered, a tracking shot may follow a character from room to room, or a crane shot may pursue a rising balloon. In such cases frame mobility functions primarily to keep our attention fastened on the subject of the shot, and it subordinates itself to that subject's movement.

Fig. 7.143

Following shots can become quite complex. Michelangelo Antonioni's *Cronaca di un amore (Story of a Love Affair)* contains many scenes in which several characters are present. Typically the camera follows one figure moving to meet another, then follows the second character's movement to another spot, where he or she meets someone else, then traces the third character's movement, and so on. The card-party sequence in *Cronaca* is a superb example of the camera's restlessly following character after character in rapid succession.

Still, the mobile frame need not be subordinate to the movement of figures at all. It can move independently of them, too. Often, of course, the camera moves away from the characters to reveal something of significance to the narrative. The most banal examples are movements that point out an overlooked clue, a sign that comments on the action, an unnoticed shadow, or a clutching hand. The moving camera can establish a locale the characters will eventually enter. This is what happens at the start of Otto Preminger's *Laura*, when the camera glides through Waldo Lydecker's sitting room, establishing him as a man of wealth and taste, before revealing the detective MacPherson. In Renoir's *Crime of M. Lange* the moving camera characterizes Lange by leaving him and panning around to survey his room, complete with six-guns, Western hats, and a map with Arizona outlined (Figs. 7.143–7.147).

Fig. 7.144

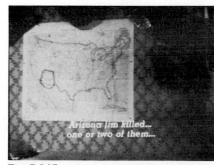

Fig. 7.145

Fig. 7.146

Fig. 7.147

Lange is shown to be a fantasist, living in the world of Western lore he draws on for his cowboy stories.

Whether dependent on figure movement or independent of it, the mobile frame can profoundly affect how we perceive the space within the frame and offscreen. Different sorts of camera movements create different conceptions of space. In *Last Year at Marienbad* Resnais often tracks into corridors and through doorways, turning a fashionable resort hotel into a maze. Alfred Hitchcock has produced some of the most famous single camera movements in film history. One track-and-crane shot moves from a high-angle long shot of a ballroom over the heads of the dancers to an extreme close-up of a drummer's blinking eyes (*Young and Innocent*). In *Vertigo,* an especially tricky combination track-*out* and zoom-*in* plastically distorts the shot's perspective. (The device reappears in Spielberg's *Jaws,* when Sheriff Brody at the beach suddenly realizes that the shark has attacked a child. Tracking and zooming simultaneously in opposite directions is rapidly becoming a cliché of modern Hollywood filmmaking.) In films such as *The Red and the White, Agnus Dei,* and *Red Psalm* Miklós Jancsó has specialized in very lengthy camera movements that roam among groups of people moving across a plain. His shots use all of the resources of tracking, panning, craning, zooming, and racking focus to shape our perception of spatial relations.

For his film *La Région centrale* Michael Snow built the machine pictured in Figure 7.148. Since all of the moving arms could pivot the camera in several ways in response to a remote-control device, the machine produced a varied series of rotational camera movements—everything from elaborate corkscrew spiralings to huge, Ferris-wheel spins. Snow set up his machine in a barren Canadian landscape, and the film that resulted transforms that landscape into a series of uniquely mobile views. A set of variations on the possibilities of the camera's speed and direction of movement provides the basis of this film's abstract form. This is an example of how one filmic technique can largely determine the form of a long and complex film.

All of these examples illustrate various ways in which frame mobility affects our sense of space. Of any mobile framing we can ask: How does it function to reveal or conceal offscreen space? Is the frame mobility dependent on figure movement or independent of it? What particular trajectory does the camera pursue? Such questions will best be answered by considering how spatial effects of the camera movement function with respect to narrative or nonnarrative form.

Fig. 7.148

2. *The mobile frame and time.* Frame mobility involves time as well as space, and filmmakers have realized that our sense of duration and rhythm is affected by the mobile frame. The importance of duration in camera movement, for example, can be sensed by comparing two Japanese directors, Yasujiro Ozu and Kenji Mizoguchi. Ozu prefers short, unidirectional camera movements, as in *Early Summer* and *The Flavor of Green Tea over Rice.* Mizoguchi, on the other hand, cultivates the leisurely, drawn-out tracking shot, often combining it with panning. That camera movements simply take less time in Ozu's films than in Mizoguchi's constitutes a major difference between the two directors' styles.

Since a camera movement consumes time on screen, it can create an arc of expectation and fulfillment. In the pan shot across M. Lange's study (Figs. 7.143–7.147 above), Renoir makes us wonder why the camera strays from the main character, then answers the question by indicating Lange's fascination with the American West. Later in this chapter we shall examine how our expectations are manipulated over time in the opening camera movement of Welles's *Touch of Evil.*

The velocity of frame mobility is important too. A zoom or a camera movement may be relatively slow or fast. Richard Lester's *A Hard Day's Night* and *Help!* started a fad in the 1960s for very fast zoom-ins and -outs. By comparison, one of the most impressive early camera movements, D. W. Griffith's monumental crane shot in Belshazzar's feast in *Intolerance,* gains majesty and suspense through its inexorably slow descent toward the immense set pictured in Figure 6.11 (p. 174).

In general, a camera movement may create significant effects of its own. If the camera pans quickly away from an event, we may be prompted to wonder what has happened. If the camera abruptly tracks back to show us something in the foreground which we had not expected, we are taken by surprise. If the camera slowly moves in on a detail, gradually enlarging it but delaying the fulfillment of our expectations, the camera movement has contributed to suspense. In a narrative film, the velocity of mobile framing can be motivated by narrational needs. A quick track-in to a significant object can underline a key piece of story information.

Sometimes the speed of the mobile framing functions rhythmically. In Will Hindle's *Pastorale d'été* a gentle, bouncing beat is created by zooming in and slightly tilting up and down in time to Honegger's music. Often musical films make use of the speed of camera movement to underline qualities of a song or dance. During the "Broadway Rhythm" number in *Singin' in the Rain,* the camera cranes quickly back from Gene Kelly several times and the speed of the movement is timed to accentuate the lyrics. Frame velocity can also create expressive qualities—a camera movement can be fluid, staccato, hesitant, and so forth. In short, the duration and velocity of the mobile frame can significantly control our perception of the shot over time.

3. *Patterns of mobile framing.* The mobile frame can create its own specific motifs within a film. For example, Hitchcock's *Psycho* begins and ends with a forward movement of the frame. At the beginning of the film, the camera pans right and zooms in on a building in a cityscape. Several forward movements finally carry us under a window blind and into the darkness of a

cheap hotel room. The camera's movement inward, the penetration of an interior, is repeated throughout the film, often motivated as a subjective point of view as when various characters move deeper and deeper into Norman Bates's mansion. The next-to-last shot of the film shows Norman sitting against a blank white wall, while we hear his interior monologue. The camera again moves forward into a close-up of his face. This shot is the climax of the forward movement initiated at the start of the film; the film has traced a movement into Norman's mind. Another film that relies heavily on a pattern of forward, penetrating movements is *Citizen Kane*, which depicts the same inexorable drive toward the revelation of a character's secret.

Other kinds of movements can repeat and develop across a film. Max Ophuls's *Lola Montès* uses both 360° tracking shots and constant upward and downward crane shots to contrast the circus arena with the world of Lola's past. In Michael Snow's ⟷ (usually called *Back and Forth*), the constant panning to and fro across a classroom, Ping-Pong fashion, determines the basic formal pattern of the film. It comes as a surprise when near the very end, the movement suddenly becomes a repeated tilting up and down. In these and many other films the mobile frame sets up marked repetitions and variations.

In these examples, repetitions and variations of camera-movement motifs interact with the film's narrative or nonnarrative form. By way of summary we can look at two films that illustrate possible relations of the mobile frame to narrative form. These two films constitute a pertinent contrast in that one uses the mobile frame in order to strengthen and support the narrative, whereas the other subordinates narrative form to an overall frame mobility.

Jean Renoir's *Grand Illusion* is a war film in which we almost never see the war. Heroic charges and doomed battalions, the staple of the genre, are absent. World War I remains obstinately offscreen. Instead, Renoir concentrates on life in a German POW camp to suggest how relations between nations and social classes are affected by war. The prisoners Maréchal and Boeldieu are both French; Rauffenstein is a German. Yet the aristocrat Boeldieu has more in common with Rauffenstein than with the mechanic Maréchal. The film's narrative form traces the death of the Boeldieu-Rauffenstein upper class and the precarious survival of Maréchal and his pal Rosenthal—their flight to Elsa's farm, their interlude of peace there, and their final escape back to France and presumably back to the war as well.

Within this framework, camera movement has several functions, all directly supportive of the narrative. First, and least unusual, is its tendency to adhere to figure movement. When a character or vehicle moves, Renoir often pans or tracks to follow. The camera follows Maréchal and Rosenthal walking together after their escape; it tracks back when the prisoners are drawn to the window by the sound of marching Germans below. But it is the movements of the camera *independent* of figure movement that make the film more unusual.

When the camera moves on its own in *Grand Illusion*, we are conscious of it actively interpreting the action, creating suspense or giving us information of which the characters are ignorant. For example, when a prisoner is digging in the escape tunnel and pulls on the string to signal to be pulled

Fig. 7.149

Fig. 7.150

Fig. 7.151

Fig. 7.152

Fig. 7.153

Fig. 7.154

out, the camera frames the can being tugged over (Fig. 7.149), then pans left to reveal that the characters do not notice it (Figs. 7.150, 7.151). Camera movement thus helps create a somewhat unrestricted narration.

Sometimes the camera is such an active agent that Renoir will use repeated camera movements to create patterns of narrative significance. One such pattern is the movement to link characters with details of their environment. Often a sequence begins on a close-up of some detail, and the camera moves back to anchor this detail in its larger spatial and narrative context. When Renoir begins the scene of Boeldieu and Maréchal's discussion of escape plans with a close-up of a caged squirrel (Fig. 7.152) before tracking back to reveal the men (Fig. 7.153) beside the cage, the narrative parallel is apparent.

Fig. 7.155

More complicated is the scene of the Christmas celebration at Elsa's which begins on a close-up of the crêche and tracks back to show, in several stages, the interplay of reactions among the characters. Such camera movements are not simply decoration; beginning on a scenic detail before moving to the larger context makes narrative points economically, constantly emphasizing relationships among elements of Renoir's mise-en-scene. So does the rarer track-*in* to a detail at the *end* of a scene, as when after Boeldieu's death, Rauffenstein goes to cut the geranium, the one flower in the prison (Fig. 7.154), and Renoir tracks in to a final close shot of the flower pot by the window (Fig. 7.155).

Characters are tied to their environment by some even more ambitious moving-camera shots, which function to stress important narrative parallels.

Fig. 7.156

Fig. 7.157

Fig. 7.158

Fig. 7.159

Fig. 7.160

Fig. 7.161

In the first scene, as Maréchal leaves the officers' bar (Fig. 7.156), Renoir pans and tracks left from the door to reveal pin-ups (on the right in Fig. 7.157) and a poster (Fig. 7.158). One scene later, in the German officers' bar, a similar camera movement (this time in the opposite direction) leaves the characters and explores, on its own, a similar collection of decorations (Figs. 7.159–7.161). Through his camera movements Renoir indicates a similarity between the two warring sides, blurring their national differences and stressing common desires. The camera movements, repeated in a systematic pattern, create the narrative parallel.

Or consider how two parallel tracking shots compare the war of the aristocrats and the war of the lower-class people. We are introduced to Rauffenstein's new position as commander of a prisoner-of-war camp through a lengthy tracking shot that begins on a cross (ironic, since the chapel has been commandeered as a bivouac) and tracks along whips, spurs, weapons, and gloves to a servant preparing Rauffenstein's gloves and finally to Rauffenstein himself (Figs. 7.162–7.169). In this shot Renoir presents, wordlessly, the military mystique of grace on the battlefield that characterizes the aristocrat's war.

Late in the film, however, a parallel shot criticizes this one. Again the shot begins on an object—a picture of Elsa's dead husband (Fig. 7.170)—and tracks back to reveal pictures of other of Elsa's relatives as she recites offscreen where they were killed. The camera tracks left (Fig. 7.171) to the kitchen table, where the child Lotte sits alone (Fig. 7.172) as Elsa explains

Fig. 7.162

Fig. 7.163

Fig. 7.164

Fig. 7.165

Fig. 7.166

Fig. 7.167

Fig. 7.168

Fig. 7.169

Fig. 7.170

Fig. 7.171

Fig. 7.172

Fig. 7.173

Fig. 7.174

Fig. 7.175

Fig. 7.176

Fig. 7.177

Fig. 7.178

Fig. 7.179

offscreen: "Now the table is too large." That Elsa's war has none of Rauffen-stein's glory is conveyed chiefly through a parallel created by the repeated camera movement. Moreover, these camera movements work together with mise-en-scene, as the narrative parallel is reinforced by the subtle use of objects as motifs—the crucifixes in Figures 7.162 and 7.172, the photographs in Figures 7.163 and 7.170, and the tables that end both shots.

Another function of moving the camera independently of figure move-ment is to link characters with one another. Again and again in the prison camps, the camera moves to join one man to his comrades, spatially indicating their shared condition. When the prisoners ransack the collection of women's clothes, one man decides to dress up in them. When he appears, a stillness falls over the men. Renoir tracks silently over the prisoners' faces, each one registering a reticent longing.

A more elaborate linking movement occurs in the scene of the prison vaudeville show, when the men learn that the French have recaptured a city. The camera moves among them as they begin defiantly to sing the "Marseil-laise." Renoir presents the shot as a celebration of spatial unity, tracking right from the musicians (Fig. 7.173) along the singing performers (Figs. 7.174, 7.175) to a pair of worried German guards (Fig. 7.176). The camera then pans left to reveal a row of the audience of prisoners on their feet, singing (Fig. 7.177). The camera tracks forward past the musicians again (Fig. 7.178), then pans quickly left to face the entire audience (Fig. 7.179). This very complex camera movement circulates among the prisoners as they join together in defiance of their captors.

Fig. 7.180

Fig. 7.181

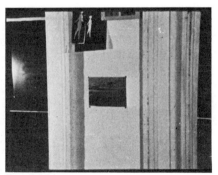
Fig. 7.182

In Elsa's cottage as well as in the prison, camera movement links characters. Recall the shot that moves from Elsa and Rosenthal inside through the window to Maréchal outside. The culmination of the linking movement comes near the film's end, when Renoir pans from the Germans on one side of the border (Fig. 7.180) to the distant French escapees on the other (Figs. 7.181, 7.182). Even on this scale, Renoir's camera refuses to honor national divisions.

A remark of André Bazin's is pertinent here: "Jean Renoir found a way to reveal the hidden meaning of people and things without destroying the unity that is natural to them." By placing emphasis and making comparisons, the mobile frame in *Grand Illusion* becomes as important as the mise-en-scene. The camera carves into space to create connections that enrich the film's narrative form. Renoir has found imaginative ways to make the mobile frame sustain and elaborate a system of narrative relationships.

Fig. 7.183

In Michael Snow's *Wavelength* the relation of narrative to the mobile frame is almost exactly the inverse. Instead of supporting narrative form, frame mobility dominates narrative, even deflecting our attention from narrative. The film begins with a long-shot framing of a loft apartment, facing one wall and window (Fig. 7.183). In the course of the film the camera zooms in abruptly a short distance, then holds that framing. It zooms in a bit more, then holds that (Fig. 7.184). And so it goes throughout the film's forty-five minute length. By the end a photograph of ocean waves on the distant wall fills the frame in close-up.

Thus *Wavelength* is structured primarily around a single kind of frame mobility—the zoom-in. Its pattern of progression and development is not a narrative one, but that of an exploration, through deliberately limited means, of how the zoom transforms the space of the loft. The sudden zooms create frequent abrupt shifts of perspective relations. In excluding parts of the room, the zoom-in also magnifies and flattens what we see; every change of focal length gives us a new set of spatial relations. The zoom places more and more space offscreen. The sound track, for the most part, reinforces the basic formal progression by emitting a single humming tone that rises consistently in pitch as the zoom magnifies more and more.

Within *Wavelength*'s basic pattern, though, there are two contrasting subsystems. The first is a series of filtered tints that plays across the image as abstract fields of color. These tints often work against the depth represented in the shot of the loft.

Fig. 7.184

Fig. 7.185

The second subsystem evokes a sketchy narrative. At various intervals characters enter the loft and carry on certain activities (talking, listening to the radio, making phone calls). There is even a mysterious death (a body lies on the floor in Fig. 7.185). But these events remain unexplained in cause-effect terms and inconclusive as to closure (although at the film's end we do hear a sound that resembles a police siren). Furthermore, none of these actions swerves the mobile framing from its predetermined course. The jerkily shifting and halting zoom continues, even when it will exclude important narrative information. Thus *Wavelength* pulls in bits and pieces of narrative, but these fragments of action remain secondary, operating within the temporal progression of the zoom.

From the standpoint of the viewer's experience, *Wavelength*'s use of frame mobility arouses, delays, and gratifies unusual expectations. What plot there is arouses curiosity (What are the people up to? What has led to the man's death, if he does die?) and surprise (the apparent murder). But in general, a story-centered suspense is replaced by a *stylistic* suspense: What will the zoom eventually frame? From this standpoint, the colored tints and even the plot work with the spasmodic qualities of the zoom to delay the forward progress of the framing. When the zoom finally reveals its target, our stylistic anticipations have come to fulfillment. The film's title stands revealed as a multiple pun, referring not only to the steadily rising pitch of the sound track but also to the distance which the zoom had to cross in order to reveal the photo—a "wavelength."

Grand Illusion and *Wavelength* illustrate, in different ways, how frame mobility can guide and shape our perception of a film's space and time. Frame mobility may be motivated by larger formal concerns, as in Renoir's film, or it may itself become the principal formal concern, motivating other systems, as in Snow's film. What is important to realize is that by attention to how filmmakers utilize the mobile frame within specific contexts, we can gain a fuller understanding of how our experience of a film is created.

DURATION OF THE IMAGE: THE LONG TAKE

In our consideration of the film image, we have emphasized spatial qualities— how photographic transformations can alter the properties of the image, how framing defines the image for our attention. But cinema is an art of time as well as of space, and we have seen already how mise-en-scene and frame mobility operate in temporal as well as spatial dimensions. What we need to consider now is how the duration of the shot affects our understanding of it.

There is a tendency to consider the shot as recording "real" duration. A runner takes three seconds to clear a hurdle. If we film the runner, our projected film will also consume three seconds—or so the assumption goes. One film theorist, André Bazin, made it a major tenet of his aesthetic that cinema records "real time." (See Notes and Queries for a discussion of Bazin's position.) What must be noted, though, is that the relation of shot duration to the time consumed by the filmed event is not so simple.

First, obviously, the duration of the event on the screen may be manipulated by adjustments in the camera's or printer's drive mechanism, as we discussed earlier in this chapter. Slow-motion or fast-motion techniques may present the runner's jump in twenty seconds or two. Second, narrative films often permit no simple equivalence of "real duration" with screen duration. As Chapter 4 pointed out (p. 97), story duration can differ considerably from plot duration and screen duration.

Consider a shot from Ozu's *Only Son*. It is well past midnight and we have just seen a family awake and talking; this shot shows a dim corner of the family's apartment, with none of the characters onscreen (Fig. 7.186). But soon the light changes. The sun is rising. By the end of the shot it is morning (Fig. 7.187). This transitional shot consumes about a minute of screen time. It plainly does not record the "real" duration of the story events; that duration would be at least five hours. To put it another way, by manipulating screen duration, the film's plot has condensed a story duration of several hours into a minute or so. In the next chapter we shall examine how editing one shot with another can expand or contract screen duration. Here we need only note that it is just as possible to manipulate screen duration *within a single shot* as well. There need be no one-to-one correspondence between the onscreen duration of the shot and the duration of the story events represented.

Fig. 7.186

Fig. 7.187

■ THE LONG TAKE

Every shot has some measurable screen duration, but in the history of cinema, directors have varied considerably in their choice of short or lengthy shots. In general, early cinema (1895–1905) tended to rely on shots of fairly long duration, since there was often only one shot in each film. With the emergence of continuity editing in the period 1905–1916, shots became shorter. In the late teens and early twenties, an American film would have an average shot length of about five seconds. After the coming of sound, the average stretched to about ten seconds.

But throughout the history of the cinema, some filmmakers have consistently preferred to utilize shots of greater duration than the average. In various countries in the mid-1930s there was a tendency to increase the length of the shots, and this tendency continued throughout the next 20 years. The causes of this change are complex and not fully understood, but film scholars agree that the use of unusually lengthy shots—*long takes*, as they are called—constitutes a major resource for the filmmaker.

"Long take" is not the same as "long shot"; the latter term refers to the apparent distance between camera and object. As we saw in examining film production (p. 17), a *take* is one run of the camera that records a single shot. Calling a shot of notable length a "long take" rather than a "long shot" prevents ambiguity, since the latter term refers to a distanced framing, not to shot duration. In the films of Jean Renoir, Kenji Mizoguchi, Orson Welles, Carl Dreyer, or Miklós Jancsó, a shot may go on for several minutes, and it would be impossible to analyze these films without an awareness of how the long take can contribute to form and style. One long take in Andy Warhol's

Fig. 7.188

My Hustler follows the seductive exchange of two gay men as they groom themselves in a bathroom (Fig. 7.188). The shot, which runs for about thirty minutes, constitutes virtually the second half of the film.

Usually, we can regard the long take as an alternative to a series of shots. The director may choose to present a scene in one or a few long takes or to present the scene through several shorter shots. When an entire scene is rendered in only one shot, the long take is known by the French term *plan-séquence,* or "sequence shot."

Most commonly, filmmakers use the long take selectively. One scene will rely heavily on editing, another will be presented in a long take. This permits the director to associate certain aspects of narrative or nonnarrative form with the different stylistic options. A vivid instance occurs in the first part of Humberto Solanas and Octavio Getiño's *Hour of the Furnaces.* Most of the film relies upon editing of newsreel and staged shots to describe how European and North American ideologies penetrate developing nations. But the last shot of the film is a slow zoom-in to a photograph of the corpse of Che Guevera, symbol of guerrilla resistance to imperialism. Solanas makes the shot a long take, holding it for three minutes to force the viewer to dwell on the cost of resistance.

Mixing long takes and shorter shots also creates parallels and contrasts among scenes. André Bazin pointed out that *Citizen Kane* oscillates between long takes in the dialogue scenes and rapid editing in the "News on the March" sequence and other sequences. Hitchcock, Mizoguchi, Renoir, and Dreyer often vary shot duration, depending on the scene's function in the entire film.

Alternatively, the filmmaker may decide to build the entire film out of long takes. Hitchcock's *Rope* is famous for containing only eight shots, each running the full length of a reel of film in the camera. Similarly, each scene in *Winterwind, Agnus Dei, Red Psalm,* and other films by Miklós Jancsó is a *plan-séquence.* In such cases, the long take becomes a large-scale part of a film. And in such a context editing can have great force. After a seven- or eight-minute shot, an elliptical cut can prove quite disorienting, as Jancsó's films show.

If the long take often replaces editing, it should surprise no one that the long take is frequently allied to the mobile frame. The long take may use panning, tracking, craning, or zooming to present continually changing vantage points that are comparable in some ways to the shifts of view supplied by editing.

Very often frame mobility breaks the long-take shot into significant smaller units. In Mizoguchi's *Sisters of Gion,* one long take begins with Omocha and the older man seated (Fig. 7.189). Preparing to lure him into becoming her patron, she moves to the opposite end of the room, the camera following her (Figs. 7.190, 7.191). Now a second phase of the scene occurs: She starts to appeal to his sympathy. He comes over to console her (Figs. 7.192, 7.193); the camera moves into a tighter shot of the two as he succumbs to her advances (Fig. 7.194). Though there is no cutting, the camera and figure movements have demarcated important stages of the scene's action.

As in this example, long takes tend to be framed in medium or long shots. Thus as the camera lingers on a fairly "full" visual field, the spectator

Fig. 7.189

Fig. 7.190

Fig. 7.191

Fig. 7.192

Fig. 7.193

Fig. 7.194

has more opportunity to scan the shot for particular points of interest. This is recognized by Steven Spielberg, not himself a director who exploits lengthy takes:

> I'd love to see directors start trusting the audience to be the film editor with their eyes, the way you are sometimes with a stage play, where the audience selects who they would choose to look at while a scene is being played. . . . There's so much cutting and so many closeups being shot today I think directly as an influence from television.

As we have seen in the previous chapter, however, the director can still guide the audience's scanning of the frame through all of the technical resources of mise-en-scene. This is another way of saying that utilizing the long take often puts more emphasis on performance, setting, lighting, and other mise-en-scene factors.

The example from *Sisters of Gion* illustrates another important feature of the long take. Mizoguchi's shot reveals a complete internal logic—a beginning, middle, and end. As a large-scale part of a film, the long take can have its own formal pattern, its own development, its own trajectory and shape. Suspense develops; we start to ask how the shot will continue and when it will end.

The classic example of how the long take can constitute a formal pattern in its own right is the opening sequence of Welles's *Touch of Evil*. The shot begins with a close-up of a hand setting the timer of a bomb (Fig. 7.195). The camera tracks immediately right to follow first the shadow and then the

Fig. 7.195

figure of an unknown assassin planting the bomb in a car (Figs. 7.196, 7.197).

The camera cranes up to a high angle as the assassin flees and the victims arrive and set out in the car (Fig. 7.198). As the car goes around the corner, the camera circles back, rejoins the car, and tracks back to follow it (Fig. 7.199).

The car passes Vargas and his wife, Susan, and the camera starts to follow them. The camera loses the car and tracks diagonally backward with the couple as they move through the crowd (Fig. 7.200).

The camera tracks backward until both the occupants of the car and Susan and Vargas meet again, this time at the border post. A brief scene with the border guard ensues (Figs. 7.201, 7.202).

Fig. 7.196

Fig. 7.197

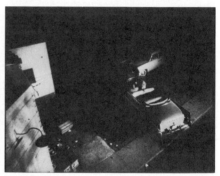

Fig. 7.198

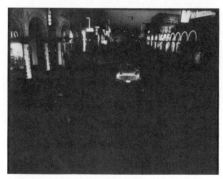

Fig. 7.199

Fig. 7.200

Fig. 7.201

Fig. 7.202

Fig. 7.203

Fig. 7.204

Fig. 7.205

Fig. 7.206

After tracking left with the car, the camera again encounters Susan and Vargas (Fig. 7.203) and tracks forward toward them. The shot ends as Susan and Vargas are about to kiss (Fig. 7.204). Their embrace is interrupted by the offscreen sound of an explosion. The couple turns to stare (Fig. 7.205). The next shot zooms in to show the car in flames (Fig. 7.206).

This opening shot makes plain most of the features of the long take. It offers an alternative to building the sequence out of many shots, and it stresses the cut that finally comes (the sudden cut on the sound of the explosion to the burning car). Most important, the shot has its own internal pattern of development. We expect that the bomb shown at the beginning will explode at some point, and we wait for that explosion through the duration of the long take. The shot establishes the geography of the scene (the border between Mexico and the United States). The camera movement, alternately picking up the car and the walking couple, weaves together two separate lines of narrative cause and effect that intersect at the border station. Vargas and Susan are thus drawn into the action involving the bombing. Our expectation is fulfilled when the end of the shot coincides with the explosion (offscreen) of the bomb. The shot has guided our response by taking us through a suspenseful process of narrative development. The long take's ability to present, in a single chunk of time, a complex pattern of events moving toward a goal makes shot duration as important to the image's effect as photographic qualities and framing are.

SUMMARY

The film shot, then, is a very complex formal unit. Mise-en-scene fills the image with material, arranging setting, lighting, costume, and figure behavior within the formal context of the total film. Within that same formal context, the filmmaker also controls the cinematographic qualities of the shot—how the image is photographed and framed, how long the image lasts on the screen.

You can sensitize yourself to these cinematographic qualities in much the same way that you worked on mise-en-scene. Trace the progress of a single technique—say, camera angle—through an entire film. Become conscious of when a shot begins and ends, observing how the long take may function to shape the film's form. Watch for camera movements, especially those that follow the action (since those are usually the hardest to notice). In short, once we are aware of cinematographic qualities, we can move to an understanding of their various possible functions within the total film.

Film art offers still other possibilities for choice and control. Chapters 6 and 7 have focused on the shot. The filmmaker may also juxtapose one shot with another through editing, and that is the subject of Chapter 8.

NOTES AND QUERIES

■ GENERAL WORKS

The standard contemporary references on cinematography are Fred H. Detmers, ed., *The American Cinematographer Manual,* 7th ed. (Hollywood: A.S.C., 1993); and Kris Malkiewicz, *Cinematography: A Guide for Film Makers and Film Teachers* (New York: Prentice-Hall, 1989). An excellent introduction to all phases of 8 and 16mm cinematography is David Cheshire, *The Book of Movie Photography* (New York: Knopf, 1979). For historical information, see Brian Coe, *The History of Movie Photography* (London: Ash & Grant, 1981); Leonard Maltin, *The Art of the Cinematographer* (New York: Dover, 1978); and David Bordwell, Janet Staiger, and Kristin Thompson, *The Classical Hollywood Cinema: Film Style and Mode of Production to 1960* (New York: Columbia University Press, 1985). *American Cinematographer* and *The Journal of the Society of Motion Picture and Television Engineers* continually publish articles on the subject.

Alternative points of view on cinematography may be found in Stan Brakhage, "A Moving Picture Giving and Taking Book," *Film Culture* **41** (Summer 1976): 39–57; Dziga Vertov, *Kino-Eye: The Writings of Dziga Vertov,* ed. Annette Michelson (Berkeley: University of California Press, 1984); and Maya Deren, "An Anagram of Ideas on Art, Form, and Film," and "Cinematography," in George Amberg, ed., *The Art of Cinema* (New York: Arno, 1972).

■ COLOR VERSUS BLACK AND WHITE

Today most films are shot on color stock and most viewers have come to expect that movies will be in color. At many points in film history, however, color and black-and-white film have been used to carry different meanings. In 1930s and 1940s American cinema, color tended to be reserved for fantasies (for example, *The Wizard of Oz*), historical films or films set in exotic locales *(Becky Sharp, Blood and Sand),* or very lavish musicals *(Meet Me in St. Louis).* Black and white was then considered more "realistic." But now that most films are in color, filmmakers can call on black and white to suggest a historical period (as witnessed by two such different films as Straub and Huillet's *Chronicle of Anna Magdalena Bach* and Tim Burton's *Ed Wood*). Such rules of thumb as "color for realism" have no universal validity; as always, it is a matter of context, the function of color or black-and-white tonalities within a specific film.

For more data on the principles of color photography, see Society of Motion Picture and Television Engineers, *Elements of Color in Professional Motion Pictures* (New York: SMPTE, 1957). A brief but well-illustrated history of color in motion pictures may be found in Roger Manvell, ed., *The International Encyclopedia of Film* (New York: Crown, 1972); this article demonstrates conclusively that radically different color ranges can all be accepted as "realistic." A basic history is R. T. Ryan, *A History of Motion Picture Color Technology* (New York: Focal Press, 1977). The most influential early process is considered in Fred E. Basten's *Glorious Technicolor: The Movies' Magic Rainbow* (San Diego: A. S. Barnes, 1980). See also Edward Branigan, "Color and Cinema: Problems in the Writing of History," *Film Reader* **4** (1979): 16–34. Len Lye explains the elaborate process behind the color design of *Rainbow Dance* in Wystan Curnow and Roger Horrocks, eds., *Figures of Motion: Len Lye/Selected Writings* (Auckland: Auckland University Press, 1984), pp. 47–49.

Film theorists have debated whether color film is artistically more impure than black and white. One argument against color may be found in Rudolf Arnheim, *Film as Art* (Berkeley: University of California Press, 1957). How is Arnheim's argument disputed by V. F. Perkins in *Film as Film* (Baltimore: Penguin, 1972)?

■ PERSPECTIVE AND THE CINEMA

On the history of perspective in painting, see John White, *The Birth and Rebirth of Pictorial Space* (New York: Harper, 1972) and Lawrence Wright, *Perspective in Perspective* (London: Routledge and Kegan Paul, 1983). Psychological aspects are discussed in Margaret A. Hagen, ed., *The Perception of Pictures*, 2 vols. (New York: Academic Press, 1980). A handy and informative guide is Fred Duberty and John Willat, *Perspective and Other Drawing Systems* (New York: Van Nostrand Reinhold, 1983).

■ SPECIAL EFFECTS

Part of the reason that major film studios tout themselves as "the magic factories" is that special-effects cinematography demands the complexity and expense that only a big firm can support. Special effects—rear projection, matte work, superimposition, and other procedures—require the time, patience, and rehearsal afforded by control over mise-en-scene. It is, then, no surprise that Méliès, the first person to exploit fully the possibilities of studio filmmaking, excelled at special-effects cinematography. Nor is it surprising that when UFA, the gigantic German firm of the 1920s, became the best-equipped film studio in Europe, it invested heavily in new special-effects processes. Similarly, as Hollywood studios grew from the midteens on, so did their special-effects departments. Engineers, painters, photographers, and set designers collaborated to contrive fantastic visual novelties. In these "magic factories" most of the history of special effects has been made.

But such firms were not motivated by sheer curiosity. The costs of elaborate back projection and matte work were usually investments. First, expensive as they were, such tricks often saved money in the long run. Instead of building a huge set, one could photograph the actors through a glass with the setting painted on it. Instead of taking cast and crew to the pyramids, one could film them against a back projection. Second, special effects made certain film genres possible. The historical epic—whether set in Rome, Babylon, or Jerusalem—was unthinkable unless special effects were devised to create huge vistas and crowds. The fantasy film, with its panoply of ghosts, flying horses, and invisible or incredibly shrinking people, demanded the perfection of superimposition and matte processes. The science-fiction film genre could scarcely exist without a barrage of special effects. For the major studios, the "factory" principle was responsible for the "magic." The main early work on the subject is Raymond Fielding's *The Technique of Special Effects Cinematography* (New York: Hastings House, 1974). See also Harold Schechter and David Everitt, *Film Tricks: Special Effects in the Movies* (New York: Dial, 1980); John Culhane, *Special Effects in the Movies: How They Do It* (New York: Ballantine, 1981); and Christopher Finch's lavishly illustrated *Special Effects: Creating Movie Magic* (New York: Abbeville, 1984). Illuminating case studies can be found in Linwood G. Dunn and George E. Turner, eds., *The ASC Treasury of Visual Effects* (Hollywood: American Society of Cinematographers, 1983). Articles on particular films' use of special effects appear regularly in *American Cinematographer* and *Cinefex*.

■ ASPECT RATIO

In Jean-Luc Godard's film *Contempt,* the director Fritz Lang (playing himself) laments that "CinemaScope is good only for filming funerals and snakes." *Contempt,* of course, is an anamorphic widescreen film (though it uses the Franscope widescreen system).

The aspect ratio of the film image has been debated since the inception of cinema. The Edison-Lumière ratio (1.33:1) was not generally standardized until 1911, and even after that other ratios were explored. Many cinematographers believed that 1.33:1 was the perfect ratio (perhaps not aware that it harks back to the "golden section" of academic painting). With the large-scale innovation of widescreen cinema in the early 1950s, cries of distress were heard. Most camera operators hated it. Lenses often were not sharp, lighting became more complicated, and as Lee Garmes put it, "We'd look through the camera and be startled at what it was taking in." Yet some directors—Nicholas Ray, Akira Kurosawa, Samuel Fuller, François Truffaut, Jean-Luc Godard—created unusual and fascinating compositions in the widescreen ratio. The systems are exhaustively surveyed in Robert E. Carr and R. M. Hayes's *Wide Screen Movies: A History and Filmography of Wide Gauge Filmmaking* (Jefferson, N.C.: McFarland, 1988). The most detailed defense of the aesthetic virtues of the widescreen image remains Charles Barr's "CinemaScope: Before and After," *Film Quarterly* **16,** 4 (Summer 1963): 4–24. To what extent does Barr's argument rest on an assumption that new technological possibilities create new formal and functional possibilities? *The Velvet Light Trap* **21** (1985) contains several articles on the history and aesthetics of widescreen cinema, including an article on Barr's essay and second thoughts by Barr. See Notes and Queries for Chapter 1 (pp. 39–40) for sources on widescreen films on video.

During the 1980s, two variants on traditional film gauges were designed in response to widescreen demands. One innovation is Super-35mm, which expands the image area within the traditional 35mm format. Tried out on *The Abyss, Black Rain,* and a few other titles, it promises to allow filmmakers to make a release print at either 2.35:1 (anamorphic) ratio or 1.85:1 matted. This format is discussed in Brett G. Sherris, "Subjectivision: Choose Your Own Aspect Ratio," *The Perfect Vision* **2,** 8 (Summer 1990): 100–107. More widely adopted was Super-16mm, which is superior to regular 16mm in its capacity for being blown up to make 35mm release prints. Super-16mm provides 40 percent more image area and creates a wider frame which can be matted to the 1.85:1 aspect ratio favored in 35mm exhibition. Pioneered on Robert Young's *Ballad of Gregorio Cortez* and Robert Altman's *Come Back to the Five and Dime, Jimmy Dean, Jimmy Dean,* Super-16mm proved successful for such independent projects as Lizzie Borden's *Working Girls* and Spike Lee's *She's Gotta Have It.* See "Shooting 16mm for Blowup to 35mm Film," *American Cinematographer* **62,** 7 (July 1981): 680–681, 720–724. Super-16mm has been used frequently during the 1990s, as on Mike Figgis's *Leaving Las Vegas.*

■ THE SUBJECTIVE SHOT

Sometimes the camera, through its positioning and movements, invites us to see events "through the eyes" of a character. Some directors (Howard Hawks, John Ford, Kenji Mizoguchi, Jacques Tati) seldom use the subjective shot, but others (Alfred Hitchcock, Alain Resnais) use it constantly. As Figure 7.128 indicated, Samuel Fuller's *Naked Kiss* starts with shocking subjective shots:

> We open with a direct cut. In that scene, the actors utilized the camera. They held the camera; it was stripped on them. For the first shot, the pimp has the camera strapped on his chest. I say to [Constance] Towers, "Hit the camera!" She hits the camera, the lens. Then I reverse it. I put the camera on her, and she whacks the hell out of him. I thought it was effective. [Quoted in Eric Sherman and Martin Rubin, *The Director's Event* (New York: Signet, 1969), p. 189.]

Historically, filmmakers began experimenting with the "first-person camera" or the "camera as character" quite early. *Grandma's Reading Glass* (1901) features subjective point-of-view shots. Keyholes, binoculars, and other apertures were often used to motivate optical point of view. In 1919 Abel Gance used many subjective shots in *J'accuse.* The 1920s saw many filmmakers taking an interest in subjectivity, seen in such films as Jean Epstein's *Coeur fidèle* (1923) and *La Belle nivernaise* (1923), E. A. Dupont's *Variety* (1925), F. W. Murnau's *The Last Laugh* (1924), with its famous drunken scene, and Abel Gance's *Napoleon* (1927). Some believe that in the 1940s the subjective shot—especially the subjective camera movement—got completely out of hand in Robert Montgomery's *Lady in the Lake* (1946). For almost the entire film the camera represents the vision of the protagonist, Philip Marlowe; we see him only when he glances in mirrors. "Suspenseful! Unusual!" proclaimed the advertising. "YOU accept an invitation to a blonde's apartment! YOU get socked in the jaw by a murder suspect!"

The history of the technique has teased film theorists into speculating about whether the subjective shot evokes identification from the audience. Do we think we *are* Philip Marlowe? The problem of audience "identification" with a point-of-view shot remains a difficult one in film theory. A useful discussion is Edward Branigan's *Point of View in the Cinema: A Theory of Narration and Subjectivity in Classical Film* (New York: Mouton, 1984).

■ CAMERA MOVEMENT AND ZOOM

A statement of the classical Hollywood cinema's position on camera movement may be found in Herb A. Lightman, "The Fluid Camera," *American Cinematographer* **27,** 3 (March 1946): 82, 102–103: "The intelligent director or cinematographer moves the camera only when the demands of the filmic situation motivate that movement." Compare the Soviet filmmaker Dziga Vertov: "I am kino-eye, I am a mechanical eye. . . . Now and forever, I free myself from human immobility, I am in constant motion" ("Kinoks: A Revolution," in *Kino Eye: The Writings of Dziga Vertov,* cited earlier, p. 17). For a historical treatment, see Jon Gartenberg, "Camera Movement in Edison and Biograph Films, 1900–1907," *Cinema Journal* **19,** 2 (Spring 1980): 1–16.

The Steadicam process, which uses complex gyroscopes to compensate for any tremble or jitter, has become a favorite way to save money on elaborate tracking shots. Cinematographer Allen Daviau also used the device in George Miller's episode of *The Twilight Zone* to create the impression of an airplane lurching during a storm. "I said to Garrett [Brown], 'Can you adjust your gyros to make it an unsteady cam?' . . . And I said to John Toll, hand holding his camera, 'Take the darn thing and shake it' " [*Moviemakers at Work,* ed. David Chell (Redmond, Wash.: Microsoft Press, 1987), p. 28]. Jean-Pierre Geuens discusses the aesthetics of the Steadicam in "Visuality and Power: The Work of the Steadicam," *Film Quarterly* **47,** 2 (Winter 1994–95): 8–17.

During the 1960s, the zoom lens became a common shooting technique. Some discussions have compared zooming with camera movement (usually unfavorably). See Arthur Graham, "Zoom Lens Techniques." *American Cinematographer* **44,** 1 (January 1963): 28–29; Paul Joannides, "The Aesthetics of the Zoom Lens," *Sight and Sound* **40,** 1 (Winter 1970–71): 40–42; and Stuart M. Kaminsky, "The Use and Abuse of the Zoom Lens," *Filmmakers Newsletter* **5,** 12 (October 1972): 20–23. To what extent do these three authors agree about the "proper" utilization of the zoom? The most thorough historical and aesthetic discussion is John Belton, "The Bionic Eye: Zoom Esthetics," *Cinéaste* **9,** 1 (Winter 1980–81): 20–27.

Hitchcock's *Vertigo* innovated the combination of zooming in and tracking out. Discussing his use of this device in *Le Samourai,* Jean-Pierre Melville remarked, "Instead of simply resorting to the now almost classical technique of a track back compensated by a zoom forward, I used the same movement but with stops." [Quoted in Rui Nogueira, ed., *Melville* (New York: Viking, 1971), p. 130.] The effect is not unlike the spasmodic flattening of depth in

Wavelength. On the latter film, see William C. Wees, "Prophecy, Memory and the Zoom: Michael Snow's *Wavelength* Re-Viewed," *Ciné-tracts* **14/15** (Summer/Fall 1981): 78–83.

■ "REAL TIME" AND THE LONG TAKE

When the camera is running, does it record "real time"? If so, what artistic implications follow from that?

It was André Bazin who took the theoretical initiative in viewing cinema as an art which depends on "real time." Like photography, Bazin argued, cinema is a *recording process.* The camera registers, photochemically, the light reflected from the object. Like the still camera, the movie camera records space. But unlike the still camera, the movie camera can also record *time.* "The cinema is objectivity in time. . . . Now, for the first time, the image of things is likewise the image of their duration, change mummified as it were" [*What Is Cinema?* vol. 1 (Berkeley: University of California Press, 1966), pp. 14–15]. On this basis, Bazin saw editing as an intrusive interruption of the "natural" continuity of duration. He thus praised long-take directors such as Jean Renoir, Orson Welles, William Wyler, and Roberto Rossellini as artists whose styles respected concrete moment-to-moment life.

Bazin shoud be credited with calling our attention to the possibilities latent in the long take at a time when other film theorists considered it "theatrical" and "uncinematic." Yet the problem of "real time" in film seems more complicated than Bazin thought. The most productive avenues which Bazin's ideas opened up have involved the analysis of different directorial *styles* rather than analysis of the most "realistic" ways to shoot a scene. That is, analysts no longer tend to ask whether Renoir's long takes arc more faithful to reality than Eisenstein's short shots; we ask instead about the shots' different formal functions in each director's films. Incidentally, Eisenstein himself—*before* Bazin—proposed shooting an entire scene from *Crime and Punishment* in one long take. See "Mise-en-shot," in Vladimir Nizhny, *Lessons with Eisenstein* (New York: Hill & Wang, 1969), pp. 93–139.

Our quotation from Steven Spielberg [p. 261, from Roger Ebert and Gene Siskel, *The Future of the Movies* (Kansas City: Andrews and McMeel, 1991), p. 73] is consistent with a widespread belief that the long take, like deep-space mise-en-scene, gives the audience more freedom than does a heavily edited scene. This idea also stems from Bazin, who explored it in his writings on Orson Welles and William Wyler. See André Bazin, *Orson Welles,* trans. Jonathan Rosenbaum (New York: Harper & Row, 1978).

Representative stylistic analyses of the long take include V. F. Perkins, *"Rope," The Movie Reader* (New York: Praeger, 1972), pp. 35–37; David Thomson, *Movie Man* (New York: Stein and Day, 1967); Brian Henderson, "The Long Take," in *A Critique of Film Theory* (New York: Dutton, 1980); and Barry Salt, "Statistical Style Analysis of Motion Pictures," *Film Quarterly* **28,** 1 (Fall 1974): 13–22.

EIGHT

THE RELATION OF SHOT TO SHOT: EDITING

Since the 1920s, when film theorists began to realize what editing can achieve, it has been the most widely discussed film technique. This has not been all to the good, for some writers have mistakenly found in editing the key to good cinema (or even *all* cinema). Yet many films, particularly in the period before 1904, consist of only one shot and hence do not depend on editing at all. Experimental films sometimes deemphasize editing by making each shot as long as the amount of film a camera will hold, as with Michael Snow's *La Région centrale* and Andy Warhol's *Eat, Sleep,* and *Empire.* Such films are not necessarily less "cinematic" than others that rely heavily on editing.

Still, one can see why editing has exercised such an enormous fascination for film aestheticians, for as a technique it is very powerful. The ride of the Klan in *The Birth of a Nation,* the Odessa Steps sequence in *Potemkin,* the "degradation of the gods" episode in *October,* the shower murder in *Psycho,* the train crash in *La Roue,* the diving sequence of *Olympia,* the "News on the March" segment of *Citizen Kane,* the tournament sequence in *Lancelot du Lac*—all of these celebrated moments derive much of their effect from editing.

Perhaps even more important, however, is the role of editing within an entire film's stylistic system. An ordinary Hollywood film typically contains between eight hundred and twelve hundred shots; a film centering on rapid action can have two thousand or more. This fact alone suggests that editing strongly shapes viewers' experiences, even if they are not aware of it. Editing contributes a great deal to a film's organization and its effects on spectators.

WHAT EDITING IS

Editing may be thought of as the coordination of one shot with the next. As we have seen, in film production a shot is one or more exposed frames in a series on a continuous length of film stock. The film editor eliminates unwanted footage, usually by discarding all but the best take. The editor also cuts superfluous frames, such as those showing the clapboard (p. 18), from the beginnings and endings of shots. She or he then joins the desired shots, the end of one to the beginning of another.

Fig. 8.1

These joins can be of different sorts. A *fade-out* gradually darkens the end of a shot to black, and a *fade-in* accordingly lightens a shot from black. A *dissolve* briefly superimposes the end of shot A and the beginning of shot B, as at the beginning of *The Maltese Falcon* (Figs. 8.1–8.3). In a *wipe*, shot B replaces shot A by means of a boundary line moving across the screen, as in *Seven Samurai* (Fig. 8.4). Here both images are briefly on the screen at the same time, but they do not blend, as in a dissolve. In the production process, fades, dissolves, and wipes are "optical effects" and are marked as such by the editor. They are typically executed in the laboratory.

Fig. 8.2

The most common means of joining two shots is the *cut*. In the production process a cut is usually made by splicing two shots together by means of cement or tape. Some filmmakers "cut" during filming by planning that the film will emerge from the camera ready for final showing. Here the physical junction from shot to shot is created in the act of shooting. Such "editing in the camera," however, is rare and is mainly confined to experimental and amateur filmmaking. Editing after shooting is the norm. Today much editing is done by means of video transfers stored on videotape or disc, so that the cuts (or *edits*, in video terminology) can be made without touching film. Nevertheless the final version of the film will be prepared for printing by cutting and splicing the negative footage.

Fig. 8.3

As viewers, we perceive a shot as an uninterrupted segment of screen time, space, or graphic configurations. Fades, dissolves, and wipes are perceived as gradually interrupting one shot and replacing it with another. Cuts are perceived as instantaneous changes from one shot to another.

Consider an example of cutting, four shots from the first attack on Bodega Bay in Alfred Hitchcock's film *The Birds* (see Figs. 8.5–8.8):

Fig. 8.4

Fig. 8.5

Fig. 8.6

Fig. 8.7

Fig. 8.8

1. *Medium shot, straight-on angle.* Melanie, Mitch, and the Captain standing by the restaurant window talking. Melanie on extreme right, bartender in background (Fig. 8.5).

2. *Medium close-up.* Melanie by Captain's shoulder. She looks to right (out offscreen window) and up, as if following with eyes. Pan right with her as she turns to the window and looks out (Fig. 8.6).

3. *Extreme long shot.* Melanie's point of view. Gas station across street, phone booth in left foreground. Birds dive-bomb attendant, right to left (Fig. 8.7).

4. *Medium close-up.* Melanie, profile. Captain moves right into shot, blocking out bartender; Mitch moves right into extreme foreground. All in profile look out window (Fig. 8.8).

Each of these four shots presents a different segment of time, space, and graphic materials. The first shot shows three people talking. An instantaneous change—a cut—shifts us to a medium close-up shot of Melanie. (Hitchcock could have utilized a fade, dissolve, or wipe instead, with a slower change from shot to shot, or he could have handled the scene as one continuous shot, as we shall see presently.) In the second shot, space has changed (Melanie is isolated and larger in the frame), time is continuous, and the graphic configurations have changed (the arrangements of the shapes and colors vary). Another cut takes us instantly to what she sees. The gas station shot (Fig. 8.7) presents a very different space, a successive bit of time, and a different graphic configuration. Another cut returns us to Melanie (Fig. 8.8), and again we are shifted instantly to another space, the next slice of time, and a different graphic configuration. Thus the four shots are joined by three cuts.

Hitchcock could have presented the *Birds* scene without editing. Imagine a camera movement that frames the four people talking, tracks in and rightward to Melanie as she turns, pans rightward to the window to show the dive-bombing gull, and pans leftward back to catch Melanie's expression. This would constitute one shot, for we would not have the disjunctions afforded by editing; the camera movements, no matter how fast, would not present the marked and abrupt shifts that cuts produce. Now imagine a deep-space composition that presents Mitch in the foreground, Melanie and the window in the middle ground, and the gull attack in the distance. Again, the scene could now be played in one shot, for we would have no abrupt change of time or space or graphics. And the movements of the figures would not yield that disjunction of the screen material that is provided by editing. In this sequence, then, Hitchcock could have presented the action in a single shot, either by means of a camera movement or by means of a deep-space composition. Instead, he presents it in *more* than one shot—that is, through editing.

Viewers sometimes assume that films are shot with several cameras running simultaneously, and that editing is principally a matter of picking the best shot to show at a given moment. It is true that most television programs are shot with this *multiple-camera* technique, but it is still fairly rare in cinema. Sometimes a filmmaker will use several cameras to capture a performance from several different angles and distances; such was the case with Marlon Brando's scenes in *Apocalypse Now*. Contemporary filmmakers may employ an "A" camera for a master shot and a "B" camera for closer views, as James Cameron frequently does. More often, multiple-camera shooting is used for recording spectacular or unrepeatable action, such as explosions or complicated stunts.

Nevertheless, throughout film history, most sequences have been shot with only one camera. In *The Birds* scene, for example, the shots were taken at different times and places—one (shot 3) outdoors, the others in a sound stage (and these perhaps on different days). A film editor thus must assemble a large and varied batch of footage. To ease this task, most filmmakers plan for the editing phase during the preparation and shooting phases. Shots are taken with an idea of how they will eventually fit together. In fictional filming, scripts and storyboards help plan cuts and other transitions. Even documentary filmmakers usually frame and film with an eye to how the shots will cut together. In examining continuity editing, we will see that the director controls the staging and framing of the action so that changes of shot will be smooth and unobtrusive.

DIMENSIONS OF FILM EDITING

Editing offers the filmmaker four basic areas of choice and control:

1. Graphic relations between shot A and shot B
2. Rhythmic relations between shot A and shot B
3. Spatial relations between shot A and shot B
4. Temporal relations between shot A and shot B

Graphic and rhythmic relationships are present in the editing of any film. Spatial and temporal relationships may be irrelevant to the editing of films using abstract form, but they are present in the editing of films built out of nonabstract images (that is, the great majority of motion pictures). Let us trace the range of choice and control in each area.

■ GRAPHIC RELATIONS BETWEEN SHOT A AND SHOT B

The four shots from *The Birds* may be considered purely as graphic configurations, as patterns of light and dark, line and shape, volumes and depths, movement and stasis—*independent of* the shot's relation to the time and space of the story. For instance, Hitchcock has not drastically altered the overall brightness from shot to shot. But he could have cut from the uniformly lit second shot (Fig. 8.6, Melanie turning to the window) to a shot of the gas station swathed in darkness. Moreover, Hitchcock has usually kept the most important part of the composition roughly in the center of the frame. (Compare Melanie's position in the frame with that of the gas station in Fig. 8.7.) He could, however, have cut from a shot in which Melanie was in, say, upper frame left to a shot locating the gas station in the lower right of the frame.

Hitchcock has also played off certain color differences. Melanie's hair and outfit make her a predominantly yellow and green figure, whereas the shot of the gas station is dominated by drab bluish grays set off by touches of red in the gas pumps. Alternatively, Hitchcock could have cut from Melanie to another figure composed of similar colors. Furthermore, the movement in Melanie's shot—her turning to the window—does not blend into the movements of either the attendant or the gull in the next shot, but Hitchcock could have echoed Melanie's movement in speed, direction, or frame placement by movement in the next shot.

In short, editing together any two shots permits the interaction, through similarity and difference, of the *purely pictorial* qualities of those two shots. The four aspects of mise-en-scene (lighting, setting, costume, and the behavior of the figures in space and time) and most cinematographic qualities (photography, framing, and camera mobility) all furnish potential graphic elements. Thus every shot provides possibilities for purely graphic editing, and every cut creates some sort of graphic relationship between two shots.

At one level we perceive all film images as configurations of graphic material, and every film manipulates those configurations. Indeed, even in a film that is not pure abstraction, graphic editing can be a source of interest to filmmaker and audience.

Graphics may be edited to achieve smooth continuity or abrupt contrast. The filmmaker may link shots by graphic similarities, thus making what we can call a *graphic match.* Shapes, colors, overall composition, or movement in shot A may be picked up in the composition of shot B. A minimal instance is the cut that joins the first two shots of David Byrne's *True Stories,* where the horizon line of the Texas prairie (Fig. 8.9) is graphically matched by the waterline of ancient seas (Fig. 8.10). Similarly, in the "Beautiful Girl" song in Stanley Donen and Gene Kelly's *Singin' in the Rain,* amusing graphic matches are achieved through dissolves from one fashionably dressed woman to another, each figure posed and framed quite similarly from shot to shot.

More dynamic graphic matches appear in Akira Kurosawa's *Seven Samurai.* After the samurai have first arrived at the village, an alarm sounds and they race to discover its source. Kurosawa cuts together six shots of different running samurai, which he dynamically matches by means of composition, lighting, setting, figure movement, and panning camera movement (Figs. 8.11–8.16).

Fig. 8.9

Fig. 8.10

Fig. 8.11

Fig. 8.12

Fig. 8.13

Fig. 8.14

Fig. 8.15

Fig. 8.16

Fig. 8.17

Fig. 8.18

Fig. 8.19

Fig. 8.20

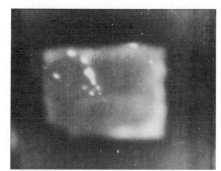

Fig. 8.21

Fig. 8.22

Filmmakers often call attention to graphic matches at transitional moments. In *Aliens* a dissolve creates a graphic match between Ripley's sleeping face and the curve of the Earth (Figs. 8.17–8.19). Satyajit Ray's *World of Apu* moves from one scene to another by dissolving from a movie screen (Fig. 8.20) to the rectangular window of a taxicab (Fig. 8.21) and then moving the camera back to show Apu and his wife riding home from the theater (Fig. 8.22).

Such precise graphic matching is relatively rare. Still, an approximate graphic continuity from shot A to shot B is typical of most narrative cinema. The director will usually strive to keep the center of interest roughly constant across the cut, to maintain the overall lighting level, and to avoid strong color clashes from shot to shot. In Souleymane Cissé's *Finye* (*The Wind*), the grandfather confronts a corrupt official, who is lying in a hammock. Alter-

Wim Wenders

Fig. 8.23

Fig. 8.24

Fig. 8.25

Fig. 8.26

nating shots (Figs. 8.23, 8.24) keep each man's face in the upper left center of the screen.

Editing need not be graphically continuous. Mildly discontinuous editing may appear in widescreen compositions organized around characters facing one another. (Later we will study this editing pattern as "shot/reverse-shot" cutting.) A scene from Wim Wenders's *Paris, Texas,* filmed in 1.75:1 aspect ratio, shows two brothers confronting one another in the southwest desert (Figs. 8.25, 8.26). Each man is framed somewhat off center, so that the empty space in each shot implies the other man's presence offscreen. Compared to the *Finye* example, the cut here creates greater graphic discontinuity. Note, however, that the cut does balance the frame area from shot to shot: each man fills the space left empty in the previous shot. In addition, each man's face is just above the horizontal center of each frame, so that the spectator's eye can easily adjust to the changing composition. If asked afterward, many viewers would probably not recall that these compositions were unbalanced.

Graphically discontinuous editing can be more noticeable. Orson Welles frequently strives for a clash from shot to shot, as in *Citizen Kane* when the dark long shot of Kane's bedroom is followed by the bright opening title of the "News on the March" reel. Similarly, in *Touch of Evil,* Welles dissolves from a shot of Menzies looking out a window on frame right (Fig. 8.27) to a shot of Susan Vargas looking out a different window on frame left (Fig. 8.28). The clash is further accentuated by contrasting screen positions of the window reflections. Alain Resnais's *Night and Fog* began something of a fad by utilizing an extreme but apt graphic conflict: Color footage of an abandoned concentration camp is cut together with black-and-white newsreel shots of the camps in the period 1942–1945. Even here, though, Resnais found striking similarities in shape, as when a tracking shot of fence posts graphically matches a low-angle shot of marching Nazi legs.

A director may call upon editing to create a graphic conflict between color qualities. Later in *Paris, Texas,* the protagonist discovers his wife working in an erotic peepshow. Wenders follows the couple's conversation by cutting from the customer's side of the glass to the performer's (Color Plates 60, 61). Although both people are visible in each shot, the cutting stresses their separation by harsh color contrasts. The wife's light-blue, almost

Fig. 8.27

Fig. 8.28

washed-out stage setting, as seen from the husband's side of the glass, clashes with the blackness and the aluminum-foil reflections in the next shot.

Later in the *Birds* sequence discussed above, Hitchcock puts graphic conflict to good use. Gasoline spurting from the pump has flowed across the street to a parking lot, and Melanie, along with several other people at the restaurant window, has seen a man accidentally set the gasoline alight. His car ignites, and an explosion of flame engulfs him. What we see next is Melanie watching helplessly as the flame races along the trail of gas toward the station. Hitchcock cuts the shots as shown in Figures 8.29–8.39:

30.	(ls)	High angle. Melanie's POV. Flaming car, spreading flames.	73 frames
31.	(mcu)	Straight-on angle. Melanie, immobile, looking off left, mouth open.	20 frames
32.	(ms)	High angle. Melanie's POV. Pan with flames moving from lower right to upper left of trail of gasoline.	18 frames
33.	(mcu)	as 31. Melanie, immobile, staring down (center).	16 frames
34.	(ms)	High angle. Melanie's POV. Pan with flames moving from lower right to upper left.	14 frames
35.	(mcu)	as 31. Melanie, immobile, looking off right, staring aghast.	12 frames
36.	(ls)	Melanie's POV. Gas station. Flames rush in from right. Mitch, sheriff, and attendant run out left.	10 frames

Fig. 8.29   Shot 30

Fig. 8.30   Shot 31

Fig. 8.31   Shot 32

Fig. 8.32   Shot 33

Fig. 8.33   Shot 34

Fig. 8.34   Shot 35

Fig. 8.35   Shot 36

Fig. 8.36   Shot 37

Fig. 8.37   Shot 38

Fig. 8.38   Shot 39

Fig. 8.39   Shot 40

37. (mcu) as 31. Melanie, immobile, stares off extreme right.   8 frames

38. (ls) as 36. Melanie's POV. Cars at station explode.   34 frames

39. (mcu) as 31. Melanie covers her face with her hands.   33 frames

40. (els) Extreme high angle on city, flaming trail in center. Gulls fly into shot.

In graphic terms, Hitchcock has exploited two possibilities of contrast. First, although each shot's composition centers the action (Melanie's head, the flaming trail), the movements thrust in different directions. In shot 31 Melanie looks to the lower left, whereas in shot 32 the fire moves to the upper left. In shot 33 Melanie is looking down center, whereas in the next shot the flames still move to the upper left, and so on.

More important—and what makes the sequence impossible to recapture on the printed page—is a crucial contrast of mobility and stasis. The shots of the flames present movement of both the subject (the flames rushing along the gas) and of the camera (which pans to follow). But the shots of Melanie could almost be "stills," since they are absolutely static. She does not turn her head within the shots, and the camera does not track in or away from her. Interestingly too, instead of showing her turning to watch the flames, Hitchcock presents only static stages of her action, and so we must infer the progress of her attention. By making movement conflict with countermovement and with stillness, Hitchcock has powerfully exploited the graphic possibilities of editing.

■ RHYTHMIC RELATIONS BETWEEN SHOT A AND SHOT B

Each shot, being a strip of film, is of a certain length, measured in frames, feet, or meters. And the shot's physical length corresponds to a measurable duration onscreen. As we know, at "sound speed" 24 frames last one second in projection. A shot can be as short as a single frame, or it may be thousands of frames long, running for many minutes when projected. Editing thus allows the filmmaker to determine the duration of each shot. When the filmmaker adjusts the length of shots in relation to each other, she or he is controlling the *rhythmic* potential of editing.

As we have already seen (pp. 196–197), rhythm in cinema includes many factors—principally accent, beat, and tempo. And cinematic rhythm as a whole derives not only from editing but from other film techniques as well. The filmmaker also relies on movement in the mise-en-scene, camera position and movement, the rhythm of sound, and the overall context to determine the editing rhythm. Nevertheless, the patterning of shot lengths contributes considerably to what we intuitively recognize as a film's rhythm.

Sometimes the filmmaker will use shot duration to create a stressed, accented moment. In one sequence of *The Road Warrior,* a ferocious gang member butts his head against that of a victim. At the moment of contact director George Miller cuts in a few frames of pure white. The result is a sudden flash that suggests violent impact. Conversely, a shot's duration can be used to deaccentuate an action. In editing *Raiders of the Lost Ark,* Steven Spielberg discovered that after Indiana Jones shoots the gigantic swordsman, several seconds had to be added to allow the audience's reaction to die down before the action could resume.

More commonly, however, the rhythmic possibilities of editing emerge when several shot lengths form a discernible pattern. A steady, metrical beat can be established by making all of the shots approximately the same length. The filmmaker can also create a dynamic pace. Steadily lengthening shots can generate a gradually slowing tempo, while successively shorter shots can create an accelerating one.

Consider how Hitchcock handles the tempo of the first gull attack in *The Birds.* Shot 1, the medium shot of the group talking (Fig. 8.5), consumes almost a thousand frames, or about 41 seconds. But shot 2 (Fig. 8.6), which shows Melanie looking out the window, is much shorter—309 frames (almost 13 seconds). Even shorter is shot 3 (Fig. 8.7), which lasts only 55 frames (about 2$\frac{1}{3}$ seconds). The fourth shot (Fig. 8.8), showing Melanie joined by Mitch and the Captain, lasts only 35 frames (about 1$\frac{1}{2}$ seconds). Clearly Hitchcock is accelerating the pace at the beginning of what will be a tense sequence.

In what follows, Hitchcock makes the shots fairly short, but subordinates the length of the shot to the internal rhythm of the dialogue and the movement in the images. As a result, shots 5 through 29 (not illustrated here) have no fixed pattern of lengths. But once the essential components of the scene have been established, Hitchcock returns to strongly accelerating cutting.

In presenting Melanie's horrified realization of the flames racing from the parking lot to the gas station, shots 30 through 40 (Figs. 8.29–8.39) climax the rhythmic intensification of the sequence. As the description on pp. 277–278 shows, after the shot of the spreading flames (no. 30, Fig. 8.29), each shot decreases in length by two frames, from 20 frames (4/5 of a second) to 8 frames (1/3 of a second). Two shots, 38 and 39, then punctuate the sequence with almost identical durations (a little less than 1$\frac{1}{2}$ seconds apiece). Shot 40 (Fig. 8.39), a long shot that lasts over 600 frames, functions as both a pause and a suspenseful preparation for the new attack. The scene's variations in rhythm alternate between rendering the savagery of the attack and generating suspense as we await the next onslaught.

We have had the luxury of counting frames on the actual strip of film. The theater viewer cannot do this, but she or he does feel and recognize the accelerating and decelerating tempo in this sequence because of the changing shot durations. In general, by controlling editing rhythm, the filmmaker controls the amount of time we have to grasp and reflect on what we see. A series of rapid shots, for example, leaves us little time to think about what we are watching. In the *Birds* sequence, Hitchcock's editing impels the viewer's perception to move at a faster and faster pace. Quickly grasping the progress of the fire and understanding Melanie's changes in position become essential factors in the rising excitement of the scene.

Hitchcock is not, of course, the only director to utilize rhythmic editing. Its possibilities were initially explored by such directors as D. W. Griffith (especially in *Intolerance*) and Abel Gance. In the 1920s the Hollywood cinema, the Soviet montage school, and the French "Impressionist" filmmakers explored the rhythmic possibilities of strings of short shots. When sound films became the norm, pronounced rhythmic editing survived in dramas such as Lewis Milestone's *All Quiet on the Western Front* as well as in musical comedies and fantasies such as René Clair's *À Nous la liberté* and *Le Million*, Rouben Mamoulian's *Love Me Tonight*, and Busby Berkeley's *42nd Street* and *Footlight Parade*. In classical Hollywood cinema the rhythmic use of dissolves became crucial to the "montage sequence," which we shall discuss shortly. Rhythm remains a fundamental resource of the editor, most notably in the use of fast cutting to build up excitement during an action sequence, a television advertisement, or a music video.

■ SPATIAL RELATIONS BETWEEN SHOT A AND SHOT B

Editing usually serves not only to control graphics and rhythm but to construct film space as well. Exhilaration in this newly discovered power can be sensed in the writings of such filmmakers as the Soviet director Dziga Vertov: "I am Kino-eye. I am builder. I have placed you . . . . in an extraordinary room which did not exist until just now when I also created it. In this room there are twelve walls, shot by me in various parts of the world. In bringing together shots of walls and details, I've managed to arrange them in an order that is pleasing."

Such elation is understandable. Editing lets an omniscient range of knowledge become visible as omnipresence, the ability to move from one spot to any other. Editing permits the filmmaker to relate *any* two points in space through similarity, difference, or development.

The director might, for instance, start with a shot that establishes a spatial whole and follow this with a shot of a part of this space. This is what Hitchcock does in shot 1 and shot 2 of the *Birds* sequence described above (Figs. 8.5, 8.6): a medium long shot of the group of people followed by a medium shot of only one, Melanie. Such analytical breakdown is a very common editing pattern, especially in classical continuity editing.

Alternatively, the filmmaker could construct a whole space out of component parts. Hitchcock does this later in the *Birds* sequence. Note that in Figures 8.5 through 8.8 and in shots 30–39 (Figs. 8.29–8.38) we do not see an establishing shot including Melanie *and* the gas station. In production the restaurant window need not have been across from the station at all; they could have been filmed in different cities or countries. (Shooting "out of continuity," Hitchcock probably filmed the restaurant shots on a sound stage and the gas station shots in an outdoor set.) Yet we are compelled to "see" Melanie as being across the street from the gas station. The bird cry offscreen and the mise-en-scene (the window and Melanie's sideways glance) contribute considerably as well. It is, however, primarily the editing that creates the spatial whole of restaurant-and-gas-station.

Such spatial manipulation through cutting is fairly common. In documentaries compiled from newsreel footage, for example, one shot might show a cannon firing, and another shot might show a shell hitting its target; we infer that the cannon fired the shell (though the shots may show entirely different battles). Again, if a shot of a speaker is followed by a shot of a cheering crowd, we assume a spatial coexistence.

The possibility of such spatial manipulation was examined by the Soviet filmmaker Lev Kuleshov, who during the 1920s shot and cut "experiments" in constructing spatial relations by eliminating establishing shots. The most famous of these involved the cutting of neutral shots of an actor's face with other shots (variously reported as shots of soup, nature scenes, a dead woman, a baby). The reported result was that the audience immediately assumed not only that the actor's expression changed but also that the actor was reacting to things present in the same space as himself. Similarly, Kuleshov cut together shots of actors, "looking at each other" but on Moscow streets miles apart, then meeting and strolling together—and looking at the White House in Washington. Although filmmakers had used such cutting before Kuleshov's work, film scholars call "the Kuleshov effect" any series of shots that *in the absence of an establishing shot* prompts the spectator to infer a spatial whole on the basis of seeing only portions of the space.

The Kuleshov effect can conjure up robust cinematic illusions. In Corey Yuen's *Legend of Fong Sai-Yuk*, a martial-arts bout between the hero and an adept woman begins on a platform but then moves into the audience—or rather, onto the audience, for the two fight while balancing on the heads and shoulders of the crowd! Yuen's rapid editing conveys the scene's point by means of the Kuleshov effect. A shot of the woman's upper body (Fig. 8.40) is followed by a shot of her legs and feet, supported by unwilling spectators (Fig. 8.41). (In production the actress hung from wires or a bar suspended out of the frame.) In a sequence of many shots, Yuen provides only a few brief full-figure framings showing Fong Sai-Yuk and the woman in combat.

While the viewer doesn't normally notice the Kuleshov effect, a few films call attention to it. Carl Reiner's *Dead Men Don't Wear Plaid* mixes footage filmed in the present with footage from Hollywood movies of the 1940s. Thanks to the Kuleshov effect, *Dead Men* creates unified scenes in which Steve Martin converses with characters who were originally featured in other films. In *A Movie*, Bruce Conner makes a joke of the Kuleshov effect by cutting from a submarine captain peering through a periscope to a woman gazing at the camera, as if they could see each other (Figs. 5.51, 5.52, p. 160).

In the Kuleshov effect, editing cues the spectator to infer a single locale. Editing can also emphasize action taking place in separate places. In *Intol-*

Fig. 8.40

Fig. 8.41

erance D. W. Griffith cuts from ancient Babylon to Gethsemane, from France in 1572 to America in 1916. Such parallel editing, or *crosscutting*, is a common way films construct a variety of spaces.

More radically, the editing can present spatial relations as being ambiguous and uncertain. In Carl Dreyer's *La Passion de Jeanne d'Arc*, for instance, we know only that Jeanne and the priests are in the same room. Because the neutral white backgrounds and the numerous close-ups provide no orientation to the entire space, we can seldom tell how far apart the characters are or precisely who is beside whom. We shall see later how *October* and *Last Year at Marienbad* create even more extreme spatial discontinuities.

■ TEMPORAL RELATIONS BETWEEN SHOT A AND SHOT B

Like other film techniques, editing can control the time of the action denoted in the film. In a narrative film especially, editing usually contributes to the plot's manipulation of story time. You will recall that Chapter 4 pointed out three areas in which plot time can cue the spectator to construct the story time: order, duration, and frequency. Our *Birds* example (Figs. 8.5–8.8) shows how editing reinforces all three areas of control.

First, there is the *order* of presentation of events. The men talk, then Melanie turns away, then she sees the gull swoop, then she responds. Hitchcock's editing presents these story events in the 1-2-3-4 order of his shots. But he could have shuffled the shots into a different order. Transposing shot 2 and shot 3 would be unusual, but it is possible to put the shots in any order at all, even reverse (4-3-2-1). This is to say that the filmmaker may control temporal succession through the editing.

As we saw in Chapter 4, such manipulation of events leads to changes in story-plot relations. We are most familiar with such manipulations in *flashbacks,* which present one or more shots out of their presumed story order. In *Hiroshima mon amour,* for instance, Resnais cuts from a shot of the hand of the protagonist's Japanese lover to a shot of the hand of her German lover years earlier (with memory motivating the violation of temporal order). In contemporary cinema, brief flashbacks to key events may brutally interrupt present-time action. *The Fugitive* uses this technique to return obsessively to the murder of Dr. Kimball's wife, the event which initiated the story's action. In Errol Morris's documentary *The Thin Blue Line,* present-day interrogations of suspects and witnesses are interspersed with reenactments which function as flashbacks to the central crime.

A much rarer option for reordering story events is the *flashforward.* Here the editing moves from the present to a future event and then returns to the present. A small-scale instance occurs in *The Godfather.* Don Vito Corleone talks with his sons Tom and Sonny about their upcoming meeting with Sollozzo, the gangster who is asking them to finance his narcotics traffic. As the Corleones talk in the present, shots of them are interspersed with shots of Sollozzo going to the meeting in the future. The editing is used to provide exposition about Sollozzo while also moving quickly to the Don's announcement, at the gangsters' meeting, that he will not involve the family in the drug trade.

Filmmakers may use flashforwards to tease the viewer with glimpses of the eventual outcome of the story action. The end of *They Shoot Horses, Don't They?* is hinted at in brief shots which interrupt scenes in the present. Such flashforwards create a sense of a narration with a powerful range of story knowledge.

We may assume, then, that if a series of shots traces a 1-2-3 order in the presentation of story events, it is because the filmmaker has chosen to do that, not because of any necessity of following this order. Editing also offers ways for the filmmaker to alter the *duration* of story events as presented in the film's plot.

In our sample sequence, the duration of the story events is presented whole. Melanie's act of turning consumes a certain length of time, and Hitchcock does not alter the duration of the event in his editing. Nevertheless, he could have. Imagine cutting from shot 1 (the men talking and Melanie standing by) to a shot of Melanie already turned and looking out the window. The time it took her to turn to the window would be eliminated by the cut. Thus editing can create a temporal *ellipsis*.

Fig. 8.42

Elliptical editing presents an action in such a way that it consumes less time on the screen than it does in the story. The filmmaker can create an ellipsis in three principal ways.

Suppose that a director wants to show a man climbing a flight of stairs, but does not want to show the entire duration of his climb. Most simply, the director could use a conventional *"punctuation"* shot change, such as a dissolve or a wipe or a fade; in the classical filmmaking tradition, such a device signals that some time has been omitted. Our director could simply dissolve from a shot of the man starting at the bottom of the stairs to a shot of him reaching the top.

Alternatively, the filmmaker could show the man at the bottom of the staircase and let him walk up out of the frame, hold briefly on the empty frame, then cut to an empty frame of the top of the stairs and let the man enter the frame. The *empty frames* on either side of the cut cover the elided time.

Fig. 8.43

Finally, the filmmaker can create an ellipsis by means of a *cutaway:* a shot of another event elsewhere that will not last as long as the elided action. In our example, the director might start with the man climbing but then cut away to a woman in her apartment. We could then cut back to the man much further along in his ascent.

In our *Birds* example, Hitchcock could also have controlled the duration of the action by *expansion,* the opposite of ellipsis. For example, he might have extended shot 1 so as to include the beginning of Melanie's act of turning, then shown her beginning to turn in shot 2 as well. This would have prolonged the action, stretching it out past its story duration. The Russian filmmakers of the 1920s made frequent use of temporal expansion through such *overlapping editing,* and no one mastered it more thoroughly than Sergei Eisenstein. In *Strike* when factory workers bowl over a foreman with a large wheel hanging from a crane, two shots expand the action (Figs. 8.42–8.44). In *October* Eisenstein overlaps several shots of rising bridges in order to stress the significance of the moment. In *Ivan the Terrible* friends pour golden coins down on the newly crowned Ivan in a torrent that seems never to cease.

Fig. 8.44

In all of these sequences the duration of the action is prolonged through noticeably overlapping the movements from shot to shot.

Returning once more to the temporal relations in the *Birds* segment, we note that in the story Melanie turns to the window only once and the gull swoops only once. And Hitchcock presents these events on the screen the same number of times that they occur in the story. But, of course, Hitchcock could have repeated any of these shots. Melanie could have been shown turning to the window several times; this would be not merely overlapping a phase of an action but rather full-scale repetition.

If this sounds peculiar, it is doubtless because we are overwhelmingly accustomed to seeing a shot present the action only once. Yet its very rarity may make repetition a powerful editing resource. In Bruce Conner's *Report* there is a newsreel shot of John and Jacqueline Kennedy riding a limousine down a Dallas street. The shot is systematically repeated, in part or in whole, again and again, building up tension in our expectations as the shot seems to move by tiny increments closer to the moment of the inevitable assassination. Occasionally in *Do The Right Thing*, Spike Lee cuts together two takes of the same action, as when we twice see a garbage can fly through the air and break the pizzeria window at the start of the riot. *Frequency* is another area of choice and control that, like order and duration, gives the filmmaker considerable temporal possibilities in editing.

Graphics, rhythm, space, and time, then, are at the service of the filmmaker through the technique of editing. Our brief survey should suggest that the potential range of these areas of control is virtually unlimited. Yet most films we see make use of a very narrow set of editing possibilities—so narrow, indeed, that we can speak of a dominant editing style throughout Western film history. This is what is usually called *continuity editing*, and because of its prevalence we will examine it. But the most familiar way to edit a film is not the only way to edit a film, and so we will also consider some alternatives to continuity editing.

CONTINUITY EDITING

Editing might appear to present a dilemma to the filmmaker. On one hand, the physical break between one shot and another may seem to have a disturbing effect, interrupting the viewer's flow of attention. For example, an abrupt change of vantage point might confuse the spectator as to where or when the action of shot B is taking place after an action is presented in shot A. But on the other hand, editing is undeniably a primary means for constructing a film. How can one use editing and yet control its potentially disruptive force?

This problem (though not stated in these terms) first confronted filmmakers around 1900–1910. The solution eventually adopted was to plan the cinematography and mise-en-scene with a view to editing the shots according to a specific system. The purpose of the system was *to tell a story* coherently and clearly, to map out the chain of characters' actions in an undistracting way. Thus editing, supported by specific strategies of cinematography and mise-en-scene, was used to ensure *narrative continuity*. So powerful is this style that, even today, anyone working in narrative filmmaking around the world is expected to be thoroughly familiar with it. How does this stylistic system work?

The basic purpose of the continuity system is to create a smooth flow from shot to shot. All of the possibilities of editing we have already examined are bent to this end. First, graphic qualities are usually kept continuous from shot to shot. The figures are balanced and symmetrically deployed in the frame; the overall lighting tonality remains constant; the action occupies the central zone of the screen.

Second, the rhythm of the cutting is usually made dependent on the camera distance of the shot. Long shots are left on the screen longer than medium shots, and medium shots are left on longer than close-ups. The assumption is that the spectator needs more time to take in the shots containing more details. In scenes of physical action like the fire in *The Birds*, accelerated editing rhythms may be present, but the shorter shots will still tend to be closer views.

Since the continuity style seeks to present a narrative action, however, it is chiefly through the handling of space and time that editing furthers narrative continuity.

■ SPATIAL CONTINUITY: THE 180° SYSTEM

In the continuity style the space of a scene is constructed along what is called variously the *"axis of action,"* the "center line," or the "180° line." The scene's action—a person walking, two people conversing, a car racing along a road— is assumed to take place along a discernible, predictable line. This axis of action determines a half-circle, or 180° area, where the camera can be placed to present the action. Consequently, the filmmaker will plan, film, and edit the shots so as to respect this center line. The camera work and mise-en-scene in each shot will be manipulated to establish and reiterate the 180° space.

A bird's-eye view (Fig. 8.45) will clarify the system. We have a girl and a boy conversing. The axis of action is that imaginary line connecting the two people. Under the continuity system, the director would arrange the mise-en-scene and camera placement so as to establish and sustain this line. The camera can be put at any point as long as it stays on the same *side* of the line (hence the 180° term). A typical series of shots would be: (1) a medium shot of the girl and boy; (2) a shot over the girl's shoulder, "favoring" the boy; (3) a shot over the boy's shoulder, favoring the girl. But to cut to a shot from camera position X, or from any position within the tinted area, would be considered a violation of the system because it *crosses* the axis of action. Indeed, some handbooks of film directing call shot X flatly "wrong." To see why, we need to examine what this 180° system does.

It ensures some common space from shot to shot. As long as the axis of action is not crossed, portions of the space will tally from shot to shot. In our example, assume that there is a wall with pictures and shelves behind the girl and boy. If we follow shot 1 with shot 2, not only will one side of the boy reappear as a common factor but so will at least part of the wall, the pictures,

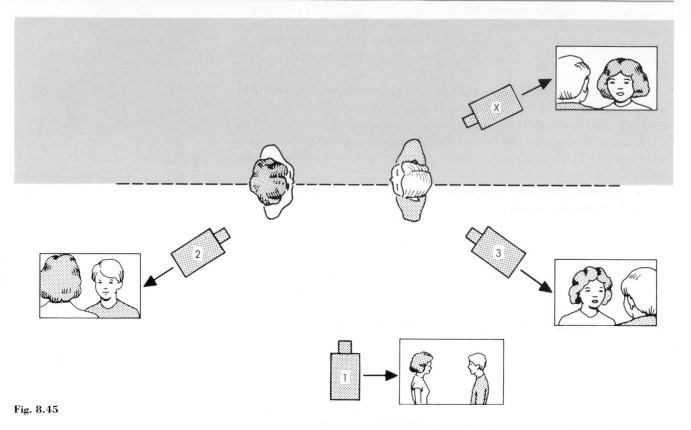

Fig. 8.45

and shelves. We are thus oriented to the space presented in shot 2: It includes part of the space of shot 1, observed from a new position. But if we follow shot 2 with shot X, we see both a new side of the boy and an entirely different background (another wall, a door, or whatever). A defender of traditional continuity would claim that this disorients us; has the boy moved to another locale? Thus the 180° rule generates a common area from shot to shot, which stabilizes space and orients the viewer within the scene.

It ensures constant screen direction. Note that in the three shots taken from camera positions 1, 2, and 3, the characters remain in the same position relative to each other. That is, the girl is always on the left of the frame and the boy is always on the right, even though we see them from various angles as the cuts shift our vantage points. Moreover, what screen direction exists is given by the direction of the characters' glances, with the girl looking right and the boy looking left. In this example, then, the characters' fixed positions and eyelines determine screen direction. Shot X violates screen direction by shifting the girl to the right of the boy and making her look leftward.

Screen direction is most obvious when the figures in the shots are moving. Assume now that the girl is walking left to right; her path constitutes the axis of action. As long as our shots do not cross this axis, cutting them together will keep the screen direction of the girl's movement constant, from left to right. But if we *cross* the axis and film a shot from the other side, not only will the background change but also the girl will now appear on the screen as moving from *right to left*. Such a cut could be disorienting.

Consider a similar situation to that in Figure 8.45, a standard scene of two cowboys meeting for a shootout on a town street (Fig. 8.46). Cowboy A and Cowboy B form the 180° line, but here A is walking from left to right and B is approaching from right to left, both seen in the shot taken from camera position one. A closer view, from camera position two, shows B still moving from right to left. A third shot, from camera position three, shows A walking, as he had been in the first shot, from left to right.

But imagine that this third shot was instead taken from position X, on the opposite side of the line. A is now seen as moving from right to left. Has he taken fright and turned around while the second shot, of B, was on the screen? The filmmakers may want us to think that he is still walking toward his adversary, but the change in screen direction could make us think just the opposite. A cut to a shot taken from any point in the colored area would create this change in direction. Such breaks in continuity can be confusing.

Even more disorienting would be crossing the line while establishing the scene's action. In our shootout, if the first shot shows A walking from left to right and the second shot shows B (from the other side of the line) also walking left to right, we would probably not be sure that they were walking toward each other. The two cowboys would seem to be walking in the same direction at different points on the street, as if one were following the other. We would very likely be startled if they suddenly came face to face within the same shot.

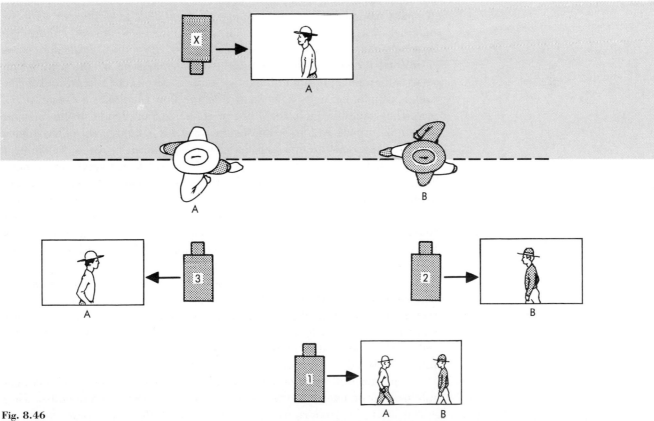

Fig. 8.46

Fig. 8.47

Fig. 8.48

Though we shall examine some stratagems for getting "across the line," it is enough for now to see that adhering to the 180° system ensures consistent screen direction from shot to shot. Still, many continuity-style films occasionally violate the 180° rule without confusing the viewer. Take the situation shown in Figure 8.45. Cutting from shot 1 to shot 3 to shot X would be considered very disruptive because shot X gives no new narrative information and is a jolting change of composition. But if the editing moved from shot 1 to shot 2 to shot X, you would probably still understand that the boy and girl are conversing face to face. Similarly, there is a cut in John Ford's *Stagecoach* that jumps across the center line without disorienting the viewer. In a long shot, the hero begins leaping from the driver's seat down onto the horse team; both he and the coach are moving to the right (Fig. 8.47). After a cut to a closer view, coach and hero are now moving leftward (Fig. 8.48). Because the action is simple and clear, we have no problem grasping the spatial relations of these shots.

The 180° system prides itself on delineating space clearly. The viewer should always know where the *characters* are in relation to one another and to the setting. More important, the viewer always knows *where he or she is* with respect to the story action. The space of the scene, clearly and unambiguously unfolded, does not jar or disorient, because such disorientation, it is felt, will distract the viewer from the center of attention: the narrative chain of causes and effects.

We saw in Chapter 4 that the classical Hollywood mode of narrative subordinates time, motivation, and other factors to the cause-effect sequence. We also saw how mise-en-scene and camera work may present narrative material. Now we can note how continuity editing also works to subordinate space to causality. On the basis of the 180° principle, filmmakers have developed the continuity system as a way to build up a smoothly flowing space which remains subordinate to narrative action. Let us consider a concrete example, the opening of John Huston's film *The Maltese Falcon*.

The scene begins in the office of detective Sam Spade. In the first two shots this space is established in several ways. First, there is the office window (shot 1a, Fig. 8.49) from which the camera tilts down to reveal Spade (shot 1b, Fig. 8.50) rolling a cigarette. As Spade says, "Yes, sweetheart?" shot 2 (Fig. 8.51) appears. This is important in several respects. It is an *establishing shot*, delineating the overall space of the office: the door, the intervening area, the desk, and Spade's position. Note also that shot 2 establishes a 180° line between Spade and his secretary, Effie; Effie could be the girl in Figure 8.45, and Spade could be the boy. The first phase of this scene will be built around staying on the same side of this 180° line.

Once laid out for us in the first two shots, the space is analyzed into its components. Shots 3 (Fig. 8.52) and 4 (Fig. 8.53) show Spade and Effie talking. Because the 180° line established at the outset is adhered to (each shot presents the two from the same side), we know their location and spatial relationships. In cutting together medium shots of the two, however, Huston relies on two other common tactics within the 180° system.

The first is the *shot/reverse-shot* pattern. Once the 180° line has been established, we can show first one end point of the line, then the other. Here

Fig. 8.49   Shot 1a

Fig. 8.50   Shot 1b

Fig. 8.51   Shot 2

we cut back and forth from Effie to Spade. A reverse shot is not literally the "reverse" of the first framing. It is simply a shot of the opposite end of the axis of action, usually showing a three-quarters view of the subject. In our bird's-eye view diagram (Fig. 8.45), shots 2 and 3 form a shot/reverse-shot pattern, as Figures 8.52 and 8.53 do here. Earlier examples in this chapter of shot/reverse-shot cutting are Figures 8.23, 8.24 and 8.25, 8.26.

The second tactic Huston uses here is the *eyeline match*. That is, shot A presents someone looking at something offscreen; shot B shows us what is being looked at. In neither shot are *both* looker and object present. In the *Maltese Falcon* opening, the cut from the shot of Effie (shot 3, Fig. 8.52) to the shot of Spade at his desk (shot 4, Fig. 8.53) is an eyeline match. The shots from *The Birds* of Melanie watching the bird attack and fire also create eyeline matches, as do the examples of editing balancing frame compositions (Figs. 8.23, 8.24 and 8.25, 8.26).

Note that shot/reverse-shot editing need not employ eyeline matches. You could film both ends of the axis in a shot/reverse-shot pattern without showing the characters looking at each other. One character might have her hands over her eyes, the other might have his back to the camera. On the whole, however, most shot/reverse-shot cuts also utilize the eyeline match.

The eyeline match is a simple idea but a powerful one, since the *directional* quality of the eyeline creates a strong spatial continuity. To be looked at, an object must be near the looker. The eyeline match presumably created the effects Kuleshov identified in his construction of false spaces through editing. That is, the expressionless actor seems to be looking at whatever is in the next shot, and the audience assumes that the actor is reacting accordingly.

Within the 180° system, the eyeline match, like constant screen direction, can stabilize space. Note how in shot 3, Effie's glance off right reiterates Spade's position even though he is not onscreen. And though Spade does not look up after the cut to shot 4, the camera position remains adamantly on the same side of the axis of action (indeed, the position is virtually identical to that in shot 1b). We know that Effie is offscreen left. Thus the breakdown of the scene's space is completely consistent, this consistency ensured by adherence to the 180° system. Thanks to the shot/reverse-shot pattern and the eyeline match, we understand the characters' locations even when they are not in the same frame.

Fig. 8.52   Shot 3

Fig. 8.53   Shot 4

Fig. 8.54   Shot 5a

Fig. 8.55   Shot 5b

Fig. 8.56   Shot 6a

Fig. 8.57   Shot 6b

The spatial consistency is reaffirmed in shot 5, which presents the same framing as did shot 2. The office is shown again (shot 5a, Fig. 8.54), when the new character, Brigid O'Shaughnessy, enters. Spade stands to greet her, and the camera reframes his movement by a slight tilt upward (shot 5b, Fig. 8.55). Shot 5 is a *reestablishing shot,* since it reestablishes the overall space that was analyzed into shots 3 and 4. The pattern, then, has been *establishment/breakdown/reestablishment*—one of the most common patterns of spatial editing in the classical continuity style.

Let us pause to examine how this pattern has functioned to advance the narrative. Shot 1 has suggested the locale and, more importantly, has emphasized the protagonist by linking him to the sign on the window. Offscreen sound and Spade's "Yes, sweetheart?" motivate the cut to shot 2. This establishing shot firmly anchors shot 1 spatially. It also introduces the source of the offscreen sound—the new character, Effie. The shot changes at precisely the moment when Effie enters. We are thus unlikely to notice the cut, because our expectations lead us to want to see what happens next. The space near the door has been shown when the cause-effect chain makes it important, not before.

Shots 3 and 4 present the conversation between Spade and Effie, and the shot/reverse shot and the eyeline match reassure us as to the characters' locations. We may not even notice the cutting, since the style works to emphasize the dramatic flow of the scene—what Effie says and how Spade reacts. In shot 5 the overall view of the office is presented again, precisely at the moment when a new character enters the scene, and this in turn situates her firmly in the space. Thus the narrative—the dialogue, the entrance of new characters—is emphasized by adhering to the 180° system. The editing subordinates space to action.

We can trace the same procedures, with one additional variation, in the shots that follow. In shot 5 Brigid O'Shaughnessy enters Spade's office. Shot 6 presents a reverse angle on the two of them as she comes toward him (shot 6a, Fig. 8.56). She sits down alongside his desk (shot 6b, Fig. 8.57). Up to this point the 180° line ran between Spade and the doorway. Now the axis of action runs from Spade to the client's chair by his desk. Once established, this new line will not be violated.

The extra factor here is a third tactic for ensuring spatial continuity—the *match on action,* a very powerful device. Assume that a person starts to stand up in shot 1. We can wait until the character is standing up and has stopped moving before cutting to shot 2. But we can instead show the person's movement *beginning* in shot 1, and then we can cut to shot 2, which shows the continuation of the movement. We would then have a match on action, the editing device that carries a movement across the break between two shots.

To appreciate the skill involved in making a match on action, recall that most films are shot with a single camera. In filming shots whose action will be matched at the editing stage, it is possible that the first shot, the one in which the movement starts, will be filmed hours or days apart from the second, in which the movement is continued. Thus matching action is not simply a matter of cutting together two complete versions of the same scene from different vantage points. The process involves keeping notes about matters of camera work, mise-en-scene, and editing so that all the details can be fitted together in the assembly phase of production.

In the *Maltese Falcon* scene the cut from the end of shot 5 (Fig. 8.55) to the beginning of shot 6 (Fig. 8.56) uses a match on action, the action being Brigid's walk toward Spade's desk. Again, the 180° system aids in concealing the match, since it keeps screen direction constant: Brigid moves from left to right in both shots. As one would expect, the match on action is a tool of narrative continuity. It takes a practiced eye to spot a smooth match on action; so powerful is our desire to follow the action flowing across the cut that we ignore the cut itself. The similarity of movement from shot to shot holds our attention more than the differences resulting from the cut.

Except for the match on action, the editing in the rest of the scene uses the same tactics we have already seen. When Brigid sits down, a new axis of action has been *established* (shot 6b, Fig. 8.57). This enables Huston to break down the space into closer shots (shots 7 through 13, Figs. 8.58–8.64). All of these shots use the shot/reverse-shot tactic: The camera frames, at an oblique angle, one end point of the 180° line, then frames the other. (Note the shoulders in the foreground of shots 7, 8, and 10—Figs. 8.58, 8.59, and 8.61.) Here again, the editing of space presents the dialogue action simply and unambiguously.

Beginning with shot 11, Huston's cuts also create eyeline matches. Brigid looks off right at Spade (shot 11, Fig. 8.62). She looks off left as the door is heard opening (shot 13, Fig. 8.64). Archer, just coming in, looks off

Fig. 8.58   Shot 7

Fig. 8.59   Shot 8

Fig. 8.60   Shot 9

Fig. 8.61   Shot 10

Fig. 8.62   Shot 11

Fig. 8.63   Shot 12

Fig. 8.64   Shot 13

Fig. 8.65   Shot 14

Fig. 8.66   Shot 15

right at them (shot 14, Fig. 8.65), and they both look off at him (shot 15, Fig. 8.66). The 180° rule permits us always to know who is looking at whom.

What is the function of the analytical cutting in this part of the scene? Huston could have played the entire conversation in one long take, remaining with shot 6b (Fig. 8.57). Why has he broken the conversation into seven shots? Most evidently, the analytical breakdown controls our attention. We will look at Brigid or Spade at exactly the moment Huston wants us to. In the long take and the more distant framing, Huston would have to channel our attention in other ways, perhaps through composition or sound.

Furthermore, the shot/reverse-shot pattern emphasizes the development of Brigid's story and Spade's reaction to it. As she gets into details, the cutting moves from over-the-shoulder shots (Figs. 8.58, 8.59) to framings that isolate Brigid (Figs. 8.60 and 8.62) and eventually one that isolates Spade (Fig. 8.63). These shots come at the point when Brigid, in an artificially shy manner, tells her story, and the medium close-ups arouse our curiosity about whether she is telling the truth. The shot of Spade's reaction (Fig. 8.63) suggests that he is skeptical. In short, the analytical editing cooperates with framing and figure behavior to focus our attention on Brigid's tale, to let us study her demeanor, and to get a hint as to Spade's response.

When Archer enters, the breakdown of the space stops for a moment, and Huston *reestablishes* the locale. Archer is integrated into the action by means of a rightward pan shot [shots 16a and 16b (Figs. 8.67, 8.68)]. His path is consistent with the scene's first axis of action, that running between Spade and the doorway. Moreover, the framing on him is similar to that used for Brigid's entrance earlier. [Compare shot 16b with 6a (Figs. 8.68 and 8.56).] Such repetitions allow the viewer to concentrate on the new information, not the manner in which it is presented.

Fig. 8.67   Shot 16a

Fig. 8.68   Shot 16b

Fig. 8.69   Shot 17

Now firmly established as part of the scene, Archer hitches himself up onto Spade's desk. His position puts him at Spade's end of the axis of action (shot 17, Fig. 8.69). The rest of the scene's editing analyzes this new set of relationships without ever crossing the 180° line.

The viewer is not supposed to notice all this. Throughout, the shots present space to emphasize the cause-and-effect flow—the characters' actions, entrances, dialogue, reactions. The editing has economically organized space to convey narrative continuity.

The continuity system, in exactly these terms, remains in force today.

Most narrative films still draw upon 180° principles. In Ron Howard's *Parenthood*, for example, eyeline-matched shot/reverse shots present the conversations (Figs. 8.70, 8.71). Here the women in the foreground establish the axis of action.

The continuity system can be refined in various ways. If a director arranges several characters in a circular pattern, say, sitting around a dinner table, then the axis of action will probably run between the characters of greatest importance at the moment. In Figures 8.72 and 8.73, from *Bringing Up Baby,* the important interaction is occurring between the two men, so we can cut from one side of the woman in the foreground to the other side in order to get consistent shot/reverse shots. When one man leaves the table, however, a semicircular arrangement of figures in space is created, so that a new axis of action can be established. Now we can get shot/reverse-shot exchanges running down the length of the table (Figs. 8.74, 8.75).

Both the *Maltese Falcon* and the *Bringing Up Baby* extracts show that in the course of a scene the 180° line may shift as the characters move around the setting. In some cases, the filmmaker may create a new axis of action which allows the camera to take up a position that would have been "across the line" in an earlier phase of the scene.

A simple example occurs in Georges Franju's *Eyes without a Face.* The daughter, who wears a mask to hide her disfigured face, is talking with her father's housekeeper. The housekeeper is shown in an over-the-shoulder medium shot, with the axis of action running from the right foreground to the

Fig. 8.70

Fig. 8.71

Fig. 8.72

Fig. 8.73

Fig. 8.74

Fig. 8.75

Fig. 8.76

Fig. 8.77

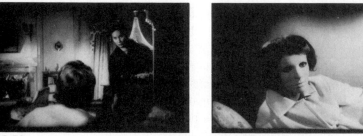

Fig. 8.78

Fig. 8.79

left middle ground (Fig. 8.76). If Franju wanted us to see the daughter's reaction, the continuity rules would oblige him to take a shot over the house-keeper's right shoulder, showing the daughter facing leftward. Instead, the housekeeper moves rightward into depth, the camera panning to keep her in the frame (Fig. 8.77). From the right rear she turns to look leftward at the daughter (Fig. 8.78). This creates an axis of action running from the fore-ground left to the background right. Now Franju gives us a three-quarter reverse shot of the young woman looking rightward (Fig. 8.79). Had Franju cut from the first camera position (Fig. 8.76) to this position, he would have violated the original axis of action. (This would essentially present us with shot X in Fig. 8.45.) The housekeeper's move to the right created a new axis that made this angle and eyeline permissible.

The power of the axis of action and the eyelines it can create is so great that the filmmaker may be able to eliminate an establishing shot, thus relying on the Kuleshov effect. In Spike Lee's *She's Gotta Have It,* Nola Darling holds a Thanksgiving dinner for her three male friends. The scene is treated without any shot showing all four in the same frame. Instead Lee presents medium long shots including all the men (for example, Fig. 8.80), over-the-shoulder shot/reverse shots among them (for example, Fig. 8.81), and eyeline-matched medium close-ups of them. Nola is given her own medium close-ups (Fig. 8.82).

Through eyelines and body orientations, the editing keeps the spatial relations completely consistent. For example, each man looks in a different direction when addressing Nola (Figs. 8.83, 8.84). This cutting pattern en-hances the dramatic action by making all the men equal competitors for her. They are clustered at one end of the table, and none is shown in the same frame with her. In addition, by organizing the angles around her overall orientation to the action (as in Fig. 8.85), Lee reinforces Nola as the pivotal

Fig. 8.80

Fig. 8.81

Fig. 8.82

Fig. 8.83

Fig. 8.84

Fig. 8.85

character. Finally, the longer shot and her separate medium close-ups intensify the progression of the scene: The men are on display, and Nola is coolly judging each one's behavior.

Another felicity in the 180° system is the *cheat cut*. Sometimes a director may not have perfect continuity from shot to shot because he or she has composed each shot for specific reasons. Must the two shots match perfectly? Again, narrative motivation decides the matter. Given that the 180° system emphasizes narrative causality, the director has some freedom to "cheat" mise-en-scene from shot to shot, that is, to mismatch slightly the positions of characters or objects.

Consider two shots from William Wyler's *Jezebel*. Neither character moves during either shot, but Wyler has blatantly cheated the position of Julie: In the first shot the top of her head is even with the man's chin (Fig. 8.86), but in the second shot she seems to have grown several inches (Fig. 8.87). Yet the great majority of viewers would not notice the discrepancy since it is the dialogue that is of paramount importance in the scene; here again, the similarities between shots outweigh the differences of position. Moreover, a change from a straight-on angle to a slightly high angle helps hide the cheat. There is, in fact, a cheat in the *Maltese Falcon* scene, too, between shots 6b and 7. In 6b (Fig. 8.57), as Spade leans forward, the back of his chair is not near him. Yet in shot 7 (Fig. 8.58), it has been cheated to be just behind his left arm. Here again, the primacy of the narrative flow overrides such a cheat cut.

Fig. 8.86

In several of our examples so far, continuity editing has proved itself well-suited for portraying the interactions of two or more characters. But the same techniques can be used when a character is alone. Hitchcock's *Rear Window* includes many scenes of the solitary photographer Jeff watching events occurring in an apartment across the courtyard from him. Hitchcock

Fig. 8.87

Fig. 8.88   Fig. 8.89

uses a standard pattern: He cuts from a shot of Jeff looking at something offscreen to a shot of what Jeff sees. (Since usually there is no establishing shot, the Kuleshov effect operates here.) Thus shot/reverse-shot and eyeline-match cutting are central to the film's effect. More specifically, Hitchcock uses a variety of eyeline-match editing known as *point-of-view cutting*.

Shot 1 (Fig. 8.88) shows Jeff looking out his window, and shot 2 (Fig. 8.89) is a shot of what he sees—from his optical POV. We have already discussed POV framings in Chapter 7, p. 240, and we have seen an instance of POV cutting in the *Birds* sequence discussed on pp. 277–278. Now we are in a position to see how this is consistent with the 180° continuity system. The second shot, that representing Jeff's POV, is taken from a position *on* the axis of action, from the end point Jeff occupies (see Fig. 8.90).

As *Rear Window* goes on, the subjectivity of the POV shots intensifies. Becoming more eager to examine the details of his neighbor's life, Jeff begins to use binoculars and a photographic telephoto lens to magnify his view. By using shots taken with lenses of different focal lengths, Hitchcock can show

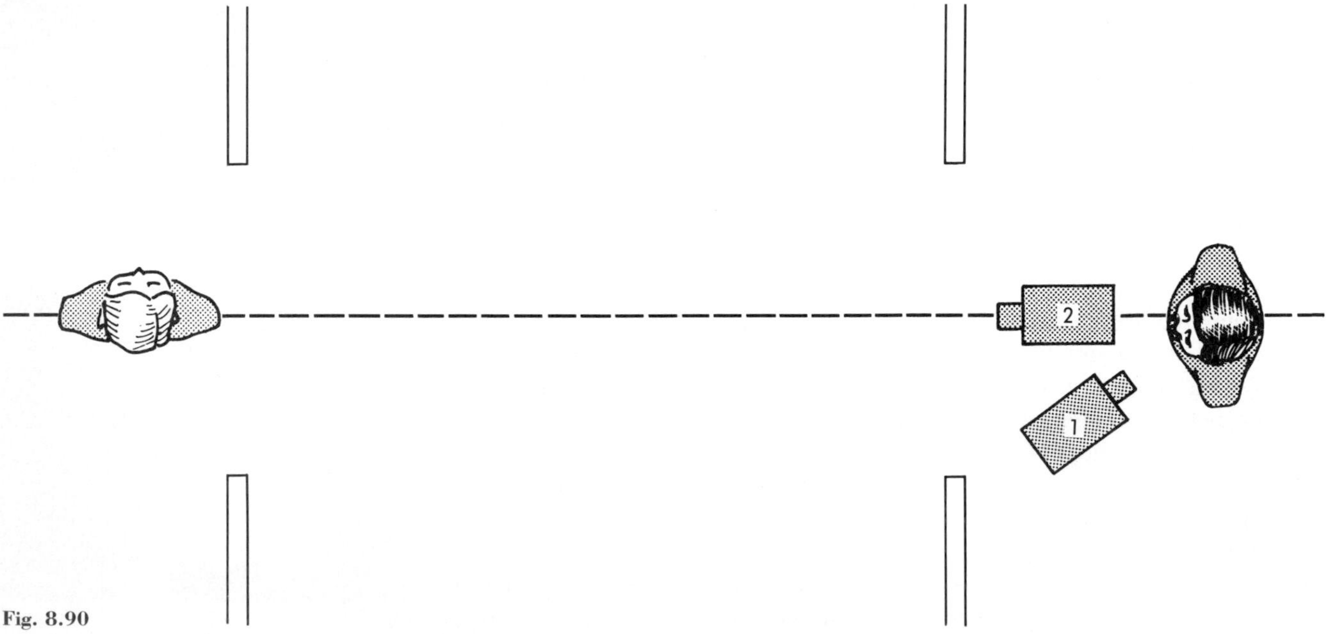

Fig. 8.90

Fig. 8.91

Fig. 8.92

Fig. 8.93

how each new tool enlarges what Jeff can see (Figs. 8.91–8.94). Even though Jeff is alone for much of the film, Hitchcock's cutting adheres to spatial continuity rules and exploits their POV possibilities in order to arouse curiosity and suspense.

Can the director ever legitimately cross the axis of action? Yes. A scene occurring in a doorway, on a staircase, or in other symmetrical settings may occasionally "break the line." Another way to get across the center line is to cut away to a character who is offscreen. By then moving that character up to the main action, perhaps following the character with a camera movement, the filmmakers can establish a quite different axis of action.

Fig. 8.94

Sometimes too the filmmakers can get across the axis by taking one shot *on the line itself* and using it as a transition. This strategy is rare in dialogue sequences, but it can sometimes be seen in chases and outdoor action. By filming on the axis, the filmmaker presents the action as moving directly toward the camera (a *head-on* shot) or away from it (a *tail-on* shot). The climactic chase of *The Road Warrior* offers several examples. As marauding road gangs try to board a fleeing gasoline truck, George Miller uses many head-on and tail-on shots of the tanker and of the driver Max. The gang launches an attack as the truck and its pursuers hurtle leftward across the screen. Miller then inserts one or more shots of the tanker moving to or from the camera. Next we see shots in which the tanker and the gangs race to the right.

When the filmmaker breaks the center line, she or he often takes extra care to make the spatial relations comprehensible. In most cases, the continuity-based director prefers not to cut across the line. Our example from *Eyes without a Face* (p. 294) has shown how moving the actors around the frame can create a new axis of action without disorienting the viewer. An alternative way to create a new axis of action is to let the camera track across the line. Since a violation of continuity editing can occur only across a shot-change, a camera movement that demarcates a new axis cannot break continuity.

Continuity editing illustrates how editing can endow the film's narration with a great range of knowledge. A cut can take us to any point on the correct side of the axis of action. Editing can even create omniscience, that godlike knowledge that some films seek to present. The outstanding technical device here is *crosscutting*, first extensively explored by D. W. Griffith in his last-minute rescue scenes. In *The Battle at Elderbush Gulch,* a cavalry troop is

Fig. 8.95

Fig. 8.96

Fig. 8.97

Fig. 8.98

riding to rescue some settlers trapped in a cabin and battling the Indians outside. Griffith cuts from a shot of the cavalry (Fig. 8.95) to a view inside the besieged cabin (Fig. 8.96), back to the cavalry (Fig. 8.97), and returning to the cabin (Fig. 8.98). After eleven additional shots of the cavalry, various parts of the cabin interior, and the Indians outdoors, a twelfth shot shows the cavalry riding in from the distance behind the cabin.

Crosscutting gives us an unrestricted knowledge of causal, temporal, or spatial information by alternating shots from one line of action in one place with shots of other events in other places. Crosscutting thus creates some spatial discontinuity, but it binds the action together by creating a sense of cause and effect and temporal simultaneity.

For example, in Fritz Lang's *M*, while the police seek the child murderer, gangsters prowl the streets looking for him as well, and we also occasionally see the murderer himself. Crosscutting ties together the different lines of action, bringing out a temporal simultaneity and the causal process of the pursuit. The crosscutting also gives us a range of knowledge greater than that of any one character. We know that the gangsters are after the murderer, but the police and the murderer do not. Crosscutting also builds up suspense, as we form expectations that are only gradually clarified and fulfilled. It may also create parallels, and Lang exploits this possibility by suggesting analogies between the police and the crooks. Whatever other functions it may have, though, crosscutting remains primarily a means of presenting narrative actions that are occurring in several locales at roughly the same time.

All the devices of spatial continuity show how film technique draws the spectator into an active process. We assume that setting, character movement, and character position will be consistent and coherent. Our prior knowledge of filmic conventions lets us form strong expectations about what shot will follow the one we are seeing. We also make inferences on the basis of cues, so that when Brigid and Spade look off left we infer that someone is entering the room and we expect to see a shot of that person. What makes the continuity system "invisible" is its ability to draw on a range of skills that we have learned so well that they seem automatic. This makes spatial continuity editing a powerful tool for the filmmaker who wishes to reinforce habitual expectations. It also becomes a central target for the filmmaker who wants to use film style to challenge or change our normal viewing activities.

■ TEMPORAL CONTINUITY: ORDER, FREQUENCY, DURATION

In the classical continuity system, time, like space, is organized according to the development of the narrative. We know that the plot's presentation of the story typically involves manipulation of time. Continuity editing seeks to support and sustain this temporal manipulation.

To get specific, recall our distinction among temporal order, frequency, and duration. Continuity editing typically presents the story events in a 1-2-3 order (e.g., Spade rolls a cigarette, then Effie comes in, then he answers her, and so on). The most common violation of this order is a flashback, signaled by a cut or dissolve. Furthermore, classical editing also typically presents only *once* what happens *once* in the story; in continuity style, it would be a gross mistake for Huston to repeat the shot of, say, Brigid sitting down (Fig. 8.57). Again, though, flashbacks are the most common way of motivating the repetition of a scene already witnessed. So chronological sequence and "one-for-one" frequency are the standard methods of handling order and frequency within the continuity style of editing. There are occasional exceptions, as we saw in our examples from *The Godfather* and *Do The Right Thing.*

What of duration? In the classical continuity system, story duration is seldom expanded; that is, screen time is seldom made greater than story time. Usually, duration is in complete continuity (plot time equaling story time) or is elided (story time being greater than plot time). Let us first consider complete continuity, the most common possibility. Here a scene occupying five minutes in the story also occupies five minutes when projected on the screen.

The first scene of *The Maltese Falcon* displays three cues for such temporal continuity. First, the narrative progression of the scene has no gaps. Every movement by the characters and every line of dialogue is presented. There is also the sound track. Sound issuing from the story space (what we shall later call "diegetic" sound) is a standard indicator of temporal continuity, especially when, as in this scene, the sound "bleeds over" each cut. Finally, there is the match on action between shots 5 and 6. So powerful is the match on action that it creates both spatial *and* temporal continuity. The reason is obvious: If an action carries across the cut, the space and time are assumed to be continuous from shot to shot. In all, an absence of ellipses in the story action, diegetic sound overlapping the cuts, and matching on action are three primary indicators that the duration of the scene is continuous.

Sometimes, however, a second possibility will be explored: *temporal ellipsis.* The ellipsis may, of course, omit seconds, minutes, hours, days, years, or centuries. Some ellipses are of no importance to the narrative development and so are concealed. To take a common example: A classical narrative film typically does not show the entire time it takes a character to dress, wash, and breakfast in the morning. Shots of the character going into the shower, putting on shoes, or frying an egg might be edited so as to eliminate the unwanted bits of time, with the plot presenting in seconds a process that might have taken an hour in the story. As we saw on p. 283, optical punctuations, empty frames, and cutaways are frequently used to cover short temporal ellipses.

But other ellipses are important to the narrative. The viewer must recognize that time has passed. For this task the continuity style has built up a varied repertory of devices. Often, dissolves, fades, or wipes are used to indicate an ellipsis between shots. Thus from the last shot of one scene we dissolve, fade, or wipe to the first shot of the next scene. (The Hollywood "rule" is that a dissolve indicates a brief time lapse and a fade indicates a much longer one.) In some cases contemporary filmmakers use a cut for such transitions. For example, in *2001* Kubrick cuts directly from a bone spinning in the air to a space station orbiting the earth, one of the boldest graphic matches in narrative cinema. The cut eliminates thousands of years of story time.

In other cases it is necessary to show a large-scale process or a lengthy period—a city waking up in the morning, a war, a child growing up, the rise of a singing star. Here classical continuity uses another device for temporal ellipsis: the *montage sequence.* (This should not be confused with the concept of "montage" in Sergei Eisenstein's film theory.) Brief portions of a process, informative titles (for example, "1865" or "San Francisco"), stereotyped images (e.g., the Eiffel Tower), newsreel footage, newspaper headlines, and the like, can be swiftly joined by dissolves and music to compress a lengthy series of actions into a few moments.

We are all familiar with the most clichéd montage ellipses—calendar leaves fluttering away, newspaper presses churning out an Extra, clocks ticking portentously—but in the hands of deft editors such sequences become small virtuoso pieces in themselves. Slavko Vorkapich's montages of American life in *Mr. Smith Goes to Washington,* Jack Killifer's tracing of a society across two decades in *The Roaring Twenties,* and Edward Curtis's brutal depictions of a gangster's rise in *Scarface* illustrate the powers of the device. The montage sequence is still utilized in Hollywood films, though it tends to be more restrained stylistically than in the 1930s and 1940s. *Jaws,* for example, simply uses a series of unmatched shots of vacationers arriving at the beach to indicate a time shift to the beginning of the tourist season. Music is still used as an accompaniment, however, as when a song accompanies a series of magazine covers in a scene from *Tootsie* that traces the hero's rise to success as a soap-opera star. A montage sequence in *The Silence of the Lambs* juxtaposes brief glimpses of Clarice Starling training at the FBI academy and researching Hannibal Lecter's past.

In sum, the continuity style uses the temporal dimension of editing primarily for narrative purposes. Through prior knowledge, the spectator expects the editing to present story events in chronological order, with only occasional rearrangement through flashbacks. The viewer expects that editing will respect the frequency of story events. And the viewer assumes that actions irrelevant to story causality will be omitted or at least abridged by judicious ellipses. At least, this is how the classical Hollywood continuity system has conceived storytelling. Like graphics, rhythm, and space, time is organized to permit the unfolding of cause and effect, the arousal of curiosity, suspense, and surprise. But there are many alternatives to the continuity style of editing, and these are worth a look.

ALTERNATIVES TO CONTINUITY EDITING

▪ GRAPHIC AND RHYTHMIC POSSIBILITIES

Powerful and pervasive as it is, the continuity style remains only *one* style, and many filmmakers have explored other editing possibilities.

Films using abstract or associational form have frequently granted the graphic and rhythmic dimensions of editing great weight. Instead of joining shot 1 to shot 2 primarily on the basis of the spatial and temporal functions that the shot fulfills in presenting a story, you could join them on the basis of purely graphic or rhythmic qualities—independent of the time and space they represent. In films such as *Anticipation of the Night, Scenes from under Childhood,* and *Western History,* experimentalist Stan Brakhage uses purely graphic means of joining shot to shot: continuities and discontinuities of light, texture, and shape motivate the editing. Interested in the very surface of the film itself, Brakhage has scratched the image, painted on it, even taped moth wings to it, in search of abstract graphic combinations. Similarly, parts of Bruce Conner's *Cosmic Ray, A Movie,* and *Report* cut together newsreel footage, old film clips, leader, and black frames on the basis of graphic patterns of movement, direction, and speed.

Fig. 8.99

Many nonnarrative films have completely subordinated the space and time presented in each shot to the rhythmic relations among shots. "Single-frame" films (in which each shot is only one frame long) are the most extreme examples of this overriding rhythmic concern. Two famous examples are Robert Breer's *Fist Fight* (Color Plate 4) and Peter Kubelka's *Schwechater.*

The preeminence of graphic and rhythmic editing in nonnarrative cinema is not, however, as recent a phenomenon as these examples might suggest. As early as 1913, some painters were contemplating the pure-design possibilities offered by film, and many works of the European avant-grade movements of the 1920s combined an interest in abstract graphics with a desire to explore rhythmic editing. Perhaps the most famous of these is the Fernand Léger–Dudley Murphy film *Ballet mécanique* (see Chapter 5, pp. 148–154). In Chapter 10 we shall see how *Ballet mécanique* juxtaposes its shots on the basis of graphic and rhythmic qualities.

Fig. 8.100

Important as the graphic and rhythmic possibilities of editing have been to the nonnarrative film, their powers have not been wholly neglected in the narrative film. Although the continuity style seeks an overall graphic continuity, this is usually subordinated to a concern with mapping narrative space and tracing narrative time. Some narrative filmmakers, however, occasionally subordinate narrative concerns to graphic pattern. The most famous examples are probably the films for which Busby Berkeley choreographed elaborate dance numbers. In *42nd Street, Golddiggers of 1933, Footlight Parade, Gold-diggers of 1935,* and *Dames,* the narrative periodically grinds to a halt and the film presents intricate dances that are arranged, shot, and edited with a concern for the pure configuration of dancers and background. (See Fig. 6.81, p. 197, from *42nd Street.*)

Fig. 8.101

More complexly related to the narrative is the graphic editing of Yasujiro Ozu. Ozu's cutting is often dictated by a much more precise graphic continuity than we find in the classical continuity style. In *An Autumn Afternoon* Ozu cuts from one man drinking *sake* (Fig. 8.99) directly to another (Fig. 8.100) caught in almost exactly the same position, costume, and gesture. Later in the film, he cuts from one man to another (Figs. 8.101, 8.102), keeping the composition very similar across the cut. Even a beer bottle (a different one in each shot) sits precisely in the same position on frame left, its label in a constant position as well. In *Ohayu* Ozu uses color for the same purpose, cutting from laundry on a line to a domestic interior and matching on a red shape in the upper left of each shot (a shirt, a lamp). (See Color Plates 62, 63.)

Graphic continuity is, of course, a matter of degree, and in narrative films the spectrum runs from Hollywood's approximate graphic continuity to Ozu's precise matching, with two shots like these from Eisenstein's *Ivan the*

Fig. 8.102

Fig. 8.103

Fig. 8.104

Terrible, Part I, coming somewhere in the middle. (See Figs. 8.103, 8.104.) The lighting (darkness on frame left, brightness on frame right) and the triangular shape on frame right of shot 1 are picked up in shot 2, with Anastasia's headdress and body now closely matching the tapering chair. If such graphic editing motivates the entire film's form, however, narrative will tend to recede, and the film will become more abstract in form.

Some narrative films have momentarily subordinated spatial and temporal editing factors to rhythmic ones. In the 1920s both the French "Impressionist" school and the Soviet avant-garde frequently made narrative secondary to purely rhythmic editing. In such films as Abel Gance's *La Roue,* Jean Epstein's *Coeur fidèle* and *La Glace à trois faces,* and Ivan Mosjoukin's *Kean,* accelerated editing renders the tempo of an onrushing train, a whirling carousel, a racing automobile, and a drunken dance. In Epstein's *Fall of the House of Usher* a poetic sequence of Usher strumming a guitar and singing organizes the length of the shots in accord with a songlike pattern of verse and refrain. Kuleshov's *The Death Ray* and, as we shall see, Eisenstein's *October* occasionally make rhythm dominate narrative space and time. More recently, we can find strong passages of rhythmic editing in the Busby Berkeley musicals, Rouben Mamoulian's *Love Me Tonight,* René Clair's *Le Million,* and several films of Ozu and Hitchcock. There has been a revival of rhythmic editing in the "New Hollywood" (see pp. 468–471), as exemplified by *Assault on Precinct 13, The Terminator, True Romance,* and films influenced by the pulsating cutting of music videos, such as *Flashdance* and *The Crow.* As we saw with graphics, rhythmic editing may override the spatial and temporal dimensions; when this happens, narrative becomes proportionately less important.

■ SPATIAL AND TEMPORAL DISCONTINUITY

Nonnarrative films may sometimes avoid using the continuity style, for that style is founded on the cogent presentation of a story. But what of *narrative* alternatives to the continuity system? How can one tell a story without adhering to the continuity rules? Let us sample some ways particular filmmakers have created distinct editing styles by use of what might be considered spatial and temporal discontinuities.

One option is to use spatial continuity in ambiguous ways. In *Mon Oncle d'Amérique,* Resnais constantly intercuts the stories of his three main characters with shots of each character's favorite star, taken from French films of

Fig. 8.105

Fig. 8.106

Fig. 8.107

the 1940s. At one point, as René's pesky office mate calls to him, we get the coworker in one shot (Fig. 8.105). But Resnais cuts to a shot of Jean Gabin in an older film, turning to him in reverse shot (Fig. 8.106). Only then does Resnais supply a shot of René turning to meet his questioner (Fig. 8.107). The film does not definitely present the Gabin shot as a fantasy image; we cannot tell whether René imagines himself as his star confronting his coworker, or whether the film's narration draws the comparison independent of René's state of mind. The cut relies upon the cues of shot/reverse shot, but uses them to create a momentarily jarring discontinuity that triggers narrational ambiguity.

Fig. 8.108

More drastically, a filmmaker could violate or ignore the 180° system. The editing choices of filmmakers Jacques Tati and Yasujiro Ozu are based on what we might call 360° space. Instead of an axis of action that dictates that the camera be placed within an imaginary semicircle, these filmmakers work as if the action were not a line but a point at the center of a circle and as if the camera could be placed at any point on the circumference. In *Mr. Hulot's Holiday, Play Time,* and *Traffic* Tati systematically films from almost every side; edited together, the shots present multiple spatial perspectives on a single event. Similarly, Ozu's scenes construct a 360° space that produces what the continuity style would consider grave editing errors. Ozu's films often yield no consistent background spaces and no consistent screen direction; the eyeline matches are out of joint and the only consistency is the *violation* of the 180° line. One of the gravest sins in the classical continuity style is to match on action while breaking the line, yet Ozu does this comfortably in *Early Summer* (see Figs. 8.108, 8.109). (See Part IV for a discussion of space and time in Ozu's *Tokyo Story.*)

Fig. 8.109

Such spatially discontinuous editing offers intriguing insights into the spectator's experience as well. The defender of classical continuity would claim that spatial continuity rules are necessary for the clear presentation of a narrative. But anyone who has seen a film by Ozu or Tati can testify that no narrative confusion arises from their continuity "violations." Though the spaces do not flow as smoothly as in the Hollywood style (this is indeed part of the films' fascination), the cause-effect chains remain intelligible. The inescapable conclusion is that the continuity system is only *one* way to render a narrative. Historically, this system has been the dominant one, but aesthetically it has no priority over other styles.

Fig. 8.110

There are two other noteworthy devices of discontinuity. In *Breathless* Jean-Luc Godard violates conventions of spatial, temporal, and graphic continuity by his systematic use of the *jump cut.* Though this term is often loosely used, its primary meaning is this. When two shots of the same subject are cut together but are not sufficiently different in camera distance and angle, there will be a noticeable jump on the screen. Classical continuity avoids such jumps by generous use of shot/reverse shots and by the "30° rule" (advising that every camera position be varied by at least 30° from the previous one). But an examination of shots from *Breathless* suggests the consequences of Godard's jump cuts. Between the first shot of Patricia riding in the car and the second, the background has changed and some story time has gone by (Fig. 8.110, 8.111). Far from flowing smoothly, such cuts disorient the spectator.

Fig. 8.111

Fig. 8.112

Fig. 8.113

Fig. 8.114

Fig. 8.115

Fig. 8.116

A second prevalent violation of continuity is that created by the *non-diegetic insert*. Here the filmmaker cuts from the scene to a metaphorical or symbolic shot that is not part of the space and time of the narrative. Clichés abound here. In *Fury* Lang cuts from housewives gossiping (Fig. 8.112) to shots of clucking hens (Fig. 8.113). More complex examples occur in the films of Eisenstein and Godard. In Eisenstein's *Strike* the massacre of workers is intercut with the slaughter of a bull. In Godard's *La Chinoise*, a character tells an anecdote about the ancient Egyptians who, he claims, thought that "their language was the language of the gods." As he says this (Fig. 8.114), Godard cuts in two close-ups of gold relics from the tomb of King Tutankhamen (Figs. 8.115, 8.116). As nondiegetic inserts, coming from outside the story world, they construct a running, often ironic, commentary on the action, and they prompt the spectator to search for implicit meanings. (Do the relics corroborate or challenge what Henri says?)

Though both the jump cut and the nondiegetic insert can be utilized in a narrative context (as in the *Fury* example), they tend to weaken narrative continuity. The jump cut interrupts it with abrupt gaps, while the nondiegetic insert suspends story action altogether. It is no accident that both devices have been prominently used by the contemporary filmmaker most associated with the challenge to classical narrative, Jean-Luc Godard. In Part IV we shall examine the nature of this challenge by analyzing *Breathless*.

There are still other alternatives to classical continuity, especially in the temporal dimension. Although the classical approach to order and frequency of story events may seem the best option, it is only the most familiar. Story events do not have to be edited in 1-2-3 order. In Resnais's *La Guerre est finie,* scenes cut in conventional continuity are interrupted by images that may represent flashbacks, or fantasy episodes, or even future events. Editing can also play with variable frequency for narrative purposes; the same event can be shown repeatedly. In *La Guerre est finie,* the same funeral is depicted in different hypothetical ways (the protagonist is present, or he is not).

Again, Godard offers a striking example of how editing can manipulate both order and frequency. In *Pierrot le fou,* as Marianne and Ferdinand leave her apartment fleeing gangsters, Godard scrambles the order of the shots. First, Ferdinand jumps into the car as Marianne pulls away (Fig. 8.117). Then the couple are seen back in their apartment (Fig. 8.118). Then the car races down a street (Fig. 8.119). Then Marianne and Ferdinand climb onto a rooftop (Fig. 8.120). The shots that follow continue to scramble the action. Godard also plays with frequency by repeating one gesture—Ferdinand jumping into the car—but showing it *differently* each time. Such manipulation of editing blocks our normal expectations about story and forces us to concentrate on the very process of piecing together the film's narrative action.

The editing may also take liberties with story duration. Although complete continuity and ellipsis are the most common ways of rendering duration, expansion—stretching a moment out, making screen time greater than story time—remains a distinct possibility. Truffaut uses such expansions in *Jules and Jim* to underscore narrative turning points (Catherine lifting her veil or jumping off a bridge). In Chabrol's *La Femme infidèle,* when the outraged husband strikes his wife's lover with a statuette, Chabrol overlaps shots of the victim falling to the floor.

Filmmakers have found creative ways to rework the most basic tenets of the continuity system. We have indicated, for example, that a match on action strongly suggests that time continues across the cut. Yet Alain Resnais

Fig. 8.117

Fig. 8.118

Fig. 8.119

Fig. 8.120

Fig. 8.121

Fig. 8.122

creates an "impossible" continuous action in *Last Year at Marienbad*. Small groups of guests are standing around the hotel lobby; one medium shot frames a blonde woman beginning to turn away from the camera (Fig. 8.121). In the middle of her turn, there is a cut to her, still turning but in a different setting (Fig. 8.122). The smooth match on action, along with the woman's graphically matched position in the frame, imply that she is moving continuously, yet the change of setting contradicts this impression. In Chapter 2, we saw how Deren's *Choreography for Camera* cuts together two shots of a dancer's leap; as in *Marienbad,* we have a match on action—yet in two different locales (see Figs. 2.14, 2.15, p. 50).

Our examples indicate that certain discontinuities of temporal order, duration, and frequency can become perfectly intelligible in a narrative context. On the other hand, with the jump cut, the nondiegetic insert, and the inconsistent match on action, such temporal dislocations can also push away from traditional notions of "story" altogether and create ambiguous relations among shots.

As an example of the power of spatial and temporal discontinuities in editing, we shall look at a single example: Sergei Eisenstein's *October*.

■ DISCONTINUITY EDITING: *OCTOBER*

For many Soviet filmmakers of the 1920s, editing was a major means of organizing the entire form of the film; it did not simply serve the narrative progression, as in the continuity system. Eisenstein's early films—*Strike, Potemkin, October,* and *Old and New*—all constitute attempts to build a film on the basis of certain editing devices. Rather than subordinate his editing patterns to the mapping out of a story, Eisenstein conceives of these films as editing constructions.

Eisenstein deliberately opposed himself to continuity editing, seeking out and exploiting what Hollywood would call discontinuities. He staged, shot, and cut his films for the maximum *collision* from shot to shot, sequence to sequence, since he believed that only through being forced to synthesize such conflicts could the viewer participate in actively understanding the film.

To this end, Eisenstein "wrote" his film by a juxtaposition of shots. No longer bound by conventional dramaturgy, Eisenstein's films roam freely through time and space to construct an intricate pattern of images calculated to stimulate the viewer's senses, emotions, and thinking. He dreamed of filming Marx's *Das Kapital,* of writing an essay by means of film editing. Needless to say, the intricacy of Eisenstein's editing cannot be wholly conveyed here; even a single sequence of an Eisenstein film is properly the subject of a chapter in itself. Let us, however, briefly indicate how Eisenstein uses editing discontinuities in a short sequence from *October.*

The sequence is the third one in the film (and comprises no fewer than 125 shots!). The story action is simple. The bourgeois Provisional Government has taken power in Russia after the February Revolution, but instead of withdrawing from World War I, the government has continued to support the Allies. This maneuver has left the Russian people no better off than under the czar. Now in classical Hollywood cinema, this story might be shown through a "montage sequence" of newspaper headlines smoothly linked to a scene wherein a protagonist complains that the Provisional Government has not changed a thing. *October*'s protagonist, though, is not one person but the entire Russian people, and the film does not usually use dialogue scenes to present its story points. Rather, *October* seeks to go beyond a simple presentation of story events by making the audience actively *interpret* those events. To this end, the film confronts the audience with a disorienting and disjunctive set of images.

The sequence begins with shots showing the Russian soldiers on the front casting down their rifles and fraternizing freely with their German "enemies"—talking, drinking, laughing together (Fig. 8.123). Eisenstein then cuts back to the Provisional Government, where a flunky extends a document to an unseen ruler (Fig. 8.124); this document pledges the government to aid the Allies. The soldiers' fraternization is suddenly disrupted by a bombardment (Fig. 8.125). The soldiers run back to the trenches and huddle as dirt and bomb fragments rain down on them. Eisenstein then cuts to a series of shots of a cannon being lowered off a factory assembly line. For a time the narration crosscuts these images with the soldiers on the battlefield (Figs. 8.126, 8.127). In the last section of the sequence, the shots of the cannon are crosscut with hungry women and children standing in breadlines in the snow (Fig. 8.128). The sequence ends with two intertitles: "All as before . . ."/"Hunger and war."

Graphically, there are some continuities and many strong discontinuities. When the soldiers fraternize, many shots closely resemble one another graphically, and one shot of a bursting bomb is graphically matched in its movement with men bustling into a trench. But the graphic *dis*continuities

Fig. 8.123

Fig. 8.124

Fig. 8.125

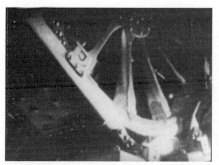

Fig. 8.126

Fig. 8.127

Fig. 8.128

Fig. 8.129

Fig. 8.130

Fig. 8.131

Fig. 8.132

Fig. 8.133

Fig. 8.134

are more noteworthy. Eisenstein cuts from a laughing German soldier facing right to a menacing eagle statue (facing left) at the government headquarters (Figs. 8.129, 8.130). There is a bold jump cut from the flunky bowing to him standing up (Figs. 8.131, 8.132). A static shot of rifles thrust into the snow cuts to a long shot of a bursting shell (Figs. 8.133, 8.134). When the soldiers race back to the trenches, Eisenstein often opposes their direction of movement from shot to shot. Moreover, the cutting contrasts shots of the men crouching in the trenches looking *upward* with shots of the cannon slowly *descending* (Figs. 8.126, 8.127). In the last phase of the sequence, Eisenstein juxtaposes the misty, almost completely static shots of the women and children with the sharply defined, dynamically moving shots of factory workers lowering the cannon. Such graphic discontinuities recur throughout the film, especially in scenes of dynamic action, and stimulate perceptual conflict in the audience. To watch an Eisenstein film is to submit oneself to such percussive, pulsating graphic editing.

Eisenstein also makes vigorous use of temporal discontinuities. The sequence as a whole is opposed to Hollywood rules in its refusal to present the order of events unambiguously. Does the crosscutting of battlefield and government, factory and street indicate simultaneous action? (Consider, for example, that the women and children are seen at night, whereas the factory appears to be working in the daytime.) It is impossible to say if the battlefield events take place before or after or during the women's vigil. Eisenstein has sacrificed the delineation of 1-2-3 order so that he can present the shots as emotional and conceptual units.

Duration is likewise variable. The soldiers fraternize in relative continuity, but the Provisional Government's behavior is elided drastically; this permits Eisenstein to identify the government as the unseen cause of the bombardment that ruptures the peace. At one point, Eisenstein utilizes one of his favorite devices, a temporal expansion: There is an overlapping cut as a soldier drinks from a bottle. (Later in *October*, such durational expansions create the famous bridge-raising sequence.) At another point, the gradual collapse of the women and children waiting in line is elided. We see them standing, then later lying on the ground. Even frequency is made discontinuous: It is difficult to say if we are seeing several cannons lowered off the assembly line or only one descending cannon shown several times. Again, Eisenstein seeks a specific *juxtaposition* of elements, not obedience to a temporal chain. Editing's manipulation of order, duration, and frequency subordinates straightforward story time to specific logical relationships. Eisenstein creates these relationships by juxtaposing disparate lines of action through editing.

Fig. 8.135

Spatially, the *October* sequence runs from rough continuity to extreme discontinuity. Although at times the 180° rule is respected (especially in the shots of women and children), never does Eisenstein begin a section with an establishing shot. Reestablishing shots are rare, and usually the major components of the locales are never shown together in one shot.

Throughout, the classical continuity of space is broken by the intercutting of the different locales. To what end? By violating space in this manner, the film invites us to make emotional and conceptual connections. For example, crosscutting to the Provisional Government makes it the source of bombardment, a meaning reinforced by the way the first explosions are followed by the jump cut of the government flunky.

More daringly, by cutting from the crouching soldiers to a descending cannon, Eisenstein powerfully depicts the men visually crushed by the warmaking apparatus of the government. This is reinforced by a *false* eyeline match from soldiers looking upward, *as if* at the lowering cannon—false because of course the two elements are in entirely separate settings (Figs. 8.126, 8.127). By then showing the factory workers lowering the cannon (Fig. 8.135), the cutting links the oppressed soldiers to the oppressed proletariat. Finally, as the cannon hits the ground, Eisenstein crosscuts images of it with the shots of the starving families of the soldiers and the workers. They too are shown as crushed by the government machine. As the cannon wheels come slowly to the floor, we cut to the women's feet in the snow, and the machine's heaviness is linked by titles ("one pound," "half a pound") to the steady starvation of the women and children. Although all of the spaces are in the story, such discontinuities make the film's plot a running political commentary on the story events.

In all, then, Eisenstein's spatial editing, like his temporal and graphic editing, constructs correspondences, analogies, and contrasts that *interpret* the story events. The interpretation is not simply handed to the viewer; rather, the editing discontinuities force the viewer to work out implicit meanings. This sequence, like others in *October*, demonstrates that there are powerful alternatives to the principles of classical continuity.

SUMMARY

When any two shots are joined, we can ask several questions:

1. How are the shots graphically continuous or discontinuous?
2. What rhythmic relations are created?
3. Are the shots spatially continuous? If not, what creates the discontinuity? (Crosscutting? Ambiguous cues?) If the shots are spatially continuous, how does the 180° system create the continuity?
4. Are the shots temporally continuous? If so, what creates the continuity? (For example, matches on action?) If not, what creates the discontinuity? (Ellipsis? Overlapping cuts?)

More generally, we can ask the question we ask of every film technique. How does this technique *function* with respect to the film's narrative or nonnarrative form? Does the film utilize editing to lay out the narrative space, time, and cause-effect chain in the manner of classical continuity? Or does the film utilize other editing patterns that enter into a different interplay with the narrative? If the film is not a narrative one, how does editing function to engage our formal expectations?

Some practical hints: You can learn to notice editing in several ways. If you are having trouble noticing cuts, try watching a film or television show and tapping with a pencil each time a shot changes. Once you recognize editing easily, watch any film with the sole purpose of observing one editing aspect—say, the way space is presented or the control of graphics or time. Sensitize yourself to rhythmic editing by noting cutting rates; tapping out the tempo of the cuts can help. Watching 1930s and 1940s American films can introduce you to classical continuity style; try to predict what shot will come next in a sequence. (You will be surprised at how often you are right.) When you watch a film on video, try turning off the sound; editing patterns become more apparent this way. When there is a violation of continuity, ask yourself whether it is accidental or serves a purpose. When you see a film that does not obey classical continuity principles, search for its unique editing patterns. If it is feasible, sit down at an editor or viewer or use the slow-motion, freeze, and reverse controls on a videocassette machine to analyze a film sequence as this chapter has done. (Almost any film will do.) In such ways as these, you can considerably increase your awareness and understanding of the power of editing.

NOTES AND QUERIES

◼ WHAT EDITING IS

Professional reflections on the work of the film editor include Ralph Rosenblum, *When the Shooting Stops . . . The Cutting Begins: A Film Editor's Story*

(New York: Penguin, 1980); Edward Dmytryk, *On Film Editing* (Boston: Focal Press, 1984); Bernard Balmuth, *Introduction to Film Editing* (Boston: Focal Press, 1989); Vincent Lo Brutto, *Selected Takes: Film Editors on Film Editing* (New York: Praeger, 1991); Gabriella Oldham, *First Cut: Conversations with Film Editors* (Berkeley: University of California Press, 1992); and Roy Thompson, *Grammar of the Edit* (Boston: Focal Press, 1993). An amusing essay on the powers of editing is William K. Everson, "Movies out of Thin Air," *Films in Review* **6**, 4 (April 1955): 171–180.

General discussions of film editing may be found in Rudolf Arnheim's *Film as Art* (Berkeley: University of California Press, 1967), pp. 87–102; Erwin Panofsky, "Style and Medium in the Moving Pictures," in Daniel Talbot, ed., *Film: An Anthology* (Berkeley: University of California Press, 1970), pp. 15–31; Béla Balázs, *Theory of the Film* (New York: Dover, 1970), pp. 118–138; Noël Carroll, "Toward a Theory of Film Editing," *Millennium Film Journal* **3** (1978): 79–99. For a wide-ranging examination of editing aesthetics, see also Ken Dancyger, *The Technique of Film and Video Editing* (Boston: Focal Press, 1993). We await an authoritative history of editing, but at least one historical pattern has been sketched in André Bazin, "The Evolution of the Language of Cinema," in *What Is Cinema?* vol. 1 (Berkeley: University of California Press, 1967), pp. 23–40.

Editing has often been seen as an alternative to mise-en-scene and camera work. Instead of cutting to a close-up of the hero's face, we can have him come closer to the camera, or we can track into a close-up. Early film theory argued that editing was more inherently "cinematic" than the more "theatrical" technique of mise-en-scene; see in this connection Arnheim, Panofsky, and Balázs, cited above. But the aesthetic prominence of editing was disputed by the film theorist André Bazin, who argued that editing ruptures and falsifies the spatiotemporal continuum of reality. (See not only the Bazin essay cited above but also "The Virtues and Limitations of Montage," pp. 41–52 of the same volume.) Bazin claimed that concrete reality is better respected by cinematography and mise-en-scene techniques. This debate has been taken up by others, notably Charles Barr in "CinemaScope: Before and After," *Film Quarterly* **16**, 4 (Summer 1963): 4–24, and Christian Metz in *Film Language* (New York: Oxford University Press, 1974), pp. 31–91.

Professional filmmakers' views of editing are invariably interesting. Roberto Rossellini and Jean Renoir, in a famous interview with André Bazin, minimize it ["Cinema and Television," *Sight and Sound* (Winter 1958–59): 26–29]. Alfred Hitchcock, in an equally famous interview with François Truffaut, swears by it [*Hitchcock* (New York: Simon & Schuster, 1967), *passim*]. For Jean-Luc Godard, "Editing can restore to actuality that ephemeral grace neglected by both snob and filmlover, or can transform chance into destiny" ["Montage My Fine Care," *Godard on Godard* (New York: Viking, 1972), p. 39]. For V. I. Pudovkin, "Editing is the basic creative force, by power of which the soulless photographs (the separate shots) are engineered into living, cinematographic form" [*Film Technique* (New York: Grove, 1960), p. 25]. An editor has recalled that John Ford shot so little footage that Ford would not have to involve himself in editing: "By and large, the film that an editor would get would almost *have* to go into the picture. After the shooting, [Ford] would often go off to his boat and not come back until after the picture was cut" [Peter Bogdanovich, *John Ford* (Berkeley: University of California Press, 1968), p. 9].

Documentary films characteristically rely upon editing, perhaps more than fictional films do. A set of cutting conventions has developed. For example, it is common to intercut talking-head shots of experts as a way of representing opposing points of view. Interestingly, in making *The Thin Blue Line*, Errol Morris instructed his editor Paul Barnes to avoid cutting between the two main suspects. "He didn't want the standard documentary good guy/ bad guy juxtaposition. . . . He hated when I intercut people telling the same story, or people contradicting or responding to what someone has just said" (Oldham, *First Cut*, p. 144). Morris apparently wanted to give each speaker's version a certain integrity, letting each stand as an alternative account of events.

■ DIMENSIONS OF FILM EDITING

Very little has been written on graphic aspects of editing. See Vladimir Nilsen, *The Cinema as a Graphic Art* (New York: Hill & Wang, 1959); Sergei Eisenstein, "The Dramaturgy of Film Form," in Richard Taylor, ed., *Selected Works, Vol. I: Writings 1922–1934* (Bloomington: Indiana University Press, 1988), pp. 161–180; and Jonas Mekas, "An Interview with Peter Kubelka," *Film Culture* 44 (Spring 1967): 42–47.

What we are calling "rhythmic editing" comprises the categories of "metric" and "rhythmic" montage discussed by Eisenstein in "The Fourth Dimension in Cinema," in *Selected Works, Vol. I*, pp. 181–194. For a sample analysis of a film's rhythm, see Lewis Jacobs, "D. W. Griffith," in *The Rise of the American Film* (New York: Teachers College Press, 1968), chap. 11, pp. 171–201. Television commercials are useful to study for rhythmic editing, for their highly stereotyped imagery permits the editor to cut the shots to match the beat of the jingle on the sound track.

For a good discussion of spatial and temporal editing, see Noël Burch, *Theory of Film Practice* (Princeton: Princeton University Press, 1981), especially pp. 3–16, 32–48; and Vladimir Nizhny, *Lessons with Eisenstein* (New York: Hill & Wang, 1962), pp. 63–92.

The Kuleshov experiments have been variously described. The two most authoritative accounts are in V. I. Pudovkin, *Film Technique* (New York: Grove, 1960), *passim,* and Ronald Levaco, trans. and ed., *Kuleshov on Film: Writings of Lev Kuleshov* (Berkeley: University of California Press, 1974), pp. 51–55. For a summary of Kuleshov's work, see Vance Kepley, Jr., "The Kuleshov Workshop," *Iris* 4, 1 (1986): 5–23. André Bazin attacks the Kuleshov effect in "The Virtues and Limitations of Montage," *What Is Cinema?,* pp. 44–52. Can the effect actually suggest an expressionless character's emotional reaction? Two film researchers tried to test it, and their skeptical conclusions are set forth in Stephen Prince and Wayne E. Hensley, "The Kuleshov Effect: Recreating the Classic Experiment," *Cinema Journal* 31, 2 (Winter 1992): 59–75.

◼ CONTINUITY EDITING

For a historical discussion of continuity editing, see Chapter 12 and the chapter's bibliography. The hidden selectivity that continuity editing can achieve is well summarized in a remark of Thom Noble, who edited *Fahrenheit 451* and *Witness*: "What usually happens is that there are maybe seven moments in each scene that are brilliant. But they're all on different takes. My job is to try and get all those seven moments in and yet have it look seamless, so that nobody knows there's a cut in there." [Quoted in David Chell, ed., *Moviemakers at Work* (Redmond, Wash.: Microsoft Press, 1987), pp. 81–82].

Since the continuity system was guided by explicit "rules," many sources enumerate the principles of continuity. See Karel Reisz and Gavin Millar, *The Technique of Film Editing* (New York: Hastings House, 1973); Daniel Arijohn, *A Grammar of the Film Language* (New York: Focal Press, 1978); and Edward Dmytryk, *On Screen Directing* (Boston: Focal Press, 1984). Our diagram of a hypothetical axis of action has been adapted from Edward Pincus's concise discussion in his *Guide to Filmmaking* (New York: Signet, 1969), pp. 120–125.

For analyses of the continuity style, see Ramond Bellour, "The Obvious and the Code," *Screen* **15,** 4 (Winter 1974/75): 7–17; Vance Kepley, Jr., "Spatial Articulation in the Classical Cinema: A Scene from *His Girl Friday*," *Wide Angle* **5,** 3 (1983): 50–58; André Gaudreault, "Detours in Film Narrative: The Development of Cross-Cutting," *Cinema Journal* **19,** 1 (Fall 1979): 35–59; and William Simon, "An Approach to Point of View," *Film Reader* **4** (1979): 145–151. Joyce E. Jesionowski presents a detailed study of Griffith's distinctive version of early continuity editing in *Thinking in Pictures: Dramatic Structure in D. W. Griffith's Biograph Films* (Berkeley: University of California Press, 1987).

Literally thousands of films can be studied for their use of continuity editing, but here are a few classics: *Bringing Up Baby* (Hawks, 1938); *Trouble in Paradise* (Lubitsch, 1932); *The Wizard of Oz* (Fleming, 1939); *Singin' in the Rain* (Donen–Kelly, 1952); *Mildred Pierce* (Curtiz, 1945); *Roaring Twenties* (Walsh, 1939); *White Heat* (Walsh, 1949); *Winchester 73* (Mann, 1950); *The Philadelphia Story* (Cukor, 1940); *The General* (Keaton, 1927); *Mr. Smith Goes to Washington* (Capra, 1939). In all of these films, watch for occasional violations of the continuity rules. The second scene of *Mr. Smith* is especially instructive in this regard; do Capra's frequent continuity breaks serve a function or are they simply errors? Are the continuity rules obeyed in such non-American films as *Children of Paradise* (Carné, 1945); *The Blue Angel* (von Sternberg, 1930); *M* (Lang, 1931); and *Persona* (Bergman, 1965)?

Contemporary Hollywood directors, many of whom learned continuity editing in film schools, usually practice it scrupulously. But Paul Schrader, director of *American Gigolo* and *Mishima,* suggests that his generation does not like to repeat shot/reverse shot without varying camera angle or distance. "Audiences today want an incessant flow of new visual information. That old technique of the master shot and coverage back and forth, back and forth is basically a stage idea. . . . What separates film-makers of my generation from those before is that one of the things we try to do is to make every cut a new cut so you're constantly moving forward. . . . Every shot is a new set-up" [Gavin Smith, "A Man of Excess," *Sight and Sound* **5,** 1 (January 1995): 28]. How accurate is Schrader's claim? Do the dialogue sequences in his own films change the camera position drastically within shot/reverse-shot passages?

■ ALTERNATIVES TO CONTINUITY EDITING

Eisenstein remains the chief source in this area. A highly introspective filmmaker, he bequeathed us a rich set of ideas on the possibilities of non-narrative editing; see the essays in Selected Works, Vol. I. For further discussion of editing in *October,* see the essays by Annette Michelson, Noël Carroll, and Rosalind Krauss in the special "Eisenstein/Brakhage" number of *Artforum* **11,** 5 (January 1973): 30–37, 56–65, and Marie Claire Ropars, "The Overture of *October,*" *Enclitic* **2,** 2 (Fall 1978): 50–72, and **3,** 1 (Spring 1979): 35–47. For a more general view of Eisenstein's editing, see David Bordwell, *The Cinema of Eisenstein* (Cambridge, Mass.: Harvard University Press, 1993). The writings of another Russian, Dziga Vertov, are also of interest. See Annette Michelson, ed., *Kino-Eye: The Writings of Dziga Vertov* (Berkeley: University of California Press, 1984); our quotation on p. 280 comes from p. 17 of this volume. Good discussions of Vertov's montage practice are Stephen Crofts and Olivia Rose, "An Essay toward *Man with a Movie Camera,*" *Screen* **18,** 1 (Spring 1977): 9–58, and Seth R. Feldman, *Evolution of Style in the Early Work of Dziga Vertov* (New York: Arno, 1977). For a detailed consideration of Godard's play with continuity cues, see Jacques Aumont, "This Is Not a Textual Analysis (Godard's *La Chinoise*)," *Camera Obscura* 8-9-10 (1982): 131–161. On Ozu's manipulation of discontinuities, see David Bordwell, *Ozu and the Poetics of Cinema* (Princeton: Princeton University Press, 1988); Kristin Thompson, "*Late Spring* and Ozu's Unreasonable Style," in *Breaking the Glass Armor: Neoformalist Film Analysis* (Princeton: Princeton University Press, 1988), pp. 317–352; and Edward Branigan, "The Space of *Equinox Flower,*" in Peter Lehman, ed., *Close Viewings: An Anthology of New Film Criticism* (Sarasota: University of Florida Press, 1990), pp. 73–108.

Experimental and avant-garde filmmakers have taken the biggest steps toward constructing alternatives to the continuity style. Apart from the sources listed in the Notes and Queries for Chapters 2 and 4, see David Curtis's *Experimental Cinema* (New York: Delta, 1971) and Gregory Battcock, ed., *The New American Cinema* (New York: Dutton, 1967).

NINE

SOUND
IN THE CINEMA

Most films create a strong impression that the people and things pictured simply produce an appropriate noise. But as we have seen in Chapter 1, in the process of film production the sound track is built up separately from the images, and it can be manipulated independently. This makes sound as flexible and wide-ranging as other film techniques.

Yet sound is perhaps the hardest of all techniques to study. We are accustomed to ignoring many of the sounds in our environment. Our primary information about the layout of our surroundings comes from sight, and so in ordinary life sound is often simply a background for our visual attention. Similarly, we speak of "watching" a film and of being movie "viewers" or "spectators"—all terms which suggest that the sound track is a secondary factor. We are strongly inclined to think of sound as simply an accompaniment to the real basis of cinema, the moving images.

Moreover, we cannot stop the film and freeze an instant of sound, as we can study a frame to examine mise-en-scene and cinematography. Nor can we lay out the sound track for our inspection as easily as we can examine the editing of a string of shots. In film, the sounds and the patterns they form are elusive. This elusiveness accounts for part of the power of this technique: Sound can achieve very strong effects and yet remain quite unnoticeable. To study sound, we must learn to listen to films.

Fortunately, many viewers are becoming more sensitive to the way movies sound. The film industry has heavily promoted improvements in sound recording, mixing, and reproduction. These developments include Dolby noise-reduction processes and four- and six-track theater sound. *Star Wars,* with its stereo and "surround" channels, demonstrated that audiences appreciated better sound tracks. During the early 1990s digital sound mixing and reproduction became routine attractions of big-budget pictures.

Although theatrical reproduction remains the weak link in the sound chain, many exhibitors are upgrading their equipment and paying more attention to the auditorium's acoustic design. George Lucas's THX theater-certification program promotes high-quality sound-design systems. Audiences who have become used to digital compact-disc music have also embraced stereo-encoded videocassettes and surround-encoded laserdiscs. Not since the first "talkies" of the late 1920s have filmgoers been so aware of cinema sound, and filmmakers now compete in creating rich and engaging sound tracks.

THE POWERS OF SOUND

Whether noticed or not, sound is a powerful film technique for several reasons. For one thing, it engages a distinct sense mode. Our visual attention is accompanied by aural attention. Even before recorded sound was introduced in 1926, the "silent" cinema recognized this by its use of accompaniment by orchestra, organ, or piano. At a minimum, the music filled in the silence and gave the spectator a more complete perceptual experience. More significantly, the engagement of hearing opens the possibility of what the Soviet director Sergei Eisenstein called "synchronization of senses"—making a single rhythm or expressive quality unify both image and sound.

Secondly, sound can actively shape how we perceive and interpret the image. In one sequence of *Letter from Siberia*, Chris Marker demonstrates the power of sound to alter our understanding of images. Three times Marker shows the same footage—a shot of a bus passing a car on a city street, three shots of workers paving a street. But each time the footage is accompanied by a completely different sound track. Compare the three versions tabulated alongside the sequence (Table 9.1). The verbal differences are emphasized by the identical images; the audience will construe the same images differently, depending on the sound track.

The *Letter from Siberia* sequence demonstrates a third advantage of sound as well. Film sound can direct our attention quite specifically within the image. When the commentator describes the "blood-colored buses," we are likely to look at the bus and not at the car. When Fred Astaire and Ginger Rogers are executing an intricate step, chances are that we watch their bodies and not the silent nightclub spectators looking on. In such ways, sound can guide us through the images, "pointing" to things to watch.

This possibility becomes even more fertile when you consider that the sound cue for some visual element may *anticipate* that element and relay our attention to it. Suppose we have a close-up of a man in a room and we hear the creaking of a door opening. If the second shot shows the door, now open, the viewer's attention will probably shift to that door, the source of the offscreen sound. But if the second shot shows the door still closed, the viewer will likely ponder his or her interpretation of the sound. (Maybe it wasn't a

Table 9.1	*LETTER FROM SIBERIA* FOOTAGE		
IMAGES	FIRST COMMENTARY	SECOND COMMENTARY	THIRD COMMENTARY
 Fig. 9.1	Yakutsk, capital of the Yakutsk Autonomous Soviet Socialist Republic, is a modern city in which comfortable buses made available to the population share the streets with powerful Zyms, the pride of the Soviet automobile industry. In the	Yakutsk is a dark city with an evil reputation. The population is crammed into blood-colored buses while the members of the privileged caste brazenly display the luxury of their Zyms, a costly and uncomfortable car at best. Bending	In Yakutsk, where modern houses are gradually replacing the dark older sections, a bus, less crowded than its London or New York equivalent at rush hour, passes a Zym, an excellent car reserved for public utilities departments on account of its scarcity.
 Fig. 9.2	joyful spirit of socialist emulation, happy Soviet workers, among them this picturesque denizen	to the task like slaves, the miserable Soviet workers, among them this sinister-looking Asiatic,	With courage and tenacity under extremely difficult conditions, Soviet workers, among them this Yakut
 Fig. 9.3	of the Arctic reaches, apply themselves	apply themselves to the primitive labor	afflicted with an eye disorder, apply themselves to
 Fig. 9.4	to making Yakutsk an even better place to live. Or else:	of grading with a drag beam. Or simply:	improving the appearance of their city, which could certainly use it.

door, after all?) Thus the sound track can clarify image events, contradict them, or render them ambiguous. In all cases, the sound track can enter into an active relation with the image track.

This example of the door opening suggests a fourth advantage of sound: It cues us to form expectations. If we hear a door creaking, we anticipate that someone has entered a room and that we will see that person in the next shot. But, if the film draws upon conventions of the horror genre, the camera might stay on the man, staring fearfully. We would then be in suspense as to the appearance of the monster offscreen. Horror and mystery films often utilize the power of sound from an unseen source to engage the audience's interest, but all types of films can take advantage of this aspect of sound. During the town meeting in *Jaws*, the characters hear a grating sound and turn to look offscreen; a cut reveals Quint's hand scraping on a blackboard— creating a dramatic introduction to this character. We shall see as well several cases in which the use of sound can creatively cheat or redirect the viewer's expectations.

In addition, as V. F. Perkins has pointed out, sound brings with it a new sense of the value of silence. "Only with colour as an available resource can we regard the use of black-and-white photography as the result of a conscious artistic decision. Only in the sound film can a director use silence for dramatic effect." In the context of sound, silence takes on a new expressive function.

A final advantage: Sound bristles with as many creative possibilities as editing. Through editing, one may join shots of any two spaces to create a meaningful relation. Similarly, the filmmaker can mix any sonic phenomena into a whole. With the introduction of sound cinema, the infinity of visual possibilities was joined by the infinity of acoustic events.

FUNDAMENTALS OF FILM SOUND

■ ACOUSTIC PROPERTIES

To pursue in detail the acoustic processes that produce sound would take us on a long detour. (See Notes and Queries for reading on the subject.) We should, however, isolate certain qualities of sound as we perceive it. These qualities are familiar to us from everyday experience.

Loudness.   The sound we hear results from vibrations in the air. The amplitude, or breadth, of the vibrations produces our sense of loudness, or volume. Film sound constantly manipulates volume. For example, in many films a long shot of a busy street is accompanied by loud traffic noises, but when two people meet and start to speak, the volume of the traffic drops. Or a dialogue between a soft-spoken character and a blustery one is character- ized as much by the difference in volume as by the substance of the talk.

Loudness is also related to perceived distance; often the louder the sound, the closer we take it to be. This sort of assumption seems to be at work in the street-traffic example already mentioned: The couple's dialogue, being louder, is sensed as in the acoustic "foreground," while the traffic noise sinks to the background. In addition, a film may startle the viewer by exploiting abrupt and extreme shifts in volume (usually called changes in *dynamics*), as when a quiet scene is interrupted by a very loud noise.

Pitch. The frequency of sound vibrations governs pitch, or the perceived "highness" or "lowness" of the sound. Certain instruments, such as the tuning fork, can produce pure tones, but most sounds, in life and on film, are "complex tones," batches of different frequencies. Nevertheless pitch plays a useful role in picking out distinct sounds in a film sound track. It helps us distinguish music and speech from other sounds. Pitch also serves to distinguish among objects. Low-pitched sounds, such as thumps, can evoke hollow objects, while higher-pitched sounds (like those of jingle bells) suggest smoother or harder surfaces and more dense objects.

Pitch can also serve more specific purposes in a film. When a young boy tries to speak in a man's deep voice and fails (as in *How Green Was My Valley*), the joke is based primarily on pitch. Marlene Dietrich's vocal delivery often depends upon a long upward-gliding intonation which makes a statement sound like a question. In the coronation scene of *Ivan the Terrible*, Part I, a court singer with a deep bass voice begins a song of praise to Ivan, and each phrase rises dramatically in pitch—which Eisenstein emphasizes in the editing, with successively closer shots of the singer coinciding with each vocal change. When Bernard Herrmann obtained the effects of shrill, birdlike shrieking in Hitchcock's *Psycho*, even many musicians could not recognize the source: violins played at extraordinarily high pitch.

Timbre. The harmonic components of a sound give it a certain "color" or tone quality—what musicians call timbre. Timbre is actually a less fundamental acoustic parameter than amplitude or frequency, but it is indispensible in describing the texture or "feel" of a sound. When we call someone's voice nasal or a certain musical tone mellow, we are referring to timbre. In everyday life, the recognition of a familiar sound is largely a matter of various aspects of timbre.

Filmmakers manipulate timbre continually. Timbre can help articulate portions of the sound track, as when it differentiates musical instruments from one another. Timbre also comes forward on certain occasions, as in the clichéd use of oleaginous saxophone tones behind seduction scenes. More subtly, in the opening sequence of Rouben Mamoulian's *Love Me Tonight*, people starting the day on a street pass a musical rhythm from object to object—a broom, a carpet beater—and the humor of the number springs in part from the very different timbres of the objects. In preparing the sound track for Peter Weir's *Witness*, the editors drew upon sounds recorded twenty or more years before, so that the less modern timbre of the older recordings would express the rustic seclusion of the Amish community.

As fundamental components loudness, pitch, and timbre interact to define the overall sonic texture of a film. At the most elementary level, these three acoustic factors enable us to distinguish the various sounds in a film. For example, these qualities enable us to recognize different characters' voices. At a more complex level, all three components of film sound interact to add considerably to our experience of the film. For instance, both John Wayne and James Stewart speak slowly, but Wayne's voice tends to be deeper and gruffer than Stewart's querulous drawl. This difference works to great advantage in *The Man Who Shot Liberty Valance,* where their characters are sharply contrasted. In *The Wizard of Oz* the disparity between the public image of the Wizard and the old charlatan who rigs it up is marked by the booming bass of the effigy and the old man's higher, softer, more quavering voice.

Citizen Kane offers a wide range of sound manipulations. Echo chambers alter timbre and volume. A motif is formed by the inability of Kane's wife Susan to sing pitches accurately. Moreover, in *Citizen Kane* the plot's shifts between times and places are covered by continuing a sound "thread" and varying the basic acoustics. A shot of Kane applauding dissolves to a shot of a crowd applauding (a shift in volume and timbre). Leland beginning a sentence in the street cuts to Kane finishing the sentence in an auditorium, his voice magnified by loudspeakers (a shift in volume, timbre, and pitch).

Recent noise-reduction techniques, multitrack reproduction, and digital sound have yielded wider ranges of frequency and volume, as well as crisper timbres.

■ SELECTION, ALTERATION, AND COMBINATION

Sound in the cinema is of three types: *speech, music,* and *noise* (also called *sound effects*). Occasionally a sound may cross categories—is a scream speech or noise? is electronic music also noise?—and filmmakers have freely exploited these ambiguities. In *Psycho,* when a woman screams, we expect to hear a human voice and instead hear "screaming" violins. Nevertheless, in most cases the distinctions hold. Now that we have an idea of some basic acoustic properties, we must consider how speech, music, and noise are selected and combined for specific functions within films.

The creation of the sound track resembles the editing of the image track. Just as the filmmaker may pick the best image from several shots, he or she may choose what exact bit of sound will best serve the purpose. Just as footage from disparate sources may be blended into a single visual track, so too sound that was not recorded during filming may be added freely. Moreover, just as a shot may be rephotographed on the optical printer or tinted in color or jigsawed into a composite image, so too may a bit of sound be processed to change its acoustic qualities. And just as the filmmaker may link or superimpose images, so may he or she join any two sounds end to end or place one "over" another (as with commentary "over" music). Though we are not usually as aware of sonic manipulations, the sound track demands as much choice and control as does the visual track.

Animated films depend on careful sound planning, since drawings and puppets cannot make sounds themselves. Studio-made animated cartoons typically record music, dialogue, and sound effects *before* the images are filmed, so that the figures may be synchronized with the sound frame by frame. For many years Carl Stalling created frantically paced jumbles of familiar tunes, weird noises, and distinctive voices for the adventures of Bugs Bunny and Daffy Duck.

Experimental films, especially those using abstract form, also frequently build their images around a preexisting sound track. Some filmmakers have even argued that abstract cinema is a sort of "visual music" and have tried to create a synthesis of the two media.

As with other film techniques, sound guides the viewer's attention. Normally, this means clarifying and simplifying the sound track so that important material stands out. Dialogue, the transmitter of story information, is usually recorded and reproduced for maximum clarity. Important lines should not have to compete with music or background noise. Sound effects are usually less important. They supply an overall sense of a realistic environment and are seldom noticed; yet if they were missing, the silence would be distracting. Music is also subordinate to dialogue, entering during pauses in dialogue or effects.

Dialogue does not always rank highest in importance. Sound effects are usually central to action sequences, while music can dominate dance scenes, transitional sequences, or emotion-laden moments without dialogue. And some filmmakers have shifted the weight conventionally assigned to each type of sound. Charles Chaplin's *City Lights* and *Modern Times* eliminate dialogue, letting sound effects and music come to the fore. The films of Jacques Tati and Jean-Marie Straub retain dialogue but still place great emphasis on sound effects. Later in this chapter we will consider how music and noise in Robert Bresson's *A Man Escaped* fill out a sparse dialogue track by evoking offscreen space and creating thematic associations.

In creating a sound track, then, the filmmaker must select sounds that will fulfill a particular function. In order to do this, usually the filmmaker will provide a clearer, simpler sound world than that of everyday life. Normally, our perception filters out irrelevant stimuli and retains what is most useful at a particular moment. As you read this, you are attending to words on the page and (to various degrees) ignoring certain stimuli that reach your ears. But if you close your eyes and listen attentively to the sounds around you, you will become aware of many previously unnoticed sounds—distant voices, the wind, footsteps, a radio playing. Any amateur recordist knows that if you set up a microphone and tape recorder in a "quiet" environment, all of those normally unnoticed sounds suddenly become obtrusive. The microphone is unselective; like the camera lens, it does not automatically filter out what is distracting. Sound studios, camera blimps to absorb motor noise, directional and shielded microphones, sound engineering and editing, and libraries of stock sounds all allow the filmmaker to choose exactly what the sound track requires. Unless a filmmaker actually wants the ambient noise of a scene, simply holding out a microphone while filming will rarely be selective enough.

By selecting certain sounds, the filmmaker guides our perception of the image and the action. In one scene from Jacques Tati's *Mr. Hulot's Holiday*, vacationers at a resort hotel are relaxing (Fig. 9.5). In the foreground guests quietly play cards; in the depth of the shot, Mr. Hulot is frantically playing Ping-Pong. Early in the scene, the guests in the foreground are murmuring

Fig. 9.5

quietly, but Hulot's Ping-Pong game is louder; the sound cues us to watch Hulot. Later in the scene, however, the same Ping-Pong game makes *no* sound at all, and our attention is drawn to the muttering card players in the foreground. The presence and absence of the sound of the Ping-Pong ball guides our expectations. If you start to notice how such selection of sound shapes our perception, you will also notice that filmmakers often use sound quite unrealistically, in order to shift our attention to what is narratively or visually important.

Our scene from *Mr. Hulot's Holiday* also points up the importance of how a chosen sound may have its acoustic qualities transformed for a particular purpose. Thanks to a manipulation of volume and timbre, the Ping-Pong game gains in vividness and clarity. Similarly, a character speaking will usually sound about as loud in long shot as in close-up, even though this is a flagrant violation of realism.

At the limit, wholly new sounds may be made of old ones. The noises emitted by the demonically possessed girl in *The Exorcist* blended screams, animal thrashings, and English spoken backward. To create the roar of a Tyrannosaurus Rex for *Jurassic Park,* sound engineers fused a tiger's roar, a baby elephant's trumpeting at midrange frequencies, and an alligator's growl for the lower tones.

Nowadays, film sound is normally reprocessed to yield exactly the qualities desired. A "dry recording" of the sound in a fairly nonreflective space will be manipulated electronically to yield the desired effect. For instance, the voice of someone on the telephone is typically treated with filters to make it more tinny and muffled. (In Hollywood parlance, this is called "futzing" the sound.) The almost nonstop rock-and-roll music of *American Graffiti* used two recordings of the music: a "dry" one for moments when the music was to dominate the scene and had to be of high sonic quality, and a more ambient one for background noise. The latter was derived from a tape recorder simply playing the tune in a backyard.

Guiding the viewer's attention, then, depends on selecting and reworking particular sounds. It also depends on *combining* them. It is useful to think of the sound track not as a set of discrete sound units but as an ongoing stream of auditory information. Each sonic event takes its place in a specific pattern. This pattern involves linking events in time as well as "layering" them at any given moment.

We can easily see how the sound track offers a stream of auditory information by considering a scene cut according to classical continuity principles. When filmmakers edit conversations in shot/reverse shot, they often utilize a *dialogue overlap* to smooth down the visual change of shot. In a dialogue overlap the filmmaker continues a line of dialogue across a cut. During a conversation in John McTiernan's *Hunt for Red October,* we get the following shots and dialogue:

1. (ms) Over political officer's shoulder, favoring Captain Ramius (Fig. 9.6).
    Officer: "Captain Tupalev's boat."
    Ramius: "You know Tupalev?"
    Officer: "I know he descends . . ."

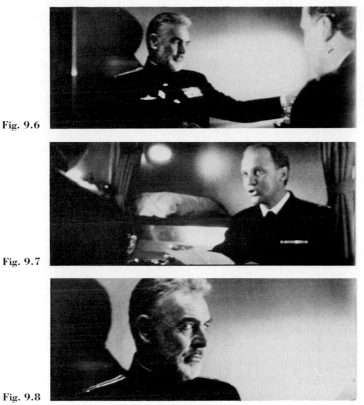

Fig. 9.6

Fig. 9.7

Fig. 9.8

2. (ms) Reverse angle over Ramius's shoulder, favoring officer (Fig. 9.7).

Officer (continuing): ". . . from aristocracy, and that he was your student. It's rumored he has a special . . ."

3. (mcu) Reverse angle on Ramius (Fig. 9.8).

Officer (continuing): ". . . place in his heart for you."

Ramius: "There's little room in Tupalev's heart for anyone but Tupalev."

Here the officer's chatter provides an auditory continuity that distracts from the shot changes. Moreover, by cutting to the listener before a sentence is finished, the sound and editing concentrate our attention on Ramius's response. As a Hollywood editor puts it: "The minute a telling word or a question is posed . . . I go for a reaction to see . . . how they are trying to formulate the answer in their face or dialogue." The principle of dialogue overlap can be used with noise as well. In the *Red October* scene just mentioned, sounds of a spoon clinking in a tea cup and of papers being riffled also carry over certain cuts, providing a continuous stream of sonic information.

This stream can involve more than simply linking one line of dialogue or bit of noise to another. We have already seen that in production, combining sounds is usually done after shooting, in the mixing process. The mixer can precisely control the volume, duration, and tone quality of each sound. In modern filmmaking, a dozen or more separate tracks may be mixed in layers at any moment. The mix can be quite dense, as when an airport scene combines the babble of several distinct voices, footsteps, luggage trolleys, Muzak, and plane engines. Or the mix can be very sparse, with an occasional sound emerging against a background of total silence. Most cases will fall somewhere in between these extremes. In our *Red October* scene, distant throbbing engines and slight brushings of fabric form a muted background to the dialogue exchange.

The filmmaker may create a mix in which each sound blends smoothly with the others. This is commonly the case when music and effects are mixed with speech. In classical Hollywood cinema of the 1930s, the musical score may become prominent in moments in which there is no dialogue, and then it is likely to fade unnoticeably down just as the characters begin to talk. (In studio parlance, this is called "sneaking in" and "sneaking out.") Alternatively, the acoustic stream may contain much more abrupt contrasts. Contemporary Hollywood films often exploit the dynamic range of Dolby technology to fill chase sequences with startling shifts between low, rumbling engines and whining sirens or squealing tires.

The ways in which sounds may combine to create an ongoing stream of information is well illustrated by the final battle sequence of Akira Kurosawa's *Seven Samurai*. In a heavy rain, marauding bandits charge into a village defended by the villagers and the samurai. The torrent and wind form a constant background noise throughout the scene. Before the battle, the conversation of the waiting men, footsteps, and the sound of swords being drawn are punctuated by long pauses in which we hear only the drumming rain. Suddenly distant horses' hooves are heard offscreen. This draws our attention from the defenders to the attackers. Then Kurosawa cuts to a long shot of the bandits; their horses' hooves become abruptly louder. (The scene employs conventional "sound perspective": the closer the camera is to a source, the louder the sound.) When the bandits burst into the village, yet another sound element appears—the bandits' harsh battle cries, which increase steadily in volume as they approach.

The battle begins. The muddy, storm-swept mise-en-scene and rhythmic cutting gain impact from the way in which the incessant rain and splashing are explosively interrupted by brief noises—the screams of the wounded, the splintering of a fence one bandit crashes through, the whinnies of horses, the twang of one samurai's bowstring, the gurgle of a speared bandit, the screams of women when the bandit chieftain breaks into their hiding place. The sudden intrusion of certain sounds marks abrupt developments in the battle. Such frequent surprises heighten our tension, since the narration frequently shifts us from one line of action to another.

The scene climaxes after the main battle has ended. Offscreen horses' hooves are cut short by a new sound—the sharp crack of a bandit's rifle shot, which fells one samurai. A long pause, in which we hear only the driving rain, emphasizes the moment. The samurai furiously throws his sword in the direction of the shot and falls dead into the mud. Another samurai races toward the bandit chieftain, who has the rifle; another shot cracks out and he falls back, wounded; another pause, in which only the relentless rain is heard. The wounded samurai kills the chieftain. The other samurai gather. At the scene's end, the sobs of a young samurai, the distant whinnies and hoofbeats of riderless horses, and the rain all fade slowly out.

The relatively dense mix of this sound track gradually introduces sounds which turn our attention to new narrative elements (hooves, battle cries) and then modulates these sounds into a harmonious stream. This stream is then punctuated by abrupt sounds of unusual volume or pitch associated with crucial narrative actions (the archery, women's screams, the gunshots). Overall, the combination of sounds enhances the unrestricted, objective narration of this sequence, which shows us what happens in various parts of the village rather than confining us to the experience of a single participant.

The choice and combination of sonic materials can also create patterns which run through the film as a whole. This is most readily seen by examining how the filmmaker uses a musical score. Sometimes the filmmaker will select preexisting pieces of music to accompany the images, as Bruce Conner does in using portions of Respighi's *Pines of Rome* as the sound track for *A Movie*. In other cases the music will be composed for the film, and here the filmmaker and the composer make several choices.

The rhythm, melody, harmony, and instrumentation of the music can strongly affect the viewer's emotional reactions. In addition, a melody or musical phrase can be associated with a particular character, setting, situation, or idea. *Local Hero*, a film about a confused young executive who leaves Texas to close a business deal in a remote Scottish village, uses two major musical themes. A rockabilly tune is heard in the urban Southwest, while a slower, more poignantly folkish melody is associated with the seaside village. In the final scenes, after the young man has returned to Houston, he recalls Scotland with affection, and the film plays the two themes simultaneously. By contrast, a single musical theme can change its quality when associated with different situations. In *Raising Arizona*, the hapless hero has a terrifying dream in which he envisions a homicidal biker pursuing him, and the accompanying music is appropriately ominous. But at the film's end, the hero dreams of raising dozens of children, and now the same melody, reorchestrated and played at a lilting tempo, conveys peace and comfort.

By reordering and varying musical motifs, the filmmaker can subtly compare scenes, trace patterns of development, and suggest implicit meanings. A convenient example is Georges Delerue's score for François Truffaut's *Jules and Jim*. Overall, the film's music reflects the Paris of 1912–1933, during which the action takes place; many of the melodies resemble works by Claude Debussy and Erik Satie, two of the most prominent French composers of that era. Virtually the entire score consists of melodies in ¾ meter, many of them in waltz time, and all the main themes are in keys related to A major. These rhythmic and harmonic decisions help unify the film.

More specifically, musical themes are associated with particular aspects of the narrative. For instance, Catherine's constant search for happiness and freedom outside conventional boundaries is conveyed by her singing the "Tourbillon" ("whirlwind") song, which says that life is a constant changing of romantic partners. Settings are also evoked in musical terms. One tune is heard every time the characters are in a café. As the years go by, the tune changes from a mechanical player-piano rendition to a jazzier version played by a black pianist.

The characters' relations become more strained and complicated over time, and the score reflects this in its development of major motifs. A lyrical melody is first heard when Jules, Jim, and Catherine visit the countryside and bicycle to the beach. This "idyll" tune will recur at many points when the characters reunite, but as the years pass it will become slower in tempo, more sombre in instrumentation, and shifted from a major to a minor mode. Another motif that reappears in different guises is a "dangerous love" theme associated with Jim and Catherine. This grave, shimmering waltz is first heard when he visits her apartment and watches her pour a bottle of vitriol down the sink. (The acid, she says, is "for lying eyes.") Thereafter, this harmonically unstable theme, which resembles one of Satie's *Gymnopédies* for piano, is used to underscore Jim and Catherine's vertiginous love affair. At times it accompanies scenes of passion, but at other times it accompanies their growing disillusionment and despair.

The most varied theme is a mysterious phrase first heard on the flute when Jules and Jim encounter a striking ancient statue. Later they meet Catherine and discover that she has the statue's face; a repetition of the musical motif confirms the comparison. Throughout the film, this brief motif is associated with the enigmatic side of Catherine. In the film's later scenes, this motif is developed in an intriguing way. The bass line (played on harpsichord or strings) that softly accompanied the woodwind tune now comes to the fore, creating a relentless, often harsh pulsation. This "menace" waltz underscores Catherine's fling with Albert and accompanies her final vengeance on Jim: driving her car, with him as passenger, into the river.

Once musical motifs have been selected, they can be combined to evoke associations. During Jim and Catherine's first intimate talk after the war, the bassline-dominated version of the "enigma" waltz is followed by the love theme, as if the latter could drown out the menacing side of Catherine's character. The love theme accompanies long tracking shots of Jim and Catherine strolling through the woods. But at the scene's end, as Jim bids Catherine farewell, the original woodwind version of her theme recalls her mystery and the risk he is running by falling in love with her. Similarly, when Jim and Catherine lie in bed, facing the end of their affair, the voice-over narrator says: "It was as if they were already dead" as the "dangerous love" theme plays. This sequence associates death with their romance and foreshadows their fate at the film's end.

A similar sort of blending can be found in the film's final scene. Catherine and Jim have drowned, and Jules is overseeing the cremation of their bodies. As shots of the coffins dissolve into detailed shots of the cremation process, the "enigma" motif segues into its sinister variant, the "menace" motif. But as Jules leaves the cemetery and the narrator comments that Catherine had wanted her ashes to be cast to the winds, the string instruments glide into a sweeping version of the "whirlwind" waltz. The film's musical score thus concludes by recalling the three sides of Catherine that attracted the men to her: her mystery, her menace, and her vivacious openness to experience. In such ways, a musical score can create, develop, and associate motifs that enter into the film's overall formal system.

DIMENSIONS OF FILM SOUND

We have seen what sounds consist of and how the filmmaker can take advantage of the widely different kinds of sounds available. In addition, the way in which the sounds relate to other film elements gives them several other dimensions. First, because sound occupies a duration, it has a *rhythm*. Second, sound can relate to its perceived source with greater or lesser *fidelity*. Third, sound conveys a sense of the *spatial* conditions in which it occurs. And fourth, the sound relates to visual events that take place in a specific time, and this relationship gives sound a *temporal* dimension. These categories reveal that sound in film offers a great many creative possibilities to the filmmaker.

RHYTHM

Rhythm is one of the most complex features of sound. We have already considered it briefly in relation to mise-en-scene (p. 196) and editing (p. 278). As we suggested, rhythm involves, minimally, a *beat* or pulse, a pace or *tempo*, and a pattern of *accents*, or stronger and weaker beats. In the realm of sound, all of these features are naturally most recognizable in film music, since there beat, tempo, and accent are basic compositional features. In our examples from *Jules and Jim* (p. 325), the motifs can be characterized as having a ¾ metrical pulse, putting an accent on the first beat, and displaying variable tempo—sometimes slow, sometimes fast.

Speech also has rhythm. People can be identified by "voice prints" which show not only characteristic frequencies and amplitudes but also distinct patterns of pacing and syllabic stress. In fictional films, speech rhythm is a matter for the performer's control, but the sound editor can also manipulate it at the dubbing phase.

Sound effects have distinct rhythmic qualities as well. The plodding hooves of a farmhorse differ from a cavalry company riding at full speed. The reverberating tone of a gong may offer a slowly decaying accent, while a sudden sneeze provides a brief one. In a gangster film, a machine gun's fire creates a regular, rapid beat, while the sporadic reports of pistols may come at irregular intervals.

Any consideration of the rhythmic uses of sound is complicated by the fact that the movements in the images have a rhythm as well, distinguished by the same principles of beat, speed, and accent. In addition, the editing has a rhythm. As we have seen, a succession of short shots helps create a rapid tempo, whereas shots held longer tend to slow down the rhythm.

In most cases the rhythms of editing, of movement within the image, and of sound all cooperate. Possibly the most common tendency is for the filmmaker to match visual and sonic rhythms to each other. In a dance sequence in a musical, the figures move about at a rhythm determined by the music. But variation is always possible. In the "Waltz in Swing Time" number in *Swing Time*, the dancing of Astaire and Rogers moves quickly in time to the music. But no fast cutting accompanies this scene. Indeed, the scene consists of a single long take from a long-shot distance.

Another prototype of close coordination between screen movement and sound comes in the animated films of Walt Disney in the 1930s. Mickey Mouse and the other Disney characters often move in exact synchronization with the music, even when they are not dancing. (As we have seen, such exactness was possible because the sound track was recorded in advance of the drawing of the cels.) Such matching of nondance movement with music in fact came to be known as "Mickey Mousing."

The filmmaker may also choose to create a disparity among the rhythms of sound, editing, and image. One of the most common options is to edit dialogue scenes in ways that "cut against" natural speech rhythms. In our specimen of dialogue overlap from McTiernan's *Hunt for Red October* (Figs. 9.6–9.8), the editing does not coincide with accented beats, cadences, or pauses in the officer's speech. By cutting "against" the rhythm of his lines, the editing smoothes over the changes of shot and emphasizes the words and facial expressions of Captain Ramius. If the filmmaker wants to emphasize the speaker and the speech, the cuts usually come at pauses or natural stopping points in the line. McTiernan uses this sort of rhythmic cutting at other points in the film.

The filmmaker may contrast the rhythm of sound and picture in more noticeable ways. For instance, if the source of sound is primarily offscreen, the filmmaker can utilize the behavior of onscreen figures to create an expressive counter-rhythm. Toward the end of John Ford's *She Wore a Yellow Ribbon,* the aging cavalry captain, Nathan Brittles, watches his troops ride out of the fort just after he has retired. He regrets leaving the service and desires to go with the patrol. The sound of the scene consists of two elements: the cheerful title song sung by the departing riders, and the quick hoofbeats of their horses. Yet only a few of the shots show the horses and singers, who ride at a rhythm matched to the sound. Instead, the scene concentrates our attention on Brittles, standing almost motionless by his own horse. The contrast of brisk musical rhythm and the static images of the solitary Brittles functions expressively, to emphasize his regret at having to stay behind for the first time in many years.

At times, accompanying music might even seem rhythmically inappropriate to the images. At intervals in *Four Nights of a Dreamer* Robert Bresson presents shots of a large, floating nightclub cruising the Seine. The boat's movement is slow and smooth, yet the sound track consists of lively calypso music. (Not until a later scene do we discover that the music comes from a band aboard the boat.) The strange combination of fast music with the slow passage of the boat creates a languorous, mysterious effect.

Jacques Tati does something similar in *Play Time.* In a scene outside a Parisian hotel, tourists climb aboard a bus to go to a nightclub. As they file slowly up the steps, raucous, jazzy music begins. The music again startles us because it seems inappropriate to the images. In fact, it primarily accompanies action in the next scene, in which some carpenters awkwardly carrying a large plate-glass window seem to be dancing to the music. By starting the fast music over an earlier scene of slower visual rhythm, Tati creates a comic effect and prepares for a transition to a new locale.

In Chris Marker's *La Jetée* the contrast between image and sound rhythms dominates the entire film. *La Jetée* is made up almost entirely of still

shots; except for one tiny gesture, all movement within the images is eliminated. Yet the film utilizes voice-over narration, music, and sound effects of
a generally rapid, constantly accented rhythm. Despite the absence of movement, the film does not seem "uncinematic," partly because it offers a dynamic interplay of audio-visual rhythms.

These examples suggest some of the ways in which rhythms may be
combined. But of course most films also vary their rhythms from one point to
another. A change of rhythm may function to shift our expectations. In the
famous battle on the ice in *Alexander Nevsky,* Sergei Eisenstein develops the
sound from slow tempos to fast and back to slow. The first twelve shots of
the scene show the Russian army anticipating the attack of the German
knights. The shots are of moderate length, and they contain very little movement. The music is comparably slow, consisting of short, distinctly separated
chords. Then, as the German army rides into sight over the horizon, both the
visual movement and the tempo of the music increase quickly, and the battle
begins. At the end of the battle Eisenstein creates another contrast with a
long passage of slow, lamenting music, majestic tracking shots, and little
figure movement.

FIDELITY

By fidelity we do not mean the quality of recording. In our sense, fidelity
refers to the extent to which the sound is faithful to the source as we conceive
it. If a film shows us a barking dog and we hear a barking noise, that sound
is faithful to its source; the sound maintains fidelity. But if the picture of the
barking dog is accompanied by the sound of a cat meowing, there enters a
disparity between sound and image — a lack of fidelity.

From our standpoint, fidelity has nothing to do with what originally
made the sound in production. As we have seen, the filmmaker may manipulate sound independently of image. Accompanying the image of a dog with
the meow is no more difficult than accompanying the image with a bark. If
the viewer takes the sound to be coming from its source in the diegetic world
of the film, then it is faithful, regardless of its actual source in production.

Fidelity is thus purely a matter of expectation. Even if our dog emits a
bark on screen, perhaps in production the bark came from a different dog or
was electronically synthesized. We do not know what a laser gun "really"
sounds like, but we accept the whang they make in *Return of the Jedi* as
plausible. (In production, their sound was made by hammering guy wires that
anchored a radio tower.)

When we do become aware that a sound is unfaithful to its source, that
awareness is usually used for comic effect. In Jacques Tati's *Mr. Hulot's
Holiday* much humor arises from the opening and closing of a dining-room
door. Instead of simply recording a real door, Tati inserts a twanging sound
like a plucked cello string each time the door swings. Aside from being
amusing in itself, this sound functions to emphasize the rhythmic patterns
created by waiters and diners passing through the door. Because many of the
jokes in *Mr. Hulot's Holiday* and other Tati films are based on quirkily
unfaithful noises, his films are good specimens for the study of sound.

Another master of comically unfaithful sound is René Clair. In several scenes of *Le Million* sound effects occur that are not faithful to their sources. When the hero's friend drops a plate, we hear not shattering crockery but the clash of cymbals. Later, during a chase scene, when characters collide, the impact is portrayed by a heavy bass drum beat. Similar manipulations of fidelity commonly occur in animated cartoons.

But as with low- or high-angle framings, we have no recipe that will allow us to interpret every manipulation of fidelity as comic. Some nonfaithful sounds have serious functions. In Hitchcock's *The Thirty-Nine Steps* a landlady discovers a corpse in an apartment. A shot of her screaming face is accompanied by a train whistle; then the scene shifts to an actual train. Though the whistle is not a faithful sound for an image of a screaming person, it provides a dramatic transition.

In some cases fidelity may be manipulated by a change in volume. A sound may seem unreasonably loud or soft in relation to other sounds in the film. Curtis Bernhardt's *Possessed* alters volume in ways that are not faithful to the sources. The central character is gradually falling deeper into mental illness. In one scene she is alone, very distraught, in her room on a rainy night, and the narration restricts us to her range of knowledge. But sound devices enable the narration to achieve subjective depth as well. We begin to hear things as she does; the ticking of the clock and dripping of raindrops gradually magnify in volume. Here the shift in fidelity functions to suggest a psychological state, a movement from the character's heightened perception into sheer hallucination.

SPACE

Sound has a spatial dimension because it comes from a *source*. Our beliefs about that source have a powerful effect on how we understand the sound.

Recall that for purposes of analyzing narrative form, we described events taking place in the story world as *diegetic* (p. 92). For this reason, *diegetic sound* is sound which has a source in the story world. The words spoken by the characters, sounds made by objects in the story, and music represented as coming from instruments in the story space are all diegetic sound.

Diegetic sound is often hard to notice as such. It may seem to come naturally from the world of the film. But as we saw in the sequence of the Ping-Pong game in *Mr. Hulot's Holiday*, the filmmaker may manipulate diegetic sound in ways that are not at all realistic.

On the other hand there is *nondiegetic sound*, which is represented as coming from a source outside the story world. Music added to enhance the film's action is the most common type of nondiegetic sound. When Roger Thornhill is climbing Mount Rushmore in *North by Northwest* and tense music comes up, we do not expect to see an orchestra perched on the side of the mountain. Viewers understand that the "movie music" is a convention and does not issue from the world of the story. The same holds true for the so-called omniscient narrator, the disembodied voice that gives us information but does not belong to any of the characters in the film. An example is *The Magnificent Ambersons*, in which the director Orson Welles speaks the nondiegetic narration.

Nondiegetic sound effects are also possible. In *Le Million* various characters all pursue an old coat with a winning lottery ticket in the pocket. The chase converges backstage at the opera, where the characters race and dodge around one another, tossing the coat to their accomplices. But instead of putting in the sounds coming from the actual space of the chase, Clair fades in the sounds of a football game. Because the maneuvers of the chase do look like a football game, with the coat serving as a ball, this enhances the comedy of the sequence. Although we hear a crowd cheering and a referee's whistle, we do not assume that the characters present are making these sounds. (Thus this is not a manipulation of fidelity, as with the earlier cases from *Le Million.*) The nondiegetic sounds create comedy by making a sort of audio-visual pun.

Entire films may be made with completely nondiegetic sound tracks. Conner's *A Movie*, Kenneth Anger's *Scorpio Rising*, and Derek Jarman's *War Requiem* use only nondiegetic music. Similarly, many compilation documentaries include no diegetic sound; instead, omniscient voice-over commentary and orchestral music guide our response to the images.

As with fidelity, the distinction between diegetic and nondiegetic sound does not depend on the real source of the sound in the filmmaking process. Rather, it depends on our understanding of the conventions of film viewing. We know that certain sounds are represented as coming from the story world, while others are represented as coming from outside the space of the story events. Such viewing conventions are so common that we usually do not have to think about which type of sound we are hearing at any moment. At many points in this chapter, however, we will find that the film's narration deliberately blurs boundaries between different spatial categories. Such a play with convention can be used to puzzle or surprise the audience, to create humor or ambiguity, or to achieve other purposes.

Let us survey some possibilities of diegetic sound. We know that the space of the narrative action is not limited to what we can see on the screen at a given moment. If we already know that several people are present in a room, we can see a shot that shows only one person without assuming that the other people have left. We simply have a sense that those people are offscreen. And if one of those offscreen people speaks, we still assume that the sound is coming from part of the story space. Thus diegetic sound can be either *onscreen* or *offscreen*, depending on whether its source is within the frame or outside the frame.

A shot shows a character talking, and we hear the sound of his or her voice. Another shot shows a door closing, and we hear a slam. A person plays a fiddle, and we hear its notes. In each case the source of the sound is in the story—diegetic—and visible within the frame—onscreen. But the shot may show only a person listening to a voice without the speaker being seen; another shot might show a character running down a corridor and the sound of an unseen door slamming; lastly, an audience is shown listening while the sound of a fiddle is heard. In all of these instances, the sounds come from within the story—again diegetic—but are now in a space outside the frame—offscreen.

At first this may seem a trivial distinction, but we know from our study of framing in Chapter 7 how powerful offscreen space can be. Offscreen sound can suggest space extending beyond the visible action. In *American*

Graffiti, a film that plays heavily on the distinction between diegetic and nondiegetic music, offscreen sounds of car radios often suggest that all of the cars on a street are tuned to the same radio station.

Offscreen sound may also control our expectations about offscreen space. In *His Girl Friday* Hildy goes into the press room to write her final story. As she chats with the other reporters, a loud clunk comes from an unseen source. Hildy glances offscreen left, and immediately a new space comes to our attention. She walks to the window and sees a gallows being prepared for an execution. Here offscreen sound initiates the discovery of a new area of action.

Offscreen sound can make the film's narration less restricted. In John Ford's *Stagecoach,* the stagecoach is desperately fleeing from a band of Indians. The ammunition is running out, and all seems lost until a troop of cavalry suddenly arrives. Yet Ford does not present the situation this baldly. He shows a medium close-up of one of the passengers, Hatfield, who has just discovered that he is down to his last bullet (Fig. 9.9). He glances off right and raises his gun (Fig. 9.10). The camera pans right to a woman, Lucy, praying. During all this, orchestral music, including bugles, plays nondiegetically. Unseen by Lucy, the gun comes into the frame from the left as Hatfield prepares to shoot her to prevent her from being captured by the Indians (Fig. 9.11). But before he shoots, an offscreen gunshot is heard, and Hatfield's hand and gun drop down out of the frame (Fig. 9.12). Then the bugle music becomes somewhat more prominent. Lucy's expression changes as she says, "Can you hear it? Can you hear it? It's a bugle. They're blowing the charge" (Fig. 9.13). Only then does Ford cut to the cavalry itself racing toward the coach.

Rather than showing the cavalry riding to the rescue, the film's narration uses offscreen sound to restrict our awareness to the initial despair of the passengers and their growing hope as they hear the distant sound. The sound of the bugle also emerges imperceptibly out of the nondiegetic music. Only Lucy's line tells us that this is a diegetic sound that signals their rescue, at which point the narration becomes far less restricted.

Diegetic sound harbors other possibilities. Often a filmmaker uses sound to represent what a character is thinking. We hear the character's voice speaking his or her thoughts even though that character's lips do not move; presumably other characters cannot hear these thoughts. Here the narration

Fig. 9.9

Fig. 9.10

Fig. 9.11

Fig. 9.12

Fig. 9.13

uses sound to achieve subjectivity, giving us information about the mental state of the character. Such spoken thoughts are comparable to mental images on the visual track. A character may also remember words, snatches of music, or events as represented by sound effects. In this case the technique is comparable to a visual flashback.

The use of sound to enter a character's mind is so common that we need to distinguish between *internal* and *external* diegetic sound. External diegetic sound is that which we as spectators take to have a physical source in the scene. Internal diegetic sound is that which comes from "inside" the mind of a character; it is subjective. (Nondiegetic and internal diegetic sounds are often called *sound over* because they do not come from the real space of the scene.) In the Laurence Olivier version of *Hamlet*, for example, the filmmaker presents Hamlet's famous soliloquies as interior monologues. Hamlet is the source of the thoughts we hear represented as speech but the words are only in his mind, not in his objective surroundings.

Fig. 9.14

A more complex use of internal diegetic sound occurs in Wim Wenders's *Wings of Desire*. Dozens of people are reading in a large public library. As the camera tracks along past them, we hear their thoughts as a throbbing murmur of many voices in many languages (Fig. 9.14). Incidentally, this sequence also constitutes an interesting exception to the general rule that one character cannot hear another's internal diegetic sound. The film's premise is that Berlin is patrolled by invisible angels who can tune in to humans' thoughts. This is a good example of how the conventions of a genre (here, the fantasy film) and the film's specific narrative context can modify a traditional device.

To summarize: Sound may be diegetic (in the story space) or nondiegetic (outside the story space). If it is diegetic, it may be onscreen or offscreen, and internal ("subjective") or external ("objective").

One characteristic of diegetic sound is the possibility of suggesting the *sound perspective*. This is a sense of spatial distance and location analogous to the cues for visual depth and volume which we get with visual perspective. "I like to think," remarks sound designer Walter Murch, "that I not only record a sound but the space between me and the sound: The subject that generates the sound is merely what causes the surrounding space to resonate."

Sound perspective can be suggested by volume. A loud sound tends to seem near; a soft one, more distant. The horses' hooves in the *Seven Samurai* battle and the bugle call from *Stagecoach* exemplify how rising volume suggests closer distance. Sound perspective is also created by timbre. The combination of directly registered sounds and sounds reflected from the environment creates a timbre specific to a given distance. Such timbre effects are most noticeable with echoes. In *The Magnificent Ambersons* the conversations that take place on the baroque staircase have a distinct echo, giving the impression of huge, empty spaces around the characters.

Multichannel recording and reproduction tremendously increase the filmmaker's ability to suggest sound perspective. In most 35mm theaters equipped with multitrack sound systems, three speakers are located behind the screen. The center speaker transmits most of the onscreen dialogue, as well as the most important effects and music. The left and right speakers are stereophonic, carrying not only important dialogue but also sound effects, music, and minor dialogue. These channels can suggest a region of sound within the frame or just offscreen. Surround channels principally carry minor sound effects, and they are divided among several speakers arranged along the sides and in the back of the theater.

By using stereophonic and surround tracks, a film can more strongly imply a sound's distance and placement. In farcical comedies like *The Naked Gun* and *Hot Shots,* stereophonic sound can suggest collisions and falls outside the frame. Without the greater localization offered by the stereophonic channels, we might scan the frame for sources of the sounds.

In addition, stereo reproduction can specify a moving sound's direction. In David Lean's *Lawrence of Arabia,* for instance, the approach of planes to bomb a camp is first suggested through a rumble occurring only on the right side of the screen. Lawrence and an officer look off right, and their dialogue identifies the source of the sound. Then, when the scene shifts to the besieged camp itself, the sound slides from channel to channel, suggesting the planes swooping overhead.

With stereophonic and surround channels, a remarkably convincing three-dimensional sound environment may be created within the theater. Sound sources can alter in position as the camera pans or tracks through a locale. The *Star Wars* series uses multiple-channel sound to suggest space vehicles whizzing not only across the screen but also above and behind the spectators.

Like other techniques, sound localization in the theater need not be used for realistic purposes. *Apocalypse Now* divides its six-track sound among three channels in the rear of the theater and three in the front. In the film's first sequence, the protagonist Ben Willard is seen lying on his bed. Shots of his feverish face are superimposed on shots of U.S. helicopters dropping napalm on the Vietnamese jungle. The sound oscillates between internal and external status, as Willard's mind turns the whoosh of a ceiling fan into the whir of helicopter blades. These subjective sounds issue from both the front and the back of the theater.

Abruptly, a POV shot tracking toward the window suggests that Willard has gotten to his feet and is walking. As the camera moves, the noises fade from all rear speakers and become concentrated in the front ones at screen left, right, and center. Then, as Willard's hand opens the venetian blinds to reveal his vision of the street outside, the sound fades out of the left and right front speakers and is heard only from the center channel. Our attention has been narrowed: As we leave Willard's mind, the sound steers us back to the outside world, which is rendered as unrealistically monophonic. In addition, the disparity in acoustic dimensions suggests that the protagonist's wraparound memory of jungle destruction is richer than the pallid environment of Saigon.

In most films, the sources of the sounds are clearly diegetic or nondiegetic. But some films blur the distinction between diegetic and nondiegetic sound, as we saw in the cavalry-rescue scene of *Stagecoach.* Since we are used to identifying a sound's source easily, a film may try to cheat our expectations.

At the beginning of Mel Brooks's *Blazing Saddles*, we hear what we think is nondiegetic musical accompaniment for a cowboy's ride across the prairie—until he rides past Count Basie and his orchestra. This joke depends on a reversal of our expectations about the convention of nondiegetic music. A more elaborate example is the 1986 musical version of *Little Shop of Horrors*. There a trio of female singers strolls through many scenes, providing musical commentary on the action without any of the characters noticing them. (To complicate matters, the three singers also appear in minor diegetic roles and only then do they interact with the main characters.)

More complex is a moment in *The Magnificent Ambersons* when Welles creates an unusual interplay between the diegetic and nondiegetic sounds. A prologue to the film outlines the background of the Amberson family and the birth of the son, George. We see a group of townswomen gossiping about the marriage of Isabel Amberson, and one predicts that she will have "the worst spoiled lot of children this town will ever see." This scene has presented diegetic dialogue. After the last line, the nondiegetic narrator resumes his description of the family history. Over a shot of the empty street, he says: "The prophetess proved to be mistaken in a single detail merely; Wilbur and Isabel did not have *children*. They had only one." But at this point, still over the shot of the street, we hear the gossiper's voice again: "Only one! But I'd like to know if he isn't spoiled enough for a whole carload." After her line, a pony cart comes up the street, and we see George for the first time. In this exchange the woman seems to reply to the narrator, even though we must assume that she cannot hear what he says. (After all, she is a character in the story and he is not.) Here Welles playfully departs from conventional usage to emphasize the arrival of the story's main character and the hostility of the townspeople to him.

This passage from *The Magnificent Ambersons* juxtaposes diegetic and nondiegetic sounds in an ambiguous way. In other films a single sound may be ambiguous because it could fall into either category. In the *Apocalypse Now* sequence already mentioned, the throbbings of the ceiling fan and the helicopter blades are clearly diegetic, but Coppola accompanies these with Jim Morrison's song, "The End." This might be taken as either a subjective part of Willard's fantasy or as nondiegetic, an external commentary on the action in the manner of normal "movie music."

A more disturbing uncertainty about whether a sound is diegetic or not often crops up in the films of Jean-Luc Godard. He narrates some of his films in nondiegetic voice-over, but in other films, such as *Two or Three Things I Know About Her*, he seems also to be in the story space, whispering questions or comments whose sound perspective makes them seem close to the camera. Godard does not claim to be a character in the action, yet the characters on the screen sometimes behave as though they hear him. This uncertainty as to diegetic or nondiegetic sound sources enables Godard to stress the conventionality of traditional sound usage.

The distinction between diegetic and nondiegetic sound is important for understanding particular films, as we shall see in some cases discussed at the end of the chapter.

TIME

Sound also permits the filmmaker to represent time in various ways. This is because the time represented on the sound track may or may not be the same as that represented in the image.

The most straightforward audio-visual relations involve sound-image synchronization. The matching of sound with image in projection creates *synchronous sound*. When a sound is synchronized with the image, we hear it at the same time as we see the source produce the sound. Dialogue between characters is normally synchronized so that the lips of the actors move at the same time that we hear the appropriate words.

When the sound does go out of synchronization during a viewing (often through an error in projection or lab work), the result is quite distracting. But some filmmakers have obtained imaginative effects by putting out-of-sync, or *asynchronous*, sound into the film itself. One such effect occurs in a scene in the musical by Gene Kelly and Stanley Donen, *Singin' in the Rain.* In the early days of Hollywood sound filming, a pair of silent screen actors have just made their first talking picture, *The Dueling Cavalier.* Their film company previews the film for an audience at a theater. In the earliest days of "talkies," sound was often recorded on a phonograph record to be played along with the film; hence the chances of the sound's getting out of synchronization with the picture were much greater than they are today. This is what happens in the preview of *The Dueling Cavalier.* As the film is projected, it slows down momentarily, but the record keeps running. From this point all the sounds come several seconds before their sources are seen in the image. A line of dialogue begins, *then* the actor's lips move. A woman's voice is heard when a man moves his lips and vice versa. The humor of this disastrous preview in *Singin' in the Rain* depends on our realization that the synchronization of sound and image is an illusion produced by mechanical means.

A lengthier play with our expectations about synchronization comes in Woody Allen's *What's Up Tiger Lily?* Allen has taken an Asian spy film and dubbed a new sound track on, but the English-language dialogue is not a translation of the original. Instead, it creates a new story in comic juxtaposition with the original images. Much of the humor results from our constant awareness that the words are not perfectly synchronized with the actors' lips. Allen has turned the usual problems of the dubbing of foreign films into the basis of his comedy.

Synchronization relates to screen duration, or *viewing* time. As we have seen in Chapter 4, narrative films can also present *plot* and *story* time. To recall the distinction: Story time consists of the order, duration, and frequency of all the events pertinent to the narrative, whether they are shown to us or not. Plot time consists of these temporal qualities (order, duration, and frequency) of the events actually represented in the film. Plot time shows us selected story events but only refers to others. Thus it usually covers a shorter span than the complete story does.

Story and plot time can be manipulated by sound in two principal ways. If the sound takes place at the same time as the image in terms of the story events, it is *simultaneous sound*. This is by far the most common usage. When characters speak onscreen, the words we hear are occurring at the same moment in the plot's action as in story time.

But it is possible for the sound we hear to occur earlier or later in the story than the events which we see in the image. In this manipulation of story order, the sound becomes *nonsimultaneous*. The most common example of this is the sonic flashback. For instance, we might see a character onscreen in the present but hear another character's voice from an earlier scene. By means of nonsimultaneous sound, the film can give us information about story events without showing them to us. And nonsimultaneous sound may, like simultaneous sound, have either an external or an internal source—that is, a source in the "objective" world of the film or the "subjective" realms of the character's mind.

As these categories suggest, temporal relationships in the cinema are complex. To help distinguish them, Table 9.2 sums up the possible temporal and spatial relationships that image and sound can display.

Diegetic sound. Because the first and third of these possibilities are comparatively uncommon, we start by commenting on the second, most normal option.

2. *Sound simultaneous in story with image.* This is by far the most common temporal relation which sound has in fiction films. Noise, music, or speech that comes from the space of the story almost invariably occurs at the same time as the image. Like any other sort of diegetic sound, simultaneous sound can be either external (objective) or internal (subjective).

1. *Sound earlier in story than image.* Here the sound comes from an earlier point in the story than the action currently visible onscreen. A clear example occurs at the end of Joseph Losey's *Accident*. Over a shot of a driveway gate, we hear a car crash. The sound represents the crash that occurred at the *beginning* of the film. Now if there were cues that the sound was internal—that is, that a character was recalling it—it would not strictly

Table 9.2   TEMPORAL RELATIONS OF SOUND IN CINEMA

| | SPACE OF SOURCE | |
TIME	DIEGETIC (STORY SPACE)	NONDIEGETIC (NONSTORY SPACE)
1. Nonsimultaneous: sound from *earlier* in story than image	Sound flashback; image flashforward; sound bridge	Sound marked as past put over images (e.g., sound of a John Kennedy speech put over images of United States today)
2. Sound *simultaneous* in story with image	*External:* dialogue, effects, music *Internal:* thoughts of character heard	Sound marked as simultaneous with images put over images (e.g., a narrator describing events in the present tense)
3. Nonsimultaneous: sound from *later* in story than image	Sound flashforward; image flashback with sound continuing in the present; character narrates earlier events; sound bridge	Sound marked as later put over images (e.g., reminiscing narrator of *The Magnificent Ambersons*)

be coming from the past, since the memory of the sound would be occurring in the present. But here no character is remembering the scene, so we have a fairly pure case of a "sonic flashback." In this film, an unrestricted narration makes an ironic final comment on the action. Similarly, early in Ron Howard's *The Paper,* we see images of two teenagers inspecting bloody corpses in a car while the sound of gunfire provides a flashback to the murders.

Sound may belong to an earlier time than the image in another way. The sound from one scene may linger briefly while the image is already presenting the next scene. This is called a *sound bridge.* Sound bridges of this sort may create smooth transitions by setting up expectations that are quickly confirmed. One scene of Jonathan Demme's *The Silence of the Lambs* ends with the heroine talking on the phone, identifying a location as the "Your Self Storage facility. . . ." Her over-the-phone description continues on the sound track (". . . right outside central Baltimore") while the image track presents a medium shot of the Your Self Storage facility sign, introducing the next scene.

Sound bridges can also make our expectations more uncertain. In Tim Hunter's *The River's Edge,* three high-school boys are standing outside school, and one of them confesses to having killed his girlfriend. When his pals scoff, he says, "They don't believe me." There is a cut to the dead girl lying in the grass by the river, while on the sound track we hear one of his friends respond to him by calling it a crazy story that no one will believe. For an instant we cannot be sure whether a new scene is starting or we are seeing a cutaway to the corpse, which could be followed by a shot returning to the three boys at school. But the shot dwells on the dead girl, and after a pause we hear, with a different sound ambience: "If you brought us. . . ." Then there is a cut to a shot of the three youths walking through the woods to the river, as the same character continues, ". . . all the way out here for nothing. . . ." The friend's remark about the crazy story belongs to an earlier time than the shot of the corpse, and it is used as an unsettling sound bridge to the new scene.

3. *Sound later in story than image.* Nonsimultaneous diegetic sound may also occur at a later time than that depicted by the images. Here we are to take the images as occurring in the past and the sound as occurring in the present or future. A simple prototype occurs in many trial dramas. The testimony of a witness in the present is heard on the sound track, while the image presents a flashback to an earlier event. The same effect occurs when the film employs a reminiscing narrator, as in John Ford's *How Green Was My Valley.* Aside from a glimpse at the beginning, we do not see the protagonist Huw as a man, only as a boy, but his narration accompanies the bulk of the plot, which is set in the distant past. Huw's voice on the sound track creates a strong nostalgia for the past and constantly reminds us of the pathetic decline that the characters will eventually suffer.

Since the late 1960s, it has become somewhat common for the sound from the next scene to begin while the images of the last one are still on the screen. Like the instances mentioned above, this transitional device is called a *sound bridge.* In Wim Wenders's *American Friend,* a nighttime shot of a little boy riding in the back seat of a car is accompanied by a harsh clacking.

There is a cut to a railroad station, where the timetable board flips through its metal cards listing times and destinations. Since the sound over the shot of the boy comes from the space of the later scene, this portion is nonsimultaneous.

If the sound bridge is not immediately identifiable, it can surprise or disorient the audience, as in this *American Friend* transition. A more recognizable sonic lead-in can create more clear-cut expectations about what we will see in the next scene. Federico Fellini's *8½* takes place in a town famous for its health spa and natural springs, and several scenes have shown an outdoor orchestra playing to entertain the tourists and guests. Midway through the film a scene ends with the closing of a window on a steam bath. Near the end of the shot, we hear an orchestral version of the song "Blue Moon." There is a cut to an orchestra playing the tune in the center of the town's shopping area. Even before the new scene has established the exact locale of the action, we can reasonably expect that the musical bridge is bringing us back to the public life of the spa.

In principle, one could also have a sound flashforward. The filmmaker could, say, use the sounds that belong with scene 5 to accompany the images in scene 2. In practice, such a technique is very rare. In Godard's *Band of Outsiders*, the sound of a tiger's roar is heard as sound "over," not as sound "off," several scenes before we see the tiger. A more ambiguous case can be found in Godard's *Contempt*. A husband and wife quarrel, and the scene ends with her swimming out to sea while he sits quietly on a rock formation. On the sound track we hear her voice, closely miked, reciting a letter in which she tells him she has driven back to Rome with another man. Since the husband has not yet received the letter, and perhaps the wife has not yet written it, the letter and its recitation presumably come from a later point in the story. Here the sound flashforward sets up strong expectations which a later scene confirms: We see the wife and the husband's rival stopping for gas on the road. In fact we never see a scene in which the husband receives the letter.

Nondiegetic sound.   Most nondiegetic sound has no relevant temporal relationship to the story. When "mood" music comes up over a tense scene, it would be irrelevant to ask if it is happening at the same time as the images, since the music has no place in the world of the action. But occasionally the filmmaker may use a type of nondiegetic sound that does have a defined temporal relationship to the story. Welles's narration in *The Magnificent Ambersons*, for instance, speaks of the action as having happened in a long-vanished era of American history.

■ SUMMARY

As we watch a film, we do not mentally slot each sound into each of these spatial and temporal categories. But our categories do assist us in analysis. They offer us ways of noticing important aspects of films—especially films that play with our expectations about sounds. By becoming aware of the rich range of possibilities, we are less likely to take a film's sound track for granted and are more likely to notice unusual sound manipulations.

One such manipulation comes early in Alain Resnais's *Providence*. As the film begins, we see a mysterious house and men hunting down a wounded old man. Suddenly we are in a courtroom, where a witness is being interrogated. These abrupt transitions give us little time to form expectations. Apparently a prosecutor is questioning a young man accused of the mercy killing of the old man during the hunt. The young man justifies his act by saying that the man was not only dying but turning into an animal. (We had seen the man's hairy face and clawlike hands, so now we begin to see the links between the scenes.) The prosecutor pauses, astonished: "Are you suggesting some kind of actual metamorphosis?" He pauses again, and a man's voice whispers, "A werewolf." The prosecutor then asks, "A werewolf, perhaps?"

The whispered words startle us, for we cannot immediately account for them. Are they whispered by an unseen character offscreen? Are they perhaps even nondiegetic, coming from outside the story world? Only much later in the film do we find out whose voice whispered these words, and why. The whole opening of *Providence* provides an excellent extended case of how disorienting an ambiguity of sound sources can be when the filmmaker departs from conventional usage.

In the *Providence* sequence, we are aware of the ambiguity immediately, and it points our expectations forward, arousing curiosity as to how the whisperer can be identified. The filmmaker can also use sound to create a retrospective awareness of how we have *mis*interpreted something earlier. This occurs in Francis Ford Coppola's *The Conversation*, a film that is virtually a textbook on the manipulation of sound and image.

The plot centers on Harry Caul, a sound engineer specializing in surveillance. Harry is hired by a mysterious corporate executive to tape a conversation between a young man and woman in a noisy park. Harry cleans up the garbled tape, but when he goes to turn over the copy to his client, he suspects foul play and refuses to relinquish it.

Now Harry obsessively replays, refilters, and remixes all his tapes of the conversation. Flashback images of the couple—perhaps in his memory, perhaps not—accompany his reworking of the tape. Finally Harry arrives at a good dub, and we hear the man say, "He'd kill us if he could."

The overall situation is quite mysterious. Harry does not know who the young couple are (is the woman his client's wife or daughter?). Nevertheless Harry suspects that they are in danger from the executive. Harry's studio is ransacked, the tape is stolen, and he later finds that the executive has it. Now more than ever Harry feels that he is involved in a murder plot. After a highly ambiguous series of events, including Harry's bugging of a hotel room during which a killing takes place, Harry learns that the situation is not as he had thought.

Without giving away the revelation of the mystery, we can say that in *The Conversation* the narration misleads us by suggesting that certain sounds are objective when at the film's end we are inclined to treat them as subjective, or at least ambiguous. The film's surprise, and its lingering mysteries, rely on unsignaled shifts between external and internal diegetic sound.

The two films just discussed point to a second justification for our set of categories. These categories seem to correspond to tacit assumptions and inferences which spectators actually make. The films and our reactions to them suggest that we quickly learn to distinguish between internal and external, diegetic and nondiegetic, simultaneous and nonsimultaneous sound. We are surprised or amused when films violate these categories; we are puzzled or misled when a sound source shifts from one category to another. If these categories did not tally with our assumptions, such films as *Providence* and *The Conversation* would not have the power to undermine our expectations, to create suspense or surprise or ambiguity. Our taxonomy, then, is offered both as a tool for film analysis and as a systematic outline of viewers' ordinary intuitions.

FUNCTIONS OF FILM SOUND: *A MAN ESCAPED*

Robert Bresson's *A Man Escaped (Un Condamné à mort c'est échappé)* illustrates how a variety of sound techniques can function throughout an entire film. The story takes place in France in 1943. Fontaine, a Resistance fighter arrested by the Germans, has been put in prison and condemned to die. But while awaiting his execution, he works at an escape plan, loosening the boards of his cell door and making ropes. Just as he is ready to put his plan in action, a boy named Jost is put into his cell. Deciding to trust that Jost is not a spy, Fontaine reveals his plan to him, and they are both able to escape.

Throughout the film, sound has many important functions. As in all of his films, Bresson emphasizes the sound track, rightly believing that sound may be just as "cinematic" as images. At certain points in *A Man Escaped,* Bresson even lets his sound technique dominate the image; throughout the film, we are compelled to *listen.* Indeed, Bresson is one of a handful of directors who create a complete interplay between sound and image.

A key factor in guiding our perception of the action is the commentary spoken over by Fontaine himself. The voice-over is nonsimultaneous, since it occurs at a time later than the images. But it could be either internal or external sound, since we never learn whether he is simply thinking back over these events or telling them to someone.

Fontaine's narration has several functions. First, the commentary helps clarify the action. Certain temporal cues suggest how long Fontaine spends in prison. As we see him working at his escape plan, his voice-over tells us, "One month of patient work and my door opened." At other points he gives us additional indications of time. His commentary is particularly important during the final escape scene, where hours of action occupy only 15 minutes of viewing time and the narration is narrowly limited to what Fontaine could know. Fontaine's voice calmly tells us of his and Jost's patient, cautious progress toward freedom.

We receive other vital information through the commentary. Sometimes the narration simply states facts: that the pin Fontaine obtains came from the women's wing of the prison or that certain prison officials' quarters were at various places in the building. More strikingly, Fontaine often tells what his thoughts had been. After being beaten and put in his first cell, he wipes the blood from his face and lies down. On the track we hear his voice say: "I'd have preferred a quick death." Often the actor does not register such thoughts visually.

At some points the sound even corrects an impression given by the image. After Fontaine has been sentenced to death, he is led back to his cell and flings himself down on the bed. We might take him to be crying, but the commentary says, "I laughed hysterically. It helped." Thus the commentary adds a degree of depth to the film's narration by allowing us glimpses into Fontaine's mental states.

Yet at first much of the commentary may seem unnecessary, since it often tells us something that we can also see in the image. In one scene Fontaine wipes the blood from his face, and his voice tells us, "I tried to clean up." Again and again in the film Fontaine describes his actions as we see him perform them or just before or after them. But this use of sound is not redundantly supporting the visuals. One major function of the past-tense commentary and even the apparently redundant remarks is to emphasize the prison event as having *already* happened. Instead of simply showing a series of events in the present, the commentary places the events in the past.

Indeed, certain phrases emphasize the fact that the commentary is a remembering of events. As we see Fontaine lie down in his cell after having been beaten, his commentary says, "I believe that I gave up and wept," as if the passage of time has made him uncertain. After meeting another prisoner, Fontaine narrates, "Terry was an exception; he was allowed to see his daughter. I learned this later." Again we are aware that the meeting we see on the screen occurred at a point in the past.

Because of this difference in time between image and commentary, the narrative indicates to us that Fontaine will eventually escape rather than be executed. (The title also indicates this.) This final *effect* of the narrative cause-effect chain is known. As a result, our suspense is centered on the *cause*—not *whether* Fontaine will escape, but *how* he will escape. The film guides our expectations, first of all, toward the minute details of Fontaine's work to break out of prison. The commentary and the sound effects draw our attention to tiny gestures and ordinary objects that become crucial to the escape.

Furthermore, the narrative stresses that work alone is not enough, that Fontaine and the other prisoners can survive, both mentally and physically, only through their efforts to help one another. Fontaine receives aid and comfort from his fellow prisoners. His neighbor Blanchet gives him a blanket to make his ropes; another prisoner who also tries to escape, Orsini, provides vital information about how to get over the walls. Finally, Fontaine himself must extend trust to his new cellmate, Jost, by taking him along in spite of suspicions that he may be a spy planted by the Germans.

The interplay between the sounds and images in *A Man Escaped* does not pertain solely to the commentary. The ability to focus our attention on details works with sound effects as well, where each object gains a specific timbre. In the long middle portion of the film, in which Fontaine works on breaking through his door and making the implements of escape, this concentration on details becomes particularly prominent. A close-up shows Fontaine's hands sharpening a spoon handle into a chisel; the loud scraping intensifies our perception of this detail. We hear distinctly the rubbing of the spoon against the boards of the door, the ripping of cloth with a razor to make ropes, even the swish of straw against the floor as Fontaine sweeps up slivers of wood. We also become intensely aware that such sounds could alert the guards to Fontaine's activities.

The concentration on details follows a general pattern in the narration of *A Man Escaped*. The narration is unusually restricted. We learn nothing that Fontaine does not know. As Fontaine looks around his cell for the first time he names the items it contains— a slop bucket, a shelf, a window. *After* he mentions each, the camera moves to give us a glimpse of it. At another point Fontaine hears a strange sound outside his cell. He moves to the door, and we get a point-of-view shot through the peephole in his door; a guard is winding the crank of a skylight in the hall. For the first time Fontaine becomes aware of the skylight, which eventually becomes his escape route.

Indeed, at times we know less than Fontaine does. When he attempts to escape from the car in the opening scene, the camera holds on his empty seat rather than moving to follow him and show his recapture. Sound aids in restricting our knowledge by controlling what we see. Later, in prison, Fontaine's neighbor Blanchet falls down during their daily walk to empty their slop buckets. We first hear the sound of his fall as the camera remains on a medium shot of Fontaine reacting in surprise. Then there is a cut to Blanchet as Fontaine moves to help him up. While the image restricts our knowledge, the sound anticipates and guides our expectations.

At times, sound in *A Man Escaped* goes beyond controlling the image; sometimes it partially *replaces* it. Several of the film's scenes are so dark that sound must play a large part in conveying information about the action. After Fontaine falls asleep in prison for the first time, there is a fade-out. While the screen is still dark, we hear his voice-over saying, "I slept so soundly, my guards had to awaken me." This is followed by the loud sound of a bolt and hinge. The light let in by the door allows us to see a faint image of a guard's hand shaking Fontaine, and we hear a voice tell him to get up. In general, the film contains many fade-outs in which the sound of the next scene begins before the image does. By putting sound over a black screen or dark image, Bresson allows the sound track an unusually prominent place in his film.

The reliance on sound culminates in the final escape scene. During much of the last 15 or 20 minutes of the film, the action takes place outdoors at night. There are no establishing shots to give us a sense of the space of the roofs and walls which Fontaine and Jost must scale. We get glimpses of gestures and settings, but often sound is our main guide to what is happening. This has the effect of intensifying the spectators' attention greatly. We must strain to understand the action from what we can glimpse and hear. We judge the pair's progress from the church bells heard tolling the hour. The train outside the walls helps cover the noise the fugitives make. Each strange noise suggests an unseen threat.

In one remarkable shot Fontaine stands in darkness by a wall, listening to the footsteps of a guard walking up and down offscreen. Fontaine knows that he must kill this man if his escape is to succeed. We hear his voice-over explaining where the guard is moving and mentioning how hard his own heart is beating. There is little movement. All we see is Fontaine's dim outline and a tiny reflection of light in his eye. Again, throughout this scene the sound concentrates our attention on the characters' most minute reactions and gestures.

We have discussed how a filmmaker controls not only what we hear, but also the qualities of that sound. Bresson has achieved a considerable variety in *A Man Escaped.* Every object in the film is assigned a distinct pitch. The volumes of sounds range from very loud to almost inaudible, as the opening scene illustrates. The first few shots of Fontaine riding to prison in a car are accompanied only by the soft hum of the motor. But as a streetcar blocks the road, Fontaine seeks to use the streetcar's uproar to conceal his dash from the car. The moment Fontaine leaps from the car, Bresson eliminates the streetcar noise, and we hear running feet and gunshots offscreen. Later, in the final escape, the film alternates sounds offscreen (trains, bells, bicycle, and so on) with stretches of silence. The film's sparse sound mix effectively isolates specific sounds for our attention.

Certain sounds not only are very loud but also have an echo effect added to give them a distinctive timbre. The voices of the German guards as they give Fontaine orders are reverberant and harsh compared to the voices of the French prisoners. Similarly, the noises of the handcuffs and bolts of the cell doors are magnified for the same echo effect. These manipulations suggest Fontaine's own perceptual subjectivity. Thus our reactions to Fontaine's imprisonment are intensified through the manipulation of timbre.

These devices all help focus our attention on the details of Fontaine's prison life. But there are other devices that help unify the film and sustain its narrative and thematic development. These are the sound *motifs,* which come back at significant moments of the action.

One set of sound motifs emphasizes the space outside Fontaine's cell. We see a streetcar in the opening scene, and the bell and motor of a streetcar are heard offscreen every time Fontaine speaks to someone through his cell window. We are always aware of his goal of reaching the streets beyond the walls. During the second half of the film the sounds of trains also become important. When Fontaine is first able to leave his cell and walk in the hall unobserved, we hear a train whistle. It returns at other moments when he leaves his cell clandestinely, until the train provides the noise to cover the sounds Fontaine and Jost make during their escape.

Since the prisoners depend upon one another, certain sound motifs call attention to Fontaine's interactions with the other men. For example, the daily gathering of the men to wash in a common sink becomes associated with running water. At first, the faucet is seen onscreen, but later Bresson presents the scrubbing of the prisoners in closer shots, with the sound of the water offscreen.

Some sound motifs become associated with defiance of the prison rules. Fontaine uses his handcuffs to tap on the wall to signal his neighbors. He coughs to cover the sound of scraping, and coughs among the prisoners become signals. Fontaine defies the guards' orders and continues to talk to the other men. There are other sound motifs in the film (bells, guns, whistles, children's voices), which share certain functions already noted: dynamizing Fontaine's escape, calling our attention to details, and guiding what we notice.

Yet another motif involves the only nondiegetic sound in the film, passages from a Mozart mass. The music is motivated clearly enough, since the film's plot action refers continually to religious faith. Fontaine tells another prisoner that he prays but does not expect God to help him if he does not work for his own liberty. But the pattern of the uses of the music is less clear.

We may be unable at first to form any consistent expectations about the music, and its recurrences are likely to take us by surprise. After it is heard over the credits, the music does not return for some time. Its first use over the action occurs during the first walk Fontaine takes with the men to empty their slop buckets. As the music plays, Fontaine's commentary explains the routine: "Empty your buckets and wash, back to your cell for the day." The juxtaposition of ceremonial church music with the emptying of slop buckets in a prison is an incongruous one. Yet the contrast is not ironic. Not only are these moments of movement important to Fontaine's life in the prison but they also provide his main means of direct contact with other prisoners.

The music, which comes back seven more times, emphasizes the narrative development. Fontaine meets the other men, wins their support, and finally plans to share his escape. The music reappears whenever Fontaine makes contact with another prisoner (Blanchet, Orsini) who will affect his escape. Later washing scenes have no music; these are scenes in which Fontaine's contact is cut off because Orsini decides not to go along. The music returns as Orsini attempts his own escape plan. He fails but is able to give Fontaine vital information he will need in his own attempt. The music reappears when Blanchet, once opposed to Fontaine's plan, contributes his blanket to the rope making.

Eventually the music becomes associated with the boy, Jost. It plays again as Fontaine realizes that he must either kill Jost or take him along. The final use of music comes over the very end of the film, as the two leave the prison and disappear into the night. The nondiegetic music has traced Fontaine's developing trust in the other men on whom his endeavor depends.

The musical motif constitutes the only major appearance of a relatively unrestricted narrational element—the principal moments when we move briefly outside of our limitation to Fontaine's knowledge. Thus the music is crucial in suggesting a general implicit meaning beyond what Fontaine tells us explicitly. If we follow the pattern of the music's recurrences, we might interpret the motif as suggesting the importance of trust and interdependence among the people of the prison. It is not simply the conventional "mood" music that accompanies the action of many films. Indeed, its very incongruity as an accompaniment to mundane actions should cue us to seek an implicit meaning of this type.

Let us look at a brief scene from *A Man Escaped* in order to see how silence and shifts between sounds that are internal and external, simultaneous and nonsimultaneous, guide our expectations. The eleven shots indicated by Figures 9.15 through 9.25 in Table 9.3 constitute the scene in which the boy Jost is put into Fontaine's cell.

The use of silence and the oscillations between Fontaine's internal and external speech dominate the scene. We have not seen Jost before and do not know what is happening as the scene begins. Fontaine's internal commentary tells us that a new threat has appeared. Offscreen footsteps and

Table 9.3   SOUND AND SILENCE IN *A MAN ESCAPED*

SHOT	VOICE	EFFECTS	ACTION/CAMERA
(1) 27 sec 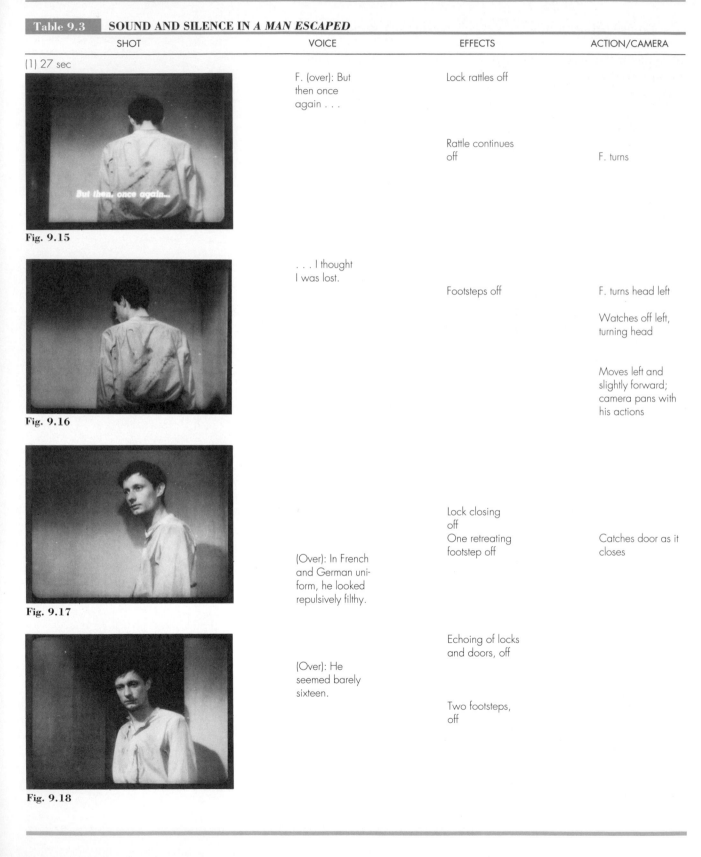 **Fig. 9.15**	F. (over): But then once again . . .	Lock rattles off Rattle continues off	F. turns
Fig. 9.16	. . . I thought I was lost.	Footsteps off	F. turns head left Watches off left, turning head Moves left and slightly forward; camera pans with his actions
Fig. 9.17	(Over): In French and German uniform, he looked repulsively filthy.	Lock closing off One retreating footstep off	Catches door as it closes
Fig. 9.18	(Over): He seemed barely sixteen.	Echoing of locks and doors, off Two footsteps, off	

Table 9.3	SOUND AND SILENCE IN *A MAN ESCAPED* (continued)		
SHOT	VOICE	EFFECTS	ACTION/CAMERA

	F. (aloud): Are you German?		
Fig. 9.19			
(2) 10 sec	French? What is your name?		
			Jost lifts head, looks off right
Fig. 9.20			
	Jost: Jost, François Jost. F. (over): Had they planted a spy?		
Fig. 9.21			
(3) 10 sec			
	F. (over): Did they think I was ready to talk?		F. lowers eyes
Fig. 9.22			

Table 9.3   **SOUND AND SILENCE IN *A MAN ESCAPED* (continued)**

SHOT	VOICE	EFFECTS	ACTION/CAMERA
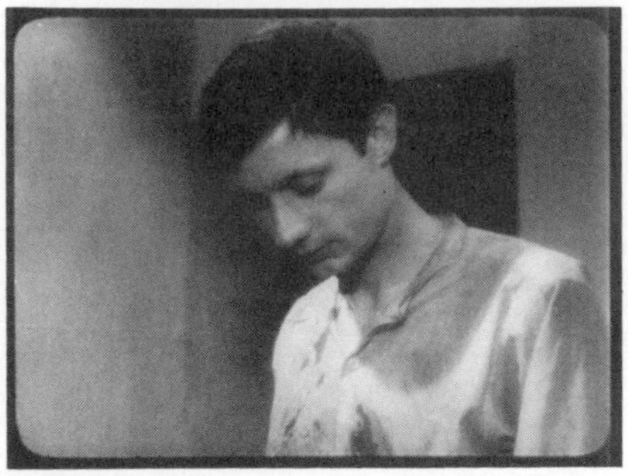 Fig. 9.23		Sound of one footstep (F.'s) on cell floor	F. moves left and forward, camera pans to follow
 Fig. 9.24	F. (aloud): Give me your hand, Jost.		F. stretches right arm out
(4) 7 sec			
 Fig. 9.25	F. (aloud): There isn't much room.	Sound of Jost rising Shoes against floor	Jost stands, they shake hands F. looks right They both look around
Dissolve			

Fontaine's gaze indicate that someone has entered his room, but the camera lingers on Fontaine. Bresson delays the cut to the newcomer for a surprisingly long time. (This first shot is as long as the other three shots combined.) The delay creates several effects. It restricts the narration considerably, since we do not know what Fontaine is reacting to. Our access to his mental state through the commentary only hints at the threat: The "he" referred to could be either a guard or another prisoner. This is one of the many small moments of suspense the narration creates.

The fact that we wait to see Jost also functions to emphasize the importance of his appearance. It directs our expectations to Fontaine's reaction (conveyed largely through his nonsimultaneous diegetic commentary) rather than to the new character. By the time we actually see Jost, we know that Fontaine feels threatened by him and disturbed by his part-German uniform. The first words Fontaine speaks in the scene emphasize his doubt. Rather than stating a decisive attitude, he simply seeks information. Again his commentary returns as he makes clear the dilemma he is in: Jost may be a spy planted by the prison officials. Yet his words to Jost contrast with this inner doubt as he shakes hands and converses in a friendly fashion. Thus the interplay of simultaneous dialogue and nonsimultaneous narration allows the filmmaker to present contrasting psychological aspects of the action.

The sound effects mark significant actions and develop the narrative progression. Fontaine's footstep is heard as he moves toward Jost after his initial reserve, and Jost's rising accompanies their first gesture of trust, the handshake. Finally, their shoes scrape against the floor as they relax and begin to speak of their situation.

This scene is very brief, but the combination of different types of sound within a few shots indicates the complexity of the film's sound track. The track, though, cannot be considered apart from its place in the entire film, functioning in interaction with other techniques and with narrative form. Through Bresson's control of what sounds we hear, what qualities these sounds have, and what relationships exist among those sounds and between sound and image, he has made this technique an important factor in shaping our experience of the film.

SUMMARY

As usual, both extensive viewing and intensive scrutiny will sharpen your capacity to notice the workings of film sound. You can get comfortable with the analytical tools we have suggested by asking several questions about a film's sound:

1. What sounds are present—music, speech, noise? How are loudness, pitch, and timbre used? Is the mixture sparse or dense? Modulated or abruptly changing?
2. Is the sound related rhythmically to the image? If so, how?
3. Is the sound faithful or unfaithful to its perceived source?
4. *Where* is the sound coming from? In the story's space or outside it? Onscreen or offscreen?
5. *When* is the sound occurring? Simultaneously with the story action? Before? After?
6. How are the various sorts of sounds organized across a sequence or the entire film? What patterns are formed, and how do they reinforce aspects of the film's overall formal system (narrative or nonnarrative)?
7. For each of questions 1–6, what *purposes* are fulfilled and what *effects* are achieved by the sonic manipulations?

Practice at trying to answer such questions will familiarize you with the basic uses of film sound. As always, though, it is not enough to name and classify. These categories and terms are most useful when we take the next step and examine how the types of sound we identify *function* in the total film.

NOTES AND QUERIES

For material on how sound is created in film production, see Notes and Queries to Chapter 1.

Articles on particular aspects of sound recording and reproduction in Hollywood are published in *Recording Engineer/Producer.* See also Jeff Forlenza and Terri Stone, eds., *Sound for Picture* (Winona, Minn.: Hal Leonard, 1993) and Vincent Lo Brutto, *Sound-on-Film: Interviews with Creators of Film Sound* (New York: Praeger, 1994). Walter Murch, Hollywood's principal sound designer, explains many contemporary sound techniques in Roy Paul Madsen, *Working Cinema: Learning from the Masters* (Belmont, Calif.: Wadsworth, 1990), pp. 288–313. Our quotation on p. 333 comes from the latter source, p. 294.

■ THE POWER OF SOUND

"The most exciting moment," claims Akira Kurosawa, "is the moment when I add the sound. . . . At this moment, I tremble."

Of all directors Sergei Eisenstein has written most prolifically and intriguingly about sound technique. See in particular his discussion of audiovisual polyphony in *Nonindifferent Nature,* trans. Herbert Marshall (Cambridge: Cambridge University Press, 1987), pp. 282–354. (For his discussion of music in particular, see below.) In addition, there are cryptic comments in Robert Bresson's *Notes on Cinematography,* trans. Jonathan Griffin (New York: Urizen, 1977), such as this: "The eye solicited alone makes the ear impatient, the ear solicited alone makes the eye impatient. *Use these impatiences"* (p. 28).

The aesthetic potential of film sound is discussed in two anthologies: John Belton and Elizabeth Weis, eds., *Film Sound: Theory and Practice* (New York: Columbia University Press, 1985) and Rick Altman, ed., *Sound Theory Sound Practice* (New York: Routledge, 1992). Critical analyses of sound in particular films and filmmakers include Noël Carroll, "Lang, Pabst, and Sound," *Cinétracts* **5** (Fall 1978): 15–23; Kristin Thompson, *Eisenstein's "Ivan the Terrible": A Neoformalist Analysis* (Princeton: Princeton University Press, 1981), pp. 203–260; Alan Williams, "Godard's Use of Sound," *Camera Obscura* 8-9-10 (1982): 193–208; Robert Self, "The Sounds of *MASH,"* in Peter Lehman, ed., *Close Viewings: Readings in New Film Criticism* (Sarasota: University of Florida Press, 1990), pp. 141–157; and Donald Kirihara, "Sound in *Les Vacances de Monsieur Hulot,"* in ibid., pp. 158–170. Lindley Handlon's *Fragments: Bresson's Film Style* (Rutherford, N.J.: Fairleigh Dickinson University Press, 1986) has chapters on sound in *Mouchette* and *Lancelot du Lac.*

The most prolific researcher into aesthetics of film sound is the French scholar Michel Chion. His several books on the subject are summarized in his *Audio-Vision,* trans. Claudia Gorbman (New York: Columbia University Press, 1994). This book provides many insights into particular sound devices.

Our quotation about dialogue overlap on p. 323 comes from Tom Rolf, in Vincent Lo Brutto's book of interviews *Selected Takes* (New York: Praeger, 1991), p. 95. Dialogue overlap is explained in detail in Edward Dmytryk, *On Film Editing* (Boston: Focal Press, 1984), pp. 47–70.

As the *Letter from Siberia* extract suggests, documentary filmmakers have experimented a great deal with sound. For other cases, see Basil Wright's *Song of Ceylon* and Humphrey Jennings's *Listen to Britain* and *Diary for Timothy.* Analyses of sound in these films may be found in Paul Rotha, *Documentary Film* (New York: Hastings House, 1952), and Karel Reisz and Gavin Millar's *Technique of Film Editing* (New York: Hastings House, 1968), pp. 156–170.

Voice-over narration is discussed in Bill Nichols, "Documentary Theory and Practice," *Screen* **17,** 4 (Winter 1976–77): 34–48, and Eric Smoodin, "The Image and the Voice in the Film with Spoken Narration," *Quarterly Review of Film Studies* **8,** 4 (Fall 1983): 19–32. The most detailed study of fictional cinema's use of voice-over commentary is Sarah Kozloff's *Invisible Storytellers: Voice-Over Narration in American Fiction Film* (Berkeley: University of California Press, 1988).

Experimental films also exploit unusual aspects of sound. See Norman McLaren's "Notes on Animated Sound," *Film Quarterly* **7,** 3 (Spring 1953): 223–229 (an article on hand-drawn sound tracks), and Robert Russell and Cecile Starr, *Experimental Animation* (New York: Van Nostrand, 1976).

A wide-ranging discussion of various sound recording and reproducing systems is Stephen Handzo's "A Narrative Glossary of Film Sound Technology," in Belton and Weis, *Film Sound: Theory and Practice.* On stereophonic technology see also Michael Arick, "The Sound of Money: In Stereo!" *Sight and Sound* **57,** 1 (Winter 1987–88): 35–42, and Ronald Haver, "The Saga of Stereo in the Movies," *The Perfect Vision* **1,** 1 (Winter 1986/87): 64–73. *The Perfect Vision* and *Widescreen Review* are two journals that review developments in modern sound reproduction.

■ ACOUSTIC PROPERTIES

On the physics of sound, see John R. Pierce, *The Science of Musical Sound,* 2d ed. (New York: Freeman, 1992). A useful introduction to the psychology of listening is Robert Sekuler and Randolph Blake, *Perception,* 2d ed. (New York: McGraw-Hill, 1990).

■ SILENT FILM VERSUS SOUND FILM

On the transition from silent to sound film in American cinema, see Harry M. Geduld, *The Birth of the Talkies: From Edison to Jolson* (Bloomington: Indiana University Press, 1975); Alexander Walker, *The Shattered Silents* (New York: Morrow, 1979); and chap. 23 of David Bordwell, Janet Staiger, and Kristin Thompson, *The Classical Hollywood Cinema: Film Style and Mode of Production to 1960* (New York: Columbia University Press, 1985).

It has long been assumed that cinema is predominantly a visual medium, with sound forming at best a supplement and at worst a distraction. In the late 1920s many film aestheticians protested against the coming of "talkies," feeling that synchronized sound spoiled a pristine mute art. In the bad sound film, René Clair claimed, "The image is reduced precisely to the role of the illustration of a phonograph record, and the sole aim of the whole show is to resemble as closely as possible the play of which it is the 'cinematic' reproduction. In three or four settings there take place endless scenes of dialogue which are merely boring if you do not understand English but unbearable if you do" [*Cinema Yesterday and Today* (New York: Dover, 1972), p. 137]. Rudolf Arnheim, who saw the artistic potential of cinema as its inability to reproduce reality perfectly, asserted that "the introduction of the sound film smashed many of the forms that the film artists were using in favor of the inartistic demand for the greatest possible 'naturalness' (in the most superficial sense of the word)" [*Film as Art* (Berkeley: University of California Press, 1957), p. 154].

It is easy to find such beliefs anachronistic, but we must recall that many early sound films relied simply on dialogue for their novelty; both Clair and Arnheim welcomed sound effects and music but warned against talkiness. In any event, the inevitable reaction was led by André Bazin, who argued that a greater overall realism was possible in the sound cinema. See his essays "The Evolution of the Language of Cinema," "In Defense of Mixed Cinema," and "Theatre and Cinema," all to be found in *What is Cinema?* vol. 1 (Berkeley: University of California Press, 1967). See also V. F. Perkins, *Film as Film* (Baltimore: Penguin, 1972); our quotation on p. 318 is taken from p. 54 of this book.

Even Bazin, however, seemed to believe that sound was secondary to vision in cinema. This view is also put forth by Siegfried Kracauer in *Theory of Film* (New York: Oxford University Press, 1965). "Films with sound live up to the spirit of the medium only if the visuals take the lead in them" (p. 103). Today, many filmmakers and filmgoers would agree with Francis Ford Coppola's remark that sound is "half the movie . . . at least" (quoted in Larry Blake, "Sound Recording and Post Production for *One from the Heart*," in Blake, *Film Sound Today*, p. 11). One of the major advances of film scholarship of the 1970s and 1980s was the increased and detailed attention to the sound track. The results can be seen in writings cited throughout these Notes and Queries.

■ FILM MUSIC

Of all the kinds of sound in cinema, music has been most extensively discussed. The literature is voluminous, and with a recent surge of interest in film composers, many more recordings of film music have become available. A survey of the field, with bibliography and discography, may be found in Harry Geduld, "Film Music: A Survey," *Quarterly Review of Film Studies* **1**, 2 (May 1976): 183–204.

A basic introduction to music useful for film study is William S. Newman, *Understanding Music* (New York: Harper, 1961). Classic studies of film music are Kurt London, *Film Music* (New York: Hastings House, 1970); Aaron Copland, "Film Music," in *What to Listen for in Music* (New York: Signet, 1957), pp. 152–157; and Hanns Eisler's attack on Hollywood film scoring, *Composing for the Films* (London: Dobson, 1947). A more up-to-date and detailed production guide is Fred Karlin and Rayburn Wright's *On the Track: A Guide to Contemporary Film Scoring* (New York: Schirmer, 1990). Karlin's *Listening to Movies* (New York: Schirmer, 1994) offers a lively discussion of the Hollywood tradition.

The history of film scoring is reviewed in Roy M. Prendergast, *Film Music: A Neglected Art* (New York: Norton, 1977). Music for silent films is discussed in Charles Hofmann, *Sounds for Silents* (New York: DBS Publications/Drama Book Specialists, 1970). In English, the principal study of the theory of film music is Claudia Gorbman, *Unheard Melodies: Narrative Film Music* (Bloomington: Indiana University Press, 1987). A highly informed, wide-ranging meditation on the subject is Royal S. Brown, *Overtones and Undertones: Reading Film Music* (Berkeley: University of California Press, 1994). See also Chuck Jones, "Music and the Animated Cartoon," *Hollywood Quarterly* **1,** 4 (July 1946): 364–370. A sampling of Carl Stalling's amazing cartoon sound tracks (p. 320) is available on compact disc (Warner Bros. 9-26027-2).

Despite the bulk of material on film music, there have been fairly few analyses of music's functions in particular films. The most famous (or notorious) is Sergei Eisenstein's "Form and Content: Practice," in *The Film Sense* (New York: Harcourt, Brace, 1942), pp. 157–216, which examines sound/image relations in a sequence from *Alexander Nevsky*. (See also Thompson, *Eisenstein's "Ivan the Terrible,"* cited above.) Claudia Gorbman has offered detailed image/sound analyses in "Music as Salvation: Notes on Fellini and Rota," *Film Quarterly* **28,** 2 (Winter 1974–75): 17–25; in *"Cleo from Five to Seven:* Music as Mirror," *Wide Angle* **4,** 4 (1981): 38–49; and in several chapters of her book *Unheard Melodies,* cited above. For other sensitive and scrupulous work on film music, see Graham Bruce, *Bernard Herrmann: Film Music and Narrative* (Ann Arbor: University of Michigan, 1985) and Kathryn Kalinak, *Settling the Score: Music and the Classical Hollywood Film* (Madison: University of Wisconsin Press, 1992). See also the supplement, "Sound and Music in the Movies," *Cinéaste* **21,** 1–2 (1995): 46–80.

■ DUBBING AND SUBTITLES

People beginning to study cinema may express surprise (or annoyance) that films in foreign languages are usually shown with subtitled captions translating the dialogue. Why not, some viewers ask, use "dubbed" versions of the films, i.e., versions in which the dialogue has been rerecorded in the audience's language? In many countries dubbing is very common. (Germany and Italy have traditions of dubbing almost every imported film.) Why, then, do most people who study movies prefer subtitles?

There are several reasons. Dubbed voices usually have a bland "studio" sound. Elimination of the original actors' voices wipes out an important component of their performance. (Partisans of dubbing ought to look at dubbed versions of English-language films to see how a performance by Katharine Hepburn, Orson Welles, or John Wayne can be hurt by a voice that does not fit the body.) With dubbing, all of the usual problems of translation are multiplied by the need to synchronize specific words with specific lip movements. Most important, with subtitling viewers still have access to the original sound track. By eliminating the original voice track, dubbing simply destroys part of the film.

STYLE AS A
FORMAL SYSTEM

At the beginning of Part II, we saw how the different parts of a film relate to one another within the dynamic we call its *form*. We have already examined one major aspect of a film's form: its organization into a categorical, rhetorical, abstract, associational, or narrative system. Now, having examined each category of techniques of the film medium, we may go on to see how these techniques interact to create another formal system of the film, its *style*. These two systems—style and narrative/nonnarrative form—in turn interact within the total film.

    At this point we can recall the diagram we introduced at the start of Part III:

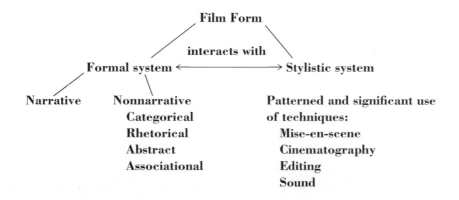

Film Form

interacts with

Formal system ⟷ **Stylistic system**

Narrative   **Nonnarrative**   **Patterned and significant use**
           Categorical   **of techniques:**
           Rhetorical   **Mise-en-scene**
           Abstract   **Cinematography**
           Associational   **Editing**
                                      Sound

No single film uses all the technical possibilities we have discussed. For one thing, historical circumstances limit the choices that filmmakers have open to them. Before 1928, for example, most filmmakers did not have the choice of using synchronized dialogue. Even today, when the range of technical choices seems far broader, there are still limits. Filmmakers cannot use the now obsolete orthochromatic film stock of the silent era, although in some respects it was superior to contemporary stocks. Similarly, a successful system for creating three-dimensional cinema images without the necessity for spectators to wear 3-D glasses has not yet been invented.

There is a second reason why only some technical possibilities may be realized within a single film. Within a concrete production situation, the filmmaker must choose what techniques to employ. Typically, the filmmaker makes certain technical choices and adheres to them throughout the film. Across the film, a filmmaker will characteristically use three-point lighting, or continuity editing, or diegetic sound. A few segments might stand out as varying from the film's normal usage, but in general a film tends to rely on consistent usage of certain techniques. The film's style results from a combination of historical constraints and deliberate choice.

The spectator has a relation to style as well. Although we are seldom conscious of the fact, we tend to have expectations about style. If we see two characters in a long shot, we expect a cut-in to a closer view. If the actor walks rightward, as if about to leave the frame, we expect the camera to pan or track right to keep the person in the shot. If a character speaks, we expect to hear diegetic sound that is faithful to its source.

Like other kinds of expectations, stylistic ones derive both from our experience of the world generally (people talk, they don't tweet) and our experience of film and other media. The specific film's style can confirm our expectations, or modify them, or cheat or challenge them.

Many films use techniques in ways that conform to our expectations. For example, the conventions of the classical Hollywood cinema and specific genres provide a firm basis for reinforcing our prior assumptions. Other films ask us to readjust our expectations somewhat. Keaton's *Our Hospitality* accustoms us to expect deep-space manipulations of figures and objects, while Renoir's *Grand Illusion* builds up specific expectations about the likelihood of camera movements. Still other films make highly unusual technical choices, and to follow them we must construct stylistic expectations to which we are unaccustomed. The editing discontinuities in Eisenstein's *October* and the use of minute offscreen sounds in Bresson's *A Man Escaped* ask us to notice stylistic manipulation. In other words, a director directs not only the cast and crew. A director directs us, directs our attention, shapes our reaction. Thus the filmmaker's technical decisions make a difference in what we perceive and how we respond.

We can speak not only of the individual *film*'s style but also of the *filmmaker*'s style. Then we are principally referring to the particular techniques that person typically employs and the distinctive ways these techniques relate to one another in the filmmaker's works. When we discussed sound in *A Man Escaped*, we characterized Bresson as a director who makes sound particularly important in his films; we analyzed several important ways in which sound related to image in *A Man Escaped*. This use of sound is one aspect of Bresson's unique style. Similarly, we looked at *Our Hospitality* in terms of how its comic mise-en-scene is organized around a consistent use of long shots; this is part of Keaton's style in other films too. Both Bresson and Keaton have distinctive filmmaking styles, and we can become familiar with those styles by analyzing the way in which they utilize techniques within whole filmic systems.

Finally, we can also speak of a *group style*—the consistent use of techniques across the work of several filmmakers. We can speak of a German Expressionist style, or a Soviet Montage style. In Part V, we will consider some significant group styles that have emerged in film history.

Style, then, is that formal system of the film that organizes film techniques. Any one film will tend to rely on particular technical options in creating its style, and these are chosen by the filmmaker within the constraints of historical circumstances. We may also extend the term "style" to describe the characteristic use of techniques made by a single filmmaker or group of filmmakers. The spectator may not consciously notice film style, but it nonetheless makes an important contribution to the film's ongoing effect and overall meaning.

ANALYZING FILM STYLE

As viewers, we register the effects of film style but seldom notice it. If we want to understand how these effects are achieved, we need to look and listen more carefully than we usually do. Since the previous four chapters have shown how we can pay attention to stylistic features, we can now set forth four general steps in analyzing style.

1. *Determine the organizational structure of the film, its narrative or nonnarrative formal system.*

The first step is to understand how the film is put together as a whole. If it is a narrative film, it will draw on all the principles we have discussed in Chapters 3 and 4. That is, it will have a plot that cues us to construct a story; it will manipulate causality, time, and space; it will have a distinct pattern of development from opening to closing; it may use parallelism; its narration will choose between restricted and more unrestricted knowledge at various points.

If the film is not a narrative, the analyst should seek to understand what other type of formal organization it uses. (See Chapters 3 and 5.) Is the film unified as a set of categories, or an argument, or a stream of associations? Or is it structured by an abstract set of technical features? In understanding either narrative or nonnarrative form, making a segmentation is usually helpful. Grasping the logic that underlies the whole film supplies a context for its use of film techniques.

2. *Identify the salient techniques used.*

Here the analyst will draw upon our survey of technical possibilities in Chapters 6 through 9. You need to be able to spot things such as color, lighting, framing, cutting, and sound, which most viewers don't consciously notice. Once you notice them, you can identify them as techniques—as nondiegetic music or as a low-angle framing.

But noting and naming are only the beginning of stylistic analysis. The analyst must develop an eye for *salient* techniques. Salience will partly be determined by what techniques the film relies heavily on. The jerky forward zoom in *Wavelength* and the rapid, discontinuous editing of *October* invite scrutiny because they play a central role in creating the overall effect of the film.

In addition, what is salient depends on the analyst's purpose. If you want to show that a film's style is typical of one approach to filmmaking, you may focus on how the technique conforms to stylistic expectations. The 180° editing of *The Maltese Falcon* is not obvious or emphasized, but adherence to rules of classical continuity is a characteristic aspect of the film's style. Our purpose in Chapter 8 was to show that the film is typical in this respect. If, however, you want to stress unusual qualities of the film's style, you can concentrate on the more unexpected technical devices. Bresson's use of sound in *A Man Escaped* is unusual, representing choices that few filmmakers would make. It was the originality of these sonic devices that we chose to stress in Chapter 9. From the standpoint of originality, costume in *A Man Escaped* is not as salient a stylistic feature as sound because it is more in accord with conventional practice. The analyst's decision about what techniques are salient will thus be influenced partly by what the film emphasizes and partly by the analyst's purpose.

3. Trace out patterns of techniques within the whole film.

Once you have identified salient techniques, you can notice how they are patterned. Techniques will be repeated and varied, developed and paralleled, across the whole film or within a single segment. Chapters 6 through 9 have shown how this occurs in some films.

You can "zero in" on stylistic patterns in two ways. First, you can reflect upon your responses. If a scene begins with a track-in, do you expect that it will end with a track-out? If you see a character looking left, do you assume that someone or something is offscreen and will be revealed in the next shot? If you feel a mounting excitement in an action scene, is that traceable to a quickening tempo in the music or to accelerating editing?

A second tactic for noticing stylistic patterns is to look for ways in which style reinforces patterns of nonnarrative or narrative organization. In any film, "punctuation" between segments utilizes stylistic features (fades, cuts, dissolves, color shifts, sound bridges). A scene in a narrative film will usually have a dramatic pattern of encounter, conflict, and outcome, and the style will often reflect this, with the cutting becoming more marked and the shots coming closer to the characters as the scene progresses. In *The Silence of the Lambs,* for example, the scenes between Clarice Starling and Hannibal Lecter tend to begin with conventional shot/reverse-shot conversations. The characters, filmed in plan américain, look off to the right or left of the camera (Figs. 10.1, 10.2). As their conversations become more intense and intimate, the camera positions move closer to each one and shift subtly toward the axis of action until each person is looking directly into the lens (Figs. 10.3, 10.4).

Fig. 10.1

Fig. 10.2

Fig. 10.3

Fig. 10.4

As we saw in *Grand Illusion,* style may create associations between situations, as when the camera movements suggest the prisoners' unity. It may also reinforce parallels, as do the tracking shots comparing Rauffenstein's war trophies and Elsa's. Later we shall see how style can also reinforce the organization of nonnarrative films.

Sometimes, however, stylistic patterning will not respect the nonnarrative or narrative structure of the film. Style can claim our attention in its own right. Since most stylistic devices have several functions, a technique may interest the analyst for different reasons. In Color Plates 62 and 63, a cut from a washline to a living room acts as a transition between scenes. But the cut is of more interest for other reasons, since we do not expect that a narrative film will treat objects as flat patches of color to be compared across shots. Such attention to graphic play is a convention of abstract form. Here, in a passage from Ozu's *Ohayu,* a stylistic choice "comes forward" because it goes beyond its narrative function. Even here, though, stylistic patterns continue to call on the viewer's expectations and to draw the spectator into a dynamic process. Anyone who notices the graphic match on red objects in *Ohayu* will most likely be delighted and amused at such an unconventional way of editing. And, if stylistic patterns do swerve off on their own, we still need a sense of the film's narrative or nonnarrative organization in order to show how and when that happens.

4. *Propose functions for the salient techniques and the patterns they form.*
Here the analyst looks for the role that style plays in the film's overall form. Does the use of camera movement tend to create suspense by delaying the revelation of story information, as in the opening of *Touch of Evil*? Does the use of discontinuous editing create a narrational omniscience, as in the sequence we analyzed in *October*? Does the arrangement of the shot tend to make us concentrate on a particular detail (as in Figure 6.78, the shot of Anne's face in *Day of Wrath*)? Does the use of music or noise create surprise?

A direct route to noticing function is to notice the effects of the film. Style may enhance *emotional* aspects of the film. Rapid cutting in *The Birds* evokes shock and horror, while the Mozart music in *A Man Escaped* ennobles the communal routine of emptying slop buckets.

Style also shapes *meaning.* For example, in *Grand Illusion* the contrast between Rauffenstein and Elsa is heightened by Renoir's parallel tracking shots. We should, however, avoid "reading" isolated elements atomistically, taking them out of context. As we argued on p. 239, a high angle does not automatically mean "inferiority," just as a low angle does not automatically mean "power." There is no dictionary to which you can turn to look up the meaning of a specific stylistic element. Instead the analyst must scrutinize the whole film, the patterns of the techniques in it, and the specific effects of film form. Meaning is only one type of effect, and there is no reason to expect that every stylistic feature will possess a thematic significance. One part of a director's job is to direct our attention, and so style will often function simply *perceptually*—to get us to notice things, to emphasize one thing over another, to misdirect our attention, to clarify, intensify, or complicate our understanding of the action.

One way to sharpen our sense of the functions of specific techniques is to *imagine alternatives* and reflect on what differences would result. Suppose the director had made a different technical choice; how would this create a different effect? *Our Hospitality* creates its gags by putting two or more elements into the same shot and letting us observe the comic juxtaposition. Suppose Keaton had instead isolated each element in a single shot and then linked the two elements by editing. The meaning might be the same, but the perceptual effects would vary: Instead of a simultaneous presentation that lets our attention shuttle to and fro, we would have a more "programmed" pattern of building up the gags and paying them off. Or, suppose that Huston had handled the opening scene of *The Maltese Falcon* as a single take with camera movement. How would he then have drawn our attention to Brigid O'Shaughnessy's and Spade's facial reactions, and how would this have affected our expectations? By focusing on effects and imagining alternatives to the technical choices that were made, the analyst can gain a sharp sense of the particular functions of style in the given film.

The rest of this chapter provides a series of illustrations of how we can analyze film style. Our specimens are the films whose narrative and nonnarrative systems were analyzed in Chapters 4 and 5: *Citizen Kane* (narrative form); *Olympia,* Part 2 (categorical form); *The River* (rhetorical form); *Ballet mécanique* (abstract form); and *A Movie* (associational form). Our analyses are the results of following all four steps in stylistic analysis. Since these earlier chapters have discussed the films' organizational structures, we will concentrate here on identifying salient techniques, locating patterns, and proposing some functions for style in each case.

STYLE IN *CITIZEN KANE*

In analyzing *Citizen Kane*'s narrative, we discovered that the film is organized as a search; a detectivelike figure, the reporter Thompson, tries to find the significance of Kane's last word, "Rosebud." But even before Thompson appears as a character, we, the spectators, are invited to ask questions about Kane and to seek their answers.

The very beginning of the film sets up a mystery. After a fade-in reveals a "No Trespassing" sign, in a series of craning movements upward, the camera travels over a set of fences, all matched graphically in the slow dissolves that link the shots. There follows a series of shots of a huge estate, always with the great house in the distance (Fig. 10.5). (This sequence depends largely on special effects; the house itself is a series of paintings, combined through matte work with three-dimensional miniatures in the foreground.) The gloomy lighting, the deserted setting, and the ominous music give the opening of the film the eerie uncertainty that we associate with mystery stories. These opening shots are connected by dissolves, making the camera seem to draw closer to the house although there is no forward camera movement. From shot to shot the foreground changes, yet the single lighted window remains in almost exactly the same position on the screen. Graphically matching the window

Fig. 10.5

Fig. 10.6

Fig. 10.7

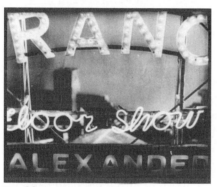

Fig. 10.8

Fig. 10.9

from shot to shot already focuses our attention on it; we assume (rightly) that whatever is in that room will be important in initiating the story.

This pattern of our penetration into the space of a scene returns at other points in the film. Again and again, the camera moves toward things that might reveal the secrets of Kane's character. In the scene in which Thompson goes to interview Susan Alexander, the camera begins not on the reporter but on the poster of Susan on a wall outside (Fig. 10.6). Then in a spectacular crane shot the camera moves up the wall, over the roof (Fig. 10.7), through the "El Rancho" sign (Fig. 10.8), and over to the skylight (Fig. 10.9). At that point a dissolve and a crack of lightning shift the scene inside to another craning movement down to Susan's table. (Actually, some of what seem to be camera movements were created in the laboratory using special effects; see Notes and Queries.)

The opening scene and the introduction to El Rancho have some striking similarities. Each begins with a sign ("No Trespassing" and the publicity poster), and each moves us into a building to reveal a new character. The first scene uses a series of shots, whereas the second depends more on camera movement, but these different techniques are working to create a consistent pattern that becomes part of the film's style. Later, Thompson's second visit to Susan repeats the crane shots of the first. The second flashback of Jed Leland's story begins with another movement into a scene. The camera is initially pointed at wet cobblestones. Then it tilts up and tracks in toward

Fig. 10.10

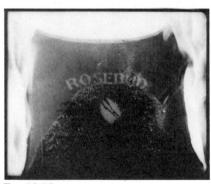

Fig. 10.11

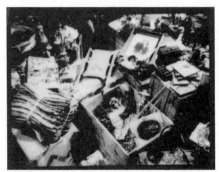

Fig. 10.12

Susan coming out of a drugstore. Only then does the camera pan right to reveal Kane standing, splashed with mud, on the curb. This pattern of gradual movement into the story space not only suits the narrative's search pattern but uses film technique to create curiosity and suspense.

As we have seen, films' endings often contain variations of their beginnings. Toward the end of *Citizen Kane*, Thompson gives up his search for Rosebud. But after the reporters leave the huge storeroom of Xanadu, the camera begins to move over the great expanse of Kane's collections. It cranes forward high above the crates and piles of objects (Fig. 10.10), then moves down to center on the sled from Kane's childhood (Fig. 10.11). Then there is a cut to the furnace, and the camera again moves in on the sled as it is tossed into the fire. At last we are able to read the word "Rosebud" on the sled (Fig. 10.12). The ending continues the pattern set up at the beginning; the film techniques create a penetration into the story space, probing the mystery of the central character.

After our glimpse of the sled, however, the film reverses the pattern. A series of shots linked by dissolves leads us back outside Xanadu, the camera travels down to the "No Trespassing" sign again, and we are left to wonder whether this discovery really provides a resolution to the mystery about Kane's character.

Our study of *Kane*'s organization in Chapter 4 also showed that Thompson's search was, from the standpoint of narration, a complex one. At one level, our knowledge is restricted principally to what Kane's acquaintances know. Within the flashbacks, the style reinforces this restriction by avoiding crosscutting or other techniques that would move toward a more unrestricted range of knowledge. Many of the flashback scenes are shot in fairly static long takes, strictly confining us to what participants in the scene could witness. When the youthful Kane confronts Thatcher during the *Inquirer* crusade, Welles could have cut away to the reporter in Cuba sending Kane a telegram or could have shown a montage sequence of a day in the life of the paper. Instead, because this is Thatcher's tale, Welles handles the scene in a long take showing Kane and Thatcher in a face-to-face standoff, which is then capped by a close-up of Kane's cocky response.

We have also seen that the film's narrative requires us to take each narrator's version as objective within his or her limited knowledge. Welles reinforces this by avoiding shots that suggest optical or mental subjectivity. (Contrast Hitchcock's optical point-of-view angles in *The Birds* and *Rear Window*, pp. 277–278 and 296.)

Welles also utilizes deep-focus cinematography that yields an external perspective on the action. The shot in which Kane's mother signs her son over to Thatcher is a good example. Several shots precede this one, introducing the young Kane. Then there is a cut to what at first seems a simple long shot of the boy (Fig. 10.13). But the camera tracks back to reveal a window, with Kane's mother appearing at the left and calling to him (Fig. 10.14). Then the camera continues to track back, following the adults as they walk to an adjoining room (Fig. 10.15). Mrs. Kane and Thatcher sit at a table in the foreground to sign the papers, while Kane's father remains standing farther away at the left, and the boy plays in the distance (Fig. 10.16).

Welles eliminates cutting here. The shot becomes a complex unit unto itself, like the opening of *Touch of Evil* discussed in Chapter 7. Most Hol-

Fig. 10.13

Fig. 10.14

Fig. 10.15

lywood directors would have handled this scene in shot/reverse shot, but Welles keeps all of the implications of the action simultaneously before us. The boy, who is the subject of the discussion, remains framed in the distant window through the whole scene; his game leads us to believe that he is unaware of what his mother is doing.

The tensions between the father and mother are conveyed not only by the fact that she excludes him from the discussion at the table but also by the overlapping sound. His objections to signing his son away to a guardian mix in with the dialogue in the foreground, and even the boy's shouts (ironically "The Union Forever!") can be heard in the distance. The framing also emphasizes the mother in much of the scene. This is her only appearance in the film. Her severity and tensely controlled emotions help motivate the many events that follow from her action here. We have had little introduction to the situation prior to this scene, but the combination of sound, cinematography, and mise-en-scene conveys the complicated action with an overall objectivity.

Fig. 10.16

Every director directs our attention, but Welles does so in unusual ways. *Kane* offers a good example of how a director chooses between alternatives. By giving up cutting, Welles cues our attention by using deep-space mise-en-scene (figure behavior, lighting, placement in space) and sound. We can watch expressions because the actors play frontally (Fig. 10.16). In addition, the framing emphasizes certain figures by putting them in the foreground or in dead center (Fig. 10.17). And of course our attention bounces from one character to another as they speak lines. Even if Welles avoids the classical Hollywood convention of cutting in such scenes, he still uses film techniques to prompt us to make the correct assumptions and inferences.

Kane's narration also embeds the narrators' objective but restricted versions within broader contexts. Thompson's investigation links the various tales, so we learn substantially what he learns. Yet he must not become the protagonist of the film, for that would remove Kane from the center of interest. Welles makes a crucial stylistic choice here. By the use of low-key selective lighting and patterns of staging and framing, Thompson is made virtually unidentifiable. His back is to us, he is tucked into the corner of the frame, and he is usually in darkness. The stylistic handling makes him the neutral investigator, less a character than a channel for information.

More broadly still, we have seen that the film encloses Thompson's search within a more omniscient narration. Our discussion of the opening

Fig. 10.17

Fig. 10.18

Fig. 10.19

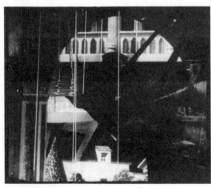

Fig. 10.20

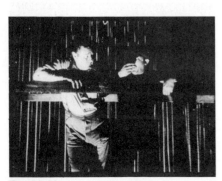

Fig. 10.21

shots of Xanadu is relevant here: Film style is used to convey a high degree of non-character-centered knowledge. But when we enter Kane's death chamber, the style also suggests the narration's ability to plumb characters' minds. We see shots of snow covering the frame (for example, Fig. 10.18), which hint at a subjective vision. Later in the film, the camera movements occasionally remind us of the broader range of narrational knowledge. For instance, during the first version of Susan's opera premiere (in Leland's story, Segment 6), the camera cranes up from the stage (Fig. 10.19) through the rigging above (Fig. 10.20) to reveal something neither Leland nor Susan could know about—two stagehands panning her performance (Fig. 10.21). The final sequence, which at least partially solves the mystery of "Rosebud," also uses a vast camera movement to give us an omniscient perspective. The camera cranes over objects from Kane's collection, moving forward in space but backward through Kane's life to concentrate on his earliest memento, the sled. A salient technique again conforms to pattern by giving us knowledge no character will ever possess.

In looking at the development of the narrative form of *Citizen Kane*, we saw how Kane changes from an idealistic young man to a friendless recluse. The film sets up a contrast between Kane's early life as an editor and his later withdrawal from public life after Susan's opera career fails. This contrast is most readily apparent in the mise-en-scene, particularly the settings of the *Inquirer* office and Xanadu. The *Inquirer* office is initially an efficient but cluttered place. When Kane takes over, he creates a casual environment by moving in his furniture and living in his office. The low camera angles tend to emphasize the office's thin pillars and low ceilings, which are white and evenly, brightly lit. Eventually Kane's collection of crated antiquities clutters his little office. Xanadu, on the other hand, is huge and sparsely furnished. The ceilings are too high to be seen in most shots, and the few furnishings stand far apart. The lighting often strikes figures strongly from the back or side (such as the shot of Kane descending a great staircase, in Figure 6.32), creating a few patches of hard light in the midst of general darkness. The expanded collection of antiquities and mementoes now is housed in cavernous storerooms.

The contrast between the *Inquirer* office and Xanadu is also created by the sound techniques associated with each locale. Several scenes at the newspaper office (Kane's initial arrival and his return from Europe) involve a dense sound mix with a babble of overlapping voices. Yet the cramped space is suggested by the relative lack of resonance in timbre. In Xanadu, however, the conversations sound very different. Kane and Susan speak their lines to each other slowly, with pauses between. Moreover, their voices have an echo effect that combines with the setting and lighting to convey a sense of huge, empty space.

The transition from Kane's life at the *Inquirer* to his eventual seclusion at Xanadu is suggested by a change in the mise-en-scene at the *Inquirer*. As we have just seen, while Kane is in Europe, the statues he sends back begin to fill up his little office. This hints at Kane's growing ambitions and declining interest in working personally on his newspaper. This change culminates in the last scene in the *Inquirer* office, Leland's confrontation with Kane. The office is being used as a campaign headquarters. With the desks pushed

Fig. 10.22

Fig. 10.23

Fig. 10.24

Fig. 10.25

Fig. 10.26

aside and the employees gone, the room looks larger and emptier than it had in earlier scenes there. Welles emphasizes this by placing the camera at floor level and shooting from a very low angle (see Fig. 7.101). The Chicago *Inquirer* office, with its vast, shadowy spaces, also picks up this pattern. Deep-focus photography and rear projection exaggerate the depth of the scene, making the characters seem very far apart (Fig. 10.22), as in later conversation scenes in the huge rooms of Xanadu (Fig. 10.17).

Contrast these scenes with one near the end of the film. The reporters invade Kane's museumlike storeroom at Xanadu (Fig. 10.23). Though the echo of Xanadu conveys its cavernous quality, the reporters transform the setting briefly by the same sort of dense, overlapping dialogue that characterized the early *Inquirer* scenes and the scene after the newsreel. By bringing together these reporters and Kane's final surroundings, the film creates another contrasting parallel emphasizing the changes in the protagonist.

Parallelism is an important feature throughout *Citizen Kane*, and most of the salient techniques work to create parallels in the ways we have already seen. For example, the use of deep focus and deep space to pack many characters into the frame can create significant similarities and contrasts. Late in Thatcher's account (Segment 4), a scene presents Kane's financial losses in the Depression. He is forced to sign over his newspaper to Thatcher's bank. The scene opens on a close-up of Kane's manager, Bernstein, reading the contract (Fig. 10.24). He lowers the paper to reveal Thatcher, now much older, seated opposite him. We hear Kane's voice offscreen, and Bernstein moves his head slightly, the camera reframing a little. Now we see Kane pacing beyond them in a huge office or boardroom (see Fig. 7.33). The scene is a single take in which the dramatic situation is created by the arrangement of the figures and the image's depth of field. The lowering of the contract recalls the previous scene, in which we first get a real look at the adult Kane as Thatcher puts down the newspaper that has concealed him (Figs. 10.25, 10.26). There Thatcher had been annoyed, but Kane could defy him. Now Thatcher has gained control and Kane paces restlessly, still defiant, but stripped of his power over the *Inquirer* chain. The use of a similar device to open these two scenes sets up a contrasting parallel between them.

Editing patterns can also suggest similarities between scenes, as when Welles compares two moments at which Kane seems to win public support. In the first scene, Kane is running for governor and makes a speech at a

Fig. 10.27

Fig. 10.28

Fig. 10.29

mammoth rally. This scene is principally organized around an editing pattern which shows one or two shots of Kane speaking, then one or two close shots of small groups of characters in the audience (Emily and their son, Leland, Bernstein, Gettys), then another shot of Kane. The cutting establishes the characters who are important for their views of Kane. Boss Gettys is the last to be shown in the scene, and we expect him to retaliate against Kane's denunciation.

After his defeat, Kane sets out to make Susan an opera star and thus justify his interest in her to the public. In the scene which parallels Kane's election speech, Susan's debut, the organization of shots is similar to that of the political rally. Again the figure on the stage, Susan, serves as a pivot for the editing. One or two shots of her are followed by a few shots of the various listeners (Kane, Bernstein, Leland, the singing teacher), then back to Susan, and so on (Figs. 10.27, 10.28). General narrative parallels and specific stylistic techniques articulate two stages of Kane's power quest: first on his own, then with Susan as his proxy.

As we have seen in Chapter 9, music can bring out parallels as well. For example, Susan's singing is causally central to the narrative. Her elaborate aria in the opera *Salammbo* contrasts sharply with the other main diegetic music, the little song about "Charlie Kane." In spite of the differences between the songs, there is a parallel between them, in that both relate to Kane's ambitions. The "Charlie Kane" ditty seems inconsequential, but its lyrics clearly show that Kane intends it as a political song, and it does turn up later as campaign music. In addition, the chorus girls who sing the song wear costumes with boots and Rough Rider hats, which they place on the heads of the men in the foreground (Fig. 10.29). Thus Kane's desire for war with Spain has shown up even in this apparently simple farewell party for his departure to Europe. When Kane's political ambitions are dashed, he tries to create a public career for his wife instead, but she is incapable of singing grand opera. Again, the songs create narrative parallels between different actions in Kane's career.

As we saw in examining *Citizen Kane*'s narrative, the newsreel is a very important sequence, partly because it provides a "map" to the upcoming plot events. Because of its importance, Welles sets off the style of this sequence from the rest of the film by distinctive techniques which do not appear elsewhere in *Citizen Kane*. Also, we need to believe that this is a real newsreel in order to motivate Thompson's search for the key to Kane's life. The realistic newsreel sequence also helps establish Kane's power and wealth, which will be the basis of much of the upcoming action.

Welles uses several techniques to achieve the look and sound of a newsreel of the period. Some of these are fairly simple. The music is that of actual newsreels, and the insert titles, outmoded in regular narrative films, were still a convention in newsreel films. But beyond this, Welles employs a number of subtle cinematographic techniques to achieve a "documentary" quality. Since some of the footage in the newsreel is supposed to have been taken in the silent period, he uses several different film stocks to make it appear that the different shots have been assembled from widely different sources. Some of the footage has been printed so as to achieve the jerkiness of silent film run at sound speed. Welles has also scratched and faded this footage to give it the look of old, worn film. This, combined with the make-up work, creates a remarkable impression of documentary footage of Kane with Teddy Roosevelt, Adolf Hitler (Fig. 10.30), and other historical figures. In the later scenes of Kane being wheeled around his estate, the hand-held camera, the slats and barriers (Fig. 10.31), and the high angle imitate the effects of a newsreel reporter surreptitiously filming Kane. All of these "documentary" conventions are enhanced by the use of a narrator whose booming voice also mimics the commentary typical in newsreels of the day.

Fig. 10.30

One of *Citizen Kane*'s outstanding formal features is the way its plot manipulates story time. As we have seen, this process is motivated by Thompson's inquiry and the order in which he interviews the narrators. Various techniques assist in the manipulation of order and duration. The shift from a narrator's present recounting to a past event is often reinforced by a "shock" cut. A shock cut creates a jarring juxtaposition, usually by means of a sudden shift to a higher sound volume and a considerable graphic discontinuity. *Citizen Kane* offers several instances: the abrupt beginning of the newsreel after the deathbed shot, the shift from the quiet conversation in the newsreel projection room to the lightning and thunder outside the El Rancho, and the sudden appearance of a screeching cockatoo in the foreground as Raymond's flashback begins (Fig. 10.32). Such transitions create surprise and sharply demarcate one portion of the plot from another.

Fig. 10.31

The transitions that skip over or drastically compress time are less abrupt. Recall, for instance, the languid images of Kane's sled being gradually covered by snow. A more extended example is the breakfast-table montage (Segment 6) that elliptically traces the decline of Kane's first marriage. Starting with the newlyweds' late supper, rendered in a track-in and a shot/reverse-shot series, the sequence moves through several brief episodes, consisting of shot/reverse-shot exchanges linked by whip pans. (A *whip pan* is a very rapid pan that creates a blurring sidewise motion across the screen. It is usually used as a transition between scenes.) In each episode, Kane and Emily become more sharply hostile. The segment ends by tracking away to show the surprising distance between them at the table.

Fig. 10.32

The music reinforces the sequence's development as well. The initial late supper is accompanied by a lilting waltz. At each transition to a later time, the music changes. A comic variation of the waltz follows its initial statement, then a tense one; then horns and trumpets restate the Kane theme. The final portion of the scene, with a stony silence between the couple, is accompanied by a slow, eerie variation on the initial theme. The dissolution of the marriage is stressed by this theme-and-variations accompaniment. A similar sort of temporal compression and sonic elaboration can be found in the montage of Susan's opera career (Segment 7).

Our brief examination of *Citizen Kane*'s style has pointed out only a few of the major patterns in the film. You will be able to find others: the musical motif associated with Kane's power; the "K" motif appearing in Kane's costumes and in Xanadu's settings; the way the decor of Susan's room in Xanadu reveals Kane's attitude toward her; the changes in the acting of individuals as their characters age in the course of the story; and the playful photographic devices, such as the photos that become animated or the many superimpositions during montage sequences. Again and again, in *Citizen Kane* such stylistic patterns sustain and intensify the narrative development and shape the audience's experience in particular ways.

STYLE IN *OLYMPIA*, PART 2

Although the Nazi government financed and guided Leni Riefenstahl's filming of the 1936 Olympic Games, she also had to conform to the regulations of the International Olympic Committee. Thus, in *Olympia*, she was limited in what sorts of film techniques she could employ. Cameras could not, of course, be allowed to distract the athletes during the competition. Riefenstahl overcame this limitation by creating a variety of ingenious devices that could allow her camera crew to film from a distance and from unusual angles. In this way, the solution to technical problems ended by enhancing the stylistic variety of the film.

The enormous stadium and other Olympic facilities built in and around Berlin for the games reflected the effort of the Nazi government to impress the rest of the world. In a sense, then, the settings were planned with the camera in mind. But Riefenstahl and her colleagues had little control over the arrangement of the actual events; the mise-en-scene was largely unstaged. Still, Riefenstahl knew ahead of time where and when each event was to take place, and she was able to plan out the cinematography in detail. And after shooting, her control of editing and the addition of a sound track contributed powerfully to the final effect of the film.

Although the action lay largely outside the filmmaker's control, we can speak of the manipulation of mise-en-scene at certain points. The events of Segment 1, which includes morning jogging, a sauna bath, swimming, and exercising, are arranged for the camera. The joggers run in perfect formation past the camera, and athletes outside their club smile and show off. Segment 5, showing the enormous group of women performing synchronized calisthenics before the stadium, could hardly have been filmed without the event's being staged to some degree. And certainly the final moments of the film were completely staged. The stadium with its ring of searchlights seems to be a model, and the rows of moving flags are arranged for the camera rather than for any audience at the games (Fig. 5.22). Still, the urge to shape our response to the events is far more evident in Riefenstahl's use of other film techniques.

The many cameras filming the games had to avoid interfering with the athletes' concentration. Some cameras were placed in pits dug at a distance from the track and field events. Cameras with telephoto lenses caught the action from a distance, and lens length becomes an important aspect of the film's style. For instance, we often see the athletes' bodies moving in front of a flat-looking backdrop of slightly out-of-focus faces (see Fig. 5.7). The effect is particularly apparent when the cameras are outfitted with extremely long lenses to capture a detail. In the close view of Glen Morris the crowd far

Fig. 10.33

Fig. 10.34

Fig. 10.35

Fig. 10.36

behind him becomes blobs of black and white (Fig. 5.13). Such shots contrast with the views of athletes against the sky, taken from low angles that eliminate the crowd (Figs. 5.9 and 5.21). As we saw in Chapter 5, the move toward the low-angle sky shots formed part of one pattern of development; they occurred toward the end of the gymnastics (Segment 2) and diving (Segment 11) events.

Other techniques of framing also play a role in the film's stylistic development. A very low placement of a row of yachts within the frame (Fig. 10.33) makes for a striking composition and emphasizes the sky motif once again. Some framings emphasize the juxtaposition of foreground and background planes in depth, as when a branch and the distant stadium carry through the nature motif (Fig. 5.6), or when winning French cyclists watch their flags being raised (Fig. 10.34). In the more personalized segments, certain techniques intensify the overall purpose of the segments, as when a superimposition creates a subjective effect of speed as a cyclist races for the finish line (Fig. 5.16).

With an enormous amount of footage at her disposal, Riefenstahl faced a huge editing task. In fact, the film was not released until 1938, two years after the games were held, partly because of the scale of postproduction work. But the many hours of film also offered the potential for dynamic graphic and rhythmic juxtapositions. *Olympia*, Part 2, contains a great range of editing techniques. Some moments exploit graphic similarities, as when a whole series of panning shots of different runners leaving the starting point in the pentathlon are strung together. But graphic discontinuity becomes important in other segments. The diagonals formed by the parallel bars in one shot (Fig. 10.35) contrast with those in the next shot (Fig. 10.36). We have seen how this kind of low-angle composition against the sky parallels the gymnastics and diving segments, reinforcing the film's pattern of development. Graphic discontinuity also functions to create a comparison between these two segments. Many shots of the divers contain opposed directions, culminating in the spectacular finale, when, one by one, eleven divers leap into space, with virtually every cut shifting the diver's take-off point from one side of the frame to the other (Figs. 10.37, 10.38). Combined with a quick cutting rhythm, such graphic playfulness creates an exhilarating ending for this subsegment.

The editing rhythms also cover a considerable range. Although the shots

Fig. 10.37

Fig. 10.38

Fig. 10.39

Fig. 10.40

Fig. 10.41

tend to follow a moderate or quick pattern, there are occasional lengthy shots. Riefenstahl holds, for example, on a shot of a gymnast changing position on the rings (Figs. 10.39, 10.40). His slow, controlled movements, combined with the telephoto lens that places him against the distant crowd, create a sense of tension within the shot. Similarly, some shots of the cross-country riding event linger over the amusing attempts of riders to persuade recalcitrant horses over a jump, or over the losers floundering about after falling into a water jump.

Riefenstahl tends to save quick editing rhythms for the most dynamic moments. The rowing races contain some quick alternations between shots of the shells skimming through the water and of the crowd cheering them on. Most spectacularly, the diving sequence gradually builds up its editing pace. A quick barrage of varied shots obliterates the concrete space and time of the event. We come to see a series of bodies soaring through space. Riefenstahl cuts in some shots backward, so that the divers fly *upward*, and one shot is even upside down and backward (Fig. 10.41). As divers move in all directions, gravity seems to be defied, and the sense of birdlike motion is enhanced.

The sound track of *Olympia* is simple but powerful. Romantic, Wagnerian-style music by Herbert Windt accompanies many events and is especially important during those early and late segments when the announcer is not giving us information about the events. This music cues us to react in certain ways: slow, majestic music for the opening in the woods; lighter rhythms for the exercise portions of Segment 2; grandiose, exhilarating music for the diving scene. For the sake of variety, a few scenes have no music, concentrating on the narrator's voice (as with the field-hockey portion of Segment 7). That voice also cues us how to respond, and it is crucially important to the personalized narrative segments in the central part of the film. In the pentathlon and decathlon, the narrator sets up suspense by cueing us to watch certain athletes. His slightly hushed voice suggests that he, too, is awaiting the outcomes of the contests (even though the sound track was added long after those outcomes were known). Occasionally there are effects that supposedly come from the space of the events—crowds cheering, wind, and so on—but the film concentrates on music and the narrator's words to guide our attention.

We saw in Chapter 5 how *Olympia*, Part 2, creates referential and explicit meanings that have to do with the Olympic Games themselves, while its more implicit and symptomatic meanings arise from the ideology of its Nazi makers. The film's style plays an important role in cueing symptomatic meanings. The grandiose settings and the framing and editing patterns that turn the athletes into superhuman beings support elements of the Nazi mythology of the supremacy of certain races. Framing also brings out the regimentation of the events. The Wagnerian music accords with the norms of official Nazi culture. Luckily these ideas have little appeal for us today, and a modern audience is unlikely to respond to *Olympia* in the same way that Germans might have in the late 1930s. But by demarcating the film's categories and tracing out patterns of development, the style can endow categorical form with considerable interest and emotion.

STYLE IN *THE RIVER*

As we saw in Chapter 5, *The River*'s formal development depends on a simple argument. The Mississippi Valley, we are told, was beautiful in the past, and the people's strength made it productive. That strength and productivity damaged the land. Now, with programs like the Tennessee Valley Authority, that strength can be used to repair the damage while enhancing the valley's productivity.

Stylistic systems in the film help create this argument. Motifs of camera work, sound, and editing set up the parallels we have noted among the various segments and work to suggest that by the end of the film, the TVA has helped re-create a situation similar to the pristine nature we saw at the beginning. But the film also sets up great contrasts between segments showing the country's beauty and strengths and other segments showing the problems created by careless exploitation of resources. Differences in the use of filmic technique strengthen the contrasts and contribute to the film's persuasive power.

Fig. 10.42

The River includes a large amount of information: a summary of decades of American history, explanations of the causes of erosion and flooding, a description of the situation in 1937, and a look at the activities of the TVA. Yet we are able to keep all these matters straight and grasp the relations among them because of the film's clear form and its stylistic repetitions. For example, some segments begin by combining camera work and editing to show us landscapes against a cloudy sky. The very first shots after the prologue introduce this motif, with mountains against the sky. At the beginning of Segment 3, we see low-height shots of the mule teams against more clouds, and again in Segment 4, we first see the pine forests against the sky (Fig. 5.25). This sets up an expectation that such sky shots are associated with the beauty and strength of the Mississippi Valley, and the filmmakers later use this association in order to draw parallels.

Fig. 10.43

During the flood in Segment 6 and the description of the problems flooding causes, such framings are less prominent. But after the introduction of the TVA, they return. We see men going to work, framed in low angle against the sky (Fig. 10.42). Soon after this, one shot begins on a hillside against the sky (Fig. 10.43) and then tilts down to reveal the model town (Fig. 10.44). Thus the film satisfies our expectations about this visual motif by bringing it back in association with the new beauty and strength created by the TVA. This repetition also ties the ending back to the beginning. We have returned to an idyllic land, a development which confirms the film's claim that the TVA was the correct solution to the problem.

By way of contrast, other scenes either eliminate the sky motif or vary it considerably. Thus Segment 4, on the Civil War, begins with a printed announcement quoting Robert E. Lee's surrender statement, with flames superimposed over the writing. This is very different from the earlier segments' openings, marking Segment 4 off as introducing the problems with which the film will deal. As we saw in Chapter 5, the segment devoted to

Fig. 10.44

erosion and flooding also contrasts with the earlier scenes by showing stumps against fog (Fig. 5.26)—an obvious contrast with the cloud-filled shots of trees (Fig. 5.25).

The River creates other parallels by means of rhythms within the editing and the sound track. Virgil Thomson's famous musical score plays a more active role than do the scores of most documentary films, and the careful mixing of voice and music enhances the images they accompany. After the prologue, a fanfare introduces the mountain-and-cloud shots, and then the authoritative narrator's voice enters, all combining to suggest the stateliness and splendor of nature in the Mississippi Valley. Later scenes employ faster rhythms, as when a bouncy version of "Hot Time in the Old Town Tonight" plays over shots of logs hurtling down chutes into the river. Here the music is very important in cueing us how to react. The logging shots could connote destruction of natural beauty, but the accompaniment suggests that this industry is part of the building of American strength.

In the next scene, Segment 6, the filmmakers create a sharp contrast. Now we are cued to take the logging activities as having harmful side effects. A long series of shots creates a slow, inexorable rhythm building up to the turbulent, dangerous movements of the flood waters. The segment begins with slow shots of the fog-shrouded stumps (Fig. 5.26), with little movement. Rhythmic, threatening, dissonant chords make up the musical accompaniment. The narrator speaks more slowly and deliberately. Dissolves, rather than straight cuts, connect the shots, slowing down the visual rhythm still further. The segment begins to build up tension. One shot shows a stump with icicles on it and, instead of going on to other stumps, as the sequence had been doing, the next shot is a cut-in to emphasize the icicles dripping (Fig. 10.45). A sudden dissonant trumpet chord signals us to expect some threat. Then, in a series of close shots of the earth, we see more and more water gathering, first in trickles (Fig. 10.46), later in streams, washing the unprotected soil away. By now the sound is very rhythmic; quiet tom-tom-like beats punctuate the shots. The narrator begins supplying dates, one over each shot: "Nineteen-seven" (Fig. 10.47); "Nineteen-thirteen" (Fig. 10.48); "Nineteen-sixteen" (Fig. 10.49); and so on, up to 1937. By the "1916" shot (Fig. 10.49), we see a small waterfall forming, and in successive shots the creeks become rivers swelling over their banks.

As the storm and flood sequence intensifies, brief shots of lightning bolts

Fig. 10.45

Fig. 10.46

Fig. 10.47

Fig. 10.48

Fig. 10.49

are intercut with shots of raging water. Here the dramatic music becomes overwhelmed by loud sirens and whistles. The stylistic techniques have combined to build up to a climax of rising tension, convincing us of the flood's threat. Were we not to grasp that threat, both factually and emotionally, the film's overall argument would probably affect us less. Throughout *The River*, voice, music, editing, and movement within the shot are used to build up a rhythm for just such rhetorical purposes.

Such uses of style encourage us to make comparisons between different segments of the film. In addition, *The River* employs techniques on a small scale to enhance each individual scene's impact. Since the film does not present a narrative with continuing characters and action, it need not use the continuity editing system or keep its style unobtrusive. For example, graphic discontinuity may create a striking transition. Lorentz cuts from a shot of a mud-filled, mule-drawn sledge moving from right to left (Fig. 10.50) to a similarly framed shot of a plow going from left to right (Fig. 10.51). This cut leads from the first portion of Segment 3, on the building of the dike, to a new portion on cotton farming. The differences between these shots suggest the transition, but their similarities might also lead us to expect some connection between these two topics.

Camera work can function in an equally striking way. *The River* uses canted framings occasionally, as when we see a montage sequence of workers loading cotton bales onto a steamboat (Fig. 10.52). The off-balance composition makes the bales seem to roll downhill almost effortlessly. Combined with sprightly banjo music, this series of shots cues us to take the scene as a positive depiction of the South's productivity in earlier years. Interestingly, the use of style here discourages us from considering whether these black workers are slaves. This is an important issue in U.S. history, but the film excludes it from its argument, preferring instead to speak of a general "we," a united people responsible for the despoiling of the Mississippi.

As we saw in Chapter 5, appeals to our emotions play a large part in rhetorical form. If a film can make us feel strongly about its subject, we may be more inclined to accept its arguments as valid. *The River*'s use of technique enhances its emotional impact. Even today, when the issues involved in Pare Lorentz's arguments are no longer topical, the film's style can powerfully affect us.

Fig. 10.50

Fig. 10.51

Fig. 10.52

STYLE IN *BALLET MÉCANIQUE*

When we first analyzed *Ballet mécanique* in Chapter 5, we necessarily looked at some aspects of its style—its short bursts of shots, its swinging camera movements, its graphic discontinuities. Style is crucial to the abstract organization of form. Indeed, we often refer to the emphasis on abstract qualities of recognizable objects as "stylization." But, now that we have surveyed the techniques of the film medium, we can be more specific about how style functions in *Ballet mécanique*.

In general, the film reverses our normal expectations about the nature of movement. The purpose is to make objects dance and to make human movement seem mechanistic. We have already seen how the film's form is calculated to bring out these pictorial qualities. Now we can see that the film uses each film technique in ways which function in this context.

Most of the objects are familiar from everyday life, but the mise-en-scene takes them out of their familiar context and makes us see them in a new way. For example, many of the shots show faces or objects against black or white backgrounds (Figs. 5.37 and 5.44). In a few cases, the backgrounds themselves have abstract white and black patterns, as in the shot of the swinging ball near the end of Segment 2 (Fig. 10.53). The swinging or turning objects, especially the machine movements in Segment 4, also emphasize the "mechanical ballet" pattern. Even make-up, which we usually associate with films involving characters, acts to render abstract relations more prominent. In the shot of the woman's profile (Fig. 5.39), heavy make-up combines with her lack of expression and stiff swiveling movement to point up her resemblance to a mannequin. Similarly, human figure movement imitates that of the machines.

The cinematographic properties of the shot heighten these qualities and add new abstract elements to the imagery. Any framing creates a composition, of course, but the filmmaker can emphasize or deemphasize the abstract aspects of shapes on the screen. In *Ballet mécanique*, shot scale often makes shape a prominent element of the shot. The film has a high proportion of medium close-ups, close-ups, and even extreme close-ups. In combination with the blank backgrounds, such close framings function to isolate and draw attention to shapes: the round hat (Fig. 5.44), the zerolike horse collar (Fig. 10.54), the round profile (Fig. 5.39). Such close framings also make texture easier to discern, as with the shiny pots and bottles.

Other aspects of framing work in similar ways. Masks change the screen's shape to emphasize one portion, as with the repeated shots of a woman's eye (Fig. 5.34). Upside-down framing is used to present the swinging woman in Segment 1 (Fig. 5.32) and the rows of swinging pans (Segment 6; Fig. 5.41). A special effect may organize the small-scale form of a whole segment, as when prismatic shots dominate part 2, and then recur as a motif in later portions. Finally, mobile framing functions prominently in the creation of the film's rhythm. The short, regular pans in the upside-down shot of the swinging woman begin this process, recurring in the rapid succession of brief, repetitive pan shots of fairground-ride cars in Segment 3.

Fig. 10.53

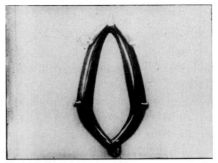

Fig. 10.54

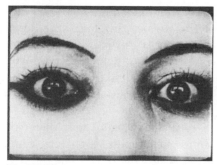

Fig. 10.55

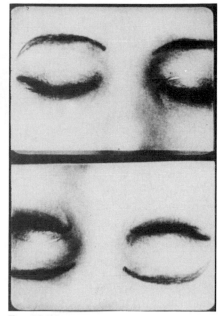

Fig. 10.56

Editing is a very important technique for creating abstract relations in *Ballet mécanique*. This film provides a good example of how filmmakers may work entirely outside the continuity editing system and create dynamic, highly organized patterns between shots. One of the film's most striking and amusing moments depends upon a precise graphic match. In Segment 2 we see an extreme close-up of a woman's wide-open eyes (Fig. 10.55). She closes them, leaving her heavily made-up eyes and brows as dark crescents against her white skin. A cut presents us with the same composition, now upside down. (Fig. 10.56 shows the last frame of the first shot and the first frame of the next.) The eyes and brows are now reversed, but in identical positions. When the eyes pop open (Fig. 10.57), we are momentarily surprised to find their positions switched; the match is so close as to make the cut almost invisible. The surprise is enhanced by a quick cutting rate that does not allow us to really examine the shots closely. Humorous touches like this occur throughout *Ballet mécanique* and make it as enjoyable to watch now as it must have been when it was first shown over seventy years ago.

Graphic matches, however, are rare in the film. Usually the shapes we are to compare do not appear in successive shots. Thus in Segment 5, the dance of intertitles and pictures, the large zero (Fig. 10.58) and the horse collar (Fig. 10.54) are graphically similar, and each recurs in many shots. Yet they are never juxtaposed in a graphic match. On the other hand, a great many cuts contrast elements through strong graphic discontinuity. The circle and triangle alternation that recurs so regularly is one example. True, the shapes are both white, and both are seen against black backgrounds. But the difference in their shapes is what we notice most readily in these passages. Such an obvious contrast cues us to look for others.

Graphic contrast can be enhanced by accelerated editing. In the hat/ shoe alternation in Segment 7 (Fig. 5.44), we see the striking differences in shape right away. But, as the lengthy series of short shots continues, we notice variations. About a third of the way through, the directions are switched: The shoe protrudes in from the left briefly, and the hat also flips. Then they return to their original positions, and the editing rhythm accelerates. By the end, the shots are so short that we seem almost to see a single white object pulsating, rapidly changing from circle to lozenge and back again. Here the filmmakers are pointing out how the apparent-motion phenomenon makes us see movement in a strip of slightly different still images. This is the process that makes cinema itself possible. (See Chapter 1.)

Fig. 10.57

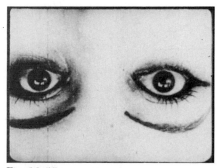

Fig. 10.58

Even when there are no specific graphic similarities or contrasts, *Ballet mécanique*'s editing suggests other comparisons. By placing a shot of a woman's eye next to that of a machine, or by punctuating a laundry woman's repeated stair-climbing with a rhythmically rotating shaft, the film creates a metaphorical similarity between human and mechanized motion. Such repeated comparisons help to organize the overall development of the film's form.

Rhythmic figure movement, rhythmic framing mobility, and rhythmic editing function to set objects scampering across the screen. It is difficult to resist seeing the quick shots of mannequins' legs (Fig. 5.43) in Segment 7 as executing a dance, even though most of the individual shots contain no movement. This passage differs greatly from the simple shot of the woman swinging that we saw at the beginning. Yet, without any use of language beyond the title itself to direct our expectations, *Ballet mécanique* has employed film techniques to guide us to see a similarity between two such contrasting moments. Random objects seem to belong together, and a mechanical rhythm pulses through objects and humans alike.

STYLE IN *A MOVIE*

We have already seen that the overall form of Bruce Conner's *A Movie* is associational. In this context, film style fulfills three general types of functions. Across the whole film, stylistic techniques help break the form into parts and create relations among those parts. On a local level, individual techniques enhance the links between different objects and draw us to form expectations on the basis of the comparison. Thirdly, the style offers us cues as to how to respond, emotionally and intellectually.

Conner controlled neither the original mise-en-scene nor the cinematography of the films from which he took the shots for *A Movie* nor the composition of the music that forms its sound track. Yet, by selection and arrangement, he made use of these elements as they already existed, and we can find techniques of mise-en-scene, camera work, sound, and editing all at work in fulfilling the three types of functions.

Perhaps the most noticeable characteristic of the mise-en-scene of *A Movie* is its great variety. By choosing material from so many different film types, Conner cues us to seek more and more generalized associations to explain the links among the objects we see. Galloping cowboys and Indians from a fiction film, atomic-bomb blasts from documentary, and nudie shots from pornography do not add up to a story or an argument, and we must find some common association, like aggressivity and disaster, to make sense of this barrage of heterogeneous images.

Our ability to follow the comparisons being made from shot to shot also depends on the fact that Conner found similar types of elements from different films and juxtaposed them, putting a stock-car crash next to a race-car crash or a water-skier's fall next to a surfer's wipe-out. *A Movie* also makes use of the mise-en-scene of its different shots to guide our emotional reaction. The plane crashes or firing-squad shots evoke horror, while the more quietly ominous sections of the film contain some images of considerable beauty, such as the first shot of the *Hindenburg* floating over a city (Fig. 5.49). Mise-en-scene elements contribute to the overall form of the film, since visual motifs are repeated and varied. As we saw in Chapter 5, motifs from Segments 2 and 3 are picked up again in the fourth and final part.

Cinematography works in similar ways in *A Movie*. On the one hand, there is a great variety in the types of techniques found in the original footage: wartime aerial photography of planes being fired upon, panning documentary shots that follow race cars and motor boats, and more static framings of staged scenes, as in the pornography shots. Again, this variety enhances the contrasts among elements and encourages us to make comparisons on a very general level. Yet *A Movie* also uses as motifs the similar types of cinematography found in different films. Thus the series of different plane disasters at the beginning of Segment 4 all use aerial photography, and this links them with the aerial shots of the *Hindenburg* early in Segment 3. Cinematography can also enhance emotional response. The series of panning shots of crashing race cars late in Segment 2 builds up a relatively regular rhythm of disasters, a pattern soon to be intensified in later parts of the film. Similarly, the long tilt down following the old car falling over a cliff at the end of this segment (Figs. 10.59, 10.60) emphasizes the length of that fall and provides an emotional climax to the series of car crashes.

At a few points in *A Movie*, Conner also manipulates cinematography by using laboratory-made special effects to alter shots. A few shots in Segment 4 begin or end with black masks that move to reveal or conceal the mise-en-scene of the shot. For example, the brief series of shots of the buckling suspension bridge begins with such a mask moving aside (Fig. 10.61). Such moments stress Conner's own manipulation of the found footage and perhaps function similarly to the repeated insertions of the titles "Movie," "Bruce Conner," and so on, at other points in the film.

There is also a brief series of shots early in Segment 4 that are linked by dissolves and optically printed zoom-ins that enlarge the frames. From the planes in front of the pyramid (Fig. 5.56), a dissolve moves us to the beginning of the first volcano shot (Fig. 10.62). You can see the edges of this frame as Conner prints it small at first, then optically enlarges it frame by frame to achieve a zooming effect (Fig. 10.63). After a straight cut to a closer volcano shot (also with an optical zoom-in), there is a dissolve to the coro-

Fig. 10.59

Fig. 10.60

Fig. 10.61

Fig. 10.62

Fig. 10.63

Fig. 10.64

Fig. 10.65

nation (Fig. 10.64), which is also optically enlarged (Fig. 10.65), followed by another dissolve to the burning *Hindenburg,* and a final dissolve and zoom-in to a moving line of army tanks. In a film that usually manipulates the original shots only through editing and sound, this brief segment stands out by contrast. The effect of the quick dissolves and zooms is partly to seem to move us in toward the disasters and other scenes. But, more strikingly, each scene seems to emerge out of the previous one—the volcano "coming forward" from the pyramid, the church official blending briefly with the smoke of the volcano and growing larger, and so on. This series creates a very strong linkage among the disparate elements, enhancing our sense of the inevitable, rhythmic flow of these ominous images.

Sound is crucial to *A Movie's* various effects. In Chapter 5 we saw how the divisions between Segments 2, 3, and 4 coincide with pauses between parts of Respighi's *Pines of Rome.* The considerable differences in tone among those parts also give us strong cues as to how to react to the images. The shots that open Segment 3—the women carrying totems, the *Hindenburg,* the acrobats—take on their eerie, slightly ominous quality almost solely because of the musical accompaniment. Moreover, the music intensifies our emotional response. While the series of disasters in Segment 4 are horrendous in themselves, the ponderous, driving music makes them merge into one plunging, apocalyptic rush.

The sound is all nondiegetic, and we hear no voices or sound effects from the individual scenes. Yet Conner has edited his shots very carefully to create corresponding rhythms in image movement, cutting, and music. For example, the frenzied build-up of the fast passage in *The Pines of Rome* toward the end of Segment 2 accompanies the series of race-car crashes. Blaring, dissonant phrases begin to punctuate the music at regular intervals. Conner times these to coincide with the individual car crashes, considerably enhancing their visual effectiveness. Later, in Segment 4, the shot of the flute player (Fig. 5.57) coincides with a passage of flute and oboe music, so that we almost sense for a moment that the sound has become diegetic. This impression enhances the idyllic quality of these exotic shots, just before the return to the disaster footage. Thus, although Conner chose an existing piece of music, he has tailored it closely to his images and used it to help create the tone and form of *A Movie.*

Editing was the only technique in *A Movie* that Conner controlled completely, and it is the source of many spectacular effects. Of course, the basic associational comparisons are made by cutting together series of shots from different sources. But Conner does not stop with juxtaposing events by cutting. He exploits the graphic, spatial, and temporal relations between shots as well.

Some cuts use principles of continuity to fit together shots that really could not be in the same space, thus creating an "impossible" continuity that gives the film much of its humor. We can see now that the joke of the submarine officer "looking" at the bikini-clad woman (Figs. 5.51, 5.52) comes from the fact that it is a false optical point-of-view shot. Similarly, the various racing horses, elephants, and tanks in the first part of Segment 2 are linked partly by their common screen direction. Most of the movement is from left to right on the screen, or coming directly toward the camera, both directions that would cut together correctly in the continuity editing system. Thus we can imagine all these vehicles and animals racing along together in some vast space. Yet the obvious impossibility of the juxtaposition makes this notion amusing. Later, in Segment 3, Conner varies this technique by cutting together various water-skiers and motor boats, some with similar directions of movement, some with opposed directions, but all compared through the general similarities of the series of shots.

Fig. 10.66

Like *Ballet mécanique*, *A Movie* uses graphic matches to create comparisons. During the same series of fast movements cut together in Segment 2, we see first a shot of a wagon moving over the camera (Fig. 10.66), then a graphically similar shot of a tank filmed from a low camera height (Fig. 10.67). Combined with the quick tempo of the editing rhythm, such moments contribute to the frenzied exhilaration that this segment generates. By finding similarities of this type between shots taken from different sources, Conner also enhances the associational connections between shots. Stylistic links cue us to find emotional and conceptual links as well.

The overall formal organization of *A Movie*, developing from humor toward a threatening tone and ultimate disaster, depends heavily on the repeated use of film techniques. Editing juxtaposes elements, mise-en-scene and cinematography emphasize the similarities and contrasts among them, and music develops and unifies the emotional tone. As a result, even a very short film can elicit a wide range of responses from the viewer. Here, as in all the types of nonnarrative form, we can see that style plays a crucial role in the total form of a film and in the spectator's experience.

Fig. 10.67

This concludes our discussion of film form and film technique. As we have emphasized, no single set of rules will allow you to understand every film automatically. Any film creates a unique form from an interplay of overall structure and film style, and each individual element (each formal part or stylistic technique) functions according to its place within that system. Analyzing the nature of that formal system and the functions of individual devices is the goal of the critic. Part IV of this book consists of a series of analyses showing how a critic may understand the workings of widely differing kinds of films.

NOTES AND QUERIES

■ THE CONCEPT OF FILM STYLE

Sometimes the concept of style is used evaluatively, to imply that something is inherently good ("Now that's got real style!"). We are using the term descriptively. From our perspective, all films have style, because all films make *some* use of the techniques of the medium, and those techniques will necessarily be organized in some way.

For discussion of the concept of style in various arts, see Monroe C. Beardsley, *Aesthetics: Problems in the Philosophy of Criticism* (New York: Harcourt, Brace & World, 1958); J. V. Cunningham, ed., *The Problem of*

Style (Greenwich, Conn.: Fawcett, 1966); and Berel Lang, ed., *The Concept of Style*, rev. ed. (Ithaca: Cornell University Press, 1987).

Pioneering studies of style in the cinema are Erwin Panofsky, "Style and Medium in the Moving Pictures" (originally published in 1937), in Daniel Talbot, ed., *Film: An Anthology* (Berkeley: University of California Press, 1970), pp. 13–32; Raymond Durgnat, *Films and Feelings* (Cambridge, Mass.: MIT Press, 1967); and Raymond Bellour, "Pour une stylistique du film," *Revue d'esthétique* **19,** 2(April–June 1966): 161–178. Most of the works cited in Notes and Queries to chapters in Part III offer concrete studies of aspects of film style.

A shot-by-shot analysis of *Ballet mécanique* may be found in Standish Lawder, *The Cubist Cinema* (Berkeley: University of California Press, 1975).

An entire book has been written on the production of *Citizen Kane*, shedding much light on how its style was created: Robert L. Carringer's *The Making of Citizen Kane* (Berkeley: University of California Press, 1985). Among other things, Carringer reveals the degree to which Welles and his collaborators used special effects for many of the film's scenes. A tribute to the film, and a reprinting of Gregg Toland's informative article on the film, "Realism for *Citizen Kane*," is available in *American Cinematographer* **72,** 8 (August 1991): 34–42. Graham Bruce illuminates Bernard Herrmann's musical score for *Kane* in *Bernard Herrmann: Film Music and Narrative* (Ann Arbor: UMI Research Press, 1985), pp. 42–57. See also Steven C. Smith, *A Heart at Fire's Center: The Life and Music of Bernard Herrmann* (Berkeley: University of California Press, 1991). A detailed analysis of the film's sound is Rick Altman, "Deep-Focus Sound: *Citizen Kane* and the Radio Aesthetic," *Quarterly Review of Film and Video* **15,** 3 (December 1994): 1–33.

PART IV

CRITICAL ANALYSIS
OF FILMS

Criticism is not an activity limited to those people who write articles or books about films. Any person who seeks actively to understand a film he or she sees is engaged in a process of criticism. You may be unsure, for example, why one scene was included in a film; your search for the function of that scene in the context of the whole is a first step in a critical examination. People who discuss a film they have seen are participating in criticism.

Up to this point, we have looked at concepts and definitions that should enable a filmgoer to analyze a film systematically. The critic approaches a film already knowing that formal patterns, such as repetitions and variations, will probably be important and should be examined. The critic will also be alert for principles of narrative and nonnnarrative form, and she or he will watch for salient uses of the various film techniques. The critic will also ground his or her claims in specific evidence from the film.

So far, we have looked at all the techniques that constitute a film; we have also laid out basic principles that govern a film's narrative or nonnarrative form. Our examples and analyses have shown how elements of a film function in an overall system. But the only way to gain an ability to analyze films is through practice in viewing and perhaps writing about films critically and through reading analyses by other critics. For this reason, we conclude our look at films as formal systems with a series of brief sample essays on individual films.

An analyst usually scrutinizes a film with some sort of purpose in view. You may want to understand a film's perplexing aspects, or reveal the process that created a pleasurable response, or convince someone that the film is worth seeing. Our sample analyses have two primary purposes. First, we want to illustrate how film form and film style work together in a variety of films. Secondly, we seek to provide models of short critical analyses, exemplars of how an essay might illuminate some aspects of a film's workings.

Because an analyst is limited by his or her purposes, there is little chance of "getting everything," of accounting for each facet of a film. As a result, these analyses do not exhaust the films. You might study any one of them and find many more points of interest than we have been able to present here. Indeed, whole books can be and have been written about single films without exhausting the possibilities for enriching our experience of those films.

ELEVEN

FILM CRITICISM: SAMPLE ANALYSES

Each of the four major sections of this chapter emphasizes different aspects of various films. First, we discuss three classical narrative films: *His Girl Friday, North by Northwest,* and *Do The Right Thing.* Since classically constructed films are very familiar to most viewers, it is important to study closely how they work.

We move to two films that represent alternatives to classical norms. *Breathless* relies on ambiguity of character motivation and on stretches of rambling action, all presented through loose, casual techniques. By contrast, *Tokyo Story* uses selective deviations from classical stylistic norms in order to create a highly rigorous style.

Documentary films can be constructed in various ways, and the third section considers two examples. Although *High School* purports to be a neutral description of a situation, it nonetheless illustrates how the filmmaker's formal and stylistic choices can create strong spectator effects and a particular range of explicit and implicit meanings. By contrast, *Man with a Movie Camera* makes no pretense of objectivity and instead flaunts the manipulative powers of the film medium.

Finally, we move to analyses that emphasize social ideology. Our first example, *Meet Me in St. Louis,* is a film that accepts a dominant ideology and reinforces the audience's belief in that ideology. By contrast, *Raging Bull* shows how a film can display ambiguity in its ideological implications.

We could have emphasized different aspects of any of these films. *Meet Me in St. Louis,* for example, is a classical narrative film and could be considered from that perspective. Similarly, *Man with a Movie Camera* could be seen as offering an alternative to classical continuity editing. And any of the films represents an ideological position which could be analyzed. Our choices suggest only certain angles of approach; your own critical activities will discover many more.

Those activities are the focus of the appendix to this part. There we suggest some ways in which you can prepare, organize, and write a critical analysis of a film. We draw on the previous sample analyses for various strategies that you can apply in your own writing.

THE CLASSICAL NARRATIVE CINEMA

■ *HIS GIRL FRIDAY*

> 1940. Columbia. Directed by Howard Hawks. Script by Charles Lederer from the play *The Front Page* by Ben Hecht and Charles MacArthur. Photographed by Joseph Walker. Edited by Gene Harlick. Music by Morris W. Stoloff. With Cary Grant, Rosalind Russell, Ralph Bellamy, Gene Lockhart, Porter Hall.

The dominant impression left by *His Girl Friday* is that of speed: It is often said to be the fastest sound comedy ever made. Let us therefore slow it down analytically. By breaking the film into parts and seeing how the parts relate to one another logically, temporally, and spatially, we can suggest how classical narrative form and specific film techniques are used to create this whirlwind experience.

His Girl Friday is built on the common unit of classical narrative cinema: the scene. Typically marked off by editing devices such as the dissolve, fade, or wipe, each scene presents a distinct segment of space, time, and narrative action. We can locate 13 such scenes in *His Girl Friday*, set in the following locales: (1) the *Morning Post* offices; (2) the restaurant; (3) the Criminal Courts pressroom; (4) Walter's office; (5) Earl Williams's cell; (6) the pressroom; (7) a precinct jail; (8) the pressroom; (9) the sheriff's office; (10) the street outside the prison; (11) the pressroom; (12) the sheriff's office; (13) the pressroom. All of these scenes are marked off by dissolves except for the transition between 8 and 9, which is simply a cut.

Within these scenes, smaller units of action occur. Note, for example, that scene 1, occupying almost 14 minutes of screen time, introduces almost all of the major characters and sets two plot lines in motion. Or, consider scene 13: Almost every major character appears in it, and it runs for about 33 minutes!

We could go on to break the longer scenes into smaller parts on the basis of changing character interactions. Thus scene 1 comprises: (a) the introduction to the newspaper office; (b) the first conversation between Hildy and Bruce; (c) Walter's discussion of the past with Hildy; (d) Walter's conference with Duffy about the Earl Williams case; (e) Hildy's telling Walter that she's remarrying; and (f) Walter's introduction to Bruce. To grasp the construction of other lengthy scenes, you may divide them into similar segments. It may be, in fact, that the somewhat theatrical feel of the film comes from its practice of segmenting its scenes by character entrances and exits (rather than, say, by frequent shifts of locale). In any event, the developing patterns of character interaction contribute a great deal to the hubbub and speed of the film.

The scenes function, as we would expect, to advance the action. As we saw in Chapter 4 (pp. 108–110), classical Hollywood cinema often constructs a narrative around characters with definite traits who want to achieve specific goals. The clash of these characters' contrasting traits and conflicting goals propels the story forward in a step-by-step process of cause and effect. *His Girl Friday* has two such cause-effect chains:

1. *The romance.* Hildy Johnson wants to quit newspaper reporting and settle down with Bruce Baldwin. This is her initial goal. But Hildy's editor and ex-husband, Walter Burns, has a different goal: He wants her to continue as his reporter and to remarry him. Given these two goals, the characters enter into a conflict in several stages. First, Walter lures Hildy by promising a nest egg for the couple in exchange for her writing one last story. But Walter also plots to have Bruce robbed. Learning of this, Hildy tears up her story. Walter continues to delay Bruce, however, and eventually wins Hildy through her renewed interest in reporting. She changes her mind about marrying Bruce and stays with Walter.

2. *Crime and politics.* Earl Williams is to be hanged for shooting a policeman. The city's political bosses are relying on the execution to ensure their reelection. This is the goal shared by the mayor and the sheriff. But Walter's goal is to induce the governor to reprieve Williams and thus unseat the mayor's party at the polls. Through the sheriff's stupidity, Williams escapes and is concealed by Hildy and Walter. In the meantime, a reprieve does arrive from the governor; the mayor bribes the messenger into leaving. Williams is discovered, but the messenger returns with the reprieve in time to save Williams from death and Walter and Hildy from jail. Presumably the mayor's machine will be defeated at the election.

The crime-and-politics line of action is made to depend on events in the romance line at several points. Walter uses the Williams case to lure Hildy back to him, Hildy chases the Williams story instead of returning to Bruce, Bruce's mother reveals to the police that Walter has concealed Williams, and so on. More specifically, the interplay of the two lines of action alters the goals of various characters. In Walter's case, inducing Hildy to write the story fulfills his goals of embarrassing the politicos and of tempting Hildy back. Hildy's goals are more greatly changed. After she destroys her article, her decision to cover Earl Williams's jailbreak marks her acceptance of Walter's goal. Her later willingness to hide Williams and her indifference to Bruce's plea firmly establish her goals as linked to Walter's. In this way the interaction of the two plot lines advances Walter's goals but radically alters Hildy's.

Within this general framework, the cause-effect sequencing is very complex and deserves a closer analysis than space permits here. But consider, for example, the various ways in which Walter's delaying tactics (involving his confederates Duffy, Louie, and Angie) set up short-term chains of cause and effect in themselves. Also interesting is the way Bruce is steadily shouldered out of the romance plot, becoming more and more passive as he is shuttled in and out of precinct jails. In this regard Earl Williams undergoes a parallel experience as he is manipulated by Hildy, the sheriff, the psychologist, and Walter. We could also consider the function of the minor characters, such as Molly Malloy (Williams's platonic sweetheart), Bruce's mother, the other reporters, and especially Pettibone, the delightful emissary from the governor.

Perhaps most important, note how the scenes "hook into" each other. An event at the end of one scene is seen as a cause leading to an effect, that is, the event that begins the next scene. For example, at the end of the first scene, Walter offers to take Bruce and Hildy to lunch; scene 2 starts with the three of them arriving at the restaurant. This exemplifies the "linearity" of classical narrative: Almost every scene ends with a "dangling cause," the effect of which is shown at the beginning of the next scene. In *His Girl Friday,* this linear pattern helps keep the plot action moving rapidly forward, setting up each new scene quickly at the end of the previous one.

The cause-and-effect logic of the film illustrates yet another principle of classical narrative structure: closure. No event is uncaused. (Even Pettibone's arrival is no lucky accident, for we know that the governor is under pressure to decide about the case.) More important, both lines of action are clearly resolved at the end. Williams is saved and the politicians are disgraced. Bruce, having gone home with mother, leaves Walter and Hildy preparing for a second honeymoon no less hectic than their first.

So much for causality. What of narrative time? Classical Hollywood cinema typically subordinates time to the narrative's cause-effect relations, and one common way is to set a deadline for the action. Thus a temporal goal is wedded to a causal one, and the time becomes charged with cause-effect significance. The deadline is, of course, a convention of the newspaper genre, adding a built-in time and suspense factor. But in *His Girl Friday* each of the two plots has its own deadlines as well. The mayor and sheriff face an obvious deadline: Earl Williams must be hanged before next Tuesday's election and before the governor can reprieve him. In his political strategizing, Walter Burns faces the other side of the same deadline: He wants Williams reprieved. What we might not expect is that the romance plot has deadlines as well.

Bruce and Hildy are set to leave on a train bound for Albany and for marriage at four o'clock that very day. Walter's machinations keep forcing the couple to postpone their departure. Add to this the fact that when Bruce comes to confront Hildy and Walter, he exits with the defiant ultimatum: "I'm leaving on the nine o'clock train!" (Hildy misses that train as well.) The temporal structure of the film, then, depends on the cause-effect sequence. If Earl Williams were to be hanged next month, or if the election were two years off, or if Bruce and Hildy were planning a marriage at some distant future date, the sense of dramatic pressure would be lacking. The numerous overlapping deadlines under which all of the characters labor have the effect of squeezing together all the lines of action and sustaining the breathless pace of the film.

Another aspect of *His Girl Friday*'s patterning of time reinforces this pace. Though the plot presents events in straightforward chronological order, it takes remarkable liberties with story duration. Of course, since the action consumes about nine hours (from around 12:30 P.M. to around 9:30 P.M.), we expect that certain portions of time *between scenes* will be eliminated. And so they have been. What is unusual is that the time *within* scenes has been accelerated.

Fig. 11.1

At the start of the very first scene, for example, the clock in the *Post* office reads 12:57. It's important to note that there have been no editing ellipses in the scene; the story duration has simply been compressed. If you clock scene 13, you will find even more remarkable acceleration. People leave on long trips and return less than 10 minutes later! Again, the editing is continuous: It is story time that "goes faster" than screen time. This temporal compression combines with frenetically rushed dialogue and occasionally accelerated rhythmic editing (for example, the reporters' cries just before Williams's capture) to create the film's breakneck pace.

Space, like time, is here subordinate to narrative cause and effect. Hawks's camera moves unobtrusively to reframe the characters symmetrically in the shot. (Watch any scene silent to observe the subtle "balancing act" that goes on during the dialogue scenes. An example is shown in Figs. 7.140–7.142.) Straight-on camera angles predominate, varied by an occasional high-angle shot down on the prison courtyard or on Williams's cell bars. Why, we might ask in passing, does the prison receive this visual emphasis in the camera angle and the lighting?

Fig. 11.2

The restriction of the action to very few locales might seem a handicap, but the patterns of character placement are remarkably varied and functional. Walter's persuading Hildy to write the story is interesting from this standpoint, as the two pace in a complete circuit around the desk and Walter assumes dynamic and comic postures (Figs. 11.1, 11.2; note the reframing). And spatial continuity in the editing anticipates each dramatic point by judiciously cutting to a closer shot or smoothly matching on action so that we watch the movements and not the cuts. In the opening scene, for example, Hildy's action of throwing her purse at Walter is matched at the cut to a more distant framing (Figs. 11.3, 11.4). The change in the position of Walter's arms, so apparent in our illustrations, goes unnoticed in the rapid action of the scene. Virtually every scene, especially the restaurant episode and the final scene, offers many fine examples of classical continuity editing. In all, space is used to delineate the flow of the cause-effect sequence.

Fig. 11.3

We might highlight for special attention one specific item of both sound and mise-en-scene. It is plausible that newspapermen in 1939 use telephones, but *His Girl Friday* makes the phone integral to the narrative. Walter's duplicity demands phones. At the restaurant he pretends to be summoned away to a call; he makes and breaks promises to Hildy via phones; he directs Duffy and other minions by phone. More generally, the pressroom is equipped with a veritable flotilla of phones, enabling the reporters to contact their editors. And, of course, Bruce keeps calling Hildy from the various police stations in which he continually finds himself. The telephones thus constitute a communications network that permits the narrative to be relayed from point to point.

Fig. 11.4

But Hawks also visually and sonically orchestrates the characters' use

Fig. 11.5

of the phones. There are many variations. One person may be talking on the phone, or several may be talking *in turn* on different phones, or several may be talking *at once* on different phones, or a phone conversation may be juxtaposed with a conversation elsewhere in the room, and so on. In scene 11, there is a polyphonic effect of reporters coming in to phone their editors, each conversation overlapping with the preceding one. Later, in scene 13, while Hildy frantically phones hospitals, Walter screams into another phone (Fig. 11.5). And when Bruce returns for Hildy, a helter-skelter din arises that eventually sorts itself into three sonic lines: Bruce begging Hildy to listen, Hildy obsessively typing her story, and Walter yelling into the phone for Duffy to clear page one ("No, no, leave the rooster story—that's human interest!"). Like much in *His Girl Friday*, the telephones warrant close study for the complex and various ways in which they are integrated into the narrative, and for their contribution to the rapid tempo of the film.

■ *NORTH BY NORTHWEST*

> 1959. MGM. Directed by Alfred Hitchcock. Script by Ernest Lehman. Photographed by Robert Burks. Edited by George Tomasini. Music composed by Bernard Herrmann. With Cary Grant, Eva Marie Saint, James Mason, Leo G. Carroll, Jesse Royce Landis.

Hitchcock long insisted that he made thrillers, not mystery films. For him, creating a puzzle was less important than generating suspense and surprise. While there are important mystery elements in films like *Notorious* (1946), *Stage Fright* (1950), and *Psycho* (1960), *North by Northwest* stands as almost a pure example of Hitchcock's belief that the mystery element can serve as merely a pretext for intriguing the audience. The film's tight causal unity enables Hitchcock to create an engrossing plot that obeys the norms of classical filmmaking. This plot is presented through a narration that continually emphasizes suspense and surprise.

Like most spy films, *North by Northwest* has a complex plot, involving two major lines of action. In one line, a gang of spies mistakes advertising-agency executive Roger Thornhill for an American agent, George Kaplan. Although the spies fail to kill him, he becomes the chief suspect in a murder which the gang commits. He must flee the police while trying to track down the real George Kaplan. Unfortunately, Kaplan does not exist; he is only a decoy invented by the United States Intelligence Agency (USIA). Thornhill's pursuit of "Kaplan" leads to the second line of action: his meeting and falling in love with Eve Kendall, who is really the mistress of Philip Van Damm, the spies' leader. The spy-chase line and the romance line further connect when Thornhill learns that Eve is actually a double agent, secretly working for the USIA. He must then rescue her from Van Damm, who has discovered her identity and has resolved to kill her. In the course of all this, Thornhill also discovers that the spies are smuggling government secrets out of the country in pieces of sculpture.

From even so bare an outline it should be evident that the film's plot presents many conventional patterns to the viewer. There is the search pattern, seen when Thornhill sets out to find Kaplan. There is also a journey pattern: Thornhill and his pursuers travel from New York to Chicago and then to Rapid City, South Dakota, with side excursions as well. In addition, the last two-thirds of the plot is organized around the romance between Thornhill and Eve. Moreover, each pattern develops markedly in the course of the film. In the course of his search, Thornhill must often assume the identity of the man he is trailing. The journey pattern gets varied by all the vehicles Thornhill uses—cabs, train, pickup truck, police car, bus, ambulance, and airplane.

Most subtly, the romance line of action is constantly modified by Thornhill's changing awareness of the situation. Believing that Eve wants to help him, he falls in love with her. But then he learns that she sent him to the murderous appointment at Prairie Stop, and he becomes cold and suspicious. When he discovers her at the auction with Van Damm, his anger and bitterness impel him to humiliate her and make Van Damm doubt her loyalty. Only after the USIA chief, the "Professor," tells him that she is really an agent does Thornhill realize that he has misjudged and endangered her. Each step in his growing awareness alters his romantic relation to Eve.

This intricate plot is made unified and comprehensible by other familiar strategies. It has a strict time scheme, comprising four days and nights (followed by a brief epilogue on a later night). The first day and a half take place in New York; the second night on the train to Chicago; the third day in Chicago and at Prairie Stop; and the fourth day at Mount Rushmore. The timetable is neatly established early in the film. Van Damm, having abducted Roger as "Kaplan," announces: "In two days you're due at the Ambassador East in Chicago, and then at the Sheraton Johnson Hotel in Rapid City, South Dakota." This itinerary prepares the spectator for the shifts in action that will occur in the rest of the film. Apart from the time scheme, the film also unifies itself through the characterization of Thornhill. He is initially presented as a resourceful liar when he steals a cab from another pedestrian. Later, he will have to lie in many circumstances to evade capture. Similarly, Roger is established as a heavy drinker, and his ability to hold his liquor will enable him to survive Van Damm's attempt to force him to kill himself when driving while drunk.

A great many motifs are repeated and help make the film cohere. Roger is constantly in danger from heights: His car hangs over a cliff, he must sneak out on the ledge of a hospital, he has to clamber up Van Damm's modernistic clifftop house, and he and Eve wind up dangling from the faces on Mount Rushmore. Thornhill's constant changing of vehicles also constitutes a motif which Hitchcock varies. A more subtle example is the motif which conveys Thornhill's growing suspicion of Eve. On the train, when they kiss, his hands close tenderly around her hair (Fig. 11.6). But in her hotel room, when she tries to embrace him after his narrow escape from death, his hands freeze in place, as if he fears touching her (Fig. 11.7).

Still, narrative unity alone cannot explain the film's strong emotional appeal. In Chapter 4's discussion of narration, we used *North by Northwest* as an example of a "hierarchy of knowledge" (pp. 103–106). We suggested that as the film progresses, sometimes we are restricted only to what Roger knows, whereas at other times we know significantly more than he does. At still other moments, our range of knowledge, while greater than Roger's, is

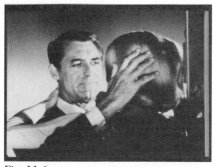

Fig. 11.6

Fig. 11.7

Fig. 11.8

Fig. 11.9

Fig. 11.10

Fig. 11.11

not as great as that of other characters. Now we are in a position to see how this constantly changing process helps create suspense and surprise across the whole film.

The most straightforward way in which the film's narration controls our knowledge is through the numerous *optical point-of-view* (POV) shots Hitchcock employs. This device yields a degree of subjective depth: We see what a character sees more or less as she or he sees it. More importantly here, the optical POV shot restricts us only to what that character learns at that moment. Hitchcock gives almost every major character a shot of this sort. The very first optical POV we see in the film is taken from the position of the two spies who are watching Roger apparently respond to the paging of George Kaplan (Figs. 11.8, 11.9). Later, we view events through the eyes of Eve, of Van Damm, of his henchman Leonard, and even of a clerk at a ticket counter.

Nevertheless, by far the greatest number of POV shots are attached to Thornhill. Through his eyes we see his approach to the Townsend mansion, the mail he finds in the library, his drunken drive along the cliff, and the airplane that is "crop dusting where there ain't no crops." Some of the most extreme uses of optical POV, such as an advancing truck or a trooper's fist coming toward the camera, give us Roger's experience directly (Figs. 11.10, 11.11).

Thornhill's opitical POV shots function within a narration that is often restricted not only to what he *sees* but to what he *knows*. The plane attack at Prairie Stop, for example, is confined wholly to Roger's range of knowledge. Hitchcock could have cut away from Roger waiting by the road in order to show us the villains plotting in their plane, but he does not. Similarly, when Roger is searching for George Kaplan's room and gets a phone call from the two henchmen, Hitchcock could have used crosscutting to show the villains phoning from the lobby. Instead, we learn that they are in the hotel no sooner than Roger does. And when Thornhill and his mother hurry out of the room, Hitchcock does not use crosscutting to show the villains in pursuit. This makes it more startling when Roger and his mother get on the elevator and discover the two men there already. In scenes like these, confining us to Thornhill's range of knowledge sharpens the effect of surprise.

Sometimes the same effect comes from the film's restricting us to Roger's range of knowledge and then giving us information that he does not at the moment have. On page 103 we suggested that this sort of surprise occurs when the plot shifts us from Roger's escape from the United Nations murder to the scene at the USIA office, where the staff discuss the case. At this point we learn that there is no George Kaplan—something that Roger will not discover for many more scenes to come.

The drifting away from Roger's range of knowledge yields a similar effect during the train trip from New York to Chicago. During several scenes, Eve Kendall helps Thornhill evade the police. Finally, they are alone and relatively safe in her compartment. At this point the narration shifts the range of knowledge. A message is delivered to another compartment. Hands unfold a note: "What do I do with him in the morning?" The camera then moves back to show us Leonard and Van Damm reading the message. Now we know that Eve is not merely a sympathetic stranger but someone working for the spy ring. Again, Roger will learn this much later. In such cases, the move to a more unrestricted range of information lets the narration put us a notch higher than Thornhill in the hierarchy of knowledge.

Such moments evoke surprise, but we have already noted that Hitchcock claimed in general to prefer to generate suspense (p. 104). Suspense is created by giving the spectator more information than the character has. In the scenes we have just mentioned, once the effect of surprise has been achieved, the narration can use our superior knowledge to build suspense across several sequences. After the audience knows that there is no George Kaplan, every attempt by Thornhill to find him will build up suspense about whether he will discover the truth. Once we learn that Eve is working for Van Damm, her message to Roger on behalf of "Kaplan" will make us uncertain as to whether Roger will fall into the trap.

In these examples, suspense arises across a series of scenes. Hitchcock also uses unrestricted narration to build up suspense within a single scene. His handling of the U.N. murder differs markedly from his treatment of the scene showing Roger and his mother in Kaplan's hotel room. In the hotel scene, Hitchcock refused to employ crosscutting to show the spies' pursuit. At the United Nations, however, he crosscuts between Roger, who is searching for Townsend, and Valerian, one of the thugs following him. Just before the murder, a rightward tracking shot establishes Valerian's position in the doorway (something of which Roger is wholly unaware). Here crosscutting and camera movement widen our frame of knowledge and create suspense as to the scene's outcome.

The sequence in Chicago's Union Station is handled very similarly. Here crosscutting moves us from Roger shaving in the men's room to Eve talking on the phone. Then another lateral tracking shot reveals that she is talking to Leonard, who is giving her orders from another phone booth. We now are certain that the message she will give Roger will endanger him, and the suspense is increased accordingly. (Note, however, that the narration does not reveal the conversation itself. As often happens, Hitchcock conceals certain information for the sake of further surprises.)

Thornhill's knowledge expands as the lines of action develop. On the third day, he discovers that Eve is Van Damm's mistress, that she is a double agent, and that Kaplan doesn't exist. He agrees to help the Professor in a scheme to clear Eve of any suspicion in Van Damm's eyes. When the scheme (a faked shooting in the Mount Rushmore restaurant) succeeds, Roger believes that Eve will leave Van Damm. Once more, however, he has been duped (as we have). The Professor insists that she must go off to Europe that night on Van Damm's private flight. Roger resists, but he is knocked out and held captive in a hospital. His escape leads to the final major sequence of the film.

Here the plot resolves all its lines of action, and the narration continues to expand and contract our knowledge for the sake of suspense and surprise. This climactic sequence comprises almost three hundred shots and runs for several minutes, but we can conveniently divide the sequence into three subsegments.

In the first subsegment, Roger arrives at Van Damm's house and reconnoiters. He clambers up to the window and learns from a conversation be-

Fig. 11.12

Fig. 11.13

Fig. 11.14

Fig. 11.15

Fig. 11.16

Fig. 11.17

tween Leonard and Van Damm that the piece of sculpture they bought at the auction contains microfilm. More important, he watches Leonard inform Van Damm that Eve is an American agent. This action is conveyed largely through optical POV as Roger watches in dismay (Figs. 11.12, 11.13) (see also Figs. 4.2–4.4, p. 106). At two moments, as Leonard and Van Damm face one another, the narration gives us optical POV shots from each man's standpoint (Figs. 11.14, 11.15), but these are enclosed, so to speak, within Roger's ongoing witnessing of the situation. For the first time in the film, Roger has more knowledge of the situation than any other character. He knows how the smuggling has been done, and he discovers that the villains intend to murder Eve.

The second phase of the sequence can be said to begin when Roger enters Eve's bedroom. She has gone back downstairs and is sitting on a couch. Again, Hitchcock emphasizes the restriction to Thornhill's knowledge by means of optical POV shots—now high-angle ones appropriate to his position at the balcony (Figs. 11.16, 11.17). In order to warn Eve, he uses his ROT monogrammed matchbook (a motif set up on the train as a joke). He tosses the matchbook down toward Eve. This initiates still more suspense when Leonard sees it, but he unconcernedly puts it in an ashtray on the coffee table. When Eve notices the matchbook, Hitchcock varies his handling of optical POV from the first subsegment. There he was willing to show us the face-off between Van Damm and Leonard (Figs. 11.14, 11.15). Now he does not show us Eve's eyes at all. Instead, through Roger's eyes, we see her back stiffen; we *infer* that she is looking at the matchbook (Fig. 11.18). Again, though, Roger's range of knowledge is the broadest, and his optical POV "encloses" another character's. On a pretext Eve returns to her room, and Roger warns her not to get on the plane.

As the spies make their way to the landing field outside, Roger starts to follow. Now Hitchcock's narration shifts again to show Van Damm's housekeeper spotting Roger's reflection in a television set. As earlier in the film, we know more than Roger does, and this generates suspense when she walks out . . . and returns with a pistol aimed at him.

The third subsegment takes place outdoors. Eve is about to get in the plane when a pistol shot distracts the spies' attention long enough for her to grab the statuette and race to the car Roger has stolen. This portion of the sequence confines us to Eve's range of knowledge, accentuating it with shots from her optical POV. The pattern of surprise interrupting a period of suspense—here, Roger's escape from the house interrupting Eve's tense walk to the plane—will dominate the rest of the sequence.

The last portion of the sequence depicts the chase across the presidents' faces on Mount Rushmore. Some crosscutting informs us of the spies' progress in following the couple, but on the whole the narration restricts us to what Eve and Thornhill know. As usual, some moments are heightened by optical POV shots, as when Eve watches Roger and Valerian roll down what seems to be a sheer drop. At the climax, Eve is dangling over the edge while Roger is clutching one of her hands and Leonard grinds his foot into Roger's other hand. It is a classic, not to say conventional, situation of suspense. Again, however, the narration reveals the limits of our knowledge. A rifle shot cracks out and Leonard falls to the ground. The Professor has arrived and captured Van Damm, and a marksman has shot Leonard. Once more, a restricted range of knowledge has enabled the narration to spring a surprise on the audience.

Fig. 11.18

The same effect gets magnified at the very end. In a series of optical POV shots, Roger pulls Eve up from the brink. But this gesture is made continuous, in both sound and image, with that of him pulling her up to a train bunk. The narration ignores the details of their rescue in order to cut short the suspense of Eve's plight. Such a self-conscious transition is not completely out of place in a film that has taken time for offhand jokes. (During the opening credits, Hitchcock himself is shown being shut out of a bus. As Roger strides into the Plaza Hotel, about to be plunged into his adventure, the Muzak is playing "It's a Most Unusual Day.") This concluding twist shows once again that Hitchcock's moment-by-moment manipulation of our knowledge yields a constantly shifting play between the probable and the unexpected, between suspense and surprise.

■ *DO THE RIGHT THING*

> 1989. Forty Acres and a Mule Filmworks (distributed by Universal). Directed and scripted by Spike Lee. Photographed by Ernest Dickerson. Edited by Barry Alexander Brown. Music by Bill Lee *et al.* With Danny Aiello, Ossie Davis, Ruby Dee, Giancarlo Esposito, Spike Lee, Bill Nunn, John Turturro, Rosie Perez.

At first viewing, Spike Lee's *Do The Right Thing*, with its many brief, disconnected scenes, restlessly wandering camera, and large number of characters without goals might not seem a classical narrative film. And indeed, as we shall see, in some ways it does depart from classical usage. Yet it has the redundantly clear action and strong forward impetus to the plot that we associate with classical filmmaking. It also fits into a familiar genre of American cinema—the social problem film. Moreover, closer analysis reveals that Lee has also drawn upon many traits of classicism to give an underlying unity to this apparently loosely constructed film.

Do The Right Thing takes place in the predominantly African-American Bedford-Stuyvesant section of Brooklyn during a heat wave. Sexual and racial tensions rise as Mookie, an irresponsible pizza delivery man, tries to get along with his Puerto-Rican girlfriend, Tina, and with his Italian-American boss, Sal. An elderly drunk, Da Mayor, sets out to ingratiate himself with his sharp-tongued neighbor, Mother Sister. An escalating quarrel between Sal and two customers, Buggin' Out and Radio Raheem, leads to a fight in which Radio Raheem is killed by police. The pizzeria is burned in the ensuing riot.

Do The Right Thing has many more individual sequences than, say, *His Girl Friday,* with its neatly delineated 13 scenes (p. 384). Even lumping together some of the very briefest scenes, there are at least 42 segments! Laying out a detailed segmentation of *Do The Right Thing* might be useful for another analysis, but here we want to concentrate on how Lee weaves his many scenes into a whole.

One important means of unifying the film is its setting. The entire narrative is played out on one block in Bedford-Stuyvesant. Sal's Famous Pizzeria and the Korean market opposite create a spatial anchor at one end of the block, and much of the action takes place there. Other scenes are played out in or in front of the brownstone buildings that line most of the rest of the street. Encounters among members of this neighborhood provide the causality for the narrative.

To match the limited setting, the action takes place in a restricted time frame—from one morning to the next. Structuring a film around a brief slice of the life of a group of characters is rare but not unknown in American filmmaking, as with *Street Scene, Dead End, American Graffiti,* and *Nashville.*

The radio DJ, Mister Señor Love Daddy, provides a running motif that also binds the film's events together. He appears in close-up in the first shot of the opening scene, and this initial broadcast provides important information about the setting and the weather—a heat wave which will intensify the characters' tensions and contribute to the final violent outbreak. As the DJ speaks, the camera tracks slowly out and cranes up to reveal the street, still empty in the early morning. At intervals throughout the film, Mister Señor Love Daddy also provides commentary on the action, as when he tells a group of characters spewing racist diatribes to "chill out." The music he plays creates sound bridges between otherwise unconnected scenes, since the radios in different locations are often tuned to his station. The end of the film echoes the beginning, as the camera tracks with Mookie in the street and we hear the DJ's voice giving a similar spiel to the one on the previous morning, then dedicating the final song to the dead Radio Raheem.

As the setting and the use of the neighborhood radio station suggest, *Do The Right Thing* centers more on the community as a whole than upon a few central characters. On the one hand, there are older traditions which are worth preserving, represented by the elderly characters: the moral strength of the matriarch Mother Sister, the decency and courage of Da Mayor, the wit and common sense of the three chatting men, ML, Sweet Dick Willie, and Coconut Sid. On the other hand, the younger people need to create a new community spirit by overcoming sexual and racial conflict. The women are portrayed as trying to make the angry young African-American men more responsible. Tina pressures Mookie to pay more attention to her and to their son; Jade lectures both her brother Mookie and the excitable Buggin' Out, telling the latter he should direct his energies toward doing "something positive in the community." The emphasis on community is underscored by the fact that most of the characters address each other by their nicknames.

One of the main conflicts in the film arises when Sal refuses to add some pictures of African-American heroes to his "Hall of Fame" photo gallery of Italian-Americans. Sal might have become a sort of elder statesman in the community, where he has run his pizzeria for 25 years. He seems to like the kids who eat his pizza, but he also views the restaurant as entirely his domain, emphatically declaring that he's the boss. Thus he reveals his lack of real integration into the community and ends by goading the more hot-headed elements into attacking him.

In creating its community, *Do The Right Thing* includes an unusually large number of characters for a classical film. Again, however, a closer examination shows that only eight of them provide the main causal action: Mookie, Tina, Sal, Sal's son Pino, Mother Sister, Da Mayor, Buggin' Out, and Radio Raheem. The others, intriguing or amusing as they may be, are more peripheral, mainly reacting to the action set in motion by these characters' conflicts and goals. (Some modern American screenwriting manuals recommend seven to eight important characters as the maximum for a clearly comprehensible film, so Lee is not departing from tradition as much as it might seem.) Moreover, the main causal action falls into two related lines, as in traditional Hollywood films: one involves the community's relations to Sal and his sons, the other deals with Mookie's personal life. Mookie becomes the pivotal figure, linking the two lines of action.

We have suggested that *Do The Right Thing* departs from classical narrative conventions in some ways. One such departure comes with respect to characters' goals. Usually the main characters of a film formulate clear-cut, long-range goals that bring them into conflict with each other. In *Do The Right Thing*, most of the main eight characters create goals only sporadically; the goals are sometimes introduced fairly late in the film, and some are vague.

Buggin' Out, for example, demands that Sal put up pictures of some black heroes on the pizzeria wall. When Sal refuses and throws him out, he shouts to the customers to boycott Sal's. Yet a little while later, when he tries to persuade his neighbors to participate in the boycott, they all refuse, and his project seems to sputter out. Then, later in the film, Radio Raheem and the mentally retarded Smiley agree to join him. Their visit to the pizzeria to threaten Sal then precipitates the climactic action. Ironically, Buggin' Out's goal is briefly achieved when Smiley puts a photograph of Malcolm X and Martin Luther King Jr. on the wall of the burning pizzeria—but by that point Buggin' Out is on his way to jail.

Mookie's goal is hinted at when we first see him. He is counting money, and he constantly emphasizes that he just wants to work and get paid. His repeated reference to the fact that he is due to be paid in the evening creates the film's only appointment, helping to emphasize the compressed time scheme. Yet his purpose remains unclear. Does he simply want the money so that he can move out of his sister's apartment, as she demands? Or does he also plan to help Tina care for their son?

Sal's goal is similarly vague—to keep operating his pizzeria in the face of rising tensions. Da Mayor articulates one of the few really clear-cut goals in the film when he tells Mother Sister that someday she will be nice to him. After he persistently acts courteously and bravely, she does in fact relent and become his friend. Sal's virulently racist son Pino has a goal—trying to convince his father that they should sell the pizzeria and get out of the black neighborhood. Perhaps he will get his desire at the end, although the narrative leaves open the question of whether Sal will rebuild.

In traditional classical films, clear-cut goals generate conflict, since the characters' desires often clash with each other. Lee neatly reverses this pattern by playing down goals but creating a community which is full of conflict from the very beginning of the film. Racial and sexual arguments break out frequently, and insults fly. Such conflict is tied to the fact that *Do The Right Thing* is a social problem film. Its didactic message gives it much of its overall unity. Everything that happens relates to a central question: With the community riven with such tensions, what can be done to heal it?

The characters' goals and actions suggest some of the possible ways of reacting to the situation. Some of the characters desire simply to avoid or escape this tense atmosphere—Pino by leaving the neighborhood, Da Mayor by overcoming Mother Sister's animosity. Mookie attempts to stay out of trouble by not siding with either Sal or his black friends in their escalating quarrel; only the death of Radio Raheem drives him to join in, and indeed initiate, the attack on Sal's pizzeria.

Other characters attempt to solve their problems. One central goal is Tina's desire to get Mookie to behave more responsibly and spend time with her and with their child. There is a suggestion at the end that she may be succeeding to some extent. Mookie gets his pay from Sal and says that he will get another job and that he's going to see his son. The last shot shows him walking down the now-quiet street, hinting that he may really visit his son more regularly in the future.

The central question in the film, however, is not whether any one character will achieve his or her goals. It is whether the pervasive conflicts can be resolved peacefully or violently. As the DJ says on the morning after the riot, "Are we gonna live together—together are we gonna live?"

Do The Right Thing leaves unanswered questions at the end. Will Sal rebuild? Is Mookie really going back to see his son? Most importantly, though the conflict that flared up has died down, it is still present in the community, waiting to resurface. The old problem of how to tame it remains, and so the film does not achieve complete closure. Indeed, such an ending is typical of the social problem film. While the immediate conflict may be resolved, the underlying dilemma that caused it remains.

That is also why there is a deliberate ambiguity at the end. Just as we are left at the end of *Citizen Kane* to wonder whether the revelation of the meaning of "Rosebud" explains Kane's character, in *Do The Right Thing* we are left to ponder what "the right thing" is. The film continues after the final story action, with two nondiegetic quotations from Martin Luther King Jr. and Malcolm X. The King passage advocates a nonviolent approach to the struggle for civil rights, while Malcolm X condones violence in self-defense.

Do The Right Thing refuses to suggest which leader is right—although the narrative action and the use of the phrase "By any means necessary" at the end of the credits seems to weight the film's position in favor of Malcolm X. Still, the juxtaposition of the two quotations, in combination with the open-ended narrative, also seems calculated to spur debate. Perhaps the implication is that each position is viable under certain circumstances. The line of action involving Sal's pizzeria ends in violence; yet at the same time Da Mayor is able to win Mother Sister's friendship gently and patiently.

As in its narrative structure, the style of *Do The Right Thing* stretches the traditional techniques of classical filmmaking. It begins with a credits sequence during which Rosie Perez performs a vigorous and aggressive dance to the rap song "Fight the Power." The editing here is strongly discontinuous, as she wears sometimes a red dress, sometimes a boxer's outfit, and sometimes a jacket and pants. One moment she is on the street, then she suddenly appears in an alley. This brief sequence, which is not part of the narrative, is very like a music video, employing the flashy style made familiar by MTV and television commercials.

Nothing in the rest of *Do The Right Thing* is quite as discontinuous or extreme as the credits sequence, but Lee uses a looser version of the traditional continuity system. Veteran film editor Dede Allen has referred to "an extreme MTV cutting" in some modern Hollywood films. Lee himself has made both music videos and commercials in addition to his feature films. He draws upon a broad range of techniques, handling some scenes in virtuosic long takes, others with shot/reverse shot, others with extensive camera movements. In two cases, he even cuts together two takes of the same action, so that the plot presents a single important story event twice: when Mookie first kisses Tina and when the garbage can hits Sal's window. One result of this varied style is a suggestion of the vigor and variety of the community itself.

Fig. 11.19

Despite the many quick changes of locale, Lee uses continuity devices to establish space clearly. As we saw in Chapter 8, he is adept at using shot/reverse shot without breaking the axis of action (see Figs. 8.80–8.85, from *She's Gotta Have It*, p. 295). *Do The Right Thing* similarly contains many shot/reverse-shot conversations where the eyelines are consistent, as when Jade chats with Buggin' Out in the street (Figs. 11.19, 11.20). Yet Lee opts to handle other conversations without any editing. The lengthy conversation in which Pino asks Sal to sell the pizzeria is handled in one long take, beginning with a track in on them (Figs. 11.21, 11.22) and lasting until Smiley appears outside (Fig. 11.23) and Pino chases him away.

Cinematic technique frequently emphasizes the community as a whole. Indeed, one reason why the film has so many segments is because there are frequent cuts from one action to another. The narration is largely unrestricted,

Fig. 11.20

Fig. 11.21

Fig. 11.22

Fig. 11.23

flitting from one group of characters to another, seldom lingering with any individual. Similarly, complex camera movements follow characters through the street, catching glimpses of other activities going on in the background. Other camera movements slide away from one line of action to another. For example, on the morning after the riot, Da Mayor wakes up in Mother Sister's apartment (Fig. 11.24). They talk and move out into her front room, the camera tracking back in front of them. As they reach the window, the camera passes through it (Fig. 11.25) and cranes down to a close view of Mookie, on his way to the pizzeria (Fig. 11.26).

The dense sound track also helps characterize the community. As Mookie walks past a row of houses, the sounds of radios turned to different stations fade up and down, hinting at the offscreen presence of the inhabitants. The music broadcast by the DJ plays a large role in drawing the many brief scenes together, with the same song carrying over various exchanges of dialogue. The different ethnic groups are characterized by the types of music they listen to.

Style also stresses the underlying problems in the community. Radio Raheem's threatening demeanor is emphasized in some scenes by his direct address into a wide-angle lens, as when he orders a slice of pizza from Sal, who has ordered him to turn his radio off (Fig. 11.27). Mookie's self-absorption and lack of interest in the neighborhood is suggested in a visual motif

Fig. 11.24

Fig. 11.25

Fig. 11.26

Fig. 11.27

of high-angle views showing him stepping unheedingly on a cheerful chalk picture of a house that a little girl is drawing on the pavement (Fig. 11.28). Sound contributes to the racial tensions, as in the scenes where Radio Raheem annoys people by playing his rap song at high volume.

Thus *Do The Right Thing*, despite its stretching of traditional Hollywood conventions, remains a good example of a contemporary approach to classical filmmaking. Its style reflects the looser techniques which became conventions of post-1960s cinema—an era when the impact of television and European art films inspired filmmakers to incorporate somewhat more variety into the Hollywood system. Even the plot's departures from tradition are somewhat motivated because Lee adopts the basic purpose of the social problem film— to make us think and to stir debate.

Fig. 11.28

NARRATIVE ALTERNATIVES TO CLASSICAL FILMMAKING

■ *BREATHLESS (À BOUT DE SOUFFLE)*

1960. Les Films Georges de Beauregard, Impéria Films and Société Nouvelle de Cinéma. Directed by Jean-Luc Godard. Story outline by François Truffaut, dialogue by Godard. Photographed by Raoul Coutard. Edited by Cécile Decugis. Music by Martial Solal. With Jean-Paul Belmondo, Jean Seberg, Daniel Boulanger, Henri-Jacques Huet, Van Doude, Jean-Pierre Melville.

In some ways, *Breathless* imitates a 1940s Hollywood trend, the *film noir*, or "dark film." Such films dealt with hard-boiled detectives, gangsters, or ordinary men tempted into crime. Often a seductive *femme fatale* lured the protagonist into a dangerous mission for hidden purposes of her own (e.g., *The Maltese Falcon, Double Indemnity*). *Breathless*'s plot links it to a common *noir* vehicle—the "outlaw" movie involving young criminals on the run (e.g., *They Live by Night, Gun Crazy*).

The bare-bones story could serve as the basis of a Hollywood script. A car thief, Michel, kills a motorcycle cop and flees to Paris in order to get money to escape to Italy. He also tries to convince Patricia, an American art student and aspiring writer with whom he had a brief affair, to go with him. After equivocating for nearly two days, she agrees. Just as Michel is about to receive the cash he needs, Patricia calls the police, and they kill him.

Yet Godard's presentation of this story could never pass for a polished studio product. For one thing, Michel's behavior is presented as driven *by* the very movies that *Breathless* imitates. He rubs his thumb across his lips in imitation of his idol Humphrey Bogart. Yet he is a petty thief whose life spins out of control. He can only fantasize himself as a romantic Hollywood tough guy.

The film's ambivalent attitude toward Hollywood cinema also pervades form and technique. As we've seen, the norms of classical style and storytelling promote narrative clarity and unity. By contrast, *Breathless* appears awkward and casual, almost amateurish. It makes character motivations ambiguous and lingers over incidental dialogue. Its editing jumps about frenet-

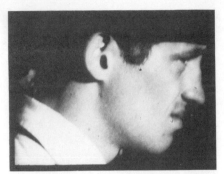

Fig. 11.29

Fig. 11.30

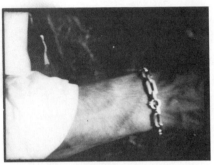

Fig. 11.31

Fig. 11.32

ically. And, whereas *films noirs* were made largely in the studio, where selective lighting could swathe the characters in a brooding atmosphere, *Breathless* utilizes location shooting with available lighting.

These strategies make Michel's story quirky, uncertain, and deglamorized. They also ask the audience to enjoy the film's rough-edged reworking of Hollywood formulas. An opening title (missing from American prints) dedicates the film to Monogram Pictures, a "Poverty Row" studio which churned out ramshackle B-movies. The title seems to announce a film which is indebted to Hollywood but not wholly bound by its norms.

Like many protagonists in classical Hollywood films, Michel has two main goals. In order to leave France, he must search for his friend Antonio, the only one who can cash a check for him. He also hopes to persuade Patricia to go with him, and it becomes apparent as the action progresses that, despite his flippant attitude, his love for her outweighs his desire to escape.

In a classical film, these goals would drive the action along fairly steadily. Yet in *Breathless* the plot moves in fits and starts. Brief scenes—some largely unconnected to the goals—alternate with long stretches of seemingly irrelevent dialogue. Most of *Breathless*'s 22 separate segments run four minutes or less. One 43-second scene consists simply of Michel pausing in front of a theater and looking at a picture of Bogart.

Scenes containing crucial action are sometimes brief and confusing. The murder of the traffic cop, an event that triggers much of what follows, is handled in a very elliptical fashion. In long shot, we see the officer approaching Michel's car, parked in a side road. In medium long shot Michel reaches into the car for the gun. A close shot of his head follows, as the cop's voice is heard saying, "Don't move or I'll drill you" (Fig. 11.29). Two very brief close-ups pan along Michel's arm and along the gun (Figs. 11.30, 11.31), with the sound of a gunshot. We then get a glimpse of the cop falling into some underbrush (Fig. 11.32), followed by an extreme long shot of Michel, running far across a field. So much action has been left out that we can barely comprehend what is happening, let alone judge whether Michel shot deliberately or by accident.

In contrast to the whirlwind presentation of this key action, a very lengthy conversation in the middle of the film brings the narrative progression almost to a standstill. For nearly 25 minutes Michel and Patricia chat in her bedroom. At some points Michel attempts to further his goals, trying vainly to phone Antonio and to persuade Patricia to come to Rome. Most of the conversation, however, is trivial, as when Michel criticizes the way Patricia puts on lipstick or when she asks whether he prefers records or the radio. The pair try to outstare each other, and they discuss Patricia's new poster. So rambling is their exchange that some critics have assumed that the dialogue was improvised (although Godard attests that it was all scripted).

At one point, Patricia suggests that she will not run off with him because she does not know if she loves him. Michel: "When will you know?" Patricia: "Soon." Michel: "What does that mean—soon? In a month, in a year?" Patricia: "Soon means soon." So although the pair make love, by the end of the long scene (which occupies nearly a third of this 89-minute film) we still do not have a definite step forward or backward in Michel's courting of

Patricia, and he has made no progress toward escaping. Such scenes make him seem more like a wandering, easily distracted delinquent than the desperate, driven hero of a *film noir*.

It is not until the scene outside the *Tribune* office that another decisive causal action occurs. A passerby (played by Godard) recognizes Michel from a newspaper photograph and tells the police. This triggers a chain of events that will lead to Michel's death. Yet immediately the plot meanders once more. In the next scene, Patricia participates in a news conference with a famous novelist, a character unrelated to the main action. Most of the questions asked by the reporters deal with the differences between men and women, but the novelist's responses seem more playful than meaningful. Finally Patricia asks him his greatest ambition, and he replies enigmatically, "To become immortal and then to die." Patricia's puzzled glance into the camera that ends the scene hints at the ambiguity that will linger at the film's end.

After Detective Vital questions Patricia at the *Tribune* office, she and Michel realize that the police are on his trail. Now *Breathless* begins to progress in a somewhat more conventional way. In the next scene, Patricia says that she loves Michel "enormously," and they steal a car. Here Michel seems to reach his romantic goal, as Patricia commits herself to fleeing with him. When Antonio agrees to bring the cash the next morning, Michel moves toward his second goal. We might anticipate possible outcomes: The pair will escape, or one or both will be killed in the attempt. The next morning, however, Patricia confounds our expectations by betraying Michel to Vital. Even then Michel has a last chance. Antonio arrives just before the police, with money and a getaway car—yet Michel cannot bring himself to leave Patricia.

The ending is particularly enigmatic. As Michel lies bleeding to death, Patricia looks down at him. He slowly makes the same playful faces at her that he had made during their bedroom conversation. Muttering "That's really disgusting" ("C'est vraiment dégueulasse"), he dies. Patricia asks Detective Vital what he said, and Vital misreports Michel's last words: "He said, 'You are really a bitch' " ("Il a dit, 'vous êtes vraiment une dégueulasse' "). (Unfortunately, the English subtitles suggest that Vital reports Michel's words accurately.) We are left to ponder what Michel thought was disgusting—Patricia's betrayal, his own last-minute failure to flee, or simply his death. In the final shot, Patricia looks out at the camera, asks what "dégueulasse" means, rubs her lips with the Bogart-inspired gesture that Michel has used throughout the film (Fig. 11.33), and abruptly turns her back on us as the image fades out.

Breathless achieves a degree of closure: Michel fails to achieve his goals. But we are left with many questions. Although Michel and Patricia talk constantly about themselves, we learn remarkably little about why they act as they do. Unlike characters in classical films, they do not have a set of clearly defined traits. The film begins with Michel saying, "All in all, I'm a dumb bastard," and in a way his actions bear this out. Yet we never learn background information which would explain his decisions. Why did he become a car thief? Since he casually leaves his female accomplice early in the film, what makes him willing to risk death to stay with Patricia, a woman

Fig. 11.33

whom he has known only briefly? Because dying for the love of an unworthy woman is what a would-be Hollywood hero is supposed to do?

Patricia's traits and goals are even more amorphous and ambiguous. When Michel first finds her selling newspapers on the Champs Elysées, she is far from welcoming. Yet at the scene's end she runs back to give him a kiss. She keeps saying she wants to get a job as a *Tribune* reporter and to write a novel, yet she seems to throw these ambitions away when she thinks she loves Michel. Patricia also tells Michel she is pregnant by him, but she has not received the final test results, and she never raises this as a reason why she should stay in Paris. She often says that she is scared, yet after she and Michel steal a car, she remarks, "It's too late now to be scared." This hints that she has resolved her own doubts and has thrown her lot definitively in with Michel. When she suddenly betrays him, she does not intend that he should be killed but simply wants to force him to leave her. Still, her speech about why she informed on Michel seems not really to explain her abrupt change of heart. Just as Michel is ill-suited to be a tough guy, Patricia is too naive and indecisive to play the role of the classic *femme fatale*.

In the outlined *film noir*, the characters are intensely committed to one another; here Michel and Patricia seem to have few strong feelings about what they do. When the treacherous woman deceives the *noir* hero, he often becomes bitterly disillusioned; but Michel apparently does not blame Patricia for betraying him. It is as if these ambivalent, diffident, confused characters are unable to play out the desperately passionate roles that the Hollywood tradition has assigned to them.

Breathless's elliptical, occasionally opaque narrative is presented through techniques that are equally unconventional. As we have seen, Hollywood films use a three-point lighting system of key, fill, and back light, carefully controlled in a film studio (pp. 181–182). *Breathless* was shot entirely on location, even for interiors. Godard and cinematographer Raoul Coutard opted not to add any artificial light in the settings. As a result, the characters' faces sometimes fall into shadow, as when Patricia sits against a window and lights a cigarette (Fig. 11.34).

Fig. 11.34

Filming on location, especially in small apartments, would ordinarily make it difficult to obtain a variety of camera angles and movements. But taking advantage of new portable equipment, Coutard was able to film while hand-holding the camera. Several lengthy tracking shots follow the characters, as in the three-minute take of Michel's first meeting with Patricia as she strolls along the Champs Elysées selling papers (Fig. 11.35). Coutard apparently sat in a wheelchair to film this shot, as well as more elaborate movements that follow the characters in interiors. When Michel visits a travel agent trying to claim his check, the framing glides and turns with ease as he moves around the desks and through the corridor (Fig. 11.36). Such shots recall the location shooting of many *films noirs*, such as the final airport scenes of Stanley Kubrick's *The Killing*, but the low camera position and the passersby who turn to look at the actors (as with the man at the right in Fig. 11.35) call attention to the technique in a way which departs from Hollywood usage.

Fig. 11.35

Even more striking than the mise-en-scene is Godard's editing. Again he sometimes follows tradition but at other points he breaks away. Standard

Fig. 11.36

Fig. 11.37

Fig. 11.38

Fig. 11.39

shot/reverse-shot cutting organizes several scenes, as when Michel pauses in front of a photograph of Bogart that seems to look back at him (Figs. 11.37, 11.38). Similarly, when Michel spots the man examining the telltale photo in the newspaper, Godard supplies correctly matched glances. Since this is a turning point in the plot, the adherence to the 180° rule makes it evident that the man has spotted Michel and may inform on him.

Yet what makes the film still quite jolting today are its violations of continuity editing. If there is one type of cut that the Hollywood editor deplores, it is the jump cut, in which a segment of time is eliminated without the camera being moved to a new vantage point (p. 303). Yet *Breathless* employs jump cuts throughout. In an early scene, when Michel visits an old girlfriend, jump cuts shift their positions abruptly. (Fig. 11.39 shows the last frame of one shot, Fig. 11.40 the first frame of the next.) We have seen another example, when Godard presents a series of jump cuts of Patricia during a conversation in a car (Figs. 8.110, 8.111, again showing the last and first frames of contiguous shots).

Fig. 11.40

Even when Godard shifts the camera position between cuts, he may drop out a bit of time or mismatch the actors' positions. At many cuts the action seems to jerk forward, like a needle skipping on a phonograph record. One effect of this jumpy editing is to enliven the rhythm. At times, as during the murder of the police officer, we have to be very alert to follow the action. This fast pace is reinforced by the fact that, as we have seen, most of the individual scenes run for under four minutes. The elliptical editing also makes certain scenes stand out by contrast: the lengthy single-take scenes with moving camera and the rambling 25-minute conversation in Patricia's apartment.

Fig. 11.41

Aside from avoiding matches on action, Godard often flaunts the moments when he does not adhere to the 180° rule. Patricia walks along reading a paper: she is moving rightward in one shot (Fig. 11.41) and leftward in the next (Fig. 11.42), flagrantly violating conventional screen direction (see p. 286). In the opening scene, as Michel's accomplice indicates a car he wants to steal, the eyelines are quite unclear, and we get little sense of where the two are in relation to each other.

The film's sound often reinforces these editing discontinuities. When the characters' dialogue and other diegetic sounds continue over the jump cuts, we are forced to notice the contradiction: Time is apparently omitted from the visual track but not from the sound track. The location shooting also

Fig. 11.42

created situations in which ambient noises intrude on the dialogue. A passing siren outside Patricia's apartment nearly overwhelms her conversation with Michel during the long central scene. Later the press conference with Parvulesco inexplicably takes place on an airport observation platform, where the loud whines of nearby planes drown out conversation. Such scenes lack the balance of volumes of the well-mixed Hollywood sound track.

Godard's break with the rules of smooth sound and picture steers *Breathless* away from the glamorous portrayals seen in the Hollywood crime film. The stylistic awkwardness suits the pseudo-documentary roughness of filming in an actual, hectic Paris. The discontinuities are also consistent with other nontraditional techniques, like the motif of the characters' mysterious glances into the camera. In addition, the jolts in picture and sound create a self-conscious narration that makes the viewer aware of its stylistic choices. In making the director's hand more apparent, the film presents itself as a deliberately unpolished revision of tradition.

Godard did not set out to criticize Hollywood films. Instead, he took genre conventions identified with 1940s America and gave them a contemporary Parisian setting and a modern, self-conscious treatment. He thereby created a new type of hero and heroine. Aimless, somewhat banal lovers on the run became central to later outlaw movies such as *Bonnie and Clyde, Badlands,* and *True Romance.* More broadly, Godard's film became a model for directors who wished to create exuberantly offhand homages to, and reworkings of, Hollywood tradition. This attitude would be central to the stylistic movement which *Breathless* helped launch, the French New Wave. (See Chapter 12, pp. 464–467.)

■ *TOKYO STORY (TOKYO MONOGATARI)*

1953. Shochiku/Ofuna, Japan. Directed by Yasujiro Ozu. Script by Ozu and Kogo Noda. Photographed by Yuharu Atsuta. With Chishu Ryu, Chieko Higashiyama, So Yamamura, Haruko Sugimura, Setsuko Hara.

We have seen how the classical Hollywood approach to filmmaking created a stylistic system ("continuity") in order to establish and maintain a clear narrative space and time. The continuity system is a specific set of guidelines which a filmmaker may follow. But some filmmakers do not use the continuity system. They may flaunt the guidelines by violating them, as Godard does in *Breathless,* creating a casual, lively film. Or they may develop a set of alternative guidelines—at least as strict as Hollywood's—which allows them to make films that are quite distinct from classical ones.

Yasujiro Ozu is one such filmmaker. His approach to the creation of a narrative differs from that used in more classical films like *His Girl Friday* or *Stagecoach.* Instead of making narrative events the central organizing principle, Ozu tends to decenter narrative somewhat. As a result, spatial and temporal structures come forward and create their own interest. *Tokyo Story,* the first Ozu film to make a considerable impression in the West, offers an enlightening introduction to some of Ozu's characteristic filmmaking strategies.

Tokyo Story presents a simple narrative of an elderly provincial couple who visit their grown children in Tokyo, only to find themselves treated as inconvenient nuisances. The narrative is quiet and contemplative, yet Ozu's style does not simply conform to some characteristically spiritual Japanese system of filmmaking. Indeed, Japanese filmmakers and critics found his nonclassical approach as puzzling as did Western audiences. By creating a systematic alternative method of shaping spatial and temporal relations, Ozu sought to engage the spectator's attention more deeply. While in Hollywood style is subservient to narrative, Ozu makes it an equal partner. We watch the narrative action, the spatial relations, and the temporal relations unfold simultaneously, and all are equally dramatic and engaging. As a result, even a simple narrative like that of *Tokyo Story* becomes fresh and fascinating.

Tokyo Story's narration is, by classical standards, rather oblique. Sometimes we learn of important narrative events only after they have occurred. The last portion of *Tokyo Story*, for example, involves a series of events surrounding the sudden illness and death of the grandmother of a family. Although the grandparents are the film's two central characters, we do not see the grandmother falling ill. We hear about it only when her son and daughter receive telegrams with the news. Similarly, the grandmother's death occurs between scenes. In one scene her children are gathered by her bedside, and in the next scene they are mourning her.

Yet these ellipses are not evidence of a fast-paced film such as *His Girl Friday*, which must cover a lot of narrative ground in a hurry. On the contrary, the sequences of *Tokyo Story* often linger over details: the melancholy conversation between the grandfather and his friends in a bar as they discuss their disappointment in their children, or the grandmother's walk on a Sunday with her grandchild. The result is a shift in the narrative balance. Key narrative events are deemphasized by means of ellipses, whereas narrative events that we do see in the plot are simple and understated.

Accompanying this shift away from a presentation of the most highly dramatic events of the narrative is a sliding away from naratively significant space. Scenes do not begin and end with shots that frame the most important narrative elements in the mise-en-scene. Instead of the usual transitional devices, such as dissolves and fades, Ozu typically employs a series of separate transitional shots linked by cuts. And these transitional shots often show spaces not directly connected with the action of the scene; the spaces are usually *near* where that action will take place. The opening of the film, for example, has five shots of the port town of Onomichi—the bay, schoolchildren, a passing train—before the sixth shot reveals the grandparents packing for their trip to Tokyo. Although a couple of important motifs make their first appearances in these first five shots, no narrative causes occur to get the action underway. (Compare the openings of *His Girl Friday* and *North by Northwest*.) Nor do these transitional shots appear only at the beginning. Several sequences in Tokyo start with shots of factory smokestacks, even though no action ever occurs in these locales.

These transitions have only a minimal function as establishing shots. Sometimes the transitions do not establish space at all but tend to confuse the space of the upcoming scene. After the daughter-in-law, Noriko, gets a phone call at work telling her of the grandmother's illness, the scene ends in a medium shot of her sitting pensively at her desk; the only diegetic sound

Fig. 11.43

Fig. 11.44

Fig. 11.45

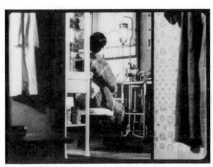

Fig. 11.46

is the loud clack of typewriters (Fig. 11.43). A nondiegetic musical transition comes up in this shot. Then there is a cut to a low-angle long shot of a building under construction (Fig. 11.44). Riveting noises replace the typewriters, with the music continuing. The next shot is another low angle of the construction site (Fig. 11.45).

A cut changes the locale to the clinic belonging to the eldest son, Dr. Hirayama. The sister, Shige, is present. The music ends and the new scene begins (Fig. 11.46). In this segment, the two shots of the construction site are not necessary to the action. The film does not give us any indication where the building under construction is. We might assume that it is outside Noriko's office, but the riveting sound is not audible in the interior shots.

As usual, we should look for the functions of such stylistic devices. It is hard to assign such transitional shots either explicit or implicit meanings. For example, someone might propose that the transitional shots symbolize the "new Tokyo" that is alien to the visiting grandparents from a village reminiscent of the old Japan. But often the transitional spaces do not involve outdoor locales, and some shots are within the characters' homes. A more systematic function, we suggest, is narrational, having to do with the flow of story information.

Ozu's narration alternates between scenes of story action and inserted portions that lead us to or away from them. As we watch the film, we start to form expectations about these "wedged-in" shots. Ozu emphasizes stylistic patterning by creating anticipation about when a transition will come and what it will show. The patterning may delay our expectations and even create some surprise.

For example, early in the film Mrs. Hirayama, the doctor's wife, argues with her son, Minoru, over where to move his desk to make room for the grandparents. This issue is dropped, and there follows a scene of the grandparents' arrival. This ends on a conversation in an upstairs room. Transitional music again comes up over the end of the scene. The next shot frames an empty hallway downstairs that contains Minoru's school desk, but no one is in the shot. There follows an exterior long shot of children running along a ridge near the house; these children are not characters in the action. Finally, a cut back inside reveals Minoru at his father's desk in the clinic portion of the house, studying. Here the editing creates a very indirect route between two scenes, going first to a place where we expect a character to be (at his own desk) but is not; then the scene moves completely away from the action, outdoors. Only then, in the third shot, does a character reappear and the action continue. In these transitional passages, a kind of game emerges, one that asks us to form expectations not only about story action but about the editing and mise-en-scene.

Within scenes, Ozu's editing patterns are as systematic as those of Hollywood, but they tend to be sharply opposed to continuity rules. For example, Ozu does not observe the 180° line, the "axis of action." Nor is his "violation" of these rules occasional, as Ford's is in *Stagecoach* (p. 288). Ozu frequently cuts 180° across the line to frame the scene's space from the opposite direction. This, of course, violates rules of screen direction, since characters or objects on the right in the first shot will appear on the left in the second, and vice versa. At the beginning of a scene in Shige's beauty

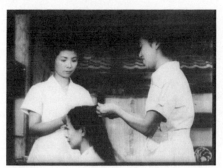
Fig. 11.47

Fig. 11.48

Fig. 11.49

Fig. 11.50

Fig. 11.51

salon, the initial interior medium shot frames Shige from opposite the front door (Fig. 11.47). Then a 180° cut reveals a medium long shot of a woman under a hair dryer; the camera now faces the rear of the salon (Fig. 11.48). Another cut 180° presents a new long shot of the room, again oriented toward the door, and the grandparents come into the salon (Fig. 11.49). Rather than being an isolated violation of continuity rules, this is Ozu's typical way of framing and editing a scene.

Ozu is a master of matching on action, but he often does so in unusual ways. For example, as Noriko and the grandmother walk toward the door of Noriko's apartment, there is a 180° cut from a head-on view (Fig. 11.50) to a tails-on framing (Fig. 11.51). The women's movements are closely matched, but because the consistent camera height and distance create such similar framings, the effect at the cut is to make it seem momentarily that the pair "bump into" themselves. Their screen positions, left to right, are also abruptly reversed, something which is usually considered an error in continuity. A classical filmmaker would most likely avoid such an unusual cut, but Ozu uses it here and in other films as part of his distinctive style.

As these examples illustrate, Ozu does not restrict his camera and editing patterns to the semicircular space on one side of the axis of action. He cuts in a full circle around the action, usually in segments of 90 or 180°. This means that backgrounds change drastically, as in both previous examples. In a Hollywood film, the camera rarely crosses the axis of action to look at the fourth wall. Because surroundings change more frequently in *Tokyo Story*, they become more prominent in relation to the action; the viewer must pay attention to setting or become confused.

Fig. 11.52

Fig. 11.53

Fig. 11.54

Fig. 11.55

Fig. 11.56

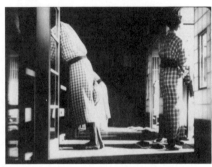

Fig. 11.57

Fig. 11.58

Fig. 11.59

The transitional shots that prolong or thwart the viewer's hypotheses and the 360° space that asks us to notice surroundings can work together. When the grandparents visit a spa at Atami, the scene begins with a long shot along a hallway (Fig. 11.52). Latin-style dance music plays offscreen, and several people walk through the hall. The next shot (Fig. 11.53) is a long shot of another hallway upstairs, with a maid carrying a tray; two pairs of slippers are just visible by a doorway at the lower left. Next comes a medium long shot of a hallway by a courtyard (Fig. 11.54). More people bustle through. A medium shot of a mah-jongg game follows (Fig. 11.55); there is a loud sound of talking and moving pieces about. Then Ozu cuts 180° across the axis, framing another mah-jongg table (Fig. 11.56). The first table is now in the background, viewed from the opposite side. The next cut returns to the medium long shot along the courtyard hallway (Fig. 11.57). In all of these shots, we have not yet seen the grandparents, who are the only major characters present at the spa. Finally, there is a medium shot of the two pairs of slippers by the door in the upper hallway (Fig. 11.58), suggesting that this is the grandparents' room. The panes of glass in the wall reflect the lively movement of the offscreen party, and the loud music and talk are still audible. A medium shot of the Hirayamas in bed, trying to sleep through the noise, finally reveals the narrative situation, and a conversation begins between the couple (Fig. 11.59). For seven shots the film slowly explores the space of the scene, gradually letting us discover the situation. The presence of the slippers in the second shot (Fig. 11.53) is almost unnoticeable. It hints that the grandparents are there, but the revelation of their whereabouts is then put off for several more shots.

In these ways Ozu draws our attention away from the strictly causal functions of space and makes space important in its own right. He does the same with the flat space of the screen as well. Figures 8.99 to 8.102 and Color Plates 62 and 63 show examples of graphic matches from Ozu films. The stylistic device is characteristic of Ozu, who seldom uses the graphic match for any narrative purpose. In *Tokyo Story* a conversation situation leads to a shot/reverse-shot pattern but again with cuts 180° across the axis of action. The two men speaking are framed so that each looks off right. (In Hollywood, upholders of the continuity system would claim that this implies that both are looking off toward the same thing.) Because they are positioned similarly in the frame, the result is a strong graphic match from one shot to another (Figs. 11.60, 11.61). In this respect, Ozu's style owes something to abstract form (see Chapter 5, pp. 146–154 and Chapter 10, pp. 373–376). It is as if he sought to make a narrative film which would still make graphic similarities as evident as they are in an abstract film like *Ballet mécanique*.

Fig. 11.60

The use of space and time in *Tokyo Story* is not willfully obscure, nor does it have a symbolic function in the narrative. Rather, it suggests a different relationship among space, time, and narrative logic than exists in the classical film. Space and time no longer simply function unobtrusively to create a clear narrative line. Ozu brings them forward and makes them into prominent aesthetic elements in their own right. A large part of the film's appeal lies in its strict but playful treatment of figures, settings, and movement. Ozu does not eliminate narrative, but he opens it out. *Tokyo Story* and his other films allow other stylistic devices to exist independently alongside narrative. The result is that the viewer is invited to look at his films in a new way, to participate in a play of space and time.

Fig. 11.61

DOCUMENTARY FORM AND STYLE

■ *HIGH SCHOOL*

1968. Produced and directed by Frederick Wiseman. Photographed by Richard Leiterman. Editor: Frederick Wiseman. Associate editor: Carter Howard. Assistant cameraman: David Eames.

Before the 1950s, most documentary filmmakers shot footage silent and added a voice-over commentary and postsynchronized music at the assembly stage. Lorentz's *The River* and Riefenstahl's *Olympia*, Part 2, analyzed in Chapters 5 and 10, are instances of this trend. After World War II, however, magnetic tape recording made it possible to record sound on location. At the same period the demands of military and television users encouraged manufacturers to develop lightweight but sophisticated 16mm cameras. These technological changes fostered a new approach to documentary filmmaking: *cinéma vérité* ("cinema truth"). In the 1950s and 1960s, many filmmakers began to use portable cameras and synchronized-sound recording equipment to capture spontaneous activity in a wide variety of situations: a political campaign (*Primary*, 1960), a legal case (*The Chair*, 1963), a folk singer's life (*Don't Look Back*, 1967), the tribulations of a Bible salesman (*Salesman*, 1969).

Some filmmakers claimed that *cinéma vérité* was more objective than traditional documentary. The older trend had relied heavily on staging, as well as on editing, music, and commentary to guide the viewer to certain conclusions. The *cinéma-vérité* film instead minimized voice-over commentary and put the filmmaker on the scene as the situation unfolded. It could, its defenders asserted, neutrally record the facts and let the audience draw its own conclusions.

Frederick Wiseman's *High School* is a good example of the *cinéma-vérité* approach. Wiseman received permission to film at Philadelphia's Northeast High School, and he acted as sound recordist while his cameraman shot footage in the hallways, classrooms, cafeteria, and auditorium of the institution. The film that resulted uses no voice-over narration and almost no nondiegetic music. Wiseman uses none of the facing-the-reporter interviews that television news coverage employs. In these ways, *High School* might seem to approach the *cinéma-vérité* ideal of simply presenting a slice of life. Yet if we analyze the film's form and style, we find that it still aims to achieve particular effects on the spectator, and it still suggests a specific range of meaning. Far from being a neutral transmission of reality, *High School* shows how film form and style, even in *cinéma vérité,* shape the event we see on film.

The *cinéma-vérité* film records reality in some sense, but like any film, it demands that the filmmaker select and arrange material. The filmmaker chooses not only the film's subject matter but also the events to be photographed. The *cinéma-vérité* filmmaker also makes decisions on the spur of the moment, choosing when to start filming during a scene, what to keep in frame, and what sounds to record. There is selection in the editing phase as well; the 80 minutes of *High School* are culled from over 40 hours of raw footage.

Fig. 11.62

The filmmaker also arranges the material, presenting it in a specific way that affects our experience. Although the *cinéma-vérité* filmmaker has surrendered control over what happens in front of the camera, she or he retains control over the film's structure, choosing what segment will follow another. The filmmaker can pick a camera position that will juxtapose various elements in the frame. (Consider Fig. 11.62, which frames the dean of discipline against the American flag; another angle, such as that of Fig. 11.67, does not make the flag visible.) The filmmaker also arranges shots through editing, by putting images and sounds into specific relations. Through selection and arrangement, the *cinéma-vérité* filmmaker utilizes film form and style no less than does a filmmaker who employs mise-en-scene and stages the action for the camera.

High School contains 37 distinct segments, each one showing an episode of high-school life. Some segments, such as chorus rehearsal, are quite brief; others involve extensive dialogue. Formally, the film presents an interesting combination of structural types. On the whole, the form is categorical. The main category is high-school life, and the subcategories consist of typical activities: classes, student/teacher confrontations, sports activities, a pep rally, and so on.

Within the activities we see, the action depends on narrative principles. Many of the segments constitute small scenes fraught with conflict. The dean of discipline insists that a boy take an unjustified detention, an administrator argues with complaining parents, and so on. Nonetheless, the overall form of the film is not narrative. The film lacks continuing characters, causality (one action does not trigger the next), and temporality (we do not know the "real" order and duration of events shown in the film). Wiseman has realized that our prior knowledge and experience will help us fill in gaps. When one segment begins with the disciplinary dean saying, "What do you mean, you can't take gym?" we will draw on our own high-school memories to create a typical context around this scene. Finally, as we shall see, the film is somewhat associational in the way it arranges and links its parts. Thus *High School,* like many documentaries, combines various principles of formal organization. The film presents typical categories of high-school life by means of small-scale narrative episodes and links them by associational factors.

The way in which categorical, narrative, and associational strategies combine becomes clearer if we look at how Wiseman has selected and arranged his material. The film is not a full cross-section of high-school life. It omits many important aspects. We never see the home life of students and faculty, and, strikingly, we never witness any conversations between students, either in class or outside it. Wiseman has concentrated on one aspect of high-school life: how the power of the authorities demands obedience from pupils and parents.

The most common strategy we see is simple drilling. The classes consist of teachers lecturing, reading aloud, or leading the students in some regimented activity, such as calisthenics, cooking, musical performance, or language drill. The filmmaker's selectivity is especially evident in one segment, in which an English teacher uses a popular song to teach poetry. Wiseman shows her reading the text aloud and then playing the song on tape, but he omits the class discussion that came in between. At other times, the authorities are shown exacting obedience through cajolery and flattery. An administrator tells one girl that she could be a leader; the disciplinary dean coaxes the boy to take his punishment like a man. If conflict breaks out, a teacher or administrator is shown taking a hard line in order to exercise discipline or win a point. In this film, no one in charge loses an argument. The narrative interest of each scene depends on our recognizing it as repeating the same pattern of the victory of authority. We come to expect that the disciplinary dean will argue down a fractious boy or that an administrator will force students to wear formal dress to the prom.

Wiseman's selectivity also gives the neutral category of high-school life some of the expressive overtones we expect of associational form. One scene may depict a drum major's march while another portrays a history class, but the important thing is that we notice the regimented quality of each one.

The arrangement of parts in the overall film betrays the mixture of formal types as well. The film's first segment evokes sketchy narrative expectations. The opening shows views of streets, highways, and eventually the school, all filmed from a car or bus. It suggests that the day begins with someone (teacher? student?) coming to school. The next sequence, apparently during homeroom period, tends to confirm the hypothesis that the school day is starting. But as the film develops, there are no cues to demarcate phases of the day. Moreover, we see another homeroom period later, as well as several

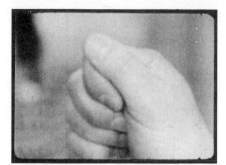

Fig. 11.63

Fig. 11.64

Fig. 11.65

Fig. 11.66

school assemblies, a simulated space flight, and other activities that would not all plausibly take place on a single day. By the last sequence, a teachers' meeting, we can't know when this event occurs—at the end of the day, the end of the semester, or at some other point. After the first two scenes, the sequences are not linked by any indications of chronology. What we see are simply categories of high-school life, restricted to the sorts of face-to-face exercises of power that we have already mentioned.

In general, *High School* lays out its categories and then links them associatively, grouping several sequences around themes. For example, several scenes concentrate on how the school teaches about sexuality and gender roles. Sequence 15 shows a boys' health class being lectured on families; this is followed by a sequence showing an assembly of girls being lectured about sexual conduct. In Sequence 17, an administrator and a teacher explain why all female students must wear formal gowns to the senior prom. In Sequence 18, as a girls' gym class practices hanging from parallel rings, the teacher calls out, "We're feminine, let's go." Later in the film, three more sex-education classes are clustered together, reinforcing the idea that the school creates models of behavior that define masculinity and femininity.

Late in the film a string of sequences associates high-school education with the military. Here we can clearly see how powerfully the order of the sequences can shape our participation in the film. A soldier home on leave talks with a coach about a wounded friend who will never play soccer again. The next sequence, which simply shows a boys' gym class bouncing an enormous ball, encourages us to imagine these boys as future soldiers, some of whom may be killed or crippled. There follows a scene of a drum corps in the auditorium, again evoking military comparisons. This is followed by the film's last scene, in which a female principal reads to the assembled teachers a letter from an ex-student about to go to Vietnam. The ordering of scenes thus encourages us to pick out emotional or conceptual qualities that a string of scenes shares—a basic convention of associational form. A film using this structure does not advance a specific *argument* about its subject (the form is not rhetorical), but the film may imply a broad *attitude* to its topic, as Conner's *A Movie* does (p. 163).

Associational linkages are stengthened by other means. For one thing, motifs reappear. Wiseman uses shots of the school hallway to demarcate the scenes. Details of student anatomy—hips and legs especially—reinforce the notion of docile bodies waiting, lining up, bent to assigned tasks. By contrast, the authorities are associated with hands. While talking to parents, one administrator makes a fist, and the framing emphasizes this with a close-up (Fig. 11.63). In the next sequence, the disciplinary dean's hand is treated in a similar framing (Fig. 11.64).

Most strikingly, the transitions between scenes depend on associations. Some are simple repetitions, as when one teacher asks, "Are there any questions?" and we cut to another teacher asking, "Any questions?" Other transitions are more figurative. A teacher concludes "Casey at the Bat" with the line "Mighty Casey has struck out." Cut to a girl in a gym glass batting a ball. A Spanish teacher waves her arms, drilling the class in a pronunciation exercise (Fig. 11.65); cut to a percussion ensemble practicing, led by a teacher conducting them (Fig. 11.66). This effectively suggests the regi-

Fig. 11.67

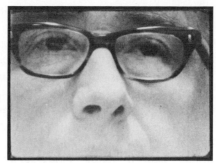

Fig. 11.68

mented nature of learning. Although the film does not supply cues for temporal order, it unifies itself through recurring motifs and transitions that reveal unexpected repetitions and similarities.

On the whole, the filmmaker's stylistic choices reinforce the overall structural features we have already mentioned. The segmentation into categories of school life is accomplished through editing and sound. Each sequence begins with an abrupt cut to a situation already in progress. Often the first shots are close-ups, so that the situation is revealed only gradually. The associative aspects of the film's form also depend upon techniques that create the sort of surprising transitions we have already considered.

Fig. 11.69

Within segments, the use of cinematography, editing, and sound supports the narrative dynamic of the individual scenes. Even though Wiseman is filming unstaged situations, he adheres to principles of classical narrative style. The zoom lens permits the camera operator to situate someone in space and then isolate details (Figs. 11.67, 11.68). More strikingly, *High School*'s scenes rely heavily on continuity editing which creates an axis of action and shot/reverse shot. In Figure 11.69, the blonde student is shown from the rear, at the far left edge of the frame. The next shot, Figure 11.70, cuts to a reverse angle on her that maintains the 180° line between her and the teacher. (Compare this cutting pattern with that in *The Maltese Falcon*, Figures 8.61–8.63, p. 291.) When filming under confined conditions, however, a *cinéma-vérité* filmmaker cannot always obtain an establishing shot. In *High School*, this makes eyelines and screen direction crucial cues for spatial continuity. For example, when the English teacher reads "Casey at the Bat," she is consistently intercut with shots of students looking to the left, even though no long shot shows both teacher and pupils in the same space.

Fig. 11.70

The use of continuity editing does more than give the scenes a narrative unity we can recognize from classical Hollywood conventions. Cutting from speaker to listener also lets Wiseman skip over action and conceal the breaks through offscreen sound. If he cuts away from the teacher to a reaction shot of the pupil listening but keeps the teacher's voice on the sound track, he can omit whole sentences before cutting back to the speaker. In the scene showing the English teacher studying the Simon and Garfunkel song, the cutaways and offscreen sound allow Wiseman to omit the class discussion of the poem. The "invisible" ellipses that cutaways and offscreen sound can yield are constantly used in television news coverage, in which a cut to a nodding reporter typically conceals omissions in the speaker's talk. This is,

Fig. 11.71

Fig. 11.72

Fig. 11.73

Fig. 11.74

in essence, a documentary application of the principle of dialogue overlap considered in Chapter 9, p. 322.

The absence of establishing shots and the reliance on eyelines can even create the sort of "imaginary geography" that Kuleshov discussed (see p. 281). We follow a teacher as he stalks the halls demanding passes. He turns (Fig. 11.71). There is a cut to a long shot of a girl walking down the corridor (Fig. 11.72). After the monitor has ordered some students to leave, he goes up to a door and peers in (Fig. 11.73). The offscreen music gradually grows louder, and we cut to a phonograph and a girls' gym class exercising, filmed to emphasize legs and torsos (Fig. 11.74).

These cuts might go unnoticed, but analysis reveals that the sequence depends upon artifice. A close study of the shot showing the girl in the corridor (Fig. 11.72) reveals that she is not in the hall that the teacher is patrolling. As for the gym class, there is no establishing shot showing both teacher and students, so we cannot know with certainty that it was really this gym class which the teacher watched through the window. In fact, if we recall the conditions of *cinéma-vérité* production, we realize that the music must have been added after the shot of the teacher was made. (If the music really was coming from the gym, there would have been a gap on the sound track when the filmmakers had to switch the camera off and go into the gym to film the students.) Thus both editing and sound create the Kuleshov effect, prompting us to connect two things that are not really adjacent. The stylistic function would seem to be to characterize the teacher as lecherous, ogling girls in the hallway and spying on them in gym class.

After analyzing how *High School* uses overall form and specific film techniques to guide our response, it may seem odd to suggest that the film is somewhat ambiguous. Yet reactions to the film varied. When *High School* was first shown to the Philadelphia Board of Education, many officials praised it. But critics from around the country have tended to see the film as criticizing the school and secondary education in general. Does this controversy mean that *cinéma vérité* has achieved its goal of a neutral capturing of reality, leaving meanings to the eye of each beholder?

We think that the varying reactions to the film illustrate how viewers can emphasize one sort of meaning over another. It is likely that school officials concentrated upon the film's *referential* and *explicit* meanings, treating it as a record of a single school (a sort of institutional home movie) and as a statement about the success of education. They may have weighted most strongly a sentiment made very explicit at the film's close, when the female principal reads a letter from the student about to go to Vietnam. Critics, however, offered an interpretation of the film that stressed an *implicit* meaning at odds with the explicit one. In this view, the school is shown as an oppressive bureaucracy. These critics could use our analysis to claim that the film's form and style, and its tactics of selection and arrangement, portray this institution as more concerned with inculcating obedience and conformity than with teaching critical thinking, independent action, and a sense of self-worth.

This interpretation could gather further evidence from the use of rock-and-roll tunes to comment on the bleakness of high-school life as well as from the final scene, in which the soldier's letter is read. Here the film's development from educational discipline to military regimentation is capped by an overt link between school and army. The boy's letter urges people not to worry, and the motif of students as docile bodies returns: "I am not worth it. I am only a body doing a job." The scene also repeats the motif of the hand of authority when the camera racks focus during the administrator's reading (Figs. 11.75, 11.76). From this interpretive stance, the film's final line—"When you get a letter like this, to me it means that we are very successful at Northeast High School. I think you will agree with me"— becomes ironic. Irony, indeed, is often defined as exactly this sort of conflict between explicit and implicit meaning.

Fig. 11.75

We could even suggest that the film's *symptomatic* meaning reinforces this interpretation. Depicting a school as a training ground for conformity is symptomatic of the period in which the film was made. In 1968, many filmmakers were questioning both specific governmental policies, such as American involvement in Vietnam, and broader values of Western society.

Frederick Wiseman's *High School* can be considered ambiguous in that its referential and explicit meanings run counter to its implicit and symptomatic ones. Nonetheless, the fact that the film can generate not vagueness but such a precise dispute about its range of meanings suggests that *cinéma vérité* is not a neutral record of the world in front of a camera and a microphone. Like other types of documentary, *cinéma vérité* is an active cinematic intervention *in* the world, another way of handling the filmmaker's inevitable choices about form, style, and effect.

Fig. 11.76

■ MAN WITH A MOVIE CAMERA (CHELOVEK S KINOAPPARATOM)

Made 1928, released 1929. VUFKU, Union of Soviet Socialist Republics. Directed by Dziga Vertov. Photographed by Mikhail Kaufman. Edited by Elizaveta Svilova.

In some ways, *Man with a Movie Camera* might seem to resemble *High School*. As a silent film, it necessarily avoids the use of music to guide our expectations (music, that is, controlled by the filmmaker, since in the theaters a piano or orchestra would have accompanied screenings). Moreover, the film does not employ intertitles to provide a commentary on the action, though most silent documentaries did use such titles. Yet, unlike *High School, Man with a Movie Camera* does not try to give the impression that the reality it documents is unaffected by the medium of film. Instead, Dziga Vertov proclaims the manipulative power of editing and cinematography to shape a multitude of tiny scenes from everyday reality into a highly idiosyncratic, even somewhat experimental documentary.

Vertov's name is usually linked to the technique of editing; in Chapter 8 (p. 280), we quoted a passage in which he equated the filmmaker with an eye, gathering shots from many places and linking them creatively for the spectator. Vertov's theoretical writings also compare the eye to the lens of the camera, in a concept he termed the "kino eye." (*Kino* is the Russian word for "cinema," and one of his earlier films is called *Kino-Glaz,* or "Cinema-Eye.")

Man with a Movie Camera takes this idea—the equation of the film-

Fig. 11.77

Fig. 11.78

Fig. 11.79

Fig. 11.80

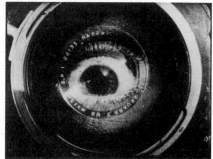

Fig. 11.81

maker's eye with the lens of the camera—as the basis for the entire film's associational form. The film becomes a celebration of the documentary film-maker's power to control our perception of reality by means of editing and special effects. The opening image shows a camera in close-up. Through a double-exposure effect, we see the cameraman of the film's title (played by Vertov's regular cinematographer, Mikhail Kaufman) suddenly climb, in extreme long shot, onto the top of the giant camera (Fig. 11.77). He sets up his own camera on a tripod and films for a bit, then climbs down again. This play with shot scale within a single image emphasizes at once the power the cinema has to alter reality in a seemingly magical way.

Cinematographic special effects of this sort appear as a motif throughout the film. These are not intended to be unnoticeable, as in a science-fiction film. Instead, they flaunt the fact that the camera can alter everyday reality. Figure 11.78 shows a typical example, with Vertov filming an ordinary street scene but altering it by exposing each side of the image separately, with the camera canted in opposite directions. Later Vertov uses pixillation to animate real objects. A crayfish on a plate executes a little dance in the course of the shot (Fig. 11.79). In another scene Vertov conveys the sound of a radio by superimposing images of a dancer and of a hand playing a piano against a single black background (Fig. 11.80). This motif of virtuosic special effects culminates in the famous final shot (Fig. 11.81), where an eye is superimposed over the lens of the camera, staring straight out at us.

At several points in the film, the camera is also personified, associated by editing with the actions of human beings. One brief segment shows the camera lens focusing and then a blurry shot of flowers coming into sharp focus. This is followed immediately by a comic juxtaposition rapidly inter-cutting two elements: a woman's fluttering eyelids as she dries her face with a towel, and a set of venetian blinds opening and closing. Finally another shot shows the camera lens with a diaphragm closing and opening. A human eye is like venetian blinds, the lens is like an eye—all can open and close, admitting or keeping out light. Later, pixillation allows the camera to move by itself, as it comes out of its box, climbs onto the tripod, demonstrates how its various parts work (Fig. 11.82), and finally walks off on three legs. Such playfulness is far from the objective tone of *High School*.

Fig. 11.82

Man with a Movie Camera belongs to a genre of documentaries that first became important during the 1920s: the "city symphony." There are many ways of making a film about a city, of course. One might use categorical form to lay out its geography or scenic attractions, as in a travelogue; rhetorical form could make arguments about aspects of city planning or government policies that need changing. A narrative might stress a city as the backdrop for many characters' actions, as in Rossellini's *Rome Open City* or Jules Dassin's semidocumentary crime drama *The Naked City*. Early city symphonies, however, established the convention of taking candid (or occasionally staged) scenes of city life and linking them, usually without commentary, through associations to suggest emotions or concepts. Associational form is evident in such early examples of the genre as Alberto Cavalcanti's *Rien que les heures* (1926) and Walter Ruttmann's *Berlin, Symphony of a Great City* (1927). More recent films like Godfrey Reggio's *Koyaanisqatsi* (1983) and *Powaqqatsi* (1988) use similar techniques, avoiding voice-over narration in favor of a musical accompaniment that along with juxtapositions of images creates particular moods and evokes certain concepts. (See pp. 154–157.)

In *Man with a Movie Camera*'s opening, we see a camera operator filming, then passing between the curtains of an empty movie theater, moving toward the screen. Then we see the theater opening, the spectators filing in, the orchestra preparing to play, and the film commencing. The film which we and the audience watch seems at first to be a city symphony of the type that lays out a typical day in the life of a town (as Ruttmann's *Berlin* does). We see a woman asleep, mannequins in closed shops, empty streets. Soon a few people appear, and the city wakes up. Indeed, much of *Man with a Movie Camera* follows a rough principle of development that progresses from waking up through work time to leisure time. But early in the waking-up portion, we also see the cameraman again, setting out with his equipment, as if starting his work day. This action creates the first of many deliberate inconsistencies. The cameraman now appears in his own film, and Vertov emphasizes this by cutting back immediately to the sleeping woman who had been the first thing we saw in the film-within-a-film.

Throughout *Man with a Movie Camera*, we will see the same actions and shots being filmed, edited, and viewed by the onscreen audience, all in scrambled order. Toward the end of the film, in fact, we see the audience in the theater watching the cameraman on the screen, filming from a moving motorcycle. Moreover, in this late portion of the film, many motifs from all the earlier parts of the day return, many now in fast motion; the simple order of the ordinary city symphony is broken and jumbled. Vertov creates an

Fig. 11.83

Fig. 11.84

impossible time scheme, once more emphasizing the extraordinary manipulative powers of the cinema. The film also refuses to show only one city, instead mixing footage filmed in Moscow, Kiev, and Riga, as if the cameraman hero can move effortlessly back and forth in space during this "day" of filming. Vertov's view of the cinema's relation to the cityscape is well conveyed in one shot which uses an extraordinary deep-focus composition to place the camera in the foreground, looming over the distant buildings as it pans madly about to capture various views on film (Fig. 11.83). In sum, *Man with a Movie Camera* may be a city symphony, but it goes beyond the genre as well.

Apart from its exuberant celebration of the powers of cinema, Vertov's film contains many explicit and implicit meanings, some of which may be missed by viewers who do not read Russian. Explicitly, the film seeks to praise and criticize aspects of Soviet society a decade after the revolution. Many of the film's juxtapositions involve machines and human labor. Under Stalin, the USSR was beginning a major push toward industrialization, and the mechanized factories are portrayed as fascinating places full of bustling movement, with the camera lingering over throbbing, gleaming machine parts (Fig. 11.84). The camera operator scales a huge factory smokestack or swings suspended over a dam to capture all this activity. Workers are seen not as oppressed, but as participating cheerfully in the country's growth, as when one young woman laughs and chats as she folds cigarette boxes on an assembly line.

Vertov also points out weak spots in contemporary life, such as lingering class inequalities. Shots in a beauty shop suggest that some bourgeois values have survived the Revolution, and the leisure-time sequence near the end contrasts workers involved in outdoor sports with chubby women exercising in a weight-loss gym. Vertov also takes pains to criticize drunkenness, a major social problem in the USSR. One of the first shots within the inner film shows a derelict sleeping outdoors, juxtaposed with a huge bottle advertising a café. A shop front which we repeatedly see advertises wine and vodka, and later there is a scene where the cameraman visits this bar. When he leaves, we see shots of workers' clubs, converted from former churches. The contrast between these two places where workers can spend their leisure time is made clear through associational crosscutting: A woman shooting at targets in one of the clubs seems to be shooting away bottles of beer that disappear (through stop-motion) from a crate in the bar. During the 1920s, government officials instituted an explicit policy whose goal was to use the cinema and workers' clubs to replace both the tavern and the church in the lives of Soviet citizens. (Since the government's biggest source of income came from its monopoly on vodka sales, the policy also aimed at making cinema a major alternative source of revenue.) Thus *Man with a Movie Camera* seems to be subtly promoting this policy by using playful camera techniques to make both the cinema and the clubs seem attractive.

Implicitly, *Man with a Movie Camera* can be seen as an argument for Vertov's view of the cinema. He opposed narrative form and the use of professional actors, preferring that films use the techniques of the camera and the editing table to create their effects upon the audience. He was not, however, entirely against controlling the mise-en-scene, and several scenes of this film—particularly the woman waking up and washing—clearly would have had to be staged. Throughout *Man with a Movie Camera*, associational juxtapositions compare the work of making a film with the other sorts of work depicted. The camera operator awakes and goes to work in the morning, like other workers. Like them, he uses a machine in his craft; the camera's crank is at various points compared with the crank on a cash register or with moving parts on factory equipment. The moving parts of the projector in the theater also resemble parts of the factory machines we see in various sequences.

Vertov further demonstrates how the film which we and the audience within the film are watching is a product of specific labor. We see the editor at work (Elizaveta Svilova, Vertov's wife and the actual editor of *Man with a Movie Camera*). Her gestures of scraping the film and putting cement on it with a brush to make a splice are cut in with shots in a beauty parlor, where a manicurist wields a nail file and a similar brush. At various times in the film we see many of the same shots in different contexts: on our screen, on the screen within the movie theater, in freeze frame, being filmed, being cut apart or spliced by the editor, in fast-motion, and so on. We must therefore view them not only as moments of recorded reality but also as pieces of a whole that is put together through much effort on the parts of these film workers. Finally, the camera operator has to resort to various means, sometimes dangerous, to obtain his shots; he not only climbs a huge smokestack but also crouches across the tracks to film an oncoming train and rides a motorcycle one-handed as he cranks the camera to capture the action of a race.

Filmmaking is thus presented as a job or craft, rather than an elite-oriented art form. Judging from the delighted reactions of the audience we see in the theater, Vertov hoped that the Soviet public would find his celebration of filmmaking interesting and entertaining.

This implicit meaning relates to a symptomatic meaning we can also see in the film. During the late 1920s, the Soviet authorities wanted films which would be easily understandable and would convey propagandistic messages to a far-flung, often illiterate populace. They were increasingly critical of filmmakers like Eisenstein and Vertov, whose films, though celebrating revolutionary ideology, were extremely complex. In Chapter 8 we saw how Eisenstein adopted a dense, discontinuous style of editing. While Vertov disagreed in many ways with Eisenstein, particularly over the latter's use of narrative form, both belonged to a larger stylistic movement called Soviet Montage, whose history we shall examine in Chapter 12 (pp. 456–459). Both used very complex editing which they hoped would create predictable reactions in their audiences. With its contradictory time scheme and rapid editing (it contains over 1700 shots, more than twice what most Hollywood films of the same period had), *Man with a Movie Camera* is unquestionably a difficult film, especially for an audience unaccustomed to the conventions of filmmaking. Perhaps more Soviet spectators would have learned over time to enjoy such films as *October* and *Man with a Movie Camera* and to react to them with the delight evident in the audience in Vertov's film. Over the next few years, however, authorities increasingly criticized Vertov and his colleagues, limiting their ability to experiment with concepts like the "film eye." Vertov in particular was constrained in his later projects, but *Man with a*

Movie Camera eventually came to be recognized, in the Soviet Union and abroad, as a classic experiment in using associational form within documentary.

FORM, STYLE, AND IDEOLOGY

■ *MEET ME IN ST. LOUIS*

> 1944. MGM. Directed by Vincente Minnelli. Script by Irving Brecher and Fred F. Finklehoffe, from the book by Sally Benson. Photographed by George Folsey. Edited by Albert Akst. Music by Hugh Martin and Ralph Blane. With Judy Garland, Margaret O'Brien, Mary Astor, Lucille Bremer, Leon Ames, Tom Drake.

Just over halfway through *Meet Me in St. Louis,* Alonzo Smith announces to his assembled family that he has been transferred to a new job in New York City. "I've got the future to think about—the future for all of us. I've got to worry about where the money's coming from," he tells the dismayed group. These ideas of family and future, central to the form and style of the film, also create an ideological framework within which the film gains meaning and impact.

All of the films we have already analyzed could be examined for their ideological standpoints. Any film combines formal and stylistic elements in such a way as to create an ideological stance, whether overtly stated or tacit. We have chosen to stress the ideology of *Meet Me in St. Louis* because it provides a clear example of a film that does not seek to change people's ways of thinking. Instead it tends to reinforce certain aspects of a dominant social ideology. In this case *Meet Me in St. Louis,* like most Hollywood films, seeks to uphold what are conceived as characteristically American values of family unity and home life.

Meet Me in St. Louis is set during the preparations for the Louisiana Purchase Exposition in St. Louis, with the fair itself becoming the culmination of the action. The film displays its form in a straightforward way, with a title card announcing each of its four sections with a different season, beginning with "Summer, 1903." In this way the film simultaneously suggests the passage of time (equated with a movement toward the spring 1904 fair, which will bring the fruits of progress to St. Louis) and the unchanging cycle of the seasons.

The Smiths, living in a big Victorian house, form a large but closely knit family. The seasonal structure allows the film to show the Smiths at the traditional times of family unity, the holidays; we see them celebrating Halloween and Christmas. At the end, the fair becomes a new sort of holiday, the celebration of the Smiths' decision to remain in St. Louis.

The opening of the film quickly introduces the idea of St. Louis as a city on the boundary between tradition and progress. The fancy candy-box title card for Summer forms a vignette of white and red flowers around an old-fashioned black-and-white photo of the Smiths' house. As the camera moves in, color fades into the photo, and it comes to life. Slow, subdued chords over the title card give way to a bouncy tune more in keeping with the onscreen movement. Horse-drawn beer wagons and carriages move along the road, but an early model automobile (a bright red, which draws our eye) passes them. Already the motif of progress and inventions becomes prominent; it will develop quickly into the emphasis on the upcoming fair.

As Lon Smith, the son, arrives home by bicycle, a dissolve inside to the kitchen launches the exposition. One by one we meet the family members as they go about their daily activities through the house. The camera follows the second youngest daughter, Agnes, as she goes upstairs singing "Meet Me in St. Louis." She encounters Grandpa, who takes up the song as the camera follows him briefly. By means of close matches on action on the characters' passing the song along, the image track yields a flow of movement that presents the house as full of bustle and music. Grandpa hears offscreen voices singing the same song. He moves to a window, and a high-angle shot from over his shoulder shows the second oldest sister, Esther, stepping out of a buggy. Her arrival brings the sequence full circle back to the front of the house.

The house remains the main image of family unity throughout most of the film. Aside from the expedition of the young people on the trolley to see the construction of the fair, the Christmas dance, and the final fairground sequence, the entire action of the film takes place in or near the Smith house. Although Mr. Smith's job provides the reason to move to New York, we never see him at his office. In the opening sequence, the family members return home one by one, until they all gather around the dinner table. Every section of the film begins with a similar candy-box title card and a move in toward the house. In the film's ideology the home appears to be a self-sufficient place; other social institutions become peripheral, even threatening.

This vision of the unified family within an idealized household places the women at the center. The narration does not restrict our knowledge to a single character's range, but it tends to concentrate on what the Smith women know. Mrs. Smith, Rose, the youngest daughter Tootie, and in particular Esther are the characters around which the narration is organized. Moreover, women are portrayed as the agents of stability. The action in the story constantly returns to the kitchen, where the mother and maid, Katie, work calmly in the midst of various small crises. The men, on the other hand, present the threat to the family's unity. Mr. Smith wants to take the family to New York, thereby destroying its ties with the past. Lon goes away to "the East," to college at Princeton. Only the grandfather, as representative of the older generation, sides with the women in their desire to stay in St. Louis. In general, the narrative's causality makes any departure from the home a threat—an example of how a narrative's principles of development can generate an ideological premise.

Within the family there are minor disagreements, but the members cooperate. The two older sisters, Rose and Esther, help each other in their flirtations. Esther is in love with the boy next door, John Truitt, and marriage to him poses no threat to the family unity. Several times in the film she gazes across at his house without having to leave her own home. First she and Rose go out onto the porch to try to attract his attention; then she sits in the window to sing, "The Boy Next Door." Finally, much later, she sits in a darkened bedroom upstairs and sees John pull his shade just after they have become engaged. That the girls might want to travel, or to educate themselves beyond high school, is never considered. By concentrating on the round of small incidents in the household and neighborhood, the film blocks consideration of any alternative way of living—except the dreaded move to New York.

Many stylistic devices build up a picture of a happy family life. The Technicolor design contributes greatly to the lushness of the mise-en-scene, making the costumes, the surroundings, and the characters' hair color stand out richly. (See Color Plates 44 and 45.) The characters wear bright clothes, with Esther often in blue. She and Rose wear red and green, respectively, to the Christmas dance. This strengthens the association of the family unity with holidays and incidentally makes the sisters easy to pick out in the swirling crowd of pastel-clad dancers. In Color Plate 45, the shot from the trolley scene, Esther is conspicuous because she is the only woman in black amidst the generally bright-colored dresses.

Meet Me in St. Louis is a musical, and music plays a large part in the family life. Songs come at moments of romance or gatherings. Rose and Esther sing "Meet Me in St. Louis" in the parlor before dinner. When the father interrupts them upon returning from work—"For heaven's sake, stop that screeching!"—he is immediately characterized as opposed to the singing and to the fair. Esther's other songs show that her romance with John Truitt is a safe and reasonable one. A woman does not have to leave home to find a husband: She can find him right in her own neighborhood ("The Boy Next Door") or by riding the trolley ("The Trolley Song"). Other songs accompany the two parties. Finally, Esther sings "Have Yourself a Merry Little Christmas" to Tootie, the youngest sister, after the Christmas dance. Here she tries to reassure Tootie that life in New York will be all right if the family can remain together.

But already there is a sense that such unity is in danger. "Someday soon we all will be together, if the Fates allow / Until then we'll have to muddle through somehow." We know already that Esther has achieved her romantic goal and become engaged to John Truitt. If the Smiths do move to New York, she will have to decide between him and her family. By this point, the plot has reached an impasse; whichever way she decides, the old way of life will be destroyed. The narrative needs a resolution, and Tootie's hysterical crying in reaction to the song leads Mr. Smith to reconsider his decision.

Tootie's destruction of the snow people after Esther's song is a striking image of the threat to family unity posed by the move to New York. As the winter season section opened, the children were building the snow people (and a dog) in the yard. In effect they had created a parallel to their own family, with statues of different sexes and sizes. At first these snow people were part of the comic scene in which Esther and Katie persuade Lon and Rose to go to the Christmas dance together. But when Tootie becomes hysterical at the prospect of leaving St. Louis, she runs down in her nightgown to smash the snow people. The scene is almost shocking, since Tootie seems to be killing the doubles of her own family. This moment has to be strong, even hysterical, because it must motivate the father's change of mind. He realizes that his desire to move to New York threatens the family's internal ties. This realization leads to his decision to stay in St. Louis.

Two other elements of the mise-en-scene create motifs which stress the family's comfortable life. The Smiths live surrounded by food. In the initial scene the women are making ketchup, which is shortly served at the family dinner. After the scene in which Rose's boyfriend fails to propose to her by phone, the tensions are reconciled, and the maid serves large slices of corned beef.

In the Halloween scene the connection between the plentiful food and family unity becomes even more explicit. At first, the children gather around to eat cake and ice cream, but the father arrives home and makes his announcement about moving to New York. The family members depart without touching their food. Only when they hear the mother and father singing at the piano do they gradually drift back to eat. The words of the song, "Time may pass, but we'll be together," accompany their actions. The use of food as a motif associates the family's life in the house with plenty and with the individuals' place as part of a group. At the fair in the last sequence, they decide to visit a restaurant together. Thus the food motif returns at the moment of their reaffirmation of their life together in St. Louis.

A second motif of family unity involves light. The house is ablaze much of the time. As the family sits together at dinner, the low evening sun sends bright yellow rays through the white curtains. Later, one of the loveliest scenes involves Esther's request that John accompany her through the downstairs to help her turn out the lights. This action is primarily accomplished in one long take, with a crane shot following the characters from room to room. At each pause, the brightly lit chandelier is framed in the upper portion of the screen (Color Plate 44). As the rooms darken and the couple moves out to the hall, the camera cranes down to a height level with their faces. The shot contains a remarkable shift of tone. It begins with Esther's comically contrived excuse ("I'm afraid of mice") to keep John with her and develops gradually toward a genuinely romantic mood.

The Halloween sequence takes place entirely at night and makes light a central motif. The camera initially moves in toward the house's glowing yellow windows. Tense, slightly eerie music makes the house seem an island of safety in the darkness. As Tootie and Agnes go out to join the other children in playing tricks, they are silhouetted against the flames of the bonfire the group has gathered around. At first the fire seems threatening, contradicting the earlier associations of light with safety and unity, but this scene actually harmonizes with the previous uses of light. Tootie is excluded from the group activities because she is "too little." After she proves herself worthy, she is allowed to help feed the flames along with the others. Note particularly the long track-back as Tootie leaves the fire to play her trick; the fire remains in the background of the shot, appearing as a haven she has left behind. Indeed, the first sequence of the Halloween section of the film becomes a sort of miniature working out of the entire narrative structure. Tootie's position as a part of the group is abandoned as she moves away from the fire, then triumphantly affirmed as she returns to it.

Similarly, light plays an important part in the resolution of the threat to the family's unity. Late on Christmas Eve, Esther finds Tootie awake. They look out the window at the snow people standing in the yard below. A strip of yellow light falls across the snow, suggesting the warmth and safety of the house they plan to leave. Tootie's hysterical crying, however, leads the father to reconsider his decision. As he sits thinking, he holds the match, with which he was about to light his cigar, unnoticed in his hand until it burns his fingers. Combined with the slow playing of the "Meet Me in St. Louis" theme, the flame serves to emphasize his distraction and his gradual change of mind.

As he calls his family down to announce his decision not to move, he turns up all the lights. The dim, bleak halls full of packing boxes become again the scene of busy activity as the family gathers. The lamps' glass shades are red and green, identifying the house with the appropriate Christmas colors. The announcement of the decision leads directly to the opening of the presents, as if to emphasize that staying in St. Louis will not create any financial hardship for the family.

As night falls in the final fair sequence, the many lights of the buildings come on, dazzlingly reflected in lakes and canals. Here the film ends, with the family gazing in awe at the view. Once more light signifies safety and family enjoyment. These lights also bring the other motifs of the film together. The father had originally wanted to move to New York as a provision for his family's future. In deciding to stay in St. Louis, he had told them: "New York hasn't got a copyright on opportunity. Why, St. Louis is headed for a boom that'll make your head swim. This is a great town." The fair confirms this. St. Louis allows the family to retain its unity, comfort, and safety, and yet have all the benefits of progress. The film ends with the following dialogue:

Mother: There's never been anything like it in the whole world.

Rose: We don't have to come here in a train or stay in a hotel. It's right in our own home town.

Tootie: Grandpa, they'll never tear it down, will they?

Grandpa: Well, they'd better not.

Esther: I can't believe it. Right here where we live. Right here in St. Louis.

These lines do not *create* the film's ideology, which has been present in the narrative and stylistic devices throughout. The dialogue simply makes explicit what has been implicit all along.

The fair solves the problems of the future and family unity. The family is able to go to a French restaurant without going away from home. The ending also restores the father's position as at least the titular head of the family. Only he is able to remember how to get to the restaurant and prepares to guide the group there.

Understanding a film's ideology typically involves analyzing how form and style create meaning. As Chapter 3 suggested, meaning can be of four general types: referential, explicit, implicit, and symptomatic. Our analysis of *Meet Me in St. Louis* has shown how all four types work to reinforce a social ideology—in this case, the values of tradition, home life, and family unity. The referential aspects of the film presuppose that the audience can grasp the difference between St. Louis and New York and that it knows about international expositions, American family customs, national holidays, and so on. These address the film to a specifically American audience. The explicit meaning of the film is formulated by the final exchange we have just considered, in which the small city is discussed as the perfect fusion of progress and tradition.

We have also traced out how formal construction and stylistic motifs contribute to one major implicit meaning: the family and home as creating a "haven in a heartless world," the central reference point for the individual's life. What, then, of symptomatic meanings?

Speaking generally, the film expresses one tendency of many social ideologies in its attempt to "naturalize" social and cultural behavior. Chapter 3 mentioned that systems of value and belief may seem unquestionable to the social groups that hold them. One way that groups maintain such systems is to assume that certain things are beyond human choice or control, that they are simply natural. Historically, this habit of thought has often been used to justify oppression and injustice, as when women, minority groups, or the poor are thought to be naturally inferior. *Meet Me in St. Louis* participates in this general tendency, not only in its characterization of the Smith women (Esther and Rose are simply presumed to want husbands) but in the very choice of a white, upper-middle-class household as an emblem of American life. A more subtle naturalization is evident in the film's overall formal organization. The natural cycle of the seasons is harmonized with the family's life, and the conclusion of the plot takes place in the spring, the period of renewal.

We can also focus on more historically specific symptomatic meanings. The film was released during 1944, late in World War II. The audience for this film would have consisted largely of women and children whose adult male relatives had been absent for extended periods, often overseas. Families were often forced apart, and the people who remained behind had to make considerable sacrifices for the war effort. At a period when many women had been required to work in defense plants, factories, and offices (and many were enjoying the experience), there appears a film which restricts the range of women's experiences to home and family, and yearns for a simpler time when family unity was paramount.

Meet Me in St. Louis can thus be seen as a symptom of a nostalgia for prewar, pre-Depression America. Parents of young fighting men in a 1944 audience would remember the 1903–1904 period as part of their own child-hoods. All of the formal devices—narrative construction, seasonal segmen-tation, songs, color, and motifs—can thus be seen as reassuring the viewers. If the women and others left at home can be strong and hold their families together against threats of disunity, harmony will eventually return. By setting forth this ideology at a time when so many people had been forced to leave home, *Meet Me in St. Louis* upholds dominant conceptions of American family life and may even propose an ideal of family unity for the postwar future.

■ *RAGING BULL*

> 1980. United Artists. Directed by Martin Scorsese. Script by Paul Schrader and Mardik Martin. From the book *Raging Bull* by Jake La Motta, with Joseph Carter and Peter Savage. Photographed by Michael Chapman. Edited by Thelma Schoonmaker. With Robert De Niro, Cathy Moriarty, Joe Pesci, Frank Vincent, Nicholas Colasanto, Theresa Saldana.

In analyzing *Meet Me in St. Louis,* we argued that the film upholds a characteristically American ideology. It is also possible for a film made in Hollywood to take a more ambivalent attitude toward ideological issues. Martin Scorsese's *Raging Bull* does so by taking violence as its central theme.

Violence is widespread in American cinema, often serving as the basis for entertainment. In recent decades, extreme violence has become central to several genres, such as science-fiction and horror films. Such genres often rely in part on making their violence very stylized, and hence minimally disturbing. A series of gory deaths, enhanced by elaborate special effects, may constitute the main narrative action. *Raging Bull* uses a different tactic, drawing upon conventions of cinematic realism to make violence visceral and disturbing. Thus even though it is in some ways less savage than many other films of its era—not a single death occurs, for instance—it contains several scenes that are hard to bear. Not only the brutal boxing matches but also the equally harsh quarrels in everyday life bring violence to the fore.

Scorsese's subject is loosely based on the actual career of boxer Jake La Motta, who became the world middleweight champion in 1949. *Raging Bull* uses the boxing scenes (based on real fights) as emblematic of the violence that pervades Jake's life. Indeed, he seems incapable of dealing with people without picking quarrels, making threats, or becoming abusive. His two marriages, especially that with his second wife, Vickie, are full of bickering and domestic abuse. Although his closest relationship is apparently to his brother Joey, who initially manages his career, he eventually thrashes Joey in a jealous rage and permanently alienates him. Moreover, while Jake's actions hurt others, he also wreaks havoc on himself, driving away everyone he loves and leading him to a pathetic career as an overweight stand-up comic and then as an actor reciting poems and speeches from famous plays and films.

How are we to understand the ideology of a film which makes such a vicious bully its hero? We might be tempted to posit either/or interpretations. Either the film celebrates Jake's murderous rage, or it condemns him as a pathological case. Yet in settling upon one of these simple notions, we would fail to confront the film's uneasy balance of sympathy and revulsion toward its central character. We suggest that *Raging Bull* uses a variety of strategies, both of narrative and style, to make Jake a case study in the role of violence in American life. Scorsese thus creates a complex context within which Jake's actions must be judged.

This context can be best approached by examining the formal structure of *Raging Bull*'s narrative. If we were to segment the film into its individual scenes, we would come up with a long list. Although there are some lengthy sequences, most are quite short. In all there are 46, including the opening credits and the closing quotation title. We can usefully group some of the shorter scenes together. This procedure yields 12 segments:

1. The opening credits, shown over a lengthy shot of Jake warming up alone in a boxing ring.
2. Backstage in a nightclub, 1964. Jake practices a poem he will recite.

   Flashback begins:

3. 1941. Expository scenes of Jake losing a match, fighting with his wife, seeing Vickie, and having his first date with her.
4. 1943. Two matches with Sugar Ray Robinson, separated by a love scene between Jake and Vickie.
5. A montage sequence alternating a series of fights, 1944 to 1947, and home movies of Jake's private life.
6. A lengthy series of scenes in 1947, including three in the Copacabana nightclub, establishing Jake's jealousy over Vickie and hatred of the mob. He ends by throwing a fight for them.
7. 1949. An argument with Vickie, followed by Jake's winning the middleweight champion bout.
8. 1950. Jake beats up Vickie and his brother Joey in an unjustified jealous rage. He defends his title and fights Robinson again.
9. 1956. Jake retires and buys a nightclub in which he does comedy routines. Vickie leaves him and he is arrested on a morals charge.
10. 1958. Jake does his comedy act in a cheap strip joint; he fails to persuade Joey to reconcile with him.

    Flashback ends.

11. 1964. Jake prepares to go onstage to perform his recital.
12. A black title with a Biblical quotation and the film's dedication.

The beginning and ending of the film are vital in shaping our attitude to Jake's career. The first image shows him warming up in the ring before an unspecified fight (Fig. 11.85). Several filmic devices create our initial impressions of the protagonist. He bounces up and down in place, in slow-motion. This slow tempo is accompanied by languid classical music, suggesting that his boxing warm-up is like a dance. The deep-space staging places the ring's ropes prominently in the foreground and makes the ring seem huge, emphasizing Jake's solitude. This long take continues through the main credits, establishing boxing as both a beautiful and a lonely sport. The image remains abstract and remote: It is the only scene in the narrative which does not take place in a year specified by a superimposed title.

Fig. 11.85

A straight cut to Segment 2 shows Jake, suddenly fat and old, again practicing. He is going over his lines for a one-man show which consists of readings from famous literature and of a poem he has written about himself: "So give me a stage / Where this bull here can rage / And though I can fight / I'd much rather recite—That's entertainment!" This episode takes place quite late in the story, after the long struggles of his boxing career. Not until Segment 11 will the plot return to this moment in the story, with Jake continuing to rehearse his lines. In Segment 11, as the manager summons him onstage, he does some boxer-style warm-up punches to build his confidence, muttering rapidly over and over, "I'm the boss, I'm the boss."

By framing most of the story as a flashback, Scorsese links violence with entertainment. Jake's gesture of spreading his arms as he says, "That's entertainment!" in Segment 2 resembles the triumphant raising of his glove-clad hands whenever he wins a fight in the lengthy central flashback. Correspondingly, *Raging Bull* ignores Jake's early life and concentrates on two periods: his boxing career and his turn to stand-up comedy and literary recitations. Both periods present him as trying to control his life and the people around him. "I'm the boss," the last line spoken in the film, sums up Jake's attitude.

The plot structure we have outlined also traces a rise-and-fall pattern of development. After Segment 7, Jake's high point, his life runs downhill and his violence appears more and more savagely self-destructive. In addition, certain motifs highlight the role of violence in his life and the lives of those around him. During a rest period in his very first prizefight (Segment 3), a fistfight breaks out in the stands—suggesting at the outset that violence spills beyond the ring. Domestic relations are expressed through aggression, as in the tough-guy shoving between Jake and Joey and in Joey's disciplining his son by threatening to stab him. Most vividly, violence is again and again turned against women. Both Jake and Joey insult and threaten their wives, and Jake's beating of both his wives forms a grim counterpoint to his battles in the ring. During the first scene at the Copacabana, women emerge as targets of abuse. Jake accuses Vickie of flirting with other men, he insults a boxer and a mob member by suggesting that both are like women, and even the comedian onstage mocks women in the audience. Scene by scene, the organization of incidents and motifs suggests that aggression and pain pervade American life.

Scorsese puts Jake's violence in context by means of film techniques. In general, by appealing to conventions of realism, the film's style makes the violence in *Raging Bull* disturbing. Many of the fights are filmed with the camera on a Steadicam brace, which yields ominous tracking movements or close shots which emphasize grimaces. Backlighting, motivated by the spotlights around the ring, highlight droplets of sweat or blood that spray off the boxers as they are struck (Fig. 11.86). Rapid editing, often with ellipses, and loud, stinging cracks intensify the physical force of punches. Special make-up creates effects of blood vessels in the boxers' faces spurting grotesquely. Scorsese treats the violent scenes outside the ring differently, favoring long shots and less vivid sound effects.

Fig. 11.86

He creates a realistic social and historical context by using other conventions. One of these is a series of superimposed titles that identify each boxing match by date, locale, and participants. This narrational ploy yields a quasi-documentary quality.

The most important factor creating realism, however, is probably the acting. Aside from Robert De Niro, the cast was chosen from virtually unknown actors or nonactors. As a result, they did not bring glamorous star associations to the film. De Niro was known mainly for his grittily realistic performances in Scorsese's *Mean Streets* and *Taxi Driver,* as well as Michael Cimino's *The Deer Hunter.* In *Raging Bull,* the actors speak with thick Bronx accents, repeat or mumble many of their lines, and make no attempt to create likeable characters. In the publicity surrounding the film, much was also made of the fact that De Niro actually gained sixty pounds in order to play Jake as an older man. The film emphasizes De Niro's transformation by cutting straight from a medium close-up of Jake at the end of Segment 2, in 1964 (Fig. 11.87), to a similar framing of him in the ring in 1941 (Fig. 11.88). Such realism in the acting and other techniques makes it difficult for us to accept the film's violence casually, as we might in a conventional horror or crime film.

Fig. 11.87

Through its narrative structure and its use of the stylistic conventions of realism, the film thus offers a criticism of violence in American life, both in the ring and in the home. Yet the film does not permit us to condemn Jake as merely a raging bull. It also presents violence as fascinating and ambiguous. Jake's brutality is made disturbingly attractive.

The main indicator of this attitude is the fact that narration concentrates far more on the perpetrators of violence than on its victims. In particular the three important female characters—Jake's first wife, Joey's wife Lenore, and Vickie—have little to do in the action except take abuse or rail ineffectually against it. We never learn why they are initially attracted to the violent men they marry or why they stay with them so long. At first Vickie seems to admire Jake for his fame and his flashy car, but her willingness to sustain their marriage for so long is not explained. Indeed, her sudden decision to leave him after eleven years has no specific motivation.

Fig. 11.88

Such victims of Jake's violence serve chiefly to provoke him to respond. One portion of the action focuses on his pummeling of a "pretty" fighter to whom he thinks Vickie is attracted. Another deals with Jake's violent reaction to his irrational belief that Joey and Vickie have had an affair. It is notable that after this crisis, when Jake beats Joey up, Joey becomes as peripheral a figure as Vickie. We glimpse him briefly watching Jake's bloody title defeat and then see a short scene of him resisting Jake's offer of reconciliation. The film thus offers no positive counterweight to Jake's excesses.

Another indication of the narration's fascination with Jake's violence is the degree to which we are encouraged to identify with him. Several scenes show events from his point of view, using slow-motion to suggest that we are seeing not just what he sees but how he reacts subjectively to it. This technique becomes especially vivid when Jake sees Vickie with other men and becomes jealous. Similarly, in the final fight with Robinson, Jake's vision of his opponent is shown via a point-of-view framing. The POV imagery also incorporates a combined track forward and zoom out to make the ring seem to stretch far into the distance, while a decrease in the frontal light makes Robinson appear even more menacing (Fig. 11.89). Other deviations from realism, such as the thunderous throbbing on the sound track during Jake's major victory bout, also suggest that we are entering Jake's mind.

Fig. 11.89

In part Scorsese justifies the film's fascination with violence by emphasizing how self-destructive Jake is. However much he hurts other people, he injures himself at least as much. He also quickly regrets having hurt people, as several parallel scenes show. In Segment 3, Jake has a vicious argument with his first wife in which he threatens to kill her, but then immediately says, "Come on, honey, let's be—let's be friends. Truce, all right?" Later,

Fig. 11.90

after he has beaten Vickie up for her imagined infidelities, he apologizes and persuades her to stay with him. These domestic reconciliations are echoed in the big title fight where he defeats the current champion Cerdon, then walks to his opponent's corner and magnanimously embraces him.

Sympathy for Jake is reinforced by other means. *Raging Bull* suggests that he is strongly masochistic, using his aggression to induce others to inflict pain on him. This notion is emphasized in the love scene in Segment 4. There he childishly asks Vickie to caress and kiss the wounds from his triumph over Sugar Ray Robinson. A close-up of the couple (Fig. 11.90) links violence and sexuality, as Jake asks Vickie to kiss his bruises. Soon Jake denies himself sexual gratification by pouring ice water into his shorts. The scene then leads directly into a fight in which Sugar Ray Robinson defeats him.

This defeat is paralleled in Segment 8, another boxing scene, when Jake simply stands and goads Robinson into beating him to a pulp. The motif of masochism comes to a climax in Segment 9, when Jake is thrown into solitary confinement in a Dade County jail. A long, disturbing take has Jake beating his head and fists against the prison wall, as he asserts that he is not an animal and berates himself as stupid.

More implicitly, the film suggests a strain of repressed homosexuality in Jake's aggressiveness. His embrace of the defeated opponent, Cerdon, in his title fight, as well as his urging of Robinson to attack him in his final bout, suggest such an interpretation. In Segment 6, when Jake sits down at a nightclub table and jokes about how pretty his upcoming opponent is, he tauntingly offers him as a sex partner to a mobster he suspects of being in love with Vickie. In Segment 8, one scene begins with an erotically suggestive slow-motion shot of seconds' hands massaging Jake's torso. In general, there is a hint that Jake's fascination with boxing, and his refusal to deal with his domestic life, stem from an unacknowledged homosexual urge. Such an implication goes against the usual ideology of Hollywood, which assumes that a heterosexual romance is the basis for most narratives.

Ultimately the ideological stance that *Raging Bull* offers is far from being as straightforward as that of *Meet Me in St. Louis.* Instead of displaying an idealized image of American society, the film criticizes one pervasive aspect of that society: its penchant for unthinking violence. Yet it also displays a considerable fascination with that violence and with its main embodiment, Jake.

The film's ambiguity intensifies at the end. In Segment 12, a Biblical quotation appears: "So, for the second time, [the Pharisees] summoned the man who had been blind and said: 'Speak the truth before God. We know this fellow is a sinner.' 'Whether or not he is a sinner, I do not know,' the man replied. 'All I know is this: once I was blind and now I can see.' "

As this quotation emerges line by line, we are cued to relate it to the protagonist. Has Jake achieved some sort of enlightenment through his experiences? Several factors suggest not. Despite being a poor actor, he continues to perform literary recitals, trying to regain his public ("I'm the boss"). Futhermore, the speech he practices at the end is the famous "I could have been a contender" passage from *On the Waterfront.* In that film, a failed boxer blamed his brother for his lack of a chance to succeed. Is Jake now blaming Joey or someone else for his decline? Or is it possible that he has become aware enough of his faults to ironically recall a film in which the hero also comes to realize his mistakes?

After the Biblical quotation, there appears Scorsese's dedication of the film: "Remembering Haig R. Manoogian, teacher, May 23, 1916–May 26, 1980, With Love and resolution, Marty." Now the Biblical quotation may equally apply to Scorsese, himself from the tough Italian neighborhoods of New York. Were it not for people like this teacher, he might have ended up somewhat like Jake. And perhaps the professor, who helped him "to see," enabled him to present Jake with a mixture of detachment and sympathy.

As a cinema student, Scorsese was well aware of alternative foreign films like *Breathless* and *Tokyo Story*, so it is not surprising that his own work invites differing interpretations. The film's ending places *Raging Bull* in a tradition of Hollywood films (such as *Citizen Kane*) which avoid complete closure and opt for a degree of ambiguity, a denial of either/or answers. Such ambiguity can render the film's ideology equivocal, generating contrasting and even conflicting implicit meanings.

APPENDIX:
WRITING A CRITICAL ANALYSIS OF A FILM

The analyses in this chapter all exemplify a sort of writing characteristic of film criticism. It may be useful for us to conclude this part of the book by discussing some general choices and strategies open to the reader who wishes to write a film analysis for a course assignment, a published article, or some related purpose. This appendix does not seek to replace a good composition manual. We simply want to suggest some particular issues that come up in writing film analyses.

■ PREPARATION

As with any sort of writing, a film analysis requires that work be done before you sit down to write the piece. First, what sort of writing will the finished product be? Broadly speaking, your analysis will probably be some sort of *argumentative* essay. You will seek to present your opinion about the film and to back that opinion up with an argument. For instance, our analysis of *High School* argues that Wiseman does not neutrally present the school's everyday events; film form and style shape our response to the subject matter. Likewise, our discussion of *Raging Bull* tries to show that the film criticizes violence as mass entertainment while still displaying a fascination with its visceral appeal.

Deciding on the film to be analyzed is probably not a great problem. Perhaps something about it attracted you, or you have heard that it is worth examining closely. More difficult is the process of thinking through in some detail what you want to say about the film. What do you find most intriguing or disturbing about the film? What makes the film noteworthy? Does it illustrate some aspect of filmmaking with special clarity? Does it have an unusual effect on the viewer? Do its implicit or symptomatic meanings seem to have particular importance?

Your answer to such questions will furnish the *thesis* of your analysis. The thesis, as in any piece of writing, is the central claim your argument advances. In our analysis of *His Girl Friday*, the thesis is that the film uses classical narrative devices to create an impression of rapid speed. In our discussion of *Man with a Movie Camera*, the thesis is that the film makes the viewer aware of how cinema manipulates the world we see on film.

Typically, your thesis will be a claim about the film's *functions*, its *effects*, or its *meanings* (or some mixture of all three aspects). For example, we argue that the various characters of *Do The Right Thing* allow Spike Lee to create interconnected plot lines and a broader theme of the problems of maintaining a community. In our discussion of *North by Northwest*, we concentrate more on how the film achieves the effects of suspense and surprise. The analysis of *Meet Me in St. Louis* emphasizes how technique carries implicit and symptomatic meanings.

The chemist who analyzes a compound breaks it into constituent elements. The orchestra conductor who analyzes a score takes it apart mentally in order to see how the melodies and motifs are organized. All analysis implies breaking something down into its component parts. Your thesis will be a general claim about the functions, effects, or meanings of the film. Your analysis will show how these arise from the interaction of the parts that make up the film's formal and stylistic systems. For example, our claim that *Raging Bull* links violence with entertainment is based partly on the evidence that the opening sequence in the boxing ring is followed immediately by Jake's rehearsal of his one-man show, ending with the line: "That's entertainment!"

In most cases, your argument will benefit if you begin with considerable preparatory work before actually beginning to write your piece. You can, as we suggest throughout Part II, make a segmentation of the film. Sometimes you will find it necessary for your argument to show your reader a scene-by-scene segmentation, as we do in the *His Girl Friday* discussion (p. 384). For other purposes, it may suffice only to show a more general breakdown into larger-scale sections. In still other cases, you may find it necessary to bring out a still finer-grained segmentation; we do this in considering the three subsegments of the final chase scene in *North by Northwest* (pp. 391–393). However much of your segmentation finally surfaces in your written analysis, we strongly recommend making a fairly detailed segmentation every time you examine a film. It will make the overall form clearer to you and thus enable you to spot the patterns of repetition, variation, and development that unify the film.

In examining a narrative film, it is usually a good idea to start by identifying the various causes and effects, the characters' goals, the principles of development, the degree of closure at the end, and other basic components of narrative form. In examining a nonnarrative film, you will need to be especially alert to its use of categorical, rhetorical, abstract, or associational principles. You probably noticed that nearly every one of our analyses includes, early on, a statement about the film's underlying formal organization. This provides a firm basis for more detailed analysis.

Another part of preparatory note taking involves jotting down accurate descriptions of various film techniques that are used. Here we can simply remind you of the suggestions for analyzing style that we set out in Chapter 10 (pp. 357–360). Once you have determined the overall organizational structure of the film, you can identify salient techniques, trace out patterns of techniques across the whole film, and propose functions for those techniques. The critic should be able to identify the techniques in isolation. Is this a case of three-point lighting? Is this a continuity cut? Just as important, the analyst should be sensitive to context—What is the function of the technique *here*?—and to patterning—Does the technique repeat or develop across the film?

Often beginning film analysts are uncertain as to what techniques are most relevant to their thesis. Sometimes they try to describe every single costume or cut or pan, and they wind up drowned in data. It is most fruitful to think in advance about what techniques stand out as most pertinent to the thesis that you want to prove. For example, the use of optical POV shots and crosscutting in *North by Northwest* is highly relevant to our general claim that Hitchcock achieves suspense and surprise by shifting from a restricted to an unrestricted range of knowledge. The performance styles, while relevant to some other thesis about the film, are not relevant to this one. By contrast, we emphasize acting technique somewhat more in our analysis of *Raging Bull*, because acting is pertinent to our analysis of the film's use of realistic conventions. Similarly, the editing in *Meet Me in St. Louis* would be interesting from the standpoint of another argument, but it is not central to the one that we are making, so it goes almost completely unmentioned.

Once you have a thesis, an awareness of the overall shape of the film, and a set of notes on the techniques relevant to your thesis, you are ready to plan the organization of your critical analysis.

■ ORGANIZATION AND WRITING

Broadly speaking, most argumentative writing has this underlying structure:

Introduction: Background information
    Statement of thesis

Body: Reasons to believe the thesis
    Evidence and examples that support the thesis

Conclusion: Restatement of thesis and discussion of its broader implications

You will notice that all of our analyses in this part of the book adhere to this basic structure. The opening portion seeks to lead the reader into the argument to come, and the thesis is set forth at the end of this introduction. Where the introduction is brief, as in the *His Girl Friday* analysis, the thesis comes at the end of the first paragraph (p. 384). Where more background material is needed, the introduction is somewhat longer and the thesis is stated a little later. In the *High School* essay, the thesis comes at the end of the fourth paragraph (p. 410).

These last remarks depend on a principle which you already know but which no writer can ever afford to forget: The building block of any piece of writing is the paragraph. Each slot in the argumentative pattern outlined above will be filled by one or more paragraphs. The introduction is at least one paragraph, the body will be several paragraphs, and the conclusion will be one or two paragraphs.

Typically, the introductory paragraphs of a film analysis consist of little concrete evidence. Instead, this is the place to initiate the thesis you want to advance. Often this involves situating the point within some pertinent background information. For example, our analysis of *Tokyo Story* situates the film in a tradition of noncontinuity editing before stating our thesis. Usually the introductory paragraph or two consist of generalizations of this sort. However, if you are adventurous, you may wish to start with a concrete piece of evidence—say, an intriguing scene or detail from the film—before you move quickly to state your thesis. Our *Meet Me in St. Louis* piece uses this sort of opening.

Writing a film analysis poses one particular problem of organization. Should the body of the argument follow the film's progress in chronological order, so that each paragraph deals with a scene or major part? In some cases this can work. By and large, however, you strengthen your argument by following a more conceptual structure of the sort indicated in our outline.

It is useful to think of the body of your essay as consisting of a series of *reasons* to believe the thesis, with those reasons buttressed by evidence and examples. An instance is our analysis of *Breathless*, which contends that Godard's film both pays homage to *film noir* outlaw movies and also revises their conventions through a rough-edged treatment. The first paragraph sketches the relevant Hollywood traditions, and the second shows how the basic story of *Breathless* is comparable to the couple-on-the-run movie. The next three paragraphs make the point that Godard's film also reworks the studio conventions. Michel himself seems to be imitating Hollywood tough guys (p. 399), while the film's form and style seem casual (p. 399), as if aiming to let the audience enjoy a new, more self-conscious version of an American crime movie (p. 400).

Since the argument involves an extended comparison-and-contrast strategy, the essay's body explores the film's similarities to and differences from Hollywood conventions. The next eleven paragraphs seek to establish the following points about the film's narrative form:

1. Michel is like a Hollywood protagonist in certain ways (p. 400).
2. The action is, however, much more choppy and digressive than in a Hollywood film (p. 400).
3. The death of the policeman offers an extended instance of an abruptly handled scene (p. 400).
4., 5. By contrast, the bedroom conversation of Patricia and Michel exemplifies a fairly static narrative situation in which little progress is made toward Michel's goals (pp. 400–401).
6. Later the plot starts moving again, but once more it stalls (p. 401).
7., 8. Moving toward resolution, the plot again picks up, but the finale remains enigmatic and open-ended (pp. 401–402).

9., 10.   Overall, Michel and Patricia remain puzzling and opaque as characters (p. 402).

11.   The characterization of the couple is thus sharply different from the romantic couple in most *film noir* plots (p. 402).

Each of these points constitutes a reason to accept the thesis.

Supporting reasons may be of many sorts. Several of our analyses distinguish between reasons based upon the film's overall narrative form and reasons based upon stylistic choices. The portion of the *Breathless* essay we have just reviewed offers evidence to support our claims about the film's reworking of Hollywood narrative conventions. The paragraphs that follow this material discuss Godard's similarly self-conscious use of stylistic strategies. In discussing *Meet Me in St. Louis*, we concentrate more on reviewing various motifs that create particular thematic effects. Here, as usual, preparation can save you time in the long run. As you start to formulate your thesis, it is a good idea to make a list of reasons that, suitably arranged, can form the body of your argument.

If you organize the essay conceptually rather than as a blow-by-blow résumé of the action, you may find it useful to acquaint your reader with the plot action at some point. A brief synopsis soon after the introduction may do the trick. (See, for example, our *North by Northwest* analysis, p. 388.) Alternatively, you may wish to cover basic plot material when you discuss segmentation, characterization, causal progression, or other topics. The crucial point is that the writer is not forced to follow the film's order. You can make the film subordinate to your argument about it.

Typically, each reason for the thesis becomes the topic sentence of a paragraph, with more detailed evidence displayed in the sentences that follow. In the *Breathless* example, each main point is followed by specific examples of how plot action, dialogue, or film techniques at once refer to Hollywood tradition and loosen up the conventions. It is in mounting such examples that the writer's detailed notes about salient scenes or film techniques will prove useful. You can select the strongest and most vivid instances of mise-en-scene, cinematography, editing, and sound to back up the reason that each paragraph explores.

The body of the analysis can be made more persuasive by several other tactics. A paragraph that compares or contrasts this film with another can help you zero in on specific aspects that are central to your argument. (See, for example, our contrast between *Man with a Movie Camera* and *High School*.) You can also include a brief in-depth analysis of a single scene or sequence that drives your argumentative point home. We use this tactic in discussing several films' endings, chiefly because a concluding segment often reveals most clearly overall principles of development. As many of our analyses suggest, a close scrutiny of the film's ending can be a strong way to end the body of your analysis.

In general, the body of the argument should progress toward stronger or subtler reasons for believing the thesis. In discussing *High School*, we suggest that the filmmaker uses formal and stylistic choices to guide our response. Only then do we raise the question as to whether the film may still be considered somewhat ambiguous. This leads us to consider how the filmmaker's choices can be interpreted in different ways. This is a fairly complex point that would probably not come across if introduced early on. Only after the analysis has worked through more clear-cut matters is it possible to consider nuances of interpretation.

As for the ending: this is the occasion to restate the thesis (skillfully, not repeating previous statements word for word) and to remind the reader of the reasons to entertain the thesis. The ending is also an opportunity for you to try for a bit of eloquence, a telling quotation, a bit of historical context, or a concrete motif from the film itself. Again, in making preparatory notes, it is wise to look for something that can create a vivid ending. Just as there is no general recipe for understanding films or interpreting them, there is no formula for writing incisive and enlightening criticism. But there are basic principles and rules of thumb that govern good writing of all sorts. Only through writing, and constant rewriting, do these principles and rules come to seem second nature to the writer. By analyzing films, we come to a better understanding of the sources of our pleasure in them, and we are able to share that understanding with others. If we succeed, the writing itself can give pleasure to ourselves and our readers.

NOTES AND QUERIES

■ SPECIMENS OF FILM ANALYSIS

Many of the critical studies we have cited in the Notes and Queries to Parts II and III repay attention as instances of film analysis. Here are some others that exemplify diverse approaches: Thomas W. Benson and Carolyn Anderson, *Reality Fictions: The Films of Frederick Wiseman* (Carbondale: Southern Illinois University Press, 1989); David Bordwell, *The Films of Carl-Theodor Dreyer* (Berkeley: University of California Press, 1981); Noël Burch, *In and Out of Sync: The Awakening of a Cine-Dreamer* (London: Scolar Press, 1991); Robert Burgoyne, *Bertolucci's "1900": A Narrative and Historical Analysis* (Detroit: Wayne State University Press, 1991); Noël Carroll, "Identity and Difference: From Ritual Symbolism to Condensation in *Inauguration of the Pleasure Dome*," *Millennium Film Journal* **6** (Spring 1980): 31–42; Philip Drummond, "Textual Space in *Un Chien andalou*," *Screen* **18,** 3 (Autumn 1977): 55–119; Stephen Heath, "Film and System: Terms of Analysis," *Screen* **16,** 1 (Spring 1975): 7–77, and **16,** 2 (Summer 1975): 91–113; Sandy Flitterman-Lewis, *To Desire Differently: Feminism and the French Cinema* (Urbana: University of Illinois Press, 1990); Lea Jacobs, *The Wages of Sin: Censorship and the Fallen Woman Film, 1928–1942* (Madison: University of Wisconsin Press, 1991); Annette Kuhn, "The Camera I—Observations on Documentary," *Screen* **19,** 2 (Summer 1978): 61–83; Thierry Kuntzel, "The Film-Work, 2," *Camera Obscura* **5** (1980): 7–68; Judith Mayne, *The Woman at the Keyhole: Feminism and Women's Cinema* (Bloomington: Indiana University Press, 1990); Vlada Petrić, "Two Lincoln Assassinations by D. W. Griffith," *Quarterly Review of Film Studies* **3,** 3 (Summer 1978): 345–369; Bill Simon, "'Reading' *Zorns Lemma*," *Millennium Film Journal* **1,** 2

(Spring–Summer 1978): 38–49; P. Adams Sitney, *Modernist Montage: The Obscurity of Vision in Cinema and Literature* (New York: Columbia University Press, 1990); and Kristin Thompson, *Breaking the Glass Armor: Neoformalist Film Analysis* (Princeton, N.J.: Princeton University Press, 1988).

Two rich collections of film analyses are *Enclitic*'s special number **5,** 2/**6,** 1 (Fall 1981/Spring 1982), and Peter Lehman, ed., *Close Viewings: An Anthology of New Film Criticism* (Tallahassee: Florida State University Press, 1990).

Feminist filmmaker Lizzie Borden's personal perspective on *Raging Bull*, "Blood and Redemption," *Sight and Sound* **5,** 2 (NS) (February 1995): 61, offers an interesting supplement to our analysis.

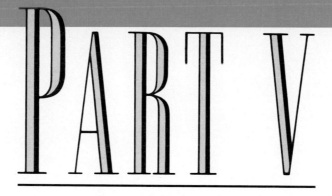

PART V

FILM HISTORY

TWELVE

FILM FORM
AND
FILM HISTORY

"Not everything is possible at all times." This aphorism of art historian Heinrich Wölffin might serve as a slogan for the final chapter of this book. So far, our survey of film art has examined various formal and stylistic possibilities, and we have drawn our examples from the entire range of film history. But film forms and techniques do not exist in a timeless realm, equally accessible to all filmmakers. In particular historical circumstances, certain possibilities are present while others are not. Griffith could not make films as Godard does, nor could Godard make films as Griffith did. This chapter asks: What are some ways in which film art has been treated in some particular historical contexts?

These contexts will be defined, first, by period and by nation. Although there are other equally good tools for tracing change, period and nation remain useful ways of organizing historical problems. Second, in some of our cases, we shall look for what are typically called *film movements*. A film movement consists of:

1. Films that are produced within a particular period and/or nation and that share significant traits of style and form; and
2. Filmmakers who operate within a common production structure and who share certain assumptions about filmmaking.

There are other ways of defining a historical context (for example, biographical study, genre study), but the category of *movement* corresponds most closely to the emphasis of this book. The concepts of formal and stylistic systems permit us to compare films within a movement and to contrast them with films of other movements.

Finally, our range of choice will be narrowed still further. We are concerned with Hollywood and selected alternatives. We shall trace the development of the commercial narrative cinema while contrasting it to other approaches to style and form.

Since a film movement consists of not only films but also the activities of specific filmmakers, we must go beyond noting stylistic and formal qualities. For each period and nation, we shall also sketch relevant factors that affect the cinema. These factors include the state of the film industry, artistic theories held by the filmmakers themselves, pertinent technological features, and elements of the socioeconomic context of the period. Such factors necessarily help explain how a particular movement began, what shaped its development, and what affected its decline. However brief, such material will also provide a context for particular films we have already discussed; for example, the following section on early cinema situates Lumière and Méliès in the context of their period.

Needless to say, what follows is drastically incomplete. The writing of serious film history is in its early stages, and we must often rely on secondary sources that will eventually be superseded. This chapter reflects only current states of knowledge; there are doubtless important films, filmmakers, and movements that await discovery. Moreover, there are many unfortunate omissions. Important filmmakers who do not relate to a movement (for example, Tati, Bresson, Kurosawa) are absent, as are certain important film movements, such as French populist cinema of the 1930s and Brazil's Cinema Nôvo movement of the early 1960s. What follows simply seeks to show how certain possibilities of film form and style were explored within a few typical and well-known historical periods.

EARLY CINEMA (1893–1903)

In order to create the illusion of movement, still pictures must appear in rapid succession. To prepare them and display them at the right rate, certain technologies are necessary. Most basically, there must be a way of recording a long series of images on some sort of support. In principle one could simply draw a string of images on a strip of paper or a disk. But photography offered the cheapest and most efficient way to generate the thousands of images needed for a reasonably lengthy exhibition. Thus the invention of photography in 1826 launched a series of discoveries that made cinema possible.

Early photographs required lengthy exposures (initially hours, later minutes) for a single image; this made photographed motion pictures, which need twelve or more frames per second, impossible. Faster exposures, of about $1/25$ second, became possible by the 1870s, but only on glass plates. Glass plates were not usable for motion pictures since there was no practical way to move them through a camera or projector. In 1878 Eadweard Muybridge, an American photographer, did make a series of photographs of a running horse by using a series of cameras with glass plate film and fast exposure, but he was primarily interested in freezing phases of an action, not re-creating the movement by projecting the images in succession.

In 1882 another scientist interested in analyzing animal movement, the Frenchman Étienne-Jules Marey, invented a camera that recorded twelve separate images on the edge of a revolving disc of film. This constituted a step toward the motion-picture camera. In 1888 Marey built the first camera to use a strip of flexible film, this time on paper. Again, the purpose was only to break down movement into a series of stills, and the movements photographed lasted a second or less.

In 1889 Kodak introduced a crude flexible film base, celluloid (one type of which still forms the base of film stock today). Once this base was improved and camera mechanisms had been devised to draw the film past the lens and expose it to light, the creation of lengthy series of frames became possible.

Projectors had existed for many years and had been used to show slides and other shadow entertainments. These "magic lanterns" were modified by the addition of shutters, cranks, and other devices to become early motion picture projectors.

Fig. 12.1

One final device was needed if films were to be projected. Since the film stops briefly while the light shines through each individual frame, there had to be a mechanism to create an *intermittent* motion of the film. Marey used a Maltese cross gear on his 1888 camera, and this became a standard part of early cameras and projectors.

The combination of a flexible, transparent film base, a fast exposure time, a mechanism to pull the film through the camera, an intermittent device to stop the film, and a shutter to block off light was achieved by the early 1890s. After several years, inventors working independently in many countries had developed several different film cameras and projection devices. The two most important firms were Edison in America and Lumière in France.

By 1893 Thomas A. Edison's assistant, W. K. L. Dickson, developed a camera that made short 35mm films. Interested in exploiting these films as a novelty, Edison hoped to combine them with his phonograph to show sound movies. He had Dickson develop a peep-show machine, the *Kinetoscope* (Fig. 12.1), to display these films to individual viewers.

Since Edison believed that movies were a passing fad, he did not develop a system to project films onto a screen. This was left to the Lumière brothers, Louis and Auguste. They invented their own camera independently; it exposed a short roll of 35mm film and also served as a projector (Fig. 12.2). On December 28, 1895, the Lumière brothers held one of the first public showings of motion pictures projected on a screen, at the Grand Café in Paris.

There had been several earlier public screenings, including one on November 1 of the same year, by the German inventor Max Skladanowsky. But Skladanowsky's bulky machine required two strips of wide-gauge film running simultaneously and hence had less influence on the subsequent technological development of the cinema. Although the Lumières did not invent cinema, they largely determined the specific form the new medium was to take. Edison himself was soon to abandon Kinetoscopes and form his own production company to make films for theaters.

The first films were extremely simple in form and style. They usually

Fig. 12.2

Fig. 12.3

consisted of a single shot framing an action, usually at long-shot distance. In the first film studio, Edison's Black Maria (Fig. 12.3), vaudeville entertainers, famous sports figures, and celebrities (for example, Annie Oakley) performed for the camera. A hinged portion of the roof opened to admit a patch of sunlight, and the entire building turned on a circular rail (visible in Figure 12.3) to follow the sun's motion. The Lumières, on the other hand, took their cameras out to parks, gardens, beaches, and other public places to film everyday activities or news events, as in their *Arrival of a Train at a Station* (see Fig. 7.48).

Until about 1903 most films showed scenic places or noteworthy events, but narrative form also entered the cinema from the beginning. Edison staged comic scenes, like one copyrighted 1893 in which a drunken man struggles briefly with a policeman. The Lumières made a popular success with *L'Arroseur arrosé* (*The Waterer Watered*, 1895), also a comic scene, in which a boy tricks a gardener into squirting himself with a hose (see Fig. 6.6).

After the initial success of the new medium, filmmakers had to find more complex or interesting formal properties to keep the public's interest. The Lumières sent camera operators all over the world to show films and to photograph important events and exotic locales. But after making a huge number of films in their first few years, the Lumières' output diminished, and they ceased filmmaking altogether in 1905.

In 1896 Georges Méliès purchased a projector from the British inventor Robert William Paul and soon built a camera based on the same mechanism. Méliès's first films resembled the Lumières' shots of everyday activities. But as we have seen (p. 171), Méliès was also a magician, and he discovered the possibilities of simple special effects. In 1897 Méliès built his own studio. Unlike Edison's Black Maria, Méliès's studio was glass-sided like a greenhouse, allowing the filming to utilize sunlight coming from any direction, so that the studio did not have to move with the sun (Fig. 12.4).

Méliès also began to build elaborate settings to create fantasy worlds within which his magical transformations could occur. We have already seen how Méliès thereby became the first master of mise-en-scene technique (see Figs. 6.2–6.5). From the simple filming of a magician performing a trick or

Fig. 12.4

two in a traditional stage setting, Méliès progressed to longer narratives with a series of "tableaux." Each consisted of one shot, except when the transformations occurred. These were created by cuts designed to be imperceptible on the screen. He also adapted old stories, such as *Cinderella* (1899) or wrote his own. All these factors made Méliès's films extremely popular and widely imitated.

Fig. 12.5

During this early period, films circulated freely from country to country. The French phonograph company Pathé Frères moved increasingly to film-making from 1901 on, establishing production and distribution branches in many countries. Soon it was the largest film concern in the world, a position it retained until 1914, when the beginning of World War I forced it to cut back production. In England, several entrepreneurs managed to invent or obtain their own filmmaking equipment and made scenics, narratives, and trick films from 1895 into the early years of the twentieth century. Members of the "Brighton School" (primarily G. Albert Smith and James Williamson), as well as others like Cecil Hepworth, shot their films on location or in simple open-air studios (as in Fig. 12.5, from Smith's 1898 film, *Santa Claus*). Their innovative films circulated abroad and influenced other filmmakers. Pioneers in other countries invented or bought equipment and were soon making their own films of everyday scenes or fantasy transformations.

From about 1904 on, narrative form became the most prominent type of filmmaking in the commercial industry, and the worldwide success of the cinema continued to grow. French, Italian, and American films dominated world markets. Later, World War I was to restrict the free flow of films from country to country, and Hollywood was to emerge as the dominant industrial force in world film production. These factors contributed to the creation of distinct differences in the formal traits of individual national cinemas.

THE DEVELOPMENT OF THE CLASSICAL HOLLYWOOD CINEMA (1908–1927)

Edison's determination to exploit the money-making potential of his company's invention led him to try to force competing filmmakers out of business by bringing patents-violation suits against them. One other company, American Mutoscope & Biograph, managed to survive by inventing cameras that differed from Edison's patents. Other firms kept operating while Edison fought them in court. In 1908 Edison compromised with Biograph to bring these other companies under control by forming the Motion Picture Patents Company (MPPC), a group of ten firms based primarily in Chicago, New York, and New Jersey. Edison and Biograph were the only stockholders and patent owners. They licensed other members to make, distribute, and exhibit films.

The MPPC never succeeded in eliminating its competition. Numerous independent companies were established throughout this period. Biograph's most important director from 1908 on, D. W. Griffith, formed his own company in 1913, as did other filmmakers. The United States government brought suit against the MPPC in 1912; in 1915 it was declared a monopoly. Around 1910, film companies began to move permanently to California.

Eventually Hollywood and other small towns on the outskirts of Los Angeles became the site of widespread film production. Some historians claim that the independent companies fled west to avoid the harassment of the MPPC, but some MPPC companies also made the move. Among the advantages of Hollywood were the climate, which permitted shooting year-round, and the great variety of terrains—mountains, ocean, desert, city—available for location shooting.

The demand for films was so great that no single studio could meet it. This was one of the factors that had led Edison to accept the existence of a group of other companies, although he tried to control them as much as possible through his licensing procedure. Before 1920, the American industry assumed the structure that would continue for years: a few large studios with individual artists under contract, and a peripheral group of small independent producers. In Hollywood, the studios developed a "factory" system, with each production under the control of the producer, who usually did not work on the actual making of the films. Even an independent director like Buster Keaton, with his own studio, had a business manager and distributed his films through larger companies, first Metro and then United Artists.

Gradually, through the 1910s and 1920s the smaller studios merged to form the large firms which still exist today. Famous Players joined with Jesse L. Lasky and then formed a distribution wing, Paramount. By the late 1920s, most of the major companies existed—MGM (a merger of Metro, Goldwyn, and Mayer), Fox Film Corporation (merged with 20th Century in 1935), Warner Bros., Universal, and Paramount. Though in competition with one another, these studios tended to cooperate to a degree, realizing that no one firm could satisfy the market.

Within this system of mass-production studios, the American cinema became definitively oriented toward narrative form. One of Edison's directors, Edwin S. Porter, made some of the first films to utilize principles of narrative continuity and development (as opposed to the series of tableaux or the filmed vaudeville-style skits that made up early, preclassical narrative films). Among these was *The Life of an American Fireman* (1903), which showed the race of the fire fighters to rescue a mother and a child from a burning house. Although this film utilized several important classical narrative elements (a fireman's premonition of the disaster, a series of shots of the horse-drawn engine racing to the house), it still had not worked out the logic of temporal relations in cutting. Thus we see the rescue of a mother and her child twice, from both inside and outside the house. Porter had not realized the possibility of intercutting the two locales within the action or matching on action to convey narrative information to the audience.

In 1903, Porter made *The Great Train Robbery*, in some ways a prototype for the classical American film. Here the action develops with a clear linearity of time, space, and logic. We follow each stage of the robbery (Fig. 12.6), the pursuit, and the final defeat of the robbers. In 1905, Porter also created a simple parallel narrative in *The Kleptomaniac*, contrasting the fates of a rich woman and a starving woman who are both caught stealing.

British filmmakers were working along similar lines. Indeed, many historians now believe that Porter derived some of his editing techniques from films like James Williamson's *Fire!* (1901) and G. A. Smith's *Mary Jane's*

Fig. 12.6

Mishap (1903). The most famous British film of this era was Lewin Fitzhamon's 1905 film *Rescued by Rover* (produced by a major British firm, Cecil Hepworth), which treated a kidnapping in a linear fashion similar to that of *The Great Train Robbery*. After the kidnapping, we see each stage of Rover's journey to find the child, his return to fetch the child's father, and their retracing of the route to the kidnapper's lair. All the shots along the route maintain consistent screen direction, so that the geography of the action is completely intelligible.

In 1908, D. W. Griffith began his directing career. In the next five years, he was to make hundreds of one- and two-reelers (running about 15 and 30 minutes, respectively). These films created relatively complex narratives in short spans. Griffith certainly was not the initiator of all the devices with which he has been credited, but he did give many techniques strong narrative motivation. For example, a few other filmmakers had used simple last-minute rescues with crosscutting between the rescuers and victims, but Griffith is famous for developing and popularizing this technique (Figs. 8.95–8.98, p. 298). By the time he made *The Birth of a Nation* (1915) and *Intolerance* (1916), Griffith was creating lengthy sequences by cutting between several different locales. During the early teens, he also directed his actors in an unusual way, concentrating on subtle changes in facial expression. To catch such nuances, he set up his camera closer than did many of his contemporaries, placing his actors in medium long shot or medium shot. Griffith's films were widely influential. In addition, his dynamic, rapid editing in the final chase scenes of *Intolerance* was to have a considerable impact on the Soviet Montage style of the 1920s.

The refinement of narratively motivated cutting occurs in the work of a number of important filmmakers of the period. One of these was Thomas H. Ince, a producer and director responsible for many films between 1910 and the end of World War I. He devised a "unit system," whereby a single producer could oversee the making of several films at once. He also called for tight narratives, with no digressions or loose ends. *Civilization* (1915) and *The Italian* (1915) are good examples of films directed or supervised by Ince. He also supervised the popular Westerns of William S. Hart (p. 56), who directed many of his own films.

Another prolific filmmaker of this period (and later years as well) was Cecil B. De Mille. Not yet engaged in the creation of historical epics, De Mille made a series of feature-length dramas and comedies. His *The Cheat* (1915) reflects important changes occurring in the studio style between about 1914 and 1917. During that period, the glass-roofed studios of the earlier period began to give way to studios dependent on artificial lighting rather than mixed daylight and electric lighting. *The Cheat* used spectacular effects of chiaroscuro, with only one or two bright sources of light and no fill light. According to legend, De Mille justified this effect to nervous exhibitors as "Rembrandt" lighting. This so-called Rembrandt, or "north," lighting was to become part of the classical repertoire of lighting techniques. *The Cheat* also greatly impressed the French Impressionist filmmakers, who occasionally used similar stark lighting effects.

Like many American films of the teens, *The Cheat* also uses a linear pattern of narrative. The first scene (Fig. 12.7) introduces the hard lighting

Fig. 12.7

Fig. 12.8

Fig. 12.9

Fig. 12.10

Fig. 12.11

Fig. 12.12

Fig. 12.13

Fig. 12.14

Fig. 12.15

but also quickly establishes the Japanese businessman as a ruthless collector of objects; we see him burning his brand onto a small statue. The initial action motivates a later scene in which the businessman brands the heroine, who has fallen into his power by borrowing money from him (Fig. 12.8). *The Cheat* was evidence of the growing formal complexity of the Hollywood film.

The period 1909–1917 saw the development of the basic continuity principles. Eyeline matches occur with increasing frequency from 1910 on. The match on action developed at about the same time and was in common use by 1916. It appears in such Douglas Fairbanks films as *The Americano* (1916) and *Wild and Woolly* (1917). Shot/reverse shot was used only occasionally between 1911 and 1915, but it became widespread by 1916–1917; instances occur in such films as *The Cheat* (1915), *The Narrow Trail* (a William S. Hart Western of 1917), and Griffith's *A Romance of Happy Valley* (1919). During this period, most films seldom violated the axis-of-action rule in using these techniques.

By the 1920s, the continuity system had become a standardized style that directors in the Hollywood studios used almost automatically to create coherent spatial and temporal relations within narratives. A match on action could provide a cut to a closer view in a scene, as in *The Three Musketeers*, with Fairbanks (Figs. 12.9, 12.10; Fred Niblo, 1921). A three-way conversation around a table would no longer be handled in a single frontal shot. Note the clear spatial relations in Figures 12.11 through 12.15, shots from *Are Parents People?* (Malcolm St. Clair, 1925). The daughter sits down at the table in an establishing shot (Fig. 12.11), then looks back and forth in shot/ reverse shot at her parents, seated at the ends of the table. At the period, screen direction was usually respected, as in this case. When an awkward match might have resulted from the joining of two shots, the filmmakers could cover it by inserting a dialogue title.

Keaton's *Our Hospitality* (1923), which we examined in Chapter 6, provides another example of a classical narrative. Keaton's mastery of classical form and style are evident in the carefully motivated recurrences of the various narrative elements and in the straightforward causal development from the death of Willie McKay's father in the feud to Willie's final resolution of the feud.

By the end of the silent period, in the late 1920s, the classical Hollywood cinema had developed into a sophisticated movement, but the Hollywood "product" was remarkably standardized. All of the major studios used the same production system, with a similar division of labor at each. Independent production was less important. Some independent firms made low-budget films, often Westerns, for small and rural theaters. Even powerful Hollywood stars and producers had trouble remaining independent. Keaton gave up his small studio in 1928 to go to MGM under contract; there his career declined, due partly to the incompatibility of his old working methods with the rigid production patterns of the huge studio. Griffith, Mary Pickford, Fairbanks, and Charles Chaplin were better off. Forming a distributing corporation of their own, United Artists, in 1919, they were able to continue independent production at small companies under their umbrella corporation, though Griffith's company soon failed, and the careers of Fairbanks and Pickford declined soon after the introduction of sound.

There were alternative kinds of films being made during these years— most of them in other countries. After examining these alternative movements, we shall return to a brief examination of the classical Hollywood cinema after the coming of sound.

GERMAN EXPRESSIONISM (1919–1926)

At the start of World War I, the output of the German film industry was relatively small, though some impressive pictures were made there. Germany's 2000 movie theaters were playing mostly French, American, Italian, and Danish films. Although America and France banned German films from their screens immediately, Germany was not even in a solid enough position to ban French and American films, for then the theaters would have had little to show.

In order to combat imported competition, as well as to create its own propaganda films, the German government began to support the film industry. In 1916 film imports were banned except from neutral Denmark, whose film industry had close ties to that of Germany. Production increased rapidly; from a dozen small companies in 1911, the number grew to 131 by 1918. But government policy encouraged these companies to band together into cartels.

The war was unpopular with many in Germany, and rebellious tendencies increased after the success of the Russian Revolution in 1917. Widespread strikes and antiwar petitions were organized during the winter of 1916–1917. In order to promote pro-war films, the government, the Deutsche Bank, and large industrial concerns combined several small film firms to create the large company UFA (short for Universumfilm Aktiengesellschaft) in late 1917. Backed by these essentially conservative interests, UFA was a move toward a control of not only the German market but the postwar international market as well.

With this huge financial backing, UFA was able to gather superb technicians and build the best-equipped studios in Europe. These studios later attracted foreign filmmakers, including the young Alfred Hitchcock. During the 1920s, Germany coproduced many films with companies in other countries, thus helping to spread German stylistic influence abroad.

In late 1918, with the end of the war, the need for overt militarist propaganda disappeared. Although mainstream dramas and comedies continued to be made, the German film industry concentrated on three genres. One was the internationally popular adventure serial, featuring spy rings, clever detectives, or exotic settings. Second was a brief sex exploitation cycle, which dealt "educationally" with such topics as homosexuality and prostitution. Finally, UFA set out to copy the popular Italian historical epics of the prewar period.

This last type of film proved financially successful for UFA. In spite of continued bans and prejudice against German films in America, England, and France, UFA finally was able to break into the international market. In September 1919 Ernst Lubitsch's *Madame Dubarry,* an epic of the French Revolution (Fig. 12.16), inaugurated the magnificent UFA Palast theater in Berlin. This film helped reopen the world film market to Germany. Released as *Passion* in the United States, this film was extremely popular and won critical acclaim in many other countries as well. It was less enthusiastically received in France, however, where its premiere was considerably delayed by charges that it was anti-French propaganda. But it did well in most markets, and other Lubitsch historical films were soon exported. In 1923, he became the first German director to be hired by Hollywood.

Fig. 12.16

Some small companies briefly remained independent. Among these was Erich Pommer's Decla (later Decla-Bioscop). In 1919, the firm undertook to produce an unconventional script by two unknowns, Carl Mayer and Hans Janowitz. These young writers wanted the film to be made in an unusually stylized way. The three designers assigned to the film—Hermann Warm, Walter Reimann, and Walter Röhrig—suggested that it be done in an Expressionist style. As an avant-garde movement, Expressionism had first been important in painting (starting about 1910) and had been quickly taken up in theater, then in literature, and in architecture. Now company officials consented to try it in the cinema, apparently believing that this might be a selling point in the international market.

This belief was vindicated when the inexpensively made film, *The Cabinet of Dr. Caligari* (1920), created a sensation in Berlin, and then in the United States, France, and other countries. Because of its success, other films in the Expressionist style soon followed. The result was a stylistic movement in cinema that lasted several years.

The success of *Caligari* and other Expressionist films kept Germany's avant-garde directors largely within the industry. A few experimental film-makers made abstract films, like Viking Eggeling's *Diagonal-symphonie* (1923), or Dada films influenced by the international art movement, like Hans Richter's *Ghosts before Breakfast* (1928). Big firms such as UFA (which absorbed Decla-Bioscop in 1921) as well as smaller companies invested in Expressionist films because these films would compete with those of America. Indeed, by the mid-1920s, the most prominent German films were widely regarded as among the best in the world.

The first film of the movement, *Caligari*, is also one of the most typical examples. One of its designers, Warm, claimed, "The film image must become graphic art." *Caligari*, with its extreme stylization, was indeed like a moving Expressionist painting or woodcut print. In contrast to French Impressionism, which bases its style primarily on cinematography and editing, German Expressionism depends heavily on mise-en-scene. Shapes are distorted and exaggerated unrealistically for expressive purposes. Actors often wear heavy make-up and move in jerky or slow, sinuous patterns. Most important, all of the elements of the mise-en-scene interact graphically to create an overall composition. Characters do not simply exist within a setting but rather form visual elements that merge with the setting. We have already seen an example of this in Figure 6.58, where the character Cesare collapses in a stylized forest, his body and outstretched arms echoing the shapes of the trees' trunks and branches.

In *Caligari*, the Expressionist stylization functions to convey the distorted viewpoint of a madman. We see the world as the hero does. This narrative function of the settings becomes explicit at one point, as the hero enters an asylum in his pursuit of Caligari. As he pauses to look around, he stands at the center of a pattern of radiating black-and-white lines that run across the floor and up the walls (Fig. 12.17). The world of the film is literally a projection of the hero's vision.

Later, as Expressionism became an accepted style, filmmakers did not motivate Expressionist style as the narrative point of view of mad characters. Instead, Expressionism often functioned to create stylized situations for fantasy and horror stories (as with *Waxworks*, 1924, and *Nosferatu*, 1922) or historical epics (as with *The Nibelungen*, 1923–1924). Expressionist films depended greatly on their designers. In the German studios, a film's designer received a relatively high salary and was often mentioned prominently in the advertisements.

Fig. 12.17

A combination of circumstances led to the disappearance of the movement. The rampant inflation of the early 1920s in Germany actually favored Expressionist filmmaking, partly by making it easy for German exporters to sell their films cheaply abroad. Inflation discouraged imports, however, for the tumbling exchange rate of the mark made foreign purchases prohibitively expensive. But in 1924 the U.S. Dawes Plan helped to stabilize the German economy, and foreign films came in more frequently, offering a degree of competition unknown in Germany for nearly a decade. Expressionist film budgets, however, were climbing. The last major films of the movement, Murnau's *Faust* (1926) and Lang's *Metropolis*, were costly epics that helped drive UFA deeper into financial difficulty, leading Erich Pommer to quit and try his luck briefly in America. Other personnel were lured away to Hollywood as well. Murnau left after finishing *Faust,* his last German film. Major actors (e.g., Conrad Veidt and Emil Jannings) and cinematographers (e.g., Karl Freund) went to Hollywood as well. Lang stayed on, but after the criticisms of *Metropolis*'s extravagance on its release in early 1927, he formed his own production company and turned to other styles in his later German films. At the beginning of the Nazi regime in 1933, he too left the country.

Trying to counter the stiffer competition from imported Hollywood films after 1924, the Germans also began to imitate the American product. The resulting films, though sometimes impressive, diluted the unique qualities of the Expressionist style. Thus by 1927, Expressionism as a movement died out. But as Georges Sadoul has pointed out, an expressionist (spelled with a small "e" to distinguish it from the Expressionist movement proper) tendency lingered on in many of the German films of the late 1920s and even into such 1930s films as Lang's *M* (1930) and *Testament of Dr. Mabuse* (1932). And because so many of the German filmmakers came to the United States, Hollywood films also displayed expressionist tendencies. Horror films, such as *Son of Frankenstein* (1939), and *films noirs* have strong expressionist touches in their settings and lighting. Although the German movement lasted only about seven years, expressionism has never entirely died out as a trend in film style.

FRENCH IMPRESSIONISM AND SURREALISM (1918–1930)

During the silent era, a number of film movements in France posed major alternatives to classical Hollywood narrative form. Some of these alternatives—abstract cinema, Dada filmmaking—are not specifically French and constituted instead a part of the growing international avant-garde. But two alternatives to the American mode remained quite localized. The first, Impressionism, was an avant-garde style that operated largely within the film industry. Most of the Impressionist filmmakers started out working for major French companies, and some of their avant-garde works proved financially successful. In the mid-twenties, most formed their own independent companies but remained within the mainstream commercial industry by renting studio facilities and releasing their films through established firms. The second alternative movement, Surrealism, lay largely outside the film industry; allied with the Surrealist movement in other arts, these filmmakers relied on their own means and private patronage. France in the 1920s thus offers a striking instance of how different film movements may coexist in similar circumstances.

■ IMPRESSIONISM

World War I struck a serious blow to the French film industry. Personnel were conscripted, many film studios were shifted to wartime uses, and much export was halted. Yet since the two major firms, Pathé Frères and Léon

Gaumont, also controlled circuits of theaters, they needed to fill vacant screens, and so in 1915 American films began increasingly to flood into France. Represented by Pearl White, Douglas Fairbanks, Chaplin and Ince films, De Mille's *The Cheat,* and William S. Hart (affectionately named "Rio Jim" by the French), the Hollywood cinema dominated the market by the end of 1917. After the war, French filmmaking never fully recovered: In the 1920s, French audiences saw eight times more Hollywood footage than domestic footage. The film industry tried in several ways to recapture the market, mostly through imitation of Hollywood production methods and genres. Artistically, however, the most significant move was the firms' encouragement of younger French directors: Abel Gance, Louis Delluc, Germaine Dulac, Marcel L'Herbier, and Jean Epstein.

These directors differed from their predecessors. The previous generation had regarded filmmaking as a commercial craft. More theoretical and ambitious, the younger filmmakers wrote essays proclaiming cinema to be an art comparable to poetry, painting, and music. Cinema should, they said, be purely itself and should not borrow from the theater or literature. Impressed by the verve and energy of the American cinema, the young theorists compared Chaplin to Nijinsky and the films of "Rio Jim" to *The Song of Roland.* Cinema should, above all, be (like music) an occasion for the artist to express feelings. Gance, Delluc, Dulac, L'Herbier, Epstein, and other more tangential members of the movement sought to put this aesthetic into practice as filmmakers.

Between 1918 and 1928, in a series of extraordinary films, the younger directors experimented with cinema in ways that posed an alternative to the dominant Hollywood formal principles. Given the centrality of emotion in their aesthetic, it is no wonder that the intimate psychological narrative dominated their filmmaking practice. The interactions of a few characters, usually a love triangle [as in Delluc's *L'Inondation* (1924), Epstein's *Coeur fidèle* (1923) and *La Belle nivernaise* (1923), and Gance's *La Dixième symphonie* (1918)], would serve as the basis for the filmmaker's exploration of fleeting moods and shifting sensations.

As in the Hollywood cinema, psychological causes were paramount, but the school gained the name "Impressionist" because of its interest in giving narration considerable psychological depth, revealing the play of a character's consciousness. The interest falls not on external physical behavior but on *inner* action. To a degree unprecedented in international filmmaking, Impressionist films manipulate plot time and subjectivity. To depict memories, flashbacks are common; sometimes the bulk of a film will be one flashback or a series of them. Even more striking is the films' insistence on registering characters' dreams, fantasies, and mental states. Dulac's *The Smiling Mme. Beudet* (1923) consists almost entirely of the main character's fantasy life, her imaginary escape from a dull marriage. Despite its epic length (over five hours), Gance's *La Roue* (1922) rests essentially on the erotic relations among only four people, and the director seeks to trace the development of each character's feelings in great detail. Impressionism's emphasis on personal emotion gives the films' narratives an intensely psychological focus.

The "Impressionist" movement earned its name as well for its use of film style. The filmmakers experimented with ways of rendering mental states

Fig. 12.18

Fig. 12.19

by new uses of cinematography and editing. In Impressionist films, irises, masks, and superimpositions function as traces of characters' thoughts and feelings. In *Coeur fidèle*, the heroine looks out a window, and a superimposition of the foul jetsam of the waterfront conveys her dejection at having to work as a barmaid in a dockside tavern (Fig. 12.18). In *La Roue,* the image of Norma is superimposed over the smoke from a locomotive, representing the fantasy of the engine driver, who is in love with her.

To intensify the subjectivity, the Impressionists' cinematography and editing present characters' perceptual experience, their optical "impressions." These films use a great deal of point-of-view cutting, showing a shot of a character looking at something, then a shot of that thing, from an angle and distance replicating the character's vantage point. When a character in an Impressionist film gets drunk or dizzy, the filmmaker renders that experience through distorted or filtered shots or vertiginous camera movements. Figure 12.19, from L'Herbier's *El Dorado* (1920), shows a man drinking in a cabaret; his tipsiness is conveyed by means of a curved mirror that stretches his body sideways.

The Impressionists also experimented with pronounced rhythmic editing to suggest the pace of an experience as a character feels it, moment by moment. During scenes of violence or emotional turmoil, the rhythm accelerates—the shots get shorter and shorter, building to a climax, sometimes with shots only a few frames long. In *La Roue* a train crash is presented in accelerating shots ranging from thirteen frames down to two, and a man's last thoughts before he falls from a cliff are rendered in a blur of many single-frame shots (the first known use of such rapid editing). In *Coeur fidèle* lovers at a fair ride in whirling swings, and Epstein presents their giddiness in a series of shots four frames, then two frames, long. Several Impressionist films use a dance to motivate a markedly accelerated cutting rhythm. More generally, their comparison of cinema to music encouraged the Impressionists to explore rhythmic editing. In such ways subjective shooting and editing patterns function within Impressionist films to reinforce the narrative treatment of psychological states.

Impressionist form created certain demands on film technology. Gance, the boldest innovator in this respect, used his epic *Napoléon* (1927) as a chance to try new lenses (even a 275mm telephoto), multiple frame images (called "Polyvision"), and widescreen ratio (the celebrated triptychs; see Fig. 7.50). The most influential Impressionist technological innovation was the development of new means of frame mobility. If the camera was to represent a character's eyes, it should be able to move with the ease of a person. Impressionists strapped their cameras to cars, carousels, and locomotives. For Gance's *Napoléon,* the camera manufacturer Debrie perfected a hand-held model that let the operator move on roller skates. Gance put the machine on wheels, cables, pendulums, and bobsleds. In *L'Argent* (1928), L'Herbier had his camera gliding through huge rooms and even plummeting straight down toward the crowd from the dome of the Paris stock exchange in an effort to convey the traders' frenzied excitement.

Such formal, stylistic, and technological innovations had given French filmmakers the hope that their films could win the popularity granted to Hollywood's product. During the 1920s, the Impressionists in fact operated somewhat independently; they formed their own small production companies and leased studio facilities from Pathé and Gaumont in exchange for distribution rights. Some Impressionist films did prove moderately popular with French audiences. But by 1929 most foreign audiences had not taken to Impressionism; its experimentation was attuned to elite tastes. Moreover, although production costs were rising, the Impressionists (especially Gance and L'Herbier) became even more free-spending. As a result, filmmakers' companies either went out of business or were absorbed by the big firms. Two behemoth productions of the decade, *Napoléon* and *L'Argent*, failed and were reedited by the producers; they were among the last Impressionist films released. With the arrival of the sound film, French industry tightened its belt and had no money to risk on experiments.

Impressionism as a distinct movement may be said to have ceased by 1929. But the influences of Impressionist form—the psychological narrative, subjective camera work, and editing—were more long-lived. They continued to operate, for example, in the work of Alfred Hitchcock and Maya Deren, in Hollywood "montage sequences," and in certain American genres and styles (the horror film, *film noir*).

■ SURREALISM

Whereas the French Impressionist filmmakers worked within the commercial film industry, the Surrealist filmmakers relied on private patronage and screened their work in small artists' gatherings. Such isolation is hardly surprising, since Surrealist cinema was a more radical movement, producing films that perplexed and shocked most audiences.

Surrealist cinema was directly linked to Surrealism in literature and painting. According to its spokesperson, André Breton, "Surrealism" was "based on the belief in the superior reality of certain forms of association, heretofore neglected, in the omnipotence of dreams, in the undirected play of thought." Influenced by Freudian psychology, Surrealist art sought to register the hidden currents of the unconscious, "in the absence of any control exercised by reason, and beyond any aesthetic and moral preoccupation."

"Automatic" writing and painting, the search for bizarre or evocative imagery, the deliberate avoidance of rationally explicable form or style— these became features of Surrealism as it developed in the period 1924– 1929. From the start, the Surrealists were attracted to the cinema, especially admiring films that presented untamed desire or the fantastic and marvelous (for example, slapstick comedies, *Nosferatu*, serials about mysterious super-criminals). In due time, painters such as Man Ray and Salvador Dalí and writers such as Antonin Artaud began dabbling in cinema, while the young Spaniard Luis Buñuel, drawn to Surrealism, became its most famous film-maker.

Surrealist cinema is overtly antinarrative, attacking causality itself. If rationality is to be fought, causal connections among events must be dissolved. *The Seashell and the Clergyman* (1928; scripted by Artaud, filmed by the Impressionist Germaine Dulac) begins with the protagonist pouring liquids from flasks and then systematically breaking each one (Fig. 12.20). In Dalí and Buñuel's *Un Chien andalou* (*An Andalusian Dog*, 1928) the hero

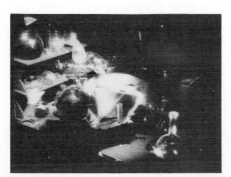

Fig. 12.20

Fig. 12.21

drags two pianos, stuffed with dead donkeys, across a parlor. In Buñuel's *L'Age d'or* (1930) a woman begins obsessively sucking the toes of a statue.

Many Surrealist films tease us to find a narrative logic that is simply absent. Causality is as evasive as in a dream. Instead, we find events juxtaposed for their disturbing effect. The hero gratuitously shoots a child (*L'Age d'or*), a woman closes her eyes only to reveal eyes painted on her eyelids (Ray's *Emak Bakia,* 1927), and—most famous of all—a man strops a razor and deliberately slits the eyeball of an unprotesting woman (*Un Chien andalou,* Fig. 12.21). An Impressionist film would motivate such events as a character's dreams or hallucinations, but in these films character psychology is all but nonexistent. Sexual desire and ecstasy, violence, blasphemy, and bizarre humor furnish events that Surrealist film form employs with a disregard for conventional narrative principles. The hope was that the free form of the film would arouse the deepest impulses of the viewer. Buñuel called *Un Chien andalou* "a passionate call to murder."

The style of Surrealist cinema is eclectic. Mise-en-scene is often influenced by Surrealist painting. The ants in *Un Chien andalou* come from Dalí's pictures, whereas the pillars and city squares of *The Seashell and the Clergyman* hark back to the Italian painter Giorgio de Chirico. Surrealist editing is an amalgam of some Impressionist devices (many dissolves and superimpositions) and some devices of the dominant cinema. The shocking eyeball slitting at the start of *Un Chien andalou* relies on some principles of continuity editing (and indeed on the Kuleshov effect). On the other hand, discontinuous editing is also commonly used to fracture any organized temporal-spatial coherence. In the same film, the heroine locks the man out of a room only to turn to find him inexplicably behind her. On the whole, Surrealist film style refused to canonize any particular devices, since that would order and rationalize what had to be an "undirected play of thought."

The fortunes of Surrealist cinema shifted with changes in the art movement as a whole. By late 1929, when Breton joined the Communist party, Surrealists were embroiled in internal dissension about whether communism was a political equivalent of Surrealism. Buñuel left France for a brief stay in Hollywood and then returned to Spain. The chief patron of Surrealist filmmaking, the Vicomte de Noailles, supported Jean Vigo's *Zéro de Conduite* (1933), a film of Surrealist ambitions, but then stopped sponsoring the avant-garde. Thus as a unified movement, French Surrealism was no longer viable after 1930. Individual Surrealists continued to work, however. The most famous was Buñuel, who continued to work in his own brand of the Surrealist style for 50 years. His later films, such as *Belle de Jour* (1967) and *The Discreet Charm of the Bourgeoisie* (1972), continue the Surrealist tradition.

SOVIET MONTAGE (1924–1930)

Despite the victory of the Russian Revolution in October of 1917, the new Soviet government faced the difficult task of controlling all sectors of life. Like other industries, the film production and distribution systems took years to build up a substantial output that could serve the aims of the new government.

Although the pre-Revolutionary Russian film industry had not figured prominently in world cinema, there were a number of private production companies operating in Moscow and Petersburg. With most imports cut off during the war, these companies had done quite well making films for the domestic market. The most distinctive Russian films made during the mid-1910s were slow-paced melodramas that concentrated on bravura performances by actors playing characters caught in extremely emotional situations. Such films showcased the talents of Ivan Mozhukin and other popular stars and were aimed mainly at the large Russian audience, seldom being seen abroad.

These film companies resisted the move made directly after the Revolution to nationalize all private property. They simply refused to supply films to theaters operating under the control of the government. In July 1918 the government's film subsection of the State Commission of Education put strict controls on the existing supplies of raw film stock. As a result, producers began hoarding their stock; the largest firms took all the equipment they could and fled to other countries. Some companies made films commissioned by the government, while hoping that the Reds would lose the Civil War and that things would return to pre-Revolutionary conditions.

In the face of shortages of equipment and difficult living conditions, a few young filmmakers made tentative moves that would result in the development of a national cinema movement. Dziga Vertov began working on documentary footage of the war; at age twenty, he was placed in charge of all newsreels. Lev Kuleshov, teaching in the newly founded State School on Cinema Art, performed a series of experiments by editing footage from different sources into a whole that creates an impression of continuity. In this sense, Kuleshov was perhaps the most conservative of the young Soviet filmmakers, since he was basically trying to systematize principles of editing similar to the continuity practices of the classical Hollywood cinema. Thus even before they were able to make films, Kuleshov and his young pupils were working at the first film school in the world and writing theoretical essays on the new art form. This grounding in theory would be the basis of the Montage style.

In 1920 Sergei Eisenstein worked briefly in a train carrying propaganda to the troops in the Civil War. He returned that year to Moscow to stage plays in a workers' theater. In May 1920, Vsevolod Pudovkin made his acting debut in a play presented by Kuleshov's State Film School. He had been inspired to go into filmmaking by seeing Griffith's *Intolerance*, which was first shown widely in Russia in 1919. American films, particularly those of Griffith, Douglas Fairbanks, and Mary Pickford, which kept circulating to fill the void left by the low output of new Soviet productions, were a tremendous influence on the filmmakers of the emerging Soviet movement.

None of the important filmmakers of the Montage style was a veteran of the pre-Revolutionary industry. All came from other fields (for example, Eisenstein from engineering, Pudovkin from chemistry) and discovered the cinema in the midst of the Revolution's ferment. The Czarist-era filmmakers who remained active in the USSR in the 1920s tended to stick to older traditions. One popular director of the Czarist period, Yakov Protazanov, went abroad briefly after the Revolution but returned to continue making films whose style and form owed almost nothing to the theory and practice of the new filmmakers.

Protazanov's return coincided with a general loosening of government restrictions on private enterprise. In 1921 the country was facing tremendous problems, including a widespread famine. In order to facilitate the production and distribution of goods, Lenin instituted the New Economic Policy (NEP), which for several years permitted private management of business. For film, the NEP meant a sudden reappearance of film stock and equipment belonging to the producers who had not emigrated. Slowly Soviet production began to grow as private firms made more films. The government attempted, with little success, to control the film industry by creating a central distribution company, Goskino, in 1922.

"Of all the arts, for us the cinema is the most important," Lenin stated in 1922. Since Lenin saw film as a powerful tool for education, the first films encouraged by the government were documentaries and newsreels such as Vertov's newsreel series *Kino-Pravda,* which began in May 1922. Fictional films were also being made from 1917 on, but it was not until 1923 that a Georgian feature, *Red Imps,* became the first Soviet film to compete successfully with the foreign films predominant on Soviet screens. (And not until 1927 did the Soviet industry's income from its own films top that of the films it had imported.)

The Soviet Montage style displayed tentative beginnings in 1924, with Kuleshov's class from the State Film School presenting *The Extraordinary Adventures of Mr. West in the Land of the Bolsheviks.* This delightful film, along with Kuleshov's next film, *The Death Ray* (1925), showed that Soviet directors could apply Montage principles and come up with amusing satires or exciting adventures as entertaining as the Hollywood product.

Eisenstein's first feature, *Strike,* was released early in 1925 and initiated the movement proper. His second, *Potemkin,* premiered later in 1925, was successful abroad and drew the attention of other countries to the new movement. In the next few years Eisenstein, Pudovkin, Vertov, and the Ukrainian Alexander Dovzhenko created a series of films that are classics of the Montage style.

The theoretical writings and filmmaking practice of these directors were based on editing. They all declared that a film does not exist in its individual shots but only in their combination through editing into a whole. We should remember here that since the primitive cinema, no national film style had yet appeared that depended on the long take. The great films that inspired Soviet filmmakers, like *Intolerance* and some French Impressionist efforts, were based largely on editing juxtapositions.

Not all of the young theoreticians agreed on exactly what the Montage approach to editing was to be. Pudovkin, for example, believed that shots were like bricks, to be joined together to build a sequence. Eisenstein disagreed, saying that the maximum effect would be gained if the shots did not fit together perfectly, if they created a jolt for the spectator. He also favored juxtaposing shots in order to create a concept, as we have already seen with his use of conceptual editing in *October* (pp. 306–309). Vertov disagreed with both theorists, favoring a "cinema-eye" approach to recording and shaping documentary reality.

Pudovkin's *Storm over Asia* makes use of conceptual editing similar to that of Eisenstein's *October*. Shots of the couple being dressed in their accessories are intercut with shots of the preparation at the temple. For example, a close-up of a necklace being fastened around the wife's neck (Fig. 12.22) leads to a medium close-up of an elaborate piece of jewelry being lowered over the head of a priest (Fig. 12.23). Then a close-up of a tiara being placed on the wife's head (Fig. 12.24) is followed by a similar framing of a large headdress being lowered onto a priest's head (Fig. 12.25). Pudovkin's parallel montage points up the absurdity of both rituals.

Fig. 12.22

The Montagists' approach to narrative form set them apart from the cinemas of other countries. Soviet narrative films tended to downplay character psychology as a cause; instead, social forces provided the major causes. Characters were interesting for the way these social causes affected their lives. Films of the Soviet Montage movement did not always have a single protagonist. Social groups could form a collective hero, as in Eisenstein's films before *Old and New* (1929). In keeping with this de-emphasis of individual personalities, Soviet filmmakers often avoided well-known actors, preferring to cast parts by searching out nonactors. This practice was called *typage*, since the filmmakers would often choose an individual whose appearance seemed at once to convey the type of character he or she was to play. Except for the hero, Pudovkin used nonactors to play all of the Mongols in *Storm over Asia.*

Fig. 12.23

By the end of the 1920s, each of the major directors of this movement had made about four important films. The decline of the movement was not caused primarily, as in Germany and France, by industrial and economic factors. Instead, government political pressures exerted a strong control which discouraged the use of the Montage style. By the late 1920s, Vertov, Eisenstein, and Dovzhenko were being criticized for their excessively formal and "esoteric" approaches. In 1929 Eisenstein went to Hollywood to study the new technique of sound; by the time he returned in 1932, the attitude of the film industry had changed. While he was away, a few filmmakers carried their Montage experiments into sound cinema in the early 1930s. But the Soviet authorities, under Stalin's direction, encouraged filmmakers to create simple films that would be readily understandable to all audiences. Stylistic experimentation or nonrealistic subject matter was often criticized or censored.

Fig. 12.24

This trend culminated in 1934, when the government instituted a new artistic policy called Socialist Realism. This policy dictated that all artworks must depict revolutionary development while being firmly grounded in "realism." The great Soviet directors continued to make films, occasionally masterpieces, but the Montage experiments of the 1920s had to be discarded or modified. Eisenstein managed to continue his work on montage, but occasionally incurred the wrath of the authorities up until his death in 1948. As a movement, the Soviet Montage style can be said to have ended by 1933, with the release of such films as Vertov's *Enthusiasm* (1931) and Pudovkin's *Deserter* (1933).

Fig. 12.25

THE CLASSICAL HOLLYWOOD CINEMA
AFTER THE COMING OF SOUND

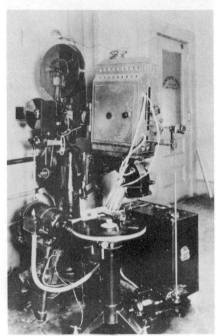

Fig. 12.26

Fig. 12.27

Fig. 12.28

The introduction of sound technology came about through the efforts of certain Hollywood firms to widen their power. During the mid-1920s Warner Bros. was in the process of investing a great deal of money to expand its facilities and holdings. One of these expansions was the investment in a sound system using records in synchronization with film images. Figure 12.26 shows an early projector with sound attachment.

By releasing *Don Juan* (1926) with orchestral accompaniment and sound effects on disc, along with a series of sound vaudeville shorts with singing and talking, Warner Bros. began to popularize the idea of sound films. In 1927, *The Jazz Singer* (a part "talkie" with some scenes accompanied only by music) had a tremendous success, and the Warner Bros. investment began to pay off.

The success of *Don Juan, The Jazz Singer*, and the shorts convinced other studios that sound contributed to profitable filmmaking. Unlike the early period of filmmaking and the Motion Picture Patents Company, there was now no fierce competition within the industry. Instead, firms realized that whatever sound system the studios finally adopted, it would have to be compatible with the projection machinery of any theater. Eventually a sound-on-film rather than a sound-on-disc system became the standard and continues so to the present. (That is, as we saw in Chapter 1, the sound track is printed on the strip of film alongside the image.) By 1930 most theaters in America were wired for sound.

For a few years, sound created a setback for Hollywood film style. The camera had to be put inside a sound booth so that its motor noise would not be picked up by the microphone. Figure 12.27, a posed publicity still, shows the components of a dialogue scene in a 1928 MGM film. The camera operator can hear only through his earphones, and the camera cannot move except for short pans to reframe. The bulky microphone, on the table at the right, also did not move. The actors had to stay within a limited space if their speech was to register on the track. The result of such restrictions was a brief period of static films resembling stage plays.

Still, from the very beginning of sound filming, solutions were found for these problems. Sometimes several cameras, all in soundproof booths, would record the scene from different angles simultaneously. The resulting footage could be cut together to provide a standard continuity editing pattern in a scene, with all the sound synchronized perfectly. The whole camera booth might be mounted on wheels to create camera movements, or a scene might be shot silent and a sound track added later. Early sound films such as Rouben Mamoulian's *Applause* (1929) demonstrate that the camera soon regained a great flexibility of movement. Later, smaller cases, enclosing only the camera body, replaced the cumbersome booths. These *blimps* (Fig. 12.28) permitted cinematographers to place the camera on movable supports. Similarly, microphones mounted on booms and hanging over the heads of the actors could also follow moving action without a loss of recording quality.

Once camera movement and subject movement were restored to sound films, filmmakers continued to use many of the stylistic characteristics developed in Hollywood during the silent period. Diegetic sound provided a powerful addition to the system of continuity editing. Overlapping dialogue with the cuts, for instance, could create smooth temporal continuity and suggest spaces outside the frame.

Fig. 12.29

Within the overall patterns of continuity style and classical narrative form, each of the large studios developed a distinctive approach of its own. Thus MGM, for example, became the prestige studio, with a huge number of stars and technicians under long-term contract. MGM lavished money on settings, costumes, and special effects, as in *The Good Earth* (1937), with its locust attack, or *San Francisco* (1936), in which the great earthquake is spectacularly re-created. Warner Bros., in spite of its success with sound, was still a relatively small studio and specialized in less expensive genre pictures. Its series of gangster films (*Little Caesar, Public Enemy*) and musicals (*42nd Street, Golddiggers of 1933, Dames*) were among the studio's most successful products. Even lower on the ladder of prestige was Universal, which depended on imaginative filmmaking rather than established stars or expensive sets in its atmospheric horror films such as *Frankenstein* (1931) and *The Old Dark House* (1932, Fig. 12.29).

One major genre, the musical, became possible only with the introduction of sound. Indeed, the original intention of the Warners when they began their investment in sound equipment was to circulate vaudeville acts on film. The form of most musicals involved separate numbers inserted into a linear narrative, although a few "revue" musicals simply strung together a series of numbers with little or no connecting narrative.

One of the major studios, RKO, made a series of musicals starring Fred Astaire and Ginger Rogers; *Swing Time* (George Stevens, 1936) illustrates how a musical can be a classically constructed narrative. Like *Our Hospitality, Swing Time* contains a set of causally important motifs that recur to create a tight narrative. Fred comes from a family of gamblers, and his skill allows him to win a night club away from a bandleader who is also a gambler. Thus Fred also wins Ginger, who works for the bandleader. As a gambler, the hero has a "lucky" quarter, the loss of which causes his initial meeting with Ginger. The Ginger Rogers character is even named Penny, which links her to the "lucky quarter" motif. Here the musical numbers are motivated by the narrative. Initially Ginger works in a dancing school; although Fred is a professional dancer, he pretends to be a beginner to get to know her. When Ginger decides to marry the bandleader, Fred persuades her to dance one last romantic dance with him. This helps to motivate the final scene, in which Ginger chooses Fred instead of the bandleader. Stylistically, the musical numbers use much lengthier shots and thus a slower editing rhythm than we find in other scenes.

During the 1930s, color film stocks became widely used for the first time. In the 1920s, a small number of films had Technicolor sequences, but the process was crude, using only two colors in combination to create all other hues. The result tended to emphasize greenish-blue and pink tones; it was also too costly to use extensively. By the early 1930s, however, Technicolor had been improved. It now used three primary colors and thus could reproduce a very large range of hues. Though still expensive, it was soon proven to add hugely to the appeal of many films. After *Becky Sharp* (1935), the first feature-length film to use the new Technicolor, and *The Trail of the Lonesome Pine* (1936), studios began using Technicolor extensively. The Technicolor process was used until the early 1970s. (For a variety of examples of Technicolor, running from the 1940s to the 1960s, see Color Plates 17–19, 27, 38, 39, 44, 45, and 57.)

Technicolor needed a great deal of light on the set, and the light had to favor certain hues. Thus, brighter lights specifically designed for color filmmaking were introduced. Some cinematographers began to use the new lights for black-and-white filming. These brighter lights, combined with faster film stocks, made it easier to achieve greater depth of field with more light and a smaller aperture. Many cinematographers stuck to the standard soft-focus style of the 1920s and 1930s, but others began to experiment. By the late 1930s, there was a definite trend toward a deep-focus style.

Mervyn Leroy's *Anthony Adverse* (1936), Alfred L. Werker's *The Adventures of Sherlock Holmes* (1939), and the Sam Wood–William Cameron Menzies *Our Town* (1940) also utilized deep focus to a considerable degree. But it was *Citizen Kane* that in 1941 brought deep focus strongly to the attention of spectators and filmmakers alike. Welles's compositions placed the foreground figures very close to the camera and the background figures deep in the space of the shot. In some cases, the "deep-focus" image was actually achieved through matting and rear projection. Overall, *Citizen Kane* helped make the tendency toward deep focus a major part of classical Hollywood style in the next decade. Many films using the technique soon appeared. *Citizen Kane*'s cinematographer, Gregg Toland, worked on some of them, such as *The Little Foxes* (William Wyler, 1941, Fig. 12.30).

The light necessary for deep focus also tended to lend a hard-edge appearance to objects. Gauzy effects were largely eliminated, and much 1940s cinema became visually quite distinct from that of the 1930s. But the insistence on the clear narrative functioning of all these techniques remained strong. The classical Hollywood narrative modified itself over the years but did not change radically.

Fig. 12.30

ITALIAN NEOREALISM (1942–1951)

There is no definitive source for the term "Neorealism," but it first appeared in the early 1940s in the writings of Italian critics. From one perspective, the term represented a younger generation's desire to break free of the conventions of ordinary Italian cinema. Under Mussolini, the motion-picture industry had created colossal historical epics and sentimental upper-class melodramas (nicknamed "white-telephone" films), and many critics felt these to be artificial and decadent. A "new realism" was needed. Some critics found it in French films of the 1930s, especially works by Jean Renoir. Other critics turned closer to home to praise films like Luchino Visconti's *Ossessione* (1942).

Yet now most historians believe that Neorealist filmmaking was not a decisive break with Italian cinema under Mussolini. Pseudo-documentaries such as Rossellini's *White Ship* (1941), even though propagandistic, prepared the way for more forthright handling of contemporary events. Other current trends, such as regional dialect comedy and urban melodrama, encouraged directors and scriptwriters to turn toward realism. Overall, spurred by both foreign influences and indigenous traditions, the postwar period saw several filmmakers beginning to work with the goal of revealing contemporary social conditions. This trend became known as the Neorealist movement.

Economic, political, and cultural factors helped Neorealism survive. Nearly all the major Neorealists—Roberto Rossellini, Vittorio De Sica, Luchino Visconti, and others—came to the movement as experienced filmmakers. They knew one another, frequently shared scriptwriters and personnel, and gained public attention in the journals *Cinema* and *Bianco e Nero*. Before 1948 the Neorealist movement had enough friends in the government to be relatively free of censorship. There was even a correspondence between Neorealism and an Italian literary movement of the same period modeled on the *verismo* of the previous century. The result was an array of Italian films which gained worldwide recognition: Visconti's *La Terra Trema* (1947); Rossellini's *Open City* (1945), *Paisan* (1946), and *Germany Year Zero* (1947); De Sica's *Shoeshine* (1946) and *Bicycle Thief* (1948); and works of Lattuada, Blasetti, and De Santis.

Neorealism created a somewhat distinctive approach to film style. By 1945 the fighting had destroyed most of Cinecittà, so studio settings were in short supply and sound equipment was rare. As a result, Neorealist mise-en-scene relied on actual locales, and its photographic work tended toward the raw roughness of documentaries. Rossellini has told of buying bits of negative stock from street photographers, so that much of *Open City* was shot on film with varying photographic qualities.

Shooting on the streets and in private buildings made Italian camera operators adept at cinematography that often avoided the "three-point" lighting system of Hollywood. (See Fig. 6.39.) Although Neorealist films often featured famous stage or film actors, they also made use of nonactors, recruited for their realistic looks or behavior. For the adult "star" of *Bicycle Thief*, De Sica chose a factory worker: "The way he moved, the way he sat down, his gestures with those hands of a working man and not of an actor . . . everything about him was perfect." The Italian cinema had a long tradition of dubbing, and the ability to postsynchronize dialogue permitted the filmmakers to work on location with smaller crews and to move the camera freely. With a degree of improvisational freedom in the acting and setting went a certain flexibility of framing, well displayed in the death of Pina in *Open City*, the final sequence of *Germany Year Zero*, and the magnificent landscapes in depth of *La Terra Trema* (Fig. 12.31). The tracking shots through the open-air bicycle market in *Bicycle Thief* illustrate the possibilities which the Neorealist director found in returning to location filming.

Perhaps even more influential was the Neorealist sense of narrative form. Reacting against the intricately plotted white-telephone dramas, the Neorealists tended to loosen up narrative relations. The earliest major films of the movement, such as *Ossessione*, *Open City*, and *Shoeshine*, contain relatively conventionally organized plots (albeit with unhappy endings). But

Fig. 12.31

Fig. 12.32

the most formally innovative Neorealist films allow the intrusion of non-causally motivated details, such as the famous scene in *Bicycle Thief* in which the hero takes shelter along with a group of priests during a rain shower (Fig. 12.32). Although the causes of characters' actions are usually seen as concretely economic and political (poverty, unemployment, exploitation), the effects are often fragmentary and inconclusive. Rossellini's *Paisan* is frankly episodic, presenting six anecdotes of life in Italy during the Allied invasion; often we are not told the outcome of an event, the consequence of a cause.

The ambiguity of Neorealist films is also a product of narration that refuses to yield an omniscient knowledge of events, as if acknowledging that the totality of reality is simply unknowable. This is especially evident in the films' endings. *Bicycle Thief* concludes with the worker and his son wandering down the street, their stolen bicycle still missing, their future uncertain. Although ending with the defeat of the Sicilian fishermen's revolt against the merchants, *La Terra Trema* does not cancel the possibility that a later revolt will succeed. Neorealism's tendency toward a slice-of-life plot construction gave many films of the movement an open-ended quality quite opposed to the narrative closure of the Hollywood cinema.

As economic and cultural forces had sustained the Neorealist movement, so they were prime causes of its cessation. When Italy began to prosper after the war, the government looked askance at films so critical of contemporary society. After 1949, censorship and state pressures began to constrain the movement. Large-scale Italian film production began to reappear, and Neorealism no longer had the freedom of the small production company. In addition, the Neorealist directors, now famous, began to pursue more individualized concerns: Rossellini's investigation of Christian humanism and Western history, De Sica's sentimental romances, Luchino Visconti's examination of upper-class milieus. Most historians date the end of the Neorealist movement with the public attacks on De Sica's *Umberto D* (1951). Nevertheless, Neorealist elements are still quite visible in the early works of Federico Fellini (*I Vitelloni*, 1954, is a good example) and of Michelangelo Antonioni (*Cronaca di un amore*, 1951); both directors had worked on Neorealist films. The movement exercised a very strong influence on individual filmmakers such as Ermanno Olmi and Satyajit Ray, and on groups such as the French New Wave.

THE FRENCH NEW WAVE (1959–1964)

The late 1950s and early 1960s saw the rise of a new generation of filmmakers around the world. In country after country there emerged directors born before World War II but grown to adulthood in the postwar era of reconstruction and rising prosperity. Japan, Canada, England, Italy, Spain, Brazil, and the United States all had their "new waves" or "young cinema" groups—some trained in film schools, many allied with specialized film magazines, most in revolt against their elders in the industry. The most generally influential of these groups appeared in France.

In the mid-1950s a group of young men who wrote for the Paris film journal *Cahiers du cinéma* made a habit of attacking the most artistically respected French filmmakers of the day. "I consider an adaptation of value," wrote François Truffaut, "only when written by a *man of the cinema*. Aurenche and Bost [the leading scriptwriters of the time] are essentially literary men and I reproach them here for being contemptuous of the cinema by underestimating it." Addressing 21 major directors, Jean-Luc Godard asserted, "Your camera movements are ugly because your subjects are bad, your casts act badly because your dialogue is worthless; in a word, you don't know how to create cinema because you no longer even know what it is." Truffaut and Godard, along with Claude Chabrol, Eric Rohmer, and Jacques Rivette, championed certain directors considered somewhat outdated (Jean Renoir, Max Ophuls) or eccentric (Robert Bresson, Jacques Tati).

More important, the young men saw no contradiction in rejecting the French filmmaking establishment while loving blatantly commercial Hollywood. The young rebels of *Cahiers* claimed that in the works of certain directors—certain *auteurs* (authors)—artistry existed in the American cinema. An *auteur* usually did not literally write scripts, but managed nonetheless to stamp his or her personality on genre and studio products, transcending the constraints of Hollywood's standardized system. Howard Hawks, Otto Preminger, Samuel Fuller, Vincente Minnelli, Nicholas Ray, Alfred Hitchcock—these were more than craftsmen. Each person's total output constituted a coherent world. Truffaut quoted Giraudoux, "There are no works, there are only *auteurs*." Godard remarked later: "We won the day in having it acknowledged in principle that a film by Hitchcock, for example, is as important as a book by Aragon. Film *auteurs*, thanks to us, have finally entered the history of art." And indeed, many of the Hollywood directors these critics and filmmakers praised gained reputations that have persisted up to the present.

Writing criticism did not, however, satisfy these young men. They itched to make movies. Borrowing money from friends and filming on location, each started to shoot short films. By 1959 they had become a force to be reckoned with. In that year Rivette filmed *Paris nous appartient* (*Paris Belongs to Us*); Godard made *À Bout de souffle* (*Breathless*); Chabrol made his second feature, *Les Cousins;* and in April Truffaut's *Les Quatre cent coups* (*The 400 Blows*) won the Grand Prize at the Cannes Festival.

The novelty and youthful vigor of these directors led journalists to nickname them *la nouvelle vague*—the "New Wave." Their output was staggering. All told, the five central directors made 32 feature films between 1959 and 1966; Godard and Chabrol made 11 apiece! So many films must of course be highly disparate, but there are enough similarities for us to identify a broadly distinctive New Wave approach to style and form.

The most obviously revolutionary quality of the New Wave films was their casual look. To proponents of the carefully polished French "cinema of quality," the young directors must have seemed hopelessly sloppy. The New Wave directors had admired the Neorealists (especially Rossellini) and in opposition to studio filmmaking, took as their mise-en-scène actual locales in and around Paris. Shooting on location became the norm. Similarly, glossy

Fig. 12.33

Fig. 12.34

studio lighting was replaced by available light and simply supplemental sources. Few postwar French films would have shown the dim, grimy apartments and corridors featured in *Paris Belongs to Us* (Fig. 12.33).

Cinematography changed too. The New Wave camera moves a great deal, panning and tracking to follow characters or trace out relations within a locale. Furthermore, shooting cheaply on location demanded flexible, portable equipment. Fortunately, Eclair had recently developed a lightweight camera that could be hand held. (That the Eclair had been used primarily for documentary work accorded perfectly with the "realistic" mise-en-scene of the New Wave.) New Wave films were intoxicated with the new freedom offered by the hand-held camera. In *The 400 Blows* the camera explores a cramped apartment and rides a carnival centrifuge. In *Breathless* the cinematographer held the camera while seated in a wheelchair to follow the hero along a complex path in a travel agency's office (Fig. 11.36, p. 402).

One of the most salient features of New Wave films is their casual humor. These young men deliberately played with the medium. In Godard's *Band of Outsiders* the three main characters resolve to be silent for a minute, and Godard dutifully shuts off *all* the sound. In Truffaut's *Shoot the Piano Player*, a character swears that he's not lying: "May my mother drop dead if I'm not telling the truth." Cut to a shot of an old lady keeling over. But most often the humor lies in esoteric references to other films, Hollywood or European. There are homages to admired *auteurs*: Godard characters allude to *Johnny Guitar* (Ray), *Some Came Running* (Minnelli), and "Arizona Jim" (from Renoir's *Crime of M. Lange*). In *Les Carabiniers* Godard parodies Lumière, and in *Vivre sa vie* he "quotes" *La Passion de Jeanne d'Arc*. Hitchcock is frequently cited in Chabrol's films, and Truffaut's *Les Mistons* recreates a shot from a Lumière short; compare Figure 12.34 with the frame from *L'Arroseur arrosé* (Fig. 6.6). Such homages even became in-jokes, as when New Wave actors Jean-Claude Brialy and Jeanne Moreau "walk on" in *The 400 Blows* or when a Godard character mentions "Arizona Jules" (combining names from *Crime of M. Lange* and *Jules and Jim*). Such gags, the New Wave directors felt, took some of the solemnity out of filmmaking and film viewing.

New Wave films also pushed further the Neorealist experimentation with plot construction. In general, causal connections became quite loose. Is there actually a political conspiracy going on in *Paris Belongs to Us?* Why is Nana shot at the end of *Vivre sa vie?* In *Shoot the Piano Player* the first sequence consists mainly of a conversation between the hero's brother and a man he accidentally meets on the street; the latter tells of his marital problems at some length, even though he has nothing to do with the film's narrative.

Moreover, the films often lack goal-oriented protagonists. The heroes may drift aimlessly, engage in actions on the spur of the moment, spend their time talking and drinking in a café or going to movies. New Wave narratives often introduce startling shifts in tone, jolting our expectations. When two gangsters kidnap the hero and his girlfriend in *Shoot the Piano Player*, the whole group begins a comic discussion of sex. Discontinuous editing further disturbs narrative continuity; this tendency reaches its limit in Godard's jump cuts (pp. 303, 403).

Perhaps most important, the New Wave film typically ends ambiguously. We have seen this already in *Breathless* (p. 401). Antoine in *The 400 Blows* reaches the sea in the last shot, but as he moves forward, Truffaut zooms in and freezes the frame, ending the film with the question of where Antoine will go from there (see Fig. 4.1, p. 96). In Chabrol's *Les Bonnes Femmes* and *Ophelia*, in Rivette's *Paris Belongs to Us*, and in nearly all the work of Godard and Truffaut in this period, the looseness of the causal chain leads to endings that remain defiantly open and uncertain.

Curiously, despite the demands that the films placed on the viewer and despite the critical rampages of the filmmakers, the French film industry was not hostile to the New Wave. The decade 1947–1957 had been good to film production: The government supported the industry through enforced quotas, banks had invested heavily, and there was a flourishing business of international coproductions. But in 1957 cinema attendance fell off drastically, chiefly because television became more widespread. By 1959 the industry was in a crisis. The independent financing of low-budget films seemed to offer a good solution. New Wave directors shot films much more quickly and cheaply than did reigning directors. Moreover, the young directors helped one another out and thus reduced the financial risk by the established companies. Thus the French industry supported the New Wave through distribution, exhibition, and eventually production.

Indeed, it is possible to argue that by 1964, although each New Wave director had his or her own production company, the group had become absorbed into the French film industry. Godard made *Le Mépris* (*Contempt*, 1963) for a major commercial producer, Carlo Ponti; Truffaut made *Fahrenheit 451* (1966) in England for Universal; and Chabrol began turning out parodies of James Bond thrillers.

Dating the exact end of the movement is difficult, but most historians select 1964, when the characteristic New Wave form and style had already become diffused and imitated (by, for instance, Tony Richardson in his 1963 English film *Tom Jones*). Certainly, after 1968 the political upheavals in France drastically altered the personal relations among the directors. Chabrol, Truffaut, and Rohmer became firmly entrenched in the French film industry, whereas Godard set up an experimental film and video studio in Switzerland, and Rivette began to create narratives of staggering complexity and length (such as *Out One*, originally about twelve hours long!). By the mid-1980s, Truffaut had died, Chabrol's films were often unseen outside France, and Rivette's output had become esoteric. Rohmer retained international attention with his ironic tales of love and self-deception among the upper-middle class [*Pauline at the Beach* (1982) and *Full Moon over Paris* (1984)]. Godard continued to attract notoriety with such films as *Passion* (1981) and his controversial retelling of the Old and New Testaments, *Hail Mary* (1983). In 1990 he released an elegant, enigmatic film ironically entitled *Nouvelle vague*—which bears little relationship to the original tendency. In retrospect, the New Wave not only offered several original and valuable films but also demonstrated that renewal in the film industry could come from talented, aggressive young people inspired in large part by the sheer love of cinema.

THE NEW HOLLYWOOD
AND INDEPENDENT FILMMAKING

Midway through the 1960s, the Hollywood industry seemed very healthy, with "blockbusters" like *The Sound of Music* (1965) and *Dr. Zhivago* (1965) yielding huge profits. But soon problems arose. Expensive studio pictures failed miserably. Television networks, which had paid high prices for broadcasting films after theatrical release, stopped bidding for pictures. American movie attendance flattened out at around one billion tickets per year (a figure that, despite home video, has remained fairly constant ever since). By 1969 Hollywood companies were losing over $200 million annually.

Producers fought back. One strategy was to produce counterculture-flavored films aimed at young people. The most popular and influential were Dennis Hopper's low-budget *Easy Rider* (1969) and Robert Altman's *M*A*S*H* (1970). By and large, however, other "youthpix" about campus revolution and unorthodox lifestyles proved not to be big box-office attractions. What did help lift the industry's fortunes was a series of immense hits made by young directors. The most successful were Francis Ford Coppola's *The Godfather* (1972); William Friedkin's *The Exorcist* (1973); Steven Spielberg's *Jaws* (1975) and *Close Encounters of the Third Kind* (1977); John Carpenter's *Halloween* (1978); and George Lucas's *American Graffiti* (1973), *Star Wars* (1977), and *The Empire Strikes Back* (1980). In addition, films by Brian De Palma (*Obsession,* 1976) and Martin Scorsese (*Taxi Driver,* 1976; *Raging Bull,* 1980) attracted critical praise.

These and other directors came to be known as the "movie brats." Instead of coming up through the ranks of the studio system, most had gone to film schools. At New York University, the University of Southern California, and the University of California at Los Angeles, they had not only mastered the mechanics of production but also learned about film aesthetics and history. Unlike earlier Hollywood directors, the movie brats often had an encyclopedic knowledge of great movies and directors. Even those who did not attend film school were admirers of the classical Hollywood tradition.

As had been the case with the French New Wave, these movie-mad directors produced some personal, highly self-conscious films. The movie brats worked in traditional genres, but they also tried to give them an autobiographical coloring. Thus *American Graffiti* was not only a teenage musical but also Lucas's reflection on growing up in California in the 1960s. Coppola imbued both *Godfather* films with a vivacious and melancholy sense of the intense bonds within the Italian-American family. Paul Schrader poured his own obsessions with violence and sexuality into his scripts for *Taxi Driver* and *Raging Bull* and his own directed films, such as *Hard Core* (1979).

Since movies had been a major part of the young directors' lives, many films of the New Hollywood were based upon the old Hollywood. De Palma's films borrowed heavily from Hitchcock, with *Dressed to Kill* (1980) an overt redoing of *Psycho*. Peter Bogdanovich's *What's Up, Doc?* (1972) was an updating of screwball comedy, with particular reference to Howard Hawks's *Bringing Up Baby*. Carpenter's *Assault on Precinct 13* (1976) derived partly from Hawks's *Rio Bravo*; the credits list as editor one "John T. Chance," the character played by John Wayne in Hawks's Western.

At the same time, many directors admired the European tradition, with Scorsese drawn to the visual splendor of Luchino Visconti and British director Michael Powell. Some directors dreamed of making complex "art films" in the European mold. The most well-known effort is probably Coppola's *The Conversation* (1974), a mystery-story reworking of Antonioni's *Blow-Up* (1966) that plays ambiguously between reality and hallucination (p. 219). Robert Altman and Woody Allen, in quite different ways, displayed creative attitudes fed by European cinema: Altman's *Three Women* (1977) and Allen's *Interiors* (1978), for example, owed a good deal to Ingmar Bergman's work.

Altman and Allen were of a slightly older generation, but the "movie brats" proved the most continuously successful directors of the era. Lucas and Spielberg became powerful producers, working together on the Indiana Jones series and personifying Hollywood's new generation. Coppola failed to sustain his own studio, but he remained an important director. Scorsese's reputation rose steadily: By the end of the 1980s he was the most critically acclaimed living American filmmaker.

During the 1980s fresh talents won recognition, creating a "New New Hollywood." Many of the biggest hits of the decade continued to come from Lucas and Spielberg, but other successful directors were somewhat younger: James Cameron (*The Terminator*, 1984; *Terminator 2: Judgment Day*, 1991), Tim Burton (*Beetlejuice*, 1988; *Batman*, 1989), and Robert Zemeckis (*Back to the Future*, 1985; *Who Framed Roger Rabbit?*, 1988). The two stupendously successful films of 1993 and 1994 emblematized successive waves of the Hollywood renaissance: Spielberg's *Jurassic Park* and Zemeckis's *Forrest Gump*.

The resurgence of mainstream film was also fed by filmmakers from outside Hollywood. Many directors came from abroad—from Britain (Tony and Ridley Scott), Australia (Peter Weir, Fred Schepisi), Germany (Wolfgang Peterson), the Netherlands (Paul Verhoeven), or Finland (Rennie Harlin). During the 1980s, more women filmmakers also became commercially successful, such as Amy Heckerling (*Fast Times at Ridgemont High*, 1982; *Look Who's Talking*, 1990), Martha Coolidge (*Valley Girl*, 1983; *Rambling Rose*, 1991), and Penelope Spheeris (*Wayne's World*, 1992).

Several directors from independent film managed to shift into the mainstream, making medium-budget pictures with widely known stars. David Lynch moved from the midnight movie *Eraserhead* (1978) to the cult classic *Blue Velvet* (1986), while Canadian David Cronenberg, a specialist in low-budget horror films such as *Shivers* (1975) won wider recognition with *The Dead Zone* (1983) and *The Fly* (1986). The "New New Hollywood" also absorbed some minority directors from independent film. Wayne Wang was the most successful Asian-American (*Chan Is Missing*, 1982; *Smoke*, 1995). Spike Lee (*She's Gotta Have It*, 1986; *Malcolm X*, 1992) led the way for young African-American directors such as Reginald Hudlin (*House Party*, 1990), John Singleton (*Boyz N the Hood*, 1991), and Mario van Peebles (*New Jack City*, 1991).

Still other directors remained independent and more or less marginal to the studios. In *Stranger than Paradise* (1984) and *Down by Law* (1986), Jim

Jarmusch presented quirky, decentered narratives peopled by drifting losers. Allison Anders treated the contemporary experiences of disaffected young women, either in small towns (*Gas Food Lodging*, 1992) or city centers (*Mi Vida Loca*, 1994). Leslie Harris's *Just Another Girl on the IRT* (1994; p. 23, Fig. 1.21) likewise focused on the problems of urban women of color.

Stylistically, no single coherent film movement emerged during the 1970s and 1980s. The most mainstream of the young directors continued the tradition of classical American cinema. Continuity editing remained the norm, with clear signals for time shifts and new plot developments. Some directors embellished Hollywood's traditional storytelling strategies with new or revived visual techniques. In films from *Jaws* onward, Spielberg utilized deep-focus techniques reminiscent of *Citizen Kane*. Lucas developed motion-control techniques for filming miniatures for *Star Wars*, and his firm Industrial Light and Magic has become the leader in new special-effects technology. With the aid of ILM, Zemeckis astutely exploited digital imaging for *Forrest Gump* (p. 46, Fig. 2.6). Spielberg and Lucas have also led the move toward digital sound and high-quality theater reproduction technology.

Several of the newest entrants into Hollywood have enriched mainstream conventions of genre, narrative, and style. We have already seen one example of this strategy in our discussion of Spike Lee's *Do The Right Thing* (Chapter 11, pp. 393–399). Another intriguing example is Wayne Wang's *The Joy Luck Club* (1993). Set among Chinese-American families, the film concentrates on four emigrant mothers and their four assimilated daughters. In presenting the women's lives the film adheres to narrative principles that recall *Citizen Kane*. At a party, the three surviving mothers recall their lives before coming to America, and a lengthy flashback is devoted to each one. Alongside each mother's flashback, however, the plot sets flashbacks tracing the experiences of each woman's daughter in the United States. The result is a rich set of dramatic and thematic parallels. Sometimes the mother/daughter juxtapositions create sharp contrasts; at other moments, they blend together to emphasize commonalities across generations (Fig. 12.35). The women's voice-over commentaries always orient the viewer to the shifts in narration while still enabling Wang and his screenwriters to treat the flashback convention in ways which intensify the emotional effect.

Fig. 12.35

More stylistically flamboyant are Scorsese's films. *Taxi Driver, Raging Bull,* and *The Age of Innocence* (1993) use camera movement and slow-motion to extend the emotional impact of a scene. De Palma has been an even more outrageous stylist; his films flaunt long takes, startling overhead compositions, and split-screen devices. Coppola has experimented with fast-motion black-and-white in *Rumble Fish* (1983), phone conversations handled in the foreground and background of a single shot (*Tucker*, 1988), and old-fashioned special effects to lend a period mood to *Bram Stoker's Dracula* (1993).

An even more experimental attitude pervades the work of other independent directors. The brothers Joel and Ethan Coen treat each film as a pretext for exploring cinema's expressive resources. In *Raising Arizona* (1987), high-speed forward and backward tracking shots cooperate with distorting wide-angle close-ups to create comic-book exaggerations (Fig. 12.36). A somewhat similar approach is taken in Gregg Araki's gay road picture *The*

Fig. 12.36

Living End (1992). In films such as *Trust* (1991), Hal Hartley mutes a melodramatic plot through slow pacing, brooding close-ups, and dynamic foreground/background compositions (Fig. 12.37).

Fig. 12.37

Independent directors have also experimented with narrative construction. The Coens' *Barton Fink* (1991) passes unnoticeably from a satiric portrait of 1930s Hollywood into a hallucinatory fantasy. Quentin Tarentino's *Reservoir Dogs* (1993) and *Pulp Fiction* (1994) juggle story and plot time in ways that recall the complex flashbacks of the 1940s. Unlike the flashbacks in *The Joy Luck Club,* moreover, the switches are not motivated as characters' memories; the audience is forced to puzzle out the purposes served by the time shifts. In *Daughters of the Dust* (1991) Julie Dash incorporates the rich Gullah dialect and explores a complex time scheme that seeks to fuse present and future. In one scene, optical effects give the characters a glimpse of a child who is as yet unborn.

In studio-based cinema, the "old" Hollywood returned in the 1970s and 1980s, as talented young directors adapted classical conventions to contemporary tastes. At the same time there emerged an energetic independent film tradition that found audiences among film fans, young people, and minorities and subcultures willing to participate in an experience significantly different from the mainstream.

BIBLIOGRAPHY
FOR CHAPTER 12

■ GENERAL

Allen, Robert C., and Douglas Gomery. *Film History: Theory and Practice.* New York: Random House, 1985.

Branigan, Edward. "Color and Cinema: Problems in the Writing of History." *Film Reader* **4,** "Metahistory of Film" (1979): 16–34.

Knight, Arthur. *The Liveliest Art.* New York: New American Library, 1957.

Luhr, William, ed. *World Cinema since 1945.* New York: Ungar, 1987.

MacGowan, Kenneth. *Behind the Screen.* New York: Dell, 1965.

"Metahistory of Film." Issue of *Film History* **4** (1979).

Mitry, Jean. *Histoire du cinéma.* Vols. 1–3. Paris: Éditions universitaires, 1967, 1969, 1973. Vols. 4–5. Paris: Jean-Pierre Delarge, 1980.

Nowell-Smith, Geoffrey. "Facts about Films and Facts of Films." *Quarterly Review of Film Studies* **1,** no. 3 (August 1967): 272–275.

Rotha, Paul. *The Film Till Now.* London: Spring, 1967.

Sadoul, Georges. *Histoire générale du cinéma.* 6 vols. Paris: Denoël, 1973–1977.

Salt, Barry. *Film Style and Technology: History and Analysis.* 2d ed., London: Starword, 1992.

Thompson, Kristin, and David Bordwell. *Film History: An Introduction.* New York: McGraw-Hill, 1994.

■ EARLY CINEMA

Abel, Richard, *The Ciné Goes to Town: French Cinema 1896–1914.* Berkeley: University of California Press, 1994.

Allen, Robert C. *Vaudeville and Film, 1985–1915: A Study in Media Interaction.* New York: Arno, 1980.

"Archives, Document, Fiction." Issue of *Iris* **2,** no. 1 (1984).

Ceram, C. W. *Archaeology of the Cinema.* New York: Harcourt, Brace & World, 1965.

Chanan, Michael. *The Dream That Kicks: The Prehistory and Early Years of Cinema in Britain.* London: Routledge & Kegan Paul, 1980.

Cherchi Usai, Paolo, and Lorenzo Codelli, eds. *Before Caligari: German Cinema, 1895–1920.* Pordenone: Edizioni Biblioteca dell'Immagine, 1990.

"Early Cinema Audiences." Issue of *Iris* **11** (Summer 1990).

Elsaesser, Thomas, ed. *Early Cinema: Space, Frame, Narrative.* London: BFI Publishing, 1990.

"Essays on D. W. Griffith." Issue of *Quarterly Review of Film Studies* **6,** no. 1 (Winter 1981).

Fell, John L., ed. *Film before Griffith.* Berkeley: University of California Press, 1983.

Gunning, Tom. *D. W. Griffith and the Origins of American Narrative Film: The Early Years at Biograph.* Urbana and Chicago: University of Illinois Press, 1991.

Hammond, Paul. *Marvelous Méliès.* New York: St. Martin's, 1975.

Hendricks, Gordon. *The Edison Motion Picture Myth.* Berkeley: University of California Press, 1961.

Kern, Stephen. *The Culture of Time and Space, 1880–1918.* Cambridge, Mass.: Harvard University Press, 1983.

Leyda, Jay, and Charles Musser, eds. *Before Hollywood: Turn-of-the-Century Film from American Archives.* New York: American Federation of the Arts, 1986.

Mayne, Judith. "Immigrants and Spectators." *Wide Angle* **5,** no. 2 (1982): 32–41.

Musser, Charles. *Before the Nickelodeon: Edwin S. Porter and the Edison Manufacturing Company.* Berkeley: University of California Press, 1991.

———. *The Emergence of Cinema: The American Screen to 1907.* New York: Scribner's, 1991.

Musser, Charles, with Carol Nelson. *High-Class Moving Pictures: Lyman H. Howe and the Forgotten Era of Traveling Exhibition, 1880–1920.* Princeton, N.J.: Princeton University Press, 1991.

Pratt, George, ed. *Spellbound in Darkness.* Greenwich, Conn.: New York Graphic Society, 1973.

Spehr, Paul C. *The Movies Begin.* Newark, N.J.: Newark Museum, 1977.

Thompson, Kristin, and David Bordwell. "Linearity, Materialism, and the Study of Early American Cinema." *Wide Angle* **5,** no. 3 (1983): 4–15.

■ CLASSICAL HOLLYWOOD CINEMA (1908–1927)

Balio, Tino, ed. *The American Film Industry.* Rev. ed. Madison: University of Wisconsin Press, 1985.

Bordwell, David, Janet Staiger, and Kristin Thompson. *The Classical Hollywood Cinema: Film Style and Mode of Production to 1960.* New York: Columbia University Press, 1985.

Bowser, Eileen. *The Transformation of Cinema, 1907–1915.* New York: Scribner's, 1990.

Brownlow, Kevin, *The Parade's Gone By.* New York: Knopf, 1968.

Cherchi Usai, Paolo, and Lorenzo Codelli, eds. *Sulla via di Hollywood 1911–1920.* (*The Path to Hollywood 1911–1920.*) Pordenone: Edizioni Biblioteca dell'Immagine, 1988. (Bilingual in Italian and English.)

"Economic and Technological History." Issue of *Cinema Journal* **18,** no. 2 (Spring 1979).

Gomery, Douglas. *Shared Pleasures: A History of American Moviegoing.* Madison: University of Wisconsin Press, 1992.

Hampton, Benjamin B. *History of the American Film Industry.* (1931) rep. New York: Dover, 1970.

Jacobs, Lewis. *The Rise of the American Film.* (1939) rep. New York: Teachers College Press, 1968.

Koszarski, Richard. *An Evening's Entertainment: The Age of the Silent Feature Picture, 1915–1928.* New York: Scribner's, 1990.

Staiger, Janet. *Interpreting Films: Studies in the Historical Reception of American Cinema.* Princeton, N.J.: Princeton University Press, 1992.

■ GERMAN EXPRESSIONISM

Barlow, John D. *German Expressionist Film.* Boston: Twayne, 1982.

Bronner, Stephen Eric, and Douglas Kellner, eds. *Passion and Rebellion: The Expressionist Heritage.* South Hadley, Mass.: J. F. Bergin, 1983.

Budd, Mike, ed. *The Cabinet of Dr. Caligari: Texts, Contexts, Histories.* New Brunswick: Rutgers University Press, 1990.

Courtade, Francis. *Cinéma expressioniste.* Paris: Henri Veyrier, 1984.

Eisner, Lotte. *F. W. Murnau.* Berkeley: University of California Press, 1983.

———. *Fritz Lang.* New York: Oxford University Press, 1977.

———. *The Haunted Screen.* Berkeley: University of California Press, 1969.

Elsaesser, Thomas. "Social Mobility and the Fantastic: German Silent Cinema." *Wide Angle* **5,** no. 2 (1982): 14–25.

Kracauer, Siegfried. *From Caligari to Hitler.* Princeton, N.J.: Princeton University Press, 1947.

Myers, Bernard S. *The German Expressionists.* New York: Praeger, 1963.

Selz, Peter. *German Expressionist Painting.* Berkeley: University of California Press, 1957.

Willett, John. *Expressionism.* New York: McGraw-Hill, 1970.

———. *The New Sobriety: Art and Politics in the Weimar Republic, 1917–1933.* London: Thames & Hudson, 1978.

■ FRENCH IMPRESSIONISM

Abel, Richard. *French Cinema: The First Wave, 1915–1929.* Princeton, N.J.: Princeton University Press, 1984.

———. *French Film Theory and Criticism, 1907–1939.* Vol. 1. Princeton, N.J.: Princeton University Press, 1988.

Bordwell, David. *French Impressionist Cinema: Film Culture, Film Theory, and Film Style.* New York: Arno, 1980.

Brownlow, Kevin. *NAPOLEON: Abel Gance's Classic Film.* New York: Knopf, 1983.

Clair, René. *Cinema Yesterday and Today.* New York: Dover, 1972.

King, Norman. *Abel Gance: A Politics of Spectacle.* London: British Film Institute, 1984.

Liebman, Stuart. "French Film Theory, 1910–1921." *Quarterly Review of Film Studies* **8,** no. 1 (Winter 1983): 1–23.

Sadoul, Georges. *The French Cinema.* London: Falcon Press, 1952.

■ SOVIET MONTAGE

Bordwell, David. *The Cinema of Eisenstein.* Cambridge, Mass.: Harvard University Press, 1993.

Bowlt, John, ed. *Russian Art of the Avant-Garde.* New York: Viking, 1973.

Carynnyk, Marco, ed. *Alexander Dovzhenko: Poet as Filmmaker.* Cambridge, Mass.: MIT Press, 1973.

Christie, Ian. "Soviet Cinema—Making Sense of Sound." *Screen* **23,** no. 2 (July–August 1982): 34–49.

Eisenstein, S. M. *S. M. Eisenstein: Writings 1922–1934,* Richard Taylor, ed. London: British Film Institute, 1988; *Eisenstein, Volume 2, Towards a Theory of Montage,* Michael Glenny and Richard Taylor, eds. London: British Film Institute, 1991.

Fuelop-Miller, René. *The Mind and Face of Bolshevism.* New York: Harper & Row, 1965.

Kepley, Vance. *In the Service of the State: The Cinema of Alexander Dovzhenko.* Madison: University of Wisconsin Press, 1986.

Kuleshov, Lev. *Kuleshov on Film.* Edited and translated by Ronald Levaco. Berkeley: University of California Press, 1974.

Leyda, Jay. *Kino.* 3rd. ed. Princeton, N.J.: Princeton University Press, 1983.

Lodder, Christina. *Russian Constructivism.* New Haven: Yale University Press, 1983.

Michelson, Annette, ed. *Kino-Eye: The Writings of Dziga Vertov.* Berkeley: University of California Press, 1984.

Nilsen, Vladimir. *The Cinema as a Graphic Art.* New York: Hill & Wang, 1959.

Petric, Vlada. *Constructivism in Film: The Man with a Movie Camera—A Cinematic Analysis.* London: Cambridge University Press, 1987.

Pudovkin, V. I. *Film Technique and Film Acting.* New York: Grove, 1960.

Schnitzer, Luda, Jean Schnitzer, and Marcel Martin, eds. *Cinema and Revolution.* New York: Hill & Wang, 1973.

Taylor, Richard. *The Politics of the Soviet Cinema, 1917–1929.* Cambridge: Cambridge University Press, 1979.

Taylor, Richard, and Ian Christie, eds. *The Film Factory: Russian and Soviet Cinema in Documents, 1896–1939.* Cambridge, Mass.: Harvard University Press, 1988.

———. *Inside the Film Factory: New Approaches to Russian and Soviet Cinema.* London: Routledge, 1991.

Thompson, Kristin. "Early Sound Counterpoint." *Yale French Studies* **60** (1980): 115–140.

Youngblood, Denise. *Soviet Cinema in the Silent Era, 1918–1933.* Ann Arbor: UMI Research Press, 1985.

■ THE CLASSICAL HOLLYWOOD CINEMA AFTER THE COMING OF SOUND

Balio, Tino, ed. *The American Film Industry.* Rev. ed. Madison: University of Wisconsin Press, 1985.

Balio, Tino. *Grand Design: Hollywood as a Modern Business Enterprise, 1930–1939.* New York: Scribner's, 1993.

Balio, Tino, ed. *Hollywood in the Age of Television.* Boston: Unwin Hyman, 1990.

Bordwell, David, Janet Staiger, and Kristin Thompson. *The Classical Hollywood Cinema: Film Style and Mode of Production to 1960.* New York: Columbia University Press, 1985.

Gomery, Douglas. *The Hollywood Studio System.* New York: St. Martin's 1986.

———. *Shared Pleasures: A History of American Moviegoing.* Madison: University of Wisconsin Press, 1992.

Koszarski, Richard, ed. *Hollywood Directors, 1914–1940.* New York: Oxford University Press, 1976.

Maltby, Richard. *Harmless Entertainment: Hollywood and the Ideology of Consensus.* Metuchen, N.J.: Scarecrow Press, 1983.

Silver, Alain, and Elizabeth Ward. *Film Noir: An Encyclopedic Reference to the American Style.* Woodstock, N.Y.: Overlook Press, 1979.

Staiger, Janet, ed. *The Studio System.* New Brunswick, N.J.: Rutgers University Press, 1995.

"The Studio System: Case Histories." *Wide Angle* **10,** 1 (1988).

Walker, Alexander. *The Shattered Silents: How the Talkies Came to Stay.* New York: Morrow, 1979.

"Widescreen." Issue of *The Velvet Light Trap* **21** (Summer 1985).

■ ITALIAN NEOREALISM

Armes, Roy. *Patterns of Realism.* New York: A. S. Barnes, 1970.

Bazin, André. "Cinema and Television." *Sight and Sound* **28,** no. 1 (Winter 1958–59): 26–30.

———. *What Is Cinema?* Vol. 2. Berkeley: University of California Press, 1971.

Bondanella, Peter. *Italian Cinema From Neorealism to the Present.* New York: Ungar, 1983.

Brunette, Peter. *Roberto Rossellini.* New York: Oxford University Press, 1987.

Leprohon, Pierre. *The Italian Cinema.* New York: Praeger, 1984.

Liehm, Mira. *Passion and Defiance: Film in Italy from 1942 to the Present.* Berkeley: University of California Press, 1984.

Marcus, Millicent. *Italian Film in the Light of Neorealism.* Princeton, N.J.: Princeton University Press, 1986.

Overbey, David, ed. *Springtime in Italy: A Reader on Neo-Realism.* London: Talisman, 1978.

Pacifici, Sergio J. "Notes toward a Definition of Neorealism." *Yale French Studies* **17** (Summer 1956): 44–53.

Sitney, P. Adams. *Vital Crises in Italian Cinema: Iconography, Stylistics, Politics.* Austin: University of Texas Press, 1995.

■ THE FRENCH NEW WAVE

Armes, Roy. *The French Cinema since 1946.* Vol. 2. New York: A. S. Barnes, 1970.

Brown, Royal S., ed. *Focus on Godard.* Englewood Cliffs, N.J.: Prentice-Hall, 1972.

Burch, Noël. "Qu'est-ce que la Nouvelle Vague?" *Film Quarterly* **13,** no. 2 (Winter 1959): 16–30.

Crisp, Colin. *The Classic French Cinema, 1930–1960.* Bloomington: Indiana University Press, 1994.

Godard, Jean-Luc. *Godard on Godard.* New York: Viking, 1972.

Graham, Peter, ed. *The New Wave.* Garden City, N.J.: Doubleday, 1968.

Hillier, Jim, ed. *Cahiers du Cinéma: The 1950s: Neo-Realism, Hollywood, New Wave.* Cambridge, Mass.: Harvard University Press, 1985.

———. *Cahiers du Cinéma: The 1960s: New Wave, New Cinema, Reevaluating Hollywood.* Cambridge, Mass.: Harvard University Press, 1986.

Insdorf, Annette. *François Truffaut.* New York: William Morrow, 1979.

Marie, Michel. "The Art of the Film in France since the 'New Wave.'" *Wide Angle* **4,** no. 4 (1981): 18–25.

Monaco, James. *The New Wave: Truffaut, Godard, Chabrol, Rohmer, Rivette.* New York: Oxford University Press, 1976.

Mussman, Toby, ed. *Jean-Luc Godard.* New York: Dutton, 1968.

■ THE NEW HOLLYWOOD AND INDEPENDENT FILMMAKING

Cones, John W. *Film Finance and Distribution: A Dictionary of Terms.* Los Angeles: Silman-James Press, 1992.

Donahue, Suzanne Mary. *American Film Distribution: The Changing Marketplace.* Ann Arbor: UMI Research Press, 1987.

Gomery, Douglas. "The American Film Industry of the 1970s: Stasis in the 'New Hollywood.'" *Wide Angle* **5,** 4 (1983): 52–59.

———. "Corporate Ownership and Control in the Contemporary US Film Industry." *Screen* **25,** 4–5 (July–October 1984): 60–69.

Goodwin, Michael, and Naomi Wise. *On the Edge: The Life and Times of Francis Coppola.* New York: Morrow, 1989.

Hillier, Jim. *The New Hollywood.* New York: Continuum, 1994.

Hoberman, J., and Jonathan Rosenbaum. *Midnight Movies.* New York: Harper & Row, 1983.

Kellner, Douglas, and Michael Ryan. *Camera Politica: The Politics and Ideology of Contemporary Hollywood Cinema.* Bloomington: Indiana University Press, 1988.

McGilligan, Patrick. *Robert Altman: Jumping Off the Cliff.* New York: St. Martin's, 1989.

Monaco, James. *American Film Now: The People, the Power, the Money, the Movies.* New York: New American Library, 1979.

Mott, Donald R., and Cheryl McAllister Saunders. *Steven Spielberg.* Boston: Twayne, 1986.

Noriega, Chon A. *Chicanos and Film: Representation and Resistance.* Minneapolis: University of Minnesota Press, 1992.

Pye, Michael, and Lynda Myles. *The Movie Brats: How the Film Generation Took Over Hollywood.* New York: Holt, Rinehart and Winston, 1979.

Reid, Mark A. *Redefining Black Film.* Berkeley: University of California Press, 1993.

Squires, Jason E. *The Movie Business Book.* 2d ed., New York: Simon & Schuster, 1992.

Welbon, Yvonne. "Calling the Shots: Black Women Directors Take the Helm." *The Independent* **15,** 2 (March 1992): 18–22.

GLOSSARY

abstract form   A type of filmic organization in which the parts relate to each other through repetition and variation of such visual qualities as shape, color, rhythm, and direction of movement.

Academy ratio   The standardized shape of the film frame established by the Academy of Motion Picture Arts and Sciences. In the original ratio, the frame was $1\frac{1}{3}$ times as wide as it was high (1.33:1); later the width was normalized at 1.85 times the height (1.85:1).

aerial perspective   A cue for suggesting represented depth in the image by presenting objects in the distance less distinctly than those in the foreground.

anamorphic lens   A lens for making widescreen films using regular *Academy ratio* frame size. The camera lens takes in a wide field of view and squeezes it onto the frame, and a similar projector lens unsqueezes the image onto a wide theater screen.

angle of framing   The position of the frame in relation to the subject it shows: above it, looking down (a high angle); horizontal, on the same level (a straight-on angle); looking up (a low angle). Also called "camera angle."

animation   Any process whereby artificial movement is created by photographing a series of drawings (see also *cel animation*), objects, or computer images one by one. Small changes in position, recorded frame by frame, create the illusion of movement.

aspect ratio   The relationship of the frame's width to its height. The standard *Academy ratio* for many years was 1.33:1.

associational form   A type of organization in which the film's parts are juxtaposed to suggest similarities, contrasts, concepts, emotions, and expressive qualities.

asynchronous sound   Sound that is not matched temporally with the movements occurring in the image, as when dialogue is out of synchronization with lip movements.

auteur   The presumed or actual "author" of a film, usually identified as the director. Also sometimes used in an evaluative sense to distinguish good filmmakers (*auteurs*) from bad ones.

axis of action   In the *continuity editing* system, the imaginary line that passes from side to side through the main actors, defining the spatial relations of all the elements of the scene as being to the right or left. The camera is not supposed to cross the axis at a cut and thus reverse those spatial relations. Also called the "180° line." (See also *180° system.*)

backlighting   Illumination cast onto the figures in the scene from the side opposite the camera, usually creating a thin outline of highlighting on those figures.

boom   A pole upon which a microphone can be suspended above the scene being filmed and which is used to change the microphone's position as the action shifts.

camera angle   See *angle of framing.*

canted framing   A view in which the frame is not level; either the right or left side is lower than the other, causing objects in the scene to appear slanted out of an upright position.

categorical form   A type of filmic organization in which the parts treat distinct subsets of a topic. For example, a film about the United States might be organized into fifty parts, each devoted to a single state.

cel animation   Animation that uses a series of drawings on pieces of celluloid, called "cels" for short. Slight changes between the drawings combine to create an illusion of movement.

cheat cut   In the *continuity editing* system, a cut which presents continuous time from shot to shot but which mismatches the positions of figures or objects.

cinematography   A general term for all the manipulations of the film strip by the camera in the shooting phase and by the laboratory in the developing phase.

close-up   A framing in which the scale of the object shown is relatively large; most commonly a person's head seen from the neck up, or an object of a comparable size that fills most of the screen.

closure   The degree to which the ending of a narrative film reveals the effects of all the causal events and resolves (or "closes off") all lines of action.

continuity editing   A system of cutting to maintain continuous and clear narrative action. Continuity editing relies upon matching screen direction, position, and temporal relations from shot to shot. For specific techniques of continuity editing, see *axis of action, crosscutting, cut-in, establishing shot, eyeline match, match on action, reestablishing shot, screen direction, shot/reverse shot.*

contrast In cinematography, the difference between the brightest and darkest areas within the frame.

crane shot A shot with a change in framing accomplished by having the camera above the ground and moving through the air in any direction.

crosscutting Editing that alternates shots of two or more lines of action occurring in different places, usually simultaneously.

cut 1. In filmmaking, the joining of two strips of film together with a splice. 2. In the finished film, an instantaneous change from one framing to another. See also *jump cut.*

cut-in An instantaneous shift from a distant framing to a closer view of some portion of the same space.

deep focus A use of the camera lens and lighting that keeps both the close and distant planes being photographed in sharp focus.

deep space An arrangement of mise-en-scene elements so that there is a considerable distance between the plane closest to the camera and the one farthest away. Any or all of these planes may be in focus.

depth of field The measurements of the closest and farthest planes in front of the camera lens between which everything will be in sharp focus. A depth of field from five to sixteen feet, for example, would mean everything closer than five feet and farther than sixteen feet would be out of focus.

dialogue overlap In editing a scene, arranging the cut so that a bit of dialogue or noise coming from shot A is heard under a shot of character B or of another element in the scene.

diegesis In a narrative film, the world of the film's story. The diegesis includes events that are presumed to have occurred and actions and spaces not shown onscreen. See also *diegetic sound, nondiegetic insert, nondiegetic sound.*

diegetic sound Any voice, musical passage, or sound effect presented as originating from a source within the film's world. See also *nondiegetic sound.*

direct sound Music, noise, and speech recorded from the event at the moment of filming; opposite of *postsynchronization.*

discontinuity editing Any alternative system of joining shots together using techniques unacceptable within *continuity editing* principles. Possibilities would include mismatching of temporal and spatial relations, violations of the *axis of action,* and concentration on graphic relationships. See also *elliptical editing, graphic match, intellectual montage, jump cut, nondiegetic insert, overlapping editing.*

dissolve A transition between two shots during which the first image gradually disappears while the second image gradually appears; for a moment the two images blend in *superimposition.*

distance of framing The apparent distance of the frame from the mise-en-scene elements. Also called "camera distance" and "shot scale." See also *close-up, extreme close-up, extreme long shot, medium close-up, medium shot, plan américain.*

distribution One of the three branches of the film industry; the process of supplying the finished film to the places where it will be shown. See also *exhibition, production.*

dolly A camera support with wheels, used in making *tracking shots.*

dubbing The process of replacing part or all of the voices on the sound track in order to correct mistakes or rerecord dialogue. See also *postsynchronization.*

duration In a narrative film, the aspect of temporal manipulation that involves the time span presented in the *plot* and assumed to operate in the *story.* See also *frequency, order.*

editing 1. In filmmaking, the task of selecting and joining camera takes. 2. In the finished film, the set of techniques that governs the relations among shots.

ellipsis In a narrative film, the shortening of *plot* duration achieved by omitting intervals of *story* duration. See also *elliptical editing, viewing time.*

elliptical editing Shot transitions that omit parts of an event, causing an *ellipsis* in plot and story duration.

establishing shot A shot, usually involving a distant framing, that shows the spatial relations among the important figures, objects, and setting in a scene.

exhibition One of the three general areas of the film industry; the process of showing the finished film to audiences. See also *distribution, production.*

exposure The adjustment of the camera mechanism in order to control how much light strikes each frame of film passing through the aperture.

external diegetic sound Sound represented as coming from a physical source within the story space and which we assume characters in the scene also hear. See also *internal diegetic sound.*

extreme close-up A framing in which the scale of the object shown is very large; most commonly, a small object or a part of the body.

extreme long shot A framing in which the scale of the object shown is very small; a building, landscape, or crowd of people would fill the screen.

eyeline match A cut obeying the *axis of action* principle, in which the first shot shows a person looking off in one direction and the second shows a nearby space containing what he or she sees. If the person looks left, the following shot should imply that the looker is offscreen right.

fade 1. *Fade-in:* A dark screen that gradually brightens as a shot appears. 2. *Fade-out:* A shot gradually darkens as the screen goes black. Occasionally fade-outs brighten to pure white or to a color.

fill light Illumination from a source less bright than the *key light,* used to soften deep shadows in a scene. See also *three-point lighting.*

film noir "Dark film," a term applied by French critics to a type of American film, usually in the detective or thriller genres, with low-key lighting and a sombre mood.

film stock The strip of material upon which a series of still photographs is registered; it consists of a clear base coated on one side with a light-sensitive emulsion.

filter A piece of glass or gelatin placed in front of the camera or printer lens to alter the quality or quantity of light striking the film in the aperture.

flashback An alteration of story order in which the plot moves back to show events that have taken place earlier than ones already shown.

flashforward An alteration of story order in which the plot presentation moves forward to future events, then returns to the present.

focal length The distance from the center of the lens to the point at which the light rays meet in sharp focus. The focal length determines the perspective relations of the space represented on the flat screen. See also *normal lens, telephoto lens, wide-angle lens.*

focus The degree to which light rays coming from the same part of an object through different parts of the lens reconverge at the same point on the film frame, creating sharp outlines and distinct textures.

following shot A shot with framing that shifts to keep a moving figure onscreen.

form The general system of relationships among the parts of a film.

frame A single image on the strip of film. When a series of frames is projected onto a screen in quick succession, an illusion of movement is created by the spectator.

framing The use of the edges of the film frame to select and to compose what will be visible onscreen.

frequency In a narrative film, the aspect of temporal manipulation that involves the number of times any *story* event is shown in the *plot*. See also *duration, order.*

front projection Composite process whereby footage meant to appear as the background of a shot is projected from the front onto a screen; figures in the foreground are filmed in front of the screen as well. This is the opposite of *rear projection.*

frontal lighting Illumination directed into the scene from a position near the camera.

frontality In staging, the positioning of figures so that they face the viewer.

function The role or effect of any element within the film's form.

gauge The width of the film strip, measured in millimeters.

genres Various types of films which audiences and filmmakers recognize by their familiar narrative conventions. Common genres are musical, gangster, and Western films.

graphic match Two successive shots joined so as to create a strong similarity of compositional elements (e.g., color, shape).

hand-held camera The use of the camera operator's body as a camera support, either holding it by hand or using a harness.

hard lighting Illumination that creates sharp edged shadows.

height of framing The distance of the camera above the ground, regardless of the *angle of framing.*

high-key lighting Illumination that creates comparatively little contrast between the light and dark areas of the shot. Shadows are fairly transparent and brightened by *fill light.*

ideology A relatively coherent system of values, beliefs, or ideas shared by some social group and often taken for granted as natural or inherently true.

intellectual montage The juxtaposition of a series of images to create an abstract idea not present in any one image.

internal diegetic sound Sound represented as coming from the mind of a character within the story space. Although we and the character can hear it, we assume that the other characters cannot. See also *external diegetic sound.*

interpretation The viewer's activity of analyzing the implicit and symptomatic meanings suggested in a film. See also *meaning.*

iris A round, moving *mask* that can close down to end a scene (iris-out) or emphasize a detail, or it can open to begin a scene (iris-in) or to reveal more space around a detail.

jump cut An elliptical cut that appears to be an interruption of a single shot. Either the figures seem to change instantly against a constant background, or the background changes instantly while the figures remain constant. See also *ellipsis.*

key light In the three-point lighting system, the brightest illumination coming into the scene. See also *backlighting, fill light, three-point lighting.*

lens A shaped piece of transparent material (usually glass) with either or both sides curved to gather and focus light rays. Most camera and projector lenses place a series of lenses within a metal tube to form a compound lens.

linearity In a narrative, the clear motivation of a series of causes and effects that progress without significant digressions, delays, or irrelevant actions.

long shot A framing in which the scale of the object shown is small; a standing human figure would appear nearly the height of the screen.

long take A shot that continues for an unusually lengthy time before the transition to the next shot.

low-key lighting Illumination that creates strong contrast between light and dark areas of the shot, with deep shadows and little *fill light.*

mask An opaque screen placed in the camera or printer that blocks part of the frame off and changes the shape of the photographed image, leaving part of the frame a solid color. As seen on the screen, most masks are black, although they can be white or colored.

masking   In exhibition, stretches of black fabric that frame the theater screen. Masking may be adjusted according to the *aspect ratio* of the film to be projected.

match on action   A continuity cut which splices two different views of the same action together at the same moment in the movement, making it seem to continue uninterrupted.

matte shot   A type of *process shot* in which different areas of the image (usually actors and setting) are photographed separately and combined in laboratory work.

meaning   1. *Referential meaning:* Allusion to particular pieces of shared prior knowledge outside the film which the viewer is expected to recognize. 2. *Explicit meaning:* Significance presented overtly, usually in language and often near the film's beginning or end. 3. *Implicit meaning:* Significance left tacit, for the viewer to discover upon analysis or reflection. 4. *Symptomatic meaning:* Significance which the film divulges, often "against its will," by virtue of its historical or social context.

medium close-up   A framing in which the scale of the object shown is fairly large: a human figure seen from the chest up would fill most of the screen.

medium long shot   A framing at a distance which makes an object about four or five feet high appear to fill most of the screen vertically. See also *plan américain,* the special term for a medium long shot depicting human figures.

medium shot   A framing in which the scale of the object shown is of moderate size; a human figure seen from the waist up would fill most of the screen.

mise-en-scene   All of the elements placed in front of the camera to be photographed: the settings and props, lighting, costumes and make-up, and figure behavior.

mixing   Combining two or more sound tracks by recording them onto a single one.

mobile frame   The effect on the screen of the moving camera, a *zoom lens,* or certain *special effects;* the framing shifts in relation to the scene being photographed. See also *crane shot, pan, tilt, tracking shot.*

monochromatic color design   Color design which emphasizes a narrow set of shades of a single color.

montage   1. A synonym for *editing.* 2. An approach to editing developed by the Soviet filmmakers of the 1920s; it emphasizes dynamic, often discontinuous, relationships between shots and the juxtaposition of images to create ideas not present in either shot by itself. See also *discontinuity editing, intellectual montage.*

montage sequence   A segment of a film that summarizes a topic or compresses a passage of time into brief symbolic or typical images. Frequently *dissolves, fades, superimpositions,* and *wipes* are used to link the images in a montage sequence.

motif   An element in a film that is repeated in a significant way.

motion control   A computerized method of planning and repeating camera movements on miniatures, models, and process work.

motivation   The justification given in the film for the presence of an element. This may be an appeal to the viewer's knowledge of the real world, to genre conventions, to narrative causality, or to a stylistic pattern within the film.

narration   The process through which the *plot* conveys or withholds *story* information. The narration can be more or less restricted to character knowledge and more or less deep in presenting characters' mental perceptions and thoughts.

narrative form   A type of filmic organization in which the parts relate to each other through a series of causally related events taking place in a specific time and space.

nondiegetic insert   A shot or series of shots cut into a sequence, showing objects represented as being outside the space of the narrative.

nondiegetic sound   Sound, such as mood music or a narrator's commentary, represented as coming from a source outside the space of the narrative.

nonsimultaneous sound   Diegetic sound that comes from a source in time either earlier or later than that of the images it accompanies.

normal lens   A lens that shows objects without severely exaggerating or reducing the depth of the scene's planes. In 35mm filming, a normal lens is 35 to 50mm. See also *telephoto lens, wide-angle lens.*

offscreen sound   Simultaneous sound from a source assumed to be in the space of the scene but in an area outside what is visible onscreen.

offscreen space   The six areas blocked from being visible on the screen but still part of the space of the scene: to each side and above and below the frame, behind the set, and behind the camera. See also *space.*

180° system   The continuity approach to editing dictates that the camera should stay on one side of the action to ensure consistent left-right spatial relations between objects from shot to shot. The 180° line is the same as the *axis of action.* See also *continuity editing, screen direction.*

order   In a narrative film, the aspect of temporal manipulation that involves the sequence in which the chronological events of the *story* are arranged in the *plot.* See also *duration, frequency.*

overlap   A cue for suggesting represented depth in the film image by placing closer objects partly in front of more distant ones.

overlapping editing   Cuts that repeat part or all of an action, thus expanding its viewing time and plot duration.

pan   A camera movement with the camera body turning to the right or left. On the screen, it produces a mobile framing which scans the space horizontally.

pixillation   A form of single-frame animation in which three-dimensional objects, often people, are made to move in staccato bursts through the use of stop-action cinematography.

plan américain   A framing in which the scale of the object shown is moderately small; the human figure seen from the shins to the head would fill most of the screen. This is sometimes referred to as a *medium long shot,* especially when human figures are not shown.

plan-séquence French term for a scene handled in a single shot, usually a *long take.*

plot In a narrative film, all the events that are directly presented to us, including their causal relations, chronological order, duration, frequency, and spatial locations. Opposed to *story,* which is the viewer's imaginary construction of all the events in the narrative. See also *duration, ellipsis, frequency, order, viewing time.*

point-of-view shot (POV shot) A shot taken with the camera placed approximately where the character's eyes would be, showing what the character would see; usually cut in before or after a shot of the character looking.

postsynchronization The process of adding sound to images after they have been shot and assembled. This can include *dubbing* of voices, as well as inserting diegetic music or sound effects. It is the opposite of *direct sound.*

process shot Any shot involving rephotography to combine two or more images into one, or to create a special effect; also called "composite shot." See also *matte shot, rear projection, special effects.*

production One of the three branches of the film industry; the process of creating the film. See also *distribution, exhibition.*

racking focus Shifting the area of sharp focus from one plane to another during a shot; the effect on the screen is called "rack focus."

rate In shooting, the number of frames exposed per second; in projection, the number of frames thrown on the screen per second. If the two are the same, the speed of the action will appear normal, while a disparity will create slow or fast motion. The standard rate in sound cinema is 24 frames per second for both shooting and projection.

rear projection A technique for combining a foreground action with a background action filmed earlier. The foreground is filmed in a studio, against a screen; the background imagery is projected from behind the screen. The opposite of *front projection.*

reestablishing shot A return to a view of an entire space after a series of closer shots following the *establishing shot.*

reframing Short panning or tilting movements to adjust for the figures' movements, keeping them onscreen or centered.

rhetorical form A type of filmic organization in which the parts create and support an argument.

rhythm The perceived rate and regularity of sounds, series of shots, and movements within the shots. Rhythmic factors include beat (or pulse), accent (or stress), and tempo (or pace).

rotoscope A machine that projects live-action motion picture frames one by one onto a drawing pad so that an animator can trace the figures in each frame. The aim is to achieve more realistic movement in an animated cartoon.

scene A segment in a narrative film that takes place in one time and space or that uses crosscutting to show two or more simultaneous actions.

screen direction The right-left relationships in a scene, set up in an establishing shot and determined by the position of characters and objects in the frame; by the directions of movement; and by the characters' eyelines. *Continuity editing* will attempt to keep screen direction consistent between shots. See also *axis of action, eyeline match, 180° system.*

segmentation The process of dividing a film into parts for analysis.

sequence Term commonly used for a moderately large segment of a film, involving one complete stretch of action. In a narrative film, often equivalent to a *scene.*

shallow focus A restricted *depth of field,* which keeps only those planes close to the camera in sharp focus; the opposite of *deep focus.*

shallow space Staging the action in relatively few planes of depth; the opposite of *deep space.*

shot 1. In shooting, one uninterrupted run of the camera to expose a series of frames. Also called a *take.* 2. In the finished film, one uninterrupted image with a single static or mobile framing.

shot/reverse shot Two or more shots edited together that alternate characters, typically in a conversation situation. In *continuity editing,* characters in one framing usually look left, in the other framing, right. Over-the-shoulder framings are common in shot/reverse-shot editing.

side lighting Lighting coming from one side of a person or object, usually in order to create a sense of volume, to bring out surface tensions, or to fill in areas left shadowed by light from another source.

simultaneous sound Diegetic sound that is represented as occurring at the same time in the story as the image it accompanies.

size diminution A cue for suggesting represented depth in the image by showing objects that are further away as smaller than foreground objects.

soft lighting Illumination that avoids harsh bright and dark areas, creating a gradual transition from highlights to shadows.

sound bridge 1. At the beginning of one scene, the sound from the previous scene carries over briefly before the sound from the new scene begins. 2. At the end of one scene, the sound from the next scene is heard, leading into that scene.

sound over Any sound that is not represented as being directly audible within the space and time of the images on the screen. This includes both nonsimultaneous diegetic sound and nondiegetic sounds. See also *nondiegetic sound, nonsimultaneous sound.*

sound perspective The sense of a sound's position in space, yielded by volume, timbre, pitch, and, in stereophonic reproduction systems, binaural information.

space Most minimally, any film displays a two-dimensional graphic space, the flat composition of the image. In films which depict recognizable objects, figures, and locales, a three-dimensional space is represented as well. At any moment, three-dimensional space may be directly depicted, as onscreen space, or suggested, as *offscreen space*. In narrative film, we can also distinguish between story space, the locale of the totality of the action (whether shown or not), and plot space, the locales visibly and audibly represented in the scenes.

special effects   A general term for various photographic manipulations that create fictitious spatial relations in the shot, such as *superimposition, matte shots,* and *rear projection.*

story   In a narrative film, all the events that we see and hear, plus all those that we infer or assume to have occurred, arranged in their presumed causal relations, chronological order, duration, frequency, and spatial locations. Opposed to *plot,* which is the film's actual presentation of certain events in the narrative. See also *duration, ellipsis, frequency, order, space, viewing time.*

storyboard   A tool used in planning film production, consisting of comic-strip-like drawings of individual shots or phases of shots with descriptions written below each drawing.

style   The repeated and salient uses of film techniques characteristic of a single film or a group of films (for example, a filmmaker's work or a national movement).

superimposition   The exposure of more than one image on the same film strip.

synchronous sound   Sound that is matched temporally with the movements occurring in the images, as when dialogue corresponds to lip movements.

take   In filmmaking, the shot produced by one uninterrupted run of the camera. One shot in the final film may be chosen from among several takes of the same action.

technique   Any aspect of the film medium that can be chosen and manipulated in making a film.

telephoto lens   A lens of long focal length that affects a scene's perspective by enlarging distant planes and making them seem close to the foreground planes. In 35mm filming, a lens of 75mm length or more. See also *normal lens, wide-angle lens.*

three-point lighting   A common arrangement using three directions of light on a scene: from behind the subjects (*backlighting*), from one bright source (*key light*), and from a less bright source balancing the key light (*fill light*).

tilt   A camera movement with the camera body swiveling upward or downward on a stationary support. It produces a mobile framing that scans the space vertically.

top lighting   Lighting coming from above a person or object, usually in order to outline the upper areas of the figure or to separate it more clearly from the background.

tracking shot   A mobile framing that travels through space forward, backward, or laterally. See also *crane shot, pan,* and *tilt.*

typage   A performance technique of Soviet Montage cinema whereby an actor is given features believed to characterize a social class or other group.

underlighting   Illumination from a point below the figures in the scene.

unity   The degree to which a film's parts relate systematically to each other and provide motivations for all the elements used.

variation   In film form, the return of an element with notable changes.

viewing time   The length of time it takes to watch a film when it is projected at the appropriate speed.

whip pan   An extremely fast movement of the camera from side to side, which causes the image to blur into a set of indistinct horizontal streaks briefly. Often an imperceptible cut will join two whip pans to create a trick transition between scenes.

wide-angle lens   A lens of short focal length that affects a scene's perspective by distorting straight lines near the edges of the frame and by exaggerating the distance between foreground and background planes. In 35mm filming, a wide-angle lens is 30mm or less. See also *normal lens, telephoto lens.*

wipe   A transition between shots in which a line passes across the screen, eliminating the first shot as it goes and replacing it with the next one.

zoom lens   A lens with a focal length that can be changed during a shot. A shift toward the *telephoto* range enlarges the image and flattens its planes together, giving an impression of moving into the scene's space, while a shift toward the *wide-angle* range does the opposite.

INTERNET RESOURCES: SELECTED REFERENCE SITES IN FILM FROM THE WORLD WIDE WEB

Due to the temporary nature of some web sites and their continually changing structure and content, we cannot guarantee that the information listed here will always be available.

1. Movie Resources
http://www.csp.it/cinema._e.html
A complete list of movie databases, reviews, film history, WWW resources, usenet groups, and commercial sites.

2. Yahoo! Entertainment: Movies and Films
http://www.yahoo.com/Entertainment/Movies_and_Films/
A very complete list of links to a wide variety of topics in film on the World Wide Web.

3. Internet Movie Database Tour
http://www.msstate.edu/Movies/tour.html
A complete listing of information about over 750,000 films, including year of release, credits, sequels, awards, etc.

4. The Wheel: Media, Music, Film, TV, and Theatre
http://www.unn.ac.uk/~isu8/media.html
Includes a movie database, film and video resources, and links to newspapers and magazines.

5. General Index of Film Resources on Web
http://www.film.com/film/misc/other.sites.html
Includes links to actors, databases, essays and magazines, institutes, and the movie industry.

6. The Cinema Connection, Journals and Magazines
http://www.webcom.com/~3e-media/TMC/zines.html
From Europe, Australia, and the United States, a list of many film resources and journals.

7. Movies.net
http://www.movies.net/index.html
Includes links to studios, news, reviews, movie clips, and stars and movie memorabilia.

8. Hollywood Online
http://www.hollywood.com/movies/
This site is a graphics-intense site that offers a movie list, trailers, sounds, photos, chat rooms, a voting booth, and more.

9. Circle of Critics' Cafe
http://useattle.uspan.com/u-movies/circleofcritics.html
Discussions of the finer points of great films.

10. Film Discussion Boards
http://www.film.com/film/hyper/filmtalk/
Includes discussion group on Quentin Tarantino, for example.

11. History on/and/in Film
http://kali.murdoch.edu.au/~cntinuum/hfilm/contenth.html
An informative site with many articles on film history.

12. The Making of Citizen Kane
http://www.voyagerco.com/CC/gh/welles/p.makingkane.html
A nice site devoted to *Citizen Kane*.

13. Millennium Film Journal
http://www.sva.edu/MFJ/
This site includes information about the Journal's articles on avant-garde and experimental cinema.

14. World Film Festival Guide
http://www.film.com/film/filmfests/
An exhaustive list of film festivals in the United States and throughout the world.

15. Film Festivals

http://www.eden.com/~delta-9/festival.html
Searchable film festival database.

16. United International Pictures

http://www.uip.com/film/html
This site comes from the distributor of MGM/United Artists, Paramount, and Universal Pictures, and includes the latest information about recent releases.

17. Twentieth Century Fox

http://www.foxhome.com
Covers the film industry from Twentieth Century Fox's early releases in the 1920s to present day.

18. Disney Animated

http://www2.best.com/~dijon/disney/movies/
This site is devoted to all the animated features produced by the Walt Disney Company, from *Snow White* to *Pocahontas.*

19. Metro-Goldwyn-Mayer/United Artists

http://www.mgmua.com
Their web site covers information on motion pictures, television, video, interactive entertainment, studio store, and their executive suite.

20. Miramax Films

http://www.miramax.com
Includes promotional material on their latest films, cash and prizes, and other information.

21. MCA/Universal Pictures

http://www.mca.com
This site allows users to sample products and entertainment, including their screening room of classic films.

22. Sony Pictures

http://www.sony.com
From Sony Entertainment, this site offers information on recent films, as well as a studio tour.

23. Digital Movie News

http://www.el-dorado.ca.us/~dmnews/dmn_toc.html
Information on how to create your own digital movies and reviews of software needed to do it.

24. Motion Picture and Video Production and Post Production

http://www.solutions.ibm.com/multimedia/production.html
An advertisement of IBM's hardware for film production, including a complete range of media services.

25. MPEG Movie Archive

http://www.eeb.ele.tue.nl/mpeg/news.html
An archive of films.

CREDITS

Frame enlargements and production stills were obtained from a variety of sources. In the following listing, the boldface numbers are the figure references. In addition, the following abbreviations are used: WCFTR (Wisconsin Center for Film and Theater Research) and MOMA (Museum of Modern Art). All illustrations not credited are from the collection of the authors.

1.9 copyright 1954, Columbia; **1.10, 1.20** copyright Universal and Amblin; **1.11** copyright 1989, Paramount; **1.14, 1.16** WCFTR; **1.17** MOMA; **1.24** copyright 1988, Geffen.

2.5 copyright 1972, Paramount; **2.6** copyright 1994, Paramount; **2.11** British Film Institute; **2.22** copyright 1943, RKO; **2.25** copyright 1956, Warner Bros.; **2.27** copyright 1942, RKO; **2.29** copyright 1932, Universal.

3.1–3.11 copyright 1939, MGM.

4.2–4.4 copyright 1959, MGM; **4.6** copyright 1941, RKO.

5.43 MOMA; **5.47–5.60** courtesy Bruce Conner.

6.10 copyright 1976, Warner Bros.; **6.31, 6.44** copyright 1958, Universal; **6.32** copyright 1931, RKO; **6.35** copyright 1932, Paramount; **6.36** copyright 1962, United Artists; **6.40** copyright 1938, Warner Bros.; **6.41–6.42** copyright 1985, Universal; **6.54** copyright 1977, United Artists; **6.55** copyright 1950, Universal; **6.62** copyright 1986, Twentieth Century Fox; **6.65** copyright 1939, 20th Century-Fox; **6.73** courtesy Norman McLaren; **6.74** copyright 1936, Warner Bros.; **6.81** copyright 1932, Warner Bros.; **6.88–6.89** copyright 1952, MGM.

7.5, 7.115–7.116 courtesy Palladium Films; **6.11** copyright 1941, Samuel Goldwyn; **7.20–7.21** courtesy Toho; **7.22–7.23** copyright 1974, Paramount; **7.26–7.27** courtesy Ernie Gehr; **7.29** copyright 1932, Paramount; **7.30** copyright 1972, Paramount; **7.33** copyright 1941, RKO; **7.35** copyright 1981, Filmways; **7.42** copyright 1982, Blade Runner Partnership; **7.38, 7.43, 7.50** MOMA; **7.59** copyright 1980, United Artists; **7.64,** copyright 1988, Twentieth Century Fox; **7.67–7.69,** copyright 1962, Columbia; **7.70–7.71** copyright 1986, Twentieth Century Fox; **7.72–7.74** copyright 1985, Universal; **7.80–7.83** copyright 1938, Warner Bros.; **7.101** copyright 1941, RKO; **7.102,** copyright 1959, MGM; **7.110** copyright 1949, Warner Bros.; **7.125–7.126** copyright 1980, Warner Bros.; **7.127** courtesy Pennebaker, Inc.; **7.130–7.132** courtesy WCFTR; **7.148** MOMA; **7.183–7.185** courtesy Michael Snow; **7.195–7.206** copyright 1958, Universal.

8.1–8.3 copyright 1940, Warner Bros.; **8.5–8.8, 8.29–8.39** copyright 1963, Universal; **8.11–8.16** courtesy Toho; **8.17–8.19** copyright 1986, Twentieth Century Fox; **8.27–8.28** copyright 1958, Universal; **8.49–8.69** copyright 1940, Warner Bros.; **8.70–8.71** copyright 1989, Universal; **8.72–8.75** copyright 1938, Warner Bros.; **8.80–8.85** copyright 1986, Island Pictures; **8.86–8.87** copyright 1938, Warner Bros.; **8.88–8.89, 8.91–8.94** copyright 1954, Patron, Inc.; **8.99–8.102** courtesy New Yorker Films; **8.114–8.116** courtesy Pennebaker Films.

9.1–9.4 courtesy New Yorker Films; **9.6–9.8** copyright 1990, Paramount; **9.9–9.13** copyright 1939, United Artists; **9.15–9.25** courtesy New Yorker Films.

10.1–10.4 copyright 1990, Orion; **10.5–10.32** copyright 1941, RKO; **10.59–10.67** courtesy Bruce Conner.

11.6–11.18 copyright 1959, MGM; **11.19–11.28** copyright 1989, Universal; **11.43–11.61** courtesy New Yorker Films; **11.62–11.76** courtesy Zipporah Films; **11.85–11.90** copyright 1980, United Artists.

12.1 George Eastman House; **12.26** MOMA; **12.27–12.28** WCFTR; **12.29** copyright 1932, Universal; **12.30** copyright 1941, Samuel Goldwyn; **12.36** copyright 1987, Circle.

INDEX